AF615659

IN SUPPORT OF LIBERTY

European Paintings
at the 1883
Pedestal Fund Art Loan Exhibition

In Support of Liberty: European Paintings at the 1883 Pedestal Fund Art Loan Exhibition has been made possible with support from

THE BETTY PARSONS FOUNDATION
THE NEW YORK STATE COUNCIL ON THE ARTS
THE SUFFOLK COUNTY OFFICE OF CULTURAL AFFAIRS
THE NEW YORK COUNCIL FOR THE HUMANITIES
THE HEARST FOUNDATION
MR. AND MRS. JACK C. MASSEY
THE EQUITABLE REAL ESTATE GROUP
THE POLYESTHER CORPORATION
THE FLORENCE J. GOULD FOUNDATION
THE LUTECE FOUNDATION
AT&T

This catalogue is published with the assistance of
THE J. PAUL GETTY TRUST

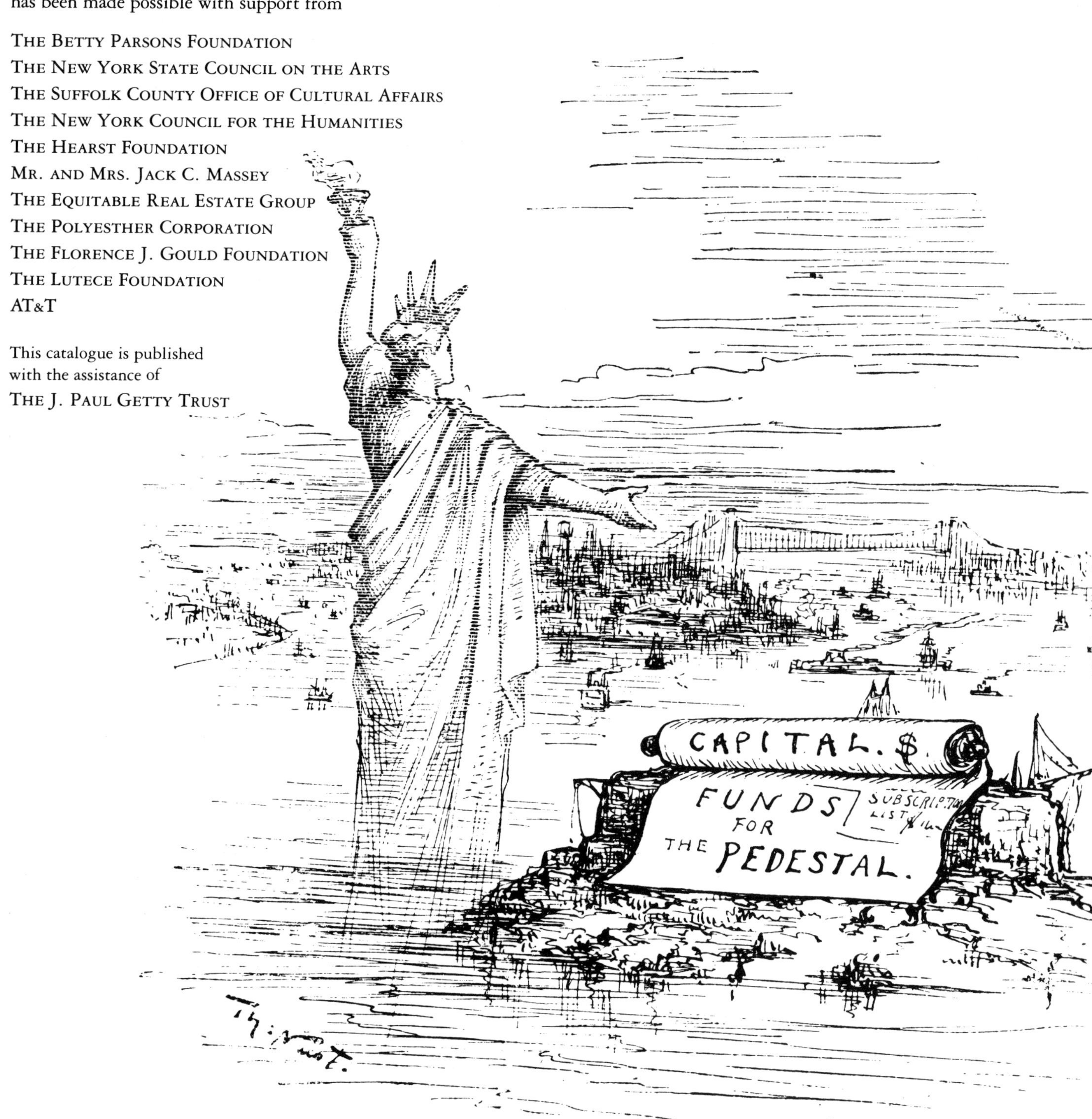

THE BARTHOLDI STATUE.
Even Liberty demands something substantial to stand upon.

Harper's Weekly, December 6, 1884

IN SUPPORT OF LIBERTY

European Paintings at the 1883 Pedestal Fund Art Loan Exhibition

Maureen C. O'Brien

THE PARRISH ART MUSEUM, Southampton, New York
June 29–September 1, 1986

NATIONAL ACADEMY OF DESIGN, New York
September 18–December 7, 1986

Cover:
Jean-François Millet
The Bather, c. 1846
Yale University Art Gallery, New Haven, Connecticut
Anonymous Gift in Honor of Alan Shestack

Library of Congress Catalog Card Number 86-60099
ISBN 943526-14-0

Contents

Lenders

Walters Art Gallery, Baltimore, Maryland
Indiana University Art Museum, Bloomington
Museum of Fine Arts, Boston
The Brooklyn Museum, Brooklyn, New York
Bowdoin College Museum of Art, Brunswick, Maine
Albright-Knox Art Gallery, Buffalo, New York
The Ackland Art Museum, University of North Carolina at Chapel Hill
The Art Institute of Chicago
Cincinnati Art Museum
The Taft Museum, Cincinnati, Ohio
The Cleveland Museum of Art
Detroit Institute of Arts
Tweed Museum of Art, Duluth, Minnesota
Glasgow Art Gallery and Museum, Glasgow, Scotland
Denison University Gallery, Granville, Ohio
The Heckscher Museum, Huntington, New York
Herbert F. Johnson Museum of Art, Cornell University, Ithaca, New York
Milwaukee Art Museum, Milwaukee, Wisconsin
The Minneapolis Institute of Arts
Montreal Museum of Fine Arts
Ball State University Art Gallery, Muncie, Indiana
Yale University Art Gallery, New Haven, Connecticut
The Metropolitan Museum of Art, New York
The New-York Historical Society, New York
The Chrysler Museum, Norfolk, Virginia
Allen Memorial Art Museum, Oberlin College, Oberlin, Ohio
National Gallery of Canada, Ottawa
The Pennsylvania Academy of the Fine Arts, Philadelphia
Philadelphia Museum of Art
Phoenix Art Museum, Phoenix, Arizona
Museum of Art, Carnegie Institute, Pittsburgh
Portland Art Museum, Portland, Oregon
Vassar College Art Gallery, Poughkeepsie, New York
Museum of Art, Rhode Island School of Design, Providence

Memorial Art Gallery of the University of Rochester, Rochester, New York
The Fine Arts Museums of San Francisco
Charles and Emma Frye Art Museum, Seattle, Washington
Museum of Fine Arts, Springfield, Massachusetts
The Toledo Museum of Art, Toledo, Ohio
Munson-Williams-Proctor Institute Museum of Art, Utica, New York
The Corcoran Gallery of Art, Washington, D.C.
National Gallery of Art, Washington, D.C.
The Phillips Collection, Washington, D.C.
Sterling and Francine Clark Art Institute, Williamstown, Massachusetts
Worcester Art Museum, Worcester, Massachusetts

Robert B. Beardsley
The FORBES Magazine Collection, New York
Mr. and Mrs. D. W. Hill, London
Robert Isaacson, New York
Stuart Pivar, New York
William B. Ruger
Lila and Herman Shickman, New York
Joey and Toby Tanenbaum, Toronto, Canada
Gretchen Theobald and Sprague Theobald
Paul Underwood, New York
Mrs. John Hay Whitney
Four private collections

Julian Hartnoll, London
M. Knoedler & Co., New York
Sacks Fine Art, New York
Schweitzer Gallery, Inc., New York
Shepherd Gallery Associates, New York

Foreword

For interpreters of the forces at play in the history of American art, it is instructive—often surprisingly so—to study exhibitions in which artists played a critical role in forcing the public to an awareness of new ideas. American artists in the nineteenth and twentieth centuries have, for the most part, presented these new ideas in small, intimate settings. A well-known exception is the Armory Show of 1913, a momentous example of artistic insurgence, where artists confronted other artists with new and fresh possibilities and where collectors and the general public were jolted from the confines of predictable taste. Nearly as momentous but far less well known is the exhibition of European paintings at the 1883 *Pedestal Fund Art Loan Exhibition*, an occasion on which the taste of a small group of American artists assumed a new significance and affected the viewing habits of other artists, dealers, collectors, and the general public. It is this event that The Parrish Art Museum and the National Academy of Design have chosen to examine and, insofar as possible, to reconstruct.

The 1883 exhibition was organized to raise money for the base of the Statue of Liberty. What better way to honor Liberty's centennial in 1986 than to focus on an event that helped make her installation a reality. Our collaboration is fitting. The audacious selections for the Pedestal Fund exhibition were primarily those of William Merritt Chase, for whom The Parrish Art Museum, as the major repository of Chase's work, has particular affection. It was the National Academy of Design, in 1883, that played host to the original *Pedestal Fund Art Loan Exhibition.*

We are especially grateful to Maureen C. O'Brien, Associate Director of The Parrish Art Museum, for bringing to light this historic event. Her investigation of this important transitional period in American art and her success in locating so many works from the original exhibition deserve great praise. We are also indebted to Ronald G. Pisano for his insight into the contributions of Chase and his colleagues; to Dr. Lois Dinnerstein for her commentary on the social and critical climate of the time; and to Christopher P. Monkhouse for his discussion of other aspects of the *Pedestal Fund Art Loan Exhibition.*

We are most thankful to have such excellent staffs, and extend them our deep appreciation for their unswerving attention to the details of the project. At the Parrish, Alicia Longwell, Registrar, has with grace and efficiency made innumerable contributions to the assembly of the exhibition. Norma Loehner and Mary McNeirney handled the exhibition's voluminous correspondence and the mysteries of preparing a complicated manuscript with precision and good humor. Anke Jackson, Associate Director for Budget and Operations, adeptly managed all aspects of budget and grants; Marsha Kenny energetically handled exhibition publicity; and Robin Box-Klopfer, Building Manager, has helped in countless ways. At the National Academy of Design, Barbara Krulik, Assistant Director, and Helen Morris, Director of Public Affairs, have been tireless in making arrangements for the New York exhibition.

We appreciate as well the great skill of the designers associated with this project. We thank Mark Hampton and Richard Franklin for enhancing the presentation of the works and Dana Levy and Tish O'Connor for their handsome catalogue design. We also thank Jane Fluegel for her perceptive and intelligent editing and Alarik Skarstrom and Pamela Barr for their assistance in proofreading. We particularly wish to recognize the lenders—collectors, art dealers, and museum directors and curators—for their support of this project and for their generosity in granting loans.

Special acknowledgment must also go to those individuals who so enthusiastically responded with financial support early on: Mr. and Mrs. Jack C. Massey, Robert B. Baird, William P. Rayner, Benjamin Halloway, John R. Hearst, Jr., and Ward Mintz. Our gratitude extends as well to our institutional sources of financial support: the Betty Parsons Foundation, the Hearst Foundation, the New York State Council on the Arts, the New York Council for the Humanities, the J. Paul Getty Trust, the Polyesther Corporation, Suffolk County Office of Cultural Affairs, the Equitable Real Estate Group, the Florence J. Gould Foundation, the Lutece Foundation, and AT&T.

And finally, we would like to thank the members of our boards, particularly Garrick C. Stephenson, Chairman of the Board of Trustees at the Parrish, and Wilbur L. Ross, Jr., Chairman of the Museum Board of the National Academy, for their collective support in encouraging original scholarly research and for providing financial resources to make this project a success.

Trudy C. Kramer
Director
The Parrish Art Museum

John H. Dobkin
Director
National Academy of Design

May 1986

Acknowledgments

This exhibition would not have been possible without the assistance of many patrons, museum colleagues, scholars, collectors, art dealers, and friends. A special debt of gratitude is owed to Kermit S. Champa, Charles F. Stuckey, and Gabriel P. Weisberg, whose advice, encouragement, and inspiration have contributed immeasurably to the success of this project.

The American Council on Germany and The Metropolitan Museum of Art, New York, through the award in 1985 of a John J. McCloy Fellowship in Art, provided valuable professional contacts and research opportunities abroad.

The J. Paul Getty Trust provided publication support that significantly broadened the scope of the exhibition catalogue.

The following museum professionals are to be thanked for their generous suggestions, cooperation, and support: Baltimore, the Walters Art Gallery, William R. Johnston, Elizabeth Binckley; Bloomington, Indiana, Indiana University Art Museum, Thomas T. Solley, Diane Drisch; Boston, Museum of Fine Arts, Patricia Loiko, Helen Hall, Barbara Stern Shapiro, Alison Hatcher; Brooklyn, The Brooklyn Museum, Robert T. Buck, Sarah Faunce, Barbara La Salle; Brunswick, Maine, Bowdoin College Museum of Art, John W. Coffey; Buffalo, Albright-Knox Art Gallery, Douglas C. Schultz; Chapel Hill, North Carolina, Ackland Art Museum, The University of North Carolina at Chapel Hill, Innis H. Shoemaker, Wanda C. Calhoon; Chicago, The Art Institute of Chicago, Susan Wise, Wallace D. Bradway, Mary Kuzniar; Cincinnati Art Museum, Millard F. Rogers, Jr.; Cincinnati, The Taft Museum, Ruth K. Mayer, David Torbet Johnson; Cleveland, The Cleveland Museum of Art, Evan H. Turner, William S. Talbot; Davenport, Iowa, Davenport Art Gallery, Ann C. Madonia; The Detroit Institute of Arts, Samuel Sachs II, J. Patrice Marandel, Iva Lisikewycz, Terry Segal; Duluth, Minnesota, Tweed Museum of Art, William G. Boyce; Elmira, New York, Arnot Art Museum, Pamela Beecher; Farmington, Connecticut, Hill-Stead Museum, Katherine Warwick, Marguerite Atkinson; Granville, Ohio, Denison Art Gallery, George Bogdanovitch, Letha Schetzsle; Hartford, Connecticut, Wadsworth Atheneum, Gregory Hedberg; Huntington, New York, The Heckscher Museum, Christopher B. Crosmann, William Titus, Anne Cohen de Pietro; Indianapolis Museum of Art, Ellen W. Lee; Ithaca, New York, Herbert F. Johnson Museum of Art, Cornell University, Thomas W. Leavitt, Cynthia Wayne, Cathy Anderson; Madison, Wisconsin,

Elvehjem Museum of Art, Russell Panczenko, Lisa Calden; Milwaukee Art Museum, Russell Bowman; Minneapolis, American Swedish Institute, John Lofgren; The Minneapolis Institute of Arts, Alan Shestack, Richard J. Campbell, Rosamond Hurrell; Montclair, New Jersey, Montclair Art Museum, Edith A. Rights; the Montreal Museum of Fine Arts, Alexander V. J. Gaudieri, Janet Brooke; Muncie, Indiana, Ball State University, Alain Joyaux; New Haven, Yale Center for British Art, Susan Casteras; New Haven, Connecticut, Yale University Art Gallery, Anne C. Hanson, Michael Komanecky, Rosalie Reed, William Cuffe; New York, Cooper-Hewitt Museum, Elaine Evans Dee; New York, the staff of The Frick Art Reference Library; New York, National Academy of Design, John Dobkin, Barbara Krulik, Robert Sawchuck; New York, The Metropolitan Museum of Art, Sir John Pope-Hennessy, Katherine Baetjer, Walter Liedtke, Jacob Bean, Susan Stein, Kathleen Luhrs, Doreen B. Burke, James L. Yarnall, Catherine Hoover, Katria Czerwoniak, Mary Doherty, Alison Yates, Linda Lawson, Marceline McKee; The New-York Historical Society, Dr. James B. Bell, Ella Foshay, Holly Hotchner, Mary Alice Mackay; The Newark Museum, Gary A. Reynolds; Norfolk, Virginia, The Chrysler Museum, Dr. David W. Steadman, Catherine Jordan; Northampton, Massachusetts, Smith College Museum of Art, Charles Chetham; Oberlin, Ohio, Allen Memorial Art Museum, Kimberlie C. Gumz; Ottawa, National Gallery of Canada, Joseph Martin, Peggy McKeever; Philadelphia, The Pennsylvania Academy of the Fine Arts, Linda Bentel, Kathleen A. Foster, Robert Harman; Philadelphia Museum of Art, Anne d'Harnoncourt, Joseph Rishel, Nancy S. Quaile; Phoenix Art Museum, James K. Ballinger, Karen Hodges, Susan Gordon; Pittsburgh, The Frick Art Museum, Kahren Hellerstedt; Pittsburgh, Museum of Art, Carnegie Institute, John R. Lane, Diana Strazdes; Portland, Oregon, Portland Art Museum, Donald Jenkins; Poughkeepsie, New York, Vassar College Art Gallery, Jan E. Adlmann, Ann Conforti; Providence, Anne S. K. Brown Military Collection, Peter Harrington; Providence, John Hay Library, Brown University, Jennifer Lee; Providence, Annmary Brown Memorial, Brown University, Catherine Denning; Providence, Museum of Art, Rhode Island School of Design, Franklin Robinson, Daniel Rosenfeld, Robert Workman, Deborah Johnson, Christopher P. Monkhouse, Maureen Harper; Rochester, Memorial Art Gallery of the University of Rochester, Patricia Anderson; The Saint Louis Art Museum,

James D. Burke, Jack Sawyer, Marie Louise Kane; San Francisco, The Fine Arts Museums of San Francisco, M. H. de Young Memorial Museum, Marion Stewart, Lynn Federle Orr, Marc C. Simpson; Seattle, Charles and Emma Frye Art Museum, Mrs. Walser S. Greathouse; Springfield, Massachusetts, Museum of Fine Arts, Nancy Swallow; The Toledo Museum of Art, Roger Mandle, William Hutton, Patricia Whitesides, Marilyn Symmes; Utica, New York, Munson-Williams-Proctor Institute, Dr. Paul D. Schweizer, Pat Serafini; Washington, D.C., The Corcoran Gallery of Art, Michael Botwinick, Edward Nygren, Elizabeth D. Beam, Rebecca T. Gregson; Washington, D.C., National Gallery of Art, J. Carter Brown, Charles F. Stuckey; Washington, D.C., National Museum of American Art, William H. Truettner; Washington, D.C., The Phillips Collection, Willem de Looper, Joseph Holbach, Janet Dorman; Williamstown, Massachusetts, Sterling and Francine Clark Art Institute, David S. Brooke, Martha Asher; Worcester Art Museum, James A. Welu, Sally Freitag.

Berlin, Nationalgalerie, Dr. Dominik Bartmann, Dr. Jiri Svestka; Berlin, Staatliche Museen, Preussicher Kulturbesitz, Dr. Wolf-Dieter Dube, Dr. Ellen Weski; Bremen, Kunsthalle Bremen, Dr. Siegfried Salzmann, Dr. Gerhard Gerkens; Cologne, Wallraf-Richartz Museum, Dr. Götz Czymmek; Dordrecht, Dordrechts Museum, Dr. G. J. Schweitzer; Düsseldorf, Kunstmuseum Düsseldorf, Dr. Rolf Andree; Edinburgh, National Gallery of Scotland, Dr. Lindsay Errington; Glasgow Museums and Art Galleries, Alasdair A. Auld, Anne Donald, Hugh T. Stevenson, Rosemary Watt, Philip S. Vainker; Glasgow, Hunterian Art Gallery, Martin Hopkinson; Hamburg, Hamburger Kunsthalle, Dr. Helmut Leppien; London, The National Gallery, Sir Michael Levey; London, Victoria and Albert Museum, Michael Darby; Melbourne, Australia, National Gallery of Victoria, Kenneth Hood, Annette Dixon; Munich, Bayerische Staatsgemäldesammlungen, Dr. Christian Lenz; Otterlo, Rijksmuseum Kröller-Müller, Dr. R. W. D. Oxenaar; Paris, Musée de l'Armée, Jean Humbert; Paris, Compagnie des Commissaires-Priseurs de Paris, Marie-Cécile Comerre; Paris, Ecole Nationale d'Administration, Françoise Renaud; Paris, Direction du Musée du Louvre, Ministère de la Culture, Hélène Toussaint; Rennes, Musée des Beaux-Arts et d'Archéologie de Rennes, Jean Aubert; Stockholm, Nationalmuseum, Pontus Grate, Per Bjurström; Warsaw, Polish Art Gallery, National Museum in Warsaw, Dr. Agnieszka Morawinska.

We would like to express our gratitude to the following individuals whose generosity and enthusiasm were among the greatest rewards of this undertaking: American Council on Germany, New York, David Klein, Jeffrey Feltman; Professor Nathaniel B. Atwater; Austrian Cultural Affairs, New York, Brigitta Agstner; Robert B. Baird; Fred Baker; Renzo Baldaccini; Robert B. Beardsley; Pamela and Julian Beck; Gretchen Bellinger; Dr. Kenneth Bendiner; Annette Blaugrund; Ursula Boekels; Professor Albert Boime; Annette Bourrut-Lacouture; Arie van Harwegen den Breems; Professor Thomas B. Brumbaugh; Frances Chaves; Pari Choate; Christie, Manson & Woods International, Inc., New York, Betty Krulik; Dr. Petra ten-Doesschate Chu; William A. Coles; David Daniels; Gloria-Gilda Deák; C. Dobczynski; Professor Lorenz Eitner; Madeleine Fidell-Beaufort; The FORBES Collection, New York, Margaret Kelly; Michael Geiger; Mr. and Mrs. Jerome Gore; The Fine Art Society, London, Andrew McIntosh Patrick, Roger Billcliffe; Grand Central Art Galleries, New York, Robert Preato; Dr. Susanne Grimm; Daniel B. Grossman Fine Art, New York, Daniel B. Grossman, Eric Baumgartner; Guarisco Gallery Ltd., Washington, D.C., Jane M. Studabaker; Dr. June Hargrove; Julian Hartnoll Gallery, London, Julian Hartnoll; Professor Robert L. Herbert; David W. Hill; Richard N. Hurley; Robert Isaacson; Mrs. Marg Jay; Joseph Keiffer; Knoedler-Modarco, S.A., Hope Davis, Nancy C. Little; Henry Koehler; Beth Kubly; Bruce P. Lenman; Lipert Gallery, Brooklyn, New York, Z. Michael Legutko; Dr. Hans Lüthy; Jeremy Maas & Co., Ltd., M. A. Ford; Margaret F. MacDonald; Dr. Laura Meixner; Dr. Joseph Malejka; John Monahan; Galerie Nathan, Zurich, Switzerland, Dr. Peter Nathan; Christopher Newall; Newhouse Galleries, New York, Clyde Newhouse; Newel Art Galleries, Inc., New York, Bruce Newman; Professor Roberta J. M. Olson; Galerie G. Paffrath, Düsseldorf, G. Paffrath; W. H. Patterson Fine Arts Ltd., London, John White; Heather B. Pattison; Phillips Auction Gallery, New York, Carolyn Madley; Stuart Pivar; Joseph A. Pulitzer, Jr.; William P. Rayner; Rembrandt Gallery, Forest Hills, New York, William Artman; Roman Galleries, New York, Herbert Roman; William B. Ruger; Dr. Eberhard Ruhmer; Peter Salm; Schweitzer Gallery, New York, M. R. Schweitzer; Professor Aaron Sheon; Shepherd Gallery, New York, Robert Kashey; Shickman Gallery, New York, Herman Shickman,

Michael Lewin; Dr. Eugene Slotkowski; Sotheby's, London, Simon Taylor; Sotheby Parke-Bernet, Buenos Aires, Mallory Hathaway de Graviere; Sotheby's, New York, Nancy Harrison; Ira Spanierman Gallery, New York, Ira Spanierman, David Henry; Stair Sainty Fine Art, Ltd., New York, Guy Stair Sainty, Janet Friedman; Hope Stefenson; Dr. Halina Stepien; Suzanne Sunshine; Carol Tabler; Eugene V. Thaw; Dana E. Tillou; Paul Underwood; Professor Kirk Varnedoe; Vose Galleries, Boston, Philip Wharton; H. Barbara Weinberg; Michael Wentworth; Wheelock Whitney & Company, New York, Wheelock Whitney; Mrs. John Hay Whitney; Wildenstein & Co., New York, Daniel Wildenstein, Joseph Baillio; Fronia E. Wissman; Christopher Wood, London.

M. C. O'B.

Introduction

The galleries of the National Academy of Design at Fourth Avenue and Twenty-third Street, New York, were nearly impassable on the night of December 3, 1883, when a thousand guests in evening attire gathered for the opening of the *Pedestal Fund Art Loan Exhibition*. Shortly before nine o'clock, the Esperance and Helvetian Singing Societies assembled on the main staircase to sing Gounod's "Hymn to Liberty," followed by the appearance of F. Hopkinson Smith, the salaried director of the event, who thanked his numerous volunteer committees, then read "The New Colossus," a poem written by Emma Lazarus for the *Portfolio* of the Art Loan Collection.[1] The Hon. William K. Evarts, chairman of the general committee to build a pedestal for Frédéric Auguste Bartholdi's statue *Liberty Enlightening the World*, due to arrive in New York harbor eighteen months later, ascended the podium next. "Here," said Evarts, "is everything charming, everything elegant, everything beautiful and everything splendid. It is such an exhibition as our country never saw before."[2] Indeed, the public had been invited to view an extraordinary array of treasures "which their owners seldom show to any save their intimates and friends."[3]

Handsomely displayed throughout the Academy's rooms, which were rented by the committee for the occasion, were loan exhibitions of paintings, old prints, missals and old books, stained glass, laces, musical instruments, miniatures, old china, costumes, arms and armor, Oriental art, aboriginal art, fans, old jewelry and silver, old furniture, metalwork, ceramics, old coins, and embroideries. They were selected by an army of New York artists, businessmen, and socialites, presided over by Allen Thorndike Rice,[4] and by a forty-eight member executive committee with representatives from New York, Boston, Philadelphia, Jersey City, Cincinnati, Louisville, and London. Cornelius Vanderbilt served on the finance committee; Richard Morris Hunt, the architect of the pedestal, chaired the committee on insurance. William Merritt Chase administered the committee on the admission of objects and directed J. Carroll Beckwith and Louis Comfort Tiffany in the decoration of the galleries. John La Farge, Augustus Saint-Gaudens, John Quincy Adams Ward, Olin Warner, Eastman Johnson, Frederick Dielman, and Frank D. Millet also made conspicuous contributions as organizers, supported by an honorary committee of eighty-four other American artists.

The purpose of this elaborate production was to raise enough money to pay for the construction of Hunt's pedestal for the statue—a cause that had secured only two-fifths of the needed revenues by December 1883, and remained in jeopardy a year later. Generous philanthropic underwriting had not been forthcoming, nor, argued the fund's managers, somewhat uneasily,[5] should the privilege of supporting Liberty be restricted to the wealthy. All citizens should be invited to contribute to the installation of a "statue that had come from more than 100 municipalities in France and from the pockets of more than 100,000 Frenchmen."[6] By attending the exhibition, "each person who pays an admittance fee or buys the handsome catalogue will have the right to feel that he has helped to build the pedestal for the magnificent gift of France to the United States."[7]

General Ulysses S. Grant, a special guest at the opening of the Pedestal Fund show, gently chided New Yorkers by directing the responsibility to those present that evening: "I know the people of this City well enough . . . to believe that all the funds necessary to complete this pedestal could be raised in one day if they thought it was necessary to do so. When we reflect that the statue is the gift of a people who gave us their warm sympathy in our struggle for national independence we should not let there be a want for a fund sufficient to complete it for a single day."[8] Grant then declared the exhibition open to the public for a four-week engagement that would attract over 40,000 visitors at a general admission fee of fifty cents (twenty-five cents on Sunday), sell 5,000 catalogues for one dollar each (2,000 of which were bought back at fifty cents and resold), earn total receipts of between $25,000 and $27,000, and net about $12,000 for the Bartholdi Pedestal Fund.[9]

The show had the excitement and variety of an international exhibition, on a smaller, more focused, and more intimate scale. There had been significant precedents for fund-raising events of this type in America,[10] but the idea of combining an art exhibition with an appeal for contributions toward the construction of a monument was one that had longer and greater currency in Europe. In the 1870s, when William Merritt Chase was a student in Munich, the weekly *Beiblatt*, or supplement, to *Kunst-Chronik* included frequent announcements of funds that had been established to build statues commemorating revered poets and artists. The Friday *Beiblatt* of January 21, 1876, for example, named Chase's teacher, Karl von Piloty, as a member of the committee that was raising funds to install a statue of Peter von Cornelius, former Academy director, in Maximilians-Platz. An even closer prototype of the Pedestal Fund show was the *Lessing-Denkmal Ausstellung* held in Hamburg in 1879—an exhibition of contemporary European paintings lent by local collectors for the purpose of raising money for the refurbishment of the monument to the German poet Gotthold Lessing.[11] Later variations on the theme included New York's *Barye Monument Fund Exhibition* of 1889–90 and the *Exposition organisée au profit du monument du centenaire de Corot*, held in Paris in 1895. Consistent references to the "Bartholdi Fund" made it clear that its support by American artists, particularly those who had recently studied in Munich and Paris, was as much an acknowledgment of the work of Bartholdi as it was an expression of gratitude for the symbol of America's independence offered in friendship by the people of France.

A glance at the committee rosters published in the *Catalògue of the Pedestal Fund Art Loan Exhibition* reveals a diversity of supporters that rivaled the variety of objects in the 1883 show. Chairmanships of subcommittees on the decorative arts were nearly equally distributed between men and women who were offered free reign in collecting objects in their particular areas of expertise. A profusion of line drawings in the catalogue documents the wide range of interests pursued by American collectors in the 1880s, and gives an indication of the strength of the market for both domestic and international antiques.

In contrast to these displays, and strikingly unified in its own expansive diversity, was the selection of modern paintings that filled the south gallery of the Academy. Here the works of seventy modern European artists, culled from New York's private collections and from the stock of a handful of dealers, introduced the American public to the painterly, nonnarrative styles that had been the focus of Europe's recent international exhibitions and Salons. A majority of the 194 paintings was French—not only in homage to Liberty's benefactors but also in acknowledgment of the incontrovertible influence of French painting throughout the nineteenth century, and in particular its impact on American artists in the 1870s and 1880s. Although the selection ran the gamut from Jean-Louis-Ernest Meissonier to Edouard Manet, it did not attempt to champion either the major Salon lights or the young turks of the Impressionist exhibitions.

Nor were the "rising young masters of France," such as Jules Bastien-Lepage and Paul Adolphe Jean Dagnan-Bouveret, represented in great number.[12]

Noting the absence of the paintings by Adolphe William Bouguereau, Alexandre Cabanel, Hugues Merle and Jean-Léon Gérôme that had been so actively sought and commissioned by America's wealthiest collectors in the last quarter of the nineteenth century, critics complained that the collection appealed to far too few picture-buyers.[13] With a few exceptions, history painting, classical subject matter, and labored draftsmanship were out; intimate landscapes, still lifes, painterly figures, and colorism and lively surface effects were in. The tone of the French selections was directed by the influence of Eugène Delacroix and Théodore Géricault, and by the landscapes of Georges Michel, "powerful, broad, and carefully painted, like the old Dutchmen, sometimes like Old Crome."[14] The choices were heavily weighted in favor of the men of 1830, and strong in their preference of J.-B.-C. Corot, Jean-François Millet—"an artist for the select"—and Gustave Courbet, "a painter whose rough brush sends a cold chill down the average American's back."[15] The impact of seventeenth-century Spanish and Dutch painting on nineteenth-century French realism was pointedly apparent in the rich surfaces of Antoine Vollon, the costume pieces of Ferdinand Roybet, and the dark figures of Louis Mettling and Théodule Ribot. And disproportionately abundant on the walls of the Academy were the landscapes and bouquets of Narcisse Diaz and the *fêtes galantes* of Adolphe Monticelli, "whom most people regard as little better than a fool and his admirers as would-be eccentrics or amiable lunatics."[16]

In addition to these painters, the exhibition also included the work of major foreign adherents to contemporary French realist styles: Giovanni Boldini, Antonio Mancini, Giuseppe de Nittis, and Alberto Pasini from Italy; C. F. Hill, Wilhelm von Gegerfelt, Alfred Wahlberg, and Oskar Törna from Sweden; Belgian artists P.-J. Clays and Alfred Stevens; Flemish landscape painter César de Cock; and Austrians Eduard Charlemont and Eugen Jettel. Whistler and Tissot also came under this umbrella, resisting identification by either country of origin or residence.

In retrospect, the absence of the German painters who were among the first to introduce this generation of young American artists to painterly realism was more glaring than the exclusion of Bouguereau and Cabanel. With the exception of Ludwig Knaus and his Hungarian student, Michael Munkácsy, by this time well established in Paris, Germany was represented only by association with Polish and Austrian artists of the Munich School. England fared only slightly better: through the sponsorship of Scottish dealer Daniel Cottier, the Scottish artists Hugh Cameron and William Lockhart and the Englishman Walter Reynolds were included in the show, along with Jules Lessore, a French watercolorist living in London. In effect, France shared the spotlight only with Holland, whose Hague School artists had begun to establish international reputations in the 1870s. Again through the efforts of Cottier, who would be responsible for the success of these artists in London and New York, Bernardus Johannes Blommers, Johannes Bosboom, Jacob and Matthew Maris, Anton Mauve, Hendrik Willem Mesdag, and Albert Neuhuys helped expand the view of contemporary European painting presented to New York in December 1883.

The current exhibition attempts to reconstruct the visual impact of the Paintings Section of the *Pedestal Fund Art Loan Exhibition*. Wherever possible, paintings that were exhibited in 1883 have been included in the show or reproduced in the opening essay. Works that have been added to the exhibition have been selected on the basis of their similarity in date, style, and subject to the original paintings, their familiarity through contemporary criticism, and their existence in American collections in the 1880s. Through the scholarship of art historians Lois Dinnerstein, Ronald G. Pisano and Christopher P. Monkhouse, the catalogue explores the critical reception of the 1883 exhibition; the extensive personal contacts of the American artist and exhibition-organizer William Merritt Chase with his European contemporaries; and the importance of the decorative arts that shared the spotlight with the exhibition's paintings. It is hoped that this reconstruction, which coincides with the centennial of the Statue of Liberty, will illuminate the taste of the period and the convictions of the artists and collectors who made the *Pedestal Fund Art Loan Exhibition* an event that would also strengthen the foundations of American art.

Maureen C. O'Brien
Associate Director for Curatorial Affairs
The Parrish Art Museum

1. "Admiring Objects of Art," *The New York Times*, December 4, 1883, p. 2. Smith was elected director of the exhibition, with a salary of $1,500, at a meeting held October 6, 1883, in the rooms of the American Art Galleries ("The Art Loan Exhibition," *The New York Times*, October 7, 1883, p. 7).

2. "Admiring Objects of Art."

3. "The Pedestal Art Loan," *The New York Times*, December 2, 1883, p. 2.

4. *The New York Times* reported that Rice had advanced the committee enough money to begin operations. See "An Art Loan Exhibition," *The New York Times*, October 19, 1883, p. 2.

5. "It is known to you all," stated Evarts, "that the greatness of the receipts of our committee does not comport with the greatness of the statue or the greatness of the generosity of the French people. I do not know how to account for this except that every man is afraid to give for fear of preventing others from giving." Quoted from "Admiring Objects of Art."

6. *Ibid.*

7. "The Pedestal Art Loan."

8. "Admiring Objects of Art."

9. "Close of the Loan Exhibition," *The New York Times*, January 2, 1884, p. 2.

10. The important exhibitions held by the Society of Decorative Art, New York, are discussed by Christopher P. Monkhouse in an essay in this catalogue entitled "Bric-a-brac at the Pedestal Fund Art Loan Exhibition."

11. The nature of this exhibition and the similarity of its selections to those of the *Pedestal Fund Art Loan Exhibition* were pointed out to the author by Dr. Helmut Leppien, Chief Curator of the Hamburger Kunsthalle.

12. "The Pedestal Art Loan," *The New York Times*, December 16, 1883, p. 5.

13. *Ibid.*

14. "The Pedestal Art Loan," *The New York Times*, December 2, 1883, p. 2.

15. "The Pedestal Art Loan," December 16, 1883.

16. *Ibid.*

PAINTINGS.

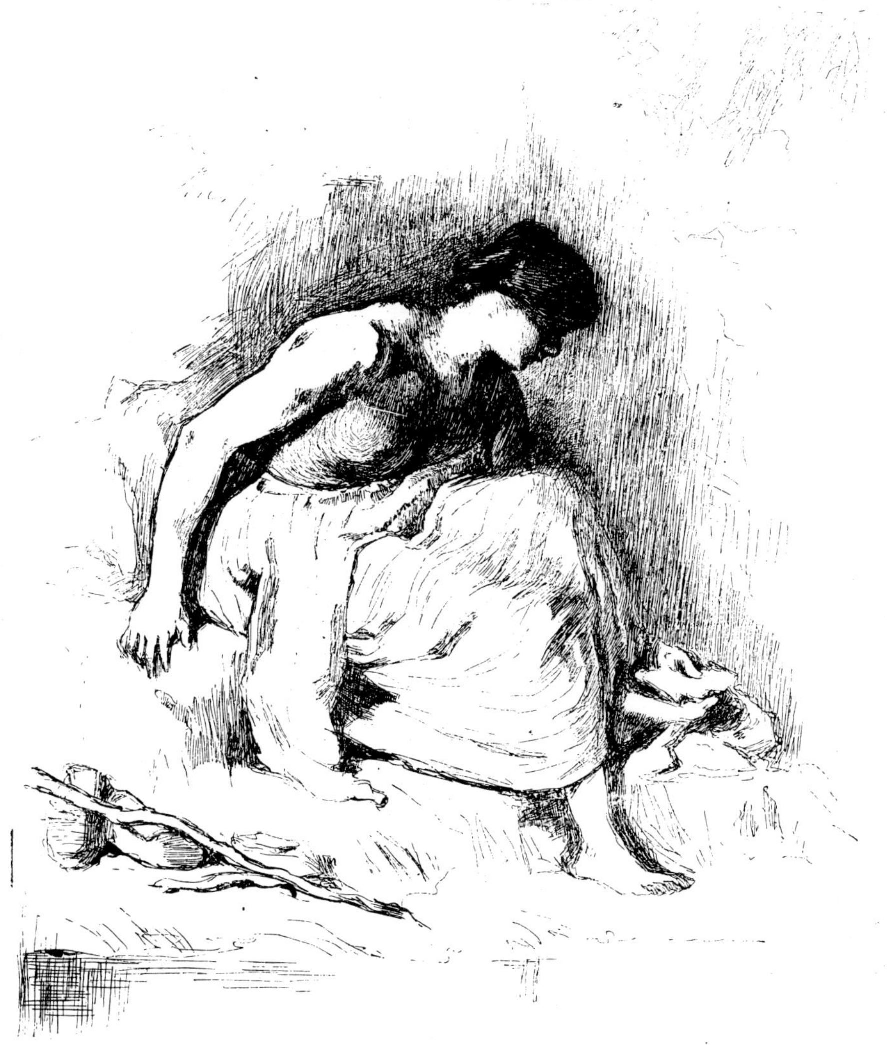

165. MILLET. WOMAN BATHING. FROM ERWIN DAVIS COLLECTION.

FIGS. 1.–9. Illustrations and checklist from the Paintings Section of the *Catalogue of the Pedestal Fund Art Loan Exhibition,* National Academy of Design, New York, 1883

FIG. 1.
JEAN-FRANÇOIS MILLET
Woman Bathing
From Erwin Davis Collection
Drawing by Frederick S. Church

PAINTINGS.

No.		Loaned by
1	MEISSONIER (J. L. E). Water Color. The Cavalier.	Mrs. R. L. Stuart.
2	MUNKACSY. In the Garden.	"
3	COROT (J. B. C.). Landscape.	"
4	DAUBIGNY (C. F.). The Cooper.	Wm. Schaus.
5	COROT (J. B. C.). La Danse des Amours.	Chas. A. Dana.
6	MILLET (J. F.). The Turkey Guardian..	"
7	JACQUE (CHAS.). Sheep and Forest.	"
8	DIAZ (N.). La Mare aux Grenouilles.	"
9	DAUBIGNY (C. F.). On the Seine.	"
10	ROUSSEAU (THEO.). Harvest.	"
11	TROYON (CONSTANT). Holland Landscape, with Cattle.	Miss Catharine Wolfe.
12	DIAZ (N.). Holy Family.	"
13	COROT (J. B. C.). Ville d'Avray.	"
14	HAMON (J. L.). Etruscan Merchant.	"
15	FORTUNY (MARIANO). Water Color. Camels Reposing.	"
16	MEISSONIER (J. L. E.). General and Adjutant.	"
17	BARGUE (C.). Bazi-Bazouk in a Turkish Café.	"
18	BONHEUR (ROSA). Staghound.	"
19	VOLLON (A.). French Farmyard.	"
20	HENNER (J. J.). Listening Nymph.	"
21	PASINI (A.). Fair Day.	Theodore Havemeyer.
22	TROYON (C.).	"
23	LAURENS (J. P.).	"
24	STEVENS (ALFRED).	"
25	CHARLEMONT (E.).	"
26	ETHOFER.	"
27	——	"
28	JETTEL.	"
29	GIERMSKY.	"
30	BRETON (JULES). Brittany Peasant.	John G. Johnson.
31	MILLET (J. F.). Hylas Tempted by the Nymphs.	I. T. Williams.

18

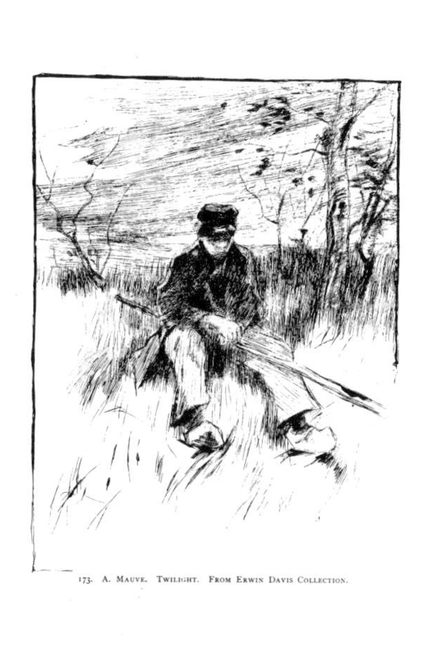

173. A. MAUVE. TWILIGHT. FROM ERWIN DAVIS COLLECTION.

FIG. 2.
ANTON MAUVE, *Twilight*
From Erwin Davis Collection
Drawing by Frederick S. Church

20

No.		Loaned by
32	HILL (C. F.). Landscape.	I. T. Williams.
33	DIAZ (N.). The Lovers.	"
34	MARIS (J.). Turkish Lady.	"
35	MONTICELLI. The Festa.	"
36	MILLET (J. F). The Quarriers.	"
37	ROUSSEAU (THEO.). Landscape.	"
38	MICHEL (GEORGES). Hills of Montmartre.	"
39	VOLLON (A.). Portrait of the Artist's Sister.	"
40	—— On the River.	"
41	JACQUE (CHAS.). Shepherdess.	"
42	MARIS (M.). Corner of the Hague.	"
43	ROYBET (F.). Moorish Captive.	"
44	MARIS (M.). The Flirtation.	"
45	RIBOT (T.). The Studio.	"
46	MILLET (J. F.). Peasant and Child.	Albert Spencer.
47	—— Nude.	"
48	KNAUS (L.). Pigs.	"
49	TROYON (C.). Landscape.	"
50	—— Animals.	"
51	DELACROIX (EUGÉNE). Descent from the Cross.	"
52	FROMENTIN (EUGÉNE). The Rest.	"
53	MONTICELLI. The Pic-nic.	I. T. Williams.
54	COROT (J. B. C.). Twilight.	"
55	DUPRÈ (JULES). Marine.	"
56	BOSBOOM. Cathedral Interior.	"
57	MARIS (J.). Holland Scene.	"
58	RIBOT (T.). The Cook's Assistant.	"
59	BOLDINI. In the Meadow.	G. Reichard.
60	HENNER (J. J.). La Nymphe.	"
61	COUTURE (THOS.). Sketch from the Courtesan.	R. M. Hunt.
62	MILLET (J. F.). Susanne.	"
63	STEVENS (ALFRED). Young Girl.	Moore & Clarke Co.
64	ROYBET (F.). En Grand Seigneur.	"
65	—— Masterless.	"
66	VOLLON (A.). Still Life.	"
67	COURBET (G.). Ocean.	"
68	—— The Valley.	"
69	PASINI (A.). Door-way in Constantinople.	George Kemp.
70	Prayer Rug, Framed. (Not properly belonging among the Paintings).	"
71	CÆSAR DE KOCK. Spring Woods near Paris.	"
72	HENNER (J. J.). The Bather.	S. P. Avery.
73	CAZIN (J. C.). Hagar and Ishmael.	"

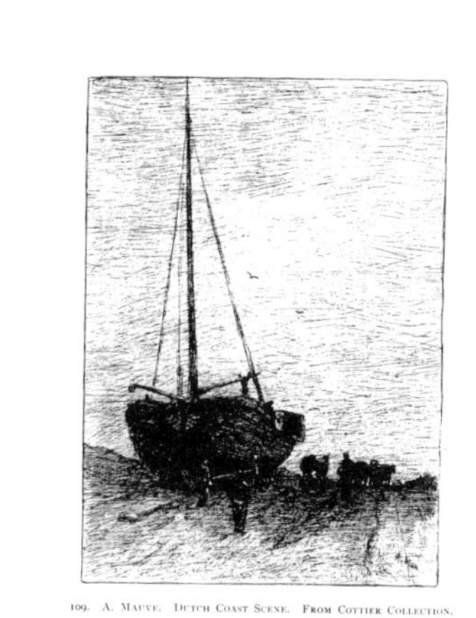

109. A. MAUVE. DUTCH COAST SCENE. FROM COTTIER COLLECTION.

FIG. 3.
ANTON MAUVE, *Dutch Coast Scene*
From Cottier Collection
Drawing by Arthur Quartley

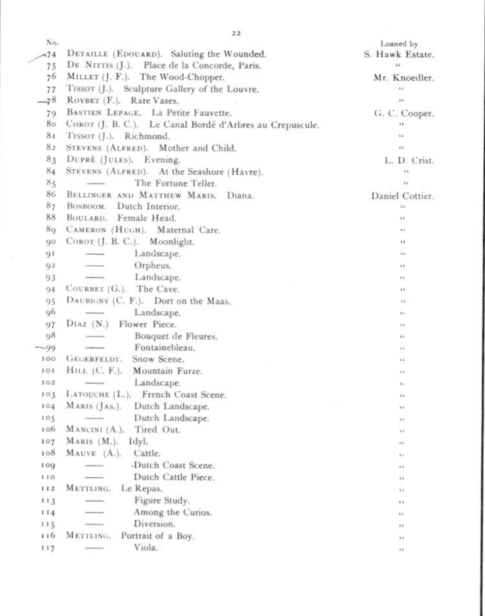

22

No.		Loaned by
74	DETAILLE (EDOUARD). Saluting the Wounded.	S. Hawk Estate.
75	DE NITTIS (J.). Place de la Concorde, Paris.	"
76	MILLET (J. F.). The Wood-Chopper.	Mr. Knoedler.
77	TISSOT (J.). Sculpture Gallery of the Louvre.	"
78	ROYBET (F.). Rare Vases.	"
79	BASTIEN LEPAGE. La Petite Fauvette.	G. C. Cooper.
80	COROT (J. B. C.). Le Canal Bordé d'Arbres au Crepuscule.	"
81	TISSOT (J.). Richmond.	"
82	STEVENS (ALFRED). Mother and Child.	"
83	DUPRÈ (JULES). Evening.	L. D. Crist.
84	STEVENS (ALFRED). At the Seashore (Havre).	"
85	—— The Fortune Teller.	"
86	BELLINGER AND MATTHEW MARIS. Diana.	Daniel Cottier.
87	BOSBOOM. Dutch Interior.	"
88	BOULARD. Female Head.	"
89	CAMERON (HUGH). Maternal Care.	"
90	COROT (J. B. C.). Moonlight.	"
91	—— Landscape.	"
92	—— Orpheus.	"
93	—— Landscape.	"
94	COURBET (G.). The Cave.	"
95	DAUBIGNY (C. F.). Dort on the Maas.	"
96	—— Landscape.	"
97	DIAZ (N.) Flower Piece.	"
98	—— Bouquet de Fleures.	"
99	—— Fontainebleau.	"
100	GEGERFELDT. Snow Scene.	"
101	HILL (C. F.). Mountain Furze.	"
102	—— Landscape.	"
103	LATOUCHE (L.). French Coast Scene.	"
104	MARIS (JAS.). Dutch Landscape.	"
105	—— Dutch Landscape.	"
106	MANCINI (A.). Tired Out.	"
107	MARIS (M.). Idyl.	"
108	MAUVE (A.). Cattle.	"
109	—— Dutch Coast Scene.	"
110	—— Dutch Cattle Piece.	"
112	METTLING. Le Repas.	"
113	—— Figure Study.	"
114	—— Among the Curios.	"
115	—— Diversion.	"
116	METTLING. Portrait of a Boy.	"
117	—— Viola.	"

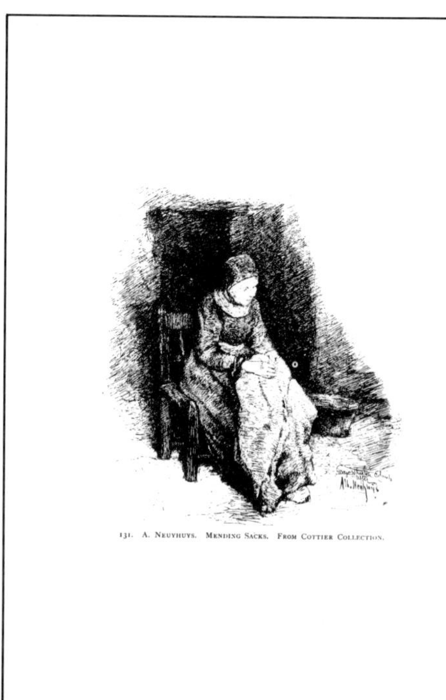

131. A. NEUYHUYS. MENDING SACKS. FROM COTTIER COLLECTION.

FIG. 4.
ALBERT NEUHUYS, *Mending Sacks*
From Cottier Collection
Drawing by George W. Edwards

24

No.		Loaned by
118	Mettling. After Rembrandt.	Daniel Cottier.
119	Michel (Georges). View in Holland.	"
120	—— Landscape.	"
121	—— Landscape.	"
122	Monticelli. Italian Scene.	"
123	—— Italian Fête.	"
124	—— Fête Musicale.	"
125	—— Landscape.	"
126	—— Italian Terrace.	"
127	—— La Festa.	"
128	—— Gateway.	"
129	—— The Barn.	"
130	Neuyhuys (A.). The Lesson.	"
131	—— Mending Sacks.	"
132	Reynolds (W.). Cathedral Town in France.	"
133	Ribot (J.). Guitarist.	"
134	—— The Vendean.	"
135	Rousseau (Philippe). Still Life.	"
136	Roybet (F.). The King's Kitchen.	"
137	—— Arab Girl.	"
138	—— Return from the Chase.	"
139	Torna (Oscar). Moonlight.	"
140	Valton. Donkey Ride.	"
141	Vollon (A.). Study of a Child.	"
142	—— Donkey.	"
143	—— Portrait of Rembrandt.	"
144	Courbet (G). Music.	Erwin Davis.
145	Diaz (N). Flowers.	"
146	Rousseau (Th.). Trees.	"
147	Ribot (T.). Head.	"
148	Wahlberg. Landscape.	"
149	Corot (J. B. C.). Landscape.	"
150	Gericault. Dead Lamb.	"
151	Michel (Georges). Landscape.	"
152	Henner (J. J.). The Bath.	"
153	Manet. Boy with Sword.	"
154	Dagnan Bouveret. Child and Vase.	"
155	Diaz. Rocky Gorge.	"
156	Kowalski. Napoleon in Russia.	"
157	Vollon (A.). Fruit.	"
158	Corot (J. B. C.). Landscape.	"
159	Ribot (T.). The Lesson.	"
160	Dupré. Landscape.	"

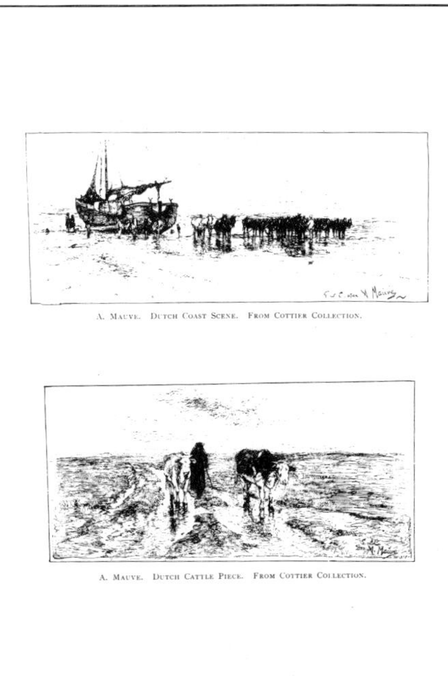

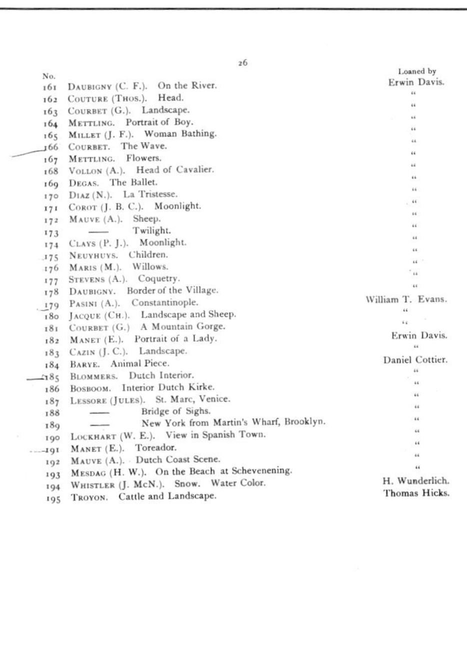

26

No.		Loaned by
161	Daubigny (C. F.). On the River.	Erwin Davis.
162	Couture (Thos.). Head.	"
163	Courbet (G.). Landscape.	"
164	Mettling. Portrait of Boy.	"
165	Millet (J. F.). Woman Bathing.	"
166	Courbet. The Wave.	"
167	Mettling. Flowers.	"
168	Vollon (A.). Head of Cavalier.	"
169	Degas. The Ballet.	"
170	Diaz (N.). La Tristesse.	"
171	Corot (J. B. C.). Moonlight.	"
172	Mauve (A.). Sheep.	"
173	—— Twilight.	"
174	Clays (P. J.). Moonlight.	"
175	Neuyhuys. Children.	"
176	Maris (M.). Willows.	"
177	Stevens (A.). Coquetry.	"
178	Daubigny. Border of the Village.	"
179	Pasini (A.). Constantinople.	William T. Evans.
180	Jacque (Ch.). Landscape and Sheep.	"
181	Courbet (G.) A Mountain Gorge.	"
182	Manet (E.). Portrait of a Lady.	Erwin Davis.
183	Cazin (J. C.). Landscape.	"
184	Barye. Animal Piece.	Daniel Cottier.
185	Blommers. Dutch Interior.	"
186	Bosboom. Interior Dutch Kirke.	"
187	Lessore (Jules). St. Marc, Venice.	"
188	—— Bridge of Sighs.	"
189	—— New York from Martin's Wharf, Brooklyn.	"
190	Lockhart (W. E.). View in Spanish Town.	"
191	Manet (E.). Toreador.	"
192	Mauve (A.). Dutch Coast Scene.	"
193	Mesdag (H. W.). On the Beach at Schevenening.	"
194	Whistler (J. McN.). Snow. Water Color.	H. Wunderlich.
195	Troyon. Cattle and Landscape.	Thomas Hicks.

Fig. 5.
Anton Mauve, *Dutch Coast Scene*
From Cottier Collection
Drawing by George W. Edwards

Fig. 6.
Anton Mauve, *Dutch Cattle Piece*
From Cottier Collection
Drawing by George W. Edwards

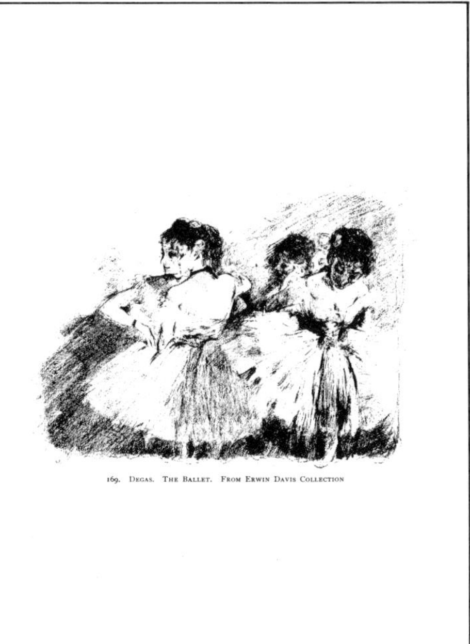

Fig. 7.
Edgar Degas, *The Ballet*
From Erwin Davis Collection
Drawing by Robert Blum

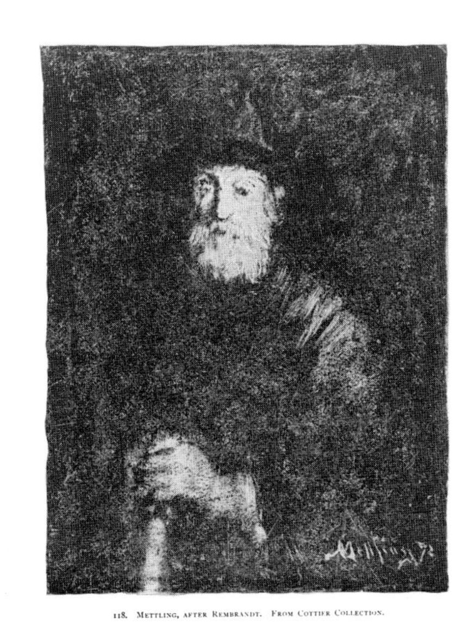

Fig. 8.
Louis Mettling, *After Rembrandt*
From Cottier Collection
Drawing by William Merritt Chase

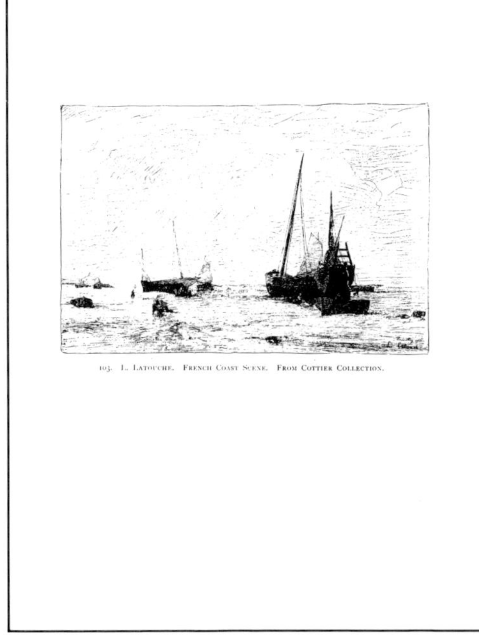

Fig. 9.
Louis Latouche
French Coast Scene
From Cottier Collection
Drawing by Arthur Quartley

European Paintings at the Pedestal Fund Art Loan Exhibition: An American Revolution in Taste

Maureen C. O'Brien

A *New York Times* critic previewing the kaleidoscope of displays at the *Pedestal Fund Art Loan Exhibition* of 1883 wrote: "No single department is so impressive as the pictures. Well may an irascible Parisian, who loves pictures and hates Americans, exclaim that we drain France of her finest works and never give them back."[1] This wry observation about the donors of the statue for which the exhibition had been organized held a certain amount of truth. In recent decades America had proved itself happy to provide a haven for French paintings of substantial importance and value and had spawned a cadre of wealthy and knowledgeable collectors who not only commissioned paintings directly from French artists, but also paid considerable sums for pictures found at the annual exhibitions in Paris. The London *Art Journal* reported that in 1883 alone, Americans spent $1,754,000[2] at the Paris Salon to add to collections that were "almost exclusively confined to modern works, the majority being of the French school."[3] Although the English journal attributed this predilection to the fact that the majority of the art dealers were French or German in origin, a more impartial observer would also have recognized as factors America's aesthetic and intellectual preferences and its perception of the investment potential (and decorative value) of French painting. Furthermore, there was a bias toward French painting among influential American dealers such as George A. Lucas and Samuel P. Avery and within the New York showrooms of M. Knoedler & Co., Messrs. Schaus, and Cottier & Co.

Ironically, even if one were to acknowledge the importance of the Barbizon paintings, now familiar to Americans and Frenchmen alike through their inclusion in the *Expositions Universelles* of 1855 and 1867 in Paris, it is unlikely that either the irascible Parisian or the average New York art amateur would have described the pictures at the Pedestal Fund exhibition as a threat to France's patrimony. The show bore so little evidence of America's Salon acquisitions that year that another reviewer was compelled to describe it as a mistake, a sacrifice to the taste of connoisseurs, a collection that appealed to "far too few picture lovers and picture buyers here."[4] These conflicting opinions offered a succinct portrayal of the critical climate that greeted modern European paintings in America in 1883. On the one hand, they were judged by popular and traditional taste that sought pictures with "intellectual" content and reliable investment value. On the other, in a small but growing sphere, they had begun to come under the scrutiny of "connoisseurs" who preferred the work of artists of the imagination, even if they were still unproven in the marketplace.

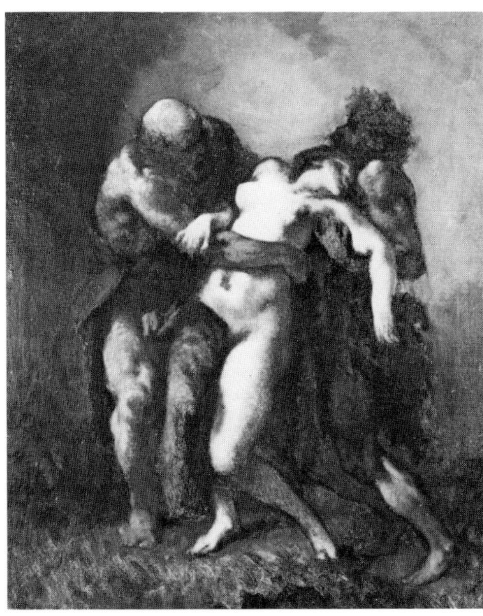

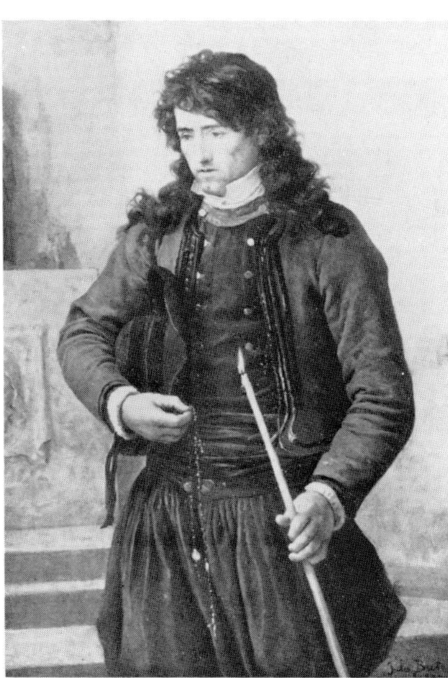

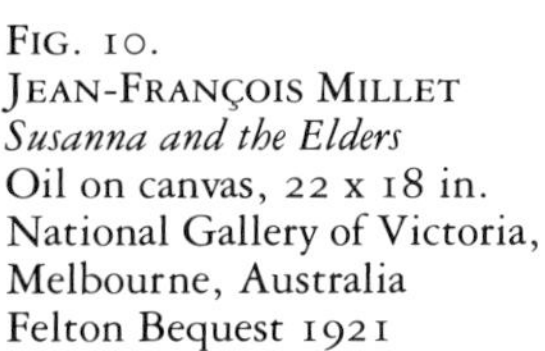

FIG. 10.
JEAN-FRANÇOIS MILLET
Susanna and the Elders
Oil on canvas, 22 x 18 in.
National Gallery of Victoria,
Melbourne, Australia
Felton Bequest 1921

FIG. 11. (*right*)
JULES BRETON, *Brittany Peasant*
Oil on canvas, 49 x 33 in.
Current location unknown

Only an enlightened New York observer, or a close reader of contemporary American art and literary periodicals, would have been aware that a small circle of dealers, collectors, and critics now shared the convictions espoused by young European-trained American artists. These were the connoisseurs responsible for the choice of paintings at the Pedestal Fund exhibition — principally, the painters William Merritt Chase and James Carroll Beckwith, collectors Erwin Davis and Ichabod T. Williams, and dealer Daniel Cottier. Their selections were not only examples from the latest French schools but also the work of Dutch, Swedish, Belgian, Austrian, Scottish, Italian, Polish, Spanish, and German artists whose participation in the currents of international modernism could be identified in qualities of imagination and color and paint handling that still eluded the average viewer.

The artists whose work dominated the paintings gallery at the *Pedestal Fund Art Loan Exhibition* were Jean-Baptiste-Camille Corot, Narcisse Diaz, Adolphe Monticelli, Antoine Vollon, Louis Mettling, Jean-François Millet, Gustave Courbet, Alfred Stevens, Ferdinand Roybet, Théodule Ribot, and Anton Mauve. There were no less than eight paintings each by Corot, Diaz, Mettling, Millet, Monticelli, and Vollon, and six or more by each of the others. The show included a representative selection of the "modern Dutchmen," Bernardus Johannes Blommers, Johannes Bosboom, Jacob and Matthew Maris, Hendrik Mesdag, and Albert Neuhuys, as well as a number of Barbizon-influenced landscape painters from Austria, Belgium, and Sweden. There was also a smattering of "'impressionists' of the most pronounced kind — Manet . . . Degas . . . and Whistler,"[5] and a handful of the less pronounced kind: James-J.-J. Tissot, Giovanni Boldini, Giuseppe de Nittis, Alfred Stevens, Jules Bastien-Lepage, Pascal Dagnan-Bouveret, Jean-Jacques Henner, and Jean-Charles Cazin. The exhibition's aesthetic imperative was established by works of Eugène Delacroix, Théodore Géricault, and Thomas Couture, the latter represented by *Sketch for The Courtesan,* loaned by Richard Morris Hunt, a painting that visually and symbolically liberated the other selections from the requirements of "finish."

Mounted nine years after the first Impressionist exhibition in Paris, the Pedestal Fund show was not avant-garde by French standards. Nor did it provide the first opportunity for Americans to view a selection of works by the Impressionists. In September 1883, seventeen paintings by Edouard Manet, Claude Monet, Camille Pissarro, Auguste Renoir, and Alfred Sisley had been shown in the French section of the International Exhibition of Art and Industry in Bos-

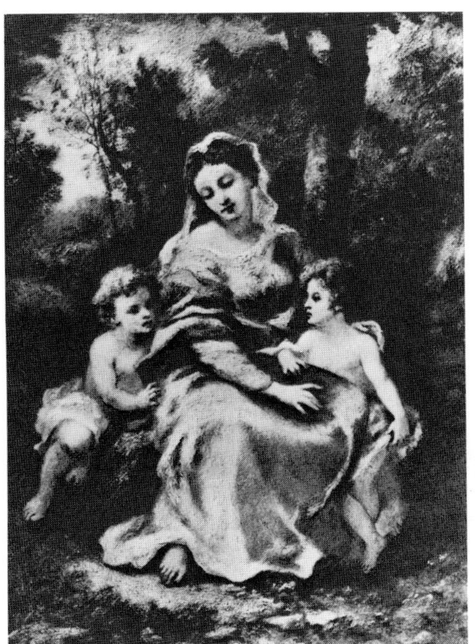

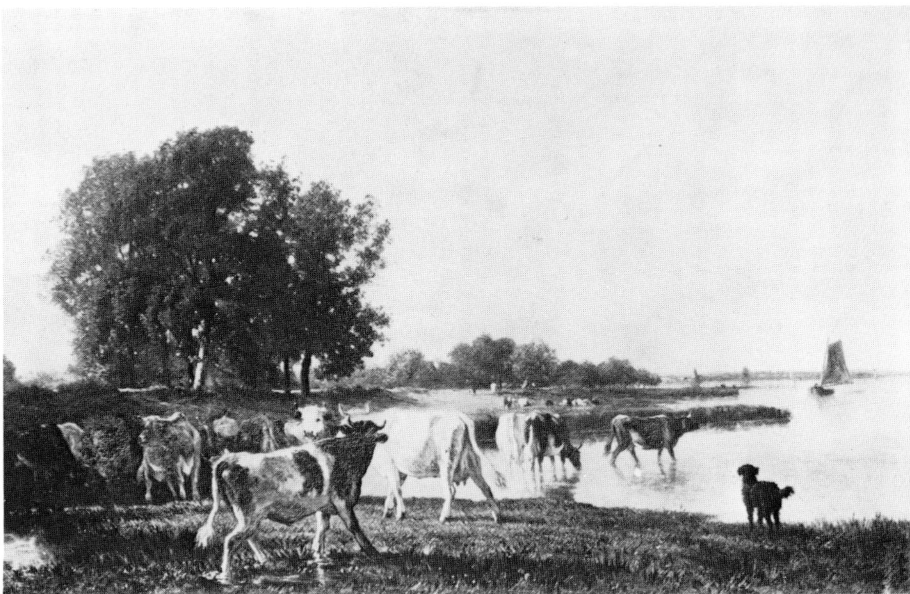

FIG. 12. (*left*)
NARCISSE VIRGILE DIAZ DE LA PEÑA, *Holy Family*
Oil on panel, 12 1/4 x 9 1/2 in.
Current location unknown

FIG. 13.
CONSTANT TROYON, *Holland Landscape with Cattle*
Oil on canvas, 40 x 59 3/8 in.
Current location unknown

ton.[6] Three years later, in 1886, the Paris dealer Durand-Ruel provided an even more dramatic opportunity for the revision of American taste by shipping some three hundred works to New York and displaying them first at the American Art Association and then at the National Academy of Design in *Special Exhibition: Works in Oil and Pastel by the Impressionists of Paris.*[7] Compared to these two events, the Pedestal Fund exhibition seems restrained to modern eyes. But examined in the light of the Philadelphia Centennial Exposition of 1876 and the international exhibitions of the preceding decade in France and Germany, the Pedestal Fund show was a strong statement of the revolution in taste underway in New York. The exhibition's organizers, unable to rely on the extensive resources of a major Paris gallery, and working in a city where special art events were traditionally and predictably arranged by a relatively closed committee of private collectors and academicians, were nevertheless able to represent artists, motives, and techniques that were not predictable and defined — and to reveal the transition from narrative to "imaginative" painting in nineteenth-century art. If their selections were not remarkable to admirers of Monet and Renoir, they were assuredly surprising to patrons of Adolphe William Bouguereau and Jean-Léon Gérôme; and this was particularly true in New York, where "advanced taste" was a frontier willingly ceded to Boston. Through the efforts of a group of young artists who combined enthusiasm and organizational skill with a distinctive, international point of view, the *Pedestal Fund Art Loan Exhibition* marked a turning point in American taste. It succeeded by relying heavily on a few lenders whose names were unfamiliar to New York's distinguished collectors and by supplementing their loans with careful selections from a number of traditional sources.

In the early 1880s, the best American collections from New York to San Francisco were lavishly documented in *The Art Treasures of America*,[8] a series of profiles by painter and art critic Earl Shinn, who wrote under the *nom de plume* of Edward Strahan. What amateurs in New York had known from newspaper articles and reproductions and had glimpsed at the 1876 *Centennial Loan Exhibition of Paintings, Selected from Private Art Galleries* and the *Loan Exhibition in Aid of the Society of Decorative Art* of 1877 and its counterpart in 1878 — all held at the National Academy of Design — had become public record, illustrated by drawings and photogravures and vividly described by Strahan in his informed and literate prose. In 1883, America's prominent collectors had substantial investments in the paintings of French Salon laureates Bouguereau, Alexandre Cabanel, Edouard Detaille, Gérôme, Jean-Louis-Ernest Meissonier, Hugues

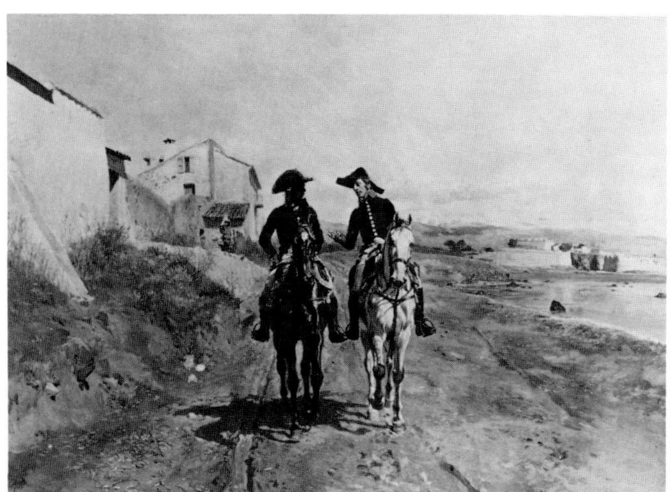

FIG. 14.
JEAN-LOUIS-ERNEST MEISSONIER
A General and His Aide-de-Camp, 1869
Oil on panel, 7 3/4 x 10 7/8 in.
The Metropolitan Museum of Art, New York, Catharine Lorillard Wolfe Bequest, 1887. Catharine Lorillard Wolfe Collection

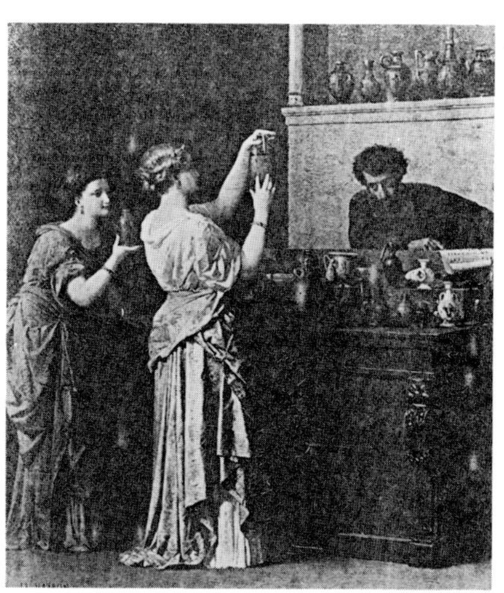

FIG. 15.
JEAN-LOUIS HAMON
Etruscan Merchant
Oil on canvas, 19 x 16 in.
Current location unknown

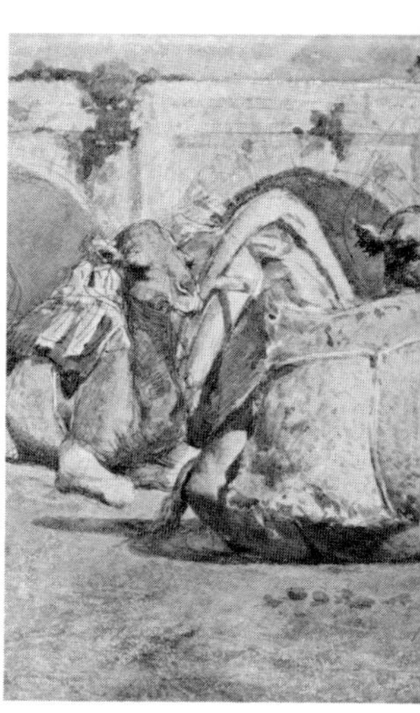

FIG. 16.
MARIANO FORTUNY Y CARBO
Camels Reposing, Tangiers
Watercolor on paper, 8 x 14 in.
The Metropolitan Museum of Art,

Merle, and Georges Vibert. They similarly preferred the landscapes and the genre and history painting of the Germans Andreas and Oswald Achenbach, Carl Becker, Ludwig Knaus, Meyer von Bremen, and Adolf Schreyer. For a less ponderous blend of anecdote, technique, and *la vie moderne,* Americans favored the popular Spanish, Venetian, and Orientalist subjects of Mariano Fortuny y Carbo, Raimundo de Madrazo y Garreta, Martin Rico y Ortega, Ignacio de Leon y Escosura, Eduardo Zamacoïs, and Felix Ziem, or the modish cabinet and conversation pieces of Florent Willems, Auguste Toulmouche, Antoine Emile Plassan, Marie-François Firmin-Girard, Charles Baugniet, Jean-Baptiste Béranger, and Edouard Frère. In sheer number, the paintings of these artists resoundingly outweighed those of their imitators in Strahan's extensive index to American collections.

Nevertheless, there was a growing market, first established in Providence and Boston in the 1850s, for French painting of the Barbizon School — in particular Millet's homages to French peasant life and Corot's tonal landscapes. By the end of the 1870s, many of the same collections that boasted sophisticated Salon subjects had also added the simpler landscapes and animal pictures of Charles-François Daubigny, Jules Dupré, Charles Jacque, Théodore Rousseau, and Constant Troyon. With the exception of Eastman Johnson and landscape painters Frederic E. Church, Albert Bierstadt, William Trost Richards, and Sanford R. Gifford, American artists appeared infrequently on the published rolls of their country's great collections.

What *The Art Treasures of America* did not reveal was the existence of an undercurrent in American art and American collecting that was slowly eroding the conservative image documented in its pages. In May 1878, following the first exhibition of the Society of American Artists, an editor of *Scribner's Monthly* commented that suddenly the future seemed full of promise for America's painters and sculptors. He quoted a letter from a young American artist in Paris who spoke of the encouragement and inspiration he now sensed coming from home: "In New York," the artist wrote, "it is like taking part in a revolution."[9] Clarence Cook, another chronicler of recent developments in painting and the decorative arts, could easily have named some of the participants in this counterculture: painter Helena de Kay, her husband Richard Watson Gilder (editor of *Scribner's*), Augustus Saint-Gaudens (the likely author of the letter from Paris), Wyatt Eaton, and Walter Shirlaw — names that would also figure in the organization of the *Pedestal Fund Art Loan Exhibition* and would help shape its presentation of European paintings.

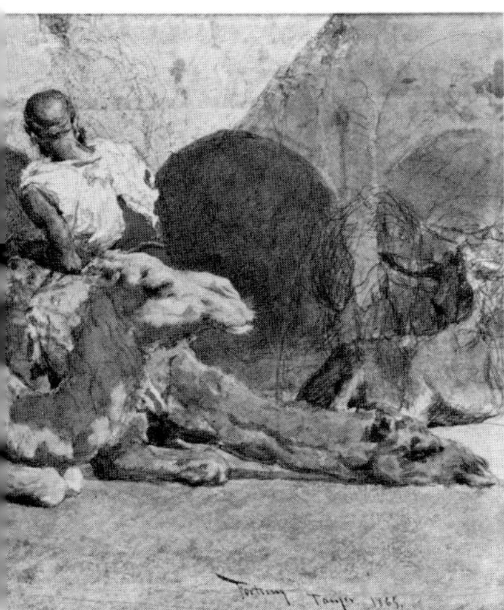

New York, Catharine Lorillard Wolfe Bequest, 1887. Catharine Lorillard Wolfe Collection

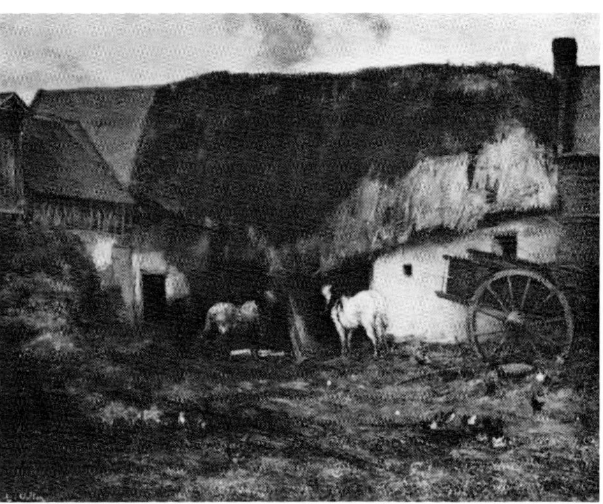

FIG. 17.
ANTOINE VOLLON
French Farmyard (La Basse Cour)
Oil on canvas, 37 7/8 x 46 3/8 in.
Current location unknown

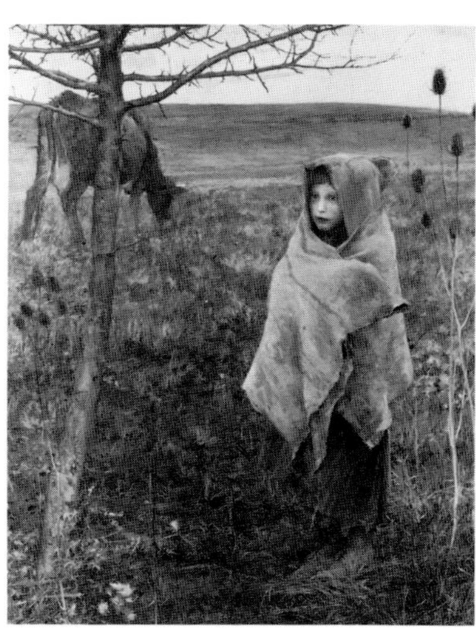

FIG. 18.
JULES BASTIEN-LEPAGE
Pauvre Fauvette
Oil on canvas
Glasgow Art Gallery and Museum, Glasgow, Scotland

The list of lenders to the paintings section of the Pedestal Fund show appears to consist of names already familiar from society benefits of this type. But closer scrutiny reveals that such noteworthy collectors as James H. Stebbins, August Belmont, Mrs. Paran Stevens, Morris K. Jesup, J. W. Pinchot, Robert L. Cutting, John Jacob and William Astor, and Jordan Mott are not mentioned — an indication that many of America's "best" paintings had not been made available. Nevertheless, the list prominently features Catharine Lorillard Wolfe, the collector and philanthropist who had served on the Special Committee on Pictures of the 1877 Society of Decorative Art exhibition and on the general committee for the Society's benefit the following year. Collectors Theodore Havemeyer, Samuel Hawk, Thomas Hicks, Robert L. Stuart, and the dealers William Schaus and Samuel P. Avery are also listed, and they had assisted the 1876 Centennial Loan Exhibition in New York, as well as subsequent shows, with loans of paintings and organizational support. Another familiar name is that of Richard Morris Hunt, who had sent his Millet, *Susanna and the Elders* (fig. 10; pl. XXVIII), "a tragedy almost too fearful to be looked at,"[10] to the Decorative Art show in 1877.

It was in the Committee on Painting and Sculpture, however, that the most dramatic shift in direction could be detected: the names of Jesup, Stebbins, Pinchot, Parke Godwin, John Taylor Johnston, John Wolfe, and Cornelius Vanderbilt were missing (the last three bumped up to Honorary Vice President), and the position owed them by birthright, education, and tradition had been ceded to a panel of artists. The reins were now in the hands of Beckwith, Chase, Saint-Gaudens, Weir, Carl Brandt, Rosina Emmet, Frederick Dielman, J. Henry Harper, Arthur Quartley, and J. Q. A. Ward — a crew that had distinct ideas about the paintings that would make the most appropriate tribute to Frédéric Auguste Bartholdi, France, and America's independence.

When the first visitors entered the south gallery of the National Academy of Design on the evening of December 3, 1883, they found not a single painting by Bouguereau, Cabanel, Gérôme, or Merle and no trace of Achenbach, Meyer von Bremen, or Schreyer. Jules Breton, whose *Pardon in Brittany*[11] was one of the great paintings in the Catharine Lorillard Wolfe collection, was represented by *Brittany Peasant*[12] (fig. 11), loaned by John G. Johnson of Philadelphia. The rough, long-haired penitent would have been more at home in Courbet's *Funeral at Ornans* than in the wholesome French countryside populated by Breton's handsome peasants. Ignoring the "masterpieces" by Cabanel, Charles Chaplin, Paul Cot, and Jules Worms that were in Miss Wolfe's power to lend, the

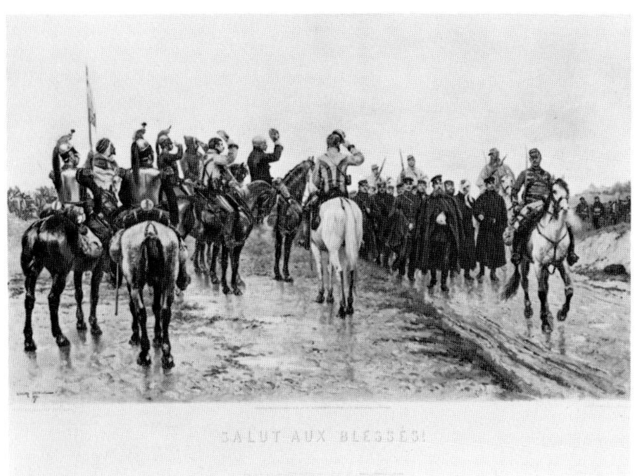

FIG. 19.
EDOUARD DETAILLE
Salut aux blessés, 1876
Current location unknown
Photogravure by Goupil & Cie;
courtesy Anne S. K. Brown Military
Collection, Providence, Rhode Island

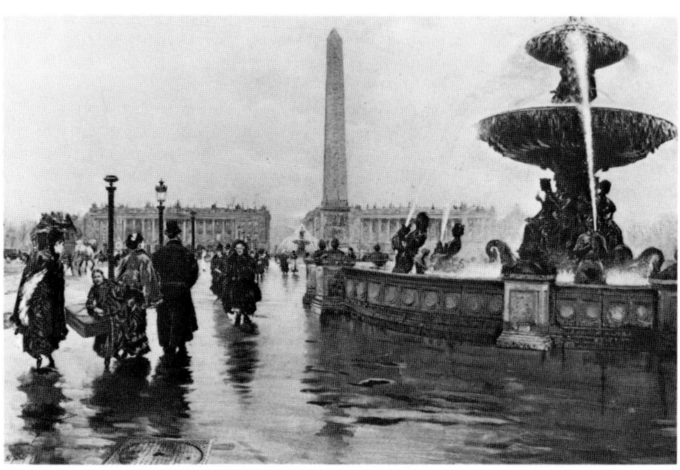

FIG. 20.
GIUSEPPE DE NITTIS
Place de la Concorde, 1875
Current location unknown
Photogravure from Armand Silvestre,
The Gallery of Contemporary Art, 1884

committee instead looked for paintings that were modern in technique and intimate in scale and intent. From Miss Wolfe's collection they selected Diaz's *Holy Family*[13] (fig. 12); Troyon's *Holland Landscape with Cattle*[14] (fig. 13); Corot's *Ville d'Avray* (cat. no. 13; pl. VIII); the small and unpretentious Meissonier study, *A General and His Aide-de-Camp,*[15] two men on horseback in the sun-drenched light of Antibes (fig. 14; pl. XXI); and Jean-Louis Hamon's painting *Etruscan Merchant*[16] (fig. 15). Charles Bargue's colorful *A Bashi-Bazouk* (cat. no. 1; pl. I) and Mariano Fortuny's delicate watercolor *Camels Reposing, Tangiers*[17] (fig. 16), formerly in the collection of Gérôme, were technically fresh and uncomplicated examples by these artists and among the few Orientalist subjects in the exhibition. Rosa Bonheur, whose grand *Horse Fair* and *Rendezvous de Chasse* were both owned by New Yorkers in 1883,[18] was represented by the painting *A Limier-Briquet Hound (Staghound)* (cat. no. 6; pl. III), depicting one of the many pets she cherished at her country estate at Chevilly, France. Jean-Jacques Henner's *A Bather (Listening Nymph)* (cat. no. 38; pl. XIV), painted with the Correggiesque *sfumato* that had won him the admiration of both French and American painters, and a stunning *French Farmyard*[19] (fig. 17) by Vollon, whom Strahan had called the "most distinguished of the 'impressionists,'"[20] completed the Wolfe contribution.

Theodore A. Havemeyer, the brother of H. O. Havemeyer and Vice President of the American Sugar Refining Company, was another lender prominent in New York society. An avid golfer and sportsman and an active supporter of The Metropolitan Museum of Art and the Museum of Natural History, Havemeyer also collected rare musical instruments.[21] Perhaps as a result of his marriage to Emilie de Losey, daughter of the Austrian Consul, and his own subsequent appointment as Consul General for the Austrian Empire, Havemeyer had built an impressive collection of Austrian and German paintings. Amid the more obvious choices of works by Hans Makart, Franz Adam, and August von Pettenkofen in the Havemeyer collection were artists little known to most American amateurs but of interest to young European-trained artists such as Chase and Beckwith. From Havemeyer they borrowed a painting by the Austrian Eugen Jettel,[22] whose lowland landscapes with cattle had won awards in 1869 at Vienna's *Grosse internationale Kunstausstellung* and the first *Internationale Kunstausstellung* in Munich, and had gone on to acclaim at the Paris Salon and the 1878 *Exposition Universelle.* Eduard Charlemont, an Austrian artist invited to participate in the 1882 *Exposition Internationale* at Georges Petit's rue de Sèze gallery, Paris, was represented by a little painting of a cavalier seated at a library

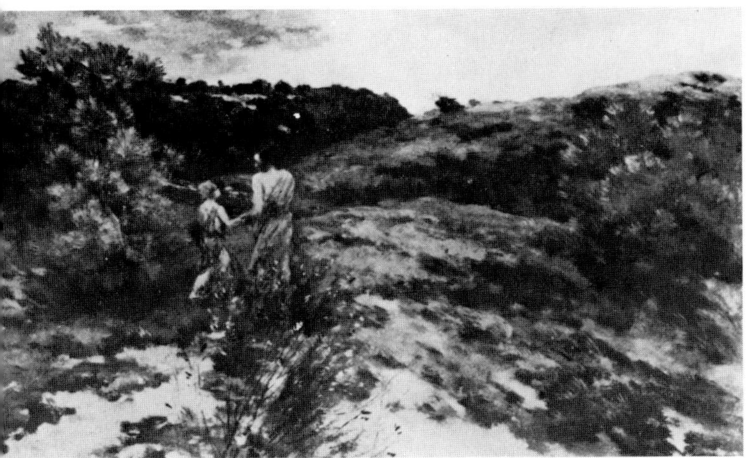

Fig. 21.
Jean-Charles Cazin
Hagar and Ishmael
Oil on canvas, 26 x 32 in.
Current location unknown

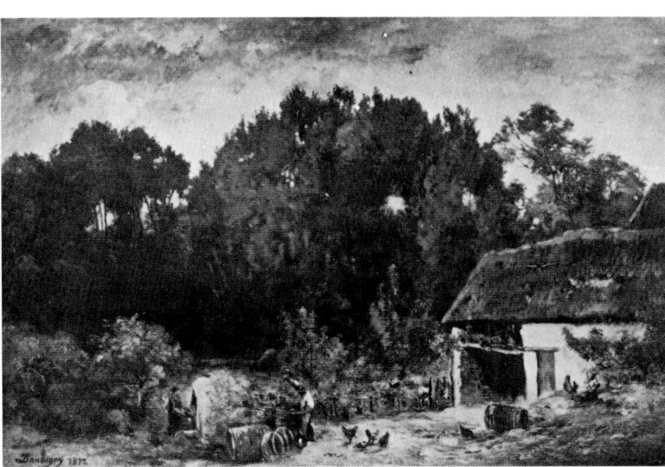

Fig. 22.
Charles-François Daubigny
The Cooper
Oil on canvas, 45 x 65 1/2 in.
Current location unknown

table.[23] Two Italian genre scenes by Theodore Ethofer,[24] another Austrian who, like Chase, had exhibited at the 1879 *Internationale Kunstausstellung* in Munich, were included, as was a work by Alberto Pasini[25] and a Troyon *Study of Sheep.*[26] Havemeyer also agreed to lend Jean-Paul Laurens's *Benvenuto Cellini Visiting Charles VII*,[27] one of his historical genre subjects, and an early painting by Stevens, *At the Pawnshop* (cat. no. 79; pl. XXXVII), which had already been shown in New York at the Centennial Loan Exhibition of 1876.

The most unusual of Havemeyer's loans was the work of a young Polish painter of the Munich School whose early death cut short a promising career. Maksymilian Gierymski's *Riding to the Hunt*[28] was similar in theme to a subject that had been exhibited by the artist at the Kaiser's Salon, Berlin, of 1870 and the Vienna international exhibition of 1871. In 1874 *Polowanie "par force" na Jelenia*, a more elaborate version of a hunt scene in the time of Louis XV, was exhibited at the *Kunstausstellung der koeniglichen Akademie der Künste* in Berlin and was acquired for the Nationalgalerie, Berlin, that year.[29] Gierymski's reputation was at its peak in 1874, the year of his death, when Chase was fully involved in Munich student life. Rare in American collections, his painting was an example of the type of work in the Pedestal Fund show that had special meaning to "young artists with 'convictions.'"[30]

Peter Cooper's nephew, George Campbell Cooper, whose sister Julia was involved in the support of the Society of Decorative Art, loaned Tissot's *Richmond Bridge* (cat. no. 83; pl. XXXVIII), a picture of the artist's companion, Mrs. Kathleen Newton, fashionably dressed and seated on a bridge at the River Thames.[31] He also sent Stevens's *Mother and Child,* possibly the one later owned by Chase (*La Jeune Mère*; cat. no. 80),[32] and a landscape by Corot entitled *Canal bordé d'arbres au crépuscule.* A member of the Grolier Club and "an authority on art matters,"[33] Cooper, whose print collection was later given to Cooper Union,[34] provided the only work by Bastien-Lepage in the 1883 exhibition. *Pauvre Fauvette*, a version of the painting that was purchased by the London collector J. Staats Forbes (fig. 18),[35] was featured along with Degas's *Ballet Dancers* (*The Ballet*) in a sketch of the exhibition's "new art" in the New York *Daily Graphic* (see fig. 5, p. 77). Critics who had seen Bastien-Lepage's monumental *Joan of Arc,*[36] then in the Erwin Davis collection, expected better work from "one of the rising young masters of France,"[37] but his popularity among American artists warranted his inclusion in the show, and few if any other examples were available in New York at that time.

Three paintings were loaned by the widow of sugar refiner Robert L. Stu-

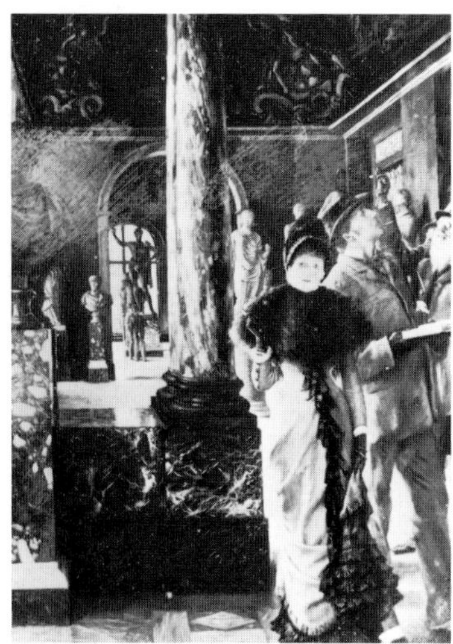

FIG. 23.
JAMES-JACQUES-JOSEPH TISSOT
Visiteurs étrangers au Louvre
Current location unknown
Photograph from an album of Tissot's paintings, vol. 3, no. 21; private collection, United States

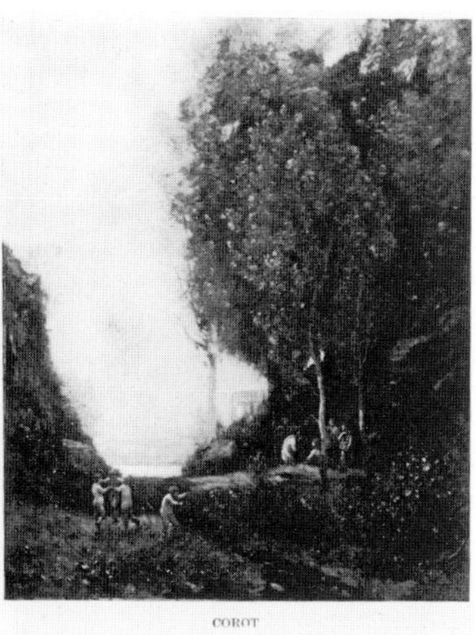

FIG. 24.
JEAN-BAPTISTE-CAMILLE COROT
Le Soir (La Danse des Amours), 1866
Oil on canvas, 54 x 44 in.
Museum Folkwang, Essen, West Germany
Photograph from John La Farge, *The Higher Life in Art*, 1908

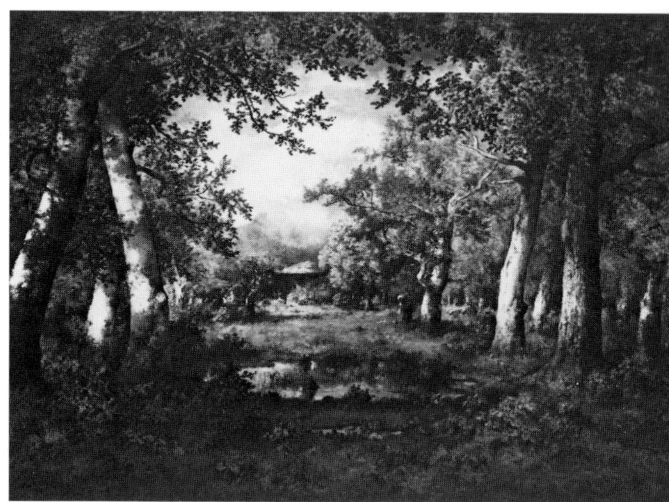

FIG. 25.
NARCISSE VIRGILE DIAZ DE LA PEÑA
La Mare aux Grenouilles
Oil on panel, 31 1/8 x 41 1/2 in.
The Corcoran Gallery of Art, Washington, D.C.,
William A. Clark Collection

art who, unlike the majority of New York's prominent art amateurs, had a considerable number of American paintings in his collection.[38] Selections from the Stuart collection included Michael Munkácsy's light-filled outdoor scene *Luncheon in the Garden* (cat. no. 68), Corot's *Landscape and Figures* (cat. no. 14), and Meissonier's 1872 watercolor self-portrait *The Cavalier* (cat. no. 54; pl. XXII), "a truculent capitaine in a morion helmet and a grey dress of Louis XIII,"[39] which Stuart had purchased at a sale of foreign paintings contributed by artists in aid of the Chicago Fire sufferers and had previously shown in New York's Centennial Loan Exhibition of 1876. Both the *Cavalier* and Miss Wolfe's *General and His Aide-de-Camp,* while chosen to demonstrate painterly qualities obscured by Meissonier's more important works, were denied a place of honor by the Pedestal Fund exhibition's hanging committee (Chase, Beckwith, and Louis Comfort Tiffany), and were installed in a corridor under the staircase at the National Academy.

Edouard Detaille's renowned portrayal of military courtesy during the Franco-Prussian War, *Salut aux blessés*[40] (fig. 19), showing French soldiers saluting wounded German troops, was loaned by the estate of Samuel Hawk, the New York hotelier who had commissioned it. Painted and sent to Hawk in 1876, the canvas was returned to Paris for the 1877 Salon, where Detaille retouched the uniforms to portray a salute to Austrian soldiers at Solferino. Hawk, the fondly remembered proprietor of the St. Nicholas Hotel, had a collection that mixed Hudson River School paintings with works by Franz Defregger, Meyer von Bremen, Wilhelm von Kaulbach, and Adolf Schreyer, balanced by the requisite examples of Bouguereau, Cabanel, and Charles Chaplin. He made two trips to Europe, in 1875 and 1878, remaining abroad for about a year each time.[41] Like the Detaille painting, Giuseppe de Nittis's *Place de la Concorde* may have been purchased during the first trip. It was not among the twelve works exhibited at the 1878 *Exposition Universelle* by de Nittis,[42] an Italian who had participated in the early Impressionist exhibitions. Already considered a "celebrated" painting when it was exhibited at the Pedestal Fund show, the *Place de la Concorde* owned by Hawk was possibly the one reproduced in a photogravure by Goupil (fig. 20).[43] Cook later described this particular work as one in which the artist "showed the vivid realism of his talent, seizing as if by instinct upon the essential character of the place, and transporting us by magic, as it were, to the remembered scene. . . . Here, as often in his pictures, it is not the place itself

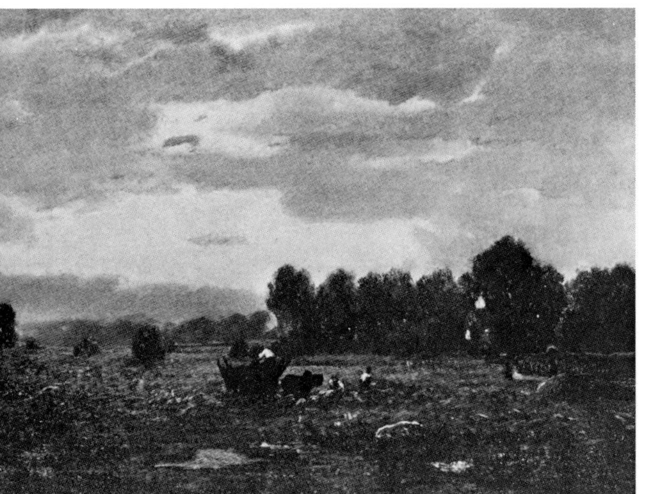

FIG. 26.
THEODORE ROUSSEAU
The Harvest Field
Oil on canvas, 16 1/2 x 24 3/4 in.
Current location unknown

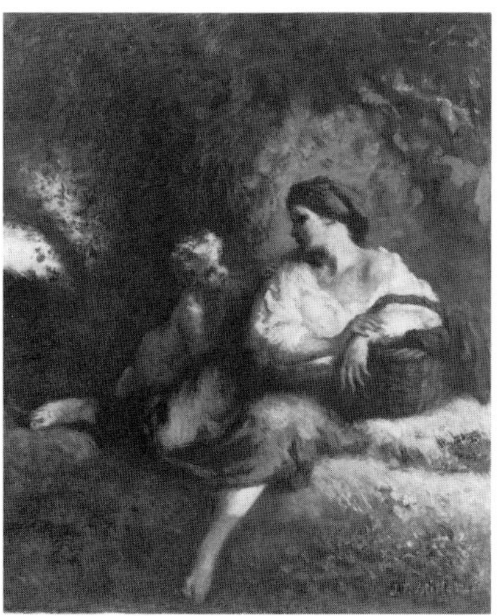

FIG. 27.
JEAN-FRANÇOIS MILLET
The Whisper (Peasant and Child)
Oil on canvas, 18 x 15 in.
National Gallery, London, Gift of George Salting, 1910

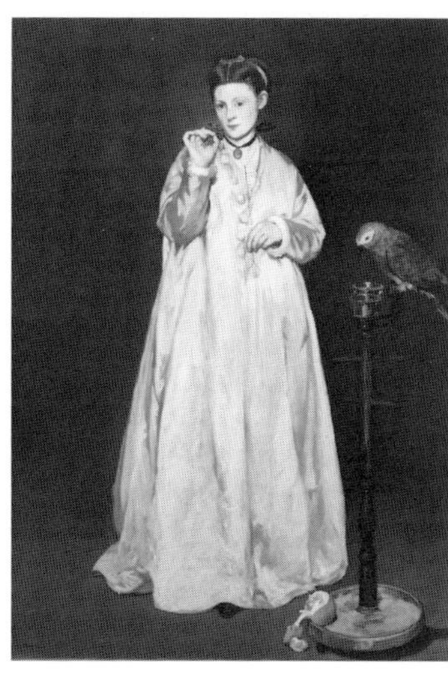

FIG. 28.
EDOUARD MANET
Woman with a Parrot
Oil on canvas, 72 7/8 x 50 5/8 in.
The Metropolitan Museum of Art, New York, Gift of Erwin Davis, 1889

that we are asked to look at; it is the way in which nature is playing with it, that is of importance."[44]

Support for the Pedestal Fund show also came from dealers Samuel P. Avery and William Schaus, who had supplied works by Bouguereau, Merle, Schreyer, Willems, and Andreas and Oswald Achenbach to the 1878 *Loan Exhibition in Aid of the Society of Decorative Art.* In 1883 their contributions were limited in number and different in style, expressing the new committee's more modern point of view. Avery sent a Henner *Bather* that he had probably acquired at the J. C. Runkle sale that year.[45] His second loan, Cazin's *Hagar and Ishmael* (fig. 21), a variation of the artist's 1880 Salon triumph on that subject,[46] was also a recent purchase, acquired at a sale in Paris in February 1883.[47] William Schaus, who with Cottier and Knoedler enjoyed the highest sales of French and Dutch paintings in New York in 1882,[48] loaned Daubigny's *The Cooper* (fig. 22), which had previously been exhibited at the Salon of 1872 and at the 1878 *Exposition Universelle.*[49] The dealer M. Knoedler, who had earlier absorbed Goupil's New York branch, loaned the Millet *Woodchopper* (cat. no. 63; pl. XXXI), which *The New York Times* considered one of the gallery's "choicest hauls during the past season,"[50] and also provided Roybet's *Rare Vases*[51] and an early oil version of Tissot's *Visiteurs étrangers au Louvre*[52] (fig. 23).

L. Crist Delmonico loaned a Dupré landscape and Stevens's *The Fortune Teller* and *At the Seashore (Havre).* From Gustave Reichard the committee chose another *Nymph* by Henner and Boldini's *In the Meadow.* George Kemp sent Alberto Pasini's *Doorway in Constantinople,* one of three scenes of this type included in the show, and *Spring Woods near Paris* by César de Cock, a Belgian artist whose soft woodland interiors, appreciated for their "manner of Corot," could also be found in the John Wolfe and Henry C. Gibson collections, as well as in smaller private collections outside New York.

Moore & Clarke Co., which in 1879 under the direction of M. E. Moore established a gallery where American artists could exhibit and sell their works,[53] sent Courbet's *Ocean* and *Valley,* Roybet's *Masterless* and *Un Grand Seigneur,* a Vollon still life, and Stevens's painting *Young Girl.*[54] H. Wunderlich, who had purchased two watercolors from Whistler in 1883,[55] sent a Whistler *Snow Scene,* a painting that gave a small indication of the esteem in which the artist was held by his younger countrymen and the only work by an American in the exhibition.

New York *Sun* editor Charles A. Dana, a former Brook Farm member and

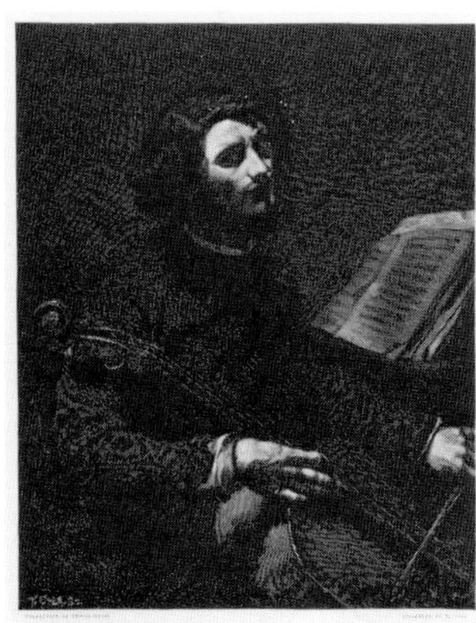

FIG. 29.
GUSTAVE COURBET, *The Musician*
Engraving by Timothy Cole from John C. Van Dyke, ed., *Modern French Masters*, 1896

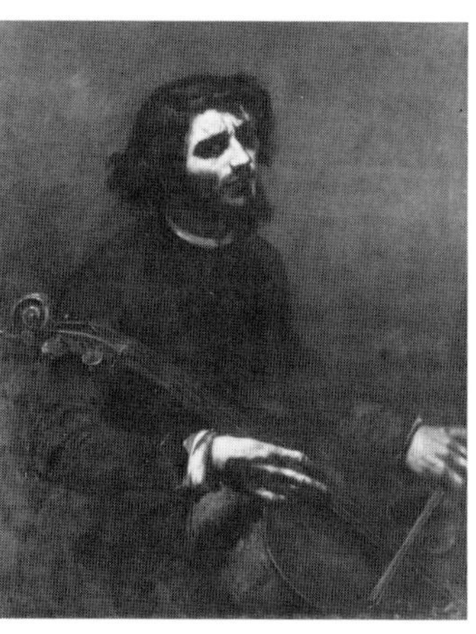

FIG. 30.
GUSTAVE COURBET
Le Violoncelliste: Portrait de l'artiste
Oil on canvas, 46 x 35 in.
Nationalmuseum, Stockholm, Sweden

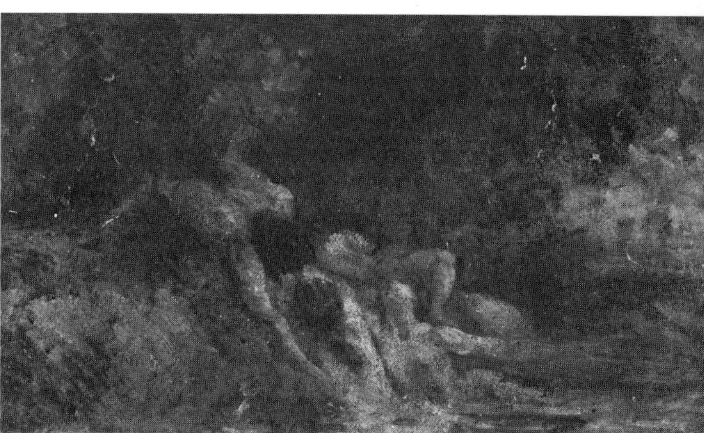

FIG. 31.
JEAN-FRANÇOIS MILLET
Hylas and the Nymphs
Oil on canvas, 10 x 16 1/4 in.
Rijksmuseum Kröller-Müller, Otterlo, the Netherlands

Abraham Lincoln's Assistant Secretary of War, loaned six of the most important works from his small but select collection of paintings.[56] Corot's *Le Soir* (*La Danse des Amours*)[57] (fig. 24; pl. VII), later loaned by Dana to the *Barye Monument Exhibition* of 1889–90[58] and by its next owner, George Gould, to the Saint Louis Exposition of 1904, was acclaimed as one of the highlights of the Pedestal Fund show. Dana also sent Millet's *Autumn Landscape with a Flock of Turkeys* (*The Turkey Guardian*) (cat. no. 64; pl. XXXII) — purchased from Samuel Avery for $6,500 and sold to Herman Schaus for $20,500 at the Dana sale of 1898 — along with the Diaz *La Mare aux Grenouilles* (fig. 25; pl. XIII), Charles Jacque's *Sheep at the Entrance to a Forest* (cat. no. 40; pl. XV), Rousseau's *The Harvest Field*[59] (fig. 26), and Daubigny's 1871 sunset view, *On the Oise.*[60]

Considering the offerings of Wolfe, Havemeyer, Cooper, Stuart, and Dana, as well as the general acceptance of Barbizon painting among New York's collectors, one would assume that the committee found this sort of material easily available. But with the exception of Corot, the artists who dominated the Pedestal Fund show were brought in from galleries and from a handful of collectors who had embraced, or were on the brink of joining, a new direction in collecting. Albert Spencer, who had held a major sale in 1879, was in 1883 accumulating a second important collection of European paintings.[61] Among these were Delacroix's moving *Le Christ au tombeau* (*Descent from the Cross*) (cat. no. 26; pl. XII), a leitmotif for the painterly romanticism that dominated the show; a small Millet nude, *Après le bain* (cat. no. 62; pl. XXIX), "a work so fine that it crushes all competition";[62] and a "most charming"[63] *Peasant and Child,* a title that obscured its subject matter, that of a pastoral Venus and Cupid (now called *The Whisper*; fig. 27; pl. XXVI).[64] Spencer also lent a rather intimate and, to American collectors, atypically loose and unsentimental scene, *Pigs and Swineherd*[65] (cat. no. 42; pl. XVI) by Professor Ludwig Knaus, an artist who had been lately rediscovered by Paris critics and included in Georges Petit's 1882 International Exhibition.[66] His other loans included *The Halt,* one of Eugène Fromentin's many scenes of Arab travelers at rest,[67] and two Troyons, *Landscape*[68] and *Drove of Cattle and Sheep.*[69] In 1888, after the highly successful sale of his second collection, Spencer directed his attention to collecting French Impressionist paintings, among them the works of Degas, Monet, and Renoir that he loaned to the World's Columbian Exposition Chicago, in 1893.[70]

Another lender to the Pedestal Fund exhibition, William T. Evans, would go on to buy American impressionist paintings that later entered the collections of the National Museum of American Art, Washington, D.C., and the Montclair Art Museum in Montclair, New Jersey.[71] In 1883, Evans, a partner in the dry-goods firm of Mills and Gibb, was one of the few private collectors in

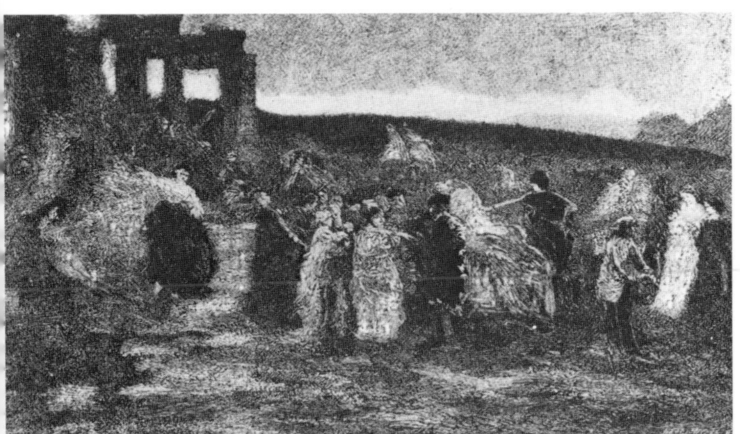

FIG. 32.
ADOLPHE MONTICELLI, *The Festa*
13 x 22 1/2 in.
Current location unknown
Photograph from Richard Muther,
The History of Modern Painting, vol. 4, 1907

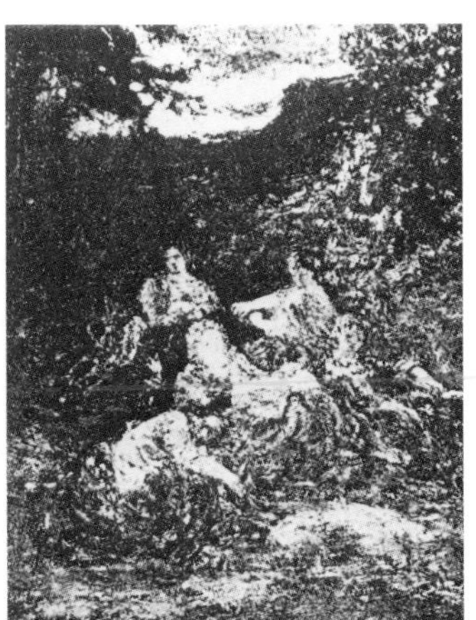

FIG. 33.
ADOLPHE MONTICELLI
The Pic-nic
18 x 13 3/4 in.
Current location unknown

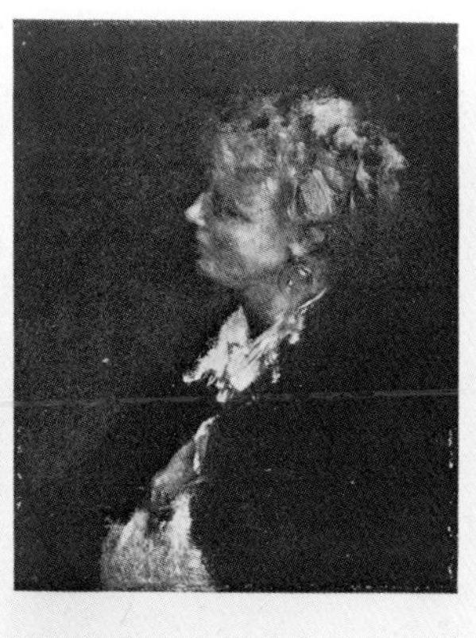

ANTOINE VOLLON

FIG. 34.
ANTOINE VOLLON
Portrait of the Artist's Sister
9 3/4 x 7 1/2 in.
Current location unknown

New York who owned the work of Courbet.[72] He loaned Courbet's *A Mountain Gorge*,[73] along with the small *Landscape and Sheep*,[74] by Jacque, and *Constantinople*,[75] another of the popular scenes by Pasini that were favored by the selections committee.

There were not many collectors in New York in the early 1880s who risked a more substantial commitment to new directions in French and Dutch painting. The ability of the paintings committee to present its own enlightened point of view would probably have failed had it not been for the involvement of the Scottish designer and art-furniture dealer Daniel Cottier and two collectors, Erwin Davis and Ichabod T. Williams, who did their business outside the shops of Avery, Schaus, and Knoedler. In the final count one hundred and twenty paintings, nearly two-thirds of the selections in the Pedestal Fund show, came from Cottier, Davis, and Williams. Davis, a New York financier with a reputation for buying either at auction or directly from artists, loaned thirty-seven paintings from a collection that was later more than ten times that size.[76] His loans comprised a generous number of Barbizon paintings, including three canvases each by Corot[77] and Diaz,[78] a Rousseau landscape,[79] and the striking Millet *The Bather* (*Woman Bathing*) (cat. no. 60; pl. XXV), formerly in the collection of Cottier and illustrated at the beginning of the Paintings Section of the Pedestal Fund exhibition catalogue (fig. 1). The Hague School was represented by the Neuhuys *Children*, Matthew Maris's painting *Willows*, and two works by Anton Mauve, *Twilight*, a solitary figure of a Dutch boy seated in a field (illustrated by a line drawing in the original catalogue, fig. 2), and the study *Sheep*.[80] In addition to landscapes by Dupré and Georges Michel, Davis also sent a painting by Géricault entitled *Dead Lamb*[81] and a Couture head, possibly the *Self-Portrait* (cat. no. 20) in the 1889 Davis sale.

Davis, who lived abroad during the 1870s, became a familiar participant at New York auctions in the early 1880s. Among the paintings he loaned to the Pedestal Fund show were Alfred von Wierusz-Kowalski's *Napoleon in Russia* and P.-J. Clays's *Moonlight*, both acquired at sale at the Leavitt Art Galleries in February 1880;[82] Mettling's *Flowers*, purchased in March 1880 at the J. Abner Harper sale;[83] and Stevens's *Coquetry*[84] from the John L. Wolfe sale of 1882. His more distinctive mode of operation was to send an agent to Paris to find pictures for him. In 1880 and 1881, his representative was the American artist J. Alden Weir, whose first important acquisition for Davis was the Bastien-Lepage *Joan of Arc*, shown in the Salon of 1880.[85] The following year, reputedly at the recommendation of Chase, Weir purchased Manet's *Boy with a Sword* (cat. no. 47; pl. XVII) and *Woman with a Parrot* (fig. 28; pl. XVIII) from the artist's dealer, Durand-Ruel, and then went on his own to Manet's studio where he bought a

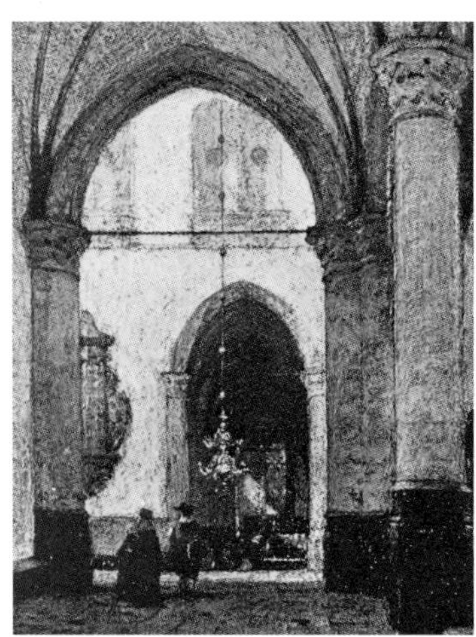

FIG. 35.
JOHANNES BOSBOOM
The Church at Alkmaar
Oil on panel, 12 1/2 x 10 1/4 in.
Saint Louis Art Museum

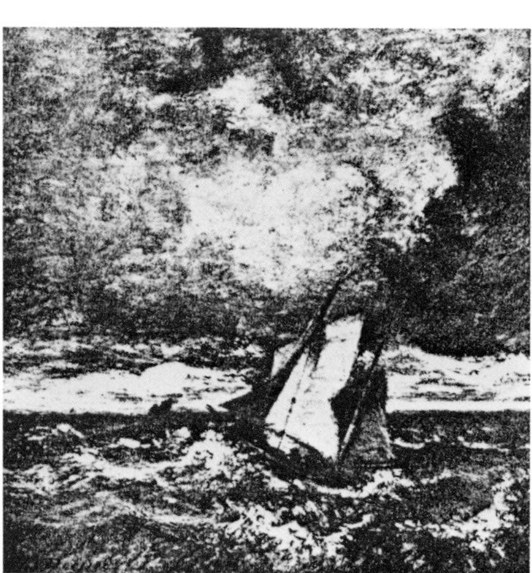

FIG. 36.
JULES DUPRÉ, *Marine*
11 1/4 x 10 1/2 in.
Current location unknown

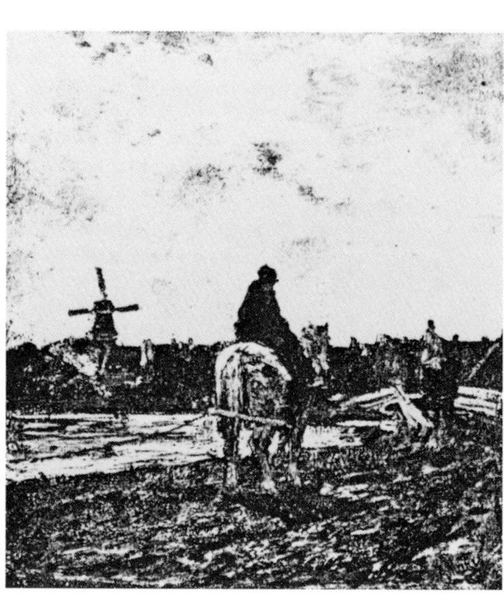

FIG. 37.
JACOB MARIS, *Holland Scene*
13 1/2 x 12 1/2 in.
Current location unknown

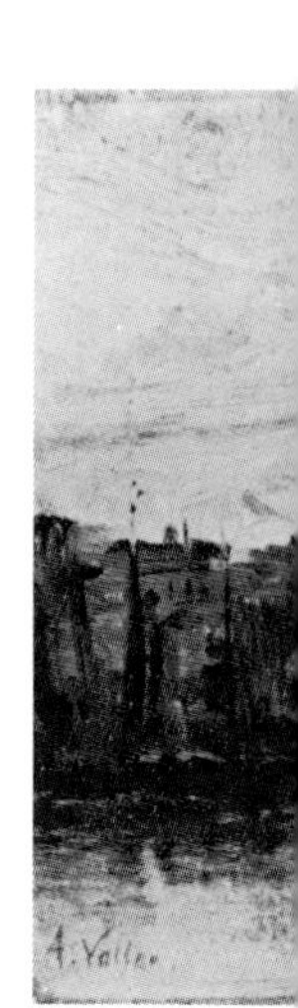

third painting, *Marine* (*Les Marsouins*),[86] which he believed to be a scene of the battle of the *Kearsarge* and the *Alabama.* The two Manet figures, emblematic of the influential role of Chase and Weir in the Pedestal Fund exhibition, proved to be show-stoppers when they were hung in the position of preference denied Meissonier and Detaille. Similarly honored, Degas's *Ballet Dancers* (*The Ballet*)[87] (fig. 7; pl. XI), described by one critic as "repulsively real ballet girls magnificently brushed in,"[88] and also acquired through Durand-Ruel, was one of the nine paintings selected for illustration in the catalogue. Courbet was represented by *Landscape*[89] and *The Wave*,[90] and by another Weir purchase, *The Violoncellist* (*Music*) (cat. no. 16; pl. IX), a portrait of the artist as a young man holding a cello (reproduced as *The Musician*, fig. 29). The musical score in the upper-right corner, an addition that is attributable to Courbet's frequent habit of revising his work, distinguishes the painting from the 1848 Salon version, *Le Violoncelliste* (fig. 30).

Of the work that had recently made a strong impression on young Americans in Paris, Davis loaned a landscape by Cazin,[91] a Henner bather,[92] and Dagnan-Bouveret's *Child and Vase.*[93] Théodule Ribot, whose dark naturalism was currently undergoing positive critical appraisal in Paris,[94] was seen in a *Head*[95] and in a painting of "heavy strong heads of his children"[96] titled *The Lesson.* Davis also loaned a landscape by Alfred Wahlberg, a Swedish artist who had considerable success in Paris in the 1870s and who was among the international selection of artists invited to the 1882 Georges Petit exhibition, and two paintings by Vollon, *Head of a Cavalier* and a still life, listed only as *Fruit,* which may have been the one described by Clarence Cook as "a magnificent example . . . a covered bowl of Dresden china, with fruit on a table — a picture sufficient for fame in itself."[97]

It was Davis's paintings that gave the exhibition the edge that challenged the New York critics, even though the pictures only suggested the impact that French Impressionism would have after Durand-Ruel's 1886 show. But the overwhelming tone of the Pedestal Fund exhibition came from Williams and Cottier, who had an understanding of "art for art's sake" and reveled in the heat of the sketch, the dark tones of Rembrandt, and the overlays of color that typified Monticelli's *paradis artificiels.*

Like Davis and Evans, Ichabod T. Williams was convinced of the value of modern American art, and he eventually incorporated into his collection of European paintings the work of Sargent,[98] Weir, John H. Twachtman, Will Low, George Fuller, Ralph Blakelock, and Albert Pinkham Ryder.[99] He had begun

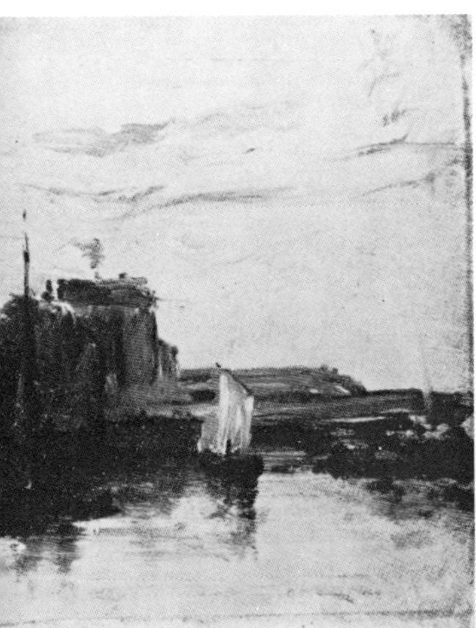

FIG. 38.
ANTOINE VOLLON, *On the River*
9 1/2 x 13 in.
Current location unknown

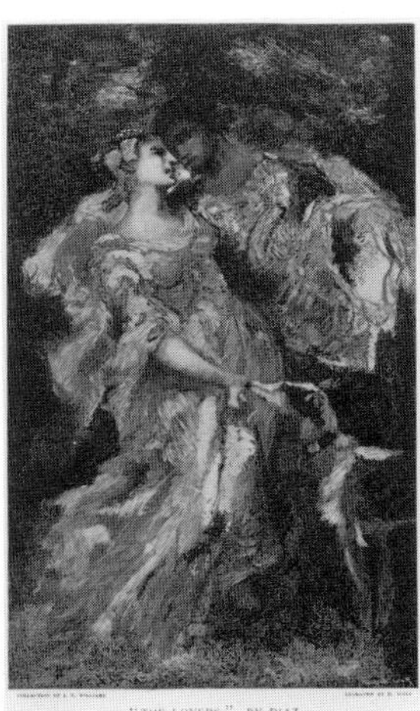

FIG. 39.
NARCISSE VIRGILE DIAZ DE LA PEÑA, *The Lovers*
12 3/4 x 7 1/4 in.
Current location unknown
Engraving by Henry Wolf from John C. Van Dyke, ed., *Modern French Masters*, 1896

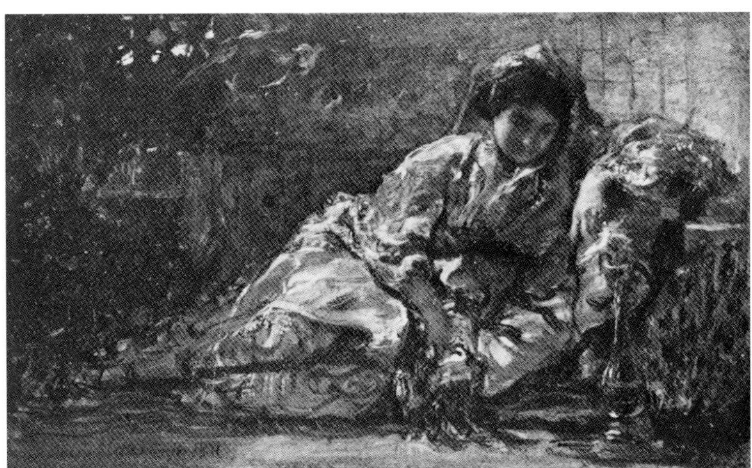

FIG. 40.
JACOB MARIS, *Turkish Lady*
8 1/4 x 13 1/4 in.
Current location unknown

collecting paintings around 1874,[100] shortly after Cottier had established his art-furniture showroom in New York. A lumber dealer specializing in cabinet woods and veneers,[101] Williams was probably a supplier to Cottier & Co., whose factory and workshops at 223 West Twenty-eighth Street eventually employed over a hundred workmen.[102] Cottier was responsible for educating Williams in contemporary French and Dutch painting and for providing him with examples from his gallery.[103]

Millet's *The Quarriers* (cat. no. 61; pl. XXX), "a rapid brusque painting expressing essentials . . . in which the reactions of the muscles to the effort is the theme of the picture"[104] (acquired from Cottier who had exhibited it in New York in 1877 and 1878), was one of the strongest paintings in the Williams collection. Its complement, Millet's sinuous and darkly scumbled *Hylas and the Nymphs* (fig. 31; pl. XXVII), also loaned by Williams, would later appear in Cottier's private collection.[105] Along with the "fearful" *Susanna and the Elders* (pl. XXVIII), the female nudes from the Spencer and Davis collections (pls. XXIX and XXV), and the shrouded *Turkey Guardian* (pl. XXXII), Williams's two pictures exposed the author of *The Angelus* to the Pedestal Fund audience as an artist of intensely emotional color, imagery, and gesture.

Like Cottier, Williams seemed to prefer paintings that were broad in arrangement and effect and quick and free in handling, imparting a sense of the artist's activity. He required no uniformity of subject or approach but owned a variety of figures, landscapes, and "fantasias." Monticelli met these criteria with glowing scenes of courtly life such as *Landscape with Figures* (cat. no. 67; pl. XXXV) and with *fêtes champêtres* such as *The Festa*[106] (fig. 32) and *The Pic-nic*[107] (fig. 33), which were among the works loaned to the Pedestal Fund exhibition. His taste developed through an appreciation of "painter's paintings," such as the little Vollon *Portrait of the Artist's Sister* (fig. 34), described as "a portrait [such] as is done by one artist for another or by a painter for himself — executed in utmost freedom, sketchy and studious at once, a serious studio diversion bespeaking the joy of doing."[108] An autographic impression was apparent in many of the small paintings Williams loaned to the show: Bosboom's *The Church at Alkmaar* (fig. 35; pl. IV), Dupré's *Marine*[109] (fig. 36), Jacob Maris's *Holland Scene*[110] (fig. 37), Vollon's *On the River*[111] (fig. 38), and Matthew Maris's *A Corner of The Hague*[112] (cat. no. 51; pl. XIX); all were purchased from Cottier and shared qualities of immediacy and freshness.[113]

Williams's figure paintings had the same intimacy of scale, frequently enlivened by brilliant color. Diaz's *The Lovers*[114] (fig. 39), entangled in a wooded

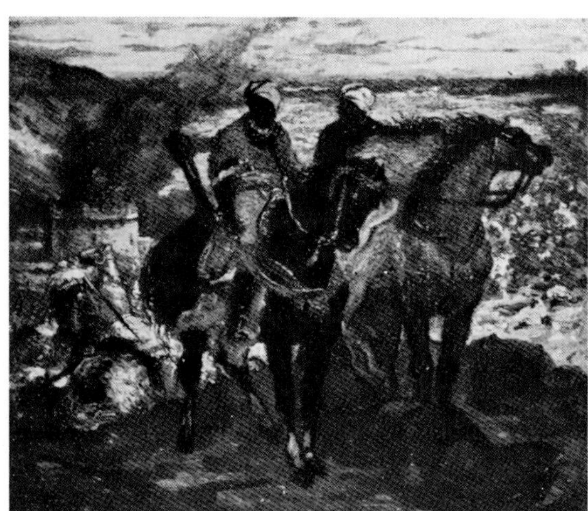

FIG. 41.
FERDINAND ROYBET
Moorish Captive
12 x 14 in.
Current location unknown

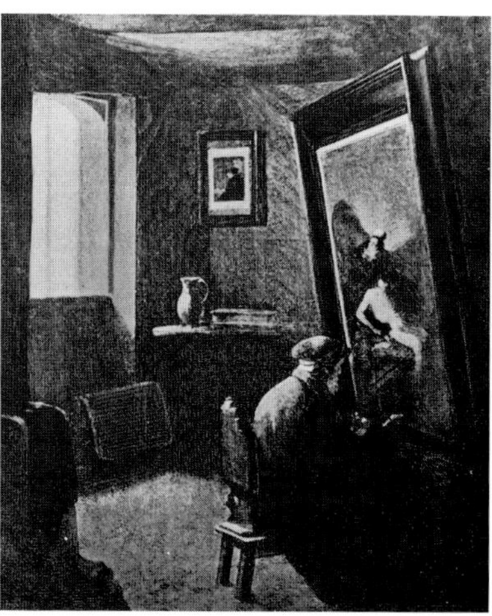

FIG. 42.
THÉODULE AUGUSTIN RIBOT
The Studio
22 x 18 1/4 in.
Current location unknown
Photograph from Clarence Cook, *Art and Artists of Our Time*, vol. 2, 1888

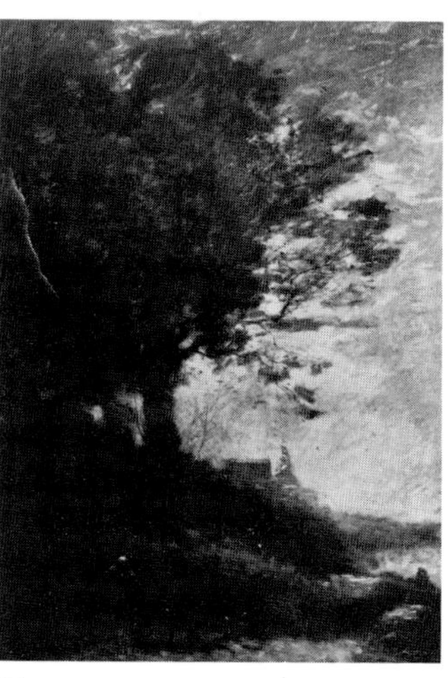

Fig 43.
JEAN-BAPTISTE-CAMILLE COROT
Twilight (Evening, Lake Nemi)
35 1/2 x 23 3/4 in.
Current location unknown

setting of green, brown, and yellow, embraced in robes of red and gold. Jacob Maris's *Turkish Lady* (fig. 40), "a glowing essay in rich mellifluous color . . . Oriental luxuriance . . . and chromatic splendor,"[115] was in frank emulation of Delacroix, as was Roybet's *Moorish Captive*[116] (fig. 41), a painting whose broad treatment lacked the sometimes fussy detail of his popular seventeenth-century-style costume pieces. In other works it was clear that Williams shared Cottier's admiration for Rembrandt, particularly in the dark tones of Ribot's *The Cook's Assistant*[117] and in the homage to Rembrandt (who appears in an etching on the wall) in *The Studio*[118] (fig. 42), described as a "picture in a million, a deep and beautiful work."[119] In several instances Williams's loans were large tonal studies, incorporating sketchiness and atmospheric effect in Corot's *Twilight,* an evening view of Lake Nemi[120] (fig. 43), and C. F. Hill's *Landscape.*[121] There was a sensation of expansiveness in Michel's *Clouds and Landscape* (*Hills of Montmartre*) (cat. no. 59; pl. XXIV), "a broad prospect of mount and plain, the distant valleys still dark, under a characteristic Michel sky of glow and thunder-gray clouds."[122]

"The power to recombine the facts of experience in a single impression"[123] was the quality shared by the artists in the Williams collection, setting it apart from the stylistically eclectic collections of the majority of his contemporaries. Although he believed that the value of his paintings would be perceived in future years, he did not acquire them in anticipation of their next round on the auction block. The paintings were kept together until ten or twelve years after his death when their public sale was hailed as the dispersal of a collection that typified "imagination in art."[124]

By far the most extensive and influential group of loans came from the collection of Daniel Cottier (fig. 44), a native of Glasgow who had apprenticed himself to a glassmaker in Scotland before becoming established as a designer of stained glass, furniture, and interiors in the 1860s.[125] By 1870, when the firm of Cottier & Co., Art Furniture Makers, Glass and Tile Painters, advertised from a studio at 2 Langham Place, London,[126] Cottier had completed interior commissions for Scottish architects J. J. Stevenson and Campbell Douglas, and had collaborated with Alexander Thomson on surface decorations for the United Presbyterian Church at Queen's Park.[127] Upon reviewing the program of Egyptian, classical, and plant motifs that Cottier executed for Thomson, Ford Madox Brown praised him as a colorist whose range of performance was beyond that of any modern artist.[128]

Cottier's London business, which provided services that ranged from fur-

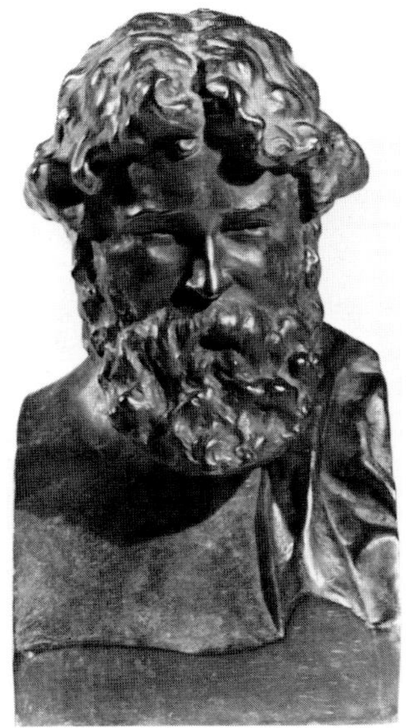

FIG. 44.
OLIN LEVI WARNER
Portrait of Daniel Cottier, 1878
Bronze, 11 x 6 x 6 in.
National Academy of Design, New York

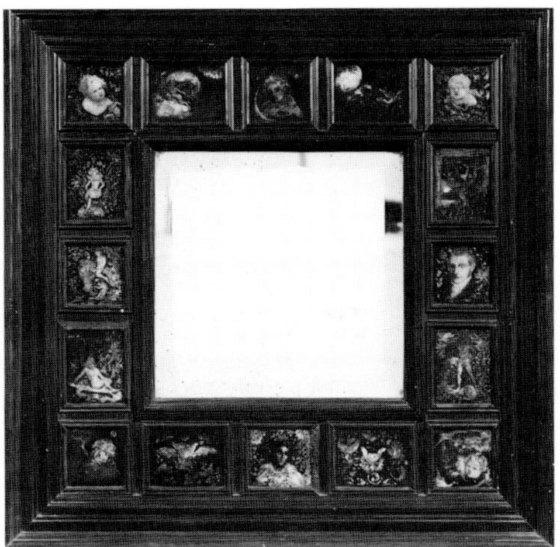

FIG. 45.
ALBERT PINKHAM RYDER
The Culprit Fay
Oil on wood (mirror frame)
20 1/4 x 20 1/4 in.
Courtesy Whitney Museum of American Art, New York

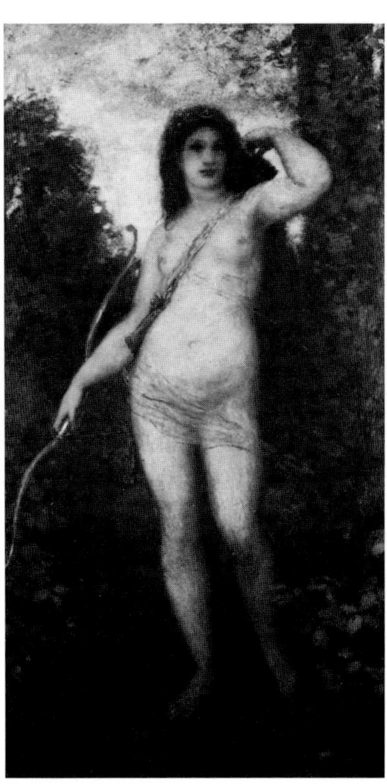

FIG. 46.
GEORGE S. BELLENGER AND MATTHEW MARIS, *Diana*
Oil on canvas, 78 x 49 in.
Glasgow Art Gallery and Museum, Glasgow, Scotland

nishings to wall, ceiling, and window decoration, flourished to such an extent that in 1873 he was able to form a new partnership in Australia with his former colleague John Lamb Lyon.[129] In the same year he also opened an American showroom that was "as strange in New York as a rose-bed with nightingales and fountain would be [if] come upon in the back yard of a First Avenue tenement house."[130] In 1874 the Cottier galleries at 144 Fifth Avenue were filled with artistic furniture described as "the chairs and tables and side-boards, the curtain-stuffs, the glass and china, that will excite the heart's desire" of people who were "bent on being in fashion . . . up to the times."[131] The firm's reputation was further enhanced by a series of articles by Cook entitled "Beds and Tables, Stools and Candlesticks," which used illustrations from Cottier & Co.'s stock to fan America's interest in the aesthetic interior.[132]

Owing to the experience Cottier had gained on domestic and ecclesiastical commissions in Great Britain and to his exceptional organizational skills, he was hired to assist John La Farge with execution of interior designs for H. H. Richardson's Trinity Church, Boston. In fact, Cook, writing for *Scribner's* in 1877, indicated that neither Richardson nor La Farge would have succeeded at the task without

> help at the right moment [from] a decorator in the person of Mr. Daniel Cottier, who, beside an intimate knowledge of the tecnics of his profession, and the control of assistants made adepts in the mixing and applying of colors by long experience, is a man of very uncommon power of perception, of first rate judgment and, what is not always the companion of these qualities, an inexhaustible enthusiasm and love for art. . . . The truth is, the debt we owe to him is not at all to be reckoned with. When all the panels, spandrels and wall spaces shall have been filled with the pictures that are now in such a slim minority, the obligation to Mr. Cottier will be more plain than ever.[133]

Although Cottier was involved in other American architectural commissions, his major interest in this country seemed to be the development of his art-furniture business and the creation of a gallery of modern pictures. Not long after establishing the New York rooms, Cottier convinced Elbert Jan van Wisselingh, a Dutch employee of the international art dealers Goupil & Cie., Paris, to work for him in London.[134] Van Wisselingh shared Cottier's enthusiasm for Barbizon painting and introduced him to the artists of the Hague School who would soon begin to find an appreciative audience in America. Paintings became an integral part of Cottier's decorative philosophy, and they were even incorporated into furniture design. An extant example of artistic

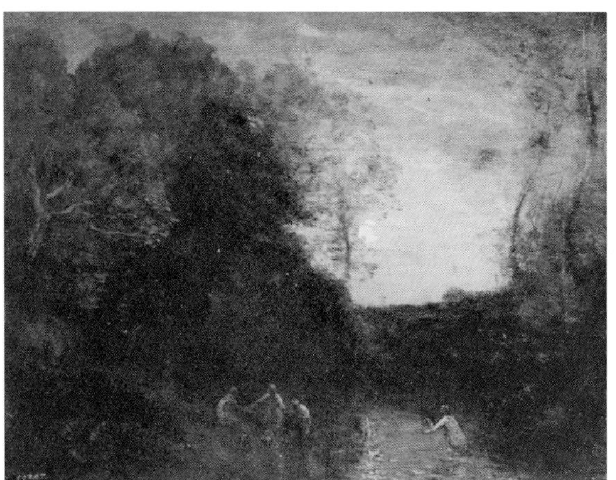

FIG. 47.
JEAN-BAPTISTE-CAMILLE COROT
Moonlight (Le Clair de lune)
Oil on canvas, 11 x 14 in.
Current location unknown

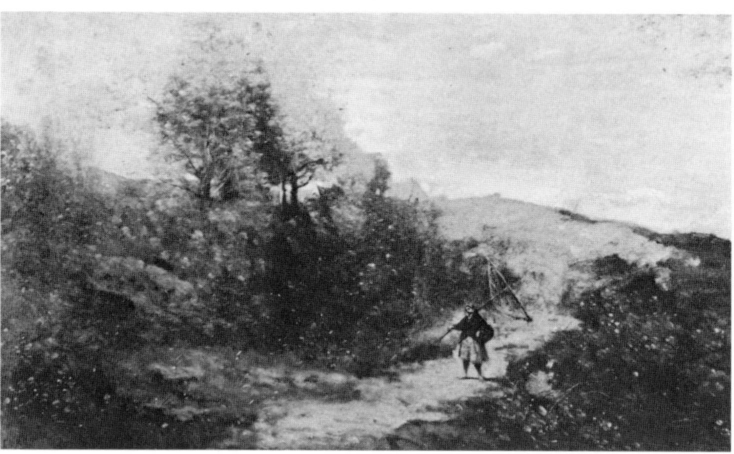

FIG. 48.
JEAN-BAPTISTE-CAMILLE COROT
The Sandhills of Zuydcoote, near Dunkirk
Oil on canvas, 29 x 50 1/4 in.
Current location unknown

collaboration of this type is a mirror frame of sixteen wooden panels (fig. 45) painted by Ryder for Cottier & Co. and exhibited at the New York gallery in 1879.[135] Matthew Maris, whom van Wisselingh had befriended in Paris, lived in Cottier's home in London and decorated gas globes[136] for Cottier & Co. in addition to "restoring" paintings by other artists (see fig. 46 and cat. no. 67). At one point even Vincent van Gogh, who had worked with van Wisselingh at Goupil's and visited him in London, commented that he thought his own drawings would have looked well in Cottier's furniture.[137]

With van Wisselingh in charge of the London business, Cottier set about making contacts with American artists in New York. A few weeks after the opening of the Annual Exhibition at the National Academy of Design in 1875, Cottier opened an exhibition of paintings "with which the Academy has little sympathy."[138] A harbinger of the exhibitions of the Society of American Artists,[139] Cottier's selection included the work of William Morris Hunt, La Farge, Ryder, Helena de Kay, Francis Lathrop, Maria Oakey, and Abbott H. Thayer. Heartened by a review that found the character of the show "grave, sincere and soothing," Cottier heeded the recommendation that frequent exhibitions of this type might keep the public apprised of the different directions being pursued by modern artists.

During the following year, the official recognition awarded to Hague School artists Mauve and Mesdag at the 1876 Centennial Exhibition in Philadelphia was one of the factors that encouraged Cottier to assemble a gallery of modern European paintings on the second floor of his New York showrooms. On the evening of February 28, 1877, he gave a small reception at which "gentlemen more especially interested in art, artists, members of the press, and others, might examine them for the first time at their leisure."[140] Ryder's rendering of a cow[141] was the only American painting noted in the exhibition of imported works by French, Dutch, and English artists. Included were "a magnificent specimen of Daubigny," a sketch by Rousseau, and paintings by Diaz, Jacob Maris, Mauve, Mettling, Theophile de Bock, M. Boks, John Constable, W. G. Orchardson, and Henry Staquet. A position of honor was given to Corot's *Orpheus Greeting the Dawn* (pl. VI) — "refined, harmonious, and elevated, as we may imagine the music of Orpheus himself to have been"[142] — a large canvas that had been part of a decorative scheme commissioned for the Paris townhouse of Prince Paul Demidoff in 1865.[143] Millet's *The Quarriers* (cat. no. 61; pl. XXX), admired for its action and coloring, was included in the show, as was a panoramic watercolor, "some 10 feet by 4," by Jules Lessore, depicting "the

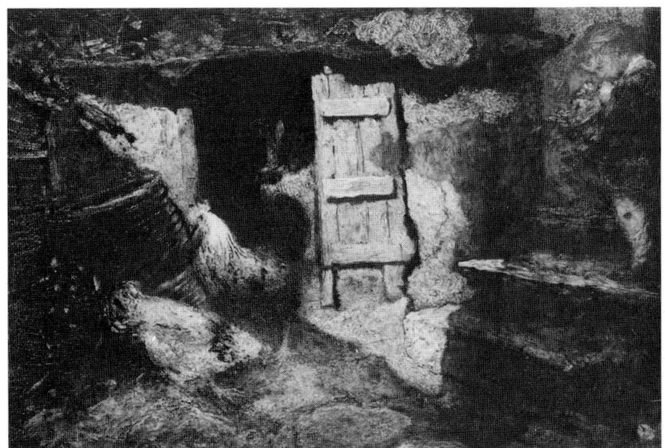

FIG. 49.
ADOLPHE MONTICELLI AND MATTHEW MARIS, *The Farmyard*
Oil on panel, 15 3/4 x 23 in.
Yale University Art Gallery, New Haven, Connecticut, Gift of Duncan Phillips

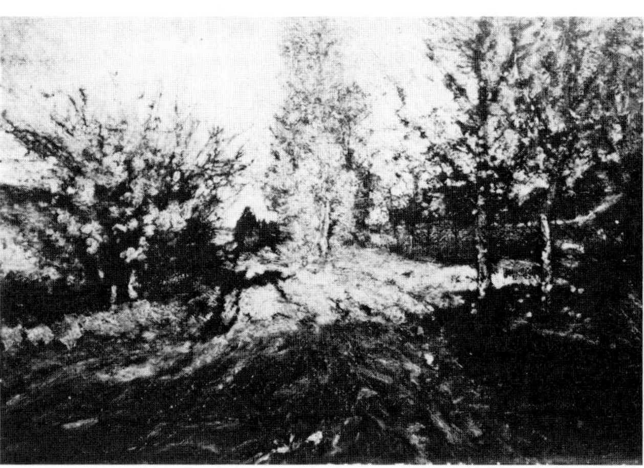

FIG. 50.
ADOLPHE MONTICELLI, *Autumn Landscape*
Oil on mahogany panel, 15 1/2 x 23 1/2 in.
Allen Memorial Art Museum, Oberlin, Ohio, Gift of Mrs. A. A. Healy

lower portion of Manhattan Island taken from a high point somewhere in the neighborhood of the Brooklyn pier of the bridge."[144] The exhibition, an event that would often be repeated, established Cottier's gallery as a gathering place for artists and amateurs.

Early in 1878, Cottier's Art-Rooms were again graced by a shipment of European paintings "noble beyond any similar collection in this country."[145] To the *Orpheus,* now on view for almost a year, were added other works by Corot, as well as Millet's *Samson and Delilah* and paintings by Bosboom, Diaz, Dupré, Jacque, Michel, Rousseau, and Troyon. Monticelli's *Don Quixote,* "a feast for the eyes and the imagination,"[146] exhibited at this time, was subsequently purchased by a Boston collector,[147] a sale that led Cottier to decide that it was a propitious moment to test the impact of his taste on the New York market. In April 1878, he consigned his paintings to Leavitt Art Galleries for sale at public auction in Association Hall. In face of a report that Cottier & Co. intended to give up this aspect of the business,[148] *The New York Times* called the paintings "the finest collection of modern masters ever brought together in this country."[149]

The 1878 sale, directed by Samuel P. Avery at Cottier's request, included one hundred and sixty-three "Fine Oil Paintings and Water Color Drawings by the Great Modern Classic Painters." Cottier himself contributed an introduction to the catalogue, in which he acknowledged the genius of Millet, Corot, Diaz, Michel, Troyon, and Daubigny, expressing hope in the art of Bonvin, Roybet, Ribot, Mettling, Jacque, Dupré, Hill, and Vollon, and singling out, in his praise of the Hague School, the imaginative painting and simple landscapes of Matthew and Jacob Maris, the cattle scenes of Mauve, and the Dutch interiors of Bosboom. No less than ten Corots and six Millets headed the two-day sale, but despite published reports that the sale realized $36,821, more than two-thirds of the paintings were bought in by Cottier and his representatives.[150] At least twenty of the paintings would be loaned to the Pedestal Fund show nearly five years later. Of these, a number were still in Cottier's collection at the time of his death in 1891, and others remained in the collection of his partner, James S. Inglis, until 1909.

As reported by the *Times:* "The picture buyers who attended the sale of the residue of the collection at Association Hall, last evening, admired the finest paintings, but went no further."[151] R. Swain Gifford purchased a Jacob Maris and a Dupré, but few of Cottier's young artist friends were in a position to buy, and the list of successful bidders lacked the names generally associated with

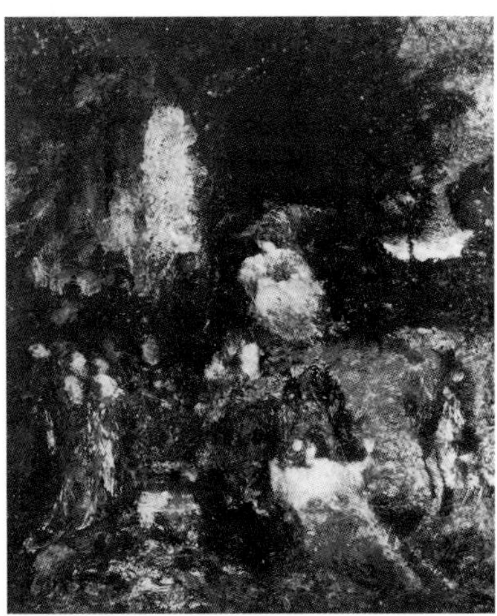

FIG. 51.
ADOLPHE MONTICELLI
The Fountain of Youth
Oil on panel, 15 3/8 x 12 3/8 in.
Museum of Art, Carnegie Institute, Pittsburgh

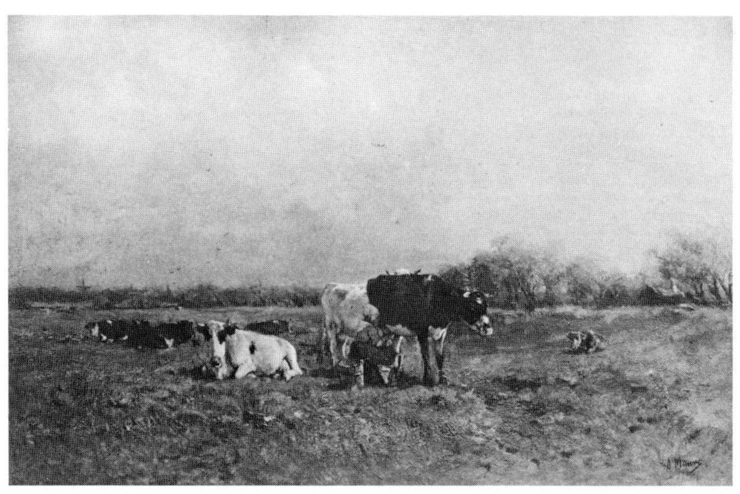

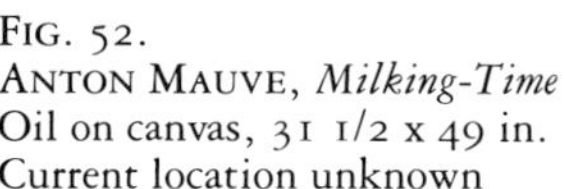

FIG. 52.
ANTON MAUVE, *Milking-Time*
Oil on canvas, 31 1/2 x 49 in.
Current location unknown

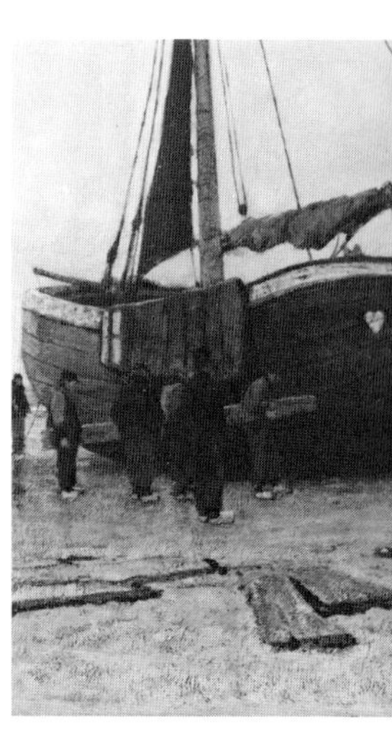

America's noteworthy collections. Despite the failure of the sale, a sympathetic art press commended Cottier's refusal to be discouraged by the lack of clients for his "Corots, Millets, and other *progresistas* of the modern art schools,"[152] and fears that he would give up the art gallery proved to be unfounded. His professional goal, to send his paintings into the quiet nooks of America "so that the brotherhood of art and art lovers may advance in all lands,"[153] was reviewed as even more audacious in the spring of 1879 when he opened an exhibition of the paintings of Monticelli. *The New York Times* said:

> Probably no other firm of dealers would venture to do what the Messrs. Cottier have done this year. As a rule, men in business of the kind follow slavishly after well-ascertained tastes of the public, fearing to embark any large amount of capital on the purchase of objects of art which are not sure of a ready sale. This firm makes an exception, in that it holds pictures which are likely to be admired by a very narrow circle of people, among whom actual purchasers are few and far between. The present gallery is chiefly composed of the vagaries of a man who was considered, even among the eccentrics of Paris, as something short of insane.[154]

But the tone of the review shifted quickly to applause, christening Monticelli the prince of Impressionists, comparing his paintings to the "vague poems of Edgar Poe thrust upon a colored surface," and questioning if it were not the cynical viewer who was lacking in sensitivity.[155]

Cottier's interest in Monticelli was in keeping with his support of Matthew Maris and Ryder: "Let but the color be right," wrote the critic W. E. Henley, "the arrangement large in purpose and effect, the handling quick and free and essential, and {Cottier's} imagination did the rest."[156] He shared this enthusiasm with his partner, Inglis, and with a circle of New Yorkers that included collector Ichabod T. Williams and artists Olin Warner, Weir, and Ryder.[157] It was probably through Weir that Cottier met Chase, although the attention given Cottier's exhibitions in the late 1870s had already made him a familiar participant in the "comradeship and 'atmosphere'"[158] that was attracting young artists back to New York from Europe. Cottier became known as a "friend in need to a host of our artists . . . never weary of pointing out that in this country we have the stuff for as good painters {as those} of France."[159]

Despite critical support and an expanding network of collector and artist friends, Cottier's gallery maintained its reputation as a source for only a limited clientele. M. Knoedler & Co. began to import works by Jacob Maris, Mauve, and Roybet in the late 1870s,[160] and Avery attempted to claim credit for discovering Monticelli,[161] but Cottier's business, unlike that of his competitors, was

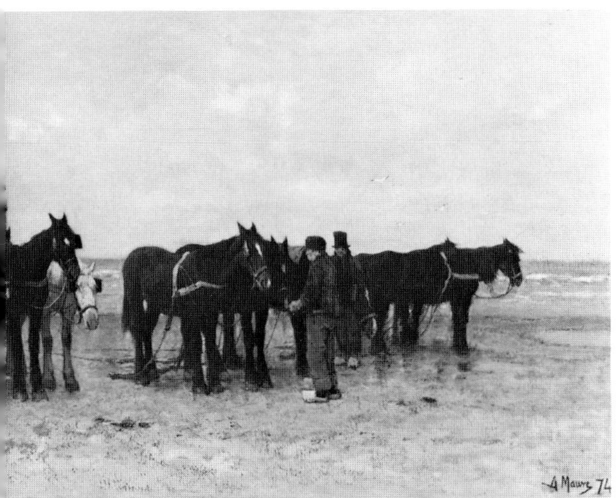

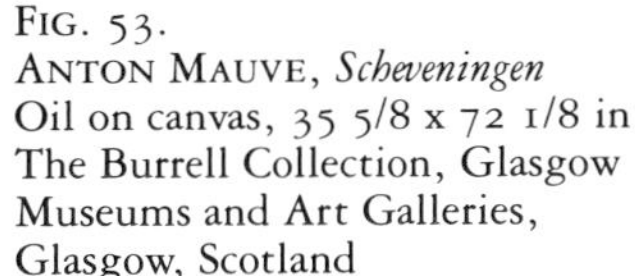

FIG. 53.
ANTON MAUVE, *Scheveningen*
Oil on canvas, 35 5/8 x 72 1/8 in.
The Burrell Collection, Glasgow Museums and Art Galleries, Glasgow, Scotland

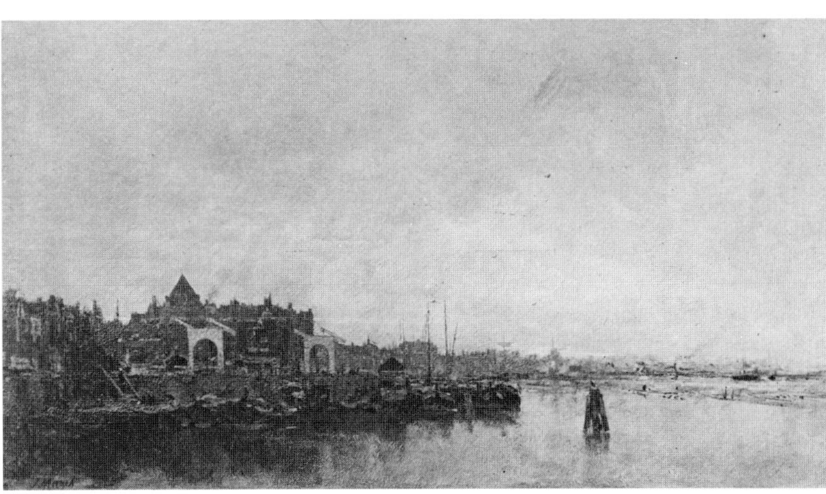

FIG. 54.
JACOB MARIS, *View of Amsterdam*
Oil on canvas, 32 x 58 in.
Current location unknown

never carried by a stock that served more traditional collectors. His unwillingness to cater to the market reflected his love for the paintings and his belief that they would one day provide for his family the "insurance policy" that his recurring rheumatic fever denied him.[162]

Although the organizers of the Pedestal Fund show had intended to show paintings never seen before by the public, a number of the lots Cottier bought in at the 1878 sale were among the sixty-seven paintings on loan from him. Corot's *Orpheus*, now in New York for over six years, and Matthew Maris's reworking of Georges Bellenger's *Diana*[163] (fig. 46) were two of the largest paintings in the show, both measuring over six feet in height. *Moonlight (Le Clair de lune)*[164] (fig. 47) and *The Sandhills of Zuydcoote, near Dunkirk*[165] (fig. 48) were probably among the three other Corots he sent.[166] There were two flower pieces[167] and a Fontainbleau landscape by Diaz, as well as eight works by his "disciple" Monticelli,[168] including *Gateway to a Fort* (cat. no. 66; pl. XXXIII), *The Farmyard*[169] (fig. 49; pl. XXXIV), and perhaps also *Autumn Landscape*[170] (fig. 50). *The Fountain of Youth*[171] (fig. 51), also shown by Cottier in 1878, may have been included, although it was not listed under this title in the Pedestal Fund exhibition catalogue.

Three landscapes by Michel, including a typical *View in Holland* (see, for example, *The Windmill,* cat. no. 58), and the *Female Head* (cat. no. 8; pl. V) by Auguste Boulard, an intimate of Corot and Daubigny, surrounded Cottier's Barbizon selections. In additions to the works of Corot and Diaz, he also loaned two paintings by Daubigny, a Dutch scene on the river Maas[172] and a landscape that may have been the "magnificent specimen" noted in Cottier's 1877 exhibition.[173]

Among the living artists, Cottier gave significant weight to the members of the Hague School. He sent two works by Bosboom,[174] *Dutch Interior* by Blommers,[175] *On the Beach at Scheveningen* by Mesdag[176] and *Idyl* by Matthew Maris.[177] Mauve, "the Dutchman whose work has been introduced here by Cottier,"[178] was seen to advantage in four paintings from his collection: two scenes on the Dutch coast (figs. 3 and 5) and two cattle pieces — *Changing Pasture* (fig. 6; pl. XX), included in the 1878 sale,[179] and a second possibly known as *Milking-Time*[180] (fig. 52). One of the coastal scenes, a team of horses drawing a boat onto the beach,[181] was a smaller version of *Scheveningen* (fig. 53), a painting for which Mauve had been awarded a medal at the Philadelphia Centennial Exhibition in 1876.[182]

Two Dutch landscapes, possibly the *View of Amsterdam*[183] (fig. 54) and

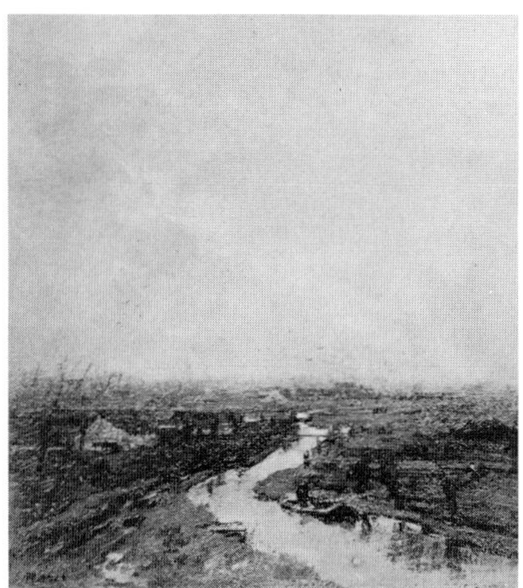

FIG. 55.
JACOB MARIS, *Canal in Holland*
Oil on canvas, 13 1/2 x 11 1/2 in.
Current location unknown

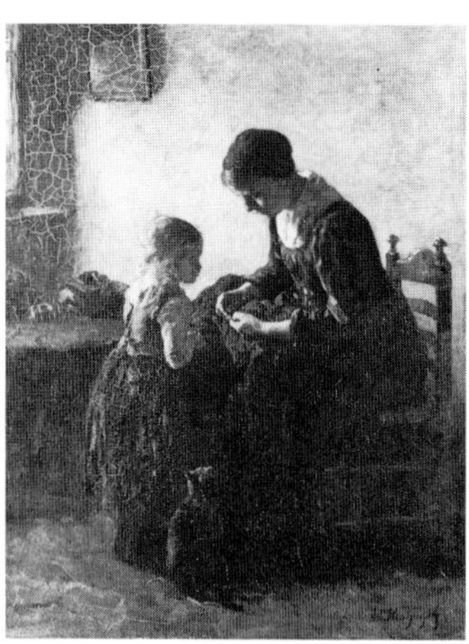

FIG. 56.
ALBERT NEUHUYS
La Première Leçon
Oil on canvas, 39 1/2 x 29 1/2 in.
Dordrechts Museum, Dordrecht, the Netherlands

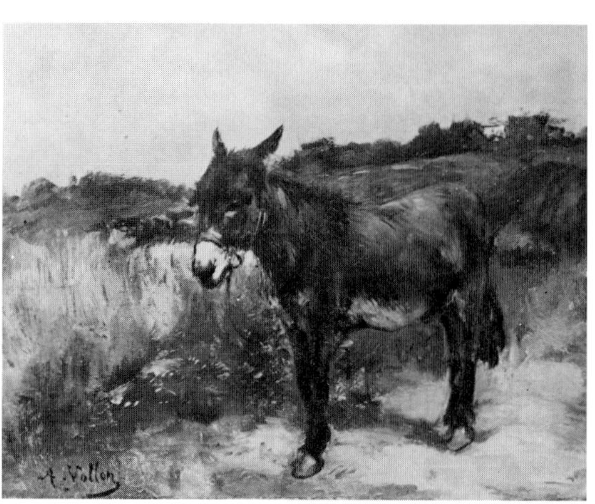

FIG. 57.
ANTOINE VOLLON, *Donkey*
Oil on canvas, 13 x 16 in.
Current location unknown

Canal in Holland[184] (fig. 55), represented Jacob Maris; Neuhuys, a young genre painter, was seen in two figure paintings, one of an old woman *Mending Sacks,* illustrated by a line drawing in the catalogue (fig. 4), and *The Lesson,* probably a Dutch interior of a peasant woman teaching a child to sew (fig. 56).[185] Cottier also sent two scenes of Venice and the view *New York from Martin's Wharf, Brooklyn,* probably watercolors, by the French artist Jules Lessore, a close friend of Matthew Maris's and a fellow expatriate to England. He also loaned a figure painting, *Tired Out*,[186] by Antonio Mancini, an Italian artist who was both admired and financially assisted by Mesdag. Louis Latouche, an artist who was included in the first Impressionist group exhibition in 1874, was represented by *French Coast Scene,* a large painting of fishing boats at Normandy that had been shown by Cottier in 1878 and was also featured in the Pedestal Fund catalogue (fig. 9).

Three Swedish painters, Wilhelm von Gegerfelt, Carl Frederik Hill, and Oskar Törna, were added to the show by Cottier. Törna, represented by "a good moonlight,"[187] had sent three paintings to the Philadelphia Centennial Exposition, and later became a founding member of the Swedish Konstnärsforbundet. Gegerfelt's *Snow Scene* and Hill's mountain views and forest interiors were the type of broad tonal landscape paintings that had brought these artists favorable Salon reviews in Paris in the 1870s.

Cottier, in keeping with his taste for paintings that imparted the spirit of the artist on a more intimate scale, loaned three small Vollons: *Portrait of Rembrandt*[188] (possibly cat. no. 88), *Study of a Child,* and a picture one critic described as a "very asinine" *Donkey*[189] (fig. 57). He also sent *Donkey Ride* by a French artist named Valton.[190] His preference for the style of Dutch and Spanish old masters was evident in two handsome Ribots, *A Young Vendean*[191] (fig. 58; pl. XXXVI) and *Guitarist* ("twanging the strings of his instrument")[192] and in three broadly drawn paintings by Roybet: *The King's Kitchen*[193] (fig. 59), *Arab Girl,* and *Return from the Chase.*[194] Mettling's *The Studio (Among the Curios)* (cat. no. 56; pl. XXIII)[195] and *After Rembrandt,* illustrated in the catalogue (fig. 8), were among seven works by the French artist whom Cottier had been promoting since the late 1870s.

Although Cottier and his firm later owned a number of paintings by Courbet, including *Autumn*[196] (fig. 60), a version of *La Grotte de la Loue*[197] (fig. 61), and a *Marine*,[198] he loaned only one work, *The Cave*,[199] to the Pedestal Fund exhibition. A Manet *Toreador,* probably a watercolor, was also listed among Cottier's loans.

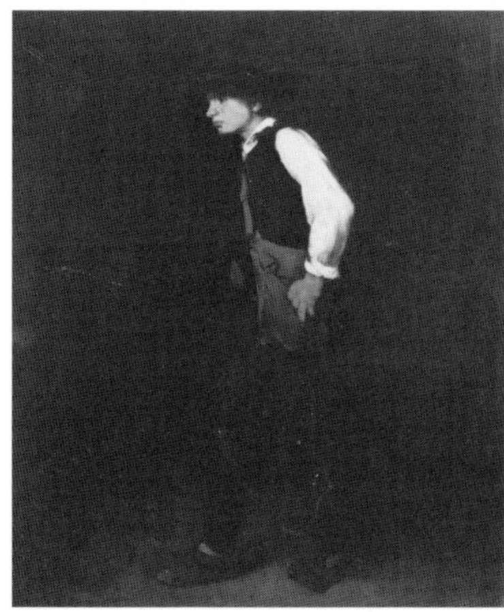

FIG. 58.
THEODULE AUGUSTIN RIBOT
A Young Vendean
Oil on canvas, 22 1/4 x 18 1/2 in.
Montreal Museum of Fine Arts,
Bequest of Miss Adaline Van Horne,
1945

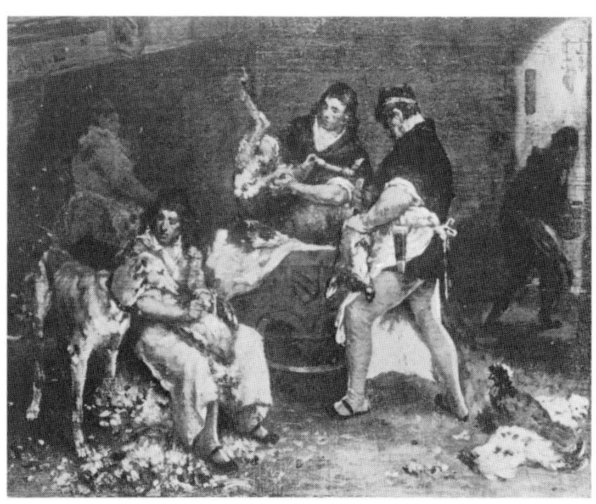

FIG. 59.
FERDINAND ROYBET
The King's Kitchen
Oil on canvas, 12 1/2 x 16 in.
Current location unknown

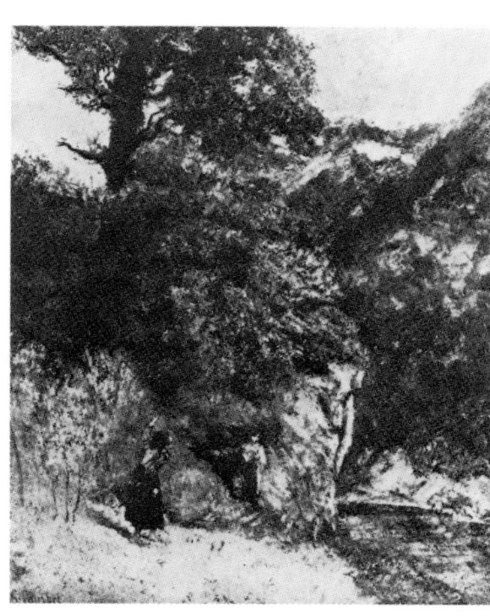

FIG. 60.
GUSTAVE COURBET, *Autumn*
Oil on canvas, 28 3/4 x 23 1/2 in.
Current location unknown

The general absence of English painting was addressed in part by Cottier, who loaned "a pleasantly toned view of a cathedral town in France" by W. Reynolds, "apparently an English artist,"[200] and works by two members of the Royal Scottish Academy: William E. Lockhart, whose *View in Spanish Town* represented a common theme in his work, and Hugh Cameron, whose *Maternal Care* reflected the penetration of Hague School genre sentiment into Scotland. A Philippe Rousseau still life[201] and one of Antoine-Louis Barye's animal pieces rounded out the sixty-seven paintings by thirty-two artists loaned by Cottier.

Despite the wide range of countries represented in the *Pedestal Fund Art Loan Exhibition*, distinctive national characteristics were relatively inconsequential factors in its selection. To the contrary, artists such as Michael Munkácsy, Eugen Jettel, Alfred Wahlberg, and Giuseppe de Nittis were included not as examples of Hungarian, Austrian, Swedish, and Italian schools, but as exponents of nonnarrative painterly styles that flourished within the Munich-Paris axis. The atmospheric landscapes and dark genre interiors of the Hague School, while quintessentially Dutch, referred to seventeenth-century prototypes that had also been revived in France and Germany in the nineteenth century. The plains and beaches within the purview of Corot and Daubigny had become familiar even to American artists through sketching trips in Holland.

Compared to the selection of international art in the 1876 Philadelphia Centennial Exhibition, the Pedestal Fund exhibition resembled a secessionist salon. Not only was there a broad representation of the Barbizon and Hague schools, but the more notorious *refusés* Courbet and Manet were given added prominence through generosity of number and placement that would have been unacceptable in an official presentation. In many respects, the Pedestal Fund show was closely keyed to the three Munich *Grosse Internationale Ausstellungen* of 1869, 1879, and 1883, the most important international exhibitions outside of Paris. In addition to featuring Courbet, whose work had made a major impact on Munich artists in 1869, the French selections were again dominated by Corot and Diaz. Antoine Vollon's still lifes and landscapes, Théodule Ribot's dark Spanish figures, and Ferdinand Roybet's seventeenth-century costume pieces preached the gospel of Hals and Velásquez, which Chase had absorbed in Munich and Beckwith had learned in the Paris atelier of Carolus-Duran. The young artists Beckwith, Chase, and Weir, who had shared the walls of the 1883 Munich exhibition with Henner, Knaus, Gegerfelt, Wahlberg, Gierymski, Pasini, and Dagnan-Bouveret, assembled a complementary company of European artists at the Pedestal Fund show that would provide the American public with a con-

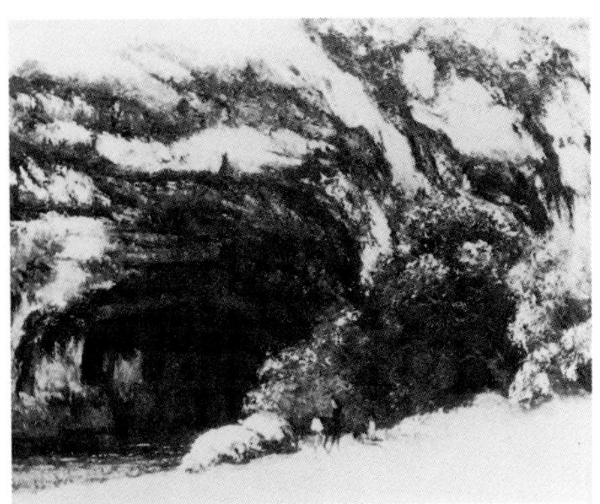

FIG. 61.
GUSTAVE COURBET
La Grotte de la Loue
Oil on canvas, 24 x 28 3/4 in.
Current location unknown

text for their own related work. The *Pedestal Fund Art Loan Exhibition* was decidedly less dramatic in impact than the exhibition of French paintings sent to America by Durand-Ruel two and a half years later, but in its revolutionary purpose, it resembled the 1913 Armory Show, a far more shocking event. For the first time in New York the direction of American art was predicted and defined by the young artists who would influence it. Their confidence and enthusiasm, their willingness to commit themselves to artistic ideals just on the brink of public acceptance, set a precedent for American participation in the future of contemporary painting that would only be matched by their own students thirty years later.

NOTES

1. "The Pedestal Art Loan," *The New York Times*, December 2, 1883, p. 2.
2. *The Art Journal* (London), 1884, p. 255.
3. *The Art Journal* (London), 1883, p. 130.
4. "The Pedestal Art Loan," *The New York Times*, December 16, 1883, p. 5.
5. *The New York Times*, December 2, 1883.
6. Hans Huth, "Impressionism Comes to America," *Gazette des Beaux-Arts,* vol. 29, per. 6 (April 1946), p. 229. He also notes that Durand-Ruel probably supplied the so-called Foreign Exhibition at Mechanic's Hall, Boston, in September 1883, with some of the Impressionist paintings represented, which included Manet's *Entombment of Christ* and *Portrait of Rouvière*; Monet's *Customhouse Station, Dieppe, My Garden*, and *Tide at Varengeville*; Pissarro's *Shepherd and Washerwoman, Suburbs of Pontoise, Goatherd, Poultrymarket, Winnowers*, and *Peasant Tending a Cow*; Renoir's *A Box at the Opera, Boatmen's Breakfast at Bougival*, and *Fisherman's Children*; and Sisley's *Barrier on the Shore, Autumn Morning St. Mammes*, and *Grande Promenade.* Although the exhibition catalogue does not name Durand-Ruel as a lender, Huth cites a letter from Pissarro to Monet of June 12, 1883 (Gustave Geffroy, *Claude Monet, sa vie, son temps, son oeuvre* [Paris: G. Crès et Cie, 1922], p. 162), mentioning that Durand-Ruel had sent some Impressionist paintings to Boston.
7. New York, National Academy of Design, *Special Exhibition: Works in Oil and Pastel by the Impressionists of Paris*, exhibition under the management of the American Art Association of the City of New York. The exhibition opened at the American Art Galleries on April 10, 1886 and moved to the National Academy of Design on May 25. See Huth, pp. 225-52, for his pioneering examination of the 1886 exhibition and for a bibliography of early Impressionist exhibitions in America.
8. Edward Strahan [Earl Shinn], ed., *The Art Treasures of America*, 3 vols. (Philadelphia: G. Barrie, 1879-82). See Albert Boime, "America's Purchasing Power and the Evolution of European Art in the Late Nineteenth Century," in Francis Haskell, ed., *Salons, Galleries, Museums and Their Influence in the Development of 19th and 20th Century Art* (Bologna, Italy: Cooperativa Libreria Universitaria, 1979), pp. 123-39.
9. "The Society of American Artists," *Scribner's Monthly,* vol. 16, no. 1 (May 1878), p. 149.
10. "The Pedestal Art Loan," *The New York Times,* December 2, 1883, p. 2.
11. Breton, *The Great Pilgrimage (Le Grand Pardon)*, 1869, Museum of Fine Arts, Havana.
12. Mme Annette Bourrut-Lacouture identified the *Brittany Peasant* in the Pedestal Fund catalogue as a male Brittany penitent (alternately titled *The Communicant* and *Breton au chapelet et au cièrge*), 1872, 49 x 33 in., owned in 1883 by John G. Johnson, Philadelphia, who purchased it from M. Knoedler, New York; later owned by Peter A. Schemm, Philadelphia. The painting, illustrated in color in S. Decatur Smith, Jr., "A Gallery of Modern Art," *The Booklovers' Magazine*, vol. 2, no. 3 (September 1903), p. 257, and by a sketch in *Les Grands Artistes français et étrangers* (Paris: H. Launette & Goupil & Cie, 1884), p. 37, was traced by Mme Bourrut-Lacouture to Buenos Aires, where it was sold at auction by Señora Clara Thisted de Diaz at Roldan y Cìa, Sale 1673, June 3-7, 1974, lot 181. Roldan's records indicate the buyer only by the initials "H. F."
13. Diaz, *Holy Family*, 12 1/2 x 9 1/2 in., ex-collection The Metropolitan Museum of Art, New York; sold New York, Sotheby Parke-Bernet, February 15, 1973.
14. Troyon, *Holland Landscape and Cattle*, 40 x 59 3/8 in., ex-collection The Metropolitan Museum of Art, New York; sold New York, Parke-Bernet, March 27, 1956.
15. Meissonier, *A General and His Aide-de-Camp*, 1869, 7 3/4 x 10 7/8 in., The Metropolitan Museum of Art, New York, Bequest of Catharine Lorillard Wolfe, 1887, Catharine Lorillard Wolfe Collection.
16. Hamon, *An Etruscan Vase Seller*, 20 1/4 x 19 in., ex-collection The Metropolitan Museum of Art, New York, Bequest of Catharine Lorillard Wolfe, 1887, Catharine Lorillard Wolfe Collection; sold New York, Parke-Bernet, March 27, 1956.

17. Fortuny, *Camels Reposing, Tangiers*, 8 x 14 in., The Metropolitan Museum of Art, New York, Bequest of Catharine Lorillard Wolfe, 1887, Catharine Lorillard Wolfe Collection.

18. Bonheur, *The Horse Fair*, 99 1/4 x 199 1/2 in., The Metropolitan Museum of Art, New York, Gift of Cornelius Vanderbilt, 1887; in 1883, Collection Mrs. A. T. Stewart. August Belmont owned the *Rendezvous de Chasse*.

19. Vollon, *French Farmyard*, 37 7/8 x 46 3/8 in., ex-collection The Metropolitan Museum of Art, New York, Bequest of Catharine Lorillard Wolfe, 1887, Catharine Lorillard Wolfe Collection; sold New York, Sotheby Parke-Bernet, February 15, 1973.

20. Strahan II, p. 133.

21. "Death of T. A. Havemeyer," *The New York Times*, April 27, 1897, p. 12.

22. Emilie de Losey Havemeyer Sale, New York, American Art Association, February 26-27, 1914; lot 58, Jettel, *In the Fall*, 1871, 23 x 43 in.: "Meadows threaded by shallow water courses are brown in the turning year, and beyond the water trees on low land in the middle distance show brown foliage above shining white trunks. Ducks swim in the foreground, near a shore where a figure huddles over a fire, cattle stand in the shallows, and gulls are flying against a cold grey sky." Jettel won a gold medal at the World's Columbian Exposition, Chicago, in 1893, and was represented in the collections of The Metropolitan Museum of Art and The Art Institute of Chicago at the turn of the century. See Heinrich Fuchs, *Eugen Jettel* (Vienna: Dr. Heinrich Fuchs Selbstverlag, 1975).

23. Strahan I, p. 140, Ed. Charlemont, *Cavalier*; Havemeyer Sale, 1914, lot 1, Edouard Charlemont, *An Interesting Letter*, 1873, 6 1/2 x 4 3/4 in.: "In buff and deep white collar and cuffs, velvet short clothes and red stockings, a thoughtful looking man is seated near a library table reading, while he smokes a long Dutch pipe. He faces the front, knees crossed, with light falling from the right, and is observed against a neutral background having rich tone." Sold to W. H. Peck for $50.

24. Havemeyer Sale, 1914, lot 39, Theodore Ethafer (*sic*), *The Pious Cobbler*, 1873, 21 3/4 x 13 1/2 in.: "A cobbler whose shop is on the stone pavement of an open court in an Italian town is seated at his bench, beneath one of the familiar outdoor shrines of Italy, under the legend 'Dite Ave Maria' and the date 1866. Crispin pauses in his work to speak to a young girl who has come up at his left and is looking on." Sold to Hoelfer for $35.

25. Havemeyer loaned Pasini's *Fair Day*, possibly the *Market Scene: Constantinople* listed in Strahan I, p. 140. Havemeyer also owned Pasini's *Venice*.

26. Havemeyer Sale, 1914, lot 11, Troyon, *Sheep and Goat*, 9 1/2 x 16 1/2 in.: "An interesting study of sheep and a goat, full of suggestion and exhibition of 'quality.' The sheep stand or lie around in various attitudes and positions, and with various expressions, and the goat rests stolidly at ease among them." Stamp: *Vente Troyon*. Sold to Martyne for $125.

27. Untitled in *Catalogue of the Pedestal Fund Art Loan Exhibition*, 1883, but listed by Strahan I, p. 140, who apparently misidentified the artist as N. A. Laurens. At the time there were few works by J.-P. Laurens in American collections (see *Honorius*, 1880, cat. no. 43), but he was admired by American artists in Paris in the 1870s and known for his often cynical selection of historical subjects.

28. Havemeyer Sale, 1914, no. 63, Max Gierymski, *Riding to the Hunt*, 26 x 46 in.: "An open forest with sparse and scattered undergrowth occupies the picture, the light bark of slender birches catching the sunshine, foliage turning to autumn hues while the ground bush remains green. Overhead the driven fleece is active in a fair blue sky. Threading the forest paths on their varied mounts the hunt is riding to the meet, with carriages visible in the distance behind the M. F. H." Sold to J. Wilbur for $80.

29. Gierymski, *Polowanie "par force" na Jelenia*, 1874, 38 5/8 x 71 7/8 in., ex-collection Nationalgalerie, Berlin, now Collection Georg Schäfer, Schweinfurt, West Germany; see Maciej Mastowski, *Maksymilian Gierymski I Jego Czasy* (Warsaw: Panstwowy Instytut Wydawniczy, 1970), fig. 91, p. 291.

30. "The Pedestal Art Loan," *The New York Times*, December 16, 1883, p. 5. Another Gierymski, *The Start for the Hunt*, was owned at this time by A. J. Drexel, Philadelphia (Strahan III, p. 18).

31. Guy Stair Sainty identified this painting as one that he had purchased at a sale at Phillips, New York, February 16, 1982, lot 164, and subsequently sold to its current owner. Michael Wentworth confirmed the painting's provenance in a conversation with the author, June 26, 1985: Knoedler had purchased it from Tissot for £100; sent it to New York on the ship *America*, November 14, 1881; and, according to Knoedler's stock books, sold it to G. C. Cooper, April 17, 1882.

32. See cat. no. 80, Stevens, *La Jeune Mère*, 25 1/6 x 16 7/8 in., Worcester Art Museum, Worcester, Massachusetts; loaned by Chase to an exhibition of the works of Stevens, at the Berlin Photographic Company, New York, February 27-March 11, 1911; no. 5, *Une Mère*.

33. "George Campbell Cooper," *The New York Times*, January 31, 1895, p. 3.

34. Cooper's prints are now in the collection of the Cooper-Hewitt Museum, New York, Smithsonian Institution. See Fitz Roy Carrington, *A Catalogue of the Engravings and Etchings formed by the late G. C. Cooper* (New York: Privately printed, 1897).

35. W. C. Brownell, "Bastien-Lepage: Painter and Psychologist," *The Magazine of Art*, vol. 6 (1883), pp. 265-71; *Pauvre Fauvette*, illus. p. 268.

36. Bastien-Lepage, *Joan of Arc (Jeanne d'Arc écoutant les voix)*, 1879, 100 x 110 in., The Metropolitan Museum of Art, New York, Gift of Erwin Davis, 1889.

37. *The New York Times*, December 16, 1883, p. 5.

38. The Robert L. Stuart Collection, described in Strahan II, pp. 117-24, was presented to the New York Public Library by his widow in 1892 and transferred to the New-York Historical Society in 1944.

39. Strahan II, p. 123.

40. According to Strahan II, p. 26, the subject of the painting was the historic and proverbial exclamation: "Hail to unsuccessful courage!" The scene Detaille had originally painted, in accordance with the sketch he submitted to Hawk, depicted wounded French soldiers saluted by a Prussian general. The artist's friends objected to his sending a picture of French prisoners to America and compelled him to reverse the identities of conqueror and vanquished. This version was sent to Hawk; but on the painting's return to France for the 1877 Salon, it was feared that this unlikely portrayal would offend the Salon's German visitors, whose participation in the coming *Exposition Universelle* was desired. Thus the artist used watercolor to paint a set of Austrian costumes for the prisoners. The watercolor was reputedly removed before the painting was returned to Hawk. The painting, widely known and frequently reproduced, has not been located by Detaille scholars.

41. "Samuel Hawk," *The New York Times*, August 2, 1882, p. 5.

42. De Nittis was represented in the collections of A. T. Stewart (see *Return from the Races*, 1875, cat. no. 70), A. E. Borie, R. L. Cutting, Darius O. Mills, Henry Hilton, C. H. Wolff, and Chauncey Blair.

43. *The New York Times*, December 16, 1883, p. 5. Goupil photogravure in Armand Silvestre, *The Gallery of Contemporary Art*, J. Eugene Reed, ed., vol. 1 (Philadelphia: Gebbie & Co., 1884), opposite p. 48. Another *Place de la Concorde* was sold at New York, American Art Association-Anderson Galleries, *Paintings of the XVI–XIX centuries from the Collection of William S. Hawk [and others]*, February 4-5, 1931, lot 25, de Nittis, *Place de la Concorde*, 1880, 16 1/2 x 19 1/2 in., panel: "Beneath a turquoise blue summer sky is a view of the Place with the fountain playing in the middle distance, and the Rue Royale and the colonnade of the Madeleine seen in perspective at right. The scene is animated with figures in picturesque costumes of the eighties."

44. Clarence Cook, *Art and Artists of Our Time*, vol. 2 (New York: Selmar Hess, 1888), p. 135, illus. p. 136.

45. J. C. Runkle Sale, New York, Leavitt Art Galleries, March 8, 1883, lot 32, Henner, *Nymph at the Fountain*, 16 x 21 in.; sold to Avery for $1,500.

46. Cazin, *Agar et Ismael*, 99 1/5 x 79 1/2 in., Musée du Louvre, Paris; on deposit at Musée des Beaux-Arts, Tours.

47. Paris, Vente de Mme R., February 3, 1883; J. Cazin, *Agar et Ismael*, 42 x 63 cm; FF 1,905. Courtesy Mme Hélène Toussaint, Musée du Louvre, Paris. Avery's version of *Hagar and Ishmael*, 26 x 32 in., was formerly in the collection of Potter Palmer of Chicago; sold New York, Parke-Bernet, March 16, 1944, for $1,100; and sold again New York, Parke-Bernet, May 15, 1946, lot 23, for $700; current location unknown.

48. *The New York Times*, December 31, 1882, p. 5.

49. Robert Hellebranth, *Charles-François Daubigny 1817-1878* (Morgues: Editions Matute, 1976), no. 498: *Le Tonnelier*, 1872, 45 x 65 1/2 in.; Mary Jane Morgan Sale, New York, American Art Galleries, March 8, 1886, lot 160, *The Cooper*, 44 x 64 in.; exhibited Museum of Fine Arts, Boston, 1933; sold New York, Parke-Bernet, December 3, 1942, lot 52, illus., to Leon Cotnareanu; current location unknown.

50. *The New York Times*, December 31, 1882, p. 5.

51. Possibly the painting recorded in Knoedler's stock book, entry no. 4372; notes that Roybet, *Le Précieux Bibelot*, was received from agent Joseph Bulla, Paris, on May 3, 1883, and sold to George I. Seney on March 12, 1884, for $1,100. William Merritt Chase owned a Roybet, *Lady in Black*, in which the central figure admires a large Oriental vase (see Ronald G. Pisano, *William Merritt Chase in the Company of Friends* [Southampton, New York: The Parrish Art Museum, 1979], no. 85, illus. p. 54).

52. Photograph courtesy Michael Wentworth, who identified the various versions and locations of this Tissot subject in nineteenth-century American collections. The Pedestal Fund version, current location unknown, was noted in Knoedler's stock book: no. 2658, *Louvre*, acquired August 1880; it was sold to Mary Jane Morgan, March 1884; Mary Jane Morgan Sale, 1886, lot 178, *In the Louvre*, 28 x 18 in.

53. "The American Art Gallery," *The New York Times*, May 7, 1879, p. 4.

54. In February 1884, Moore & Clarke Co. held a sale of its "entire stock of oil paintings and water colors." (See New York, Moore & Clarke Co., *247 High Class Paintings of the Greatest European Artists Late the Property of Moore and Clarke Co.*, February 20-23, 1884). The sale

included the following works that could be identified with loans to the *Pedestal Fund Art Loan Exhibition*: no. 87, Courbet, *Ocean*, 20 x 29 in., $200; no. 101, Roybet, *Un Grand Seigneur – 17th Century*, 30 x 19 in., $800; no. 255, Roybet, *Masterless*, 20 x 22 in., $350; and no. 171, Stevens, *Child with Flowers*, 20 x 23 in., "a great work of this Master," which sold for $3,650. The sale also included four other paintings by Courbet and three Vollon still lifes.

55. Margaret F. MacDonald, in a letter to the author dated May 1, 1985, stated: "Wunderlich's bought two watercolours from Whistler on 1 August 1883 for £50 according to a letter updating their accounts in January 1884 (Glasgow University W 1140)."

56. Charles A. Dana and his friend, the collector William T. Walters, Baltimore, were important American connoisseurs and patrons of Oriental porcelains. The renown of Dana's porcelain collection exceeded that of his paintings and may account for his not being mentioned by Strahan in *The Art Treasures of America*. For reports of the Dana sale of porcelains (New York, American Art Galleries, February 24-26, 1898), see *The New York Times*, January 21, 1898, p. 7; January 22, 1898, Saturday supplement, p. 60; February 12, 1898, p. 98; February 17, 1898, Magazine, p. 6; February 20, 1898, p. 13; February 26, 1898, p. 6.

57. A. Robaut, *L'Oeuvre de Corot, catalogue raisonné et illustré* (Paris: H. Floury, 1905), no. 1637, *La Fête de Bacchus*, 1866. Salon, Paris, 1866, no. 452, *Le Soir.*

58. *Barye Monument Exhibition*, New York, American Art Galleries, 1889-90, no. 616, Corot, *The Dance of Loves*. Three other Dana loans to the Pedestal Fund show were also loaned to the Barye exhibition: no. 614, Millet, *The Turkey Keeper*; no. 615, Daubigny, *Sunset*; no. 617, Diaz, *The Frog Pond.*

59. Dana Sale, 1898, lot 590, Rousseau, *The Harvest Field*, 16 1/4 x 25 in.; acquired by Mrs. C. A. Griscom; sold at the Griscom sale of 1916; current location unknown.

60. Dana Sale, 1898, lot 589, Daubigny, *On the Oise*, 15 x 26 in.: "An effect of grey weather . . . river in foreground . . . bank rising on right . . . opposite shore covered with trees . . . hour of sunset . . . troubled sky. One tall tree on the hill in back of the distant river rises high above its companions and shows against the sky with dramatic effect"; sold to Isidor Wormser, Jr.; current location unknown.

61. The second Albert Spencer Sale (New York, Fifth Avenue Art Galleries, February 28, 1888) realized $284,000 and was called the "sale of the season" by Walter Rowlands in "Art Sales in America," *The Art Journal*, vol. 40 (1888), pp. 318-19. See also "Spencer's Sale of Pictures," *The New York Times*, February 18, 1888, p. 4, and February 29, 1888, p. 2; "Vom Kunstmarkt," *Kunst-Chronik (Beiblatt)*, 1888, p. 454.

62. *The New York Times*, December 2, 1883, p. 2.

63. *Ibid.*

64. Identified by Robert L. Herbert, Robert Lehman Professor of the History of Art, Yale University, New Haven, Connecticut, as the Millet now titled *The Whisper*, 18 x 15 in., National Gallery, London, Gift of George Salting, 1910. The painting was owned consecutively by Alfred Sensier, Durand-Ruel, and M. Perrau, Paris, before entering the Spencer collection. Spencer Sale, 1888, lot 24, sold to S. D. Warren, Boston, for $3,500; Mrs. S. D. Warren Sale, New York, American Art Association, January 8-9, 1903, lot 78, illus.; sold to Montaignac for $11,100.

65. Located with the assistance of G. Paffrath, Galerie G. Paffrath, Düsseldorf, West Germany, and Frau Ursula Boekels. According to the catalogue of the Spencer Sale, 1888, the Knaus was "received from the artist direct." See Thomas B. Brumbaugh, "Lost in Storage: Ludwig Knaus in American Collections," *Art Journal*, vol. 27 (1968), pp. 262-65, for documentation of Knaus's popularity in America and his personal contacts with American collectors.

66. Alfred de Lostalot, "Ludwig Knaus," *Gazette des Beaux-Arts*, no. 25, per. 2 (1882), pp. 269-80.

67. The Spencer Sale, 1888, included five Fromentins: *Arab Falconer*, 42 1/2 x 28 3/4 in. (Chrysler Museum, Norfolk, Virginia); *Women of the Ouled-Nayls, Sahara*, 42 1/2 x 28 1/2 in. (Art Institute of Chicago); *The Fire*, 12 x 16 in.; *A Boar Hunt*, 15 x 23 in.; *Horse Trading in the Desert*, 8 1/2 x 10 in.

68. Possibly Spencer Sale, 1888, lot 16, *The Old Oak Early Autumn*, 21 x 18 in., from the F. J. Gsell Collection, Vienna (sold to E. Naumberg or G. Loeb for $1,900), or lot 56, *A Cloud Burst* ("shepherd and sheep"), 18 x 13 1/2 in., from the Le Roy and Rousseau collections (sold to Knoedler for $3,300).

69. Spencer Sale, 1888, lot 63, Troyon, *Drove of Cattle and Sheep*, 26 x 39 in., from the Bonnet collection, Paris; it drew one of the highest figures at the Spencer Sale, going to Cornelius Vanderbilt for $26,000. Vanderbilt subsequently loaned the painting to the *Barye Monument Exhibition*, 1889-90.

70. *The Art Amateur*, vol. 24 (1891), p. 88. Spencer loaned four paintings to the "Loan Collection. Foreign Masterpieces owned in the United States," at the World's Columbian Exposition, Chicago, 1893: Edgar Degas, *Race Horses;* Claude Monet, *Morning Fog* and *Down on the Coast of the North Sea*; and Auguste Renoir, *In the Garden*.

71. See William H. Truettner, "William T. Evans, Collector of American Painting," *American Art Journal*, vol. 3, no. 2 (Fall 1971), pp. 50-79.

72. Strahan notes paintings by Courbet in the private collections of T. Wigglesworth, Boston; Beriah Wall, Providence; S. A. Coale, Jr., Saint Louis; and Henry C. Gibson, Philadelphia. Courbet's *The Blacksmith Shop* belonged to Erwin Davis, whose collection was only briefly noted by Strahan; Evans's collection was not listed.

73. New York, American Art Association, *Sale . . . B. Stern . . . and William T. Evans,* March 6, 1890, lot 82, Courbet, *A Mountain Brook*, 19 3/4 x 28 1/4 in.: "A shallow rill breaks a channel for itself down a rocky hillside . . . cascades over a bed of stones . . . on the right a beaten path . . . trees, poor in foliage . . . sparsely clothe the hill-side. The season is early autumn . . . sky is clouded . . . wan light." The painting, current location unknown, may be related to Courbet's *The Hidden Brook*, 23 3/8 x 29 3/4 in., The Metropolitan Museum of Art, New York, or *A Mountain Stream*, 18 1/4 x 21 11/16 in., Arnot Art Museum, Elmira, New York.

74. Evans Sale, 1890, lot 67, Jacque, *On the Hillside,* 8 x 12 in.: "Under a spreading olive tree . . . the shepherd reclines . . . His flock fills the foreground . . . etc."

75. Evans Sale, 1890, lot 66, Pasini, *Constantinople,* 8 3/8 x 15 3/4 in.: "A busy day on the shores of the Bosphorus. . . . At the coffee-house in the foreground merchants and traders gather. . . . A crowd . . . fills the square beyond . . . horseman rides along the quay . . . trading vessels are moored . . . white walls of houses glow in the sunlight. . . . On the farther shore of the strait the houses of Scutari . . . with vessels at the wharves and others in the stream . . . etc."

76. Frances Weitzenhoffer, "First Manet Paintings to Enter an American Museum," *Gazette des Beaux-Arts,* vol. 6, no. 98 (March 1981), p. 126. Weitzenhoffer describes Davis as a gambler who invested in gold and silver mines in California in the 1860s, went into bankruptcy there by 1870, sold Turkish bonds in London, and divided his time between England and France in the 1870s before returning to the United States. Weitzenhoffer also notes, p. 127, that his unpopularity with New York dealers was based on the fact that he bought either at auction or directly from the artists.

77. Pedestal Fund catalogue, 1883, no. 171, Corot, *Moonlight*, may have been lot 38 in Erwin Davis Sale, New York, Fifth Avenue Art Galleries, March 19-20, 1889. Corot landscapes in the Davis Sale included lot 60, *A Summer Day*, 17 1/2 x 22 in.; lot 113, *A Woodland Path*, 19 x 27 1/2 in., "from Faure Sale, Paris, 1873, etched in Durand-Ruel catalogue, 1873"; and lot 125, *In the Woods at Marcoussis*, 23 x 31 1/2 in., "painted for Durand-Ruel, 1869." Lot 23, *The Coliseum*, 14 x 21 in. (The Corcoran Gallery of Art, Washington, D.C., Gift of William A. Clark), illustrated in an article on Corot by Mariana Griswold Van Rensselaer in *The Century Magazine* (June 1889), p. 257, was not acquired by Davis until 1886 at the Beriah Wall and John A. Brown Sale, New York, American Art Galleries, March 30-31, April 1, 1886, lot 203, "Corot, *Roman Landscape with a view of Colisseum,* 5" x 22", to Irwin Davis, $1,000."

78. Pedestal Fund catalogue, 1883, listed Davis's loans of paintings by Narcisse Diaz as nos. 145, *Flowers*; 155, *Rocky Gorge*; and 170, *La Tristesse*; not identifiable by these titles in Davis Sale, 1889.

79. Pedestal Fund catalogue, 1883, no. 146, Théodore Rousseau, *Trees*; possibly Davis Sale, 1889, lot 34, *Autumn*, 7 1/2 x 11 1/2 in., or lot 52, *Landscape and Trees*, 14 x 21 1/2 in. Since only a portion of Davis's collection was sold in 1889, the Pedestal Fund painting could have been excluded from the sale.

80. Possibly Davis Sale, 1889, lot 45, Mauve, *Watching the Flock*, watercolor, 15 x 11 in.

81. The painting was referred to only as a "dead beast" by a contemporary reviewer ("Pedestal Fund Art Loan," *The New York Times,* December 16, 1883, p. 5). Géricault scholars Lorenz Èitner and Hans Lüthy, queried independently, responded that no painting of a dead lamb is known in Géricault's oeuvre.

82. New York, Leavitt Art Galleries, *Collection of the Late Mrs. Benjamin Nathan and Others,* February 10, 1880, lot 11, Kowalski (A. W.), *The Retreat from Moscow,* 21 x 11 in., to E. Davis, 272 Clinton Ave., Brooklyn, $210; lot 64, Clays, (P. J.), *Marine, Coast of Holland,* 34 x 22 in.

83. New York, Leavitt Art Galleries, *Catalogue of Paintings . . . The Private Collection of J. Abner Harper,* March 12-13, 1880, lot 13, Mettling, *Flowers*, 14 x 16 in., to E. Davis for $120 (previously purchased by Harper at the Cottier Sale, 1878, lot 43, *Flowers*, 16 x 13 in., $145).

84. New York, Leavitt Art Galleries, *Catalogue of Mr. John Wolfe's Gallery of Valuable Paintings . . .* April 5-6, 1882, lot 88, Stevens, *Coquetrie; or, The Language of the Fan,* 18 1/4 x 13 in., $1,000; Davis Sale, 1889, lot 35, *Coquetry,* 17 x 13 in., $425.

85. The painting, described by Strahan III, p. 123, as "that superb work of expression and inspiration," was deposited by Davis in the Museum of Fine Arts, Boston, in the 1880s (see Cook, *Art and Artists of Our Time,* II, p. 254), which explains the fact that it was not available for the Pedestal Fund exhibition. Augustus Saint-Gaudens, in Homer Saint-

Gaudens, ed., *Reminiscences of Augustus Saint-Gaudens*, vol. 1, (London: Andrew Melrose, 1913), p. 215, claims that it was on his "earnest recommendation" that Davis gave it to The Metropolitan Museum of Art, New York. See Weitzenhoffer 1981, for an account of Davis's motivation for the gift.

86. Identified by Weitzenhoffer 1981, p. 129; Philadelphia Museum of Art, Thomson Bequest.

87. Paul André Lemoisne, *Degas et son oeuvre*, vol. 2 (Paris: Paul Brame et C. M. Haucke, 1946–49), no. 617, illus. p. 351, *Danseuses*, 29 x 23 1/2 in., Hill-Stead Museum, Farmington, Connecticut; identified by Weitzenhoffer, 1981, p. 129, n.7, who notes that it was bought in at the Davis Sale, 1889, and sold in 1892 to Cottier & Co. It was acquired in 1893 by Alfred Atmore Pope of Farmington, Connecticut. Davis had purchased the painting from Durand-Ruel and loaned it to Durand-Ruel's *Special Exhibition: Works in Oil and Pastel by the Impressionists of Paris,* National Academy of Design, New York, 1886, no. 304, Degas, *Ballet Dancers.* See Kenyon Cox, "The Collection of Mr. Alfred Atmore Pope," in *Noteworthy Paintings in American Private Collections,* ed. John La Farge and A. Jacacci (New York: August F. Jacacci Co., 1907), where *Ballet Dancers* was illustrated, opp. p. 296; described, pp. 281-82; and critically reviewed, pp. 343-49.

88. "The Pedestal Art Loan," *The New York Times,* December 2, 1883, p. 2.

89. Possibly Davis Sale, 1889, lot 61, Courbet, *In the Jura Mountains*, 33 1/2 x 44 in.; described as "a view of pasture and sheer sandstone cliffs," in "Sale of Work by Colorists," *The New York Times,* March 12, 1889, p. 5.

90. Davis Sale, 1889, lot 100, Courbet, *Marine,* 22 x 35 in.

91. See Davis Sale, 1889, lot 122, Cazin, *In the Garden,* 25 x 31 in. Another Cazin, *Castles at Night,* 20 1/2 x 28 in., formerly in the collection of the Walker Art Center, Minneapolis, Minnesota, was described as "painted by Cazin for Mr. Irving Davis from whose collection it comes."

92. Possibly Davis Sale, 1889, lot 80, Henner, *Eve,* 15 1/4 x 9 in.; described in "Sale of Work by Colorists," *The New York Times,* March 12, 1889, p. 5, as "a nude 'Eve' by Henner after his old patent."

93. Possibly the *Petit Bacchus à la coupe* exhibited by Dagnan-Bouveret in the 1877 Salon and listed in John D. Champlin and Charles C. Perkins, *Cyclopedia of Painters and Paintings*, vol. 1 (New York: Scribner's, 1886–87), p. 363, as *Infant Bacchus,* collection not cited.

94. See Eugène Véron, "Th. Ribot Exposition de ses oeuvres dans les galeries de l'Art," *L'Art*, vol. 21 (1880), pp. 127-31, 151-61.

95. The Davis Sale, 1889, included two works by Ribot that might be identified with this painting: lot 51, *Head*, 13 1/2 x 11 in., and lot 85, *Portrait of the Artist*, 17 1/2 x 14 in.

96. Strahan III, p. 123, cites *The Children of Ribot* in the Davis collection; Davis Sale, 1889, lot 92, Ribot, *Portraits of his Children,* 18 x 14 in.

97. Cook, *Art and Artists of Our Time,* II, p. 181.

98. Williams purchased Sargent's *Capri Girl* from the second exhibition of the Society of American Artists, 1879. Cited in "A Maris Painting Sold for $12,000," *The New York Times*, February 5, 1915.

99. See John Robinson, "Personal Reminiscences of Albert Pinkham Ryder," *Art in America*, vol. 13 (June 1925), pp. 176-87. Williams also owned paintings by Jervis McEntee, William Trost Richards, Worthington Whittredge, J. D. Smillie, and Alexander H. Wyant.

100. "A Maris Painting Sold for $12,000," *The New York Times*, February 5, 1915.

101. Moses King, *Notable New Yorkers of 1896-1899* (New York: Moses King, 1899), p. 440, illus.

102. "The Metropolis of To-day," p. 283 (page from untitled, undated periodical in Cottier file, American Arts Department, The Metropolitan Museum of Art, New York).

103. A majority of the European paintings in the Ichabod T. Williams Sale, New York, American Art Galleries, February 3-4, 1915, were listed in the catalogue as having been purchased either from the late Daniel Cottier or from Messrs. Cottier & Co.

104. "Art Notes," *The New York Times*, January 28, 1915, p. 8.

105. Cottier Collection, Paris, Galeries Durand-Ruel, May 27-28, 1892, lot 98, Millet, *L'Enlèvement de Hylas*, 10 x 16 in., illus.; sold to Boussod for FF 3,600.

106. Williams Sale, 1915, lot 90, Monticelli, *An Italian Festival*, 13 x 22 1/2 in., illus.; purchased from the late Daniel Cottier; sold to Francis R. Welch. See Richard Muther, *The History of Modern Painting*, vol. 4 (London: J. M. Dent & Co., 1907), p. 13, illus.

107. Williams Sale, 1915, lot 83, Monticelli, *Dolce Far Niente*, 18 x 13 3/4 in., illus.; purchased from the late Daniel Cottier; sold to Otto Bernet, agent, for $3,600.

108. Williams Sale, 1915, lot 69, Vollon, *Portrait of Corot's Sister*, 9 3/4 x 7 1/2 in., illus.; sold to Hugh Murray for $350.

109. Williams Sale, 1915, lot 78, Dupré, *Marine*, 11 1/4 x 10 1/2 in., illus.; purchased from the late Daniel Cottier; sold to Knoedler for $625.

110. Williams Sale, 1915, lot 70, Jacob Maris, *On the Canal: Holland*, 13 1/2 x 12 1/2 in., illus.; purchased from Messrs. Cottier & Co.; sold to William Henry.

111. Williams Sale, 1915, lot 65, Vollon, *At the Waterside*, 9 1/2 x 13 in., illus.; purchased from Messrs. Cottier & Co.; sold to Otto Bernet.

112. Williams Sale, 1915, lot 62, Matthew Maris, *A Corner of the Hague*, 7 1/2 x 11 1/2 in., illus.; purchased from the late Daniel Cottier; sold to James S. Phillips.

113. Williams also loaned a Théodore Rousseau landscape to the Pedestal Fund exhibition. There were three Rousseaus in the Williams Sale, 1915: two purchased from the late Daniel Cottier: lot 63, *Study of Sunlit Woods*, 5 3/4 x 7 3/4 in., illus., sold to Boardman, and lot 92, *The Well*, 15 1/2 x 26 in., illus.; a third, lot 97, *Pool in the Woods*, 16 x 25 1/2 in., illus., was purchased from Messrs. Cottier & Co., and sold to Mrs. Frederick Cook.

114. Williams Sale, 1915, lot 67, Diaz, *The Lovers*, 12 3/4 x 7 1/4 in., illus.; purchased from Messrs. Cottier & Co.; sold to John H. Fry for $1,625. Peter Bermingham, in *American Art in the Barbizon Mood* (Washington, D.C.: Smithsonian Institution Press, published for the National Collection of Fine Arts, 1975), p. 104, n.17, notes that a painting by Diaz entitled *The Lovers* was sold by Leeds and Company, New York, from the J. F. Beaumont collection, April 1853.

115. Williams Sale, 1915, lot 16, Jacob Maris, *The Siesta*, 1871, 8 1/4 x 13 1/4 in., illus.; purchased from the late Daniel Cottier; sold to Knoedler for $330.

116. Williams Sale, 1915, lot 18, Roybet, *Abduction of Rebecca*, 12 x 14 in., illus.; purchased from the late Daniel Cottier; sold to J. Stillwagon for $335.

117. Williams Sale, 1915, lot 6, Ribot, *The Cook*, 1853, 11 x 8 1/4 in.: "[There is] subdued light from above on the right falling upon the gray-white cap and coat of a hardy peasant who is seated beside a dark brown basket of green vegetables." Purchased from the late Daniel Cottier.

118. Williams Sale, 1915, lot 96, Ribot, *Studio of the Artist*, 22 x 18 1/4 in., illus.; purchased from Messrs. Cottier & Co.; sold to Charles M. Lea for $1,550. See Cook, *Art and Artists of Our Time*, II, p. 193, illus.: *In the Studio*; also, Muther, *The History of Modern Painting*, II, p. 429, illus. Although the catalogue of the Williams Sale indicates that the painting was signed "Ribot, '87," it is clearly the work described in reviews of the Pedestal Fund exhibition. See "The Pedestal Art Loan," *The New York Times*, December 2, 1883, p. 2: "Ribot is represented by a studio interior, with an old artist at work in a waning light"; and "The Fine Arts," *The Critic*, no. 94 (December 15, 1883), p. 504: "[There are] excellent pictures by Ribot . . . the dim interior of a studio, with an old artist at work on a very large painting in a black frame."

119. *The New York Times*, December 2, 1883, p. 2.

120. Williams Sale, 1915, lot 102, Corot, *Evening, Lake Nemi*, 35 1/2 x 23 3/4 in., illus.; purchased from the late Daniel Cottier; sold to Knoedler for $5,200; Knoedler to H. P. Eells, 1915.

121. Williams Sale, 1915, lot 29, C. F. Hill, *Landscape*, 29 x 21 in.: "On a gray day with plenty of light the bend of a river or the confluence of two streams in a wooded landscape is pictured with marked contrasts of light and shade"; purchased from Messrs. Cottier & Co.; sold to William Swift for $400. Possibly exhibited at the Cottier Sale, 1878, lot 128, Hill, *Landscape*, 28 x 20 in; bought in.

122. Williams Sale, 1915, lot 42, *The Heights of Montmartre*. Williams also loaned Jacque's *Shepherdess*, probably Williams Sale, 1915, listed under the joint authorship of Jacque and Georges Michel, lot 38, *Shepherdess, Sheep and Landscape*, 32 x 26 in., illus.; purchased from the late Daniel Cottier; sold to W. W. Seaman for $3,700.

123. "Imaginative Paintings in Current Exhibitions," *The New York Times*, Magazine, Sunday, January 31, 1915, p. 22.

124. *Ibid.*

125. See Brian Gould, *Two Van Gogh Contacts: E. J. van Wisselingh, Art Dealer; Daniel Cottier, Glass Painter and Decorator* (Bedford Park: Naples Press, 1969), and Michael Donnelly, *Glasgow Stained Glass: A Preliminary Study* (Glasgow: Glasgow Museums and Art Galleries, 1981), for discussions of Cottier as glass designer and for a history of his firm. Donnelly, p. 8, notes that Cottier was apprenticed to David Kier in the early 1850s, and that he later worked in London where he enrolled in the Working Men's College and attended lectures by John Ruskin, Dante Gabriel Rossetti, and Ford Madox Brown. After returning to Scotland, he worked in Dunfermline, became chief designer for Messrs. Field & Allen of Leith in 1862, and opened his own studio in Edinburgh at the end of 1864.

126. Gould, p. 2, states that Cottier opened the Langham Place offices in 1867. Donnelly, p. 10, places Cottier's decision to move to London late in 1869, and notes that his partners in London were architect J. Bruce Talbert, Aberdeen art-furniture designer J. M. Brydon, and another Scots designer, William Wallace.

127. Donnelly, p. 9.

128. *Glasgow Evening Times*, October 19, 1893, quoted in Donnelly, p. 9.

129. Gould, p. 3; the business, at 333 Pitt Street, Sydney, operated under the name of Lyon, Cottier & Co. Gould discusses some of the firm's Australian commissions.

130. "Cottier & Co.," *Scribner's Monthly*, vol. 8 (May-October 1874), p. 500.

131. *Ibid.*, pp. 500-501.

132. The series of eleven articles appeared in *Scribner's Monthly*, vols. 10-14 (June 1875-May 1877). Cook later published them as a book, *The House Beautiful: Essays on Beds and Tables, Stools and Candlesticks* (New York: Scribner, Armstrong & Co., 1878). Mark Girouard, *Sweetness and Light: The "Queen Anne" Movement, 1860-1900* (New York: Oxford University Press, 1977), pp. 210-11, discusses Cottier and the aesthetic movement in America; Mason Hammond, "The Stained Glass Windows in Memorial Hall, Harvard University," Cambridge, Massachusetts, 1978 (unpublished ms. in Cottier file, American Arts Department, The Metropolitan Museum of Art, New York), discusses Cottier's stained-glass work in America. Hammond cites Martin Harrison, "Contemporary Art Glass 100 Years Ago," *Glass*, vol. 6, no. 1 (January 1975), pp. 36-39, as another source on Cottier's stained glass.

133. Clarence Cook, "Recent Church Decoration," *Scribner's Monthly*, vol. 15 (1877), p. 569. Augustus Saint-Gaudens, who also assisted La Farge in the painted decoration of Trinity Church, later agreed that he didn't know what La Farge would have done without Cottier in the practical execution of the decoration, but thought that Cook had been misled on the question of art: "I know there isn't a bit of Cottier in the whole church. La Farge had every bit of Cottier's work changed to suit himself. . . . " (from a letter to Stanford White, dated Piazza Barberini, Rome, March 1878, in Homer Saint-Gaudens, ed., *The Reminiscences of Augustus Saint-Gaudens*, vol. 1 (London: Andrew Melrose, 1913), p. 257. Hammond, p. 114, n.7, cites the Trinity Church guidebook, which identified four windows by Cottier & Co.: *The Sower and the Reaper*; *The Virgins*; *The Angel Troubling the Pool*; and *Christ Saying to the Disciples in the Storm: "Peace, Be Still,"* all installed c. 1878.

134. Charles Dumas, "Art Dealers and Collectors," in The Hague, Haags Gemeentemuseum, *The Hague School*, 1983, p. 131, states that van Wisselingh joined Cottier's London firm in 1875. Van Wisselingh later took over his father's art business in The Hague, opened his own gallery in London on Old Bond Street, and set up a branch in Amsterdam in 1892. He was an active bidder at the Cottier sale of 1892 in Paris, purchasing a number of works by Corot, Courbet, Daubigny, Diaz, Jacob and Matthew Maris, Mauve, Mesdag, Mettling, Michel, Monticelli, Neuhuys, Ribot, and Roybet, some of which can be identified with paintings loaned by Cottier to the Pedestal Fund exhibition. See, Paris, Galeries Durand-Ruel, *Catalogue of Ancient and Modern Pictures: Important Works of the French, English and Dutch Schools, Sale of the Pictures of the late Mr. Cottier*, . . . sale Hôtel Drouot, May 27-28, 1892. Annotated copy, Centre de Documentation, Bureau des Commissaire-Priseurs de la Ville de Paris.

135. "The Cottier Gallery," *The New York Times*, September 1, 1879, p. 5: "An unexpected bit of fine painting is to be seen on the broad frame for a mirror which Mr. Albert Ryder has decorated for Cottier & Co. in little panels, each remarkable for its individual fantastic charm. This young artist is in appropriate company here, for his canvases offer a singular parallel in an American to the work of Monticelli."

136. Gould, p. 4.

137. *The Complete Letters of Vincent van Gogh*, vol. 2 (Greenwich, Connecticut: New York Graphic Society, n.d.), pp. 46-47, letter 289, to Theo: "Then I thought that perhaps these drawings would be something for Cottier: I imagine they would look well, placed in the panels of a large cabinet over a mantelpiece, in a wainscot — in short, framed in woodwork as they do in England, and elsewhere, too. But you know how it is with Cottier; when there is a certain degree of style in a drawing he likes it well enough, but alas, he generally pays little. Still, I believe he is one of those who would care for them; and besides, he could display the drawings favorably."

138. "Some Other Pictures," *Scribner's Monthly*, vol. 10 (1875), p. 253.

139. Lloyd Goodrich, *Albert Pinkham Ryder* (New York: George Braziller, 1959), p. 15, noted that "the show roused much interest and was one of the factors leading to the founding in 1877 of a rival to the Academy, the Society of American Artists."

140. "The Fine Arts," *The New York Times*, March 1, 1877, p. 4.

141. Ryder's *Cow in Moonlight* and *Red Cow* were in the sale of the collection of Cottier's widow, London, Christie, Manson & Woods, May 1, 1914. Combined with Ryder's *The Waste of Waters* in lot 141, the three paintings sold to Wallis for £2 2s.

142. *The New York Times*, March 1, 1877, p. 4.

143. See Fronia E. Wissman, "Corot's Hymn to the Sun," *Elvehjem Museum of Art Bulletin* (Madison, Wisconsin), 1984, pp. 9-17, for a full discussion of the Demidoff commission and decorative program.

144. *The New York Times*, March 1, 1877, p. 4.

145. "Notes," *The Art Journal*, vol. 4 (March 1878), p. 94.

146. *Ibid.*

147. "The Cottier Collection of Paintings," *The New York Times*, April 17, 1878, p. 5. Aaron Sheon, *Monticelli: His Contemporaries, His Influences* (Pittsburgh: Museum of Art, Carnegie Institute, 1978), p. 107, n.45, indicates that this might be the *Don Quichotte et Sancho Panza*, c. 1865-66, Musée du Louvre, Paris, and cites La Farge and Jacacci (n.87), p. 442, which mentions collector Herbert Terrell's purchase of the *Don Quixote* from Cottier.

148. The "rumor" was published in the introduction to the sale catalogue (New York, Leavitt Art Galleries, [The Cottier Collection]: *The Great Modern Classic Painters*, April 23-24, 1878), which stated that "Messrs. Cottier & Co., intending to discontinue this branch of their business, have requested Mr. S. P. Avery to undertake the management of a closing-out auction sale of their entire collection of Oil Paintings and Water Color Drawings."

149. *The New York Times*, April 17, 1878, p. 5.

150. Annotated copy from the collection of Samuel P. Avery, The Metropolitan Museum of Art, New York.

151. "The Cottier Collection," *The New York Times*, April 25, 1878, p. 8.

152. "An Impressionist's Work," *The New York Times*, May 20, 1879, p. 5.

153. Catalogue of Cottier Sale, New York, 1878, n.p.

154. *The New York Times*, May 20, 1879, p. 5.

155. *Ibid.*

156. W. E. Henley, "Daniel Cottier," in catalogue of Cottier Sale, Paris, 1892, p. x.

157. Dorothy Weir Young, *The Life and Letters of Julian Alden Weir* (New Haven, Connecticut: Yale University Press, 1960), p. 158, lists Cottier among the guests at Weir's wedding on April 24, 1882. Also present were Cottier's partner, Inglis, artists Chase, Beckwith, and Warner, and collector Davis. See also John Robinson (n. 99), pp. 176-87, which notes Ryder's friendship with Cottier and his family. Three of Ryder's paintings, *The Stable*, *The Lovers*, and *Eve of St. Agnes*, were later given to the Vassar College Art Gallery, Poughkeepsie, New York, by Cottier's daughter Peggy (Mrs. Lloyd Williams) in memory of her father.

158. "The Society of American Artists," *Scribner's Monthly*, vol. 16, no. 1 (May 1878), p. 147.

159. "Daniel Cottier," *The New York Times*, April 18, 1891, p. 5.

160. "Notes," *The Art Journal*, vol. 5 (January 1879), p. 32.

161. Samuel P. Avery, "The Artist Monticelli," *The New York Times*, September 29, 1879, p. 2, letter to the editor from Avery, dated New York, September 5, 1879: "Will you please do me the justice to state that I was the first person who introduced the works of this artist here, and several years before the agency of Cottier & Co. was established in this country? . . . With one exception, these were sold with much difficulty, at small prices, to Bostonians."

162. Henley, in catalogue of Cottier Sale, Paris, 1892, pp. xii-xiii.

163. Cottier Sale, New York, 1878, lot 130, Bellenger, Paris, *Diana*, 77 x 40 in., passed. Pedestal Fund catalogue, 1883, no. 86, Bellinger (*sic*) and M. Maris, *Diana*.

164. Cottier Sale, Paris, 1892, lot 26, Corot, *Le Clair de lune*, 11 x 14 in., illus.; sold to van Wisselingh for FF 6700; Robaut identifies the Cottier painting as a replica of Robaut 1138, *Clair de lune aux quatre baigneuses*, owned by Hendrik Mesdag.

165. Cottier Sale, Paris, 1892, lot 19, Corot, *Les Dunes de Zuydcoote, près Dunkerque*, 29 x 50 1/4 in., illus.; sold to Durand-Ruel, FF 65,000; Robaut 1543, *Souvenir de Zuydcoote*.

166. C. H. Stranahan, *A History of French Painting from Its Earliest to Its Latest Practice* (New York: Scribner's, 1899), p. 240, identified one of the Corot landscapes owned by Cottier: "The *Frog Pond*, exhibited by Cottier at the Loan Exhibition for the Bartholdi Pedestal Fund in New York, 1884, was insured for $25,000. It is in color one of his most pleasing pictures." There was no Corot of appropriate title or size to match this description in the 1892 Cottier sale.

167. Pedestal Fund catalogue, 1883, no. 97, Diaz, *Flower Piece;* no. 98, Diaz, *Bouquet de Fleures* [*sic*]. Cottier Sale, Paris, 1892, included lot 52, Diaz, *Fleurs*, 15 3/4 x 10 in., illus.; sold to van Wisselingh, FF 3,500.

168. "The Cottier Gallery," *The New York Times*, September 1, 1879, p. 5, referred to Monticelli's friendship with Diaz and spread the rumor that "the memory of Diaz has been reproached with a want of fair-dealing toward a companion to whose genius he owed some of his own great successes as a painter, while the insinuations have been made that the fortunate, money-making Diaz was in no hurry to bring his friend forward to reap some of the pecuniary rewards which he was at one time gaining." Samuel P. Avery, in an 1879 letter to the editor of *The New York Times*, September 5, 1879, found the judgment ludicrous, and insisted that despite the fact that Diaz knew Monticelli and took an interest in his work, he (Monticelli) was an artist of "such unsettled mind and habits as to prevent him from giving the study necessary to become an accomplished painter."

169. Yale University Art Gallery, New Haven, Connecticut, Gift of Duncan Phillips; sold by Cottier to Ichabod T. Williams; Williams Sale, 1915, no. 95, *The Farmyard*, 15 1/2 x 24 in., sold to W. W. Seaman, agent, for $1,000.

170. Monticelli, *Autumn Landscape*, 15 1/2 x 23 1/2 in., Allen Memorial Art Museum, Oberlin College, Oberlin, Ohio, Gift of Mrs. A. A. Healy.

171. Monticelli, *The Fountain of Youth*, 15 1/2 x 12 3/8 in., Museum of Art, Carnegie Institute, Pittsburgh, Museum Purchase, 1903; Cottier Sale, 1878, lot 75, bought in by Cottier.

172. The sale of the collection of Cottier's partner James S. Inglis, New York, American Art Association, March 9-10, 1909, included lot 96, Charles Daubigny, *On the River below Dordrecht*, 18 1/4 x 32 in., sold to James R. Wilson for $2,050 (Hellebranth 741). Another version of this subject (Hellebranth 742), *Moulins à Dordrecht* (*Mills at Dordrecht*, cat. no. 24), was in the Charles T. Yerkes Sale, New York, American Art Association, April 5-8, 1910, lot 34.

173. "The Fine Arts," *The New York Times*, March 1, 1877, p. 4, described the Daubigny hanging in the place of honor: "Naturally enough a green landscape, but one exceptional for depth of color and fineness of feeling. By gaslight the superb painting yields even greater charms than by day, for the gas penetrates the deepest shadows under the heavy mass of foliage and above a sleeping pond. Against the sky hovers a hawk, and to the left, on a partially leafless tree, are smaller birds on which he probably has his eye. This is a very large canvas for Daubigny, yet size has not hurt his strength a whit."

174. The two paintings by Bosboom, a church and a Dutch interior, may have been Cottier Sale, Paris, 1892, lot 12, *Interior of a Church*, 14 1/4 x 11 1/4 in., sold to van Wisselingh, or lot 13, *Interior of a Church at Alkmaar*, panel, 7 1/2 x 5 3/4 in., sold to Bruce; and lot 14, *Dutch Interior*, 14 1/2 x 10 1/4 in., sold to De St. Joachim.

175. Pedestal Fund catalogue, 1883, no. 185, *Dutch Interior*. The paintings by Blommers that were popular in America were often scenes of Dutch peasant life, with interiors populated by women and children.

176. Possibly Cottier Sale, Paris, 1892, lot 84, Mesdag, *L'Arrivée des bateaux*, 16 x 20 1/2 in.: "In the foreground two fishing boats anchored in sight of Scheveningen, waiting low tide; the fishermen are unloading their catch, and going between the boats and the shore, with baskets of fish." Sold to van Wisselingh for FF 2,200.

177. Pedestal Fund catalogue, 1883, no. 107, *Idyl*; possibly Cottier Sale, New York, 1878, lot 125, *Day Dreams*, 25 x 29 in., bought in.

178. "The Pedestal Art Loan," *The New York Times*, December 16, 1883, p. 5. A reference to the death of Mauve, in Montezuma, "My Note Book," *The Art Amateur*, vol. 18, no. 5 (April 1888), p. 104, also notes that Cottier was the first to introduce the Dutch artist's work to America.

179. Cottier Sale, New York, 1878, lot 61, Mauve, *Pastures in Holland*, 31 x 48 in., withdrawn; also noted in Montezuma, 1888, p. 104; The Metropolitan Museum of Art, New York, Bequest of Benjamin Altman.

180. Cottier Sale, Paris, 1892, lot 83, Mauve, *Milking-Time*, 31 1/2 x 49 in., illus.; sold to Boussod for FF 7,000; current location unknown.

181. Cottier Sale, Paris, 1892, lot 82, Mauve, *The Beach at Scheveningen, Holland*, 13 x 27 1/2 in., illus.; sold to van Wisselingh for FF 7,200; noted in Montezuma, 1888, p. 104; current location unknown.

182. Centennial Exhibition, Philadelphia, 1876, Department IV, Art, Netherlands, no. 109, A. Mauve, The Hague, *Hauling up the Fishing Boats*. A number of Mauve's variations on this subject, including versions in the collections of two Dutch museums, the Dordrechts Museum, Dordrecht, and the Haags Gemeentemuseum, The Hague, are cited in The Hague, Haags Gemeentemuseum, *The Hague School*, 1983, p. 236, but none corresponds to the dimensions of the Cottier painting.

183. Cottier Sale, Paris, 1892, lot 72, Jacob Maris, *View of Amsterdam*, 32 x 58 in., illus.; sold to Boussod for FF 6,000.

184. Cottier Sale, Paris, 1892, lot 73, Jacob Maris, *Canal in Holland*, 13 1/2 x 11 1/2 in., illus.; sold to van Wisselingh for FF 1,500. A nearly identical painting is the *Allotments near The Hague*, Haags Gemeentemuseum, The Hague, the Netherlands. Maris painted this scene often and under different atmospheric conditions. (See The Hague, 1983, no. 57, p. 209.)

185. Cottier Sale, Paris, 1892, lot 125, Neuhuys, *La Première Leçon*, 39 1/2 x 29 1/2 in., illus.; sold to van Wisselingh for FF 3,500; Dordrechts Museum, Dordrecht, the Netherlands.

186. This was probably lot 64, Mancini, *The Fan*, 30 1/2 x 25 1/4 in., illus., in the Inglis Sale, New York, 1909, which depicted a seated woman, resting, while holding a large feather fan. The dimensions of this painting match those of lot 26, Mancini, *Tired Out*, 30 x 25, in the Cottier Sale, New York, 1878.

187. "The Pedestal Art Loan," *The New York Times*, December 16, 1883, p. 5, referring to Pedestal Fund catalogue, 1883, no. 139, O. Törna, *Moonlight*. The three paintings in the Centennial Exhibition, Philadelphia, 1876, Department IV, Art, Sweden, were sent by O. Törna, Düsseldorf, no. 64a, *Pine Forest, Sweden*; no. 64b, *Moonrise*, Sweden; no. 64c, *Birch Forest*, Sweden.

188. Probably sold to I. T. Williams; see Williams Sale, 1915, lot 7, Vollon, *Rembrandt*, 11 1/2 x 9 in.: "Study-copy of a portrait of Rembrandt, in head and shoulders, as a young man. He is in the picturesque costume of the age, all dark, and wears a large, full, dark velvet cap, below which his dark reddish-brown hair falls to his shoulders. The subject is seen in a screened light, as though through a haze or in dusky precincts." Purchased from Messrs. Cottier & Co.

189. Cottier Sale, New York, 1878, lot 99, Vollon, *Donkey*, 13 x 16 in.; bought in. Later sold to Mary Jane Morgan; Mary Jane Morgan Sale, 1886, lot 20, *Study of a Donkey*, 13 x 16 in.; sold to Mrs. Alice Newcomb. *George Crocker. . . and others*, New York, Plaza Hotel, January 24, 1912, lot 15, 12 1/2 x 15 3/4 in., illus.; sold to H. N. Spraker for $725. Current location unknown.

190. The identity of the painter of *Donkey Ride* has not been securely determined, but he was probably the same "Valton, Paris" whose *Homely Duties* was sold in the Cottier Sale, New York, 1878, lot 32, 15 x 12 in.; sold to E. K. Sutton for $110. He may have been Edmond Eugène Valton (1836–1910), who studied with F. Fossey and at the Ecole des Beaux-Arts, Paris, and was known as a landscape and genre painter.

191. Cottier Sale, New York, 1878, lot 105, T. Ribot, *A Vendean*, 21 x 18 in.; withdrawn. Cottier Sale, Paris, 1892, lot 131, *Le Vendéen*, 1863, 21 3/4 x 17 3/4 in.: "Standing, in a soft hat and knapsack, his left hand on the barrel of his gun." Sold to van Wisselingh for FF 5,700. Montreal Museum of Fine Arts, Bequest of Miss Adaline Van Horne.

192. "The Fine Arts. The Pedestal Fund Art Loan Exhibition," *The Critic*, no. 94 (December 15, 1883), p. 504. Cottier Sale, Paris, 1892, included lot 132, Ribot, *Le Joueur au Mandoline (The Mandoline-Player)*, 21 3/4 x 18 in.: "Standing, the bust half bare, dressed in a large black cloak which makes a great fold on his left arm and shoulder, he sings to his own accompaniment on a mandoline." Sold to Inglis. Current location unknown.

193. Cottier Sale, Paris, 1892, lot 141, Roybet, *Une Cuisine au seizième siècle (A Sixteenth-Century Kitchen)*, 12 1/2 x 16 in., illus.; sold to van Wisselingh for FF 3,000. Current location unknown.

194. Cottier Sale, New York, 1878, lot 49, Roybet, *Return from the Chase*, 36 x 27 in., withdrawn. This is probably the painting in the Mary Jane Morgan Sale, 1886, lot 145, *Return from the Chase*, 36 x 26 in.; sold to H. O. Havemeyer for $2,000. Current location unknown.

195. Cottier Sale, Paris, 1892, lot 85, Mettling, *Le Recurage (Scouring)*, 1874, 18 1/2 x 15 3/4 in., illus.; sold to van Wisselingh for FF 3,700. National Gallery of Canada, Ottawa, acquired in 1911 as *The Studio*.

196. Cottier Sale, Paris, 1892, lot 32, Courbet, *L'Automne*, 28 3/4 x 23 1/2 in., illus.; sold to Durand-Ruel. Robert Fernier, *La Vie et l'oeuvre de Gustave Courbet: Catalogue raisonné*, 2 vols. (Lausanne and Paris: Fondation Wildenstein, La Bibliothèque des Arts, 1977-78), no. 567, *L'Automne*, 1866. Current location unknown.

197. Cottier Sale, Paris, 1892, lot 31, Courbet, *La Grotte de la Loue*, 24 x 28 3/4 in.: " . . . in front on the ground, covered with snow, two roebuck, one of which is lying near a thicket whose branches are touched with snow. . . . On the left, the entrance of the grotto, rendered inaccessible by a stream of water, whose bluish surface is visible. Above the grotto precipitous rock." Sold to Durand-Ruel. Fernier 966; illus. vol. 2, p. 207; Collection Luziki, 1919.

198. New York, American Art Galleries, *The Valuable Paintings and Other Art Property of the Late James S. Inglis of Cottier & Company, New York*, March 11-12, 1909, lot 90, Courbet, *The Wave*, 21 1/2 x 29 in.; sold to F. B. Pratt; given by Mrs. Frederic B. Pratt to The Brooklyn Museum (cat. no. 18). Fernier 679, *Marine, les vagues*. The dimensions of this painting are close to those of the Courbet *Ocean* in the Moore & Clarke Co. Sale, 1884 (n.54). It is presumably the painting exhibited at the Pedestal Fund show under this title.

199. Cottier Sale, Paris, 1892, lot 30, Courbet, *La Caverne (The Cavern)*, 1861, 53 x 39 1/4 in.: "In the foreground, on the right, trees stripped of their foliage by the beginning of winter. To the left, on a level with the ground, which is scattered with snow-flakes, the entrance of a cave in the hillside. Behind the trees another hill, which shuts out the horizon. Grey sky." Sold to van Wisselingh for FF 7,000. Current location unknown.

200. "The Pedestal Art Loan," *The New York Times*, December 16, 1883, p. 5. Susan Casteras, Yale Center for British Art, New Haven, Connecticut, suggests the artist may be Walter Reynolds (fl. 1859–1885; exhibited Royal Academy of Arts 1879–84).

201. Cottier Sale, New York, 1878, included three paintings by Philippe Rousseau. Lot 109, *Landscape — Evening*, 9 1/2 x 13 in., sold to J. A. Harper for $160. Lot 36, *Still Life*, 8 x 13 in., sold to Huffington for $65. Lot 103, *A Well-Provided Pantry*, 9 x 14 in., was bought in by Cottier and was possibly the painting he loaned to the Pedestal Fund show.

William Merritt Chase: Innovator and Reformer

Ronald G. Pisano

During the 1870s, William Merritt Chase (fig. 1) gained recognition as a consummate painter, influential art teacher, and international figure in the art world whose paintings won for him many coveted awards in this country and abroad. He was the epitome of success — a gentleman artist, a collector of fine art and *objets d'art,* and an arbiter of taste and fashion. An energetic spokesman for his fellow artists, Chase joined just about every art club and organization that espoused high artistic ideals, and was at the forefront of the crusade for greater art appreciation in this country — for both American and European art. It is no surprise then that when in 1883 artists were called upon to help raise money to fund the construction of a base for the Statue of Liberty, soon to be erected in New York Harbor, Chase volunteered his services. He and his friend J. Carroll Beckwith played a major role in organizing an exhibition of European art to support this worthwhile cause. Chase's motives for doing so, however, were not solely patriotic. As a controversial leader of the progressive movement in American art, Chase used this exhibition as a means of expressing his own ideas about European art. He created a scandal that drew immediate attention to his cause and served to open many American eyes to French Impressionism. By including just a few paintings by Edouard Manet, Hilaire Germain Edgar Degas, and several of their colleagues, Chase managed to strike a discordant note in what otherwise would have been received as a harmonious display of European art. In doing so, he affected the course of American art and art appreciation — one of the many ways in which his influence was felt and which contributed to his being described by a contemporary writer as "a leading spirit in American art."[1]

Although born in a small town in Indiana in 1849, Chase had aspirations well beyond a place in his father's small mercantile business. As a first step toward his goal of high artistic achievement, he studied painting under a local artist. Then, in 1870, he traveled to New York City for more formal training at the National Academy of Design. Unfortunately, Chase was forced to return to the Midwest after a year because his father's failing business would no longer support the young artist's studies. Chase was devastated, feeling that he was doomed to a life in the backwaters of nearby St. Louis, a place that he perceived as offering an artist neither inspiration nor financial rewards. In spite of the unsympathetic environment, a few serious artists were at work in the area. One, John Mulvaney, had just returned from studies in Munich and excited Chase's interest with descriptions of the art treasures of the Continent. Chase could hardly avoid dreaming and talking about having such an opportunity himself. This dream became a reality when several local businessmen raised the sum of $2,100 to finance such a trip. When approached with their offer, Chase's reply,

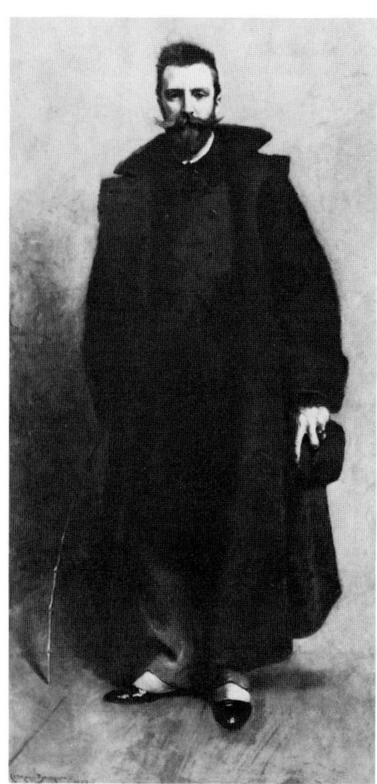

FIG. 1.
J. CARROLL BECKWITH
William Merritt Chase, 1882
Oil on canvas, 78 x 42 in.
Indianapolis Museum of Art,
Indianapolis, Gift of the Artist

now legendary, was: "My God, I'd rather go to Europe than go to heaven."[2]

Chase embarked for Munich in 1872, and there enrolled at the Royal Academy. At the Academy — where he spent the next six years — he was trained as a realist, specializing in figure paintings executed with bold, bravura brushwork. He was taught a reverence for the old masters, particularly Frans Hals and Velásquez, and developed an admiration and respect for modern European realist painters such as Wilhelm Leibl, a German, and Gustave Courbet, the great French artist. During this period he also developed an interest in contemporary Dutch, Spanish, and Italian painting. To compensate his patrons for their support during those years abroad, Chase became their agent, purchasing European paintings for their collections. In doing so he developed a discerning eye and a considerable collection of his own.

While Chase was studying in Munich, his own paintings began to attract attention from artists and critics in the United States.[3] His boldly painted figure piece *Keying Up: The Court Jester* (1875; fig. 2) won an award when it was exhibited at the 1876 Centennial Exposition in Philadelphia; and in 1878, when it was featured in the National Academy of Design's Annual Exhibition, it was singled out as "one of the most vigorous specimens of figure painting" exhibited.[4] In 1878 Chase also exhibited the subtle and masterful *Ready for the Ride* (1877) at the inaugural exhibition of the Society of American Artists, in New York. It created a sensation and was purchased by the eminent art dealer Samuel P. Avery, best known for purveying European paintings to wealthy Americans. The art critic Mariana Griswold Van Rensselaer quickly observed that this was "a strange thing . . . to happen to the work of a new American painter."[5]

These stunning successes persuaded Chase that it was time to return to the United States. He was encouraged in this decision by his mentor Karl von Piloty, who astutely predicted: "Yours will be the greatest country of artists and art lovers. . . . Italy, France, Germany, Spain, England, these have had their day, the future is to America."[6] Chase affirmed his faith in America and in his destiny there when he turned down a teaching position at the prestigious Munich Academy in order to accept a post at New York's fledgling Art Students League, which was struggling in its third year of existence with but one instructor. Chase later explained: "I was young; American art was young; I had faith in it."[7] The self-confidence conveyed by this decision would prove to be the key factor in Chase's subsequent success as an artist and as a spokesman for art and artists in America.

Brimming with optimism, Chase boarded the SS *Switzerland* on August 30, 1878, bound from Antwerp to New York. Coincidentally, another American artist was on board. James Carroll Beckwith (1852–1917), who was returning from his studies in Paris, had been offered a post at the Art Students League, as well. The two artists (figs. 3, 4), who had met earlier in Munich, renewed their friendship and discussed their plans for the future. Even in their youthful enthusiasm they could not have suspected the profound effect their joint efforts would have on the course of American art. By this time the stage had been set in New York, the nation's most prosperous city, and already its most important art center. The Art Students League had been founded in 1875 by a group of artists who objected to the restrictive policies of the National Academy's fifty-year old art school. The Society of American Artists — where Chase's painting *Ready for the Ride* had created such a stir — had also been established in 1875, in reaction to a new policy of the National Academy, which guaranteed academicians preferred placement in the annual exhibitions at the expense of less-established artists. It was a conflict of the new against the old: young artists like Chase were returning from their studies in the cosmopolitan art centers of Europe and challenging the well-established artists of the "old guard," particularly the painters of the Hudson River School. The new generation consisted largely of figure painters who stressed the aesthetic nature of painting, as well as technical virtuosity. The old guard consisted primarily of landscape and portrait painters who practiced a more literal interpretation of nature. From the start, the avant-garde painters were criticized for the overriding European influences evident in their work. There is no question that their paintings — in both subject and style — strongly reflected their experience abroad. In fact, some found it nearly impossible to exist in an America they considered philistine. America's great art museums — such as the Museum of Fine Arts in Boston, The Corcoran Gallery of Art in Washington, D.C., and The Metropolitan Museum of Art in New York — were just being formed, and their displays paled before the richness of what many young artists had seen abroad. In fact, as late as 1881, one critic appealed to the New-York Historical Society — a collection then described as "the most remarkable . . . in the country" — to lend its paintings to The Metropolitan Museum of Art so that they might be publicly seen.[8] Cultural patterns and tastes were changing fast, though. America was prosperous, and there was a new awareness and appreciation of both European art and the work of the most forward-looking American artists.

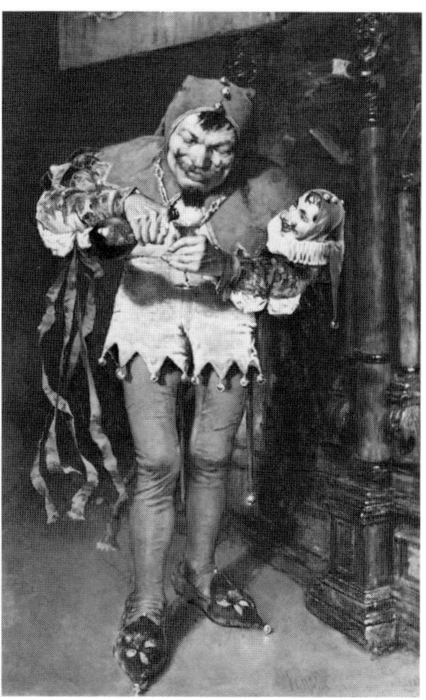

FIG. 2.
WILLIAM MERRITT CHASE
Keying Up: The Court Jester, 1875
Oil on canvas, 39 3/4 x 24 7/8 in.
The Pennsylvania Academy of the Fine Arts, Philadelphia

Notwithstanding the excitement and prosperity in the air, in 1878 these developments had not progressed sufficiently to favor such artists as Chase and Beckwith. The Hudson River School was still well established and considered by some collectors to be the traditionally American expression. Other wealthy Americans were forming impressive collections of European paintings. The uniformity of American taste in contemporary European art was amazing, with the French School and French-influenced paintings dominating. Popular artists from across Europe exhibited at the Paris Salon, including the Spanish painter Mariano Fortuny y Carbo; the Italians Giuseppe de Nittis, Giovanni Boldini, and Francesco Michetti; the Hungarian Michael Munkácsy; the Belgians Alfred Stevens and Frederik Hendrik Kaemmerer; and the Dutch artists Joseph Israels and Barend Koekkoek.[9] The awakening American interest in contemporary European art was stimulated by several factors: the extensive display of international art at the Philadelphia Centennial Exposition in 1876, the increase in foreign travel by Americans, and the promotion of European paintings — especially those exhibited at the Paris Salons — by dealers in the United States.

Where did this leave Chase and his colleagues — artists who were American by birth but whose subjects and styles were associated with the European camp? They were condemned by the proponents of the Hudson River School as "unpatriotic," yet they did not have the "pedigree" or "mystique" of the European painters, who most appealed to those collectors who had just begun to spend large sums on European art. Some of these American artists became discouraged. Will H. Low reported the failure of the Society of American Artists' third exhibition in 1880: "No one sold anything: we were popularly supposed to be producing art for art's sake, and we were left severely alone to that delightful occupation."[10]

In spite of factors that worked against many of the new generation of American artists, Chase prospered. Why? Because he was clever, resourceful, self-confident, and vital. He realized he would not be able to survive on the proceeds of the few paintings that might be sold at exhibitions. The need for additional, steady income was an important reason for his decision to take up teaching. As a teacher, he would earn enough money to continue painting without the painful sacrifice of his artistic ideals. He also hoped to become a successful painter of portraits. To attract commissions from wealthy clients, he had to create an image of himself that implied affluence, success, and artistic taste. This he achieved through his surroundings, his mode of dress, and through his engaging personality. He was determined to be the epitome of success, a gentleman artist, collector, connoisseur, and tastemaker; and the rapidity with which he accomplished these goals is astounding. As reported by his fellow artist Charles Henry Miller, Chase, "upon returning to New York, virtually took the town by storm."[11] He secured quarters for himself in the highly desirable Tenth Street Studio Building (fig. 5), bastion of the Hudson River School painters, and made his presence there known in no uncertain terms. His lavish studio was recognized, again in Miller's words, as the "sanctum sanctorum of the aesthetic

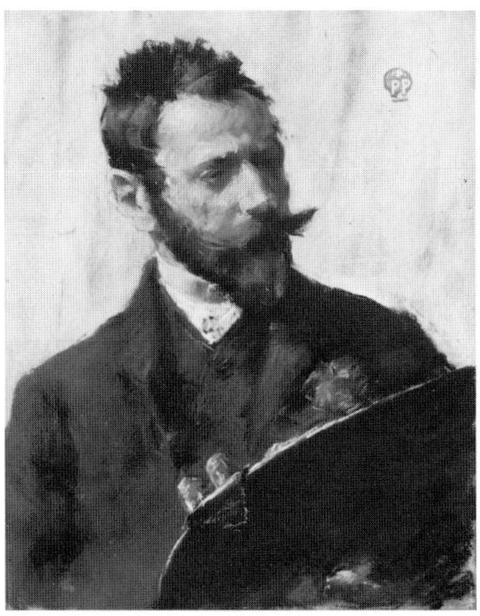

FIG. 3.
WILLIAM MERRITT CHASE, *Portrait of the Artist (Self-Portrait)*, c. 1884
Pastel on paper, 17 1/4 x 13 1/2 in.
Collection Mr. and Mrs. Raymond J. Horowitz, New York

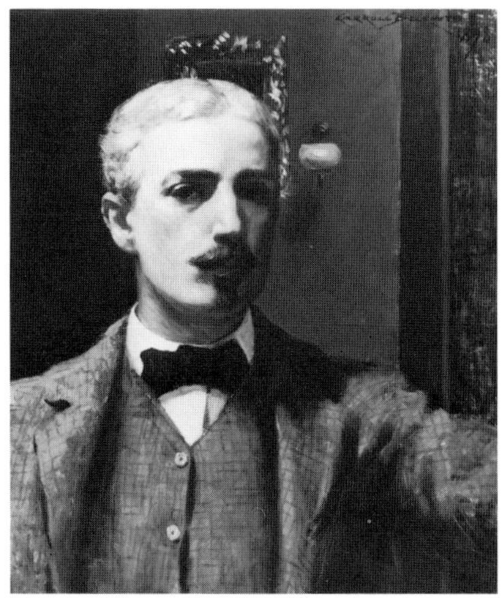

FIG. 4.
J. CARROLL BECKWITH, *Self-Portrait*
Paint on wood panel, 24 x 19 1/2 in.
The Detroit Institute of Arts

fraternity" — whose chief spokesman Chase became.[12] The decorative objects, paintings, and furniture in his home spanned continents and centuries and all were described to the public in several accounts, beginning as early as 1879.[13] His own paintings, such as *The Tenth Street Studio* (fig. 6), recreated in brilliant color the opulence of the setting. Chase's studio was even featured in a whimsical novel of the period, *Witch Winnie's Studio,* in which the author, Elizabeth Champney, provided a typical student's response to it:

> A knock at Mr. Chase's door was the "open sesame" to a magical change. A high studded room hung with tapestries and armour, and filled with beautifully carved furniture and rare old bric-a-brac, opened before us. This proved to be only an ante-room, for the servant, a Negro in buttons, who reminded the imaginative Winnie of a Nubian slave, showed us into the studio proper, formerly the picture gallery for the building.[14]

Chase himself, as can be seen in the well-known Beckwith portrait (fig. 1), attracted equal attention as he made his way down the avenues elegantly dressed in spats and cutaway coat, with a scarf threaded through a bejeweled ring and a carnation in his buttonhole. The total effect was often enhanced by a Russian hound. While artists such as Will H. Low were sulking in the background writing their memoirs, Chase was living life to the fullest.

During the late 1870s and throughout the 1880s, Chase established himself as one of this country's foremost artists and art teachers. His kindness endeared him to art students, and his sincerity, technical skill, and dedication to promoting an appreciation of art in this country gained him the respect and support of his fellow artists. His flamboyant personal style and engaging wit charmed his patrons and amused the press. No one ignored him. It is not surprising, therefore, that he played a major role in the development of American art during this period of his career. He was considered to be a reformer and an iconoclast, an advocate of change who shocked the art world on more than one occasion. Undoubtedly he knew that the intentionally jarring reds of his boldly painted *Keying Up: The Court Jester* would provoke a reaction from critics at the Centennial Exhibition. He used similar tactics in subsequent years — as in 1886 when he surprised critics and stole the show at the American Watercolor Society's annual exhibition with an egg-tempera painting that measured five and a half by six and a half feet, overwhelming all of the traditionally small entries.[15]

During the late 1870s and early 1880s, Chase was an active member of many important art organizations and artistic fraternities. He was a founding

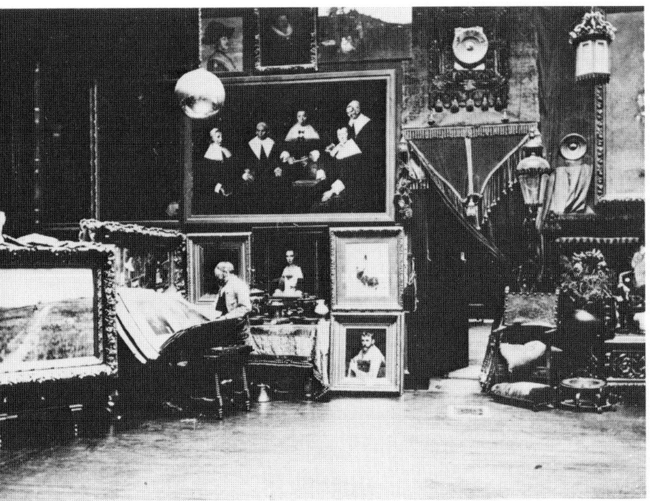

FIG. 5.
Chase's Tenth Street Studio, c. 1890
William Merritt Chase Archives
The Parrish Art Museum,
Southampton, New York

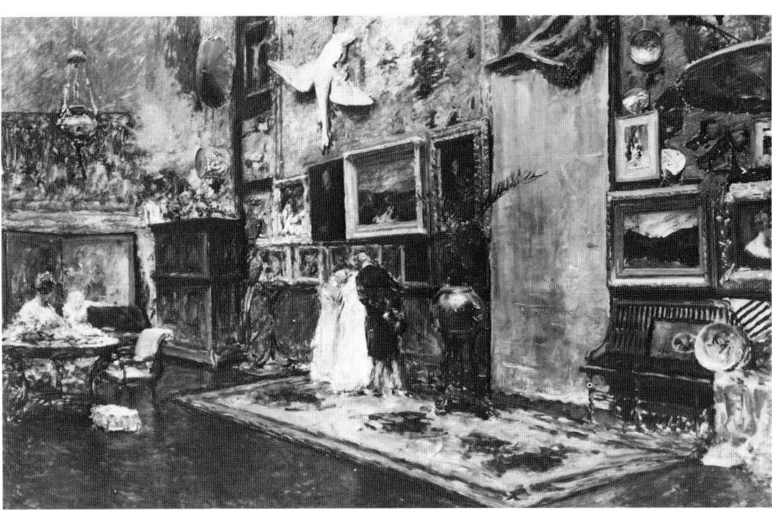

FIG. 6.
WILLIAM MERRITT CHASE
The Tenth Street Studio
Oil on canvas, 47 x 66 in.
Museum of Art, Carnegie Institute,
Pittsburgh

member of the Society of Painters in Pastel in 1882. He was also a member of the Salmagundi Club, the Art Club, and the Tile Club, the latter an informal forum for progressive artists. With other members of the Tile Club, he traveled on summer excursions to upstate New York in 1879 and to Eastern Long Island in 1881,[16] making sketches such as *A Subtle Device* (fig. 7). Most important among his memberships in artistic organizations was his participation in the Society of American Artists, which he served as president in 1880 and again from 1885 to 1895.

In addition to his involvement in all these organizations and progressive art activities at home during the 1880s, Chase, with his friend Beckwith and other colleagues, made regular pilgrimages to Europe during the summer months to study the work of the old masters, to see important contemporary exhibitions, and to renew friendships made in student days. In 1881 Chase and his associates traveled to Spain; he then went on to Paris, where his portrait of American painter Frank Duveneck, *The Smoker* (1875; reportedly later destroyed by fire), received an honorable mention at the Salon. During this trip, he met the Belgian artist Alfred Stevens, who was at the height of his career. Stevens took an interest in Chase, advising him to abandon his old-master style of painting, which he had learned in Munich, and to lighten his palette. It is likely that Stevens introduced Chase to the work of Manet and Berthe Morisot, two of his close friends. While in Paris Chase encountered his American friend J. Alden Weir, with whom he discussed his interest in the work of Manet. Perhaps at Chase's suggestion, Weir purchased two major paintings by Manet for the American collector Erwin Davis, *Boy with a Sword* (pl. XVII) and *Woman with a Parrot* (pl. XVIII).

During the summer of 1882, Chase, Beckwith, and several other artists visited Spain once again, stopping on the way in Paris, where Chase's *Portrait of Peter Cooper* (*The Burgomaster*) (c. 1882; later destroyed by fire) was on exhibition at the Salon. After visiting Madrid, Chase returned to Paris, where he met Boldini, and then proceeded to Holland before sailing for home.

The spring of 1883 was a particularly busy time for Chase and Beckwith: they were preparing for the first exhibition of the Society of Painters in Pastel, which was to be held that fall, and they met regularly to select paintings for the American section of the Munich Crystal Palace exhibition scheduled for later that year.[17] Toward the end of May, the two artists shifted their attention to the organization of the Bartholdi *Pedestal Fund Art Loan Exhibition*. Chase served on five committees for this exhibition: the Executive Committee, the Committee on the Admission of Objects (as Chairman), the Committee on Painting and Sculpture, the Committee on Decoration, and the Reception Committee. Although Painting and Sculpture, the most important committee, was chaired by Beckwith, it is obvious that Chase played an active role there, too. In fact, he and Beckwith (described as "the working members") probably made the entire selection themselves.[18] As close friends with similar artistic tastes and as fellow teachers at the Art Students League and associates in similar ventures, they worked well together and shared a thorough knowledge of the artistic movements of the Continent. Both were concerned with making an aesthetically discerning selection rather than a catholic one; and the choices they made represented without a doubt their personal tastes and convictions.

Although several meetings were held that spring before Chase left for Europe on June 2, the selection process probably did not begin until he returned. That fall, Chase and Beckwith worked tirelessly to complete arrangements for loans to the show, which was only two months away. On November 5, Beckwith noted in his diary: "[I] attended the Pedestal Fund meeting. I am heartily sick of committees and meetings."[19] On a more positive note, he wrote the following week that he had had lunch with Chase, and they had spent the afternoon gathering pictures for the show. On November 14, Beckwith and Chase visited the collector Erwin Davis, from whose collection they "selected a lot of other works," including the two Manets Chase may have been instrumental in placing in Davis's collection. Apparently the meeting went well, and three days later Beckwith took Davis and his family to Chase's studio. From November 28 until December 3, the evening the show was to open, Beckwith and Chase worked ceaselessly arranging and hanging the exhibition. Exhausted, Beckwith wrote on November 28: "All the day and evening I have been at the Academy with Chase hanging the stunning collection we have brought together. . . . I am tired out but I hope it will be a success." A very different picture was reported by the *New York Herald* the following day: "In the large south picture gallery the artists J. Carroll Beckwith and William M. Chase go gayly singing about their task of hanging the superb collection of works which they have selected."[20] The conscientious Beckwith worked up to the last minute, leaving the Academy at seven o'clock on the evening the show was to open. That night he wrote in his diary: "I have been home all evening while the crowd was disporting itself at the Academy . . . I was too tired to go back." Both Beckwith and Chase knew that their selection was daring and would create considerable commotion; Beckwith somewhat gleefully admitted: "My pictures will create quite a stir and controversy," the very elements upon which Chase particularly thrived, and it is doubtful that he missed the gala event.

To what degree did the selection reflect Chase's own taste? Before this question can be addressed, several factors must be considered: first, the committee intended from the start to restrict its selection to European (particularly French) paintings never before exhibited publicly in the United States; second, a similar (and perhaps intentionally competitive) loan exhibition scheduled to follow the New York show was being arranged for the same purpose in Brooklyn; and third, according to the press, collectors were not particularly cooperative in lending to the show. With regard to this issue, one critic commented that Chase and Beckwith had almost "extracted" the paintings, "considering the apathy of the owners."[21] Finally, one has to take into account the relatively short time devoted to the selection and the fact that both Beckwith and Chase were pressured by other commitments. Therefore, the choice was limited.

All obstacles considered, however, it is obvious that the selection did parallel Chase's and Beckwith's tastes and temperaments — not only in what was chosen, but even more in what was omitted. Although the controversy anticipated by Beckwith did ensue, most critics agreed on one thing: the show was "artistic," both in selection and installation, the two areas in which Chase played a major role. One praised Beckwith and Chase for admitting "nothing that was mediocre in execution or of low artistic aim." The same critic then credited their

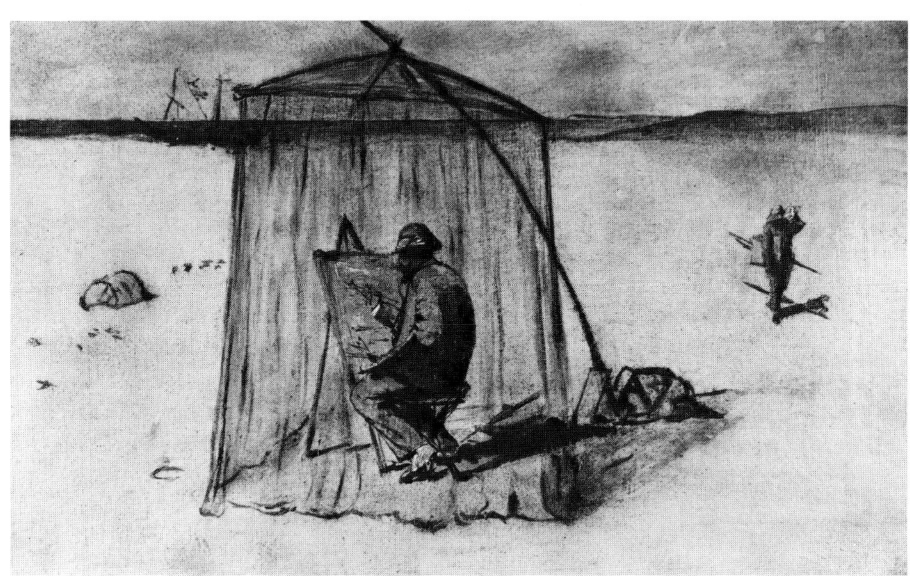

FIG. 7.
WILLIAM MERRITT CHASE
A Subtle Device, 1881
Oil on canvas, 11 1/2 x 18 1/2 in.
Baker/Pisano Collection, New York

selection as "the most purely artistic that has ever been shown in this country."[22] What was meant by the term artistic? One critic attributed the selection of paintings to the "art for art's sake" philosophy, commenting: "For those who seek in art something more than or different from a faithful rendering of nature this exhibition will be a veritable feast."[23] Another explained that the paintings "are such as are enjoyed by artists to a degree beyond that in which they can be enjoyed by the average layman. There is not a willfully amusing picture among them, and scarcely an attempt to tell a story."[24] Was this a deliberate omission on Chase's part when he participated in the selection? Indeed it was, as Chase stated himself: "I am thinking we have behind us the story-telling picture and the picture with a sentiment. Sentiment has covered up a multitude of sins in art."[25] Finally, Chase and Beckwith's obvious omission of "more popular French contemporaneous artists," such as Adolphe William Bouguereau and Alexandre Cabanel, emphasized their bias against such paintings in favor of what was described in the press as "a certain ultra-artistic class of work."[26] Therefore, it is fair to say that by contemporary standards the word artistic applied to paintings that would appeal to the taste of artists, paintings that stressed technique over faithful rendering and literal interpretation, and paintings that adhered to the philosophy of art for art's sake. This was, of course, the credo of the Society of American Artists, as opposed to that of the National Academy of Design, where, ironically, the exhibition was staged in rented space.

Further investigation of what was omitted from this exhibition (or of artists whose work was minimized) will corroborate the theory that, for the most part, this bias as it was then perceived and can now be described was no accident. There is no question that in the area of popular French art the slight was intentional. This prompted one writer to remark sarcastically: "In the corridor down the staircase, Detaille's well-known *Saluting the Wounded* [fig. 19, p. 32] has been graciously admitted, with two or three single figure Meissoniers and Hamon's *Etruscan Merchant* [fig. 15, p. 30]."[27] Commenting on this isolated placement, another writer would observe that these paintings "were somewhat out of keeping in general character with those in the chief picture gallery."[28] Chase and other American artists undoubtedly objected to the ease with which American millionaires — as if they were buying bonbons — squandered outrageous sums of money on the works of these popular French painters. One can imagine how Chase and other American portrait painters would have reacted to the following report: "Meissonier has just finished a small cabinet portrait — a miniature, it might be called — of Mrs. John W. MacKay. Few Americans own portraits by Meissonier. This American paid ten thousand dollars for hers."[29] Even at the height of his career, Chase was paid a fraction of that sum for a full-length portrait. Winslow Homer's concisely stated opinion of the work of Bouguereau best expresses the attitude of a progressive American artist with regard to the popular French artists: "I wouldn't so much as cross the street to see a Bouguereau. His pictures look false; he does not get the truth of what he wishes to represent; his light is not outdoor light; his works are waxy and artificial. They are extremely near being frauds."[30] Writers sympathetic to struggling American artists had similar feelings, expressed by one critic early in 1883: "A new painting by Bouguereau has been attracting attention at Matthew's auction rooms. . . . the picture it is said has been sold for $15,000 and has gone to Chicago. Its destination, it is hoped, is some bar-room."[31] Despite such derisive comments, the work of Bouguereau continued to be sought avidly by American collectors and admired by the public, and many were disappointed not to see it represented in the Pedestal Fund exhibition.

One critic also noted the lack of representation of the English School, and then explained: "Of course such an outrage could only be effected over the dead bodies of Messrs. Chase and Beckwith."[32] Is this criticism valid? In part it was; Chase abhorred the Pre-Raphaelites and their circle, as Chase's friend, student, and first biographer Katherine Metcalf Roof mildly put it: "Chase . . . found himself unable to discover any virtues in the Preraphaelites."[33] Referring to a painting by Sir Edward Burne-Jones, Chase commented less delicately: "If I saw a woman like that coming down the street I can tell you I'd run like a deer."[34] Although Chase greatly admired the work of the American expatriate John Singer Sargent, who was living in England, his work may have been omitted because he was thought to be an American (even though for some reason Whistler was represented). Another possible explanation for the lack of paintings by English artists may be that an adequate selection was simply not available. One contemporary writer observed: "Englishmen themselves provide a ready market for the best of their countrymen's productions. . . . An English artist, too, takes peculiar pride in keeping his masterpieces in England; he is not happy in seeing them emigrate."[35]

Another "weak" area in the show in the opinion of at least one critic was the German School; this is especially perplexing as Chase studied in Munich for six years and greatly admired the works of Munich artists such as Leibl, Hans Makart, and Franz von Lenbach.[36] It is possible that the majority of the German paintings available to Chase and Beckwith were those of the Düsseldorf School, more extensively represented in New York collections, but for the most part out of line with the taste of the two organizers. Such works would have been too detailed, too literal, and too closely associated with the detested Hudson River School painters, the "old mossy, geographical landscapes which used to crowd the holy precincts of the National Academy," as one of Chase's associates described them.[37]

Other critics complained that the Italian and Spanish schools were not sufficiently represented, but generally, Chase and Beckwith were commended for their fine work. Admittedly their selection was "a little one-sided in its views of what is best in art," as one critic noted. He maintained, however, that "the error is on the right side, and such a triumphant array of the work of the poet painters, the modern masters who rank with those of old time, will not be seen for many a long day."[38] Another writer contended: "The collection might easily have been made more widely representative of French art, but only by sacrificing the room now peopled by the pictures of men whom the best French critics now agree to call the greatest masters of the century."[39] This observation is the key to understanding the selection made by Chase and Beckwith — the quality of the art was placed above the quantity of artists represented. With this criterion in mind, an artist as important as Jean-Baptiste-Camille Corot could be represented by a dozen works and a lesser painter could be eliminated completely or consigned to an easily overlooked corner.

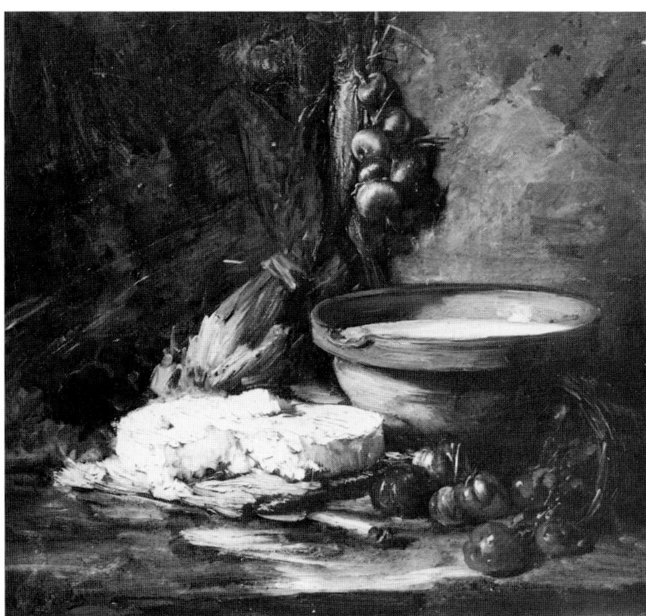

FIG. 8.
ANTOINE VOLLON, *Still Life with Cheese*
Oil on canvas, 33 3/8 x 35 3/8 in.
The Metropolitan Museum of Art, New York

In many cases this selection process correlates with Chase's own approach to collecting, as can be seen in the following chart comparing the number of works by some of the artists prominently featured in the Bartholdi Pedestal Fund exhibition with those owned by Chase:

ARTIST	NUMBER OF WORKS IN PEDESTAL FUND SHOW	NUMBER OF WORKS OWNED BY CHASE
Monticelli	10	8
Mettling	9	6
Vollon	9	20
Roybet	7	4
Mauve	6	4
Ribot	6	7
Stevens	6	9
Michel	5	5

In all, approximately forty percent of the artists included in the Pedestal Fund exhibition were also represented in Chase's collection at some point during his lifetime, and this was no coincidence.[40] Among contemporary French painters, Chase most admired the work of Antoine Vollon, which is evident from the number of paintings by Vollon in the exhibition and to an even greater extent in Chase's own collection. He particularly admired Vollon's rich, painterly still lifes. Chase stated: "Vollon . . . painted such subjects well. I have one by him which I prize highly — a big cream cheese and a bowl of milk [*Still Life with Cheese*, fig. 8]." After Vollon exhibited a still life of a pumpkin to great acclaim, Chase observed: "At the next Salon there were dozens of pumpkins but not like his. He painted it because he loved it, not because somebody else did it."[41] Chase, whose own still-life paintings were indebted to the work of Vollon, warned his students on many occasions that there is no "formula," and never himself slavishly copied or imitated Vollon's work. Two other French artists Chase admired and who were represented in the show were Jules Bastien-Lepage and Adolphe Monticelli. In 1885 Chase made a special trip to Antwerp to see Bastien-Lepage's work in an international exhibition. He was accompanied by James Abbott McNeill Whistler, who argued with Chase about the merits of this artist's paintings. At that time Whistler summed up his feeling in one word, "School!"[42] Chase, who was more interested in technical skill than innovation, disagreed — the two argued and parted ways. Monticelli, whose work

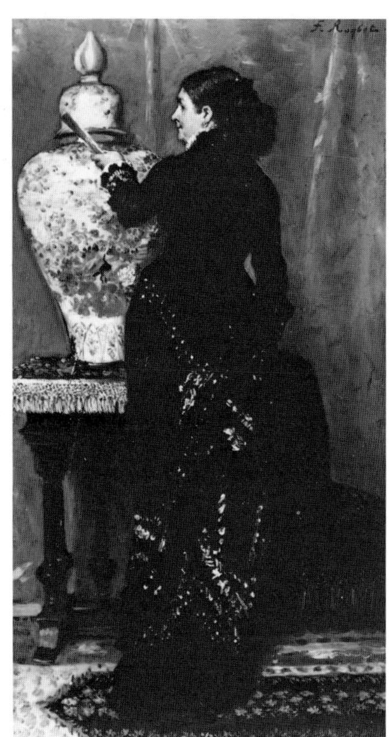

FIG. 9.
FERDINAND ROYBET, *Lady in Black*
Oil on panel, 21 1/2 x 11 1/4 in.
Private collection, Chicago

was generously represented in the show and in Chase's collection, was also admired by Chase for technical reasons, especially his ability to exploit the wide range of textural possibilities available to a robust painter in oils whose manipulative skills were virtually unlimited. Other French artists in the show whose work appealed particularly to Chase were Théodule Augustin Ribot and Ferdinand Roybet, whose *Lady in Black* (fig. 9) Chase owned. Both the painterly qualities and the strong old-master influence in the works of these two artists are directly related to Chase's own interests — especially those he cultivated as a student in Munich.

Of the Belgian artists, none could surpass the popular Alfred Stevens in Chase's estimation. Both his style of painting — as in *Portrait of Sarah Bernhardt's Sister* (fig. 10), also owned by Chase — and his style of living appealed to the American artist and had a profound influence on him. Like Stevens, Chase became a painter of his own time, beginning with his plein-air park scenes and his interiors of the mid-1880s. Stevens probably invited Chase to one of his *petits salons* in Paris in 1881 when they first met. Like Stevens, Chase soon became a tastemaker whose own elaborate studio reflected the same eclectic taste displayed by Stevens in his studio, described by a contemporary visitor in *Scribner's Monthly* (March 1881):

> The walls are old dull gold, with decorations. In the corners of the room are exquisite pieces of furniture, of Japanese work, lacquered in black and gold. . . . The window shades are white silk with rich designs, while curtains are brocade silk in old gold. . . . A Japanese picture . . . hangs upon the wall. . . . You sit upon elegant divans, cushions, and puffs, and for some time imagine yourself transported to the gorgeous and fragrant furnishings of Japanese nobility.[43]

Among the artists of the Italian School, Chase favored Alberto Pasini, Antonio Mancini, Giovanni Boldini, and Giuseppe de Nittis. Of these four artists, Chase related most closely in his own work to the bold and clever brushwork of the first three. Chase instructed his own students to "use a variety of means and mediums," and then noted: "Mancini piled on the paint so thick that one could hang a ring on it."[44] Chase owned paintings by these three Italian painters, as well as one by de Nittis. Chase's main interest in de Nittis, however, was in his pastels, which in some instances have a grand scale seldom associated with this medium. Chase admired de Nittis's dramatic compositional devices as well, such as his strong diagonals that lead the viewer into the picture plane with great force.

Chase held the contemporary Spanish painter Mariano Fortuny y Carbo in great esteem. Once again Chase's special interest in this artist is evident in the advice he gave his students: "Fortuny had a most artistic temperament. *Everything* he did was interesting. Get a complete set of photographs of Fortuny's pictures."[45] The contemporary writer G. W. Sheldon also noted an "artistic" nature in Fortuny's work: "Harmonious notes and chords in symphonies and nocturnes of color . . . the silks and satins have musical values, so to speak."[46] One might think he was analyzing the work of Whistler or, in the same art-for-art's-sake tradition, Chase.

Finally, we consider the Dutch School of artists. Chase's interest in the work of these plein-air painters far exceeded the representation they were given in the Bartholdi Pedestal Fund exhibition in deference to their French counterparts. Aside from those represented in both the show and Chase's own collection — Anton Mauve, Hendrik Willem Mesdag, and Bernardus Johannes Blommers — Chase owned paintings by Georg-Hendrik Breitner, Eugène Isabey, Jean-Barthold Jongkind, Jacob Simon Hendrik Kever, and Willem Maris. During the early to mid-1880s, these artists and their native landscape (which Chase had seen and painted during several summer trips) had a profound effect on his development as a plein-air painter. Of all the Dutch artists, he knew Mesdag the longest and the best. In fact, Mesdag very likely introduced him to the work of the others. Chase knew Mesdag's collection well, and when he showed it to one of his summer classes in Holland in 1903, Mesdag told Chase that he considered it a great compliment that they had come so far to study Dutch pictures.[47]

Although there were definite parallels between the selection made for the Bartholdi *Pedestal Fund Art Loan Exhibition* and Chase's private collecting habits, one must also consider the artists included in the show who were respected by Chase but not represented in his collection. This discrepancy can be explained by the fact that Chase was collecting with limited means and could not afford good paintings by these artists. In such cases we must rely on his statements for proof of his interest. He was especially impressed with Corot, whose delicate and lyrical treatment of trees Chase praised: "Corot's edges of foliage against sky are especially fine."[48] Some of Chase's own teaching principles were indebted to Corot, who said, for example: "Yes, yes . . . the birds must be able to fly through the branches."[49] Similarly, Chase, in criticizing one of his students who was unsuccessful in achieving such an effect, asked: "What kind of a tree is that? Could birds fly through it? Build their nests in it? They'd break their necks!"[50] Chase also revered the work of Jean-François Millet, represented by eight works in the exhibition (pls. XXV–XXXII), but whose paintings were clearly beyond Chase's means. Speaking of Millet in a lecture, Chase described him as "all heart and soul, so delightfully independent. He believed in his ideal, and insisted upon it in spite of everything, and was respected for it too!" Spiritually Chase identified with Millet, "a man whose reputation was made entirely by artists."[51] Other French Barbizon painters Charles-François Daubigny, Narcisse Virgile Diaz de la Peña, and Constant Troyon were well represented in the show but almost totally absent from Chase's holdings. Again this may be explained in part by the prohibitive cost of good paintings by these popular artists.[52]

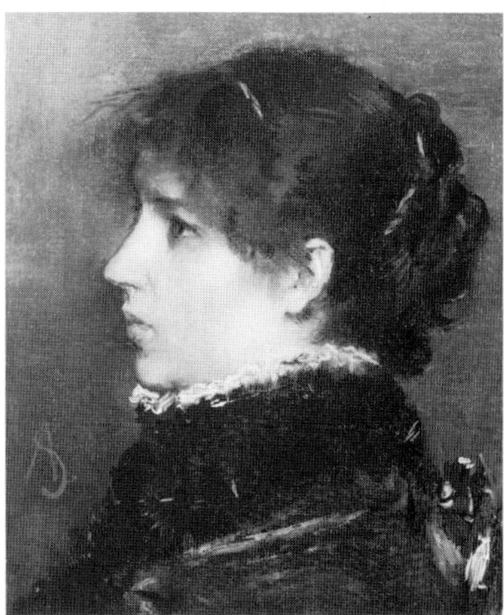

FIG. 10.
ALFRED STEVENS, *Portrait of Sarah Bernhardt's Sister*
Oil on canvas, 9 3/4 x 7 1/2 in.
Collection Ruth Emerson Cooke

The most important feature of the *Pedestal Fund Art Loan Exhibition* was the inclusion of several French Impressionist paintings and their prominent position in the main gallery. Once again, Chase set out to shock the public as a means of getting their attention, and he succeeded. He deliberately snubbed the most popular French painters such as Bouguereau and Cabanel, and insulted others such as Detaille and Meissonier (pls. XXI, XXII) by placing their work out in the corridor under the stairs. In sharp contrast, he gave the paintings of Manet (including pls. XVII, XVIII, the two purchased for Erwin Davis by Weir while he and Chase were in Paris in 1881) the place of honor. Chase, who was one of the most progressive artists in America, intended to direct attention to what he considered to be the most progressive art on the Continent and thus educate the taste of the American public (or at least that part of it with an appreciation for art, such as his own fellow artists). This was considered to be "an error of judgment" by at least one critic, who maintained that "every one will not behold them with the discriminating eye of the gentle men who are responsible. They [Chase and Beckwith] no doubt can sum up the debit and credit account for Manet and produce a correct balance sheet. But others may not be so well-equipped." He concluded that the hanging committee must expect to have on their heads "the blood of any weaker brethren" who might be hopelessly led astray "through following the will-o-the-wisp." He informed his readers that "unfortunately we have no lack of artists who are always ready to follow after strange gods."[53] This judgment, although apparently an overreaction, was actually more prophetic than it might seem. For in fact, the significance of the Bartholdi Pedestal Fund exhibition far exceeds its original goal, the raising of money for the base of the Statue of Liberty. The exhibition, along with more extensive displays of French Impressionism, had a profound effect on the direction of American art, as Chase and his colleagues adapted their means of painting under the powerful influence of this movement. Some artists adopted the style in moderation, others with blind abandon, as they formulated what is now described as American Impressionism. As the contemporary critic predicted, Chase and Beckwith could evaluate what they believed to be the advantages and limitations of the French Impressionists' approach to painting and were able to devise personal statements which were eclectic rather than slavishly derivative.

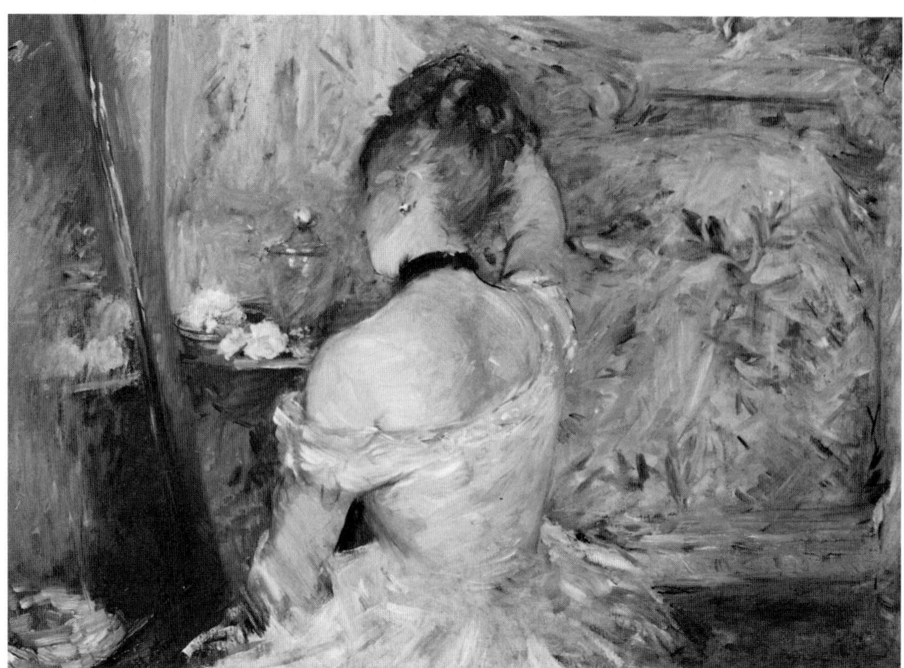

FIG. 11.
BERTHE MORISOT, *Lady at Her Toilet,* c. 1875
Oil on canvas, 23 1/2 x 31 1/2 in.
The Art Institute of Chicago

Other strong American painters were able to do the same, but many embraced a "formula" rather than understanding the theories and principles involved. Chase espoused the "ultra artistic" nature of Manet's work and admired the technical virtuosity of his painting. Manet, however, was only one of many artists Chase respected and who influenced his development. To a limited degree he respected the other French Impressionists, too, but only the more conservative ones, such as Mary Cassatt and Berthe Morisot (whose painting *Lady at Her Toilet* [fig. 11] he owned). He also accepted, with reservation, the work of Degas, who was represented in the Pedestal Fund exhibition by *Ballet Dancers* (pl. XI), one of his typical scenes. However, Chase thought that Claude Monet went too far with his "experiments" and was too scientific with regard to his treatment of light.

Therefore, as an influential artist, a spokesman for progressive art, and an arbiter of good taste, Chase played an important role in introducing French Impressionism to America. He not only included several paintings in the *Pedestal Fund Art Loan Exhibition,* but gave them the place of honor among artists already considered to be contemporary European masters. This daring and effective stunt gained immediate attention, not only for the Impressionist paintings, but for Chase as well. While many of his artistic brethren followed the will-o-the-wisp, producing hackneyed Impressionist-style paintings, Chase continued to weave a more complex and enduring fabric derived from a multitude of sources, creating a pattern all his own. He was one of the most influential artists and teachers in this country through the end of the century; by the beginning of the twentieth century, however, he had to take his place among what was becoming the "old guard." Like the Hudson River School painters before him, Chase was forced to step aside as new European movements infiltrated and influenced the mainstream of American art, and many of his own students joined the enemy camp of abstract painters.

NOTES

1. C. P. Townsley, "A Leading Spirit in American Art," *Arts and Decoration,* vol. 2, no. 8 (June 1912), pp. 285-87, 306.
2. "Janitor Brother Tells How Chance Aided W. M. Chase," *Indianapolis Star,* March 25, 1917.
3. The artist Eastman Johnson purchased Chase's painting *The Dowager* (Collection of Lewis B. Williams) when it was exhibited at the National Academy of Design in 1875, and Charles Henry Miller bought Chase's painting *The Broken Jug* (The Baltimore Museum of Art) after seeing it at the National Academy exhibition in 1877.
4. "Chase's Court Jester," *The Art Journal,* vol. 4 (1878), p. 257.

5. Mariana Griswold Van Rensselaer, "William Merritt Chase: Second and Concluding Article," *American Art Review,* vol. 2 (February 1881), p. 135.
6. "William Merritt Chase," *Fine Arts Journal,* vol. 34 (November 1916), unpaginated.
7. "Chase's Americanism," *Literary Digest,* vol. 53 (November 11, 1916), p. 1250.
8. "Topics of the Time/The Metropolitan Museum of Art," *Scribner's Monthly,* vol. 21, no. 5 (March 1881), p. 791.
9. See Albert Boime, "America's Purchasing Power and the Evolution of European Art in the Late Nineteenth Century," *Salons, Galleries, Museums and Their Influence in the Development of 19th and 20th Century Art,* ed. Francis Haskell (Bologna, Italy: Cooperativa Libreria Universitaria, 1979), pp. 123-39. These collections were celebrated in Edward Strahan [Earl Shinn], ed., *The Art Treasures of America,* 3 vols. (Philadelphia: Gebbie & Barrie, 1879-82).
10. Will H. Low, *A Painter's Progress* (New York: Charles Scribner's Sons, 1910), p. 215.
11. Quoted in Katherine Metcalf Roof, *The Life and Art of William Merritt Chase* (1917, New York: Hacker Art Books, 1975), p. 56.
12. *Ibid.*
13. John Moran, "Studio Life in New York," *The Art Journal,* vol. 5 (1879), pp. 344-45.
14. Elizabeth Champney, *Witch Winnie's Studio* (New York: Dodd, Mead & Co., 1892), p. 18.
15. *A Summer Afternoon in Holland,* possibly *Sunlight and Shadow* (Joslyn Art Museum, Omaha, Nebraska).
16. Tile Club excursions were recorded in W. MacKay Laffan and Edward Strahan [Earl Shinn], "The Tile Club at Play," *Scribner's Monthly,* vol. 17, no. 34 (February 1879), pp. 457-78; W. MacKay Laffan and Edward Strahan, "The Tile Club Afloat," *Scribner's Monthly,* vol. 19, no. 35 (March 1880), pp. 641-71; and W. MacKay Laffan, "The Tile Club Ashore," *The Century Magazine,* vol. 23, no. 34 (February 1882), pp. 481-98.
17. The Society of Painters in Pastel originally intended to hold its first show in the spring of 1883 but then announced that it had been postponed until the fall (see Montezuma, "My Note Book," *The Art Amateur,* vol. 8, no. 5 [April 1883], p. 101). Two of the key members of the group, Chase and Beckwith, were busy with the *Pedestal Fund Art Loan Exhibition* at that time, which might explain why the show did not take place until March of 1884.
18. "Two Art Exhibitions," *The New York Herald,* December 2, 1883, p. 6.
19. James Carroll Beckwith, Diary, 1883 (National Academy of Design, New York). All other references are taken from this diary.
20. "For the Bartholdi Pedestal," *The New York Herald,* November 29, 1883, p. 6.
21. *Ibid.*
22. "Two Art Exhibitions," *The New York Herald.*
23. "The Pedestal Fund Art Loan Exhibiton," *The Art Amateur,* vol. 10, no. 2 (January 1884), p. 42.
24. *Ibid.*
25. William M. Chase, "Painting," *The American Magazine of Art,* vol. 8, no. 2 (December 1916), p. 52.
26. "The Pedestal Fund Art Loan Exhibition," *The Art Amateur,* p. 43.
27. *Ibid.*
28. "Two Art Exhibitions," *The New York Herald.*
29. George W. Sheldon, *Hours with Art and Artists* (New York: D. Appleton, 1882), p. 114.
30. *Ibid.*
31. Montezuma, "My Note Book," *The Art Amateur,* vol. 8, no. 3 (February 1883), p. 56.
32. "The Pedestal Fund Art Loan Exhibition," *The Art Amateur,* p. 43.
33. Roof, *Chase,* p. 215.
34. *Ibid.*
35. Sheldon, *Hours with Art and Artists,* pp. 59-60.
36. Chase owned works by all three, including at that time Leibl's *Coquette* (Wallraf-Richartz-Museum, Cologne, West Germany), which he could have lent himself.
37. Laffan and Strahan, "The Tile Club Afloat," p. 642.
38. "For the Bartholdi Pedestal," *The New York Herald.*
39. "The Pedestal Art Loan," *The New York Times,* December 2, 1883, p. 2.
40. Based on a cumulative list compiled from various auctions held of Chase's collections. There is no way of knowing exactly when he acquired each painting.
41. Frances Lauderbach, "Notes from Talks by William M. Chase: Summer Class, Carmel by the Sea, California (Memoranda from a Student's Note Book)," *The American Magazine of Art,* vol. 8, no. 11 (September 1917), p. 437.
42. William Merritt Chase, "The Two Whistlers: Recollections of a Summer with the Great Etcher," *The Century Magazine,* vol. 80, no. 2 (June 1910), p. 225.

43. "Glimpses of Parisian Art," *Scribner's Monthly,* vol. 21, no. 5 (March 1881), p. 738.
44. Lauderbach, "Notes from Talks," pp. 437-38.
45. *Ibid.*, p. 434.
46. Sheldon, *Hours with Art and Artists,* pp. 31-32.
47. Roof, *Chase,* p. 206.
48. Lauderbach, "Notes from Talks," p. 434.
49. Sheldon, *Hours with Art and Artists,* p. 65.
50. Reynolds Beal Papers, Archives of American Art, Smithsonian Institution, Washington, D.C.
51. William M. Chase, "Address of Mr. William M. Chase before the Buffalo Fine Arts Academy, January 28, 1890," *The Studio,* vol. 5, no. 13 (March 1, 1890), p. 125.
52. A few other discrepancies appear: for example, Chase owned at least seven paintings by Eugène Boudin, an artist whose work he greatly admired, and at least four paintings by Gaston Latouche; neither artist was included in the *Pedestal Fund Art Loan Exhibition.* Perhaps Chase's serious interest in these two artists developed some time after the exhibition.
53. "Paintings at the Loan Exhibition," *New York Daily Tribune,* December 26, 1883, p. 6.

When Liberty Was Controversial

Lois Dinnerstein

"Much complaint is heard concerning the pictures," reported *The New York Times* thirteen days after the December 3, 1883, opening of the Statue of Liberty *Pedestal Fund Art Loan Exhibition* at the National Academy of Design, adding: ". . . certainly there is no lack of reason. The gentlemen who undertook the task knew the situation perfectly and expected attacks; they performed their part to the very best of their ability and according to the highest principles of art so far as they know them. Nevertheless, they made a mistake."[1] The principal organizers of the exhibition and thus the gentlemen in question were, of course, J. Carroll Beckwith (1852–1917) and William Merritt Chase (1849–1916).

Across the East River, *The Brooklyn Daily Eagle* commented: "There seems to be a determined resolve on the part of the public to withhold all sort of aid from the Bartholdi Statue Fund. They refuse absolutely to aid the scheme with their money. The exhibition is the best we have ever had in New York, but the drawback is it is a little above the heads of the people. . . ."[2] How could an exhibition, now so established as a significant moment in the creation of our national icon, have initially been viewed as so controversial?

To understand we must turn back to the year 1883 when there was a crisis of international proportions. The Statue of Liberty was nearly ready to be crated and shipped from Paris, but as yet there was nothing in New York to place it on. Or, to be more precise, less than a third of the pedestal had been erected when construction was stopped for lack of funds. By the time the exhibition opened, "only about two-fifths of the amount required had been secured," according to the Hon. William M. Evarts (fig. 1), chairman of the general committee in charge of the Pedestal Fund. As reported in *The New York Times*, Evarts had addressed the exhibition's opening assemblage: "It is known to you all . . . that the greatness of the receipts of our committee does not comport with the greatness of the statue or the greatness of the generosity of the French people."[3]

Courrier des Etats-Unis, the French-language newspaper in New York, welcomed the exhibition as a means to conclude at last the long-standing Pedestal Fund-raising efforts, which were becoming "a little embarrassing for everyone."[4] Things French had long been suspect in puritanical America, despite the fact that American artists and collectors were increasingly drawn to the art world of Paris. When receipts for the first two weeks of the Pedestal Fund exhibition proved disappointing, it was decided to keep the show open on Sundays; exhibition officials were accused of bringing the "Parisian Sunday" to America. Their opponents raised a hue and cry. In taking this step, F. Hopkinson Smith and the

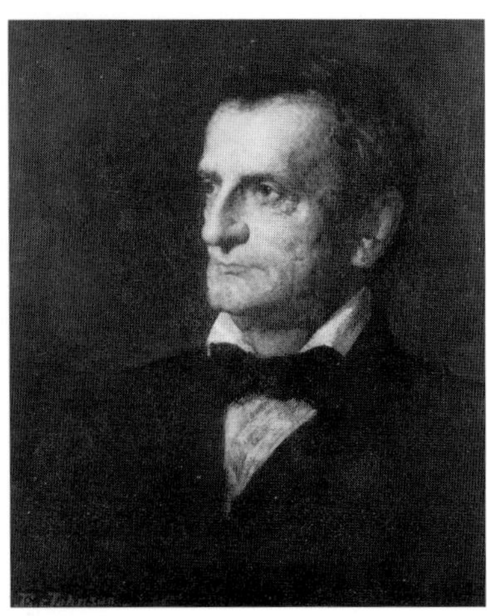

FIG. 1.
EASTMAN JOHNSON
The Hon. William M. Evarts, c. 1885
Oil on canvas, 24 x 20 in.
Harvard Law School, Cambridge, Massachusetts

other committee members were challenging the notorious blue laws (fig. 2), defying the law of the land, and they were valiantly prepared to go to jail over the issue. Charles A. Dana's *The Sun* reported the fracas with glee:

> Friday, December 21, 1883 . . .
> Exhibitions on Sunday. The Executive Committee of the Loan Exhibition for the benefit of the BARTHOLDI statue have voted to keep the exhibition open on Sundays at a reduced price of admission. . . . The two ladies who voted against the Sunday opening did not do so for the purely sentimental reasons which might have been expected from them. They did not even use the religious arguments employed by Sabbatarians. . . . Their position was not very different from that of many workingmen and labor organizations with regard to the Sunday question. . . . If the custom of keeping open places of amusement on Sunday is generally tolerated, a great many people to whom Sunday is now the only day of rest will be compelled to work.[5]

This same newspaper had noted on the day the exhibition first opened: "The delegation of fourteen workingmen from Paris, who are in this city . . . spent yesterday in visiting the various labor union meetings held every Sunday in the city."[6] The December 21 *Sun* editorial concluded: ". . . are not these ladies who voted against the Sunday opening themselves establishing the precedent to which they so strongly objected? Do they not have coachmen to drive them to church on Sunday?"[7]

The blue-laws controversy was reported to the art community in *The Studio: Devoted to Art, Artists and Their Friends,* a weekly published in New York. It began by quoting Beckwith:

> "We had a lease of the Academy for four weeks and no conditions were expressed pro or con in regard to opening it on Sunday. Our committee took a positive stand on the matter and notwithstanding the protests of the Academy committee and a letter of protest signed by many prominent citizens and contributors to the collection, we decided to throw the doors open on Sunday. We did this, believing it to be for the best interests of the public, and had the Academy committee opposed our action, they would have broken their contract with us. All places that tend to the enlightenment and education of the people should be opened on Sunday here in New York the same as in other places. The Metropolitan Museum and the libraries should be opened. They speak of New York becoming an American Paris with the significant insinuation that all of Paris is morally bad. Paris has many virtues, and one of them is the opening of its galleries, museums and libraries on Sundays, for the benefit of those who cannot go to them on week days. . . .
>
> "The primary object of opening the Academy of Design on Sunday was to give the working classes an opportunity to view the collection. No, the collection of paintings at the Academy do [*sic*] not please the public. We could not and did not attempt to please everyone. Had we done so, we would have succeeded in pleasing no one. Our object in selecting the paintings was to present to the public the very best class of art obtainable. . . . The management knew perfectly well the tastes of the committee they appointed and had they wished a more popular collection, they should have chosen other men."
>
> "Yes, the academy was open last Sunday, much to the regret of many of us," said a gentleman interested in the Academy management. "To be sure there were a great many people present, and everything was conducted in an orderly manner becoming to the day, but then, some of us older men think that the young men who have the management in charge should have treated our objections and protests with a little more respect. They had the legal right to keep the place open and defy the by-laws of the academy and ignore the wishes of many contributors to the collection, and so they did it, but they should have looked ahead to the precedent they are establishing. They are opening a door, and here-after everyone will feel justified in opening a door. We old fogies, as the young men call us, are too old to be actuated by malice in our protests. We are acting on principle and upon a belief in the sanctity of the Sabbath, and customs that have stood so long can not be tossed aside so flippantly. Yes, there is some ill-feeling in the matter, and this is to be regretted too, because art interests in this country are not so strong that it can support factions. There should be a unity."[8]

Day after day *The Sun* informed its readers about the developments at the Pedestal Fund exhibition. The following item appeared on December 24:

> Doors opened on Sunday. 3,500 citizens go to the art exhibition and 47 protest. Rooms crowded by Observant and Interested Men and Women — Sale of Catalogues Forbidden — Mr. Smith's Reply to the Protest. Across East Twenty-third street at Fourth avenue in front of the Academy of Design, a banner was flung yesterday morning bearing the words, "The Bartholdi Pedestal Fund Exhibition now open." On either side of the advertisement floated a French and an American flag. . . . Several members of the Sunday Closing League . . . called last week at the office of the Art Loan Exhibition and warned the managers not to sell catalogues. Therefore, not to deprive the Sunday visitors of any means of information . . . the catalogues were scattered about the rooms with a note written on the cover asking the user to leave it in the room when he was through with it. None of them was missing when the day was over. . . .
>
> From 9 A.M. to 6 P.M. not less than 3,500 persons attended the exhibition. Men walked around with their wives and young men with their sweethearts and pointed out the beauties which struck them. . . . Admiration and wonder were in the women's eyes at the sight of some of the rare laces or the delicate South Kensington embroidery. The most popular place, however, was the picture gallery.[9]

The story continued. On December 25 *The Sun* published interviews with the men who had signed the petition:

> Mr. William Dowd, 44 Wall Street, said: "I object to this action because it is an opening wedge. I know Director Smith says it is a wedge to let in more sunlight, but I do not see it in that way. If you allow such exhibitions to be kept open on Sunday, especially if an admission fee is charged, then I don't see why Bowery museums and shows of the lowest kinds cannot be run on Sunday on the same principle. If this breach of custom goes without a rebuke you will, in fact, see the dens open, and who knows when it will stop? Perhaps it won't stop short of a Parisian Sunday with theatre doors flapping and no Sunday anywhere."[10]

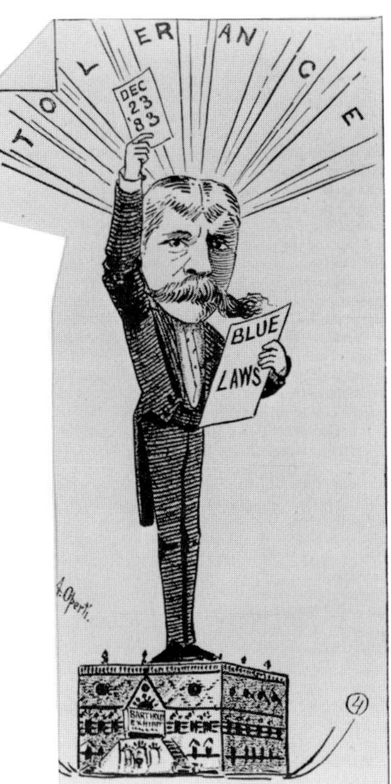

Fig. 2.
F. Hopkinson Smith as the Statue of Liberty
The Art Amateur, February 1884

Another protester warned: "All the theatres will be open on Sunday and New York will be a Paris in America." Nothing, of course, would have pleased the organizers of the *Pedestal Fund Art Loan Exhibition* more.

Perhaps the most explicit account of the anger generated by this Sunday opening was published in *The Sun* on Christmas Day. It was written by one J. Hooker Hamersley, a lawyer, who unequivocally stated:

> I have both Huguenot and English blood in my veins and I constitutionally object to bringing a Continental Sunday to these shores. I object on religious grounds chiefly. Besides, those nations which do not observe the commandment to keep the Sabbath holy soon degenerate. I do not want to see atheists and freethinkers flourish here. I don't like the notion of other people coming to these shores from abroad and making inroads on our well-established customs. Our forefathers were very strict, you know, and we have inherited their good principles. How would it look for guests who are bidden to a house to go and at once begin to dictate what should be done in the house? I look upon the oppressed of all lands as guests invited to America. They ought not to bring their Sunday with them though. They have adopted our language and customs generally, and they ought to conform in this respect.[11]

There was a particular significance in the *Pedestal Fund Art Loan Exhibition* for one group of "guests" so scorned by the above-quoted Mr. Hamersley. The *American Hebrew* critic, addressing in approximate English the immigrants who, above all else, wished to be assimilated into American culture, stressed the beneficial effects of the exhibition:

> The Bartholdi Fund Art Loan Exhibition is one of the most refined which has graced the Academy of Design since its erection. The excellence of the exhibit is not only attracting many, but also the fact that thereby may be wiped out the disgrace of so long being delayed the erection of the pedestal for Bartholdi's Statue of Liberty.[12]

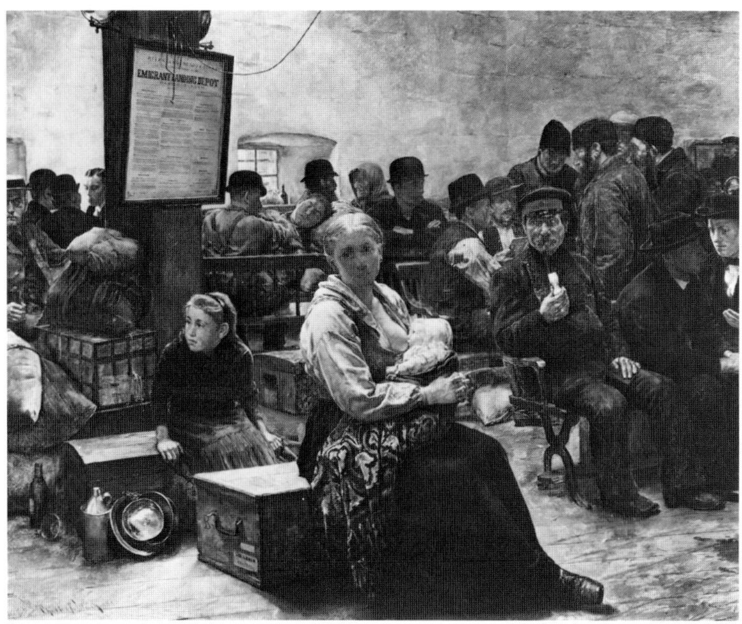

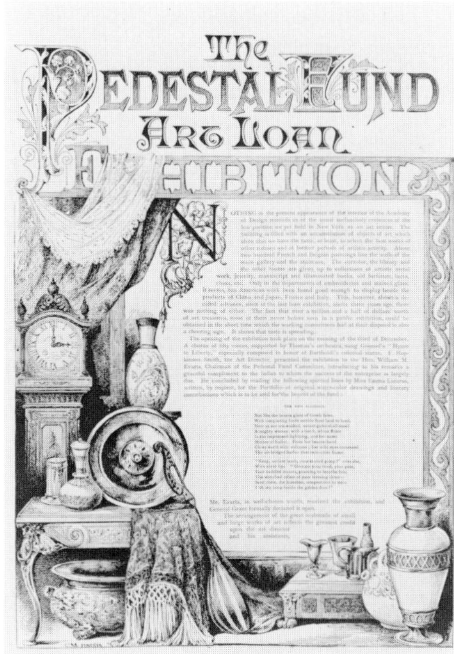

The Pedestal Fund Art Loan Exhibition

FIG. 3.
CHARLES F. ULRICH, *In the Land of Promise: Castle Garden,* 1884
Oil on panel, 28 3/8 x 35 3/4 in.
The Corcoran Gallery of Art, Washington, D.C.

FIG. 4.
The Pedestal Fund Art Loan Exhibition
The Art Amateur, December 1883

The American contribution to the Pedestal Fund exhibition, as described in *The World,* was a "handsome portfolio, which is to be sold . . . [and] contains a score or more of original water-color sketches from foremost American artists and autograph letters from the most prominent American statesmen and litterateurs."[13] The portfolio also contained "The New Colossus" by Emma Lazarus. The widely published articles on the show permanently altered the interpretation of Bartholdi's Statue of Liberty by quoting in full the words of the poem, which had been read aloud during the opening ceremonies by F. Hopkinson Smith. This sonnet, naming Liberty "Mother of Exiles," had been expressly written for the exhibition portfolio. Although it was not until 1903 that these now-famous words were bolted to the base of the pedestal, the contemporary criticism of the Pedestal Fund exhibition gave them wide currency and thus joined two previously separate issues: the Bartholdi commemoration of Liberty as a timeless, classic abstract ideal and the immediate significance of this notion in the face of the 1880s pogroms in Russia and Eastern Europe and the resulting need to shelter the dispossessed. This new consciousness was soon reflected in such paintings as the 1884 *In the Land of Promise: Castle Garden* (fig.3), by Charles Frederic Ulrich (1858–1908). A few months after the Pedestal Fund exhibition was taken off the walls, the artists taking part in the spring 1884 exhibition of the National Academy of Design voted to award this work the first Thomas B. Clarke Prize for the best figure painting of an American subject by a nonacademician.[14]

If ever there was an occasion staged as a media event, it was the *Pedestal Fund Art Loan Exhibition.* Extensive reviews (often more than one) appeared in a great variety of publications, frequently illustrated with the beautifully designed, elaborate line engravings of this period before the advent of mass-produced photographic illustrations (figs. 4–6). "A Gallery of Delights" was how the popular *Harper's Weekly* titled its second notice of the show, lest anyone otherwise miss it, after having previously covered the opening in detail. "There is no more interesting resort in the city during the holiday season, and none more worthy of the attention of citizens and strangers."[15] *The Art Interchange: A Household Journal,* published fortnightly, advised its readers:

> In character this is quite different from any other loan collection hung in New York, the selection of examples having been made with discrimination . . . so as to present in a group modern works of what is commonly regarded as the broad school, paintings that manifest the artist's personality and which, in almost every instance, are unconventional and peculiar. The result is somewhat startling, but to an art student interested in technique, theoretical treatment, conceptions as to

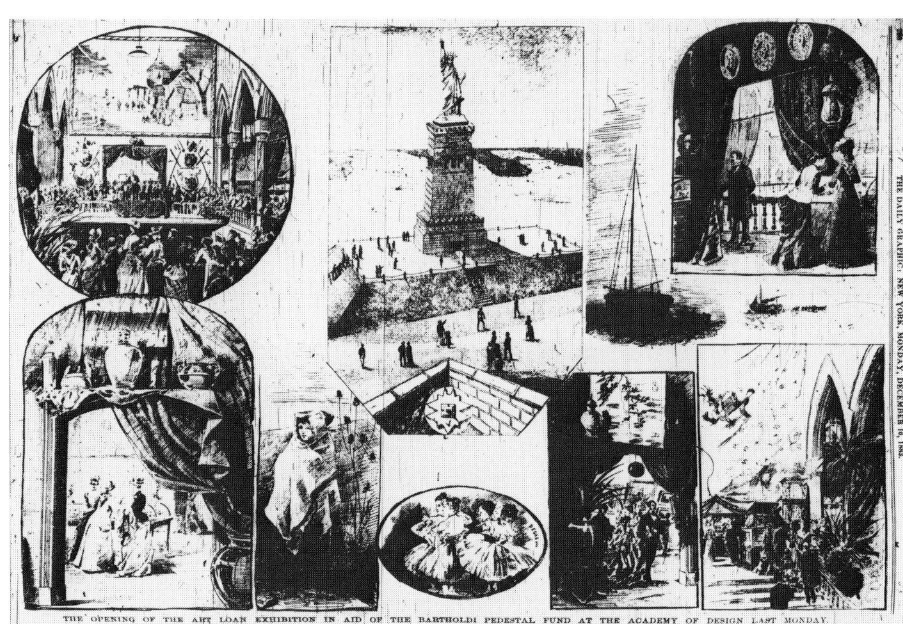

FIG. 5.
The Opening of the Art Loan Exhibition in Aid of the Bartholdi Pedestal Fund at the Academy of Design Last Monday
The Daily Graphic, December 10, 1883

> the limitations of art, the points of divergence of artistic presentation and mechanical simulation, elaboration of color at the expense of drawing or tricks of the brush that are secrets to all but one man, the gallery is more than satisfactory.[16]

Repeated reference to the exhibition also appeared in *The Studio,* but enthusiasm was tinged with ambivalence. John C. Van Dyke (1856–1932), for example, mused:

> It must be a hypercritical eye indeed that can cavil at any one of these . . . for each painting is in itself a masterpiece . . . [there] is not a single bad picture in the room, all of which reflects great credit on Mr. Chase and Mr. Beckwith. Yet, we doubt if the public will so view it. It is not a popular collection, but rather a painter's, a connoisseur's, an art student's collection.[17]

Much of the criticism focused on the great skill exhibited by these works. In stressing technique, the reviews marked a distinct shift in American criticism, for this was the very quality of French art that had been scorned, just a few years earlier, in writings about the Philadelphia Centennial Exposition of 1876. At that time, French painting had been largely censured for emphasizing technique rather than moral uplift, especially in the rendering of the nude.[18]

The late nineteenth century in America was an era of conscious professionalism in many fields. As artists and critics acquired greater expertise by virtue of travel and study abroad, they undertook the task of educating the public back home. Kenyon Cox (1856–1919), who was a critic as well as an artist and teacher, published the article "Antoine Vollon: A Painter's Painter" in December 1883, the very month of the Pedestal Fund exhibition at the National Academy. He lauded the French artist (1833–1900), who was represented by no less than nine paintings in the show, in these terms:

> Vollon cared primarily for the quality of substance; the woodenness of wood, the hardness and brilliancy of metal, the firm pliability of muscle and the like. The rendering of these qualities of substances in the best possible manner and with the least possible expenditure of labor constitutes technical excellence, and when an artist possesses any great degree of technical excellence, painters term him emphatically a *painter.* He may not be a draughtsman — he may not even be a colorist; but he is a painter. Vollon is, perhaps, the greatest *painter* living. . . . His resource is boundless and his control of his materials absolute. He can paint with anything. The brush, the palette-knife, the finger, the coat-sleeve, are all so many equally valuable tools to him, each employed in turn and each employed where it alone can do the work.
>
> There follows from this the great charm of unexpectedness in his *technique.*

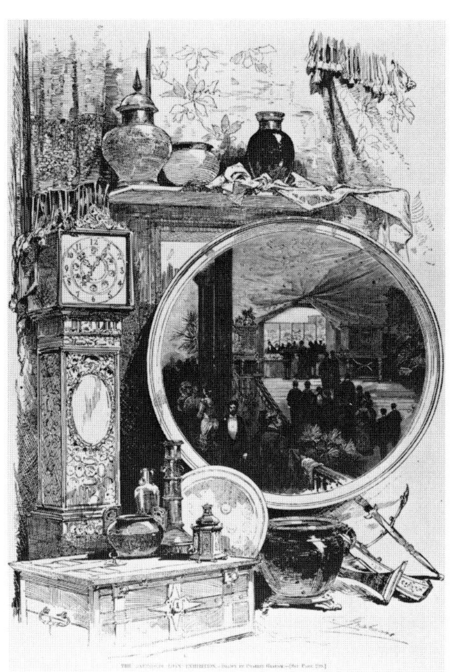

Fig. 6.
The Bartholdi Loan Exhibition
Harper's Weekly, December 15, 1883
Drawing by Charles Graham

As a friend of mine expresses it: "He seems to have *invented* upon the spur of the moment and with lightning rapidity of thought the touch which will exactly express the quality of the object which he is endeavoring to represent." The same touch may never have occurred to him before and he may never have occasion to employ it again. It is invented for its present use and for the one occasion only. . . . Study his picture, with the assurance that, however trivial his subject may seem, there was that in it which a great man thought it worth his while to express. If you cannot see it, it is your fault and not his. When Rembrandt painted the carcase of an ox hung up in a butcher's stall, or when Vollon paints a slaughtered pig, there was something there which interested *them,* and we need not think it too low to interest us.[19]

Three years after the Pedestal Fund exhibition, the critic Mariana Griswold Van Rensselaer (1851–1934) (fig.7) explained this new emphasis on technique:

This generation was born to art pretty nearly at the moment when the Republic sang the dawning of its second century: and the Centennial Exhibition played what seems an almost "providential" part in opening a path for it. . . . And, quickly following to profit by the opening thus secured, came the new band of native artists preaching a new artistic gospel . . . a like-minded, brotherly band to preach that the painter's first privilege, first task, first duty, was *to learn the art of painting.* Our elder schools had been almost entirely absorbed in the subjects of their discourse, . . . had forgotten almost entirely that in every form of human utterance, when it turns to *art,* the language itself is of primary importance.[20]

In 1889, almost six years after the Pedestal Fund exhibition, critic John Van Dyke looked back:

The point of time from which we may date the true art education of our country is at the beginning of the second century of the Republic. . . . The Centennial Exposition as a whole did a great work for America. . . . It gave us a chance to see beyond our own door-sill; it brought us into relationship with foreign nations. At this time, too, the enormous wealth of our country was suddenly developed. Business and commercial enterprises of colossal proportions started up as by magic; agriculture, manufactures, railroads, telegraphs turned the land into a nineteenth century El Dorado; and the fast ocean steamship put us in close communication with Europe. . . . And with this increased prosperity and enlightenment came the demand for higher education . . . and painting, sculpture, and decoration came into prominence. . . . The next step, and indeed the most important one, was promoted by the influence of certain young American artists who had recently returned from abroad full of Rubens, Velásquez, Corot, and Millet, and who set forth their creed and gospel in the formation and first exhibition of the Society of American Artists. . . . They led us to look at a different class of men from Sir Frederick Leighton, Holman Hunt, Cabanel, and Kaulbach. They talked Vollon and Courbet, and Bastien-Lepage and Rousseau, and we listened, and looked, and profited thereby.[21]

These were some of the artists featured in the National Academy *Pedestal Fund Art Loan Exhibition,* one of the many contemporary ventures dedicated to raising cultural standards in America. It also included certain selected predecessors, such as Théodore Géricault (1791–1824) and Eugène Delacroix (1798–1863), whose works could be better enlisted in the contemporary struggle against entrenched mediocrity in the American art world. As Mariana Griswold Van Rensselaer expressed it:

It was the proximate outcome of the great romantic movement which, under Géricault and Delacroix, burst the fetters of academic tradition, introduced the modern free, inquiring, inventive spirit into art, secured freedom of thought and practice for every painter, and proclaimed that *individuality* was, in truth, the chief claim of an artist to the world's respect.[22]

The message of the Pedestal Fund exhibition was broadcast far and wide. In Providence, Rhode Island, *The Art Folio* publicized the event,[23] and in Boston the exhibition was discussed at length in *The United States Art Directory and Yearbook of 1884.*[24] There was a special press review of the exhibition before it opened,[25] and it is likely there was some form of press release, judging by the similarity of phrasing in so many of the reviews. For example, while the *New York Herald* exclaimed: "Great credit is due [Chase and Beckwith] for not alone their efforts to secure what is elevating in art, but also for their determination to admit nothing that was mediocre in execution or of low artistic aim,"[26] the *Courrier des Etats-Unis* announced: "Aucun objet médiocre ou banal n'y a été admis."[27]

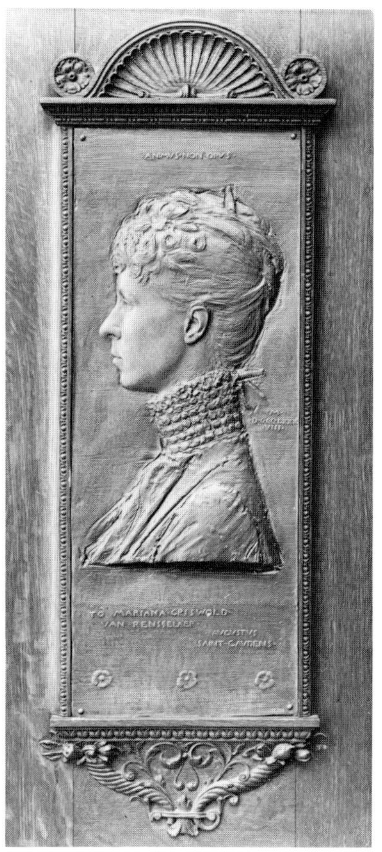

Fig. 7.
Augustus Saint-Gaudens
Mrs. Schuyler Van Rensselaer, 1888
Bronze (cast 1890), 20 7/8 x 7 1/4 in.
The Metropolitan Museum of Art, New York

This was the period that witnessed an extraordinary proliferation of art publications and art schools across the country, and Chase and Beckwith were already committed to a lifetime of teaching when they put together this exhibition, which was so clearly didactic in intent. While some 194 paintings were on display, only a few pictures were consistently prominent in the criticism. It was these images that projected the organizers' point of view most forcefully to the press by virtue of their provocative size, subject, or technique. The reviews also noted the purposeful placing of the works on the walls of the palatial National Academy of Design building, then a celebrated Twenty-third Street landmark. Even before the opening of the exhibition, the process was reported in the newspapers:

The apartments of the Venetian palace which is the home of the National Academy of Design are now in a state of much commotion incident to the arranging of the collections brought together for the Pedestal Fund Loan Exhibition. The working committees of ladies and gentlemen are occupied arranging in cases and about or on the walls the different objects which arrive in almost unceasing procession, some by the hands or under the eye of their jealous owners, and others by the usual academy carmen. . . . In the large south picture gallery the artists J. Carroll Beckwith and William M. Chase go gayly singing about their task of hanging the superb collection of works which they have selected . . . and stop now and then to ecstasize over some masterwork; while the laymen and ladies in the smaller galleries and the corridor arrange the sections and cases allotted to their care, cut up the sheets of numbers, compare lists and correct the catalogue proofs. . . .

The principal attraction of the exhibition will undoubtedly be the remarkable collection of paintings, which will be the most purely artistic that has yet been shown in this country. . . . It will be found that the committee has been perhaps a little one-sided in its views of what is best in art; but the error is on the right side, and in such a triumphant array of the work of the poet painters, the modern masters who rank with those of old time, will not be seen for many a long day.[28]

Indeed, the placement in the lesser exhibition spaces of the works of Jean-Louis-Ernest Meissonier (1815–1891) and his student, Edouard Detaille (1848–1912), painters of military subjects and favorites of the previous generation, clearly stated the position of this committee of young artists. They were out to relegate the detailed, tight style to the back galleries and favor the broadly brushed canvases, which they found to be more evocative and poetic. As the critic of the *New York Herald* expressed it:

> In addition to the large south gallery, which, by the way is admirably hung, the committee found it necessary to drape and arrange for the display of works the space under the stairway leading from the entrance to the main galleries. Here have been hung the Detaille "Salute to the wounded" [fig. 19, p. 32], the Meissoniers and many other works in oil and watercolor, which were somewhat out of keeping in the chief picture gallery — a separation generally speaking of the painters of prose from the painters of poetry.[29]

While the show was reviewed everywhere, it was particularly pertinent to the interests of the publisher Joseph Pulitzer (1847–1911). Just a few months before, Pulitzer (fig. 8) had taken over the New York City newspaper *The World.* He had seized upon the floundering campaign to raise money for the pedestal as a means of increasing the circulation of his paper. The rival *New York Times* was cool to the exhibition, but Pulitzer's *World* actively promoted it, even going so far as to publish, on the opening day, a plan of the installation (fig. 9). *The World* critic explained: "The diagram of the Academy will show intending visitors the arrangement of the exhibits in the galleries, so that they may find at once the various treasures which have the strongest individual attraction for them." Then the writer went on to rebut the negative criticism engendered by the exhibition: "The diagram will also serve to show how well the various committees have done their work and how well conceived and carried out has been their plan of arrangement."[30]

Even before the show officially opened, *The World* announced: " . . . the exhibition is the most important one of the kind ever held in New York."[31] The following day another review reiterated: "It is in many ways the most remarkable and noteworthy [exhibition] ever shown in the metropolis," and went on to explain:

> To the student of the modern French, Belgian and Dutch schools it affords opportunities of instruction never before offered in this country. Whether, however, it will meet the public and popular taste as well as one broader in its scope, and embracing the art of all periods and countries, . . . [is] another question. It is an artist's, art-student's and art connoisseur's exhibition — not a popular one: and in this sense is hardly as well fitted to please the multitude as one selected by men of other tastes and views would have been. The criticism will probably be made that an exhibition held for the purpose of stimulating public interest in America in aiding a work that should appeal to all Americans should at least have contained the works of some American artists. . . .[32]

The very day this review was published in *The World* — the opening day of the National Academy Pedestal Fund exhibition — a group of gentlemen met in Brooklyn to organize a second Pedestal Fund show "equaling anything of the kind . . . ever. . . held in this city or New York."[33] The Brooklyn event, which opened in January, included some up-and-coming young American artists as well as such popular French favorites as Alexandre Cabanel (1823–1889) and Jean-Léon Gérôme (1824–1904), who were slighted by Chase and Beckwith.[34] *The New York Times* waxed ecstatic: "Of Gérôme there is a 'Treading out the Grain' [fig. 10], an Egyptian scene, loaned by Mr. A. Healy, remarkable for the dexterous treatment of the hides of buffaloes, a very highly polished little picture."[35] "Highly polished little pictures" were exactly what Chase and Beckwith wished not to show, preferring bold, freely brushed canvases in their own work, in their teaching, and in their selections for the National Academy exhibition. Their point of view gained credence by its association with the art of the French

Barbizon School (also known for its free-flowing brushwork) then receiving great critical acclaim and record auction prices in America.

In the 1880s, a taste for French Impressionism was being cultivated in America simultaneously with an appreciation for Barbizon painting. Although a few paintings by Edouard Manet (1832–1883) and Hilaire Germain Edgar Degas (1834–1917) had been exhibited and discussed in print in America before this show, they were viewed in the context of the Barbizon School. In fact, it was in reference to Barbizon painting that American publications first came to use the term "Impressionism,"[36] and as critical evaluations of the show make clear, it was exactly in this context that Manet and Degas were presented in the Pedestal Fund exhibition.

What was already passé in Paris by 1883 had the potent force of shock in New York. The creamy flow of direct painting in the large, early, pre-Impressionist, Velásquez-inspired figures by Manet and the immediacy of Degas's touch in capturing off-stage gestures were received here with reservations, when not simply met with derision.

Critic Mariana Griswold Van Rensselaer urged an open mind, yet clearly preferred other kinds of painting. She wrote: "Degas was represented by a sketch of some ballet-girls in very vivid pink frocks [pl. XI], which was a superb bit of brush-work, but certainly nothing more." As for Manet she termed him an "aberrant talent" and "a peculiarly-endowed painter," yet she defended the decision to include both Manet and Degas in the exhibition:

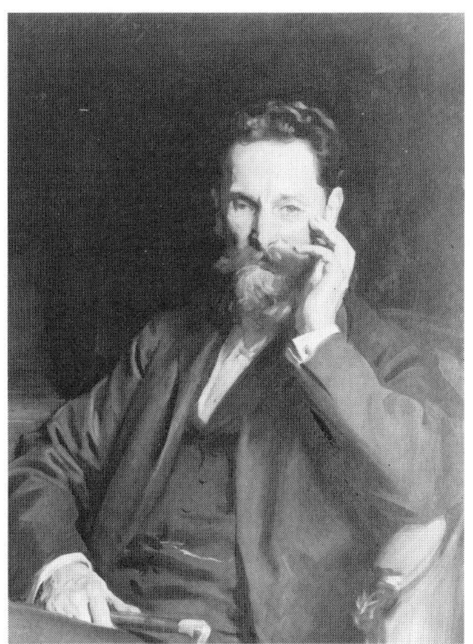

FIG. 8.
JOHN SINGER SARGENT
Joseph Pulitzer, 1905
Oil on canvas, 38 1/8 x 28 in.
Collection Mr. Joseph Pulitzer, Jr., Saint Louis

> It is curious to note that the committee has been attacked on more than one side for admitting the work of [the two painters]. . . . It must have been a surprise to be so reproached, for Mr. Chase and Mr. Beckwith were doubtless justified in believing that they would be widely thanked for this very move. No artists . . . have been more persistently talked about of recent years, and none are less familiar to our public. Gratified curiosity, if nothing else, should have ratified the course of the committee. It would not be so wonderful, perhaps, if the average visitor has found nothing gratified but curiosity in front of these pictures. Beauty, as he conceives it, is the first thing he looks for, and of sensuous beauty these pictures had nothing. They were frankly ugly in subject matter and arrangement, and their technical beauty was of so peculiar a kind that it is not strange no one but an artist could appreciate it. . . . The chief picture of the class . . . by Manet, was a large full-sized portrait of a woman in pink, with a parrot on a stand beside her [pl. XVIII]. The model was very far from beautiful, but not uninteresting in what a painter calls character. The color, also, was not beautiful in traditional ways, but had more charm for those who consent to see for a moment with the eyes of a peculiarly-endowed painter instead of with their own; and the handling was of the greatest interest to all who care at all for the painter's work as such — masterly in its way, and that way quite peculiar to this one man himself. . . . No one would have wondered had the public disliked these pictures, but it ought, at least, to have looked at them respectfully — which it did not. . . .
>
> Cazin did not attract nearly so much attention, being an original of a less noisy sort . . . one of the first among the very few really original, and at the same time poetic painters of contemporary France.[37]

Another critic referred to "an interesting Dugaz [*sic*]. . . . A Ballet Dancer"[38] and *The Brooklyn Daily Eagle* baldly maintained, "the paintings are mainly of the advanced impressionist school."[39] *The World* remarked: "It was to be expected that the French ultra-impressionists would be afforded representation from the well-known proclivities of the committee" and conceded: "Manet's 'Portrait of a Lady' . . . is an excellent example of this artist's peculiar style." It continued: "The Ballet [by Degas] . . . is a curious, but strong and important work."[40]

Van Dyke, writing in *The Studio*, concluded his discussion of the artists represented in the show by remarking:

> Prominent upon the south wall hang two Manets, which cannot fail to attract universal attention. It is almost certain that they will not please the public eye,

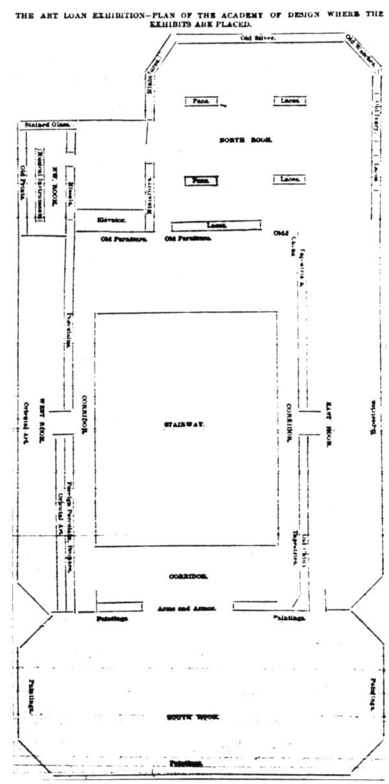

FIG. 9. *(above)*
The Art Loan Exhibition: Plan of the Academy of Design Where the Exhibits Are Placed
The World, December 3, 1883

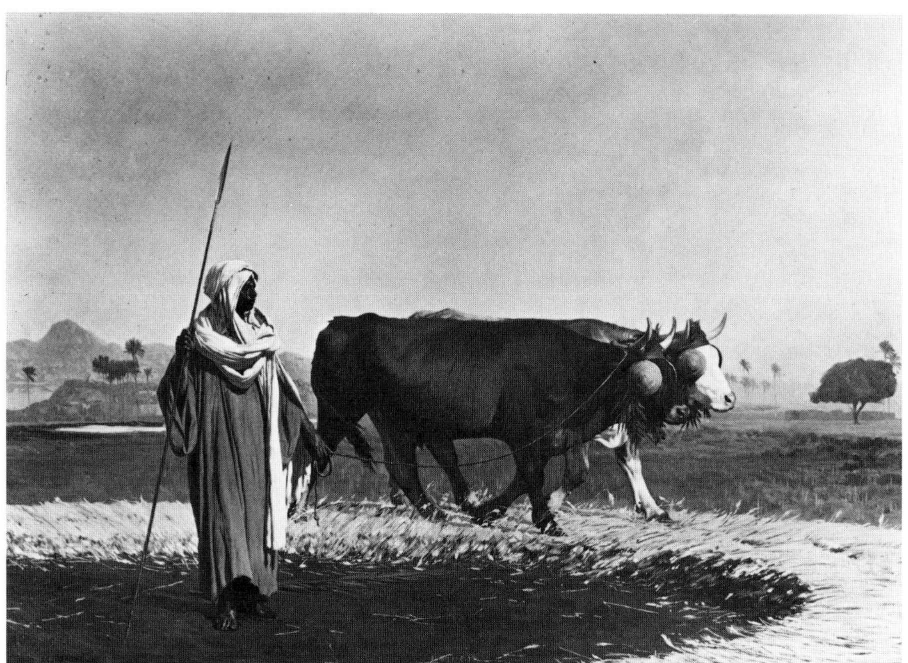

FIG. 10. *(right)*
JEAN-LÉON GÉRÔME
Dépiquage du blé en Egypte
Plate 6 from *Jean-Léon Gérôme: Oeuvres reproduites en photographie*, Paris: Goupil & Cie., 1860-63

> but, nevertheless, they must excite notice, if for no other reason then that they are from the brush of the ex-leader of the impressionists. In subject, they are both concentrated ugliness. A scrawny old maid [*sic*] with a parrot is the subject of the one, and a disreputable, dirty-looking boy holding a sword [cat. no. 47], is the other. They are repulsive looking, indeed, but it is strange how often in walking around the room the eye will wander back to study the repulsiveness and admire the ugliness. . . . Degas's 'Le Ballet,' a most pronounced example of the impressionist school, hangs upon the north wall, and must be seen from a distance to be properly appreciated. It is worthy of careful study.[41]

The writer in the *Art Amateur* opined: "Manet's 'Boy with the Sword,' and Degas's little ballet girls in pink, show that the impressionist movement means change, if not progress." Then the writer prophesied:

> There is little doubt that all the good painting of the men who will come into notice during the next ten years will be tinged with impressionism; not, perhaps, as it has been put into words by the critics, but as it has been put into paint by Manet and a few others. Looked at in this way the action of the committee in giving Manet the place of honor may be excused, although there are many much better pictures exhibited than his.[42]

Essentially the critics were far more interested in the other works in the show. The Millet *Après le bain* (cat. no. 62; pl. XXIX) "held the place of honor" for Mariana Griswold Van Rensselaer:

> Most marvelous of all was a nude study — a woman lying on a couch and seen from the back. . . . Could this exquisite work, as splendid as it was original in color and treatment, be from the same hand, we asked ourselves, as the ruder art Millet devoted to his ruder themes? It was a veritable revelation of a kind and degree of purely artistic power which could never be suspected did we only know Millet as he chose to make himself in his later years — a painter more concerned with the sentiment than with the technical perfection of his work, and treating subjects which, however high a place we may give them from the standpoint of poetry, of feeling, of intellectual force, were certainly less well adapted than this simple nude figure to display a painter's pictorial power, properly so called. Mr. Davis's collection is probably the finest on this side of the water, but with all of its treasures [including the Manets and the Degas in the Pedestal Fund exhibition] it can contain none of greater rarity and greater intrinsic worth than this.[43]

Even the engraved reproductions that accompanied these articles reveal the distinctive American attachment to more traditional realist modes. The illustration of the Degas in the New York *Daily Graphic* (fig. 5), like the one by Robert

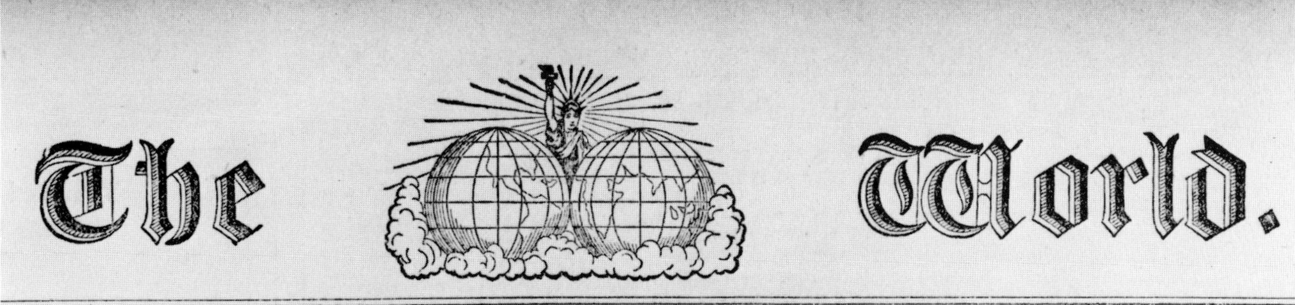

FIG. 11.
Masthead of *The World*, December 3, 1883

Blum in the exhibition catalogue, gives the figures more readable features (smiles and shadowed eyelids) in an effect that is ingratiating rather than analytic; more importantly, it focuses on the people and completely eliminates the background, which was so active a part of Degas's characteristic picture surface.

Typically, the *Daily Graphic* reproduced the Degas side by side with the Jules Bastien-Lepage (1848–1884) *Pauvre Fauvette*, in which an Impressionist high-horizon line and broken color are combined with a more traditional concern for the form and plight of the figure.[44]

The critic of *The New York Times* accurately assessed the central thrust of the exhibition in objecting:

> Was it not a mistake, considered as it must be on a purely financial basis, to pass over . . . painters . . . [such as Bouguereau and Cabanel who] are tremendously popular and nowhere more so than in New-York . . . in fact, they may be said to live on American orders . . . and take so many examples of Millet, an artist for the select; of Courbet, a painter whose rough brush sends a cold chill down the average American's back; of Monticelli, whom most people regard as little better than a fool and his admirers as would-be eccentrics or amiable lunatics?

This critic proposed that another, more inclusive, *Pedestal Fund Art Loan Exhibition* be organized (as indeed, the Brooklyn Art Association was then doing): "Whenever a French artist has found admirers and buyers in the United States he may be considered eligible as a representative; that should be the test rather than his position among the French critics or the American, or his comrades in art on either side of the ocean." Nevertheless, *The New York Times* critic concluded: " . . . nobody who delights in exquisite pictures can fail to be impressed by the . . . [paintings] which these young artists with 'convictions' have got together."[45]

One of the first things Pulitzer had done to change *The World* was to introduce illustration; another was to alter the masthead, placing the figure of *Liberty Enlightening the World* between the two hemispheres of the globe (fig. 11). Pulitzer's first editorial, under the title "The New 'World,'" stated unequivocally:

> The entire World newspaper property has been purchased by the undersigned, and will, from this day on, be under different management — different in men, measures and methods — different in purpose, policy and principles — different in objects and interests — different in sympathies and convictions — different in head and heart. . . . The new World is hereby enlisted and committed to the attention of the intelligent public. – Joseph Pulitzer[46]

In selecting the paintings for the Pedestal exhibition, Chase and Beckwith felt a similar responsibility: they were bringing the American art world under new management, as Beckwith's dapper portrait of Chase (fig. 1, p. 60), painted about this time, would suggest. As early as 1879 Chase had insisted that "there is a demand for better things in art than we have had."[47]

The generation of American artists who in 1877 had caused "a great rattling of dry bones"[48] at the National Academy with their demands for artistic liberty now tempered them with an appeal to authority in the 1883 *Pedestal Fund Art Loan Exhibition.* The works of such celebrated artists as J. B. C. Corot, Gustave Courbet, Jean-François Millet, Jules Bastien-Lepage, P. A. J. Dagnan-Bouveret, and Anton Mauve adorned the walls of the Academy, offering confirmation of the painterly values then being introduced to American art.

This is how the positive value of the exhibition was assessed by Mariana Griswold Van Rensselaer:

> The large South Gallery was filled with pictures, and these . . . were the main feature of the exhibition. They would have been so, of course, had they merely been a miscellaneous collection of good works of various sorts, such as one usually finds under similar circumstances; but they were something very different, and, I am sure, something very much better. The management of this part of the exhibition was given into the hands of Mr. Chase and Mr. Beckwith. These gentlemen, instead of merely asking for contributions in a general way and making the best of what the lenders chose to give, themselves selected the works they most desired, and they selected them along one harmonious line. . . . It has been said that as the main object of the exhibition was to attract as large a public as possible, something should have been provided to suit every taste, and that the works of "popular painters," such as Bouguereau, Gérôme, and their like, should first of all [have] been supplied. The committee did not, however, proceed from this point of view. Perhaps they were mistaken in so thinking, but it can hardly be counted against them that they *did* think the public wished to see the best things that could be got together. If the public has been disappointed, it is, it seems to me, its own fault, and not the fault of those who worked so hard and used so much discrimination for its benefit. Those who certainly were *not* disappointed, but who feel as though they owe Mr. Chase and Mr. Beckwith a debt of considerable magnitude, are the artists, art-students, and real art lovers of this city. They have delighted in this exhibition as they have never before in any other; and well they might. It is little to say that no such beautiful and instructive collection has ever before been brought together in this country — no other composed so exclusively of really first-rate works, and arranged so that each work helped its fellows, instead of hurting them, as is always the case in a more mingled exhibition. . . . I sympathize with all lovers of the best modern art who failed to see this collection. Certainly the occasion must have been very rare in Paris when such a one has been collected, and certainly in no other city but Paris, save in New York could such have been got together. Only in the private — not by any means in the public — collections of the French capital are there so many good works by these same masters to be seen. The times are seldom when they emerge into public view, and I can imagine that more than one art-student of Paris has never had such an opportunity as was here afforded to the art-students of New York. . . .
>
> The first thing one noticed on entering the room was its splendid unity of effect, so different from the spotty, mottled, distracting appearance of the average gallery wall. The decorative result, taken as a whole, was as fine as though the pictures had been placed with that sole end in view. The second point one remarked, perhaps, was the low tone preserved throughout; and the next, what an immense amount of the most splendid color existed with it. The works of the great French landscape painters of the first half of the century gave the key-note to the collection. . . . Then there was an admirable selection from that new Netherland school which Mr. Cottier should have the credit of having introduced to us . . . ; then we found Cazin, and actually Manet and Degas. Such a list cannot be called narrow. It was narrow in embracing only the best modern work, but broad enough, surely, in the kinds of this which it included. . . . To make good art has been the first concern throughout; not to make literature or morals or mere records of one sort or another.[49]

Here the critic emphasizes the spirit of reform that motivated the organizers of the Pedestal Fund painting exhibition. Chase and Beckwith rejected what they considered the moribund values of the older artists who then controlled such art institutions as the National Academy. They had allies. While the Pedestal Fund show was on the walls of the National Academy, a review of the last exhibition of members' works shown there appeared:

> The National Academy of Design appears to be in the last throes. We shall never again know it as we knew it of yore, confident in its full possession of the field, loading the walls of its exhibition rooms with scores of wretched and silly daubs, denying in the press the first principles of painting, sneering at Corot and Millet and Rousseau, and snubbing the unfortunate young men who had the conscience to get themselves taught something of art before setting up as artists. One or two more feeble efforts it may make, but the end is evidently not very far off.
>
> The nature of the present display would seem to indicate that it has at last – too late – begun to dawn upon the managers that younger men must in future produce the work that shall be known, whether at home or abroad, as American.[50]

Within a few years Chase and Beckwith, as well as many of their colleagues in reform, would themselves become members of the Academy and would be in official positions of power and influence. But in 1883, at the time of the *Pedestal Fund Art Loan Exhibition,* as the contemporary criticism makes clear, they represented the cutting edge of change.

Notes

The author gratefully acknowledges the generous cooperation of Joseph Pulitzer, Jr.; Debra Aguece, Enrico Fermi Cultural Center, Belmont Library, the Bronx, New York; and Katria Czerwoniak, The Metropolitan Museum of Art, New York.

1. "The Pedestal Art Loan," *The New York Times,* December 16, 1883, p. 5.
2. "Life in New York City. . . Art Loan Show," *The Brooklyn Daily Eagle,* December 9, 1883, p. 2.
3. Hon. William M. Evarts, quoted in "Admiring Objects of Art: Formal Opening of the Loan Exhibition for the Bartholdi Fund," *The New York Times,* December 4, 1883, p. 2.
4. "La Statue de la Liberté: L'Exposition Artistique. . . . Nul doute qu'elle ne réussisse à souhait et qu'elle ne contribué notablement à accélérer la conclusion d'une entreprise qu'il est temps de terminer, et qui ne saurait plus souffrir de grands retards sans devenir quelque peu embarrassante pour tout le monde," *Courrier des Etats-Unis,* December 3, 1883, p. 1.
5. *The Sun*, p. 2.
6. "The French Workingmen," *The Sun,* December 3, 1883, p. 4.
7. "Exhibitions on Sunday," *The Sun,* December 21, 1883, p. 2.
8. "The Listener," *The Studio,* vol. 2, no. 52 (December 29, 1883), pp. 300-301. See also David C. Huntington, in catalogue of the exhibition *The Quest for Unity: American Art between World's Fairs 1876-1893* (Detroit: The Detroit Institute of Arts, 1983), pp. 11-46.
9. *The Sun*, December 24, 1883, p. 1. Among the forty-seven signatures on the protest against the opening on Sunday, reported here as delivered that day to Director Smith's residence, were the names of Cornelius Vanderbilt, John Jay, J. Pierpont Morgan, and H. G. Marquand.
10. "Anxious about Sunday, Why They Signed a Protest against the Sunday Art Show," *The Sun,* December 25, 1883, p. 1.
11. *Ibid.*
12. *The American Hebrew*, vol. 17, no. 6 (December 21, 5644 [1883]), p. 1.
13. "Treasures in Fine Art: The Bartholdi Loan, . . . " *The World,* December 2, 1883, p. 3. See also *The New York Times,* December 4, 1883, p. 2; *New York Herald,* December 4, 1883, p. 5; *The Sun,* December 4, 1883, p. 3; "Mark Twain e Bartholdi," *Il Progresso Italo-Americano,* December 8, 1883, [p. 1]; and *The Art Amateur,* vol. 10, no. 2 (January 1884), p. 41.
14. See H. Barbara Weinberg, "Thomas B. Clarke: Foremost Patron of American Art from 1872 to 1899," *The American Art Journal,* vol. 8, no. 1 (May 1976), p. 58; Michael Quick, in catalogue of the exhibition *Munich and American Realism in the 19th Century* (Sacramento, California: E. B. Crocker Art Gallery, 1978), pp. 32-33, and in catalogue of the exhibition *Of Time and Place: American Figurative Art from the Corcoran Gallery* (Washington, D.C.: Smithsonian Institution Traveling Exhibition Service and Corcoran Gallery of Art, 1981), pp. 70-71.

15. *Harper's Weekly*, vol. 27, no. 1409 (December 22, 1883), p. 811. See also G.K., "The Bartholdi Exhibition," *Harper's Weekly*, vol. 27, no. 1408 (December 15, 1883), pp. 799 and 804; and "The Art Loan Exhibition," *The Art Folio* (Providence, Rhode Island), vol. 1, no. 8 (January 1884), p. 136.
16. "The Bartholdi Loan Exhibition — First Notice — The Paintings," *The Art Interchange: A Household Journal*, vol. 11, no. 13 (December 20, 1883), p. 160. See also vol. 12, no. 1 (January 3, 1884), p. 4, and vol. 12, no. 8 (April 10, 1884), p. 86.
17. John C. Van Dyke, "The Bartholdi Loan Collection," *The Studio*, vol. 2, no. 49 (December 8, 1883), pp. 262-63. See also vol. 2, no. 50 (December 15, 1883), p. 275, and vol. 2, no. 52 (December 29, 1883), pp. 300-301.
18. See Susan Hobbs, "Foreign Art at the Centennial," in catalogue of the exhibition *1876: American Art of the Centennial* (Washington, D.C.: Smithsonian Institution Press for the National Collection of Fine Arts, 1976), p. 10.
19. Kenyon Cox, "Antoine Vollon: A Painter's Painter," *The Manhattan*, vol. 2, no. 6 (December 1883), pp. 557-61.
20. Mariana Griswold Van Rensselaer, in *Book of American Figure Painters* (Philadelphia: J. B. Lippincott, 1886), unpaginated.
21. John C. Van Dyke, *The Increase in the Appreciation of Serious Art in America: A Paper Read Before the Rembrandt Club, February 4th 1889* (Brooklyn: Published by the Club, 1889), pp. 21-24.
22. Mariana Griswold Van Rensselaer, "French Landscape Art," *A Catalogue of Oil Paintings Exhibited by the Brooklyn Art Association in Aid of the Bartholdi Pedestal Fund*, January 1884 (New York: De Vinne Press, 1884), p. 54.
23. "The Art Loan Exhibition," *The Art Folio*, vol. 1, no. 8 (January 1884), p. 136.
24. *The United States Art Directory and Yearbook of 1884*, vol. 2, edited by Sylvester Rosa Koehler (New York, London, and Paris: Cassell and Company, Limited, 1885), p. 6.
25. "For the Bartholdi Pedestal," *New York Herald*, November 29, 1883, p. 6.
26. ". . . The Loan Collection in Aid of the Statue of Liberty Pedestal Fund: A Magnificent Display in the Academy, . . . " *New York Herald*, December 2, 1883, p. 11.
27. *Courrier des Etats-Unis*, December 3, 1883.
28. *New York Herald*, November 29, 1883.
29. *Ibid.*, December 2, 1883.
30. "The Bartholdi Art Loan," *The World*, December 3, 1883, p. 5.
31. "Treasures in Fine Art: The Bartholdi Loan . . . ," *ibid.*, December 2, 1883, p. 3.
32. *Ibid.*, December 3, p. 5.
33. "For the Bartholdi Pedestal: A Loan Exhibition to be Given by the Brooklyn Art Association," *The Brooklyn Daily Eagle*, December 4, 1883, [p. 4].
34. *Catalogue of Oil Paintings Exhibited by the Brooklyn Art Association*, 1884.
35. "The Bartholdi Statue: Brooklyn's Loan Exhibition of Paintings in Aid of the Pedestal Fund," *The New York Times*, January 13, 1884, p. 6.
36. See Peter Bermingham, "Post-Centennial Critics and Patrons," in catalogue of the exhibition *American Art in the Barbizon Mood* (Washington, D.C.: Smithsonian Institution Press, published for the National Collection of Fine Arts, 1975), pp. 70, 109 n.6-7.
37. Mariana Griswold Van Rensselaer, "The Recent New York Loan Exhibition," *American Architect and Building News*, vol. 15, no. 421 (January 19, 1884), pp. 29-30.
38. Montezuma, "My Note Book," *The Art Amateur*, vol. 10, no. 1 (December 1883), p. 2.
39. "Life in New York City, . . . " *The Brooklyn Daily Eagle*, see n.2.
40. "The Bartholdi Art Loan, . . . " *The World*, see n.30.
41. See n.17.
42. "The Pedestal Fund Art Loan Exhibition," *The Art Amateur*, vol. 10, no. 2 (January 1884): *The Art Interchange* (see n.16) mentioned Degas not at all and of Manet only stated, "Manet is seen in two [*sic*] works; but neither betray Manet, the impressionist." The Manet and Degas pictures in this show were just about ignored in *The Sun*, *The New York Commercial Advertiser*, and *Harper's Weekly*.
43. Van Rensselaer, "The Recent New York Loan Exhibition," p. 30.
44. *The Daily Graphic*, December 10, 1883, p. 298.
45. *The New York Times*, see n.1.
46. *The World*, May 11, 1883, p. 4.
47. Letter from Chase to Sylvester Rosa Koehler, editor of the short-lived *American Art Review*, December 7, 1879, Archives of American Art, Reel D30, frames 387-88.
48. Mariana Griswold Van Rensselaer used this expression in her article "American Etchers" (*The Century Magazine*, vol. 25, no. 4 [February 1883], p. 488).
49. Van Rensselaer, "The Recent New York Loan Exhibition." pp. 29-30.
50. Robert Jarvis, "Autumn Exhibition of the National Academy," *The Art Amateur*, vol. 10, no. 1 (December 1883), p. 8.

Bric-a-brac at the Pedestal Fund Art Loan Exhibition

Christopher P. Monkhouse

At the time of this country's Centennial in 1876, Americans discovered the decorative arts, then universally referred to as "bric-a-brac," which they began in earnest to collect, display, and study as a source of inspiration for new work. In 1887, Obadiah Sypher, a New York antiques dealer whose firm has been credited with introducing the bric-a-brac trade to the city, confirmed this view:

> . . . the real movement in favor of bric-a-brac dates only from 1876, that is from the Centennial year. Then it was that our fellow-citizens warmed up at the idea of collecting ancient pieces of furniture, old china, old plate, curious relics of all sorts, as well as masterpieces from artists of present and past ages. Among the early collectors I may name General S. L. M. Barlow, Robert Hoe, Esq., and several of the old Knickerbocker families.[1]

It is not coincidental that the two names Sypher singled out, Barlow and Hoe, appear along with his own among the lenders to the *Pedestal Fund Art Loan Exhibition* at the National Academy of Design in 1883. Although this exhibition occurred a scant seven years after the Centennial, the bric-a-brac mania had so seized the country that in the 1883 show the decorative arts outnumbered the fine arts by a ratio of roughly three to one. The Pedestal Fund exhibition is therefore a highly significant reflection of the first flowering of decorative-arts collecting in the wake of 1876, and its nearly 2,000 decorative-arts objects provide an invaluable frame of reference for establishing who was collecting what and from whom in and around New York. This veritable index of taste for the decorative arts includes some surprises, both in terms of what was shown as well as in what was omitted, and these will be given special attention in this survey of bric-a-brac at the *Pedestal Fund Art Loan Exhibition.*

While interest in bric-a-brac may have been comparatively recent in America, the precedent for its display with the fine arts can be found in Manchester, England, in 1857. In a country whose citizens rarely go beyond London for their cultural nourishment, Manchester was an unlikely location for the *Art Treasures Exhibition,* which was the first major loan exhibition of both decorative and fine arts assembled anywhere in the world, and it was organized on a scale that has rarely, if ever, been equaled. What is even more significant than Manchester's having set a historical precedent for the 1883 *Pedestal Fund Art Loan Exhibition* is that the artist John La Farge, one of the American show's organizers, attended the Manchester exhibition. He later acknowledged what a profound impact it had on his own work:

> After a little while I went to Manchester and spent several weeks at the great Exposition, which was the first of the special exhibitions of paintings collected from private and royal galleries. It is still remembered as the 'Manchester Exhibition' and is one of the turning points of the public's acquaintance with the art of many countries. As you know, the wealthy collections of England were poured into the great show, and certainly the pleasure of seeing, side by side, the great Titian and the great Velásquez and the great Rubens in all their contradictions, was an education for any intelligent and sympathetic mind. . . .
>
> But besides the miles of old masters, there were some of the quite new; the pre-Raphaelites, whom I knew of by reading and by some prints but whom I could now see carefully. They made a very great and important impression upon me, which later influenced me in my first work when I began to paint. But of that I had no warning.[2]

Although La Farge failed to mention Manchester's decorative-arts department, which bore the deservedly impressive title "Museum of Ornamental Art," it is reasonable to assume that memories of it later reemerged in his own decorative work and in the various decorative and fine-arts exhibitions he helped organize, including the Pedestal Fund exhibition in 1883.

Between Manchester and New York came the Centennial Exhibition in Philadelphia in 1876. Its displays of decorative and fine arts, representing every epoch and drawn from every imaginable corner of the globe, had a profound impact on American taste in general and on patterns of collecting and decorating in particular. Their importance was succinctly summed up a few years later in the introduction to the catalogue for the Pedestal Fund exhibition: "To the Exhibition of 1876, in Philadelphia, the country owes an enormous debt of gratitude, not only for the bequest in things beautiful and refining to our homes, but for practical results in fostering in America the remunerative industries of interior decoration and adornment."[3] If the writer had wanted to illustrate his remarks, he might well have singled out the display of modern embroidery arranged in Philadelphia by the Royal School of Art Needlework.

Fostered by the Arts and Crafts Movement in England, the Royal School won special praise because it addressed the need of providing dignified employment for "decayed gentlewomen" through instruction in the execution and sale of embroidery. Upon encountering the Royal School's display at the Centennial, an American society woman, Candace Wheeler, quickly perceived the advantages to be reaped by establishing similar institutions on this side of the Atlantic: "It all interested me extremely, for it meant the conversion of the common and inalienable heritage of feminine skill in the use of the needle into a means of art expression and pecuniary profit."[4] Therefore, in 1877, with some of her own money and with additional funds provided by her socially and artistically prominent friends and acquaintances, she organized the first Society of Decorative Art in New York City along the lines of the Royal School of Art Needlework, even down to the instructors who, at least initially, were graduates of the latter institution. An indication of the real void such a society filled can be discerned by noting the speed with which it spawned many auxiliary decorative-arts societies: within two years there were some thirty fledgling organizations in cities throughout the United States, including Boston, Chicago, Cincinnati, Detroit, and Philadelphia, and also in Canada. Much of Candace Wheeler's success could be attributed to her fully understanding the value of "gilt by association." She had peppered her board of managers and advisory council with such prestigious figures as Mrs. John Jacob Astor, August Belmont, and Joseph H. Choate, while her art advisors included Samuel Colman, Lockwood de Forest, John La Farge, and Louis Comfort Tiffany. Not only did the artists provide actual designs for needlework, and even instruction and criticism on occasion, but their involvement gave needed visibility to the Society and professional approbation at the highest artistic level.

As a means of raising funds to support the work of the Society of Decorative Art in New York, as well as expanding its audience, Candace Wheeler and her colleagues, perhaps with prompting from La Farge, hit upon the idea of an art-loan exhibition. Organized along the lines of Manchester, and capitalizing on the new interest in the decorative and fine arts sparked by the Centennial, their exhibition came together in record time, with the 2,000 objects fully installed for the opening on December 3, 1877; only the catalogue was late. The site of this month-long exhibition was the National Academy of Design, in its recently erected Doge's Palace on the northwest corner of Fourth Avenue and Twenty-third Street.

Built between 1863 and 1865 from the designs of Peter Bonnett Wight, the National Academy of Design had a highly ornamental facade, rich in carved details and polychromatic effects. The interior consisted of an enclosed central courtyard out of which rose a grand staircase linking the second and third stories, surrounded on three sides by an arcaded balcony of Venetian Gothic pointed arches springing from foliated capitals. By the flickering gaslight from the ivy-festooned lamp standards, cast in bronze and attached to the newel posts, the building emerged as a decorative-arts showcase in and of itself and hence a fitting backdrop for the Society of Decorative Art's loan exhibition in 1877. So much so, in fact, that the Society held yet another art-loan exhibition there in 1878, and both exhibitions were trial runs for the even more ambitious *Pedestal Fund Art Loan Exhibition* in 1883. The building was demolished in 1901; in order to see what the interior setting for the three exhibitions may have been like, it is now necessary to visit Frank Furness's 1871 Pennsylvania Academy of the Fine Arts in Philadelphia.

The rich medley of tapestries and lace, ceramics and glass, metalwork and ivories, furniture and woodwork, jewelry and fans, arms and armor, and illuminated missals and early printed books assembled in 1877 must have seemed very much at home in the exotic surroundings of the National Academy of Design. Textiles quite naturally played a dominant role because of the focus of the sponsoring organization and the zeal with which many of its members went after loans, often beginning with their own collections. Indeed, the very first object to greet visitors as they mounted the staircase was a large tapestry lent by August Belmont. Positioned over the doorway to the north gallery, it was "wrought after a picture of the old Dutch school, a work all visitors involuntarily paused to admire."[5] This arresting piece set the stage for others to come, described by the correspondent for *The New York Times* the following day: "The tapestries, of course, take more room than any other part of the exhibition. They cover the walls everywhere, hanging in graceful folds about doorways and windows and ornamenting the walls on every side. Some of the specimens are exceedingly beautiful and carry with them the shadows of fabulous prices."[6] If tapestries were not used to festoon entrances to the galleries, then arms and armor came to the fore, with the same *New York Times* correspondent comparing the resulting interiors to "the palace of some dusky Eastern Prince or the famous corridor of Sir Walter Scott's Abbotsford."[7]

Even though tapestries may have occupied more space in the galleries, antique lace received greater critical acclaim in the press, with loans from Mrs. John Jacob Astor figuring prominently in all such discussions. The heightened interest in lace can probably be explained by the fact that it had once again become a fashionable costume accessory. On the opening night of the exhibition, a reporter for *The New York Times* observed "richly dressed ladies whose costumes in many instances were made up with lace ornaments as rich as anything that was shown in the most jealously guarded cases in the exhibition."[8] Furthermore, interest in the subject had been generated earlier by an exhibition at The Metropolitan Museum of Art of the late Mrs. Andrew MacCallum's collection of antique lace. Formerly on loan to the South Kensington Museum (now the Victoria and Albert Museum) in London, it had been sent to the Metropolitan by Mrs. MacCallum's husband with an eye to interesting the museum in buying it. Given the comprehensiveness of the collection, together with the fascination with old lace on the part of the museum's influential friends, the funds for its purchase were forthcoming, and the MacCallum collection became the cornerstone of the Metropolitan's now encyclopedic holdings.

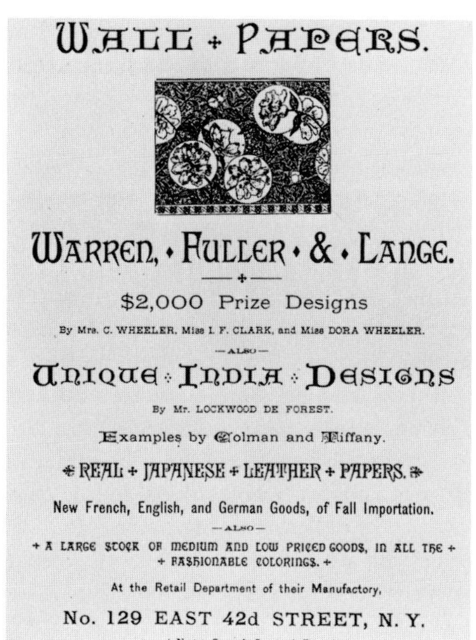

FIG 1.
Advertisement for
Warren, Fuller & Lange
Catalogue of the Pedestal Fund Art Loan Exhibition, 1883

The abundance of the lace assembled at the National Academy of Design in 1877 may actually have been a hindrance, judging from a comment that it was "exhibited in artistic confusion."[9] This same confusion appears to have been characteristic of the ceramics display, where William Cowper Prime was in charge. Although he was the leading local expert on the subject and was on the verge of publishing an authoritative text, *Pottery and Porcelain of All Times and All Nations* (1878), his display techniques were not appreciated and were totally rethought in 1878, as was noted in *The New York Times:* "The bric-a-brac room of last year will be dispensed with, and the china and porcelain will be arranged according to the dates of manufacture and the names of makers, thus affording the average visitor a practical opportunity to study ceramic art."[10]

The jewelry display appears to have been exempted from the "confusion" of the 1877 exhibition, because there were two cases "illustrating the changes in mode and manufacture from the most ancient time until the present day, arranged in chronological order."[11] Such didactic concerns had already been visible at the Manchester exhibition of 1857, and perhaps in the greater scheme of things showed the influence of Charles Darwin's theory of evolution as applied to the decorative arts.

The New York Society of Decorative Art loan exhibition for 1878 was virtually a carbon copy of 1877, with some exceptions: greater care was taken in the organization of certain displays; some recent American paintings were selected by La Farge and added to the show; a significant infusion of Oriental objects was artistically installed by Tiffany and Colman; and the date was changed from December to October. And if the press notices are to be believed, the New York Society of Decorative Art once again received much attention and praise for its efforts. Even though this was to be the last major art-loan exhibition it sponsored, some of the auxiliary societies organized their own, such as the Cincinnati Society of Decorative Art, in 1879. Such mammoth undertakings inevitably took their toll on both the organizers and the lenders, and in the case of New York, a prime mover, Mrs. Wheeler, decided to redirect her energies. In 1879 she, along with three other influential Decorative Art Society volunteers, namely Colman, de Forest, and Tiffany, came together to establish the commercial decorating firm known as Associated Artists.

When the idea of another art-loan exhibition came on the horizon in 1883 in order to raise funds for a pedestal for Frédéric Auguste Bartholdi's Statue of Liberty, Associated Artists actively participated in the selection and display of objects. The members were joined by William Merritt Chase, who had been studying in Europe between 1874 and 1878 and hence had not participated in the two earlier loan exhibitions. The influential role of Associated Artists in the *Pedestal Fund Art Loan Exhibition* is clearly evident from the very first page of the accompanying exhibition catalogue. Not by chance did a full-page advertisement appear there for the innovative wallpaper manufacturing firm of Warren, Fuller & Lange, and it listed in bold type Candace Wheeler, de Forest, Colman, and Tiffany among its contributing designers (fig. 1).

Among the many displays of decorative arts in 1883, textiles once again figured prominently, but the impressive list of lenders to the lace collection now included Mrs. Jesse Seligman's name, along with Mrs. John Jacob Astor's. Tapestries loomed as large as ever, but in place of August Belmont's name appeared some of the major tapestry dealers, such as the already mentioned Obadiah Sypher, Pottier & Stymus, and Herter Brothers, the latter firm having recently completed the construction and interior furnishings for William H. Vanderbilt's Fifth Avenue mansion. The name of Duveen was missing, as that firm had not quite arrived on the New York scene: by the end of the decade it would dominate the antique-tapestry market both here and abroad.

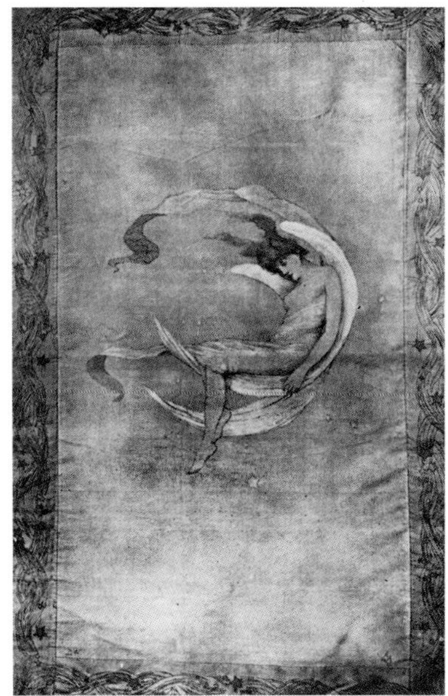

FIG 2.
DORA WHEELER
The Winged Moon
Needle-woven tapestry executed by The Associated Artists, 1883
Plate from *The Development of Embroidery in America*, 1921

While antique tapestries had become predictable fare at art-loan exhibitions, modern American tapestries, not to mention modern American stained glass, were not. Yet both were included here thanks to Associated Artists, and not surprisingly many of the loans came from its own showrooms. Its debut in the 1883 Pedestal Fund exhibition did not go unobserved:

> Only in the department of embroideries and stained glass it seems, has American work been found good enough to display beside the products of China and Japan, France and Italy. This, however, shows a decided advance, since at the last loan exhibition about three years ago, there was nothing of either.[12]

Among the forty modern American embroideries exhibited, the series of needle-woven tapestries designed by Candace Wheeler's daughter Dora, after her recent course of study with Chase, was the most notable; it was part of a commission undertaken by Associated Artists in 1882 for Cornelius Vanderbilt. This series formed the major decoration of the drawing room in Vanderbilt's Fifth Avenue mansion, only just completed from the designs of George B. Post, and it consisted of *The Winged Moon* (fig. 2), *The Water Spirit, The Birth of Psyche, The Air Spirit,* and *The Flower Girl,* each of which was executed in atmospheric tones of blue, gray, and purple on a salmon-pink ground. Other accomplished designers from Associated Artists who had work on display included Ida F. Clark, Caroline Townshend, and Rosina Emmet.

As if this exhibition of modern embroideries was not remarkable enough, Candace Wheeler also assembled a representative collection of Early American embroideries to illustrate a native precedent and to serve as a challenge to the needlewomen of her own day. Of the twenty-two embroidered pictures, samplers, and related objects shown, those worked at the Moravian School in Bethlehem, Pennsylvania, held a particular fascination for Candace Wheeler, and so she tended to emphasize them. Despite the slight imbalance favoring Bethlehem, this must assuredly be among the first serious attempts to document and display historic American needlework. Within the context of the Pedestal Fund exhibition, it was doubly exceptional because "Colonial American things" otherwise seem to have been largely ignored.

Along with its preeminence in the modern American textiles display, Associated Artists also dominated the stained glass. Out of a total of ten examples, six were contributed by Tiffany, including his *Eggplant Window* (fig. 3).[13] Tidden & Arnold and Roger Riordan & Co. contributed the four remaining examples of modern stained glass, two coming from each firm. In a detailed review of the entire exhibition in *The New York Times* for December 2, 1883, the reporter noted that Riordan had been a pupil of La Farge who was conspicuous in this display by his absence, even though his name appears as one of the selection committee for stained glass.

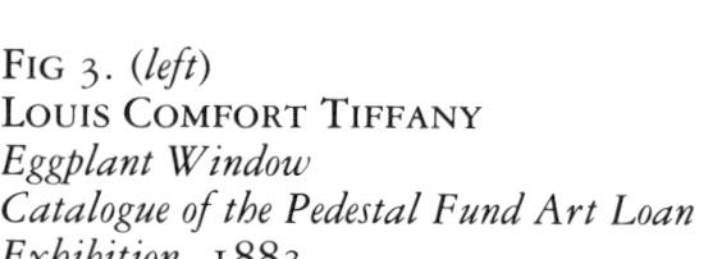

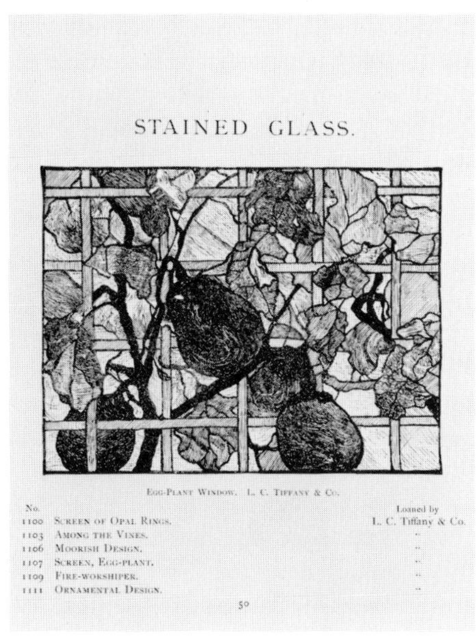

STAINED GLASS.

EGG-PLANT WINDOW. L. C. TIFFANY & CO.

No.		Loaned by
1100	SCREEN OF OPAL RINGS.	L. C. Tiffany & Co.
1103	AMONG THE VINES.	"
1106	MOORISH DESIGN.	"
1107	SCREEN, EGG-PLANT.	"
1109	FIRE-WORSHIPER.	"
1111	ORNAMENTAL DESIGN.	"

50

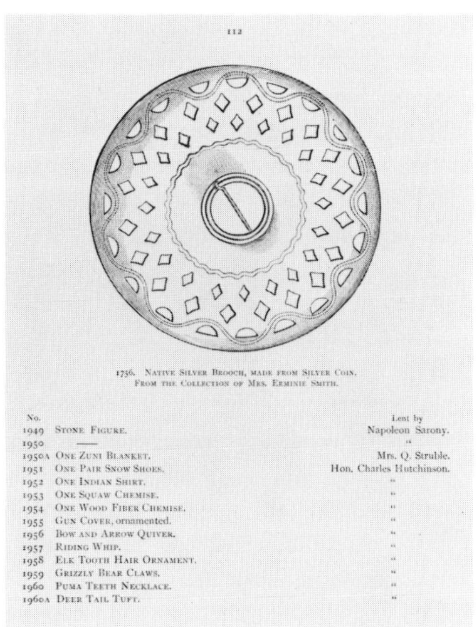

112

1756. NATIVE SILVER BROOCH, MADE FROM SILVER COIN.
FROM THE COLLECTION OF MRS. ERMINIE SMITH.

No.		Lent by
1949	STONE FIGURE.	Napoleon Sarony.
1950	——	"
1950A	ONE ZUNI BLANKET.	Mrs. Q. Struble.
1951	ONE PAIR SNOW SHOES.	Hon. Charles Hutchinson.
1952	ONE INDIAN SHIRT.	"
1953	ONE SQUAW CHEMISE.	"
1954	ONE WOOD FIBER CHEMISE.	"
1955	GUN COVER, ornamented.	"
1956	BOW AND ARROW QUIVER.	"
1957	RIDING WHIP.	"
1958	ELK TOOTH HAIR ORNAMENT.	"
1959	GRIZZLY BEAR CLAWS.	"
1960	PUMA TEETH NECKLACE.	"
1960A	DEER TAIL TUFT.	"

FIG 3. (*left*)
LOUIS COMFORT TIFFANY
Eggplant Window
Catalogue of the Pedestal Fund Art Loan Exhibition, 1883

FIG 4. (*right*)
American Indian Brooch
Catalogue of the Pedestal Fund Art Loan Exhibition, 1883

Another category included in neither of the Society of Decorative Art loan exhibitions at the National Academy of Design in 1877 and 1878, but now occupying a whole gallery on the lower floor, was costumes. Because they were essential studio props for artists, it is not surprising to discover that Napoleon Sarony, Dora Wheeler, and Rosina Emmet are listed among the lenders. A writer for *Harper's Weekly* found the trials connected with the quest for costumes an interesting commentary on American society in general:

> It is easy to fancy that Messrs. Leavitt and others on the committee of costumes had a difficult task. They were after characteristic costumes of various nations and old costumes. There are plenty of representations of other nationalities in the cosmopolitan population of New York, but a foreigner's characteristics, especially those of dress, are soon absorbed here. To obtain old costumes was still more difficult. In a Society like ours, where ancestry goes for little, and mere wealth will sooner or later lift a family into the first social rank, it is not easy to find people who would view with pride the costumes of their grandfathers or grandmothers, or those of even a nearer generation. Yet by much untiring investigation some people were found with ancestors who were not bought like those of the Major-General in *The Pirates of Penzance* and the exhibition of colonial fashions was perhaps the best evidence of the zeal with which this committee went to work. The costumes, all told, numbered about one hundred and twenty — not a large number, but intelligently arranged so as to bring the various national characteristics into most striking contrast.[14]

Although costumes and embroidery were the only two departments to include significant amounts of Colonial American material, the gallery adjacent to costumes took a step further back in time with its display of American aboriginal art (fig. 4). While exhibitions of Indian objects had occurred before, most notably at the Centennial Exhibition, they had been included for their scientific value: hence, in Philadelphia they were shown in the mineral annex. If visitors at the Centennial Exhibition took away an impression of American Indian art, it was much more likely to have been the Gorham silver centerpiece titled *Hiawatha's Barge* which so won the heart of Mrs. Ulysses S. Grant that she acquired it for the White House, where it remains today.

The change in attitude toward American Indian objects that allowed them to be seen not only in scientific and sentimental terms but also in artistic ones occurred in the early 1880s with some assistance from Associated Artists. Tiffany and Candace Wheeler in particular started to incorporate American Indian

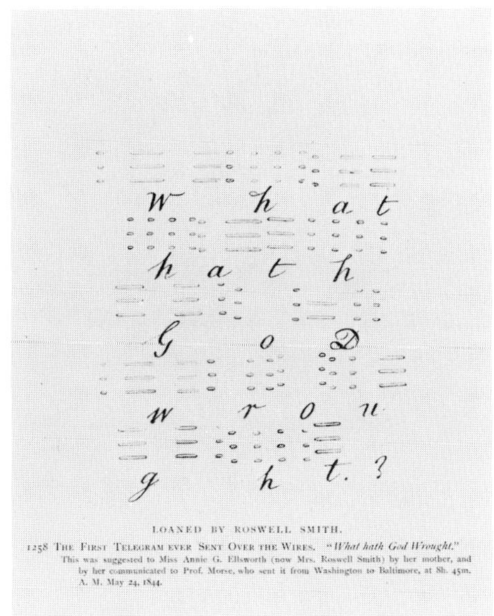

w h a t
h a t h
G o D
w r o u
g h t. ?

LOANED BY ROSWELL SMITH.

1258 THE FIRST TELEGRAM EVER SENT OVER THE WIRES. *"What hath God Wrought."* This was suggested to Miss Annie G. Ellsworth (now Mrs. Roswell Smith) by her mother, and by her communicated to Prof. Morse, who sent it from Washington to Baltimore, at 8h. 45m. A. M. May 24, 1844.

FIG 5.
SAMUEL F. B. MORSE
The First Telegram Ever Sent over the Wires, May 24, 1844
Catalogue of the Pedestal Fund Art Loan Exhibition, 1883

designs and motifs into their work with considerable aesthetic success. Whereas in the 1860s and 1870s Oriental art had been a dominant source of inspiration for Western artists and designers, who consulted it in matters of scale, color, absence of perspective, materials, and motif, in the 1880s American Indian art had the same potential. The fact that there were 300 examples of American Indian art in the Pedestal Fund exhibition and only 266 Oriental objects speaks for itself.

Of all the objects included in the Pedestal Fund exhibition, the most unlikely candidate would appear to have been the first telegram sent by Samuel F. B. Morse, on May 24, 1844, with the now-legendary message: "What hath God wrought?" (fig. 5). Although Morse had been trained initially as an artist, there seemed to be no reason for its inclusion. However, the telegram was not installed in isolation, but within the section devoted to illuminated missals and early printed books, including the magnificent Pembroke Book of Hours, then in the Brayton Ives collection. Given the Pedestal Fund exhibition's concern for illustrating the evolution of objects, the telegram showed quite literally how spreading the word of God had been dramatically transformed for the first time since Gutenberg invented movable type in the fifteenth century.

As the *Pedestal Fund Art Loan Exhibition* makes abundantly clear, artists, collectors, and the general public had an obsession at the end of the nineteenth century for acquiring objects and placing them in an historical or aesthetic context in the furnishing of their homes and studios, or, as seen here, in exhibition galleries. But the Pedestal Fund exhibition went beyond the mere celebration of collectors' material possessions, because its organizers went to some length to give craftsmen, artists, and students an opportunity to examine the exhibits. Despite New York City laws that discouraged the Sunday opening of museums and exhibitions, including The Metropolitan Museum of Art, the Pedestal Fund exhibition organizers arranged to be open on Sunday in order to attract those people who could most benefit from the exposure but would otherwise be denied it: those who worked a six-day week, with Sunday their only day off. Furthermore, Montague Marks, with the support of his fellow exhibition organizers, established a special fund to provide free admission for art students unable to afford the entrance fee of fifty cents. Given the quantity and quality of the exhibits, in which the best of the past from around the world was being shown with work of the avant-garde, the effort to make the displays accessible to artists and artisans as well as to collectors was indeed justified. In turn this effort enabled the *Pedestal Fund Art Loan Exhibition* to have a lasting significance well summarized in the following remarks published in *The New York Times:*

> In the exhibition made by the Pedestal Fund Art Loan Association there should be something acquired beyond that mere pleasure received by flash of jewels or superbness of decoration. There are to be found in every room objects which tend toward the formation of a better art judgment.[15]

NOTES

1. Obadiah Sypher, "Bric-a-Brac," *The Curio,* vol. 1, no. 2 (October 1887), p. 192.
2. Royal Cortissoz, *John La Farge: A Memoir and Study* (Boston and New York: Houghton Mifflin, 1911), pp. 97-98.
3. *Catalogue of the Pedestal Fund Art Loan Exhibition* (New York: National Academy of Design, 1883), p. 7.
4. Candace Wheeler, *Yesterdays in a Busy Life* (New York and London: Harper & Brothers, 1918), p. 211.
5. *The New York Times,* December 4, 1877, p. 5.
6. *Ibid.*, December 5, 1877, p. 4.
7. *Ibid.*
8. *Ibid.*, December 4, 1877, p. 5.
9. *Ibid.*, December 5, 1877, p. 4.
10. *Ibid.*, October 5, 1878, p. 7.
11. *Ibid.*, December 4, 1877, p. 5.
12. "The Pedestal Fund Art Loan Exhibition," *The Art Amateur,* vol. 10, no. 1 (December 1883), p. 41.
13. This window was recently included in the exhibition *The Quest for Unity: American Art between World's Fairs 1876-1893,* The Detroit Institute of Arts, 1983, no. 180.
14. *Harper's Weekly*, vol. 27, no. 1408 (December 15, 1883), p. 799.
15. *The New York Times*, December 12, 1883, p. 4.

Plates

All paintings illustrated in color were included in the 1883 *Pedestal Fund Art Loan Exhibition* with the exception of plates II, X, and XXXV, which are representative in theme or style of works by those artists in the 1883 show.

Plate I
Charles Bargue (c. 1825–1883)
A Bashi-Bazouk, 1875
Oil on canvas, 18¼ x 13⅛ in.
The Metropolitan Museum of Art, New York, Bequest of Catharine Lorillard Wolfe, 1887, Catharine Lorillard Wolfe Collection
Cat. no. 1

Plate II
Jules Bastien-Lepage (1848–1884)
Pauvre Fauvette
Watercolor on paper, 28 x 22¼ in.
The Corcoran Gallery of Art, Washington, D.C., William A. Clark Collection
Cat. no. 3

Plate III
Rosa Bonheur (1822–1899)
A Limier-Briquet Hound
Oil on canvas, 14½ x 18 in.
The Metropolitan Museum of Art, New York, Bequest of Catharine Lorillard Wolfe, 1887, Catharine Lorillard Wolfe Collection
Cat. no. 6

Plate IV
Johannes Bosboom (1817–1891)
The Church at Alkmaar
Oil on panel, 12¾ x 10½ in.
The Saint Louis Art Museum
Not in current exhibition

Plate V
Auguste Boulard (1825–1897)
Female Head (Portrait of the Artist's Niece)
Oil on canvas, 21½ x 17¾ in.
Collection Robert B. Beardsley
Cat. no. 8

Plate VI
Jean-Baptiste-Camille Corot (1796–1875)
Orpheus Greeting the Dawn, 1865
Oil on canvas, 78¾ x 54 in.
Elvehjem Museum of Art, Madison, Wisconsin, Gift in Memory of Earl William and Eugenia Brandt Quirk, Class of 1910, by Their Children (E. James Quirk, Catherine Jean Quirk, and Lillian Quirk Conley)
Not in current exhibition

Plate VII
Jean-Baptiste-Camille Corot
Le Soir (La Danse des Amours), 1866
Oil on canvas, 54 x 44 in.
Museum Folkwang, Essen, West Germany, Acquired with the support of the Landes NRW and the Eugen and Agnes von Waldhausen-Platzoff Museum Endowment
Not in current exhibition

Plate VIII
Jean-Baptiste-Camille Corot
Ville d'Avray
Oil on canvas, 21⅝ x 31½ in.
The Metropolitan Museum of Art, New York, Bequest of Catharine Lorillard Wolfe, 1887, Catharine Lorillard Wolfe Collection
Cat. no. 13

Plate IX
Gustave Courbet (1819–1877)
The Violoncellist, 1847
Oil on canvas, 45 x 35 in.
Portland Art Museum, Portland, Oregon, Gift of Col. C. E. S. Wood in Memory of His Wife, Nanny Moale Wood
Cat. no. 16

Plate X
Thomas Couture (1815–1879)
The Courtesan's Chariot, or Love Leading the World, c. 1874–76
Oil on canvas, 59⅛ x 83⅞ in.
Collection Stuart Pivar, New York
Cat. no. 21

Plate XI
Hilaire Germain Edgar Degas (1834–1917)
Ballet Dancers
Oil on canvas, 23 x 28½ in.
Hill-Stead Museum, Farmington, Connecticut
Not in current exhibition

Plate XII
Eugene Delacroix (1798–1863)
Le Christ au tombeau, c. 1847–49
Oil on canvas, 22⅛ x 18¾ in.
Phoenix Art Museum, Phoenix, Arizona, Gift of Mr. Henry R. Luce
Cat. no. 26

Plate XIII
Narcisse Virgile Diaz de la Pena (1807–1876)
La Mare aux Grenouilles
Oil on panel, 31⅛ x 41½ in.
The Corcoran Gallery of Art, Washington, D.C., Bequest of William A. Clark
Not in current exhibition

Plate XIV
Jean-Jacques Henner (1829–1905)
A Bather
Oil on canvas, 33⅛ x 27¾ in.
The Metropolitan Museum of Art, New York, Bequest of Catharine Lorillard Wolfe, 1887, Catharine Lorillard Wolfe Collection
Cat. no. 38

Plate XV
Charles-Emile Jacque (1813–1894)
Sheep at the Entrance to a Forest
Oil on canvas, 27⅜ x 39½ in.
Allen Memorial Art Museum, Oberlin College, Oberlin, Ohio, Bequest of Mrs. Elisabeth Severance Allen Prentiss
Cat. no. 40

Plate XVI
Ludwig Knaus (1829–1910)
Pigs and Swineherd, 1878
Oil on canvas, 18½ x 14 in.
Charles and Emma Frye Art Museum, Seattle, Washington
Cat. no. 42

Plate XVII
Edouard Manet (1832–1883)
Boy with a Sword, 1861
Oil on canvas, 51⅛ x 36¾ in.
The Metropolitan Museum of Art, New York, Gift of Erwin Davis, 1889
Cat. no. 47

Plate XVIII
Edouard Manet
Woman with a Parrot
Oil on canvas, 72⅞ x 50⅝ in.
The Metropolitan Museum of Art, New York,
Gift of Erwin Davis, 1889
Not in current exhibition

Plate XIX
Matthew Maris (1839–1917)
A Corner of The Hague, 1860
Oil on panel, 7⅝ x 11¾ in.
The Phillips Collection, Washington, D.C.
Cat. no. 51

Plate XX
Anton Mauve (1838–1888)
Changing Pasture
Oil on canvas, 24 x 39⅝ in.
The Metropolitan Museum of Art, New York,
Bequest of Benjamin Altman, 1913
Not in current exhibition

Plate XXI
Jean-Louis-Ernest Meissonier (1815–1891)
A General and His Aide-de-Camp, 1869
Oil on panel, 7¾ x 10⅞ in.
The Metropolitan Museum of Art, New York,
Bequest of Catharine Lorillard Wolfe, 1887,
Catharine Lorillard Wolfe Collection
Not in current exhibition

Plate XXII
Jean-Louis-Ernest Meissonier
The Cavalier: Portrait of the Artist, 1872
Gouache, watercolor, and wash on paper, 13¼ x 8⅞ in.
The New-York Historical Society, New York,
Robert L. Stuart Collection
Cat. no. 54

Plate XXIII
Louis Mettling (1847–1904)
The Studio, 1874
Oil on canvas, 17½ x 15¾ in.
National Gallery of Canada, Ottawa
Musée des beaux-arts du Canada, Ottawa
Cat. no. 56

Plate XXIV
Georges Michel (1763–1843)
Clouds and Landscape (The Hills of Montmartre), c. 1826
Oil on canvas, 33½ x 46½ in.
The Heckscher Museum, Huntington, New York,
Gift of August Heckscher
Cat. no. 59

Plate XXV
Jean-Francois Millet (1814–1875)
The Bather, c. 1846
Oil on canvas, 12⅜ x 9⅝ in.
Yale University Art Gallery, New Haven, Connecticut,
Anonymous Gift in Honor of Alan Shestack
Cat. no. 60

Plate XXVI
Jean-Francois Millet
The Whisper
Oil on canvas, 18 x 15 in.
National Gallery, London,
Gift of George Salting, 1910
Not in current exhibition

Plate XXVII
Jean-Francois Millet
Hylas and the Nymphs
Oil on canvas, 10 x 16 in.
Rijksmuseum Kröller-Müller, Otterlo, the Netherlands
Not in current exhibition

Plate XXVIII
Jean-Francois Millet
Susanna and the Elders
Oil on canvas, 22 x 18 in.
National Gallery of Victoria, Melbourne, Australia,
Felton Bequest, 1921
Not in current exhibition

Plate XXIX
Jean-Francois Millet
Après le bain, c. 1846–48
Oil on panel, 5⅜ x 6¾ in.
Private Collection, Switzerland
Cat. no. 62

Plate XXX
Jean-Francois Millet
The Quarriers, 1846–47
Oil on canvas, 29 x 23½ in.
The Toledo Museum of Art, Toledo, Ohio,
Gift of Arthur J. Secor
Cat. no. 61

Plate XXXI
Jean-Francois Millet
The Woodchopper, c. 1850
Oil on canvas, 15⅝ x 12½ in.
Ball State University Art Gallery, Muncie, Indiana,
Elisabeth Ball Collection, Permanent Loan from George and Frances Ball Foundation
Cat. no. 63

Plate XXXII
Jean-Francois Millet
Autumn Landscape with a Flock of Turkeys, c. 1870–74
Oil on canvas, 31⅞ x 39 in.
The Metropolitan Museum of Art, New York,
Bequest of Isaac D. Fletcher, 1917, Mr. and Mrs. Isaac D. Fletcher Collection
Cat. no. 64

Plate XXXIII
Adolphe Joseph Thomas Monticelli (1824–1886)
Gateway to a Fort, c. 1867
Oil on panel, 15¾ x 22⅞ in.
Montreal Museum of Fine Arts,
Musée des beaux-arts de Montreal,
Bequest of Miss Adaline Van Horne
Cat. no. 66

Plate XXXIV
Adolphe Joseph Thomas Monticelli (1824–1886) and Matthew Maris (1839–1917)
The Farmyard
Oil on panel, 15½ x 24 in.
Yale University Art Gallery, New Haven, Connecticut,
Gift of Duncan Phillips
Not in current exhibition

Plate XXXV
Adolphe Joseph Thomas Monticelli and Matthew Maris
Landscape with Figures
Oil on panel, 17½ x 31½ in.
The Phillips Collection, Washington, D.C.
Cat. no. 67

Plate XXXVI
Theodule Augustin Ribot (1823–1891)
A Young Vendean
Oil on canvas, 22¼ x 18½ in.
Montreal Museum of Fine Arts,
Musée des beaux-arts de Montréal,
Bequest of Miss Adaline Van Horne, 1945
Not in current exhibition

Plate XXXVII
Alfred Emile Leopold Stevens (1823–1906)
At the Pawnshop
Oil on panel, 39¼ x 31½ in.
Museum of Art, Rhode Island School of Design, Providence,
Gift of Mrs. Gustav Radeke
Cat. no. 79

Plate XXXVIII
James-Jacques-Joseph Tissot (1836–1902)
Richmond Bridge, c. 1878
Oil on canvas, 14⅝ x 9¼ in.
Collection William B. Ruger
Cat. no. 83

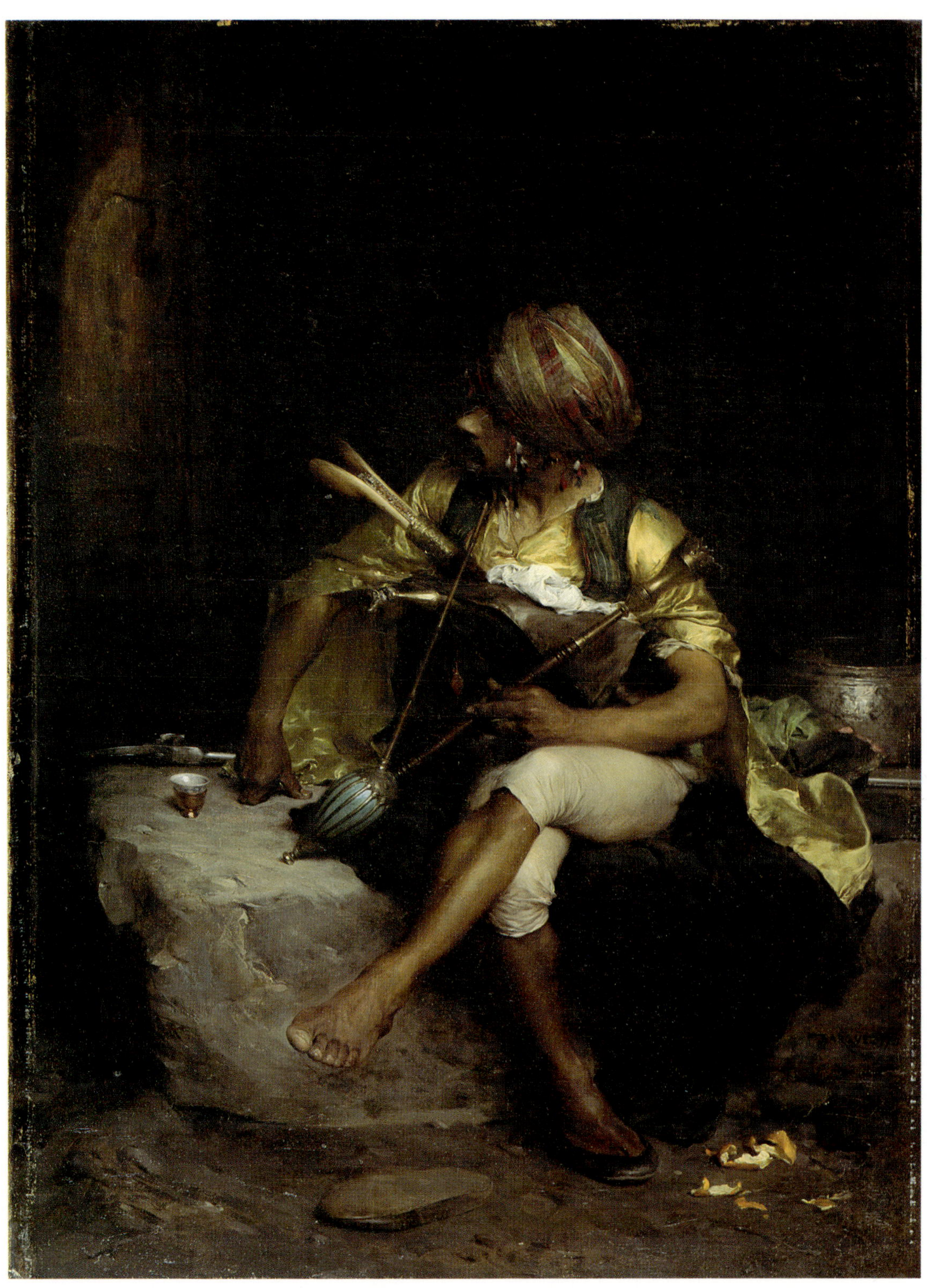

Pl. I

Charles Bargue, *A Bashi-Bazouk*, 1875

The Metropolitan Museum of Art, New York

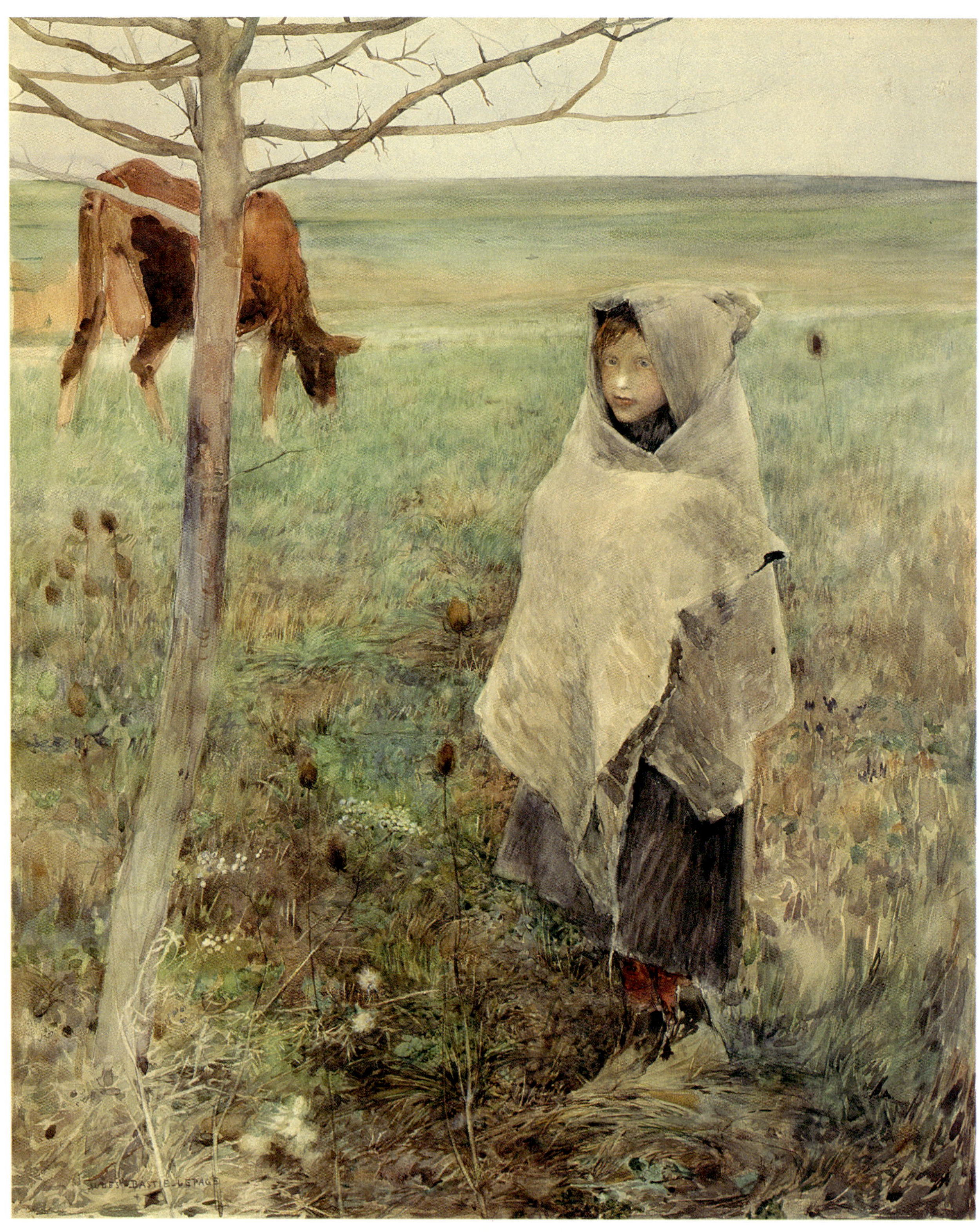

Pl. II

Jules Bastien-Lepage, *Pauvre Fauvette*

The Corcoran Gallery of Art, Washington, D.C.

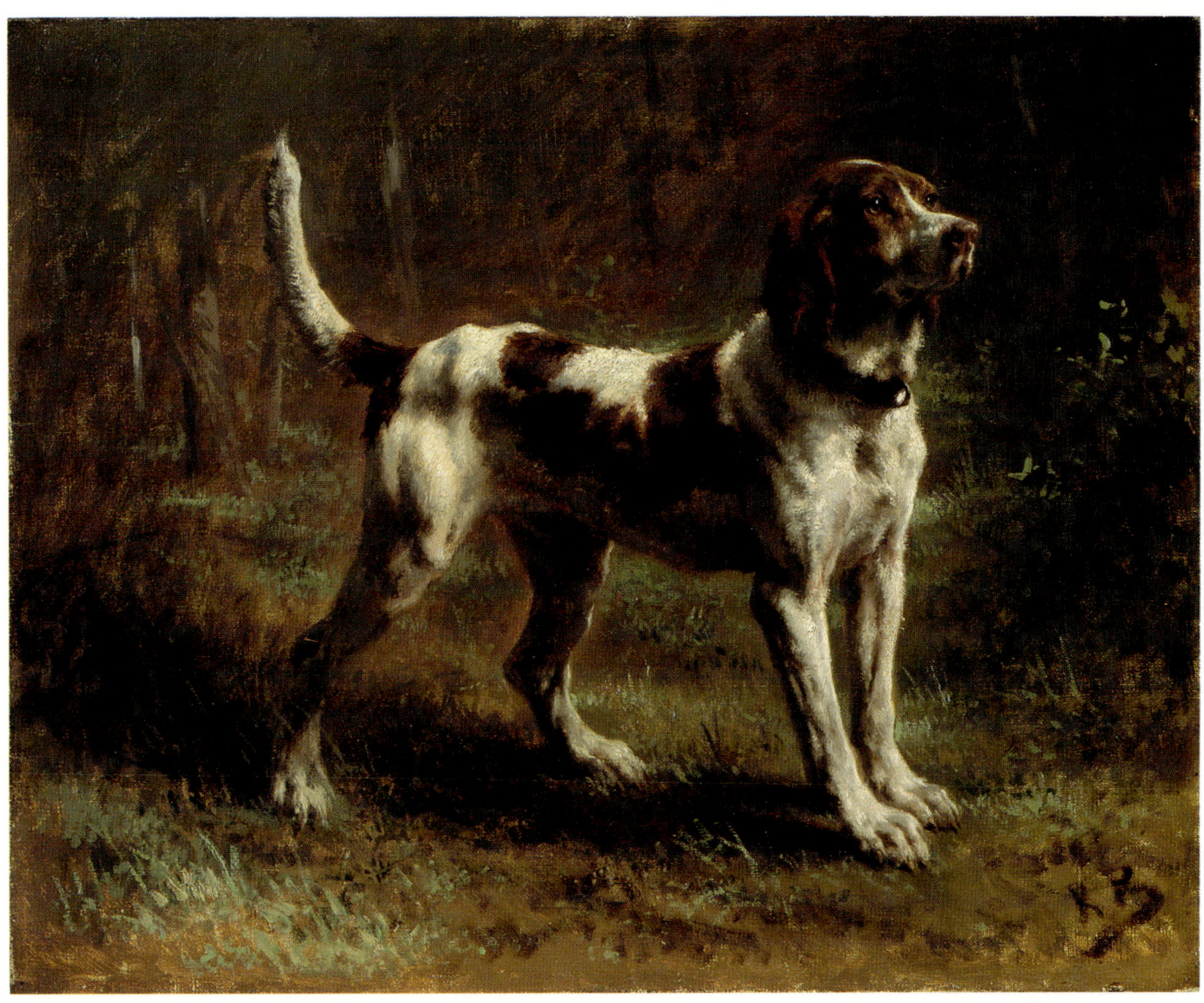

Pl. III

Rosa Bonheur, *A Limier-Briquet Hound*

The Metropolitan Museum of Art, New York

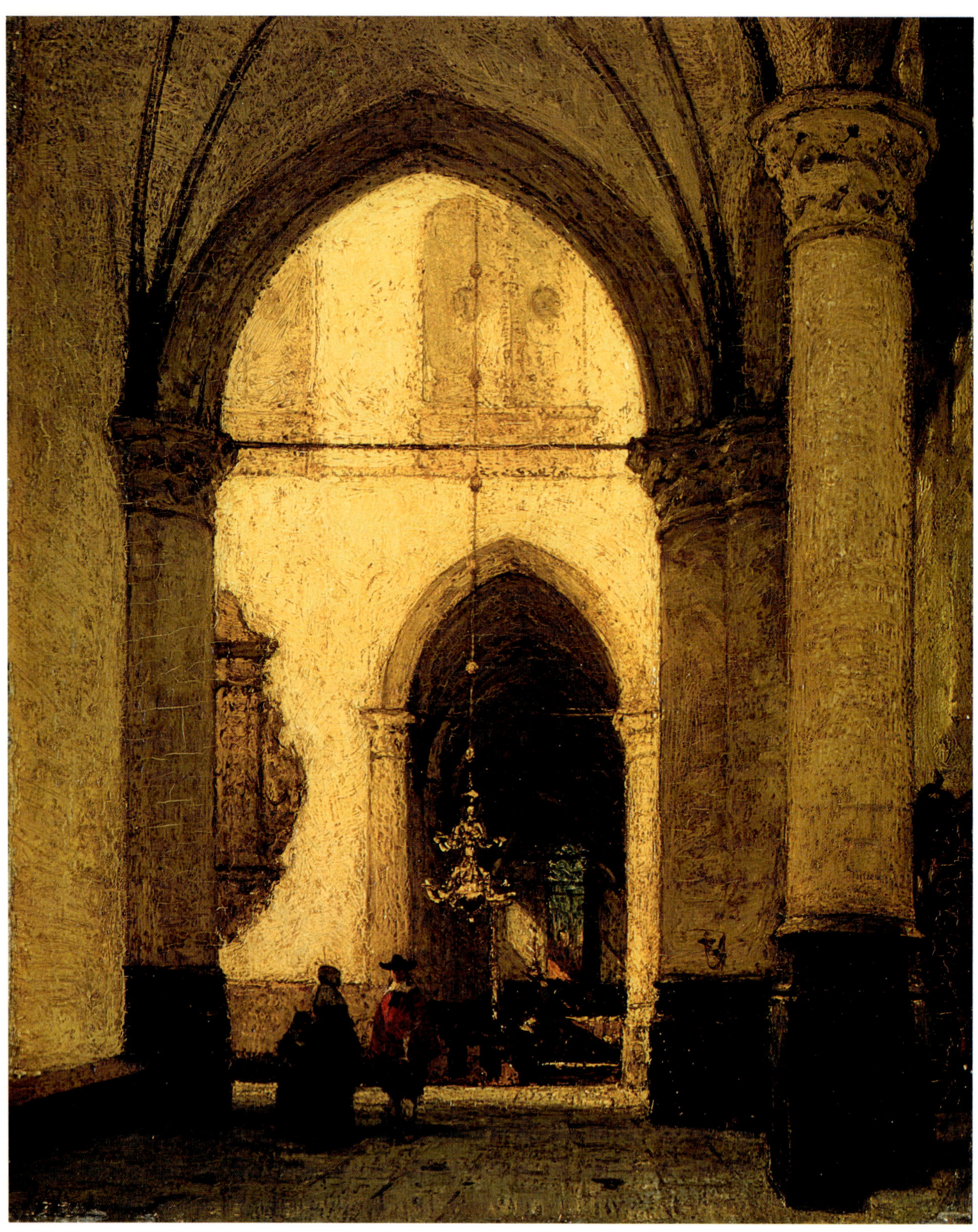

Pl. IV

JOHANNES BOSBOOM, *THE CHURCH AT ALKMAAR*

The Saint Louis Art Museum

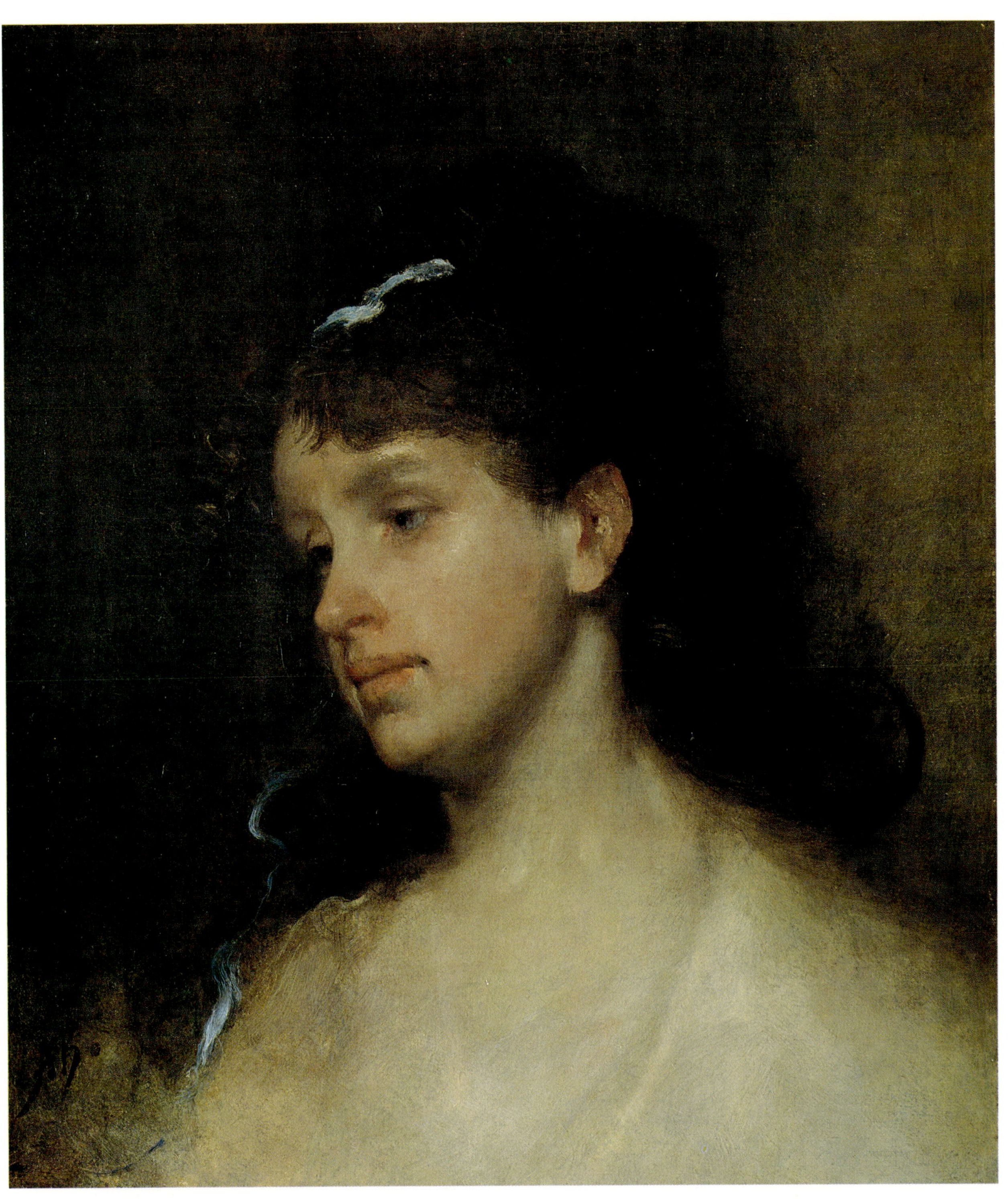

Pl. V

AUGUSTE BOULARD, *FEMALE HEAD*

Collection Robert B. Beardsley

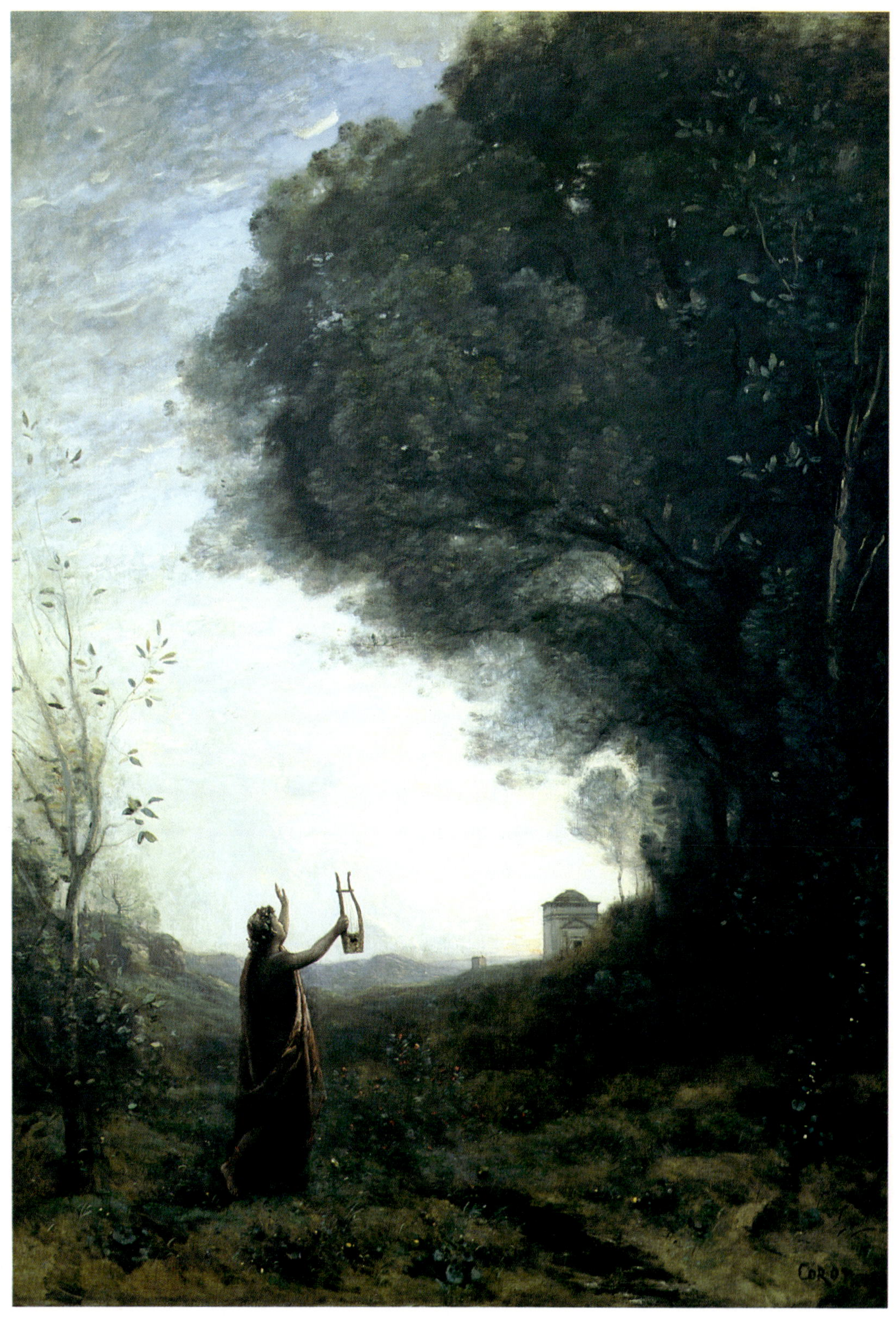

Pl. VI

JEAN-BAPTISTE-CAMILLE COROT, *ORPHEUS GREETING THE DAWN*, 1865

Elvehjem Museum of Art, Madison, Wisconsin

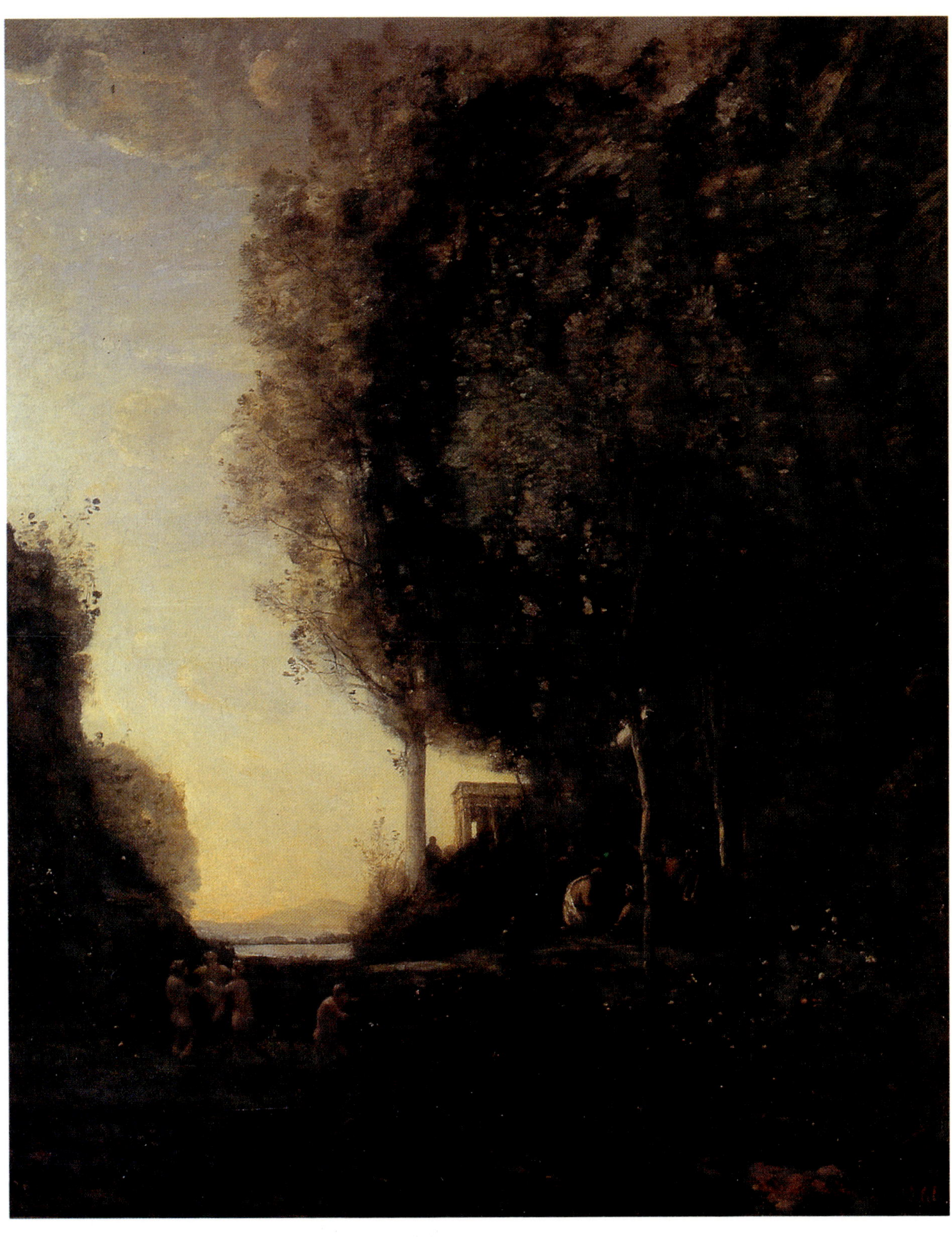

Pl. VII

JEAN-BAPTISTE-CAMILLE COROT, *LE SOIR (LA DANSE DES AMOURS)*, 1866

Museum Folkwang, Essen, West Germany

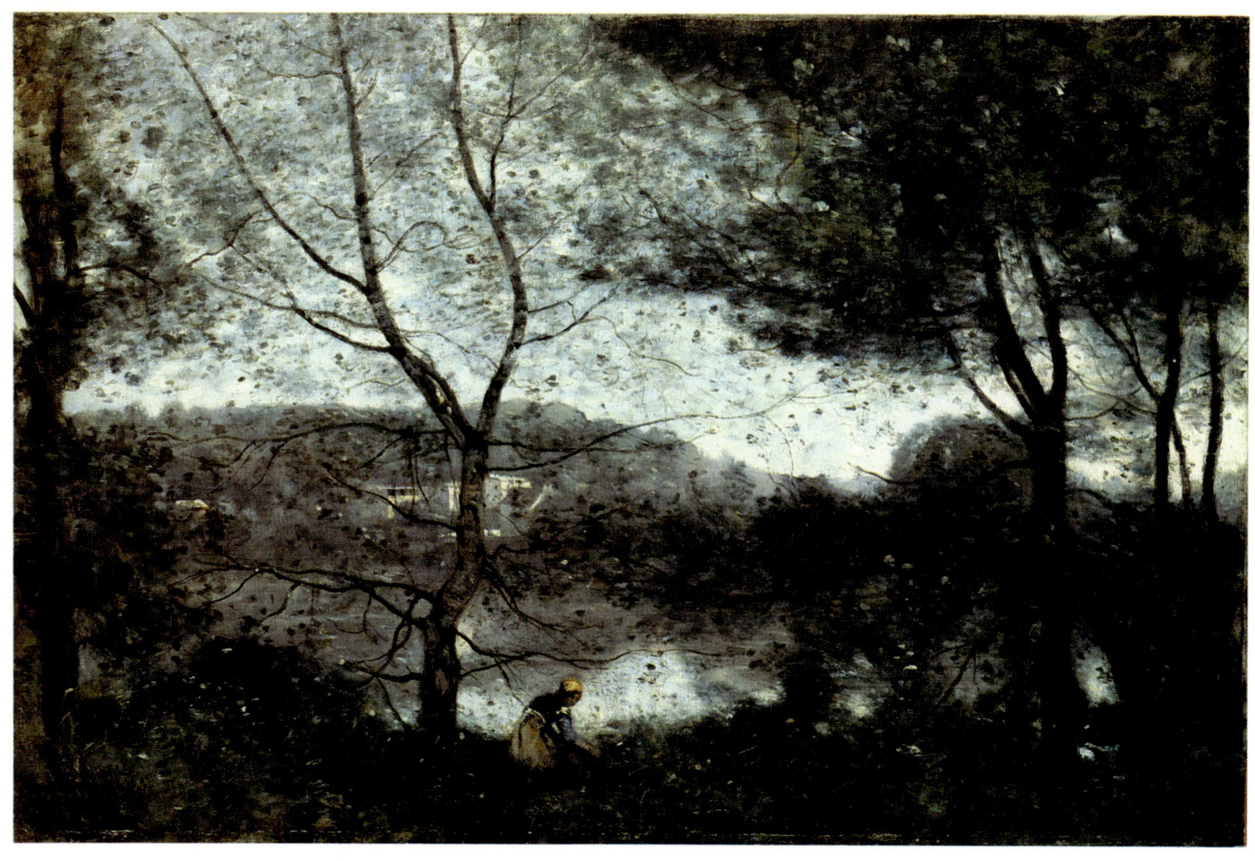

Pl. VIII

JEAN-BAPTISTE-CAMILLE COROT, *VILLE D'AVRAY*

The Metropolitan Museum of Art, New York

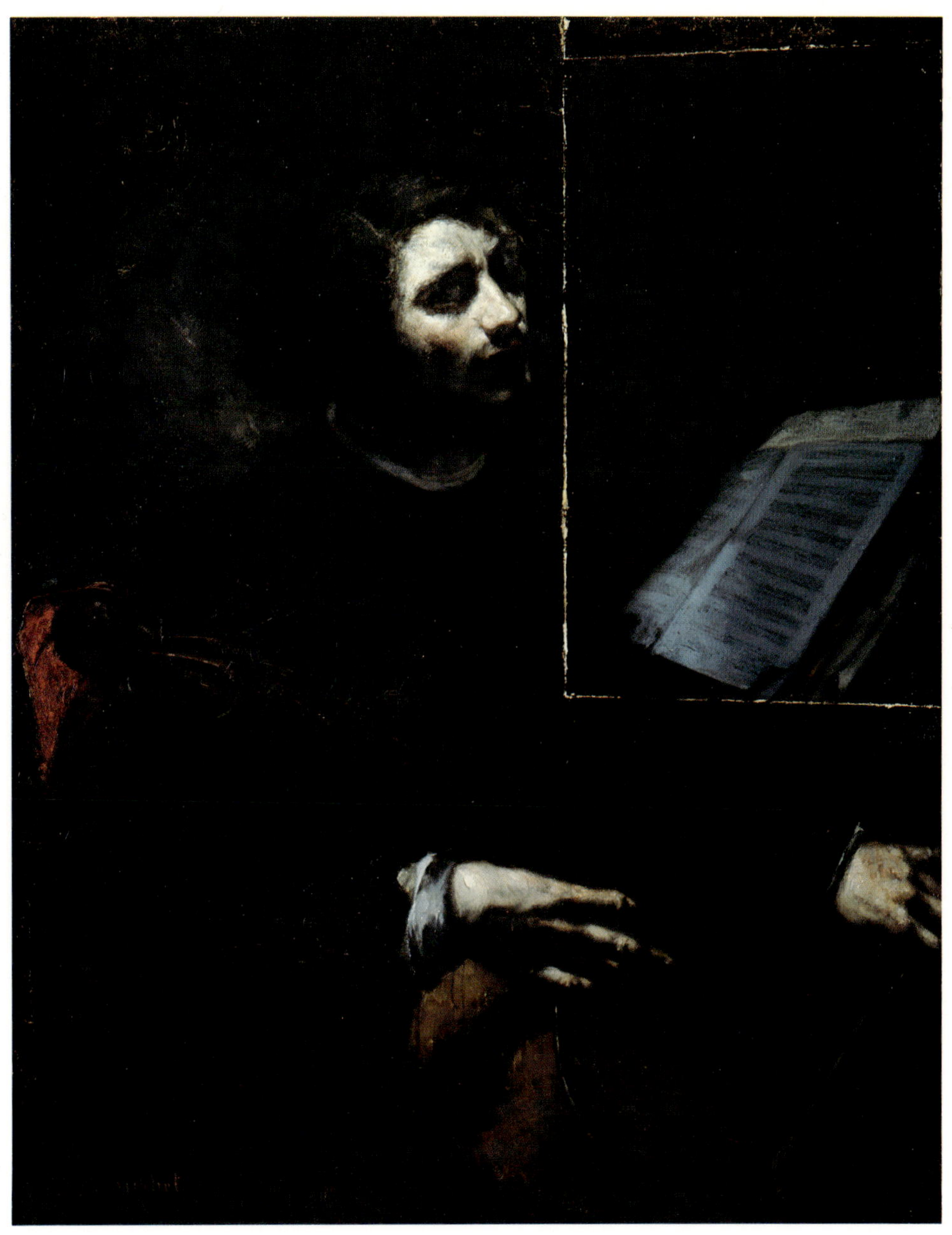

Pl. IX

Gustave Courbet, *The Violoncellist*, 1847

Portland Art Museum, Portland, Oregon

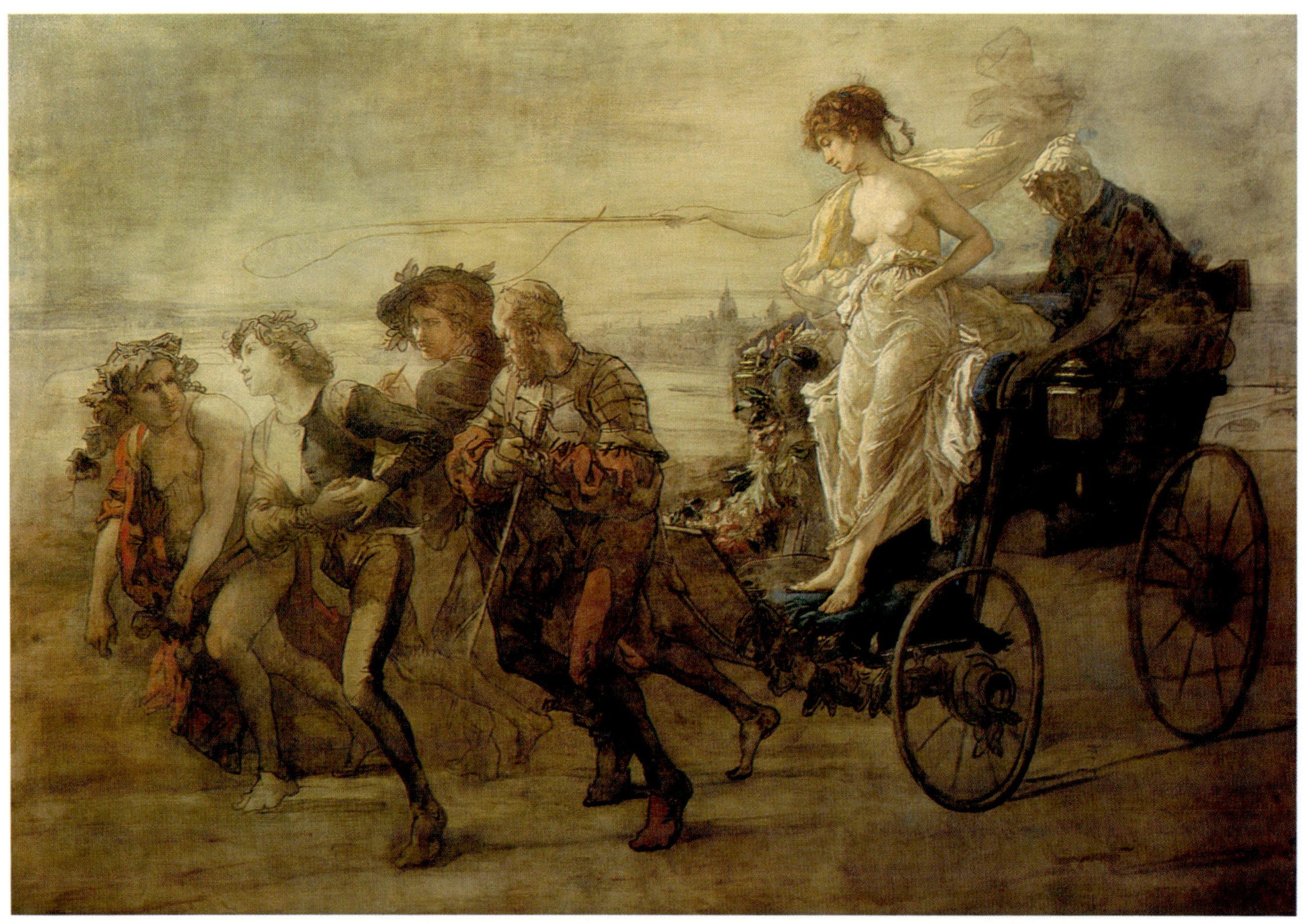

Pl. X

THOMAS COUTURE, *THE COURTESAN'S CHARIOT*, OR *LOVE LEADING THE WORLD*, c. 1874–76

Collection Stuart Pivar, New York

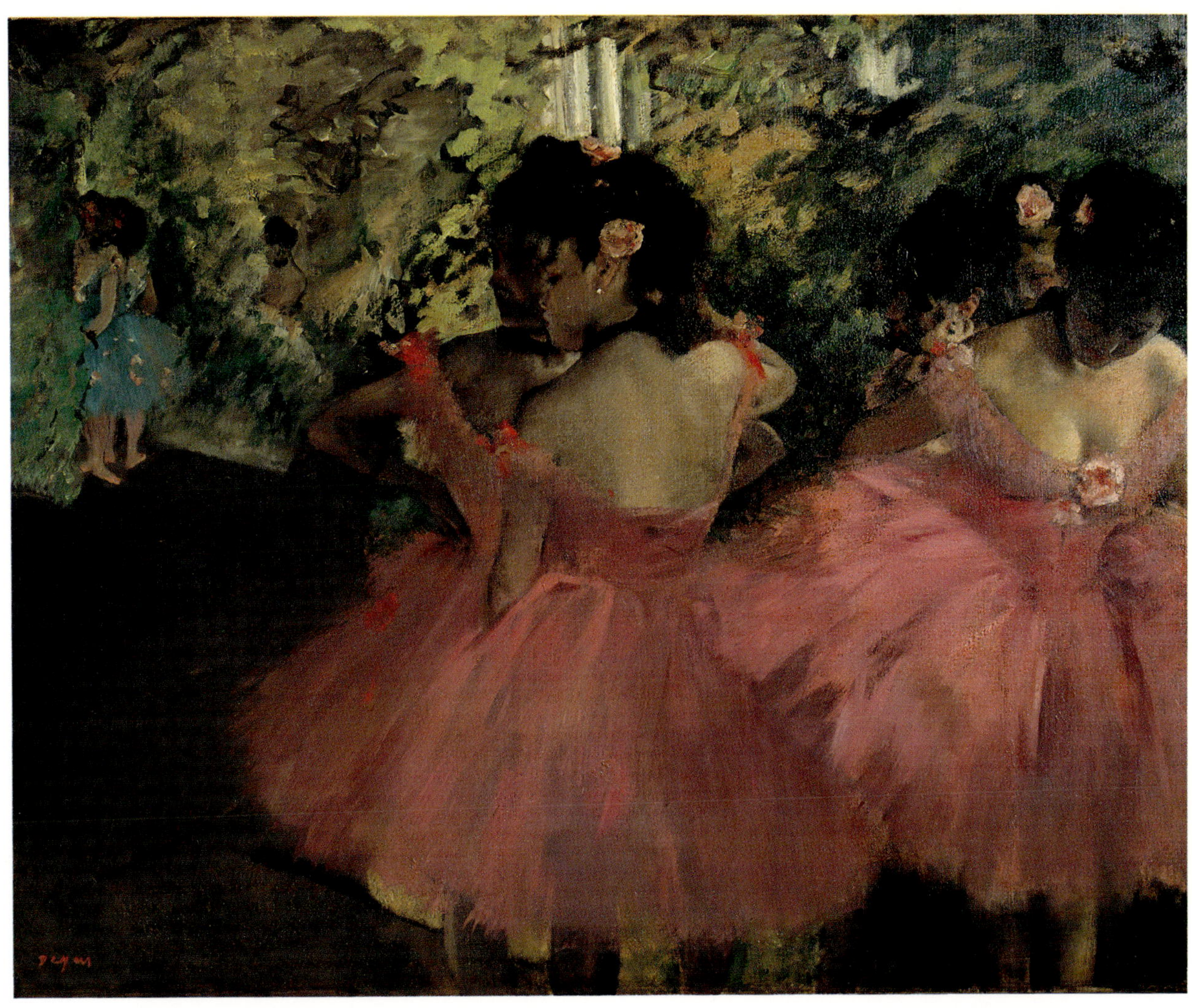

Pl. XI

Hilaire Germain Edgar Degas, *Ballet Dancers*

The Hill-Stead Museum, Farmington, Connecticut

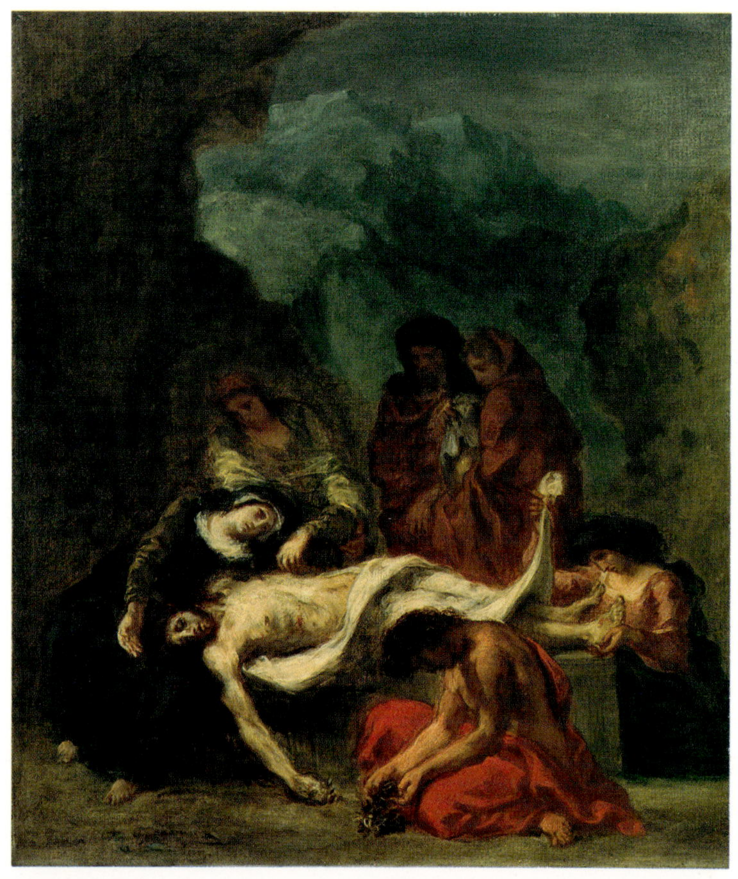

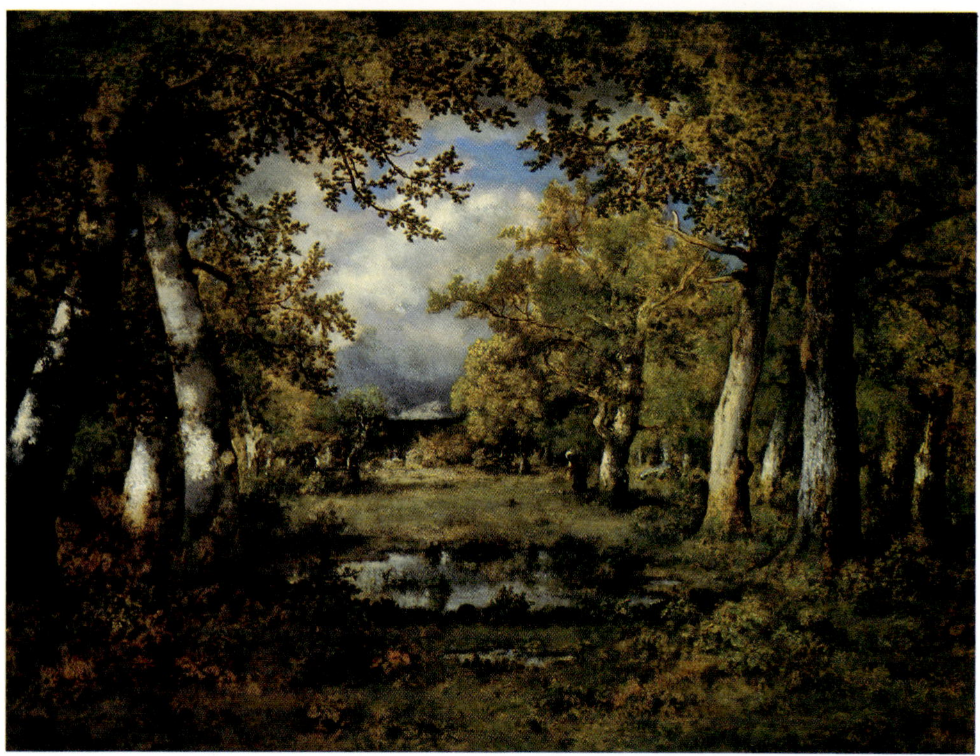

Pl. XII

Eugène Delacroix, *Le Christ au tombeau*, c. 1847–49

Phoenix Art Museum, Phoenix, Arizona

Pl. XIII

Narcisse Virgile Diaz de la Peña, *La Mare aux Grenouilles*

The Corcoran Gallery of Art, Washington, D.C.

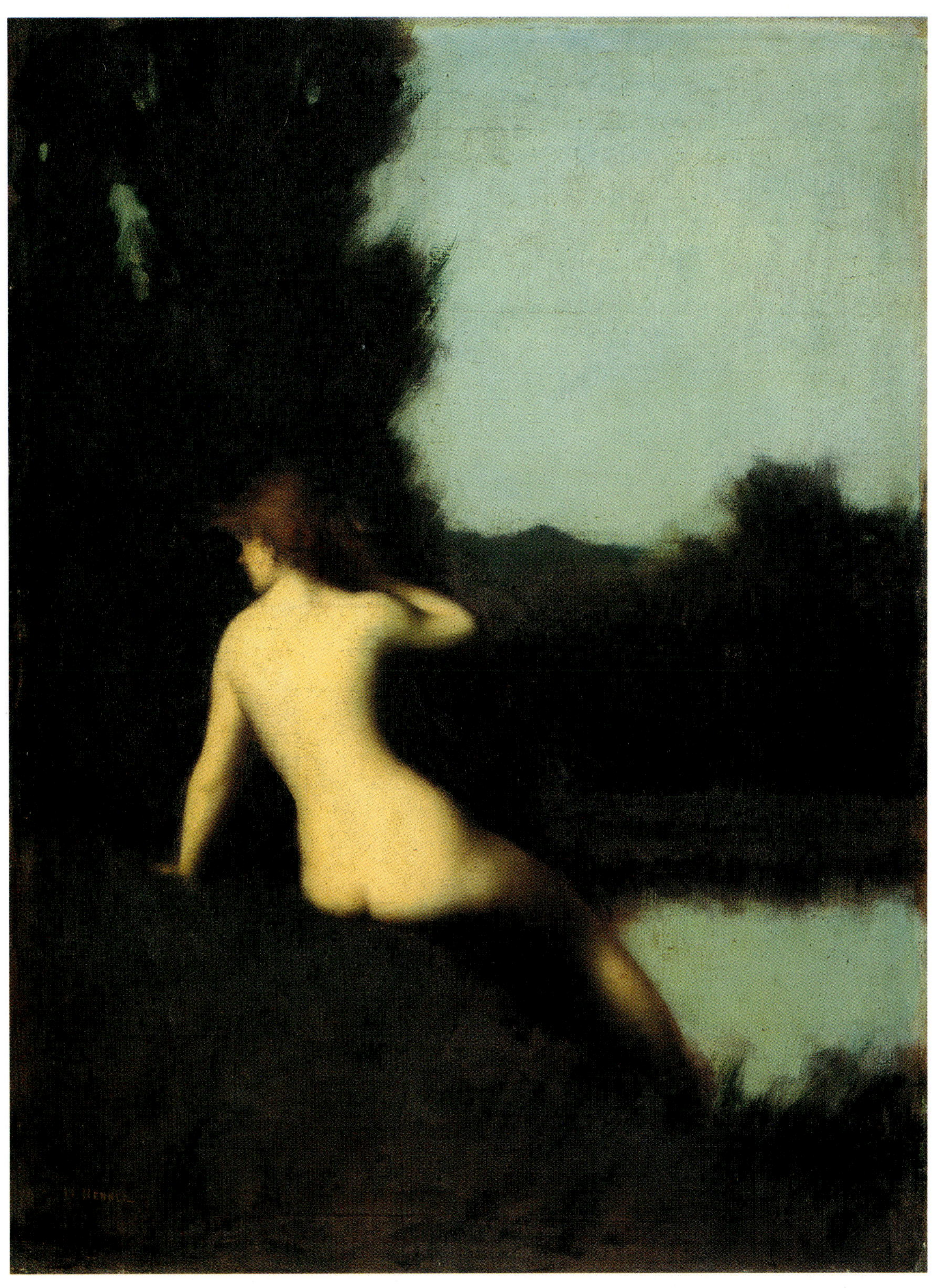

Pl. XIV

JEAN-JACQUES HENNER, *A BATHER*

The Metropolitan Museum of Art, New York

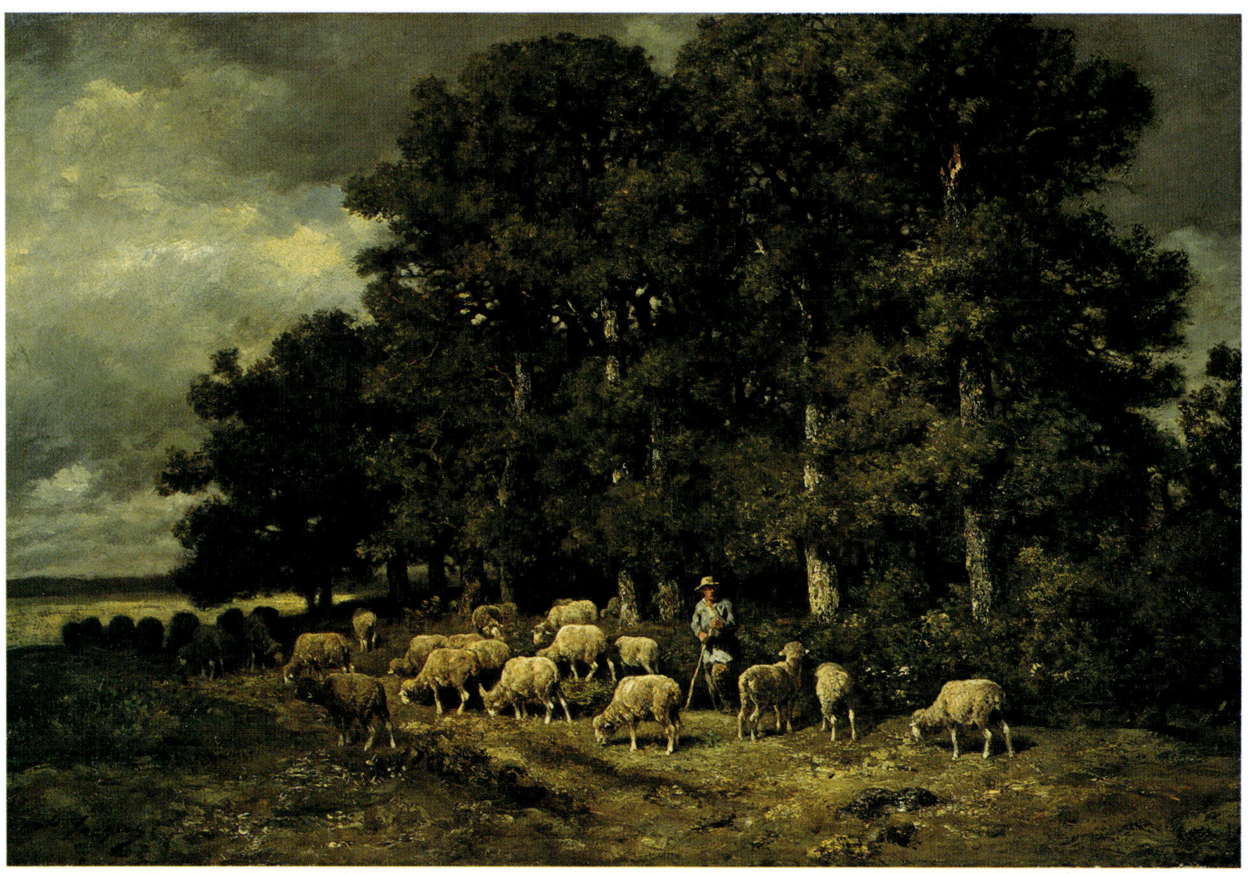

Pl. XV

CHARLES-EMILE JACQUE, *Sheep at the Entrance to a Forest*

Allen Memorial Art Museum, Oberlin College, Oberlin, Ohio

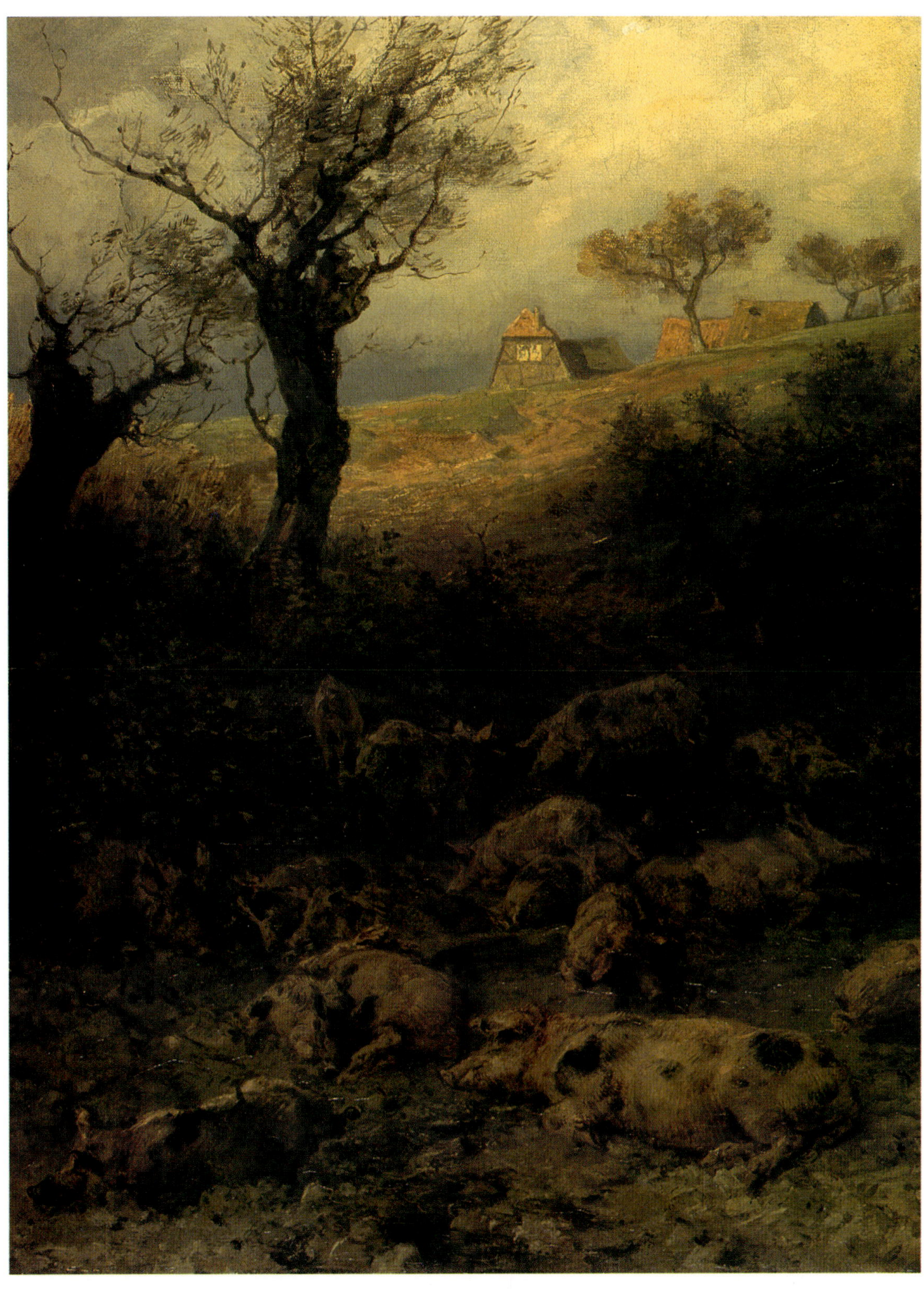

Pl. XVI

Ludwig Knaus, *Pigs and Swineherd*, 1878

Charles and Emma Frye Art Museum, Seattle, Washington

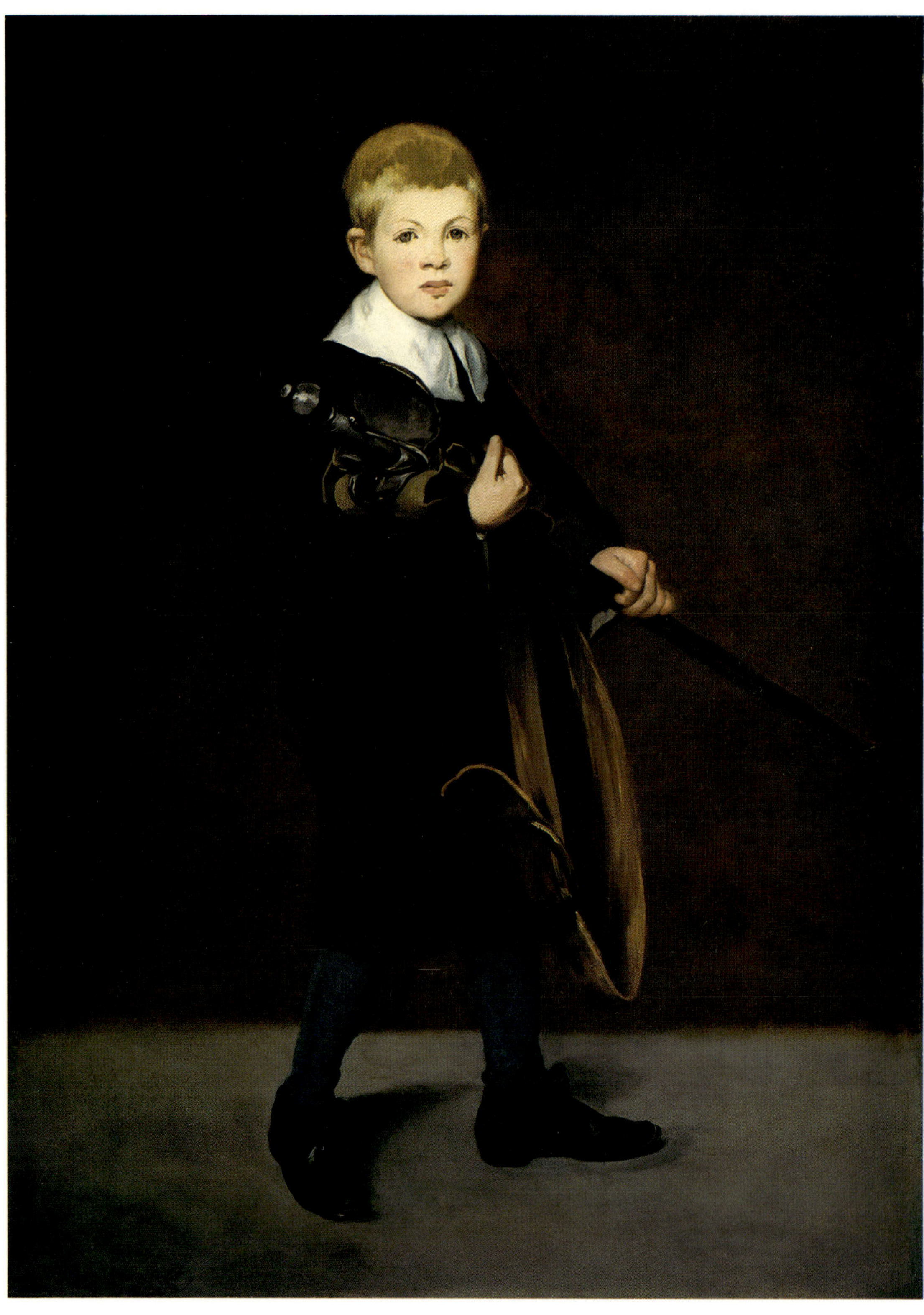

Pl. XVII

Edouard Manet, *Boy with a Sword*, 1861

The Metropolitan Museum of Art, New York

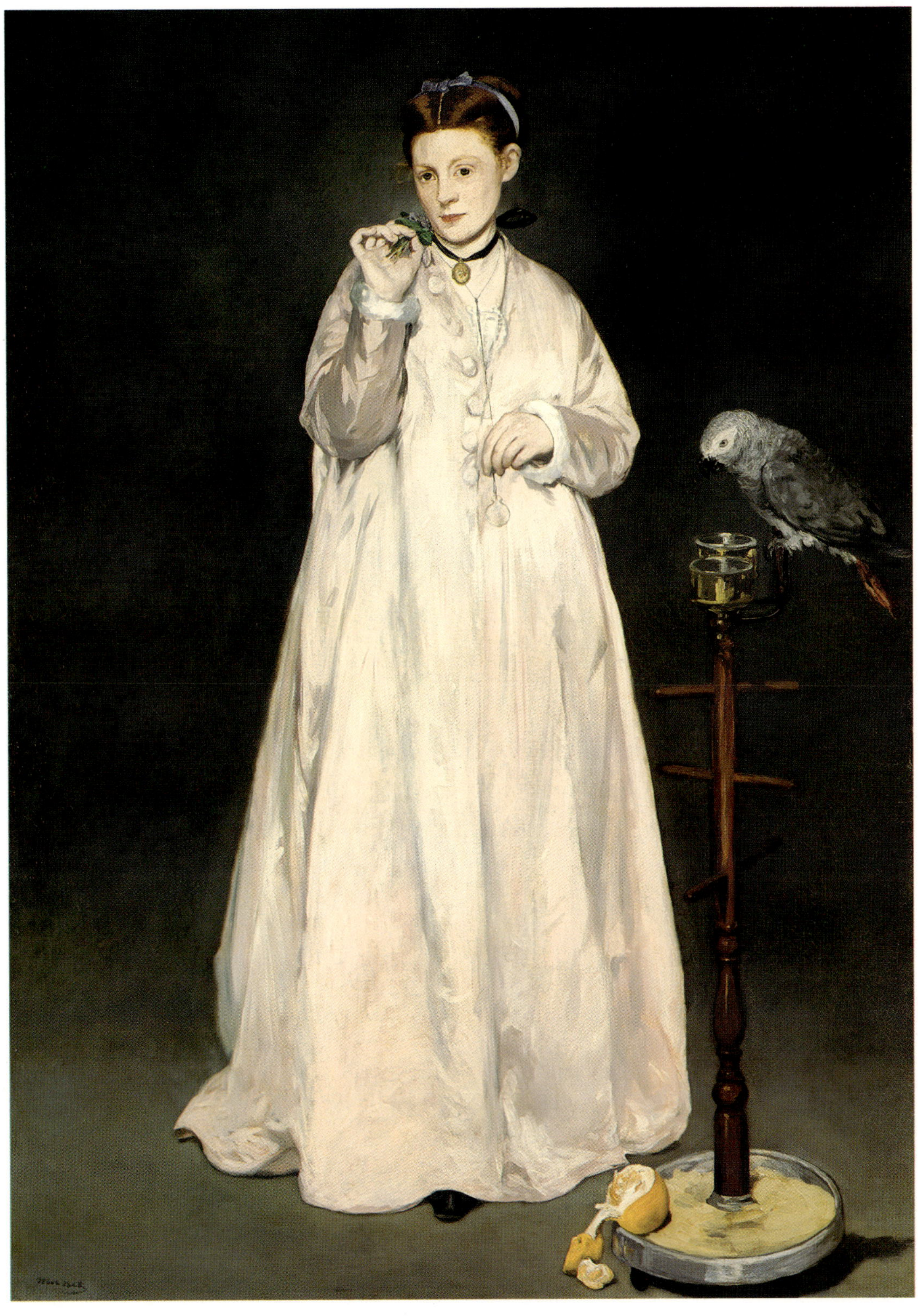

Pl. XVIII

EDOUARD MANET, *WOMAN WITH A PARROT*

The Metropolitan Museum of Art, New York

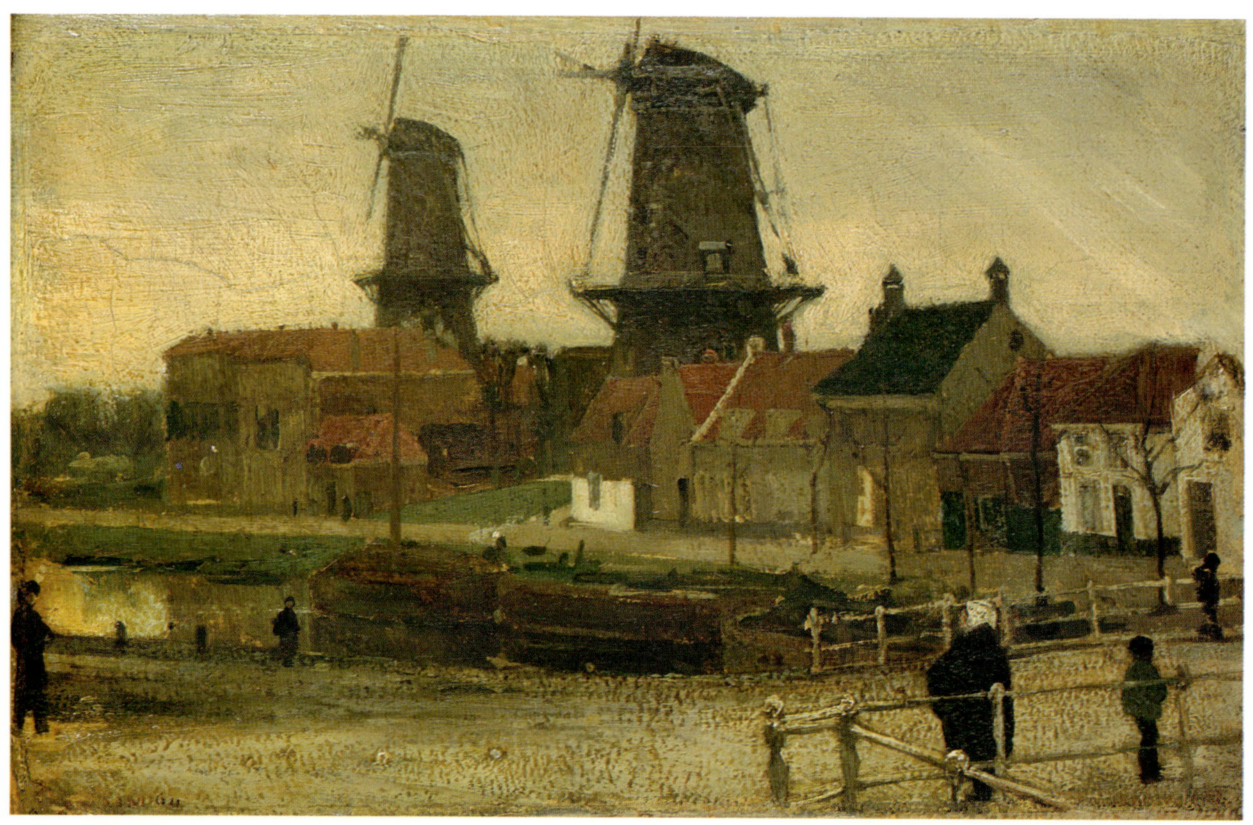

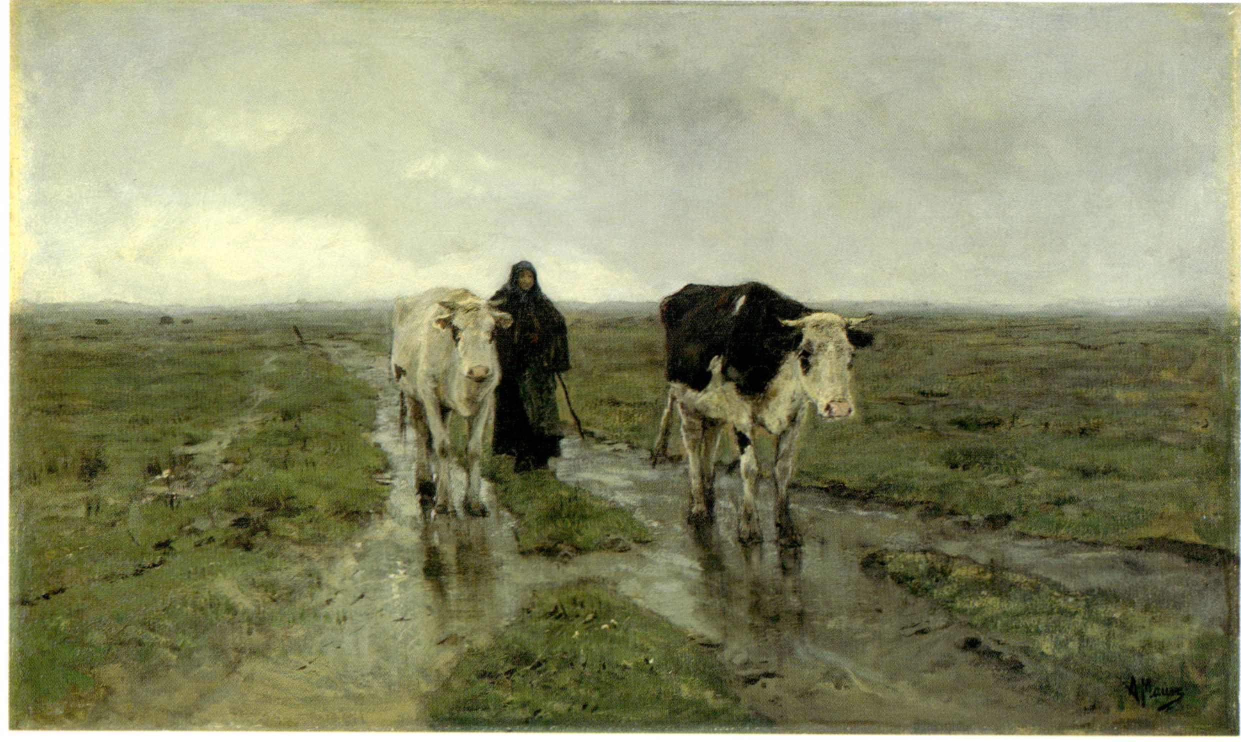

Pl. XIX

Matthew Maris, *A Corner of The Hague*, 1860

The Phillips Collection, Washington, D.C.

Pl. XX

Anton Mauve, *Changing Pasture*

The Metropolitan Museum of Art, New York

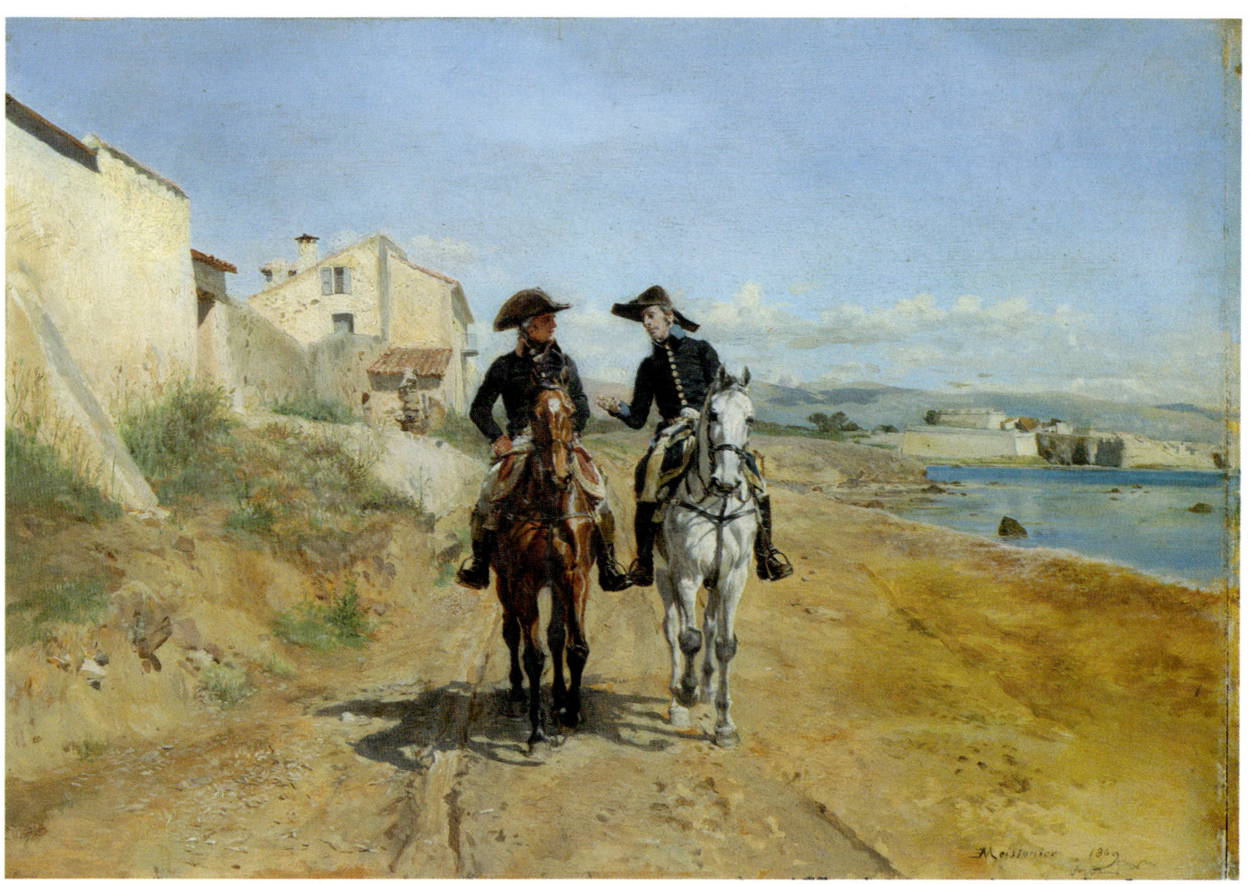

Pl. XXI

Jean-Louis-Ernest Meissonier, *A General and His Aide-de-Camp*

The Metropolitan Museum of Art, New York

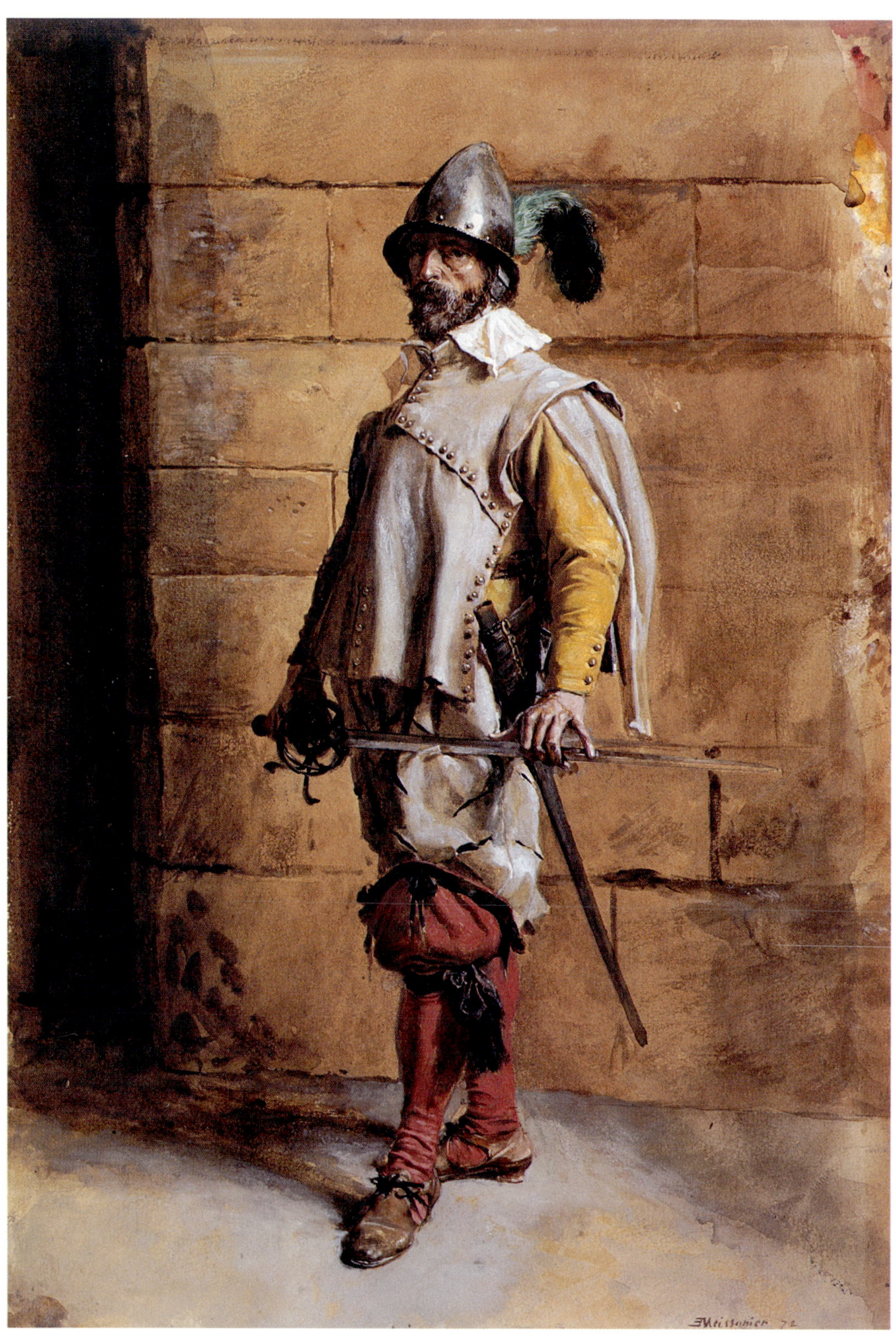

Pl. XXII

Jean-Louis-Ernest Meissonier, *The Cavalier: Portrait of the Artist*, 1872

The New-York Historical Society, New York

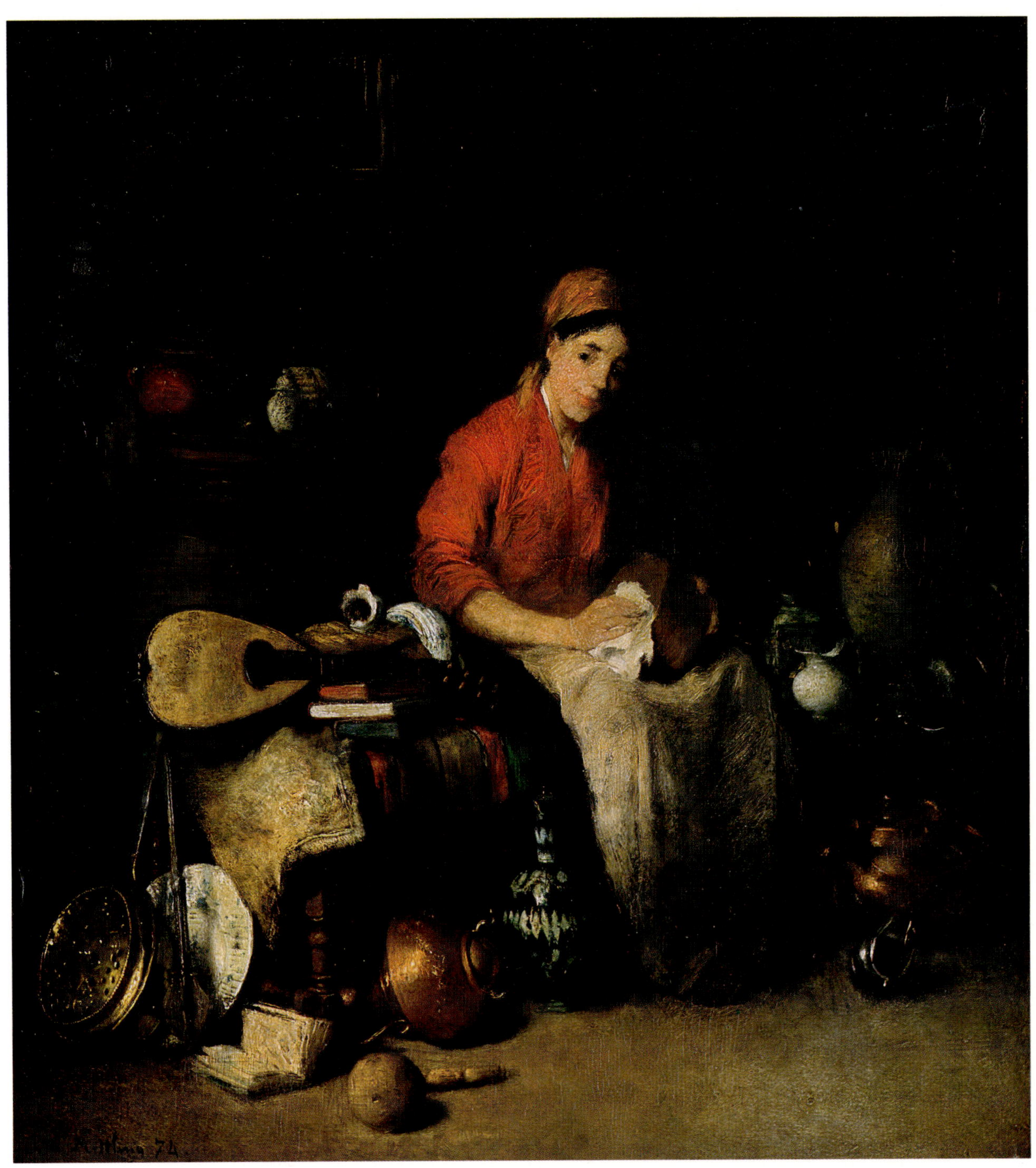

Pl. XXIII

Louis Mettling, *The Studio*, 1874
National Gallery of Canada, Ottawa
Musée des beaux-arts du Canada

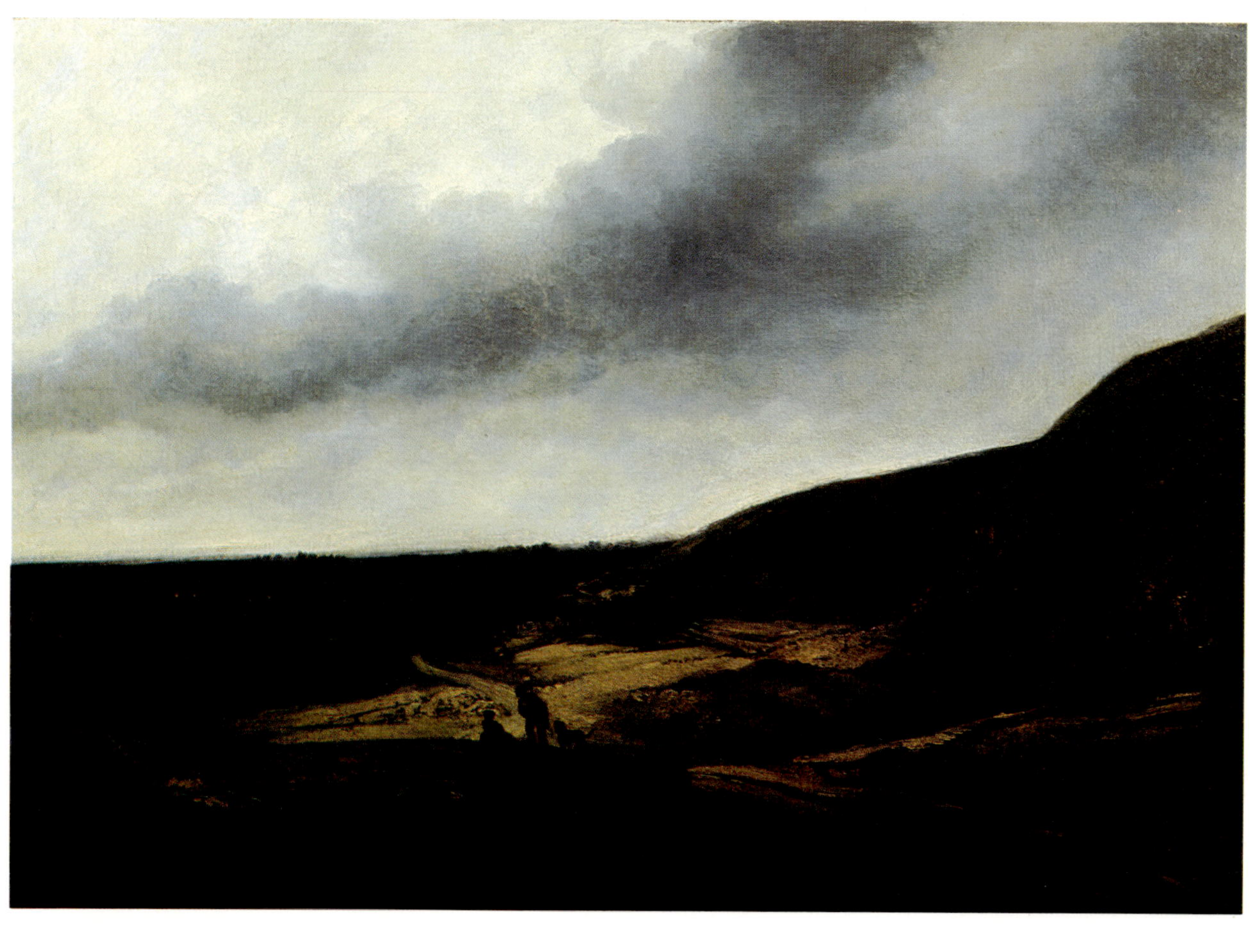

Pl. XXIV

GEORGES MICHEL, *CLOUDS AND LANDSCAPE*, c. 1826

The Heckscher Museum, Huntington, New York

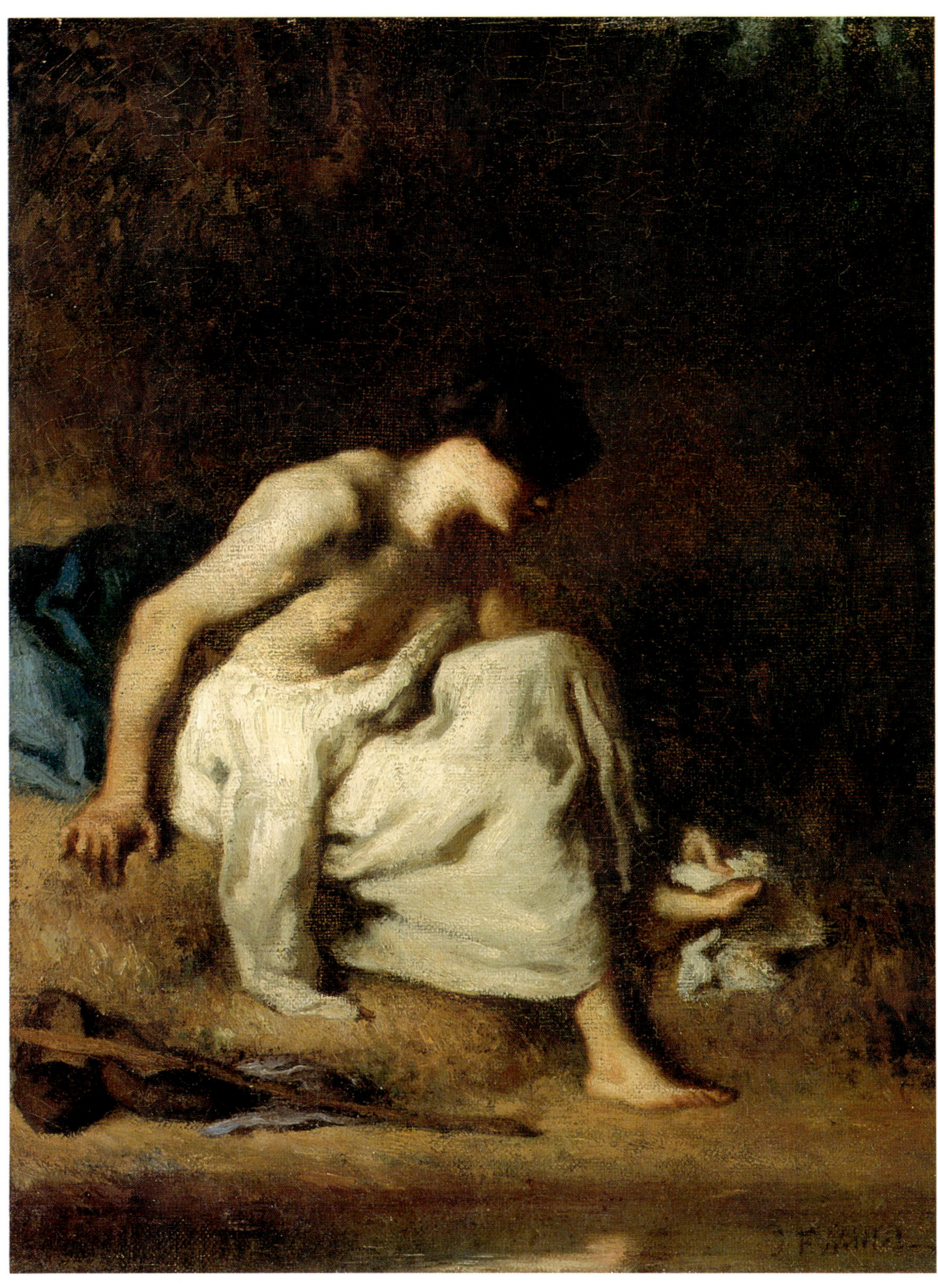

Pl. XXV

JEAN-FRANÇOIS MILLET, *THE BATHER*, c. 1846

Yale University Art Gallery, New Haven, Connecticut

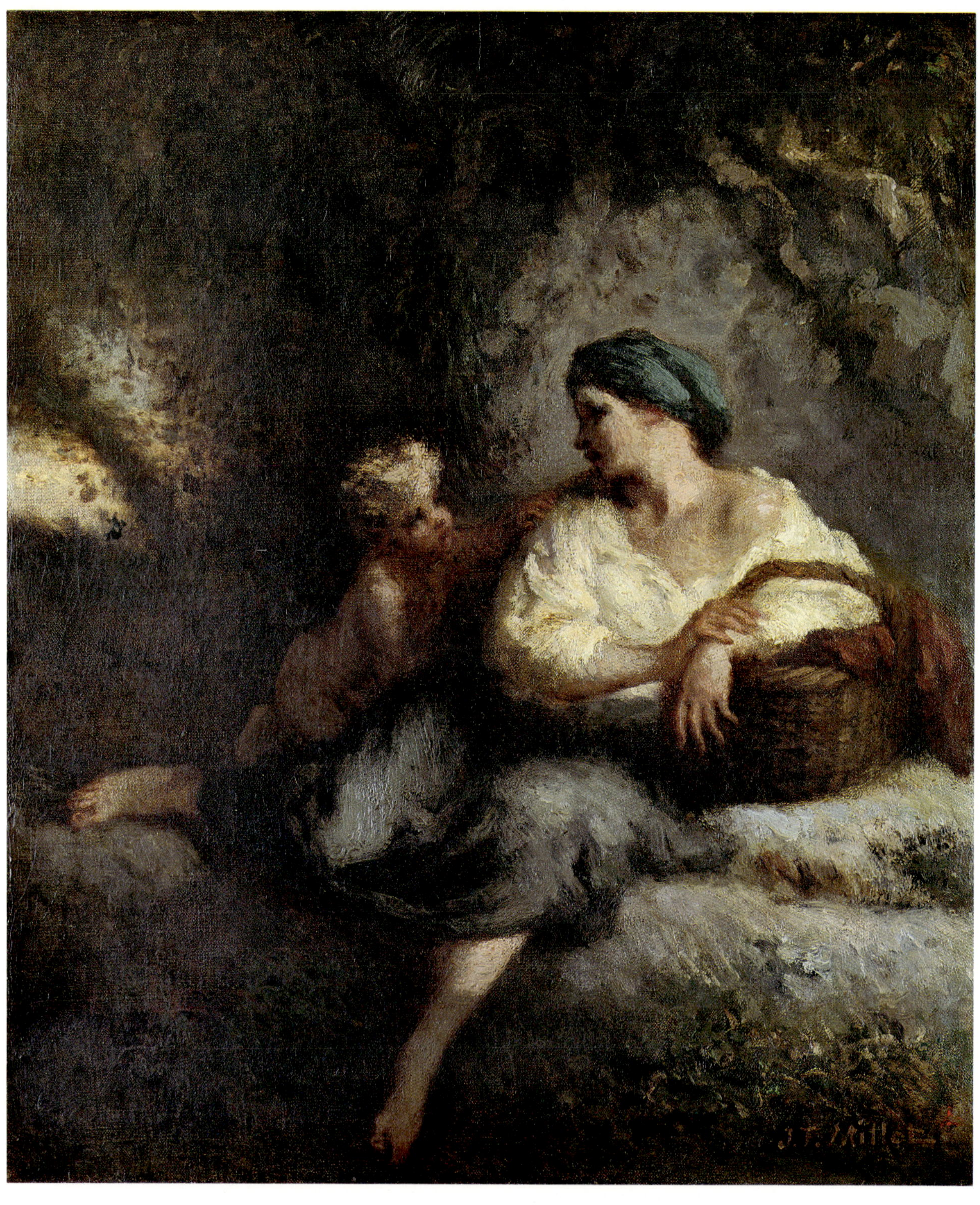

Pl. XXVI

JEAN-FRANÇOIS MILLET, *The Whisper*

National Gallery, London

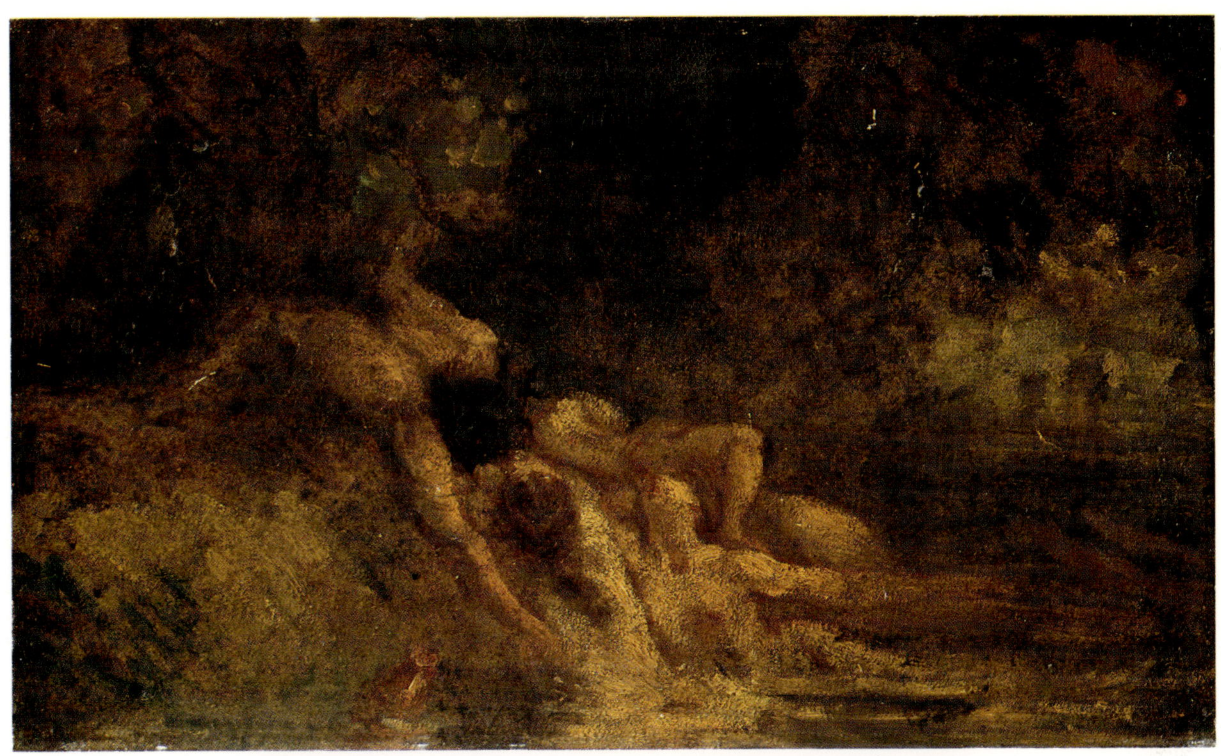

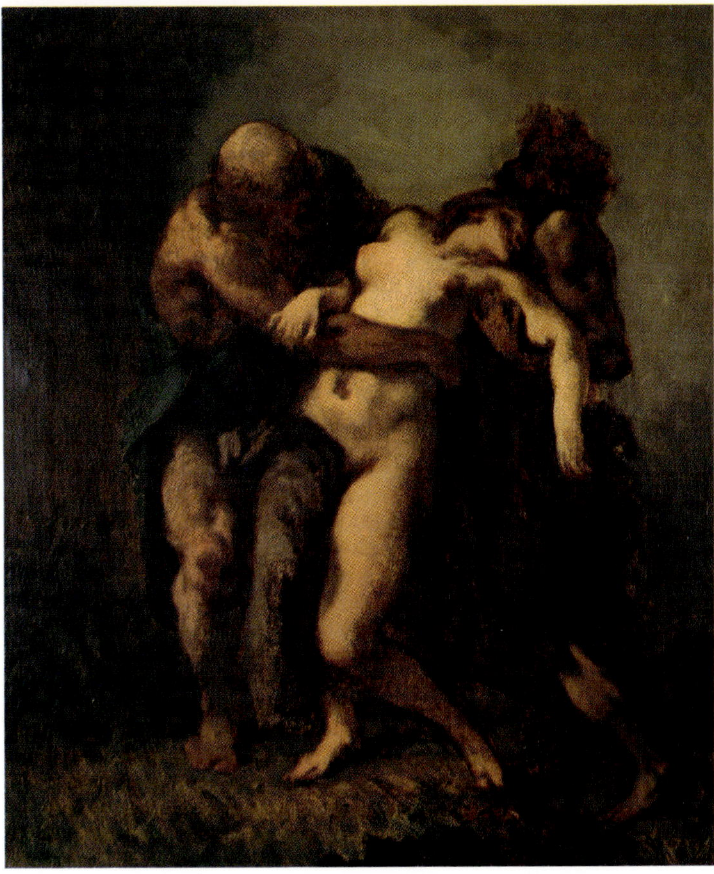

Pl. XXVII

JEAN-FRANÇOIS MILLET, *HYLAS AND THE NYMPHS*

Rijksmuseum Kröller-Müller, Otterlo, the Netherlands

Pl. XXVIII

JEAN-FRANÇOIS MILLET, *SUSANNA AND THE ELDERS*

National Gallery of Victoria, Melbourne, Australia

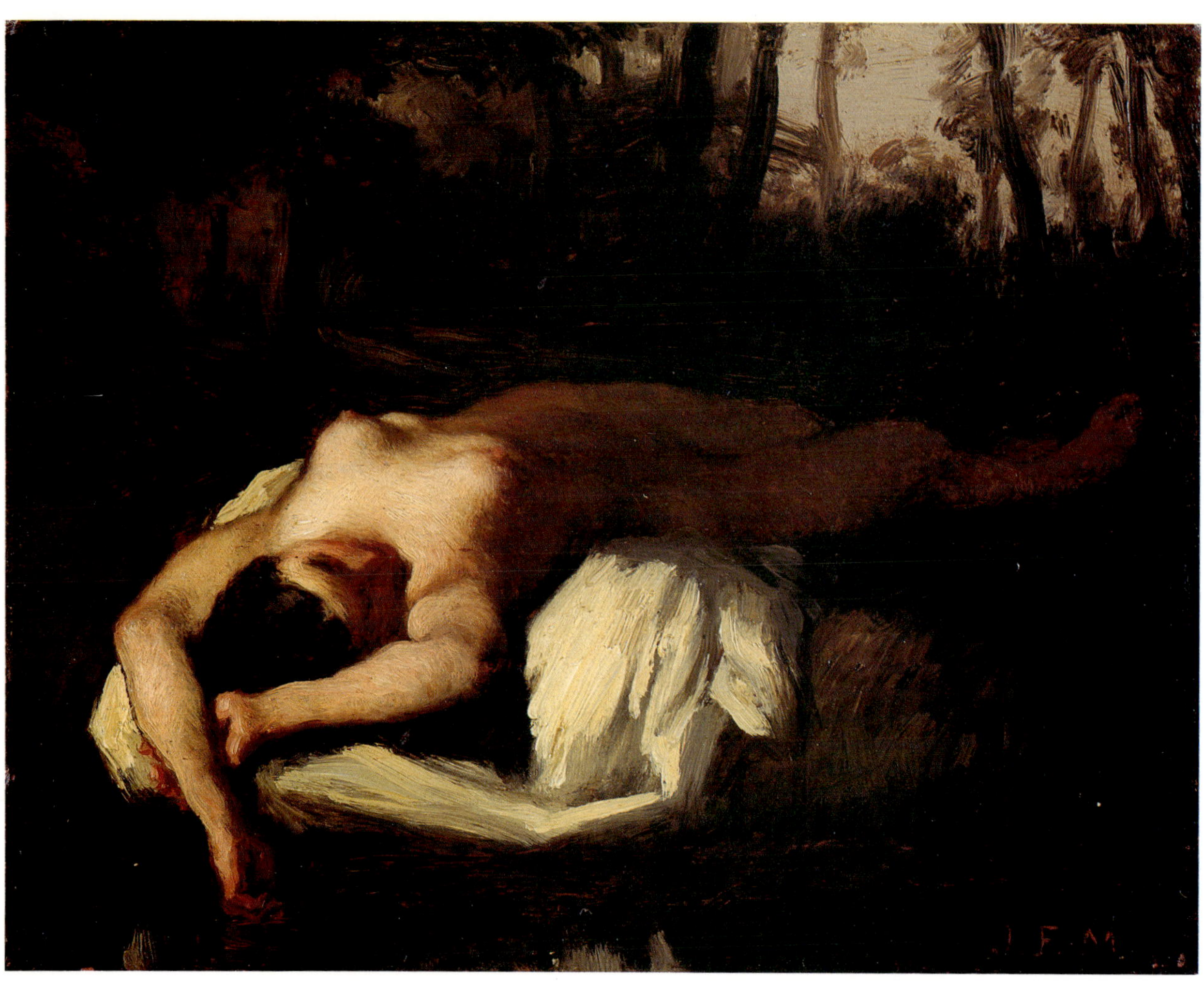

Pl. XXIX

Jean-François Millet, *Après le bain*, c. 1846–48

Private Collection, Switzerland

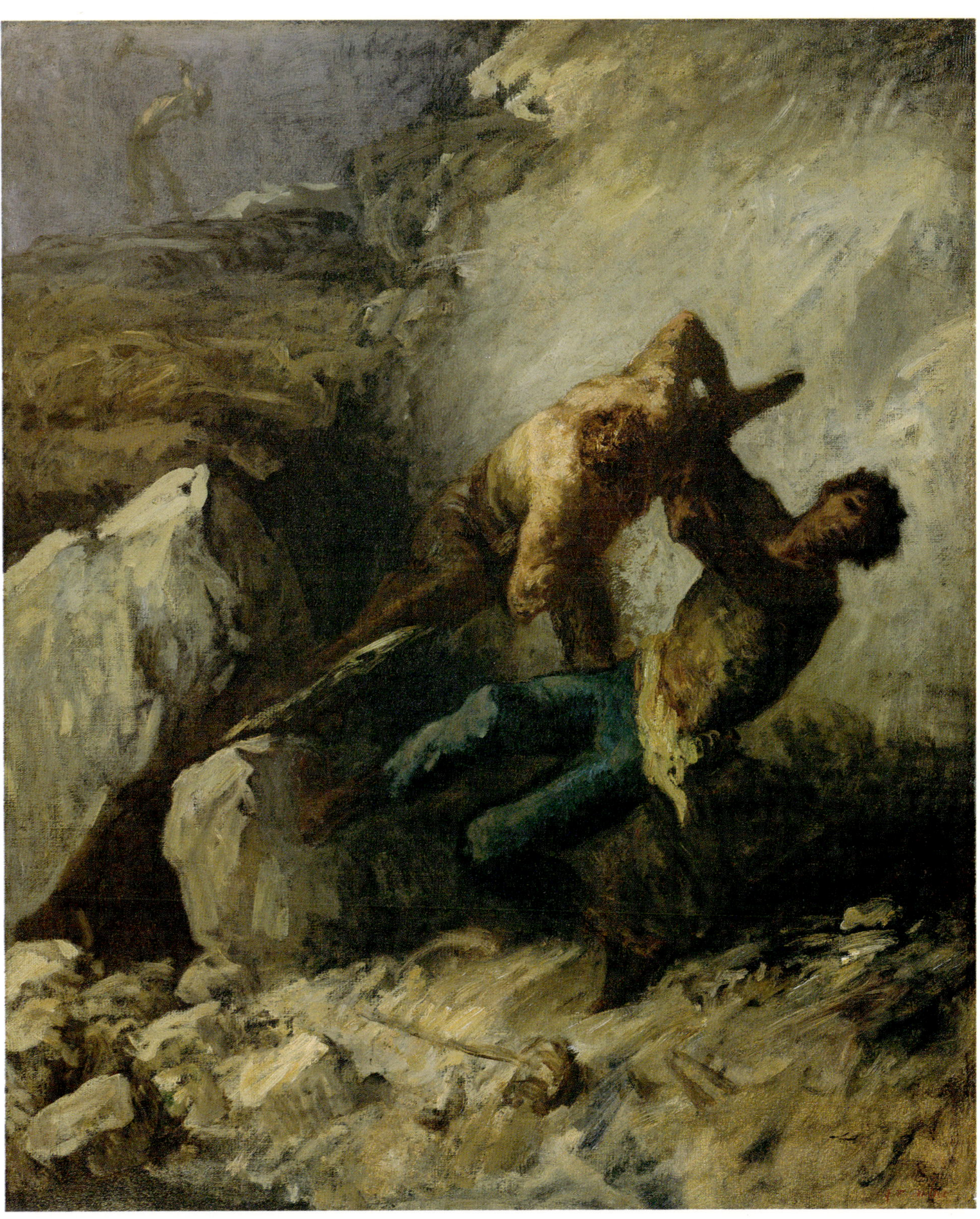

Pl. XXX

JEAN-FRANÇOIS MILLET, *THE QUARRIERS*, c. 1846–47

The Toledo Museum of Art, Toledo, Ohio

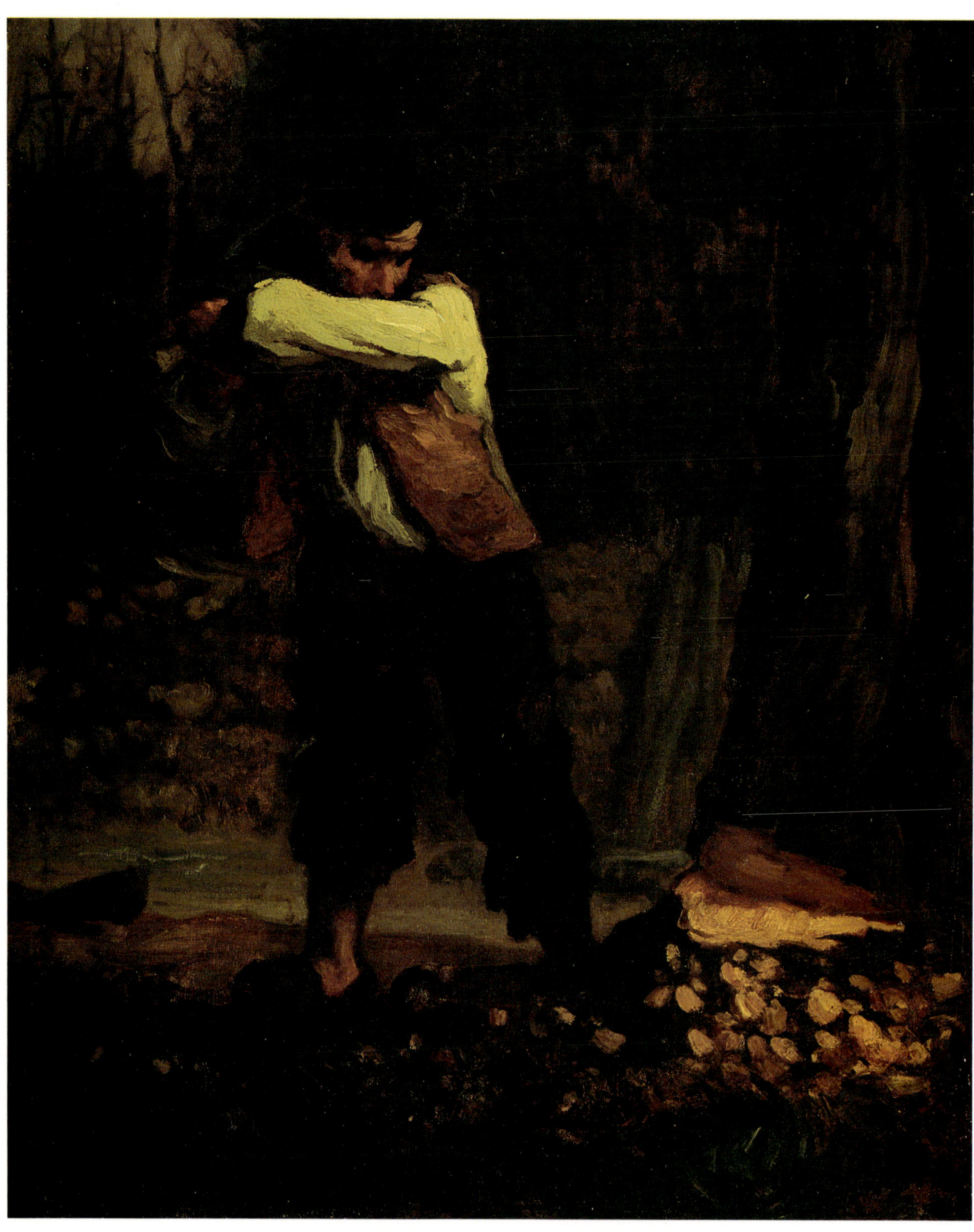

Pl. XXXI

JEAN-FRANÇOIS MILLET, *THE WOODCHOPPER*, c. 1850

Ball State University Art Gallery, Muncie, Indiana

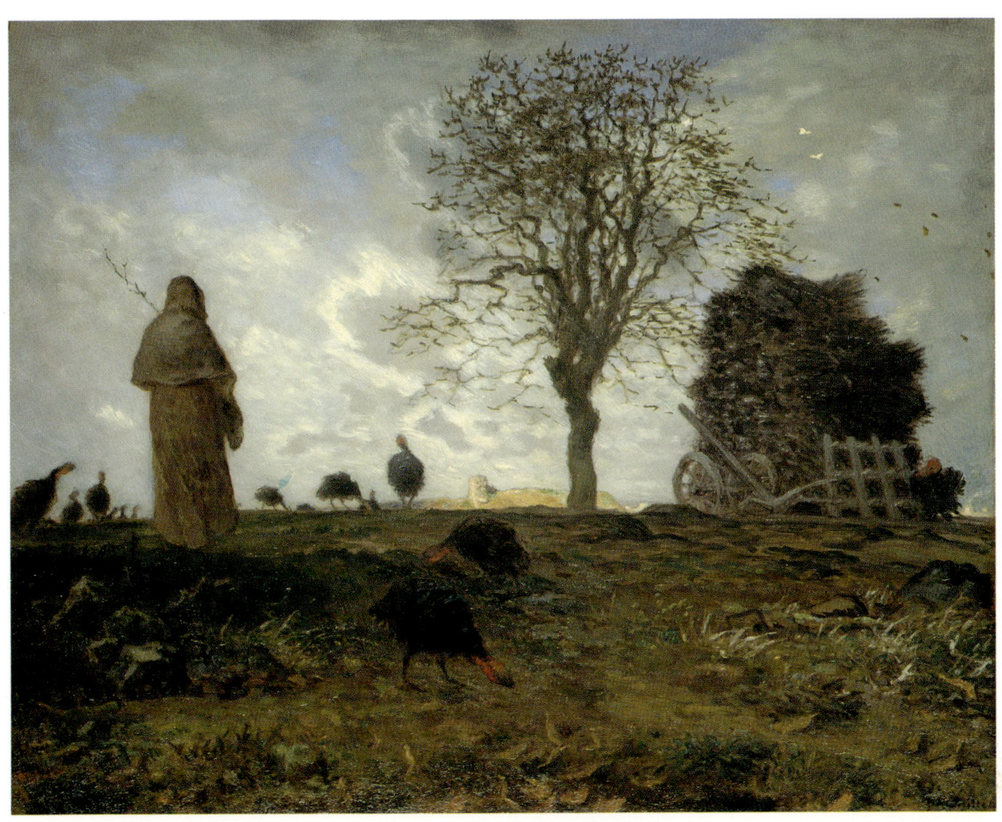

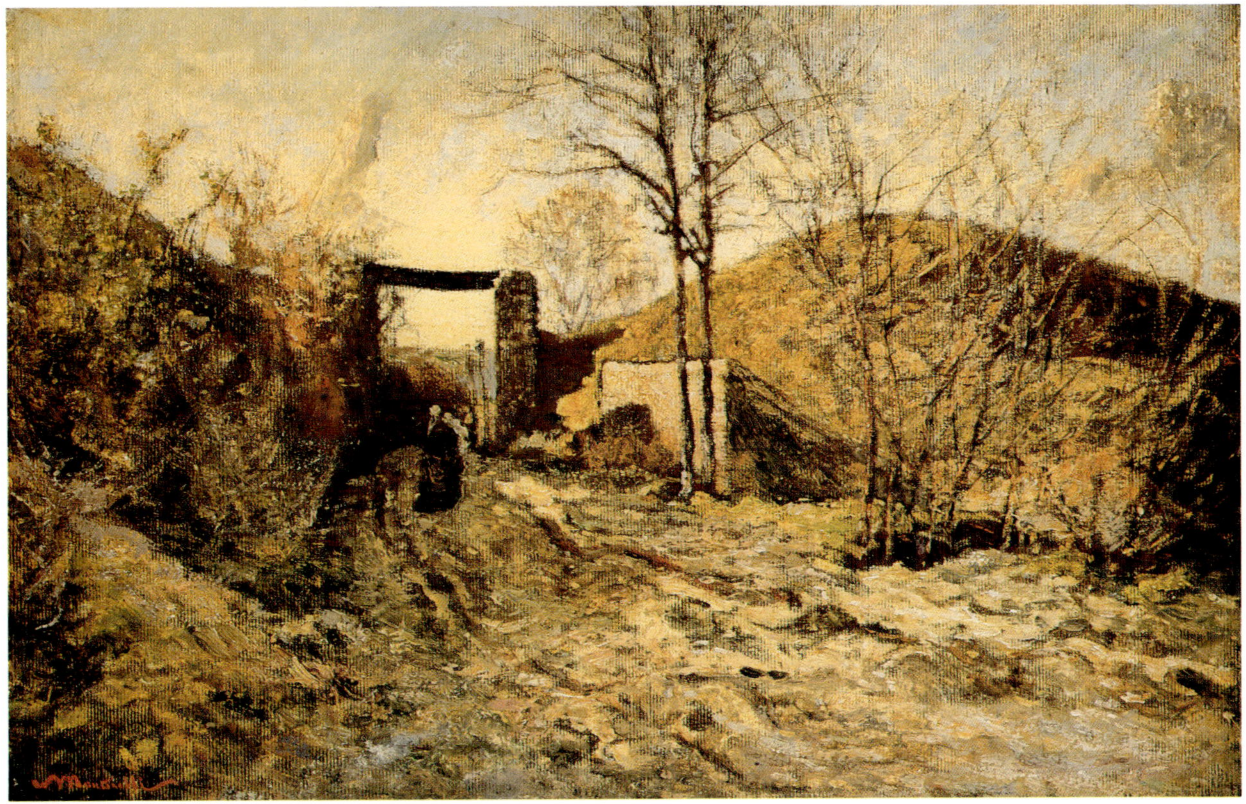

Pl. XXXII

Jean-François Millet, *Autumn Landscape with a Flock of Turkeys*, c. 1870–74

The Metropolitan Museum of Art, New York

Pl. XXXIII

Adolphe Joseph Thomas Monticelli, *Gateway to a Fort*, c. 1867

Montreal Museum of Fine Arts

Musée des beaux-arts de Montréal

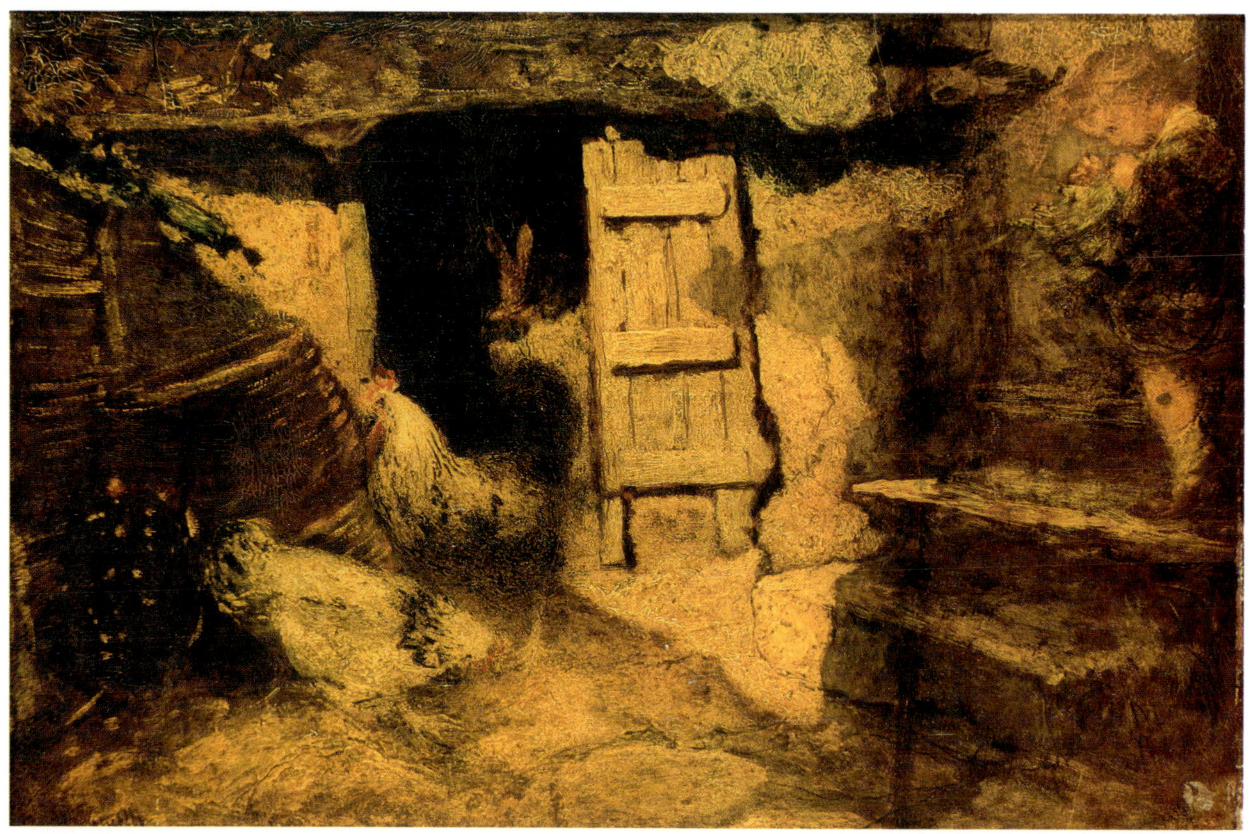

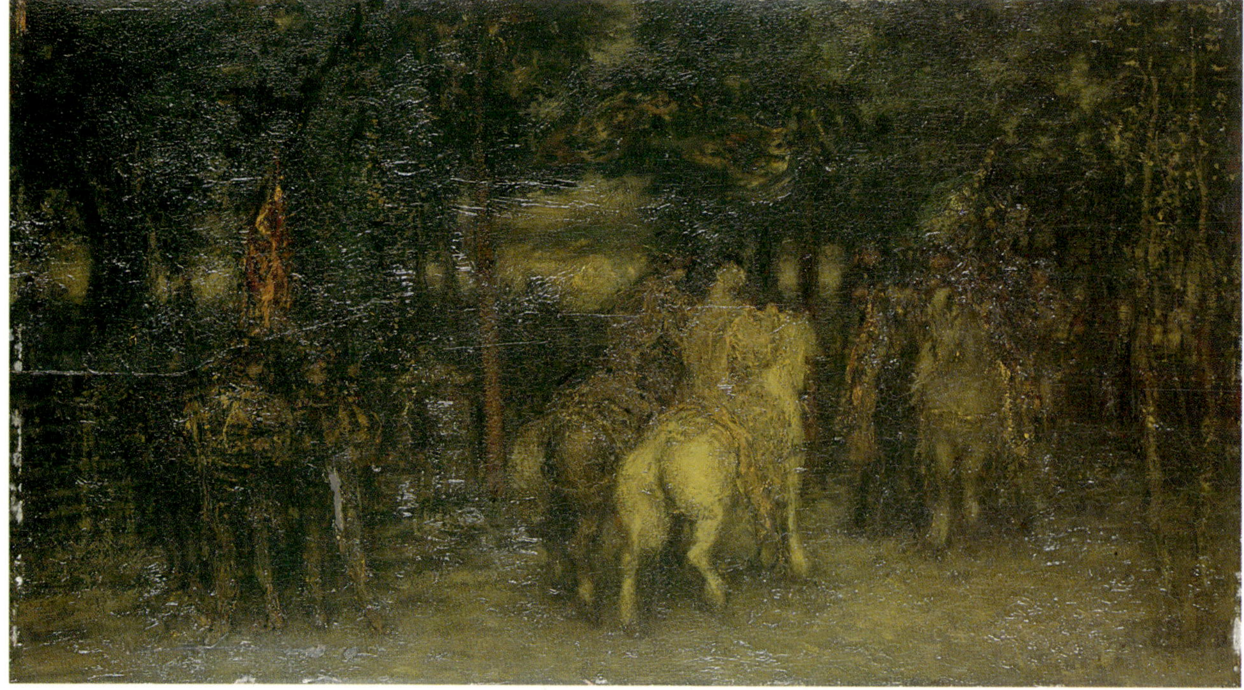

Pl. XXXIV

Adolphe Joseph Thomas Monticelli and Matthew Maris, *The Farmyard*

Yale University Art Gallery, New Haven, Connecticut

Pl. XXXV

Adolphe Joseph Thomas Monticelli and Matthew Maris, *Landscape with Figures*

The Phillips Collection, Washington, D.C.

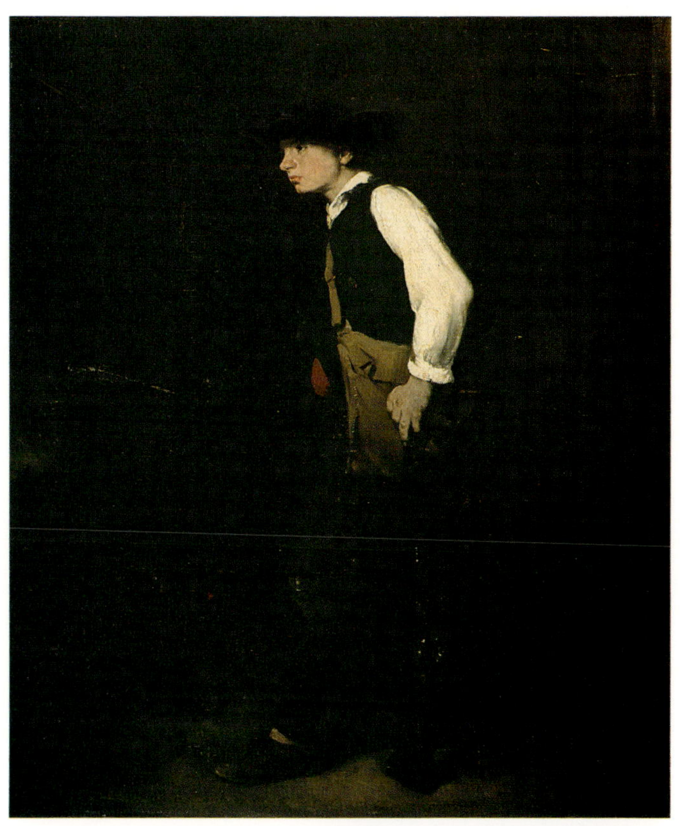

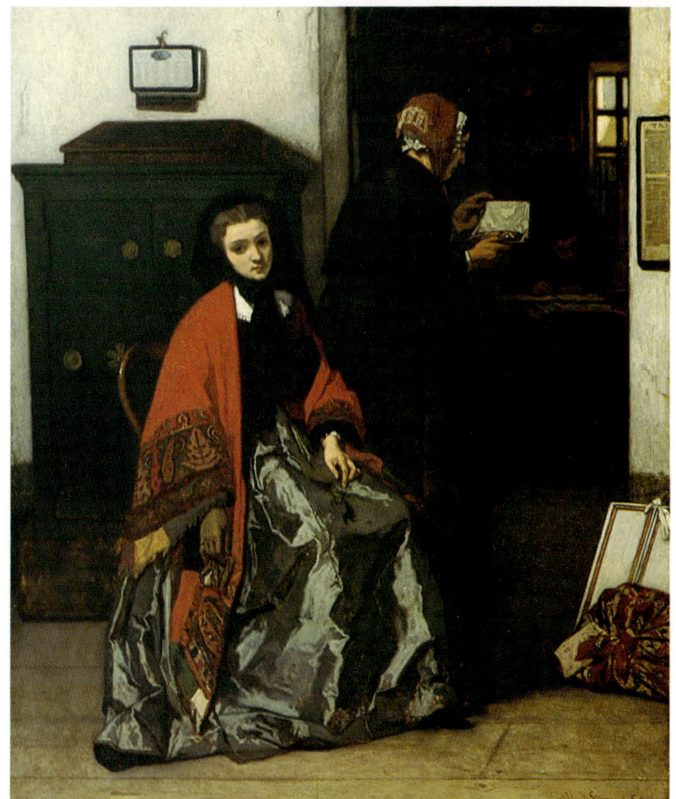

Pl. XXXVI

THÉODULE AUGUSTIN RIBOT, *A YOUNG VENDEAN*

Montreal Museum of Fine Arts

Musée des beaux-arts de Montréal

Pl. XXXVII

ALFRED EMILE LEOPOLD STEVENS, *AT THE PAWNSHOP*

Museum of Art, Rhode Island School of Design, Providence

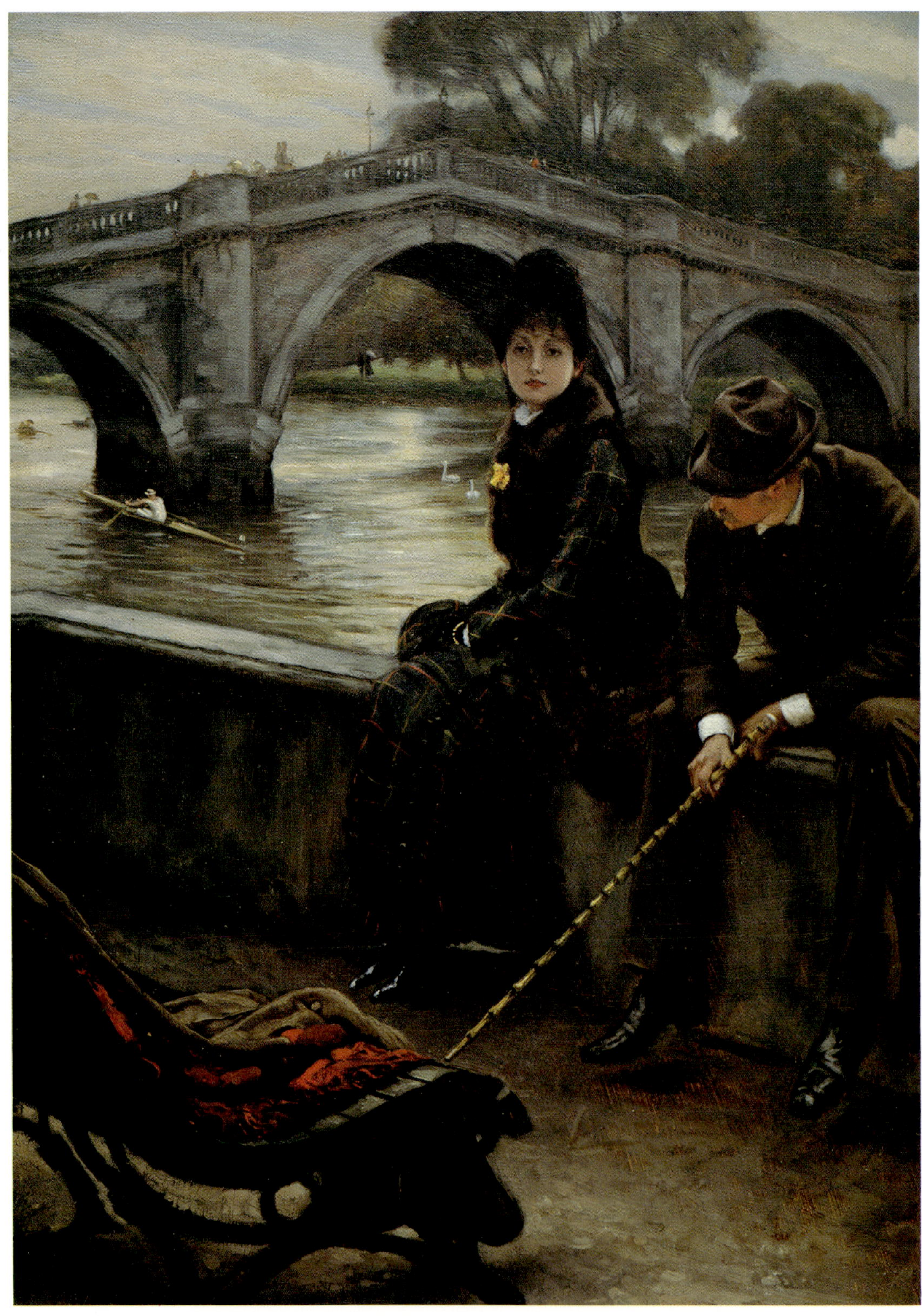

Pl. XXXVIII

James-Jacques-Joseph Tissot, *Richmond Bridge*, c. 1878

Collection William B. Ruger

Catalogue

1.
CHARLES BARGUE (French, c. 1825–1883)
A Bashi-Bazouk, 1875
Oil on canvas
18¼ x 13⅛ in.
Signed and dated l.r.: *BARGUE.75*
The Metropolitan Museum of Art, New York,
Bequest of Catharine Lorillard Wolfe, 1887,
Catharine Lorillard Wolfe Collection

Exhibited at the 1883 *Pedestal Fund Art Loan Exhibition,* no. 17, *Bazi-Bazouk in a Turkish Cafe,* loaned by Catharine Lorillard Wolfe
PLATE I

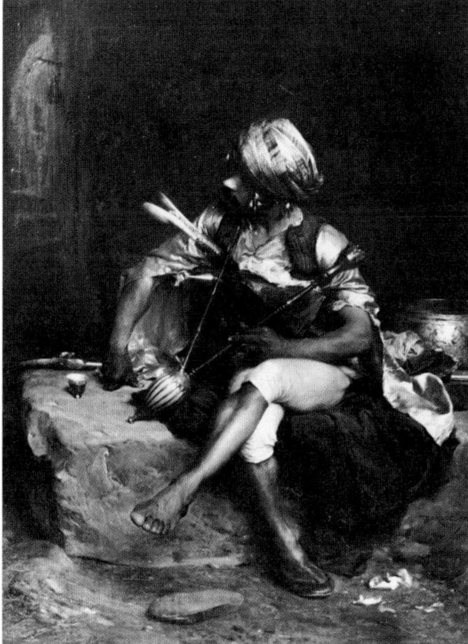

In 1889, British *Art Journal* critic Walter Rowlands described Charles Bargue's *A Bashi-Bazouk* in an article on the Catharine Lorillard Wolfe bequest to The Metropolitan Museum of Art. He elevated the artist's skills above those of Jean-Léon Gérôme, the master with whom he was most often linked: "The rich tones of a *Bashi-Bazouk,* . . . in which yellows are contrasted with the turquoise blue of a pipe-bowl, reveal a brushwork superior to Gérôme's and envelop the softer flesh tints in an atmosphere which the great French draughtsman cannot render."[1] Bargue, a lithographer who executed few paintings and exposed none at the Salon,[2] was less widely known in America than Gérôme, but the painterly qualities of his small Orientalist subjects were admired by informed collectors such as William K. Vanderbilt and S. A. Coale, Jr., who were among the few fortunate enough to have acquired them. In 1886, a French correspondent reporting on the auction of the Mary Jane Morgan collection in New York expressed astonishment at the 65,000 franc sum brought by Bargue's *The Sentinel;*[3] the prices paid by American dealers in Paris during the two years leading up to the sale clearly indicated their clients' strong interest in the rare examples of this artist's work.[4]

1. Walter Rowlands, "The Miss Wolfe Collection," *The Art Journal,* vol. 51, n.s. 41 (1889), p. 14.
2. See Meyer III, pp. 17–18; and Béraldi I, pp. 99–100.
3. Durand-Gréville 1886, p. 449.
4. George A. Lucas, acting as agent for dealer Samuel P. Avery, acquired a Bargue *Sentinel* in Paris for FF 35,000 on December 9, 1884 (Lucas II, p. 599), and initiated the sale of the artist's *Flute-player* for FF 40,000 on February 25, 1886 (Lucas II, p. 624).

2.
ANTOINE-LOUIS BARYE (French, 1796–1875)
Tiger in Its Lair
Watercolor on paper
9½ x 12⅝ in.
Museum of Fine Arts, Boston,
Bequest of Mrs. Samuel Dennis Warren, 1903

Provenance: Mrs. Samuel D. Warren, 1903
American Art Association, New York, 1892
Goupil & Cie, Paris
Barye Sale, Paris, 1876

By the early 1880s, Antoine-Louis Barye's reputation as the greatest animal sculptor of the age was well documented in the collections of Cyrus J. Lawrence and Theodore K. Gibbs of New York, W. P. Wilstach of Philadelphia, William W. Corcoran of Washington, and, most notably, William T. Walters of Baltimore.[1] Following the artist's death, American connoisseurs, including Albert Spencer and Erwin Davis, lenders to the Pedestal Fund exhibition, had also begun to appreciate his small, expressive watercolors and the even more rare landscape paintings, which had been shown in Paris at the Barye memorial exhibition at the Ecole des Beaux-Arts in 1875.[2] Contemporary critics found Barye's watercolors of animals similar to those of Eugène Delacroix, identifying the same "passionate creative nature" in both sculptor and painter.[3]

Barye's broad expressionist patterning of landscape around the exotic *Tiger in Its Lair* is not unlike the animated massing of forms in his sculpture, but it also conveys the sense of unity of all things in nature that the artist experienced in the forests of Fontainebleau. Closely associated with Barbizon painters Théodore Rousseau, Jean-Baptiste-Camille Corot, and Jean-François Millet, Barye was respected by American artists and by a phalanx of devoted collectors, who rallied to the support of a monument in his honor by organizing an important exhibition of works of Barye and his friends in New York in 1889.[4]

1. See Strahan I and III for descriptions of the Barye sculptures and watercolors in the collections of Corcoran, Walters, Wilstach, and Q. A. Shaw. Henry Eckford, "Antoine Louis

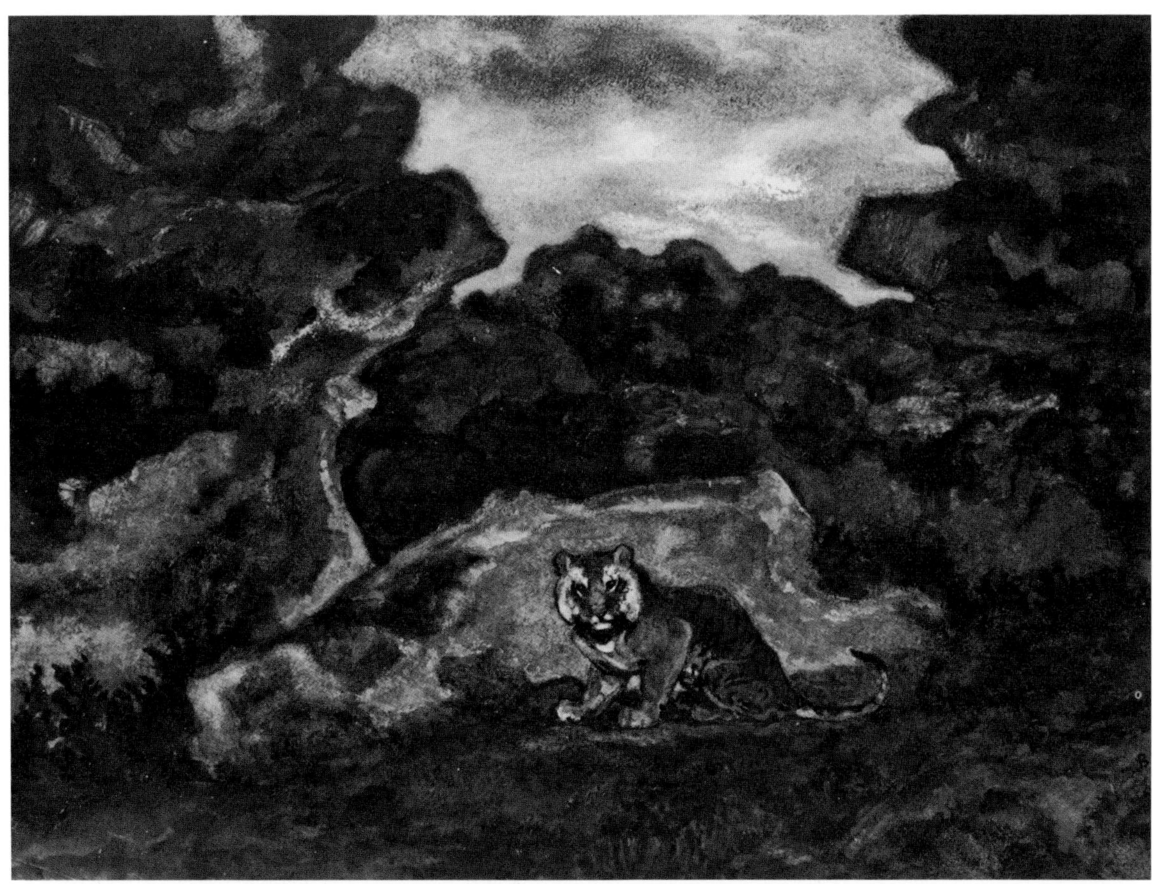

2.

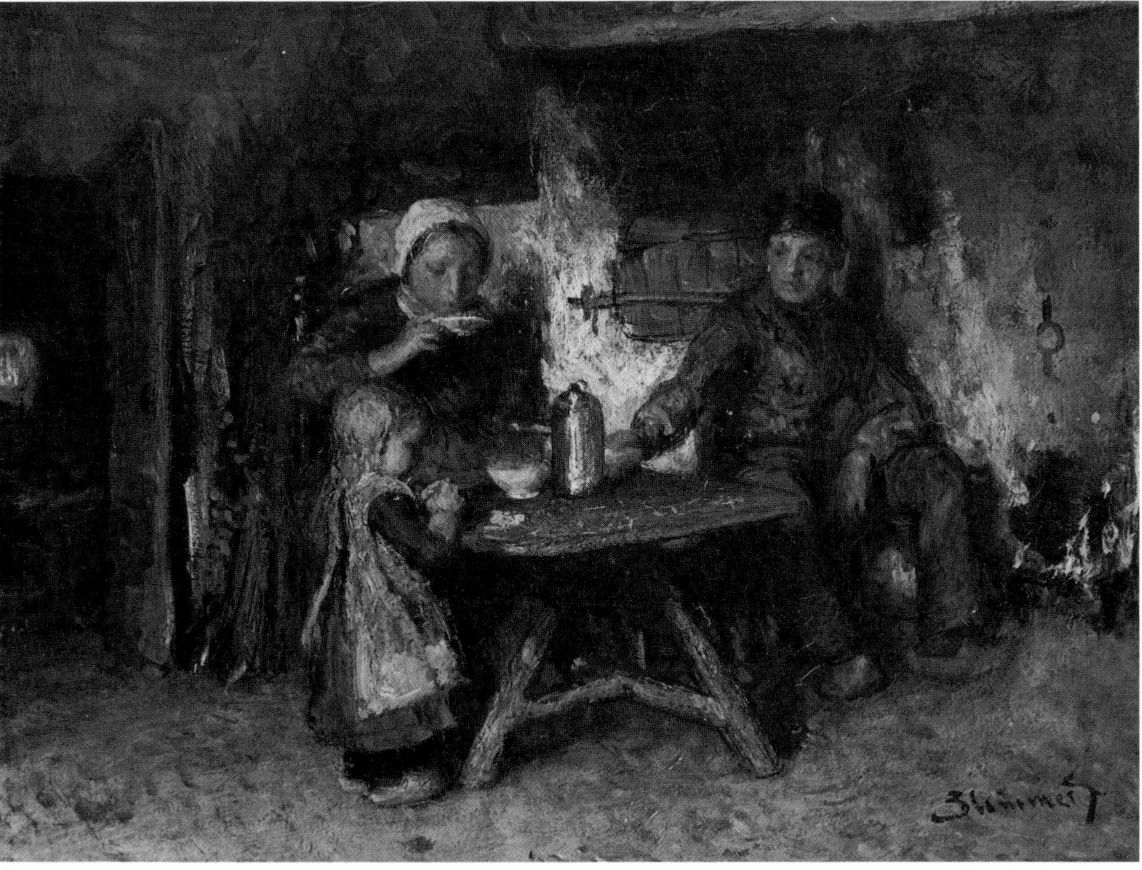

4.

Barye," *The Century Magazine,* vol. 21, no. 4 (February 1886), pp. 483–500, refers to the Gibbs and Lawrence collections, and reproduces an oil painting, *Fontainebleau Landscape,* in the possession of the latter, p. 491. See also William R. Johnston, "The Barye Collection," *Apollo,* vol. 100 (1974), pp. 56–63.

2. Paintings and drawings that were not exhibited during Barye's lifetime became available to collectors at the studio sale that followed his death. See Paris, *Oeuvres de feu Barye,* February 5–6, 1876. Objects that represented personal expressions of an artist's talent were sought by Daniel Cottier, who loaned an unidentified Barye *Animal Piece,* probably a watercolor, to the Pedestal Fund show. Erwin Davis also owned at least two Barye watercolors, *Study of a Bear* and *Study of a Tiger,* acquired at the Nathan Sale, 1880.
3. Eckford, p. 487.
4. See New York, American Art Galleries, *Catalogue of the Works of Antoine-Louis Barye... His Contemporaries and Friends for the Benefit of the Barye Monument Fund,* November 15, 1889–January 15, 1890. The *Barye Monument Exhibition* included a number of works by Corot, Daubigny, Diaz, Delacroix, Millet, and Troyon that had previously been exhibited at the Pedestal Fund show.

3.
JULES BASTIEN-LEPAGE (French, 1848–1884)
Pauvre Fauvette
Watercolor on paper
28 x 22¼ in.
Signed l.l.: *Jules Bastien-Lepage*
The Corcoran Gallery of Art, Washington, D.C., William A. Clark Collection
Provenance: Emile Bastien-Lepage
PLATE II

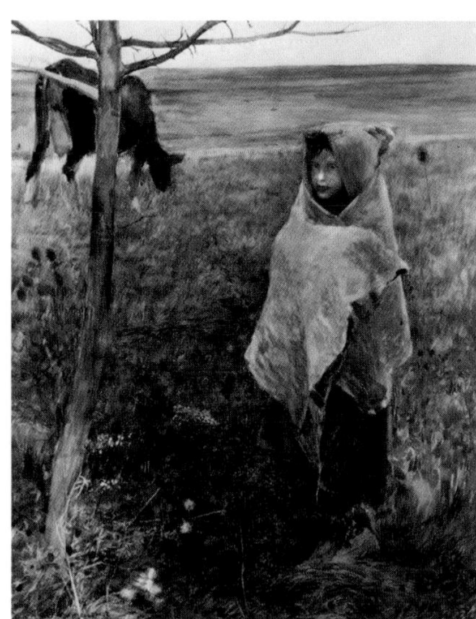

In June of 1881, *Scribner's Monthly* editor Richard Watson Gilder described the paintings of Jules Bastien-Lepage to the American public as "the vigorous work of a man of the very age of the new generation of painters; a classmate and associate of many; the very latest product of what is perhaps the best contemporary school of art."[1] Gilder's article followed the inclusion of Bastien-Lepage's *Joan of Arc* (1879) in the most recent exhibition of the Society of American Artists. Purchased for collector Erwin Davis by American artist Julian Alden Weir in the summer of 1880, it was the first important work by Bastien-Lepage to be seen in New York.

A number of American artists, including Weir, Alexander Harrison, John Singer Sargent, Will H. Low, and Augustus Saint-Gaudens, who had been friendly with Bastien-Lepage in Paris in the 1870s, confirmed Gilder's opinion and acknowledged the artist as a leader among younger French painters.[2] He was favorably reviewed for his skill as a naturalist and for the psychological attraction of his subjects by American critic William C. Brownell, whose 1883 article for *The Magazine of Art* (London) featured a full-page engraving of the artist's painting *Pauvre Fauvette,*[3] a hollow-eyed peasant child guarding a cow in a barren landscape. A critic for *The New York Times* judged the version loaned to the Pedestal Fund exhibition by George Campbell Cooper (possibly this watercolor), and listed in the Pedestal Fund catalogue as *La Petite Fauvette,* as a notch below the artist's best work, but found the little girl "all that one need ask in a disciple of Millet."[4]

1. Richard Watson Gilder, "Bastien-Lepage," *Scribner's Monthly,* vol. 22, no. 2 (June 1881), pp. 230–35.
2. See Julian Alden Weir, "Jules Bastien-Lepage," in Van Dyke 1896, pp. 227–34; Augustus Saint-Gaudens, in Homer Saint-Gaudens, ed., *Reminiscences of Augustus Saint-Gaudens,* vol. 1 (London: Andrew Melrose, 1913), pp. 217ff; and Will H. Low, *A Chronicle of Friendships 1873–1900* (New York: Charles Scribner's Sons, 1908), passim.
3. William C. Brownell, "Bastien-Lepage: Painter and Psychologist," *The Magazine of Art,* vol. 6 (1883), pp. 365–71. The oil version of *Pauvre Fauvette* reproduced by Brownell was owned by London collector J. Staats Forbes, who loaned it to the 1888 *Internationale Jubiläums Ausstellung,* Munich (currently, Glasgow Art Gallery and Museum, Purchase, 1913).
4. "The Pedestal Art Loan," *The New York Times,* December 16, 1883, p. 5. The writer took critical note of the cow, "which is badly managed in the manner of the two perspectives—namely, in the drawing of the beast and in aerial perspective. The planes occupied by the cow and the tree in front of her are not well distinguished."

4.
BERNARDUS JOHANNES BLOMMERS (Dutch, 1845–1914)
Cottage Interior
Oil on canvas
10 x 12¼ in.
Signed l.r.: *Blommers*
Museum of Fine Arts, Boston, William R. Wilson Donation, 1915

Bernardus Johannes Blommers, who studied with Christoffel Bisschop and attended the Hague Academy, achieved early success in Holland. By the late 1860s he had won recognition at exhibitions in both Amsterdam and The Hague,[1] and had established himself within the circle of artists who became known as the Hague School, including among his friends Anton Mauve and the brothers Jacob, Matthew, and Willem Maris. *Cottage Interior,* like the scenes of Scheveningen fishing folk and Dutch peasant life he painted throughout his career, shows the lasting influence of Joseph Israels, an older Hague School artist whom he met around 1865 and with whom he shared a long friendship.[2]

Like his friend Albert Neuhuys (see cat. no. 69), Blommers was relatively unknown in America in 1883, but was familiar to William Merritt Chase, Julian Alden Weir, and James Carroll Beckwith, with whom he had exhibited in Munich earlier that same year. Although Blommers was not among the Dutch artists included in the 1876 Philadelphia Centennial Exhibition, the Pedestal Fund show featured his *Dutch Interior,* loaned by the dealer Daniel Cottier,[3] and four of his paintings were seen in the Netherlands section of the World's Columbian Exposition, Chicago, in 1893. In 1904, while visiting the United States to see the Saint Louis Exposition, at which four of his works were on view, Blommers's reputation was such that even President Theodore Roosevelt received him with the courtesy due an artist of international importance.[4]

1. It is noted in *The Hague School* 1983, p. 167, that his *Scheveningen Interior* was given a place of honor at the *Amsterdam Tentoonstelling van levende Meesters* in 1865, and that he won a gold medal at the 1868 Hague exhibition.
2. *Ibid.,* states that Blommers and Israels met on the beach at Scheveningen around 1865. Cook IV, p. 324, found Blommers even more accomplished as a painter than his mentor, Israels.
3. No paintings by Blommers were in the Cottier Sale, Paris, 1892, but *A Girl Knitting* remained in the collection of Cottier's widow (Cottier Sale, London, 1914, lot 75, 16 x 9¾ in.). Blommers's reputation in Scotland, promoted by Cottier and by E. J. van Wisselingh, was crowned by honorary membership in the Royal Scottish Society of Painters in Water-Colours in 1897.
4. *The Hague School* 1983, p. 167.

5.
GIOVANNI BOLDINI (Italian, 1845–1931)
The Summer Stroll, 1872
Oil on canvas
22 x 13⅝ in.
Signed l.l.: *Boldini;* in pencil on frame verso: *Boldini 1872 / Painted for H. C. Gibson*
The Pennsylvania Academy of the Fine Arts, Philadelphia, Bequest of Henry C. Gibson, 1892
Provenance: Henry C. Gibson, Philadelphia, 1872

According to Edward Strahan, writing in *The Art Treasures of America,* Henry C. Gibson of Philadelphia housed his collection in a "series of little chapels. Each is lighted by a ceiling of glass, and the dimensions are in harmony with the pictures collected, which in hardly an instance exceed a moderate easel size."[1] The Italianate galleries, located next to a conservatory, presented the ideal setting for

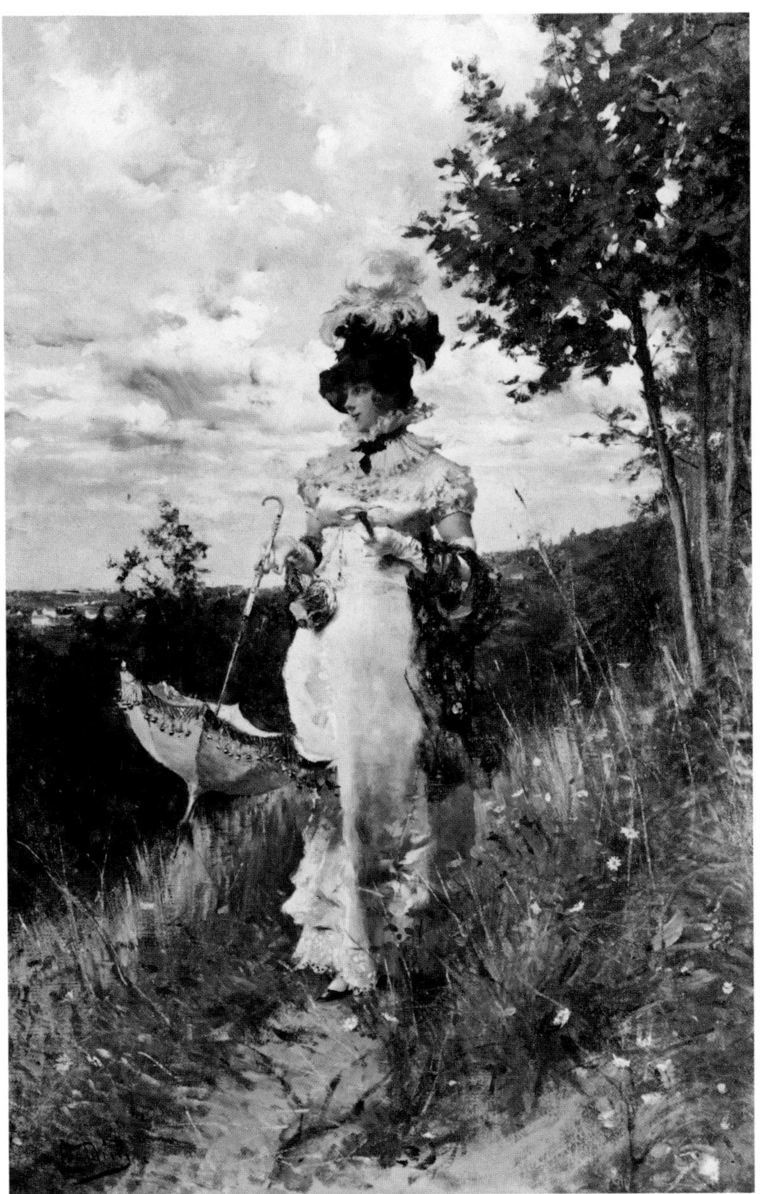

5.

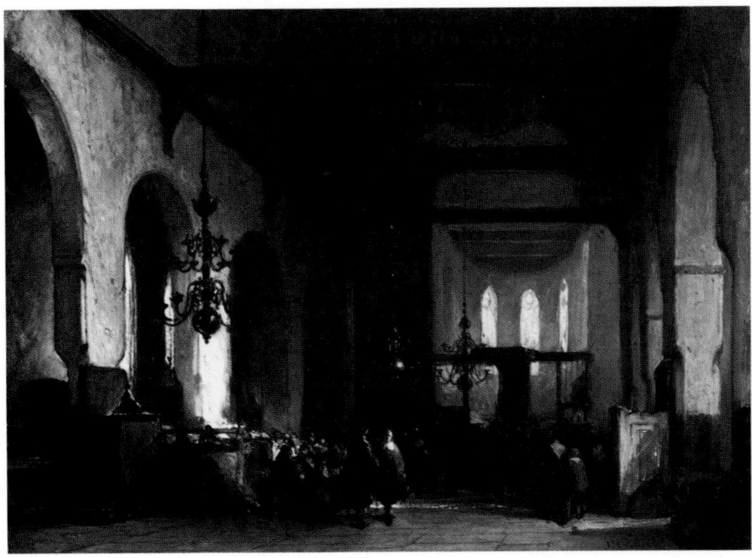

7.

Giovanni Boldini's *The Summer Stroll,* a painting that typified the Ferrarese master's landscape and genre style in the early 1870s. The high-keyed palette and close observation of light, which he had developed among the Macchiaioli, are here applied to a subject that was also of great interest to the French Impressionists, with whom Boldini first came in contact in 1867. However, *The Summer Stroll* refers not only to the sunlit, white-gowned figures in Auguste Renoir's *Lise* (1867)[2] and Claude Monet's *Women in the Garden* (1866–67),[3] but also to contemporary fashion prints and to the conversation pieces of Michael Munkácsy (cat. no. 68) and Mariano Fortuny (cat. no. 33), both popular in America in the 1880s.

1. Strahan I, p. 65. An important exception to this rule was Thomas Couture's *The Thorny Path,* 1872, 51½ x 75 in. (The Pennsylvania Academy of the Fine Arts, Bequest of Henry C. Gibson), a version of which was loaned to the *Pedestal Fund Art Loan Exhibition* by architect Richard Morris Hunt.
2. Renoir, *Lise,* 1867, 71½ x 44½ in., Folkwang Museum, Essen.
3. Monet, *Women in the Garden,* 1866–67, 100 x 80¾ in., Musée du Louvre, Paris.

6.
ROSA BONHEUR (French, 1822–1899)
A Limier-Briquet Hound
Oil on canvas
14½ x 18 in.
Signed l.r.: *R B*
The Metropolitan Museum of Art, New York,
Bequest of Catharine Lorillard Wolfe, 1887, Catharine Lorillard Wolfe Collection

Provenance: Catharine Lorillard Wolfe, New York
H. D. Newcomb, Louisville, Kentucky, 1877

Exhibited at the 1883 *Pedestal Fund Art Loan Exhibition,* no. 18, *Staghound,* loaned by Catharine Lorillard Wolfe

PLATE III

By 1883, America was rich in the paintings of Rosa Bonheur, whose country home at Chevilly, near Fontainebleau, in France, was visited by admirers who "carry off her works as soon as they are finished."[1] *The Art Treasures of America* noted that twenty-five Bonheurs were owned by American collectors in the early 1880s;[2] heading the list was *The Horse Fair* (1855), an enormous painting that had been brought to America by W. P. Wright of Weehawken, New Jersey, in 1857, and later entered the collection of A. T. Stewart, New York.[3] Far less imposing than *The Horse Fair,* which was widely known through the engraving by Thomas Landseer and an etching by J. J. Veyrassat, was Miss Wolfe's little painting of a hunting dog.[4] The study of this alert spotted hound may have been made by Bonheur in preparation for the large *Rendezvous de Chasse,* an important painting owned by another New York collector, August Belmont.[5]

1. Strahan I, p. 48.
2. Strahan III, p. 132.
3. Cook II, p. 257. The painting, which measures 99¼ x 199½ in., was sold to Cornelius Vanderbilt at the A. T. Stewart Sale of 1887 and was given by him to The Metropolitan Museum of Art, New York, that same year.
4. Wolfe owned a second Bonheur, *Weaning the Calves,* 1879, 25⅝ x 32 in., The Metropolitan Museum of Art, New York, Bequest of Catharine Lorillard Wolfe, 1887.
5. Strahan I, p. 110, illus.

7.
JOHANNES BOSBOOM (Dutch, 1817–1891)
Interior of a Church
Oil on cradled panel
10⅞ x 14⅜ in.
Signed l.r.: *J Bosboom*
Montreal Museum of Fine Arts
Musée des beaux-arts de Montréal
William John and Agnes Learmont Bequests

Early in his career, Johannes Bosboom, a leader of the Hague School, began to paint the church interiors that would become his signature subject. Three of these, *Church at Trêves, Dutch Church,* and the *New Church at Amsterdam,* were shown in the Netherlands section of the 1876 Philadelphia Centennial Exhibition, making Bosboom one of the first members of the Hague School to be introduced to the American public. As a young man he had studied with Burt van Hove, his neighbor in The Hague, assisting the painter of townscapes with stage sets and architectural views.[1] His own interpretations included detailed oil paintings of the Cathedral at Trier,[2] more modest renderings in oil or watercolor of the church at Alkmaar, and the dark synagogues that allowed him to experiment with Rembrandtesque chiaroscuro.[3] Both Daniel Cottier and Ichabod T. Williams admired Bosboom's smaller, more freely painted interiors, and each owned paintings of this description.[4]

Several works of this type, including *Church at Alkmaar* (pl. IV; Saint Louis Art Museum) from Williams's collection, were loaned to the *Pedestal Fund Art Loan Exhibition.* In the 1880s, the American critic Clarence Cook considered Bosboom's ecclesiastical interiors unequaled, a view that was shared by collectors in the United States and Canada. Recalling such paintings as *Interior of a Church* (cat. no. 7) Cook praised Bosboom's ability to "transfuse the dusky gloom of these old Dutch churches with soft splendor, filling the air with motes of floating gold, touching with magic fingers the soaring arches of the groined roof, stealing from pier to pier, or brushing silently, as with angel wings the broad fields of whitened wall, that only such a hand as his could redeem from vulgarity."[5]

1. *The Hague School* 1983, p. 171.
2. A fine example is the *Interior of Trier Cathedral,* oil on panel, 33½ x 26 in., The Toledo Museum of Art, Gift of Edward Drummond Libbey.
3. See *The Hague School* 1983, p. 178, no. 19, pl. 19, *Interior of the German Synagogue, The Hague,* oil on panel, 42 x 3 cm, Dordrechts Museum, Dordrecht.
4. In addition to church interiors, Cottier also owned a *Dutch Interior,* a scene of a master in a hall watching his servant come up from the cellar with provisions (Cottier Sale, Paris, 1892, lot 14, 14½ x 10¼ in.), possibly the *Dutch Interior* he loaned to the Pedestal Fund show.
5. Cook IV, p. 326.

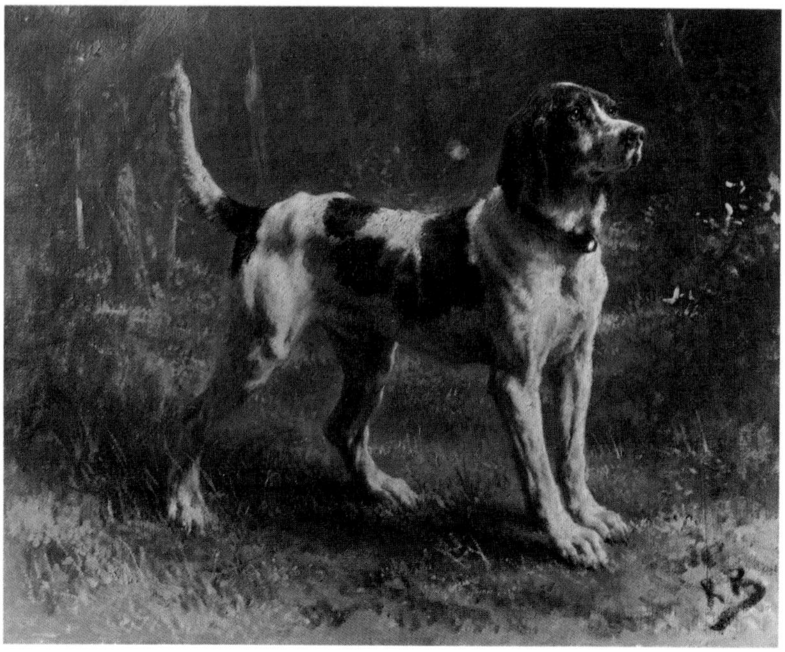

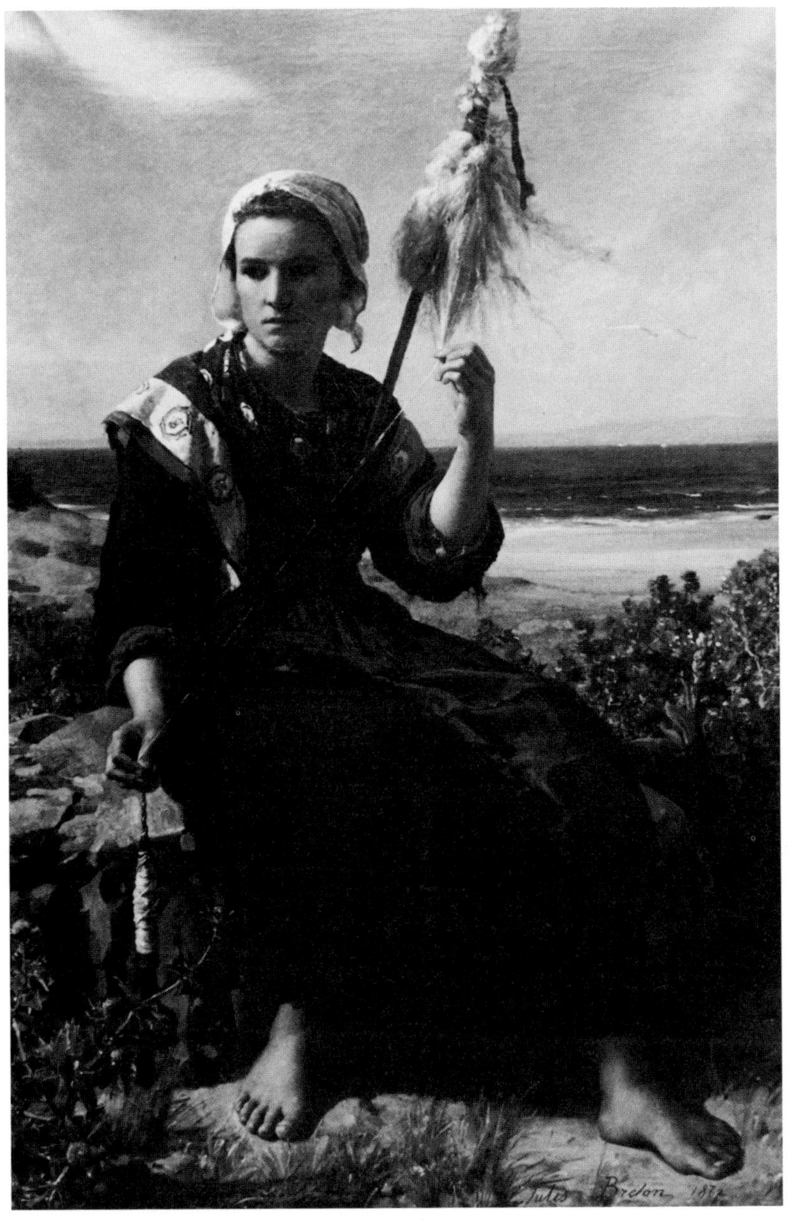

9.

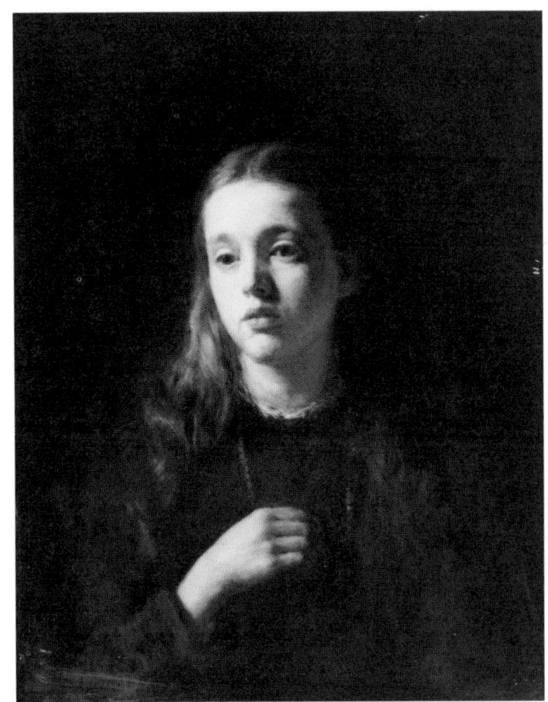

10.

8.
AUGUSTE BOULARD (French, 1825–1897)
Female Head (Portrait of the Artist's Niece)
Oil on canvas
21½ x 17¾ in.
Signed l.l.: AB
Collection Robert B. Beardsley

Provenance: Shepherd Gallery Associates, New York
Daniel Cottier, New York, 1883
Jean-Baptiste-Camille Corot

Exhibited at the 1883 *Pedestal Fund Art Loan Exhibition,* no. 88, *Female Head,* loaned by Daniel Cottier

PLATE V

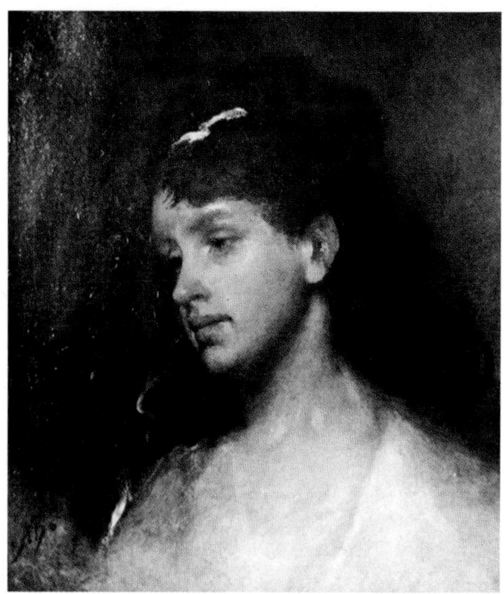

Auguste Boulard, who trained in the atelier of Léon Cogniet, Paris, in the early 1840s, was an avid student of nature who counted among his friends Jean-François Millet, Antoine-Louis Barye, Jules Dupré, and Charles Daubigny.[1] His paintings were owned by the Dutch artist Hendrik Mesdag, as well as by J.-B.-C. Corot, to whom this portrait of a woman once belonged. Although Boulard consistently exhibited his portraits, rustic genre scenes, and marines at the Paris Salons, he was not well known to American collectors, and this painting, a sensitive portrait of a young woman, failed to sell in 1878 at the New York sale of the Daniel Cottier collection.[2]

1. *American Art Annual 1898*, p. 29; Fidell-Beaufort and Bailly-Herzberg 1975, p. 85.
2. Cottier Sale, New York, 1878, no. 111; the annotated copy of the catalogue at The Metropolitan Museum of Art, New York, indicates that it was bought in by Cottier.

9.
JULES BRETON (French, 1827–1906)
Brittany Girl, 1872
Oil on canvas
63 x 42 in.
Signed and dated l.r.: *Jules Breton 1872*
Denison University Gallery, Granville, Ohio, Burke Hall of Music and Art

Provenance: Edmund G. Burke, 1945
Cornelius Vanderbilt, New York
William Henry Vanderbilt, New York, 1879
Goupil and Company, New York

In the early 1880s, Breton had no lack of admirers among New York's most prominent collectors.[1] *Brittany Girl* and *The Rainbow* (Salon of 1883) were featured in the elaborate catalogue of the collection of William Henry Vanderbilt in 1883–84.[2] Catharine Lorillard Wolfe's collection boasted Breton's *A Peasant Girl Knitting*[3] as well as *Pardon in Brittany* (Salon of 1869);[4] and Governor E. D. Morgan owned the monumental *Breton Washerwomen.*[5]

At the *Pedestal Fund Art Loan Exhibition,* Breton was represented by the painting *Brittany Peasant,* 1872 (fig. 11, p. 28), a study of a dark-haired man holding a candle and rosary and alternately described as a penitent and a communicant.[6] The choice of this rude and humble penitent, when such works as the charming and highly finished *Brittany Girl* (cat. no. 9) were available for loan, indicates the strong preference on the part of the selections committee for unsentimental realist subjects such as those painted by Courbet, Ribot, and Millet.

1. See Madeleine Fidell-Beaufort, "Jules Breton in America: Collecting in the 19th Century," in Joslyn 1982, pp. 51–61.
2. Edward Strahan [Earl Shinn], *Mr. Vanderbilt's House and Collection,* 4 vols. (Boston: G. Barrie [c. 1883–84]).
3. *A Peasant Girl Knitting,* 22⅝ x 18½, The Metropolitan Museum of Art, Catharine Lorillard Wolfe Collection.
4. Strahan I, illus. opp. p. 132; Museum of Fine Arts, Havana.
5. Strahan III, illus. opp. p. 6; current location unknown.
6. This painting was identified by Mme Annette Bourrut-Lacouture and traced as far as Buenos Aires, Sale Roldan y Cía., June 4, 1974, lot 181. Ex-collections: M. Knoedler & Co., New York; John G. Johnson, Philadelphia; Peter A. Schemm, Philadelphia; illus. in Smith 1903, p. 257; current location unknown.

10.
HUGH CAMERON (Scottish, 1835–1918)
Day Dream
Oil on canvas
27 x 21 in.
Signed l.l.: *H. Cameron*
Courtesy Sacks Fine Art, New York

Provenance: Ray Livingston Murphy, New York

Hugh Cameron, a member of the Royal Scottish Academy, was born in Edinburgh but resided in London between 1876 and 1888. He specialized in portraits and in genre scenes that depicted stages of old age or childhood, combining both in a painting entitled *Age and Infancy,* which he sent to the 1876 Philadelphia Centennial Exhibition. In contrast to the relatively extensive display of English painting at the Centennial, only Cameron, William E. Lockhart, and W. Reynolds were included in the Pedestal Fund show, each represented by a single painting loaned by dealer Daniel Cottier, who was also a native of Scotland.[1] Cameron's affectionate depictions of youth and adolescence, indicated here in *Day Dream,*[2] had much of the naturalness of the peasant figures of the Hague School, and for that reason did not seem out of place among similar works by Johannes Blommers and Albert Neuhuys at the 1883 exhibition.

1. Cottier loaned Cameron's *Maternal Care* to the Pedestal Fund exhibition; a painting by the same title was exhibited by Cameron at the Royal Scottish Academy, Edinburgh, in 1870, no. 474. In 1886, another painting by Cameron, entitled *Carrying Little Sister,* was in the New York collection of Mary Jane Morgan, an occasional client of Cottier & Co. (Mary Jane Morgan Sale, 1886, lot 33, 15 x 11 in).
2. A painting by this title was exhibited at the Royal Scottish Academy, Edinburgh, in 1875 (no. 184, lent by Alexander Curle, Esq.).

11.
JEAN-CHARLES CAZIN (French, 1841–1901)
Tobias and the Angel, 1878
Oil on canvas
23 x 33⅛ in.
Signed and dated l.l.: *J. C. Cazin 1878*
The Art Institute of Chicago, Henry Field Memorial Collection, 1894

Provenance: Henry Field, Chicago

Jean-Charles Cazin was a student of Horace Lecoq de Boisbaudran, whose method of drawing from memory required intense observation of nature and thoughtful recollection in the quiet of the studio. Cazin applied his skill as a landscape painter to Old Testament subjects in the late 1870s, achieving recognition at the Salons of 1878 and 1880 with paintings based on the stories of the Journey of Tobias and Hagar and Ishmael, respectively.[1] In 1883 the American dealer Samuel P. Avery purchased a smaller variant of the Salon *Hagar and Ishmael*[2] and loaned it to the *Pedestal Fund Art Loan Exhibition* (see fig. 21, p. 33). *Tobias and the Angel,* another interpretation of the 1878 Salon theme, was acquired by collector Henry Field and entered The Art Institute of Chicago in 1894.

With the exceptions of Avery and Erwin Davis, few New York collectors were familiar with Cazin's work in 1883. By 1893, however, Cazin's reputation reached its peak with an exhibition at the galleries of the American Art Association, where 68 of 112 works were borrowed from American collections.[3]

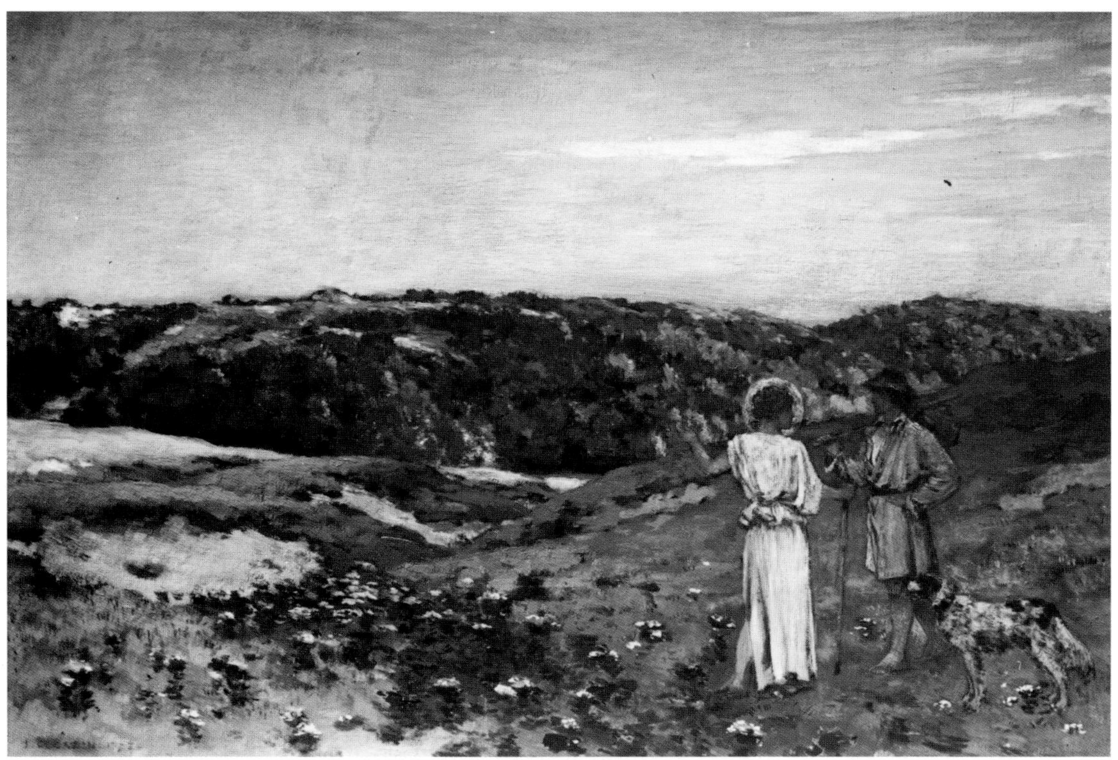
11.

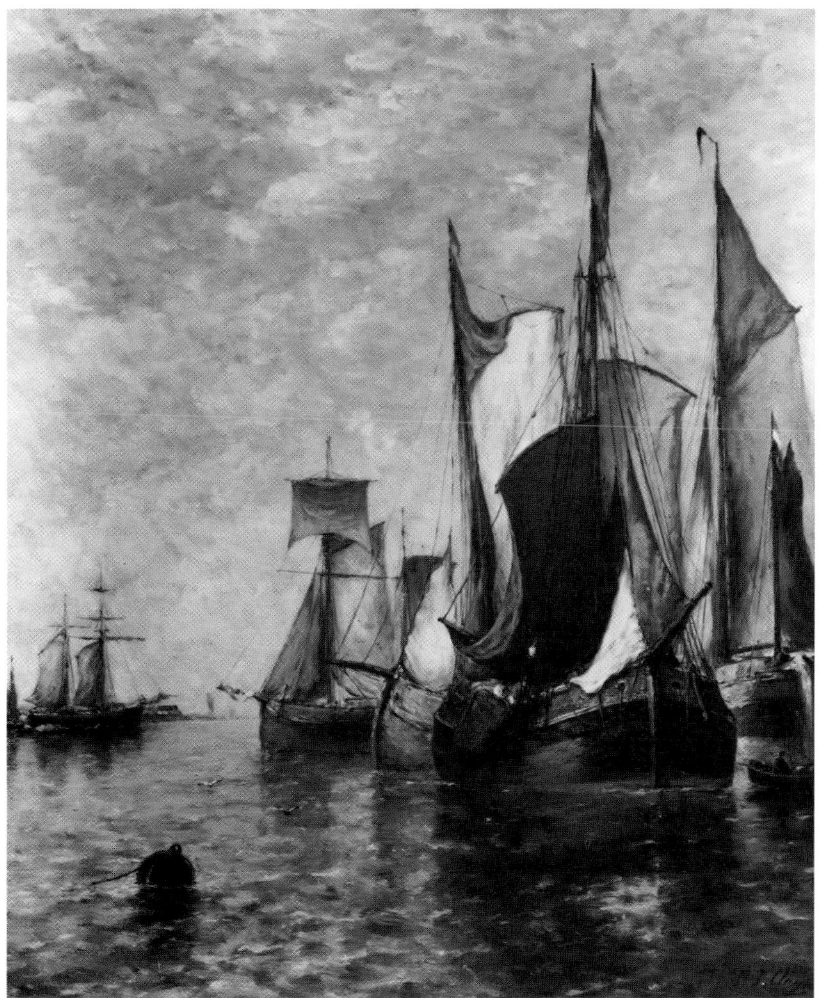
12.

1. *Hagar and Ishmael,* oil on canvas, 100¼ x 80½ in., Musée des Beaux-Arts, Tours, extended loan from the Musée du Louvre, Paris, became Cazin's best-known work in America. It was reproduced in art-study prints by Brown-Robertson, New York, and University Prints, Boston; cited in Brownell 1892, p. 106 (1901 edition, illus. opp. p. 88); and cited by William A. Coffin, "Jean-Charles Cazin," *The Century Magazine,* vol. 55, no. 50 (1898), p. 395.
2. Purchased at Vente de Mme R., 1883 (Mireur II, p. 124), and later owned by Potter Palmer of Chicago. Sold New York, Parke-Bernet, May 15, 1946, lot 23, *Hagar and Ishmael,* 26 x 32 in.
3. Coffin, p. 395.

12.
PAUL-JEAN CLAYS (Belgian, 1819–1900)
Zuyder Zee
Oil on canvas
35½ x 24¼ in.
Signed l.r.: *P. J. Clays*
Courtesy Schweitzer Gallery, Inc., New York
Provenance: M. Newman Ltd., London

Paul-Jean Clays's success at the *Expositions Universelles* of 1867 and 1878 led to wide recognition abroad by the early 1880s. Like his countryman Alfred Stevens, Clays developed a strong American following, and placed paintings in the collections of Erwin Davis of New York (who loaned a moonlit marine to the Pedestal Fund show),[1] William T. Walters of Baltimore, Henry C. Gibson of Philadelphia, and Thomas Wigglesworth of Boston, among others.[2]

Zuyder Zee, which is similar in composition to the painting in the Walters collection,[3] is typical of the calm, loosely painted maritime scenes for which Clays was best known. As a former sailor, he combined an undramatic directness of approach with a sensitivity to changes in light and atmosphere, developing a formula that established him as the foremost Belgian marine painter in the late nineteenth century.

1. The Davis loan, *Moonlight,* was probably the painting listed as lot 108, *Marine, Moonlight,* 28 x 43 in., in the Davis Sale, 1889.
2. Strahan III, p. 133, lists twenty-one of Clays's marines in American collections; characteristically they contain boats that "never go anywhere and never have anything to do. Phantasmal as the ship of the Flying Dutchman, they differ from that in never being in a hurry." Strahan II, p. 47.
3. *Moonlight in Holland,* 28⅞ x 23¼ in., probably acquired by Walters between 1880 and 1884.

13.
JEAN-BAPTISTE-CAMILLE COROT
(French, 1796–1875)
Ville d'Avray
Oil on canvas
21⅝ x 31½ in.
Signed l.r.: *Corot*
The Metropolitan Museum of Art,
New York,
Bequest of Catharine Lorillard Wolfe, 1887,
Catharine Lorillard Wolfe Collection
Provenance: Catharine Lorillard Wolfe, by 1883
Exhibited at the 1883 *Pedestal Fund Art Loan Exhibition,* no. 13, *Ville d'Avray,* loaned by Catharine Lorillard Wolfe
PLATE VIII

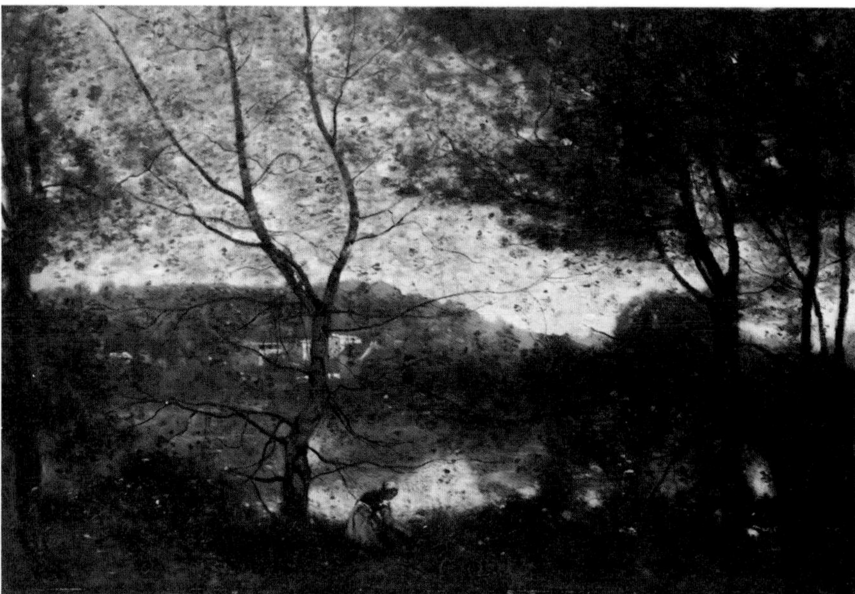

14.
JEAN-BAPTISTE-CAMILLE COROT
Landscape and Figures, 1874
Oil on canvas
19¾ x 25⅞ in.
Signed l.l.: *Corot;* dated l.r.: *1874*
The New-York Historical Society, New York,
Robert L. Stuart Collection
Provenance: The New York Public Library, 1892
Mrs. Robert L. Stuart, 1882
Robert L. Stuart, 1882
Exhibited at the 1883 *Pedestal Fund Art Loan Exhibition,* no. 3, *Landscape,* loaned by Mrs. R. L. Stuart

15.
JEAN-BAPTISTE-CAMILLE COROT
Woodland Scene
Oil on canvas
9⅝ x 7½ in.
Signed l.l.: *Corot*
Vassar College Art Gallery, Poughkeepsie, New York, Gift of Mrs. Lloyd Williams in Memory of Her Father, Daniel Cottier

Jean-Baptiste-Camille Corot, "the painter of the poets, and all who love nature not so much for her brilliant and obvious qualities as for her mystery, her poetry, and her charm,"[1] was represented by twelve paintings in the *Pedestal Fund Art Loan Exhibition.*[2] His prominence indicated the high esteem in which he was held by young artists who had trained in Paris and Munich in the 1870s, and confirmed their admiration for a treatment of landscape that was the antithesis of the linear Hudson River style still favored at the annual exhibitions of the National Academy of Design.

Appreciated by a small group of American connoisseurs since the late 1850s, when his work was introduced to New England collectors by Providence dealer Seth Vose, Corot achieved widespread recognition after his death in 1875, when a memorial exhibition of his work took place at the Ecole des Beaux-Arts, Paris. By the early 1880s Corot's works could be found not only in the hands of New York collectors of daring, such as Erwin Davis and Ichabod T. Williams, but also in the drawing rooms of J. P. Morgan, Jay Gould, William Rockefeller, and both Cornelius and William H. Vanderbilt. Loans to the Pedestal Fund show included *Landscape and Figures* (cat. no. 14), purchased a year earlier by New York sugar refiner Robert L. Stuart, and *Le Soir (La Danse des Amours)* (fig. 24, p. 34; pl. VII), a celebrated painting from the 1861 Salon owned by *The Sun* editor Charles A. Dana. *Le Soir,* one of the most acclaimed paintings by Corot in America in the late nineteenth century, was exhibited again in New York in the *Barye Monument Exhibition* of 1889–90, and, after its sale to George Gould in 1898, at the Saint Louis Exposition of 1904.

Catharine Lorillard Wolfe, whose cousin John Wolfe had also collected Corot's work in

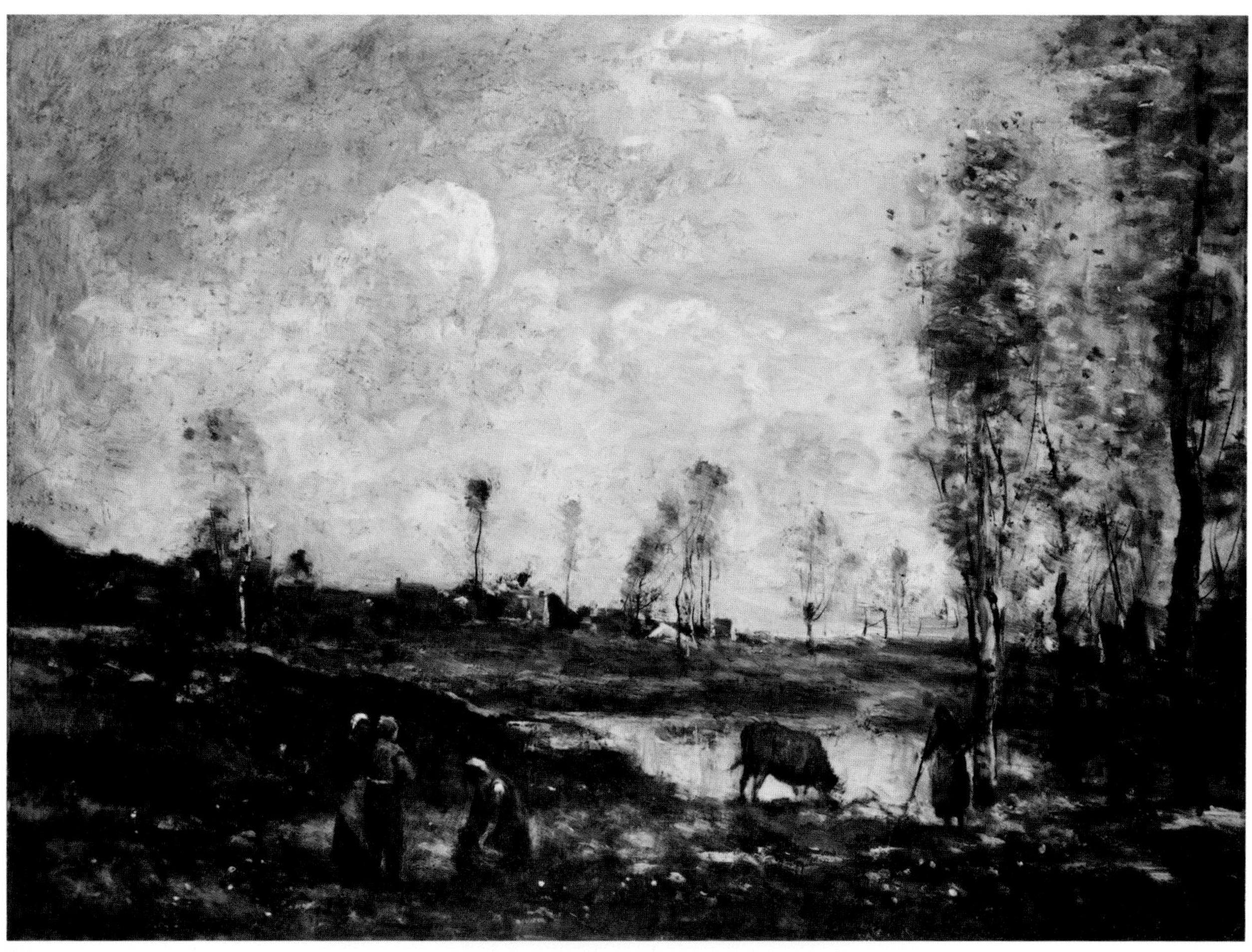
14.

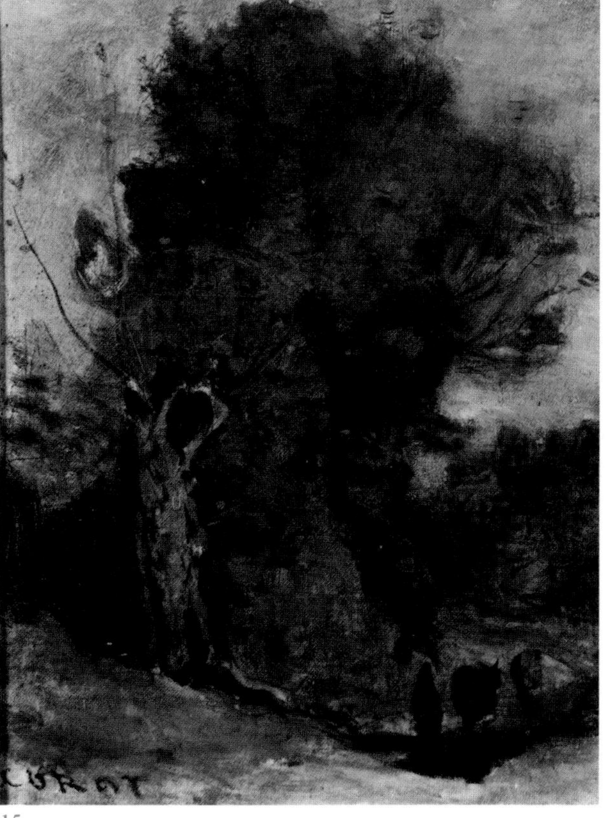

15.

the 1870s, loaned *Ville d'Avray* (cat. no. 13), exhibited in the Salon of 1870, a painting that was singled out by Theodore Robinson, an American follower of Claude Monet and one who praised the innocence of vision in Corot's intimate landscapes. Robinson's conviction that Corot's art was "painted music . . . lyric and suggestive in the highest degree"[3] was supported by dealer Daniel Cottier, who loaned the great *Orpheus Greeting the Dawn* (pl. VI; Elvehjem Museum of Art, Madison, Wisconsin), a large painting from a decorative scheme commissioned for the Paris townhouse of Prince Paul Demidoff in 1865.[4] A devoted admirer of Corot, Cottier collected works ranging from "little gems of a few inches in diameter"[5] like *Woodland Scene* (cat. no. 15) to major examples such as the *Orpheus*. Although the latter, which Cottier had exhibited in New York as early as 1877, was acclaimed by enlightened critics, it failed to attract an American buyer during Cottier's lifetime and remained in his inventory until his death in 1891.

Ironically, the artist who had been dismissed by American Pre-Raphaelites as the progenitor of a school of "daubers" became the inspiration for a posthumous oeuvre that, with only some exaggeration, supplied America with "more Corots than Corot ever painted." Although it is possible that some of these copies might have turned up at the *Pedestal Fund Art Loan Exhibition,* there is much evidence that the majority of the loans were significant examples of his work and that they documented a serious and informed appreciation of Corot on the part of New York collectors in the 1880s.

1. Theodore Robinson, "Jean-Baptiste-Camille Corot," in Van Dyke 1896, p. 116.
2. Lenders of Corot's paintings included George Campbell Cooper, Daniel Cottier, Charles A. Dana, Erwin Davis, Mrs. Robert L. Stuart, Ichabod T. Williams, and Catharine Lorillard Wolfe. Only Miss Wolfe's painting was noted among the forty or so works by Corot listed in Strahan III, p. 133.
3. Robinson, p. 113.
4. See Fronia E. Wissman, "Corot's *Hymn to the Sun*," *Elvehjem Museum of Art Bulletin* (Madison, Wisconsin), 1984, pp. 9–17, for a discussion of this commission.
5. "The Pedestal Art Loan," *The New York Times*, December 2, 1883, p. 2.

16.
GUSTAVE COURBET (French, 1819–1877)
The Violoncellist, 1847
Oil on canvas
45 x 35 in.
Signed and dated l.l.: *G Courbet 47*
Portland Art Museum, Portland, Oregon, Gift of Col. C. E. S. Wood in Memory of His Wife, Nanny Moale Wood
Provenance: Col. C. E. S. Wood, by 1906
Erwin Davis, New York, 1881
Exhibited at the 1883 *Pedestal Fund Art Loan Exhibition,* no. 144, *Music,* loaned by Erwin Davis
PLATE IX

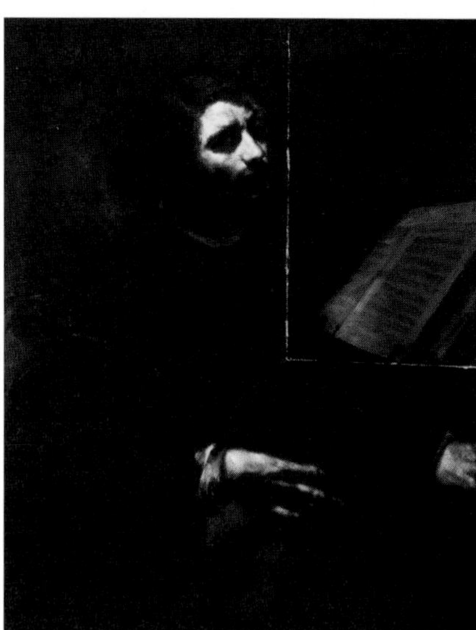

17.
GUSTAVE COURBET
The Source of the Loue, c. 1864
Oil on canvas
42¼ x 54⅛ in.
Signed l.l.: *G. Courbet*
Albright-Knox Art Gallery, Buffalo, New York,
George B. and Jenny R. Mathews Fund
Provenance: Pierre Matisse Gallery, New York, 1959
Henri Matisse, Paris, 1914
Galerie Georges Bernheim, Paris

18.
GUSTAVE COURBET
Marine, c. 1869
Oil on canvas
23¾ x 28⅛ in.
Signed l.r.: *G. Courbet*
The Brooklyn Museum, Brooklyn, New York,
Gift of Mrs. Frederic B. Pratt
Provenance: Mrs. Frederic B. Pratt, Brooklyn
Frederic B. Pratt, Brooklyn, 1909
Cottier & Co., New York, by 1909

19.
GUSTAVE COURBET
La Vague, c. 1869
Oil on canvas
29½ x 34¾ in.
Signed l.l.; *G. Courbet*
The Brooklyn Museum, Brooklyn, New York,
Gift of Mrs. H. O. Havemeyer
Provenance: H. O. Havemeyer Collection, New York
Durand-Ruel, Paris
Jean Dollfus Collection, Paris, 1912
Emil Monteaux Collection, Paris, 1884

The inclusion of seven paintings by Gustave Courbet in the 1883 *Pedestal Fund Art Loan Exhibition* was potentially the most confrontational decision made by the selections committee. In the years following Courbet's death, American critics remained wary of "the great revolutionist,"[1] describing him as an artist who "prided himself upon being the head of the realistic school in France, and who preferred ugliness to beauty, because his nature was coarse and unrefined and soulless."[2] Mention of his name only rarely failed to evoke memories of the role he was believed to have played in the destruction of the Place Vendôme column in 1871 or the political exile that followed it.[3] In Boston, where such paintings as *The Quarry* had been made available to the public by the enlightened art lovers of the Allston Club as early as 1866,[4] Courbet's "great sympathy with animals" was acknowledged but he was criticized for "faulty drawing and inexplicable perspective."[5] Appraisal of *Les Demoiselles de village,* owned by Thomas Wigglesworth of Boston,[6] was similarly ambivalent, recognizing Courbet's "supremacy of technical strength, which knows how to represent air and light and the solidity of objects as these things are only represented by the masters of art,"[7] but at the same time deploring his faults of taste.

In the early 1880s the majority of works by Courbet in American private collections were located outside New York, predominantly in New England, but also in Philadelphia and Cincinnati. Although New Yorkers seemed less interested in acquiring his paintings, they had opportunites to view them in the galleries of Cottier & Co. and Moore & Clarke Co., dealers who also encouraged the work of young American artists. Among the lenders to the Pedestal Fund exhibition, Daniel Cottier (who later owned a painting similar to *The Source of the Loue* [cat. no. 17]) sent *The Cave,*[8] and Moore & Clarke loaned paintings entitled *Ocean*[9] and *The Valley.*[10] William

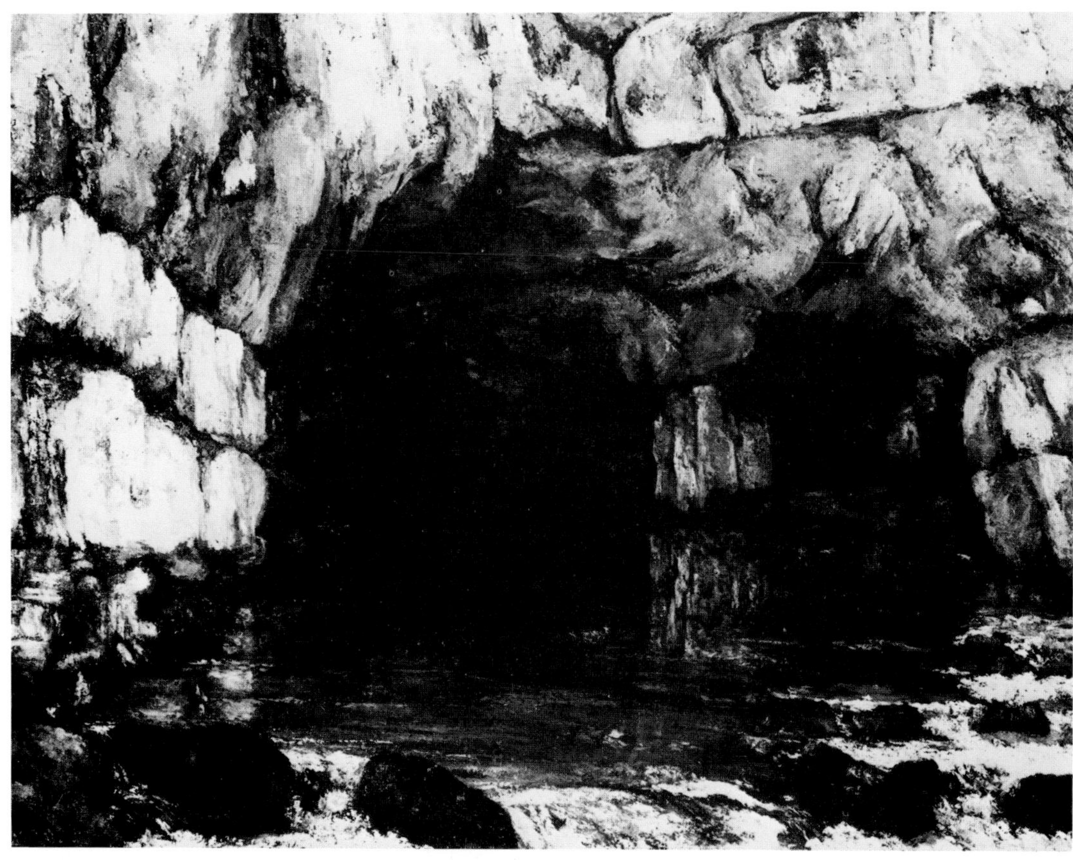

17.

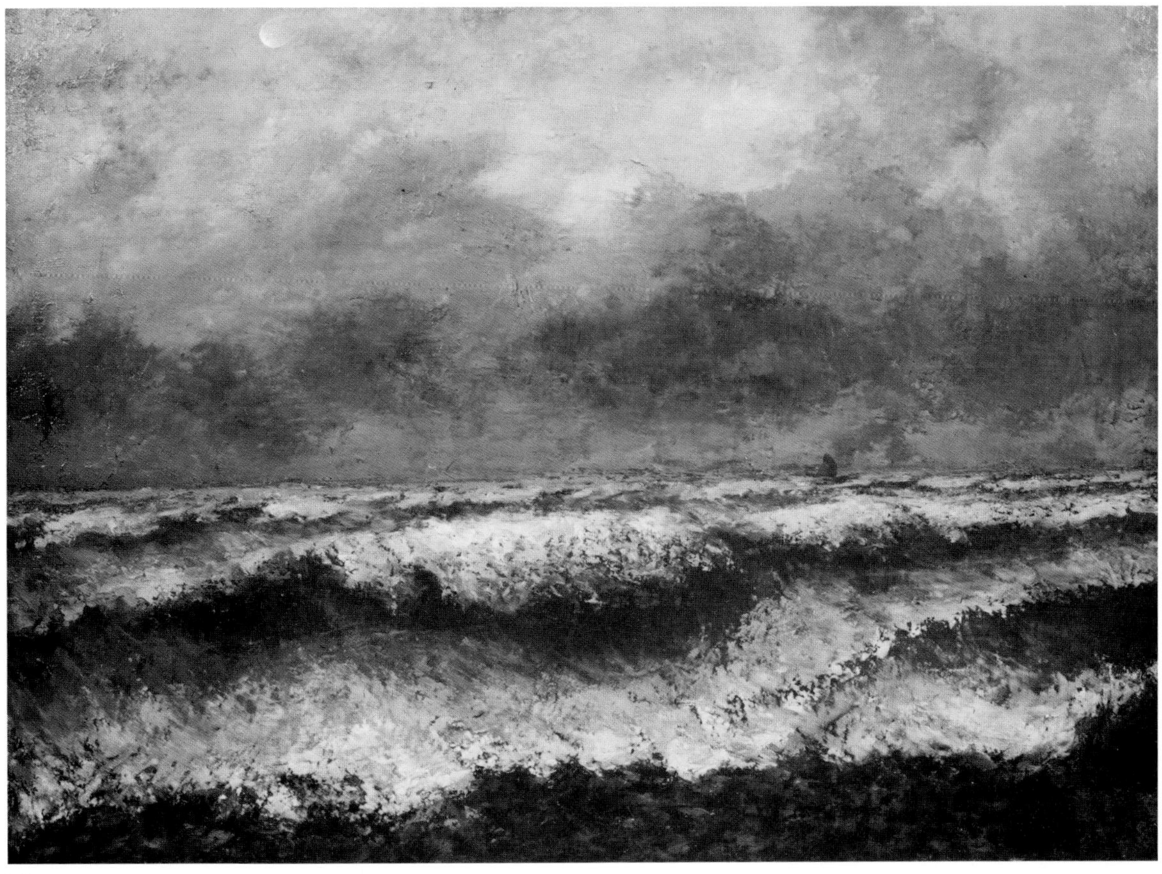

18.

T. Evans, a collector with a growing interest in contemporary American art, loaned *A Mountain Gorge,*[11] and, not surprisingly, Erwin Davis, whose two Manets were the center of critical attention, sent three Courbets: *Landscape, Music,* and *The Wave.*[12]

Although one reviewer charged the organizers with jeopardizing the financial success of the exhibition by showing so many paintings by this artist, one "whose rough brush sends a cold chill down the average American's back,"[13] another considered it a privilege to see so many Courbets—"and such magnificent ones"—in New York.[14] This view was seconded by critic Mariana Griswold Van Rensselaer, who vigorously supported Courbet in a letter to *The Century Magazine* in 1885. Recalling the impact of the Pedestal Fund show, Mrs. Van Rensselaer chided reviewers who failed to see the true painter's touch in his work. "Who but he," she queried, "has ever shown with such strong, and I must submit, poetic sympathy the majesty of the tumbling surf and overarching heaven, the beauty of the deep-green, wet, and rocky woodland glades that were Courbet's peculiar province?"[15] The selection was in fact dominated by such works, including landscapes depicting a hillside cave, a mountain brook, a view of sandstone cliffs in the Jura Mountains, and a valley scene, perhaps near Ornans. Even more accessible to viewers who found no inspiration in Courbet's realism were the two seascapes, the Davis *Wave,* apparently a singular image like *La Vague* (cat. no. 19), and the Moore & Clarke *Ocean,* a broader view similar to *Marine* (cat. no. 18). The most distinctive choice was *The Violoncellist* (cat. no. 16), a portrait of the artist as a young man playing the cello, acquired for Erwin Davis by Julian Alden Weir in 1881. A painting of the same subject was apparently submitted to the Salon of 1847, although it was not accepted until the Salon of the following year. At that time considered worthy of comparison to the paintings of Velásquez and Murillo by realist critic Champfleury,[16] *The Violoncellist* was one of a number of paintings by Courbet that exist in more than one version (see fig. 30, p. 36, *Le Violoncelliste,* Nationalmuseum, Stockholm, Sweden). As is still evident, Davis's painting, like such works as *The Quarry,* was composed of several canvases sewn together, apparently for the purpose of altering the composition by adding (or subtracting) a musical score. In the company of Théodule Ribot's *Guitarist* and several Rembrandtesque works by Louis Mettling and Antoine Vollon, the strong realist portrait succeeded in deflecting from Courbet the adverse critical reactions that were reserved at the Pedestal Fund exhibition for the paintings of Edouard Manet and Edgar Degas.

1. Strahan III, p. 84.
2. Charles Henry Hart, "The Collection of Mr. Henry C. Gibson of Philadelphia," *American Art Review,* vol. 1, part 2 (1880), p. 299. Hart reproduces, p. 299, an etching by Henri Lefort of Courbet's *Great Oak Tree of Ornans,* then owned by Gibson (now in The Pennsylvania Academy of the Fine Arts, Philadelphia).
3. See, for example, Hart, p. 299; Champlin and Perkins III, p. 341; Titus Munson Coan, "Gustave Courbet: Artist and Communist," *The Century Magazine,* vol. 27, no. 4 (February 1884), pp. 483–95.
4. *The Quarry,* 1857, 83 x 71 in., Museum of Fine Arts, Boston, was brought to America in 1866 by the French dealer Cadart and purchased by the Allston Club, a group of young artists that included William Morris Hunt. By 1873 the painting was in the collection of Henry Sayles of Boston, and, according to Strahan III, p. 87, was on loan to the Museum of Fine Arts, Boston, in the early 1880s. Strahan called the painting "the 'last word' of broad realism."
5. Coan, p. 487.
6. *Les Demoiselles de village,* 1851, 76¾ x 102¾ in., The Metropolitan Museum of Art, New York, was reproduced in Strahan III, p. 84, by a drawing in which the composition is reversed. Strahan's generally positive judgment of the painting was balanced by a suggestion that "Courbet might have better established the difference in condition between the country 'frumps' who give alms and the beggar-girl who receives them."
7. *Ibid.*
8. Cottier Sale, Paris, 1892, lot 30, *La Caverne,* 1861, 53 x 39¼ in., sold to van Wisselingh.
9. Moore & Clarke Co. Sale, 1884, lot 87, *Ocean,* 20 x 29 in.
10. *Ibid.,* possibly lot 105, *Landscape,* 20 x 36 in.
11. Evans Sale, 1890, lot 82, *The Mountain Brook,* 19¾ x 28¼ in.
12. Davis Sale, 1889, probably lot 61, *In the Jura Mountains,* 33½ x 44 in.; lot 135, *Music,* 44 x 35 in.; and lot 100, *Marine,* 22 x 35 in.
13. "The Pedestal Art Loan," *The New York Times,* December 16, 1883, p. 5.
14. "The Pedestal Art Loan," *The New York Times,* December 2, 1883, p. 2.
15. Mariana G. Van Rensselaer, "Courbet, the Artist," *The Century Magazine,* vol. 29, no. 5 (March 1885), pp. 792–94.
16. Champfleury, *Le Pamphlet,* September 28–30, 1848, reprinted in Genevieve and Jean Lacambre, *Champfleury, le Réalisme* (Paris, 1973), pp. 153–54.

20.

THOMAS COUTURE (French, 1815–1879)
Self-Portrait, c. 1848
Oil on canvas
18¼ x 15 in.
Memorial Art Gallery of the University of Rochester, Rochester, New York,
Marion Stratton Gould Fund
Provenance: Vose Galleries, Boston

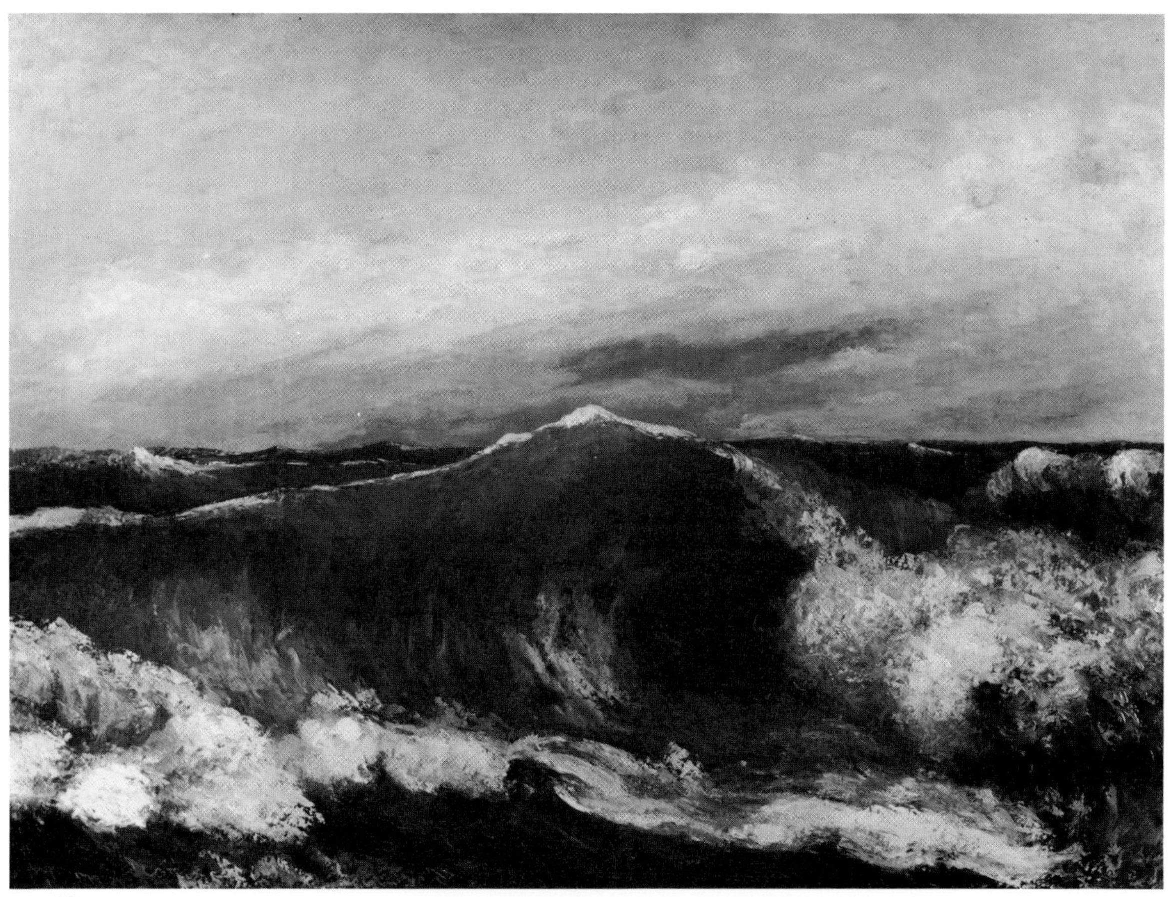

19.

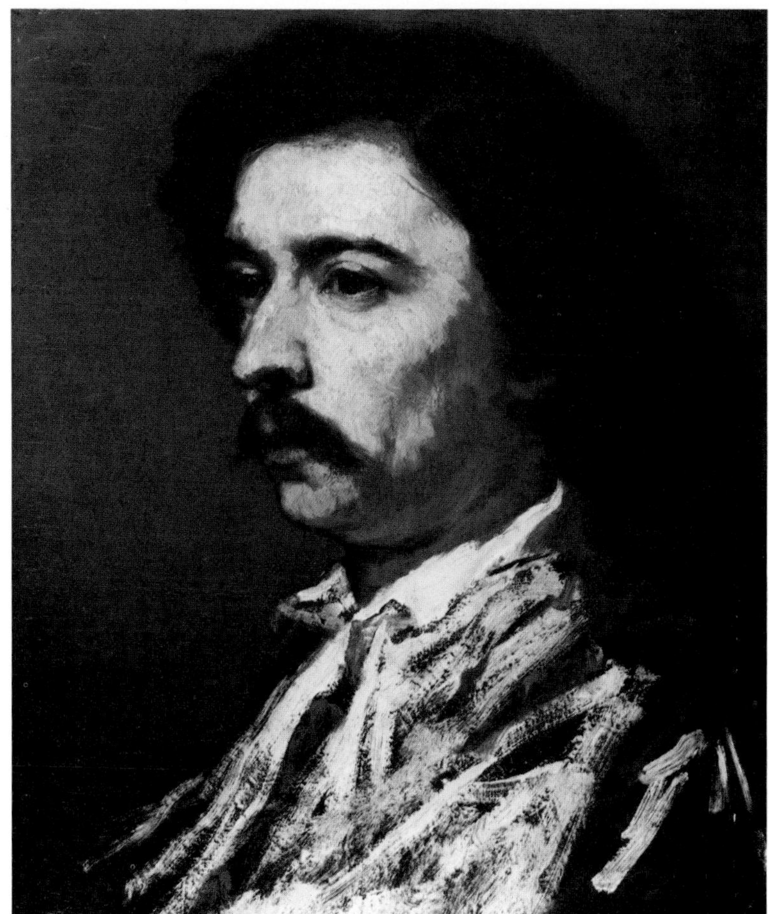

20.

21.
THOMAS COUTURE
The Courtesan's Chariot, or Love Leading the World, c. 1874–76
Oil on canvas
59⅛ x 83⅞ in.
Collection Stuart Pivar, New York
Provenance: Daniel W. Powers, Rochester, New York, 1899
Blakeslee and Co., New York, 1893
PLATE X

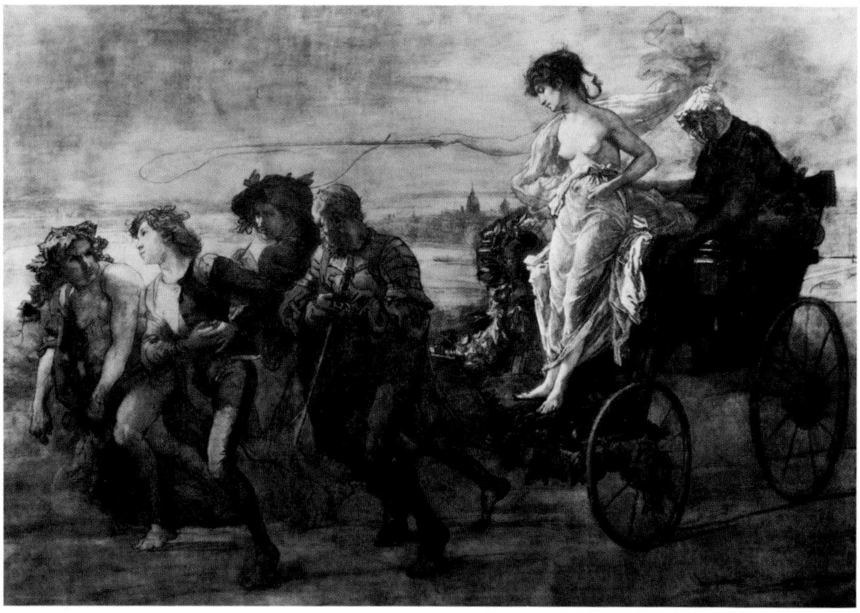

Two small works represented Thomas Couture in the *Pedestal Fund Art Loan Exhibition*: *Head* (possibly the *Self-Portrait,* cat. no. 20), from the Erwin Davis collection,[1] and a *Sketch for the Courtesan* loaned by Richard Morris Hunt, the architect of the pedestal for the Statue of Liberty. Couture's renown in America was closely linked to the Hunt family, as his most important American student had been the architect's brother, the painter William Morris Hunt.[2] Upon his return to Boston after studying with Couture in the late 1840s, William Morris Hunt had promulgated his master's methods in his own teachings by stressing the organization of a composition as an arrangement of darks and lights, and by dispelling the rigid academic distinctions between color and drawing.

By 1883 a number of important paintings by Couture were owned by Americans,[3] including *The Thorny Path* (1873), the *chef d'oeuvre* of the collection of Henry C. Gibson of Philadelphia.[4] The satiric theme of the courtesan Love enslaving Youth, Riches, Courage, and Poetry was one that had preoccupied Couture for several years.[5] In addition to Gibson's highly resolved picture, Couture had also made *The Courtesan's Chariot, or Love Leading the World* (cat. no. 21), a looser, more painterly version in which the thorny vegetation and a central figure of Priapus were excluded. This painting was also in America by the late nineteenth century and was described in the catalogue of the 1899 sale of the collection of Daniel W. Powers of Rochester, New York, as a "splendid cartoon."[6]

In spite of the relatively broad selection of Couture's works available in New York at the time of the Pedestal Fund show, the organizers included a sketch for the *Courtesan* rather than a finished painting. The choice was no doubt intentional, as it reflected the impact of the brilliant exhibition of Couture's "sketches, studies, and first impressions" that was held in Paris in September 1880,[7] and also challenged the appreciation of American collectors who admired Couture's imagery but were still unsure of their judgment when confronted with the "fascinating imperfections" of his technique.[8]

1. *Self-Portrait* was included in the Davis Sale, 1889, lot 94, *Portrait of the Artist,* 18 x 14 in., and was also cited in Strahan III, p. 123.
2. See Landgren 1970. The American painter G. P. A. Healy and Couture were students of Baron Gros in the 1830s: see George P. A. Healy, "Thomas Couture," *The Century Magazine,* vol. 44, no. 1 (May 1892), pp. 4–13.
3. Strahan III, p. 133, lists twenty-one works by Couture in American collections by 1882, at least nine of them in New York.
4. See *Le Triomphe d'une femme équivoque* (illustrated by a drawing by James D. Smillie after a photograph), in "The Collection of Mr. Henry C. Gibson of Philadelphia," *American Art Review,* vol. 1, part 1 (1880), p. 233; and republished in Montgomery 1889, p. 113. Illustrated as *The Thorny Path* in an engraving by Faust "after the original painting by Couture" in Strahan I, p. 65.
5. See Albert Boime, *Thomas Couture and the Eclectic Vision* (New Haven: Yale University Press, 1980), pp. 363–70, for a discussion of the major versions of this painting.
6. Powers Sale, 1899, lot 273, Couture, *Love Drives the World,* "From the T. J. Blakeslee Collection" (see Blakeslee Sale, 1893, lot 70, Couture, *Love Drives the World*).
7. See *Catalogue des oeuvres de Th. Couture exposées au Palais de l'Industrie* (Paris, September 1880); this exhibition included several *esquisses* and *études* for *La Courtisane moderne,* as well as a *tableau inachevé* (no. 111) of this subject from the collection of M. Barbedienne.
8. Evidence of this attitude appears in the article by Henry C. Angell, "Thomas Couture," *American Art Review,* vol. 2, part 2 (October 1881), in which the 1880 exhibition is discussed. Angell found "no artistic quality in either of the three sketches [of *La Courtisane moderne*] creditable to one of Couture's ability."

22.
PASCAL ADOLPHE JEAN DAGNAN-BOUVERET (French, 1852–1929)
Hamlet and the Gravedigger, 1883
Oil on canvas
40 x 33½ in.
Signed and dated l.l.: *P. A. J. Dagnan-B 1883*
Collection Julian Hartnoll, London
Provenance: The Metropolitan Museum of Art, New York
George F. Baker, New York, 1924
Jean-Léon Gérôme, Paris

Hamlet and the Gravedigger, a theme that was twice treated by Eugène Delacroix, was painted by Dagnan-Bouveret in 1883 for his master Jean-Léon Gérôme.[1] Although in his early career drawn to literary subjects such as *Hamlet* and *The Death of Manon Lescaut* (1878), winning the admiration of American students upon the exhibition of the latter,[2] Dagnan found his *métier* in scenes that demonstrated careful and sympathetic observation of regional customs in the Franche-Comté and Brittany. His reputation in America, which was only beginning to grow when a reviewer of the Pedestal Fund show referred to him as one of the "rising young masters of France,"[3] had been assisted by favorable comments about his 1880 Salon prizewinner *L'Accident,* a painting that described the visit of a country doctor to the home of a wounded child.[4] In the early 1880s, his paintings were relatively scarce in America, appearing in the collections of Levi P. Morton of New York, William T. Walters of Baltimore, E. B. Warren of Philadelphia, and—not surprisingly—Erwin Davis, the collector who had purchased an important work by Dagnan's close friend, Jules Bastien-Lepage.[5] During the next ten years, however, both his realist genre subjects and his portraits found expanded patronage abroad.[6] Honored throughout the 1880s and 1890s for the Brittany peasant subjects he sent to international exhibitions, Dagnan was made a member of the Institute of France in 1900. His popularity in America reached a peak the following year when he was honored by a special exhibition at The Art Institute of Chicago.[7]

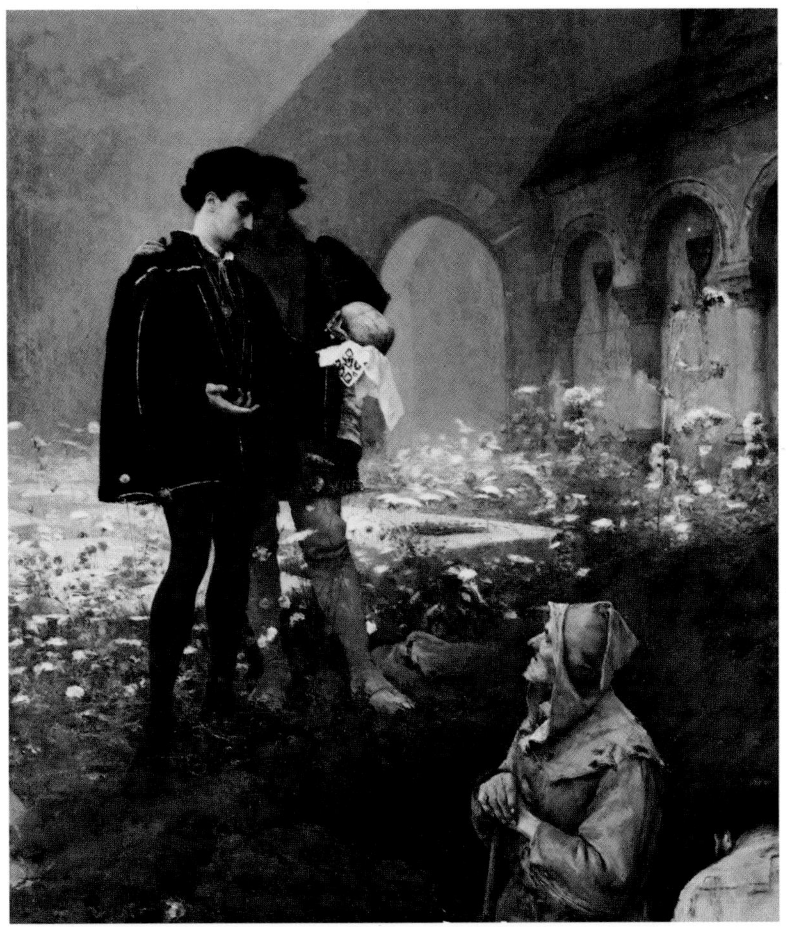

22.

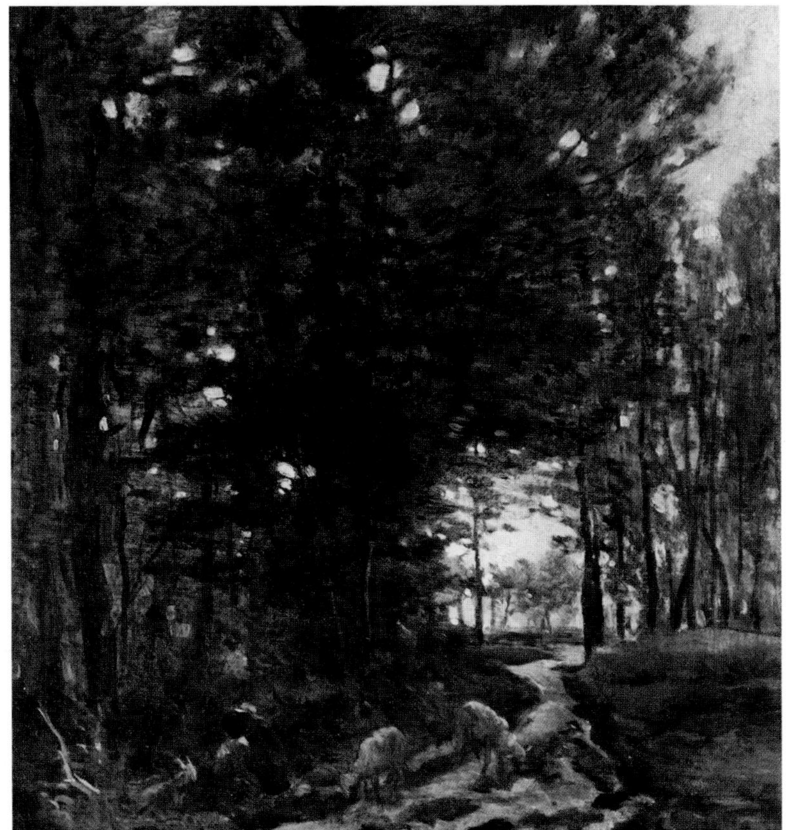

23.

1. Sterling and Salinger II, p. 219. The catalogue entry for this painting, which in 1966 was in the collection of The Metropolitan Museum of Art, notes that it had been erroneously dated 1884 in both Champlin and Perkins I, p. 363, and the *Catalogue des oeuvres de Dagnan-Bouveret* (Paris: Institut de France, 1930). William A. Coffin, "Dagnan-Bouveret," *The Century Magazine*, vol. 48, no. 1 (May 1894), p. 10, n. 1, also dates the painting 1884.
2. Coffin, p. 4, recalled that his introduction to Dagnan-Bouveret's work came after a group of students at the studio of Léon Bonnat returned from the 1878 Salon with news of the success of *Manon Lescaut*.
3. "The Pedestal Art Loan," *The New York Times*, December 16, 1883, p. 5.
4. *An Accident*, 1879, 35⅝ x 58⅛ in., Walters Art Gallery, Baltimore. The painting was noted by correspondent Lucy H. Hooper in "Art-notes from Paris," *The Art Journal*, n.s. 6 (1880), p. 253. *The New York Times* reviewer (n. 3) indicates familiarity with the painting, then in Walters's collection, by calling Dagnan-Bouveret "the painter of 'L'Accident.'"
5. Morton, the U.S. Minister to France, owned the *Manon Lescaut* but sold it at auction in New York on March 1, 1882; illustrated in Strahan III, p. 122, Strahan noted (p. 120) that it had been "bought to go back to France." Warren owned a *Lovers' Quarrel* of 1880. Davis's picture, loaned to the *Pedestal Fund Art Loan Exhibition* as *Child with Vase*, may have been the *Petit Bacchus à la coupe* in the Salon of 1877 (probably the *Infant Bacchus*, 1877, in Champlin and Perkins I, p. 363). As noted elsewhere, Davis was also the owner of Jules Bastien-Lepage's *Joan of Arc*, 1879; The Metropolitan Museum of Art, New York.
6. By 1894 his paintings were also in the collections of T. S. Clarke of Pittsburgh, John G. Johnson of Philadelphia, Potter Palmer of Chicago, and George F. Baker of New York, who purchased *Hamlet and the Gravedigger* at a later date (see Coffin, p. 10, n. 1). Dagnan-Bouveret's American portrait subjects included Mrs. George Baker and Childs Frick.
7. See *Dagnan-Bouveret, Exhibition of Works*, The Art Institute of Chicago, March 1–24, 1901.

23.
CHARLES-FRANCOIS DAUBIGNY

(French, 1817–1878)
Woodland Scene, 1851
Oil on canvas
26 x 24⅜ in.
Signed and dated l.r.: *Daubigny 1851*
Bowdoin College Museum of Art,
Brunswick, Maine
Provenance: Alexander Standish, 1941
Myles Standish

24.
CHARLES-FRANCOIS DAUBIGNY

Mills at Dordrecht, 1872
Oil on canvas
33½ x 57½ in.
Signed and dated l.l.: *Daubigny 1872*
Detroit Institute of Arts,
Gift of Mr. and Mrs. E. Raymond Field
Provenance: E. Raymond Field, Detroit
James Warren Lane
Charles T. Yerkes, New York

By the early 1880s, Charles-François Daubigny was one of the most admired of the Barbizon artists known in America and was represented by landscapes and river scenes in at least two dozen collections throughout the Northeast.[1] According to Dwight William Tryon, who met the artist in 1877, Daubigny was surprised by the extent of his fame abroad, although he had been aware that at least one of his paintings was owned in Boston.[2]

Woodland Scene and *Mills at Dordrecht* represent types of paintings owned by the New York dealer Daniel Cottier, who loaned two of the six works by Daubigny in the *Pedestal Fund Art Loan Exhibition*.[3] Both Charles A. Dana and Erwin Davis loaned river scenes inspired by the countless trips on the Seine and Oise[4] made by Daubigny on his legendary *Botin*, and the selection also included *The Cooper* (fig. 22, p. 33), which had been exhibited in the Salon of 1872 and also in the 1878 *Exposition Universelle* prior to its purchase by dealer William Schaus.[5]

Following the death of Daubigny in 1878, American critics cautioned that the demand for his paintings would encourage high prices even for works of inferior quality,[6] but he continued to be revered by younger artists for his breadth of treatment and direct observation of nature.

1. Strahan III, p. 134, names more than three dozen paintings by Daubigny in American collections between 1879 and 1882.
2. Dwight W. Tryon, "Charles-François Daubigny," in Van Dyke 1896, p. 156. According to Peter Bermingham in *American Art in the Barbizon Mood* (Washington, D.C.: Smithsonian Institution Press, published for the National Collection of Fine Arts, 1975), p. 44, Seth M. Vose was selling Daubigny's paintings in Providence, Rhode Island, as early as 1857; see also p. 104, n. 11: "From the cover of *French Masters of 1830*, catalogue of an exhibition held at R. C. and N. M. Vose Galleries, Boston, 1908."
3. Cottier loaned *Dort on the Maas*, possibly the painting in the Inglis Sale, 1909, *On the River below Dordrecht*, lot 96, sold to J. R. Wilson; Hellebranth 741. His second loan was simply titled *Landscape* and may have been the large painting he hung in a place of honor at an 1877 exhibition at his New York gallery (see "The Fine Arts," *The New York Times*, March 1, 1877, p. 4). *Woodland Scene* was also owned by Cottier and included in the Cottier Sale, Paris, 1892, lot 47, *La Bergère;* Hellebranth 900: *La Bergère sous bois*.
4. Dana's loan, *On the Seine*, was probably Dana Sale, 1898, lot 589, *On the River Oise*, 15 x 26 in., sold to Isidor Wormser, Jr., and also exhibited at the *Barye Monument Exhibition*, 1889–90, no. 615, *Sunset*.
5. *Le Tonnelier (The Cooper)* was later sold by Schaus to Mary Jane Morgan of New York, and it was included in the Mary Jane Morgan Sale, 1886, lot 160, *A Cooper's Shop*. According to French critic Paul Mantz, who reviewed the picture in "Le Salon de 1872," *Gazette des Beaux-Arts*, vol. 6, per. 2 (July 1872), p. 43, it was a painting "d'une tonalité puissante et d'une exécution magistrale."
6. Tryon, p. 164, observed that Daubigny was sometimes too easily satisfied with incomplete sketches that were "readily enough yielded up to dealers, who were only too glad to get them at small prices." Cook II, p. 222, said that "Daubigny painted too much for his fame . . . and with him, as with many a man of inferior talent, the buyer must be bid beware."

25.
HILAIRE GERMAIN EDGAR DEGAS

(French, 1834–1917)
Rehearsal before the Ballet, c. 1877
Oil on canvas
20 x 24¼ in.
Signed l.l.: *Degas*
Museum of Fine Arts, Springfield,
Massachusetts,
The James Philip Gray Collection
Provenance: Dr. Theodore Schempp, 1941
Alexander Reid, Glasgow

Rehearsal before the Ballet, a painting that is typical of the works shown by Edgar Degas in Paris at the Impressionist exhibitions of the 1870s, represents in both theme and treatment the "repulsively real ballet girls magnificently brushed in"[1] that attracted interest and scorn at the *Pedestal Fund Art Loan Exhibition*. Its brilliant counterpart, *Ballet Dancers* (pl. XI; Hill-Stead Museum, Farmington, Connecticut) was loaned to the exhibition by Erwin Davis, the New York collector whose two paintings by Manet, *Boy with a Sword* (cat. no. 47; pl. XVII) and *Woman with a Parrot* (pl. XVIII), shared with the Degas the distinction of being hung on the south wall of the paintings gallery at the National Academy of Design. Prominence of placement helped draw viewers to *Ballet Dancers*, but its high-keyed, complementary-hued palette, composed of "exquisite symphonies of arsenic green and raspberry pink,"[2] could not have failed to stand out among the landscapes of the Barbizon and Hague schools and the darker realist figures that dominated the show.

Two line drawings of *Ballet Dancers*, a charming but simplified version by Robert Blum in the exhibition catalogue (fig. 7, p. 25) and a cursory, unflattering vignette by a staff artist for the New York *Daily Graphic* (fig. 5, p. 77), reinforced the notoriety of the painting from the points of view of both advocates and detractors. Critics were confused by Degas's skewed and flattened composition and offended by his choice of subject matter (what they considered to be an inelegant behind-the-scenes view of dancers at the Paris Opera, removed from the mitigating fantasy of the spectacle). This apparent flaw in taste, a criticism frequently leveled at the Impressionists, was interpreted, at best, as an artist's attempt to "pluck beauty from the heart of ugliness."[3] At the same time, several reviewers were admittedly fascinated by Degas's technique—a confident but stenographic draftsmanship underpinning a dis-

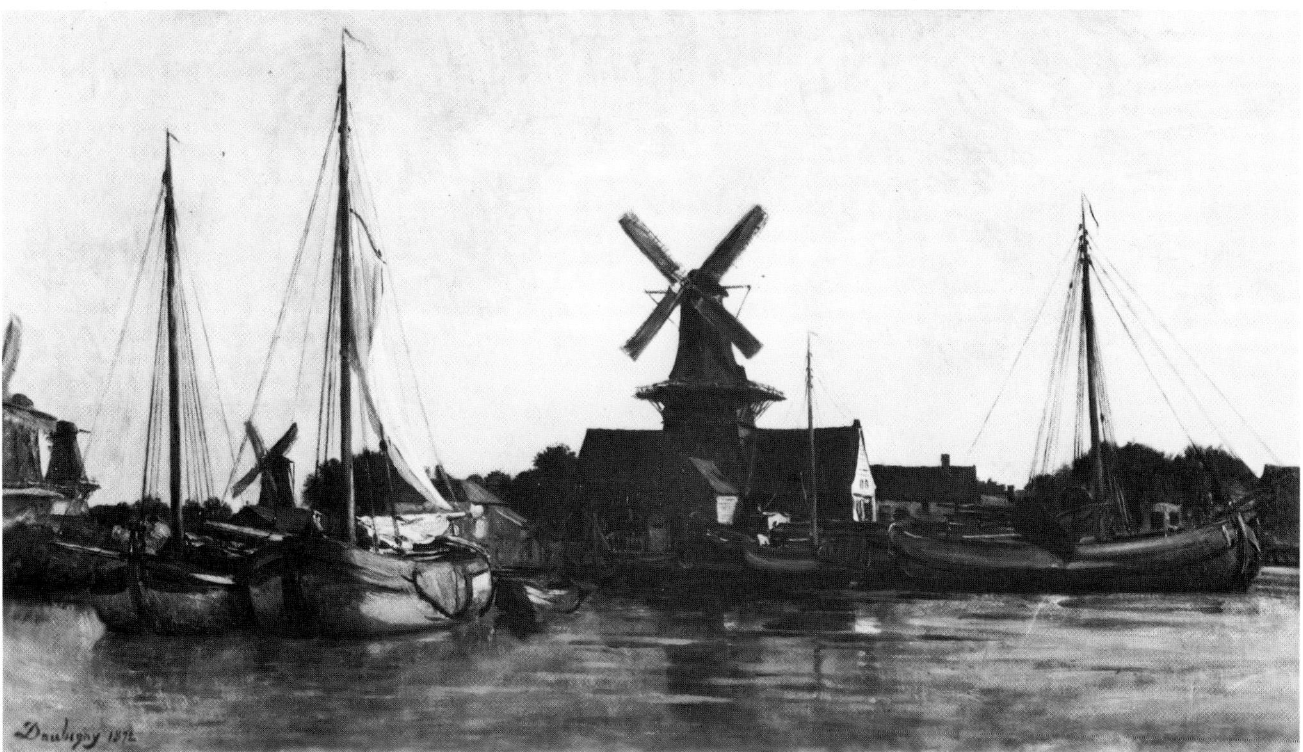

24.

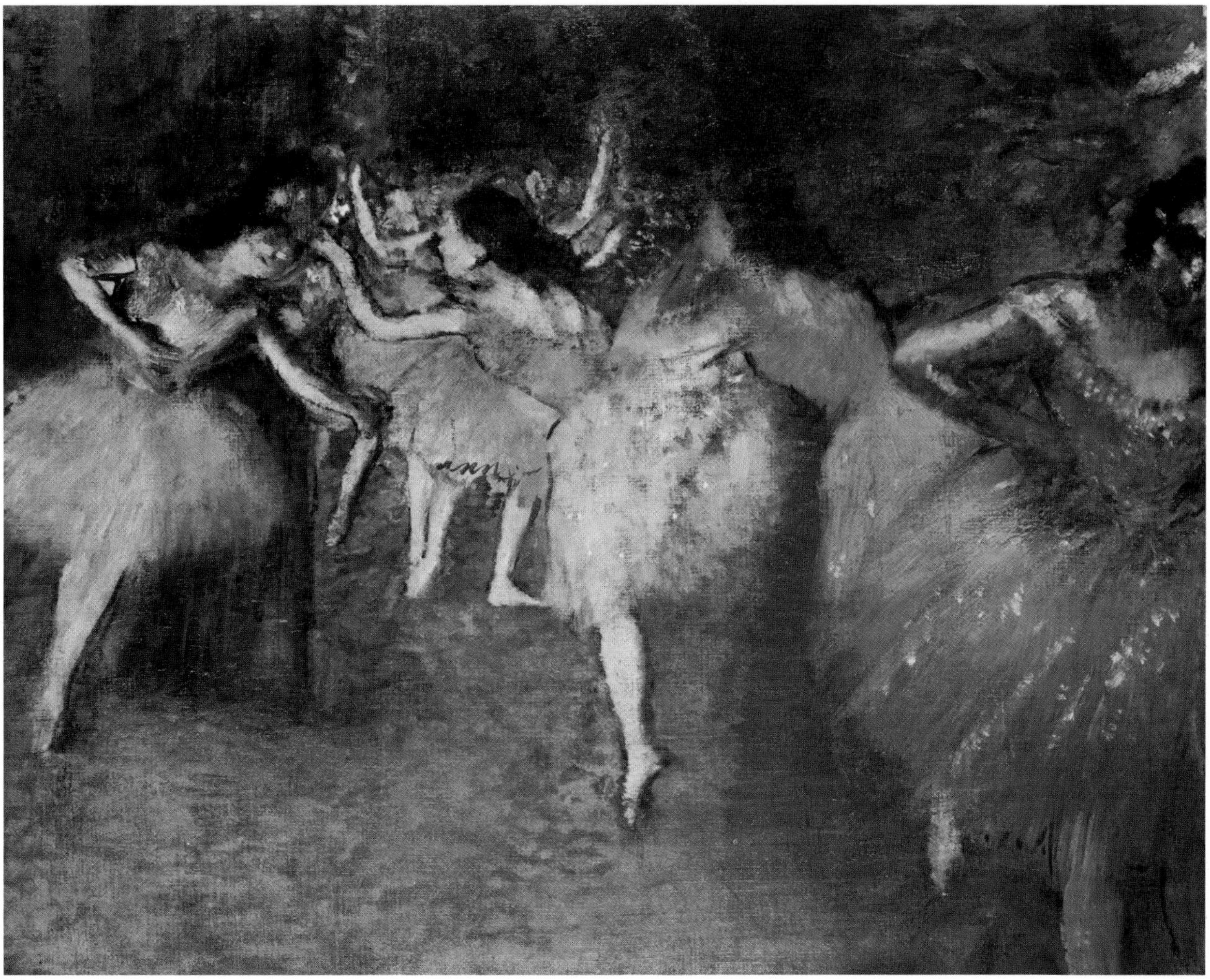

25.

solution of form that "must be seen from a distance to be appreciated."[4]

Although Degas was the one member of the Impressionist circle to have visited and painted, however briefly, in the United States,[5] he had not been included in the Foreign Exhibition held at Mechanics Hall, Boston, in September 1883,[6] and his work was virtually unknown outside a small artistic circle at the time of the Pedestal Fund show. It was not until 1886, when *Ballet Dancers* was again exhibited in New York along with twenty-two other paintings by Degas at Durand-Ruel's special exhibition of "the Impressionists of Paris," that American critics would have an opportunity to study and adequately assess the paintings of this revolutionary artist.[7]

1. "The Pedestal Art Loan," *The New York Times*, December 2, 1883, p. 2.
2. Kenyon Cox, "The Collection of Mr. Alfred Atmore Pope," in La Farge and Jacacci 1907, p. 281. Although written a number of years after the Pedestal Fund show, Cox's description of Degas's palette echoes the strident impression made on viewers in 1883.
3. *Ibid.* Critic John C. Van Dyke, in "The Bartholdi Loan Collection," *The Studio*, vol. 2, no. 49 (December 8, 1883), pp. 262–63, commented that "it is strange how often in walking around the room the eye will wander back to study the repulsiveness and admire the ugliness ...[of *Ballet Dancers*]." Mariana Griswold Van Rensselaer, in "The Recent New York Loan Exhibition," *American Architect and Building News*, vol. 15, no. 421 (January 19, 1884), pp. 29–30, called the painting a "superb bit of brushwork" but found the paintings by Manet and Degas "frankly ugly in subject matter and arrangement."
4. Van Dyke 1883, pp. 262–63.
5. With his brother René, Degas departed Liverpool for New York in October of 1872, en route to New Orleans. He remained with relatives there until mid-February 1873, when he returned to France. A painting of the cotton office of the artist's uncle, Michael Musson, in New Orleans, 1873 (Musée Municipale, Pau, France), is probably the best known of the works executed during or inspired by this visit. See John Rewald et al., *Edgar Degas, His Family and Friends in New Orleans* (New Orleans: Isaac Delgado Museum, 1965).
6. The Boston exhibition, which is discussed in Hans Huth, "Impressionism Comes to America," *Gazette des Beaux-Arts*, vol. 29, per. 6 (April 1946), pp. 225–52, included among its paintings seventeen by Manet, Monet, Pissarro, Renoir, and Sisley (see O'Brien, n.6).
7. See New York, National Academy of Design, *Special Exhibition: Works in Oil and Pastel by the Impressionists of Paris*, 1886. The exhibition opened at the galleries of the American Art Association on April 10, 1886; it was later moved to the National Academy of Design, where it reopened on May 25, 1886. In its second phase it included a number of loans from American collectors. In addition to *Ballet Dancers* from the collection of Erwin Davis, the Degas loans inlcuded *Repetition of the Dance* from the collection of A. J. Cassatt, Esq., and *Behind the Scenes* from an unidentified private collection.

26.
EUGENE DELACROIX (French, 1798–1863)
Le Christ au tombeau, c. 1847–49
Oil on canvas
22⅛ x 18¾ in.
Phoenix Art Museum, Phoenix, Arizona, Gift of Mr. Henry R. Luce

Provenance: Henry R. Luce, New York
M. Knoedler & Co., Inc., New York
William H. Taylor, West Chester, Pennsylvania, 1937
Stephen C. Clark, New York
Alfred C. Clark, New York, 1888
Albert Spencer, New York, by 1883
M. Edwards, Paris, 1881
Laurent-Richard, Paris, 1873
Adolphe Moreau, Paris, 1849

Exhibited at the 1883 *Pedestal Fund Art Loan Exhibition*, no. 51, *Descent from the Cross*, loaned by Albert Spencer

PLATE XII

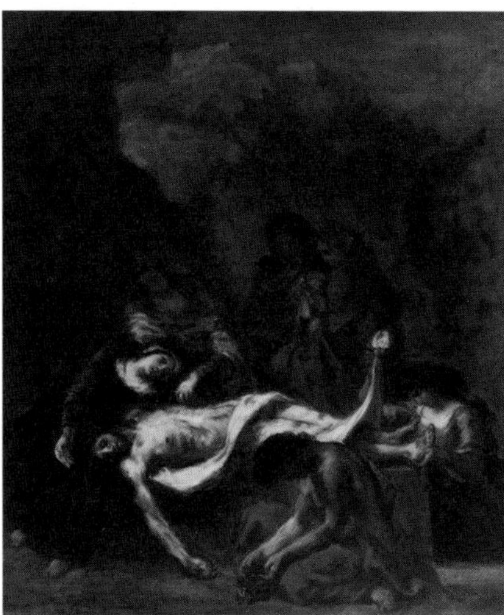

Le Christ au tombeau, "a very rich biblical scene,"[1] was included in the *Pedestal Fund Art Loan Exhibition* as an indication of Delacroix's importance for European-trained American artists who were struggling at home against a taste that preferred the classicism and linearity of Bouguereau and Gérôme. Edward Strahan described Delacroix as "the Mohammed of Romance" in *The Art Treasures of America* (1879–82), but acknowledged that he was an artist whose work was rarely seen in the salons of the United States.[2] Only a handful of Delacroix's paintings were named in Strahan's analysis of contemporary American collections: five in Philadelphia, including *The Lion Hunt*, owned by the widow of the late Secretary of the Navy, A. E. Borie, and three others in collections in Cincinnati, Boston, and Providence. Overlooked by Strahan, *Le Christ au tombeau* had been acquired in Paris by New Yorker Albert Spencer in 1881. The French journalist E. Durand-Gréville, who otherwise relied heavily on Strahan's recommendations when visiting private collections in America in the 1880s, sought out the Delacroix in Spencer's collection and characterized it for his readers as "a moving study."[3] In 1888 the painting was sold to Alfred Corning Clark for $10,600, one of the highest prices brought at the internationally publicized Spencer Sale;[4] it again came before the public eye the following year at the *Barye Monument Exhibition* in New York.[5]

1. "The Pedestal Art Loan," *The New York Times*, December 2, 1883, p. 2.
2. Strahan II, pp. 15–16.
3. E. Durand-Gréville, "La Peinture aux Etats-Unis," *Gazette des Beaux-Arts*, vol. 36, per. 2 (July 1887), p. 73. He calls the painting a "*Pietà* de Delacroix," and describes it as "analogue, non identique à la *Pietà* de la vente Beurnonville." The painting to which it is compared is now in the collection of the Museum of Fine Arts, Boston. In another article ("Correspondance d'Amérique: Le Commerce des tableaux et la vente Morgan," *Gazette des Beaux-Arts*, vol. 33, per. 2 [June 1886], p. 448), Durand-Gréville also took note of three works by Delacroix in the Mary Jane Morgan Sale, 1886. Four paintings by Delacroix were included in the sale of the collections of Beriah Wall and John A. Brown of Providence (New York, American Art Galleries, March 30–31 and April 1, 1886).
4. "A Big Sum for Paintings," *The New York Times*, February 29, 1888, p. 2. The sale of *Le Christ au tombeau* was also recorded by Walter Rowlands, "Art Sales in America," *The Art Journal* (London), vol. 50, no. 40 n.s. (1888), p. 318: "Delacroix's 'Christ at the Tomb,' from the Laurent-Richard Sale, for £2,210"; and noted in "Vom Kunstmarkt," *Kunst-Chronik (Beiblatt)* 1888, p. 454: "...'Christus im Grabe' von Delacroix erreichte den Preis von 53,000 Frs." Alfred Corning Clark also bought a second Delacroix from the Spencer Sale, 1888, *A Tiger Quenching His Thirst*, 15 x 10 in., $6,100.
5. *Barye Monument Exhibition*, 1889–90, no. 591, *Christ at the Tomb*, loaned by Alfred C. Clark, Esq.

27.
EDOUARD DETAILLE (French, 1848–1912)
Alerte!, 1880
Oil on canvas
26 x 22 in.
Signed and dated l.l.: *Edouard Detaille 1880*
The FORBES Magazine Collection, New York

Provenance: Fine Art Society, London
Anon. Sale, Guillaume Campo, Antwerp, Belgium, 1971
Goupil & Cie, Paris

Alerte!, like *Salut aux blessés* (fig. 19, p. 32), the painting that represented Edouard Detaille at the *Pedestal Fund Art Loan Exhibition*, is a scene of military life during the Franco-Prussian War.[1] Several dozen of the young French artist's military subjects were owned by Americans in 1883, closely rivaling the popularity of the work of his master, Ernest Meissonier.[2] Although the hanging committee of the Pedestal Fund show installed Detaille's painting beneath the staircase at

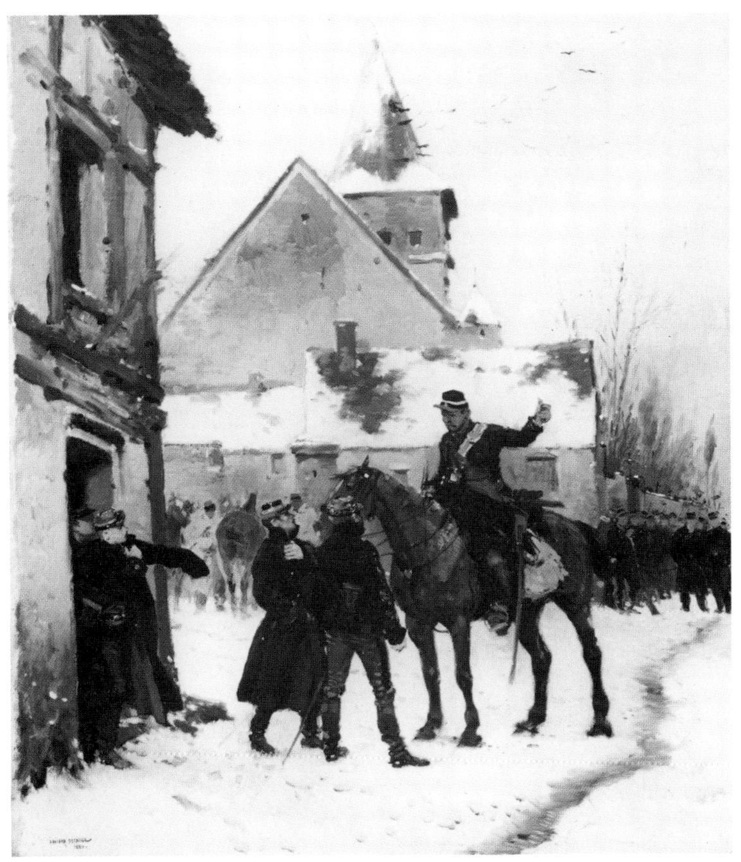
27.

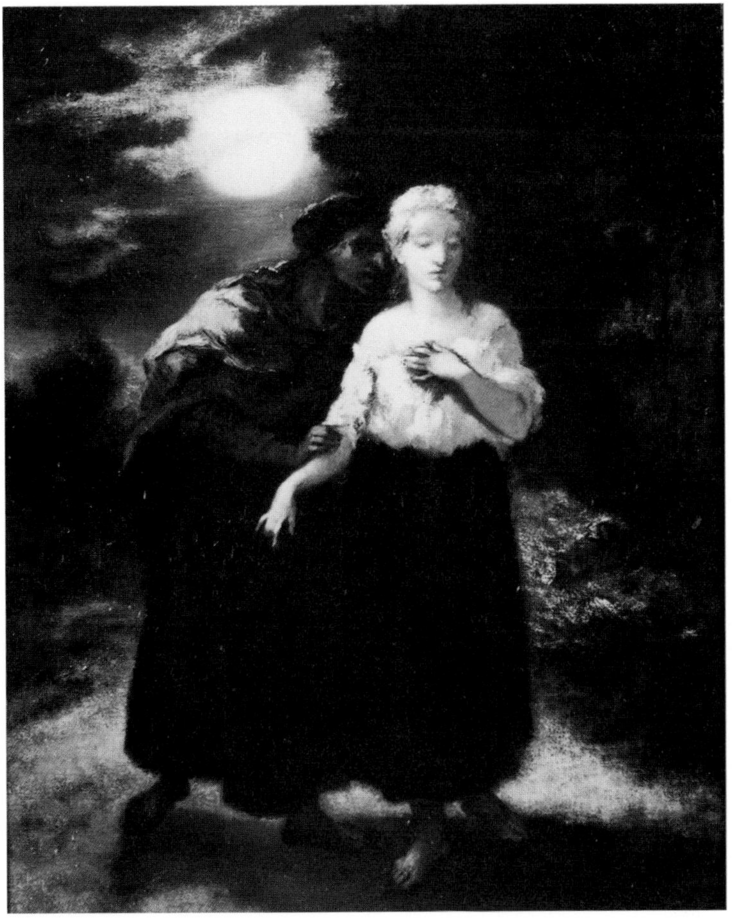
28.

the National Academy of Design, refusing him the official recognition he received in France, his work was well received by critics who were delighted to have an opportunity to view one of his most celebrated paintings.[3] Despite criticism of the "camera in his eye,"[4] which was read by some as overattention to detail, the clarity of his portrayal of events and his determination to introduce natural light to his tableaux won the grudging respect of his American contemporaries.

1. *Alerte!* is a version of a painting exhibited at the Salon in 1877, the same year as *Salut aux blessés*. See Forbes and Kelly 1975, no. 12, p. 15, illus.
2. Strahan III, p. 134.
3. "The Pedestal Art Loan," *The New York Times*, December 16, 1883, p. 5.
4. Henry Bacon, "Glimpses of Parisian Art, I," *Scribner's Monthly*, vol. 21, no. 2 (December 1880), p. 178.

28.
NARCISSE VIRGILE DIAZ DE LA PENA (French, 1807–1876)
The Sorceress (Le Maléfice), 1851
Oil on canvas
12¾ x 9¾ in.
Signed and dated l.r.: *51 N. Diaz*
Munson-Williams-Proctor Institute Museum of Art, Utica, New York, Proctor Collection
Provenance: Frederick Proctor, Utica

29.
NARCISSE VIRGILE DIAZ DE LA PENA
The Impending Storm, 1872
Oil on canvas
18¾ x 26¾ in.
Signed and dated l.l.: *N. Diaz 72*
The Heckscher Museum, Huntington, New York, Gift of August Heckscher
Provenance: August Heckscher, New York, by 1920

30.
NARCISSE VIRGILE DIAZ DE LA PENA
Flowers
Oil on canvas
14⅝ x 11½ in.
Signed l.r.: *N. Diaz*
The Fine Arts Museums of San Francisco, Jacob Stern Permanent Loan Collection

31.
NARCISSE VIRGILE DIAZ DE LA PENA
Forest
Oil on panel
4 x 6 in.
Vassar College Art Gallery, Poughkeepsie, New York, Gift of Mrs. Lloyd Williams in Memory of Her Father, Daniel Cottier
Provenance: Mrs. Lloyd Williams, New York

By the early 1880s Narcisse Virgile Diaz de la Peña, one of the artists whose work dominated the selections at the *Pedestal Fund Art Loan Exhibition,* had surpassed all of the Barbizon painters in popularity in America.[1] *The Sorceress* (*Le Maléfice*), while not in the 1883 exhibition, is typical of the imaginative, but only nominally literary, figure pieces that were favored by New York connoisseurs Erwin Davis and Ichabod T. Williams.[2] Whether painting an ostensibly religious theme, such as the *Holy Family* (fig. 12, p. 29), loaned by Catharine Lorillard Wolfe, or moody landscapes such as *The Impending Storm* (cat. no. 29) and *La Mare aux Grenouilles* (pl. XIII, The Corcoran Gallery of Art, Washington, D.C.),[3] Diaz minimized or eliminated narrative content in order to concentrate on the intertwining and dramatizing of natural forms. His skill as a colorist, often compared to that of Delacroix, and later Monticelli, was the basis of his continuing interest to the younger generation of American artists, particularly to unorthodox painters such as Albert Pinkham Ryder. Ryder's dealer, Daniel Cottier, who favored small rapid sketches like *Forest* (cat. no. 31)[4] for his personal collection, loaned a pair of the high-keyed flower pieces that were admired by Renoir but were still relatively unfamiliar to American collectors of Diaz's Eastern fantasies and woodland interiors.

1. Strahan III, p. 134, lists eighty-nine paintings by Diaz in American private collections by 1882.
2. Erwin Davis loaned *La Tristesse,* the landscape *Rocky Gorge,* and *Flowers.* Williams loaned *The Lovers* (fig. 39, p. 39), which was sold to John H. Fry at the Williams Sale, 1915, lot 67, 12¾ x 7¼ in.
3. Loaned to the Pedestal Fund exhibition and to the *Barye Monument Exhibition,* 1889–90, by Charles A. Dana.
4. *Forest,* which was given to the Vassar College Art Gallery by Daniel Cottier's daughter Peggy (Mrs. Lloyd Williams) in memory of her father, may have been one of the paintings that remained in Cottier's wife's possession after his death in 1891. See also J.-B.-C. Corot, *Woodland Scene* (cat. no. 15).

32.
JULES DUPRE (French, 1811–1889)
Fishing Boat in the Moonlight, c. 1870–72
Oil on canvas
12¾ x 19½ in.
Signed l.l.: *Jules Dupré*
Tweed Museum of Art, Duluth, Minnesota, George P. Tweed Memorial Art Collection
Provenance: Mrs. Thomas Nelson Page
Henry Field, Chicago

Jules Dupré was admired in America as "an innovator leading the public away from the epic grandeurs of nature to the quiet pastures"[1] and as an artist who "gets the spirit and lets the letter go."[2] His *Fishing Boat in the Moonlight* is similar to a *Marine* (fig. 36, p. 38) that was described by a reviewer of the Pedestal Fund show as "an inimitable little [painting], with rude fishing boat—one of those marines in which Dupré manages to seize on the charm of the old Dutch painters of the sea without adhering to that smooth-

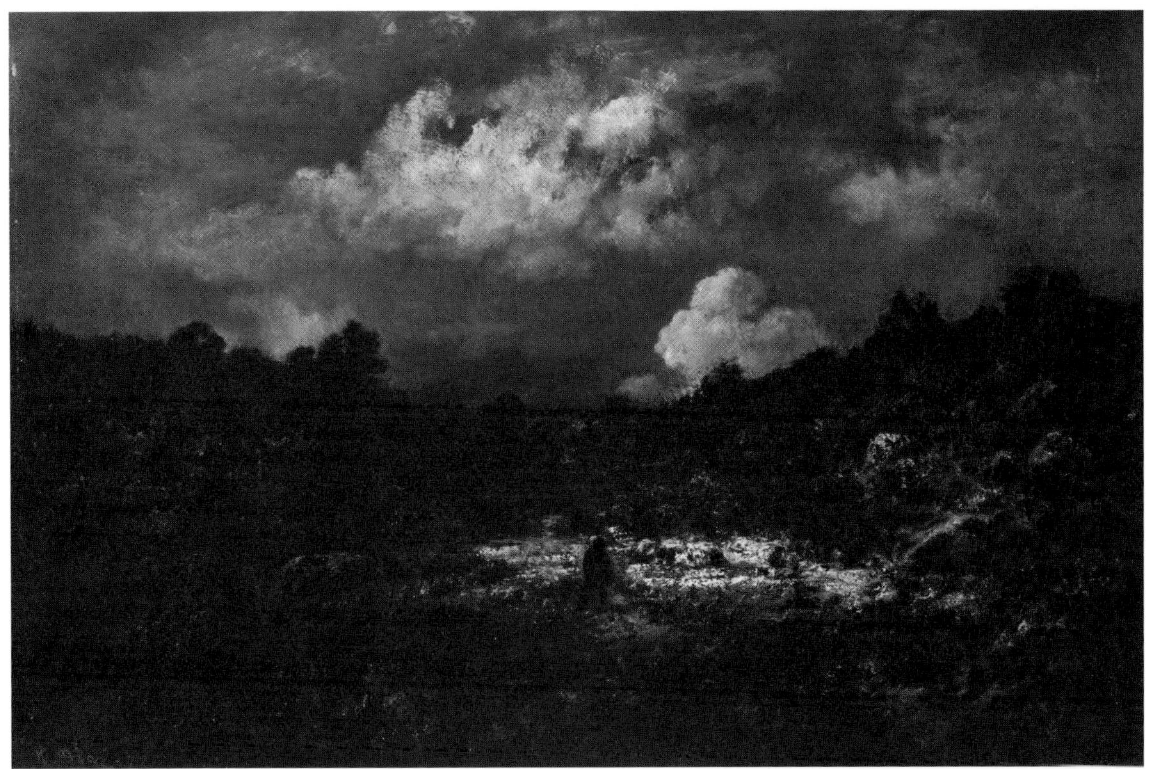

29.

30.

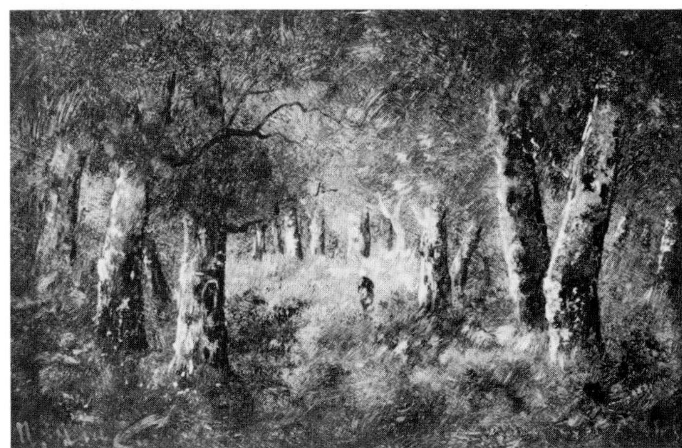

31.

ness in execution which is commonly the only thing their imitators are able to render."[3] First shown in America by the dealer Seth Vose around 1857, Dupré's work was represented in 1883 in the William W. Corcoran and William T. Walters collections, as well as in the more avant-garde collections of Ichabod T. Williams and Erwin Davis.

1. Cook II, p. 22
2. "The Pedestal Art Loan," *The New York Times*, December 16, 1883, p. 5.
3. *Ibid.*

33.
MARIANO FORTUNY Y CARBO (Spanish, 1838–1874)
A Young Lady in a Blue Dress, 1866
Watercolor and white gouache on paper
14⅛ x 9⅝ in.
The Minneapolis Institute of Arts, Minneapolis, Minnesota, The Hadlai A. Hull and David Draper Dayton Funds, 1984

The Mariano Fortuny y Carbo *A Young Lady in a Blue Dress*, a subject that captures the richness and vivacity of his style with an economy of means, is typical of the work admired by William Merritt Chase in the 1880s. Although Chase expressed appreciation of Fortuny's entire oeuvre, he chose a watercolor, *Camels Reposing, Tangiers* (fig. 16, pp. 30–31),[1] formerly in the collection of Jean-Léon Gérôme, to represent the Spaniard in the *Pedestal Fund Art Loan Exhibition;* during this period Chase produced his own series of Spanish drawings that strongly reflected the influence of Fortuny's work in pen and ink.[2]

Fortuny, who had won the patronage of the expatriate American William H. Stewart in the late 1860s,[3] established a strong following among artists and collectors before his untimely death at the age of thirty-six. Promoted by French agents Goupil & Cie., and praised as the work of an artist who was born to "teach the world his vivid perception that objects are modeled by nature in facets of luminous color,"[4] his colorful Spanish, North African, and Italian subjects were owned in America by William H. Vanderbilt and A. T. Stewart of New York, Henry C. Gibson and A. E. Borie of Philadelphia, and William T. Walters of Baltimore.

1. The Metropolitan Museum of Art, New York, Catharine Lorillard Wolfe Collection; loaned to the Pedestal Fund exhibition by Miss Wolfe. Long on exhibition in the Wolfe Galleries at the Metropolitan, this work was well known in America and frequently reproduced and cited in the late nineteenth and early twentieth centuries. See Strahan I, p. 131, illus.; Champlin and Perkins II, p.76; Walter Rowlands, "The Miss Wolfe Collection," *The Art Journal*, vol. 51, n.s. 41 (1889), p. 15; Mather 1927, p. 127, illus.
2. Pisano 1979, p. 25. Pisano noted that the drawings were later reproduced in Susan N. Carter, "Street Life in Madrid," *The Century Magazine*, vol. 39, no. 1 (November 1889), pp. 32–41.
3. See William R. Johnston, "W. H. Stewart: The American Patron of Mariano Fortuny," *Gazette des Beaux-Arts*, vol. 77, per. 6 (March 1971), pp. 183–88.
4. Strahan III, p. 135, lists twenty-four works in American collections; he describes *Camels at Rest (Camels Reposing, Tangiers)*, in the Wolfe collection as "timid and tentative" and "singularly uncharacteristic" (I, p. 132).

34.
EUGENE FROMENTIN (French, 1820–1876)
An Encampment in the Atlas Mountains
Oil on canvas
41⅜ x 56½ in.
Signed l.l.: *Eug. Fromentin*
Walters Art Gallery, Baltimore, Maryland
Provenance: Purchased by William T. Walters between 1878 and 1884

Eugène Fromentin's *Les Maîtres d'autrefois*, an account of his travels in Belgium and Holland and his discovery of and admiration for the paintings of Rembrandt, Rubens, and Frans Hals, was published in English translation in 1883.[1] His enthusiasm for these painters, as well as his respect for Delacroix and Corot, was shared by the young artists involved in the organization of the Pedestal Fund show, and may have influenced their decision to include one of his North African scenes in their selection.[2] Although recollections of trips to Africa in the 1840s and 1850s provided the subject for many of Fromentin's paintings, he was never merely a costume painter or a reporter of exotic settings and mores. His careful studies of horses and riders in sun-drenched landscapes have a naturalness and sense of direct observation that resist comparison to the more detailed and highly finished work of contemporary Orientalists.

Fromentin's work was actively sought by American collectors in the early 1880s and was represented in major museums by the end of the century. William T. Walters of Baltimore owned three paintings by 1884, including *An Encampment in the Atlas Mountains*, and Albert Spencer, who loaned a similar subject to the Pedestal Fund show, boasted five Fromentins in his prestigious collection before its dispersal in 1888.[3]

1. Eugène Fromentin, *Old Masters of Holland and Belgium (Les Maîtres d'autrefois)*, trans. Mrs. Mary C. Robbins (Boston: R. Osgood and Company, 1883).
2. The importance of Fromentin's writings on the Dutch and Flemish masters was noted by John C. Van Dyke in the preface to *Modern French Masters* (New York: The Century Co., 1896), p. v., when he called *Les Maîtres d'autrefois* "perhaps the best piece of art criticism ever written." It is also noted by Henry Eckford, "Eugène Fromentin," *The Century Magazine*, vol. 25, no. 6 (April 1883), p. 835.
3. *Women of the Ouled-Nayls* (The Art Institute of Chicago) was among the paintings in the Spencer Sale, 1888.

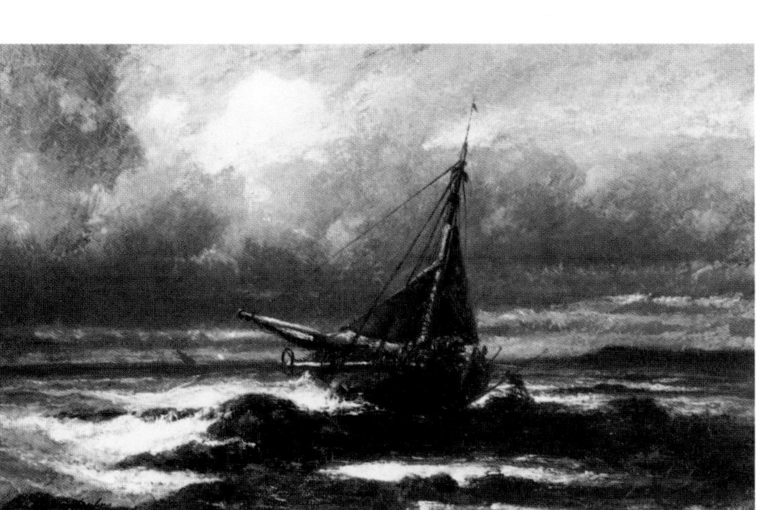

32.

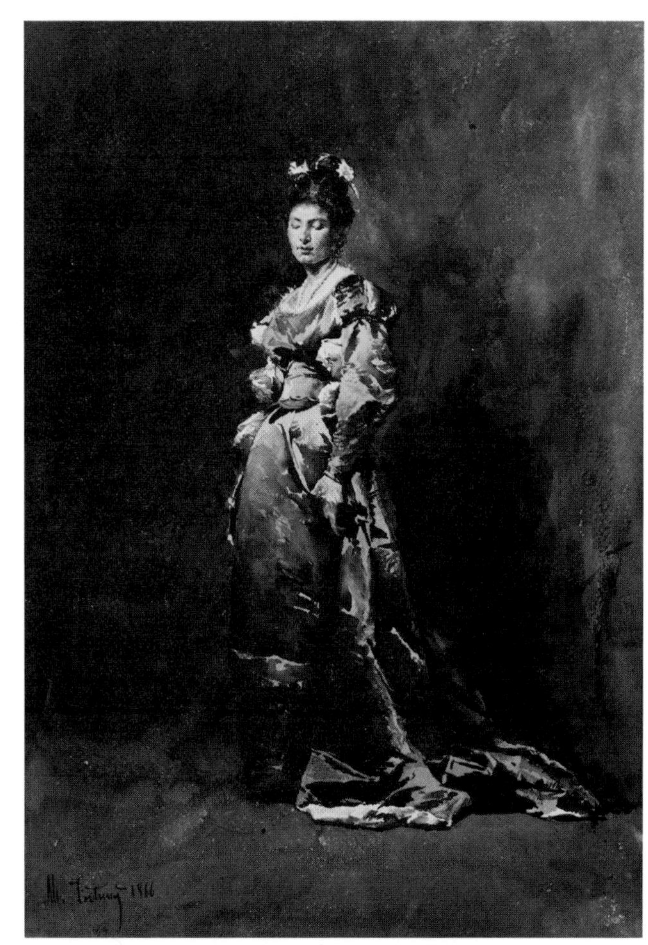

33.

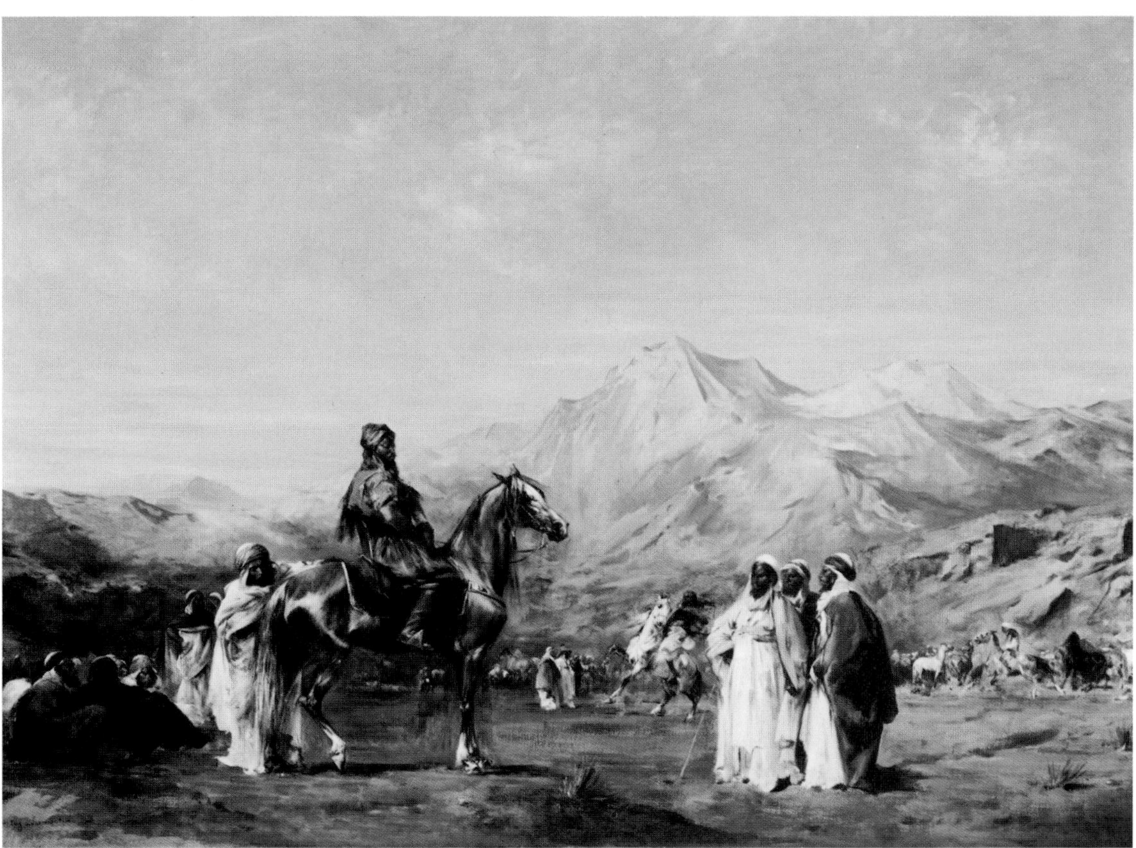

34.

35.
THEODORE GERICAULT (French, 1791–1824)
Napoleon's Horse
Oil on canvas
14¼ x 17¾ in.
Collection Mrs. John Hay Whitney

Napoleon's Horse, reputed to be a study from life of Napoleon's white Arabian stallion, was described in 1819 by Géricault's biographer Charles Clément as the painting that had won the artist a gold medal from the Empress Marie-Louise.[1] American collectors of the 1880s knew Géricault's horses through reproductions, but the scarcity of his work and the frequency of its misattribution made it difficult for them either to see or to acquire his paintings.[2] Recalled as an artist who took the public captive by his "modernness,"[3] he was primarily known through a copy of the *Raft of the Medusa* that hung, in succession, at the New-York Historical Society and The Metropolitan Museum of Art, and was determined in the twentieth century to be inauthentic.[4]

In 1883 there were few paintings by Géricault in American collections. Edward Strahan's *The Art Treasures of America* (1879–82) identified only three: a study of a youth waving a banner as he leads a horse to the Roman *corsa dei barbari,*[5] in the collection of the late A. E. Borie of Philadelphia, and the paintings *Still Life* and *Cavalry Charge* in the collection of Beriah Wall of Providence.[6] Although Erwin Davis, the adventurous collector who brought Manet's *Boy with a Sword* (cat. no. 47) and *Woman with a Parrot* (pl. XVIII) to America in 1881, presumably believed in the authenticity of the Géricault *Dead Lamb* he sent to the *Pedestal Fund Art Loan Exhibition,* there is a strong possibility that this unidentified painting was a fake.[7]

1. Charles Clément, *Géricault: Etude biographique et critique avec le catalogue raisonné de l'oeuvre du maître* (Paris: Didier, 1879), pp. 290–91. Washington, D.C., National Gallery of Art, *The John Hay Whitney Collection,* catalogue by John Rewald (1983), no. 8, pp. 28–29, illus. p. 28.
2. The scarcity of Géricault's works in America, even in the twentieth century, is discussed by Walter Pach, "Géricault in America," *Gazette des Beaux-Arts,* vol. 27, per. 6 (April 1945), pp. 227–40. In 1886–87, Champlin and Perkins II, pp. 127–28, called Géricault a "history and animal painter" and identified as noted works only the *Raft of the Medusa* and several paintings of horses and cavaliers in the Louvre.
3. Cook I, p. lxx.
4. Pach, p. 235, noted that The Metropolitan Museum of Art "unreservedly exhibited for many years a picture of the *Raft of the Medusa*" whose authenticity was later doubted. Champlin and Perkins II, p. 128, listed a *Raft of the Medusa,* presumably the same painting, in the New-York Historical Society by 1887, and it is on this work that Cook I, pp. lxix–lxx, directs his comments about Géricault.
5. A painting by this description is in the collection of Victor D. Spark, New York. Another painting related to this theme, *Riderless Races at Rome,* in the Walters Art Gallery, Baltimore, was owned by H. O. Havemeyer after 1889.
6. Four paintings by Géricault, lot 27, *Cavalry Charge;* lot 33, *The Stable;* lot 155, *Arms and Equipment;* and lot 202, *Horses in a Stable,* were included in the sale of the collections of Beriah Wall and John A. Brown of Providence (New York, American Art Galleries, March 30–31 and April 1, 1886).
7. Géricault scholars Lorenz Eitner, Stanford University (letter of January 29, 1986), and Hans A. Lüthy, The Getty Center for the History of Art and Humanities (letter of December 13, 1985), have indicated to the author that no painting of a dead lamb is known in Géricault's oeuvre.

36.
MAKSYMILIAN GIERYMSKI (Polish, 1846–1874)
Departure for the Chase, 1871
Oil on canvas
26 x 45⅞ in.
Signed and dated l.l.: *M. Gierymski 1871*
Collection Mr. and Mrs. D. W. Hill, London

The young Polish artist Maksymilian Gierymski studied at the Munich Academy and won critical attention at official exhibitions in Germany and Austria in the 1870s.[1] A specialist in hunting parties and scenes of the Polish cavalry and militia, Gierymski also excelled at incorporating figures into the natural settings of wooded forests and snowy fields. Although he often painted riders in period costume, they also appeared in modern dress, as they do in *Departure for the Chase* (1871). Gierymski sent paintings by this title to the 1870 Kaiser's Salon in Berlin and the 1871 International Exhibition in Vienna, and he was represented by *Riding to the Hunt,* loaned by Theodore Havemeyer, at the *Pedestal Fund Art Loan Exhibition.*[2] A hunting scene in the time of Louis XV, *Polowanie "par force" na Jelenia,* was shown at the Berlin Kaiser's Salon of 1874, the year of the artist's untimely death, and was immediately purchased for the collection of the Nationalgalerie, Berlin.[3]

There were few paintings by Gierymski in America in 1883,[4] presumably because his work was both unfamiliar and unavailable to collectors who did not follow the international exhibitions of Munich and Vienna. His inclusion in the Pedestal Fund show was probably the decision of Chase, who began his own studies in Munich shortly after Gierymski first achieved recognition.

1. Gierymski is included in *Münchner Maler im 19. Jahrhundert,* vol. 2 (Munich: Bruckmann, 1982). William Merritt Chase is also represented in this compendium of artists of the Munich School. See also Janus Bogucki, *Gierymscy* (Warsaw, 1959); Maciej Mastowski, *Maksymilian Gierymski I Jego Czasy* (Warsaw, 1970); Halina Stepien, *Maksymilian Gierymski 1846–1874, Malarstwo Rysunek* (Warsaw: National Museum of Warsaw, 1974).
2. Havemeyer's painting was sold in 1914 in the estate of his wife, the former Emilie de Losey, whose father was Austrian Consul in New York. See O'Brien, n.28.
3. Oil on canvas, 38⅝ x 71⅞ in.; currently Collection Georg Schäfer, Schweinfurt, West Germany.
4. Another hunt scene by Gierymski, *The Start for the Hunt,* was in the collection of A. J. Drexel of Philadelphia in the early 1880s (Strahan III, p. 18).

37.
JEAN-LOUIS HAMON (French, 1821–1874)
Vendor of Antiquities, Pompeii, 1865
Oil on canvas
10¼ x 12½ in.
Signed and dated l.l.: *J. L. Hamon 1865 Pompei*
Collection Robert Isaacson, New York

Jean-Louis Hamon won favor with American collectors in the late nineteenth century for the appeal of his scenes of everyday life during classical times. His unsentimental but occasionally coy subjects were painted in a manner that was compared to Pompeiian frescoes and had the appearance of being "seen through a veil of gauze"[1] (a technique that contrasted sharply with that of another popular painter of Greek and Roman genre, Lawrence Alma-Tadema). Hamon's paintings showed a predilection for children, putti, and pretty young women, sometimes using the same models and altering the subject only slightly. In *Vendor of Antiquities, Pompeii,* his subject is a contemporary Italian girl in native costume who appears amused by a group of small objects she has found in the ruins.

At least two related works, paintings of classically draped women admiring the wares of a local pottery merchant, were known in America in the 1880s: in *The Four-Cent Counter,* Hamon made reference to the popular interest in collecting Tanagra figures by depicting two Roman girls admiring the inexpensive terra-cotta figures at a local stand,[2] and in *Etruscan Merchant* (fig. 15, p. 30), his shoppers consider the purchase of vases. The latter was loaned to the *Pedestal Fund Art Loan Exhibition* by Catharine Lorillard Wolfe,[3] although it was apparently not a favorite of the hanging committee. Preferring gesture and sincerity to history and charm, they installed it, along with the military subjects of Meissonier and Detaille, in the corridor under the staircase at the National Academy of Design.

1. Cook I, p. 19. Jules Clarétie, *Peintres et sculpteurs contemporains,* vol. 1 (Paris: Librairie des Bibliophiles, 1882), places Hamon among the artists of "l'école néo-grec ou pompéienne." Strahan III, p. 136, lists more than a dozen paintings by Hamon in American collections by 1882.
2. Cook I, p. 21, illus.
3. Purchased by Miss Wolfe from the 1863 sale of her cousin, John Wolfe, New York; it entered the collection of The Metropolitan Museum of Art in 1887, was deaccessioned in 1956, and its current location is unknown.

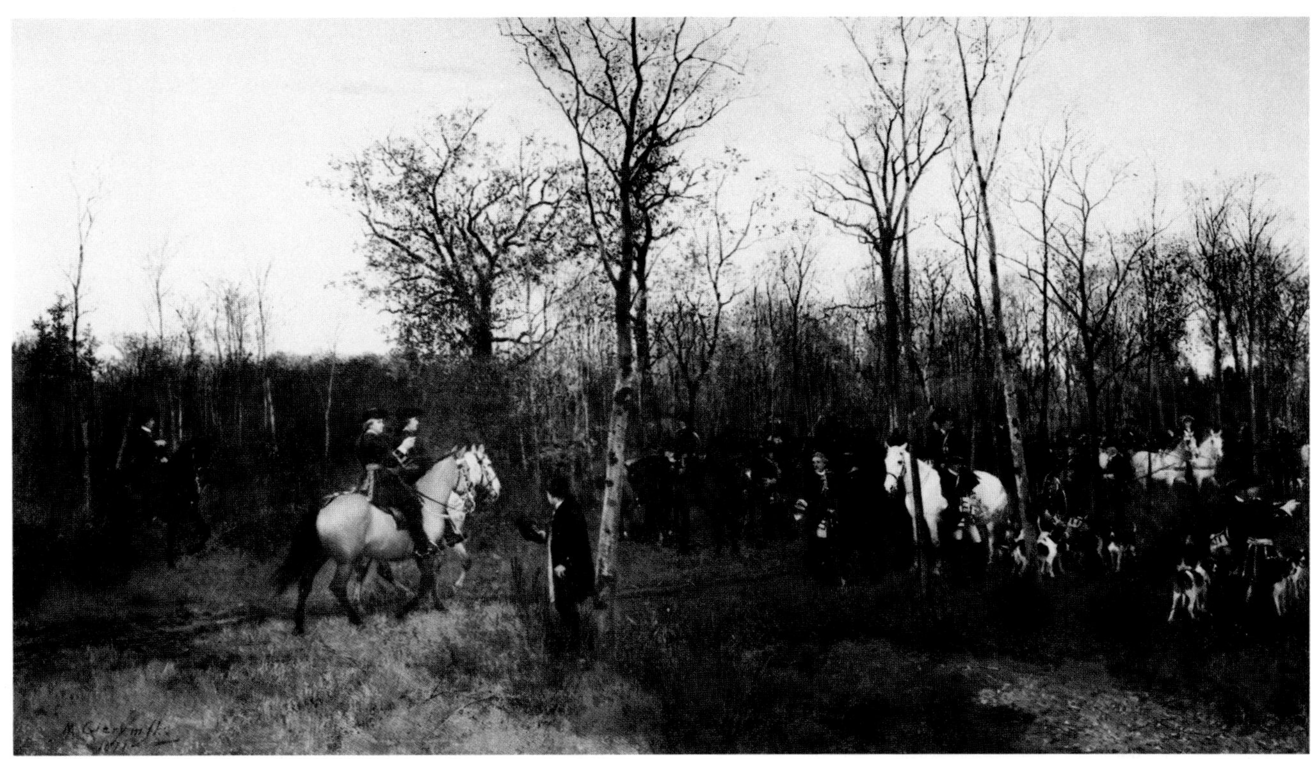

36.

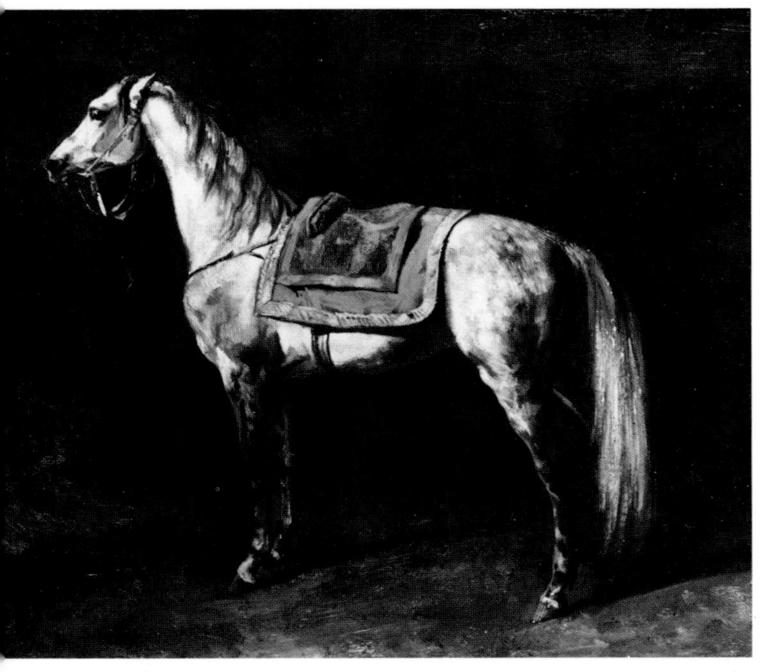

35.

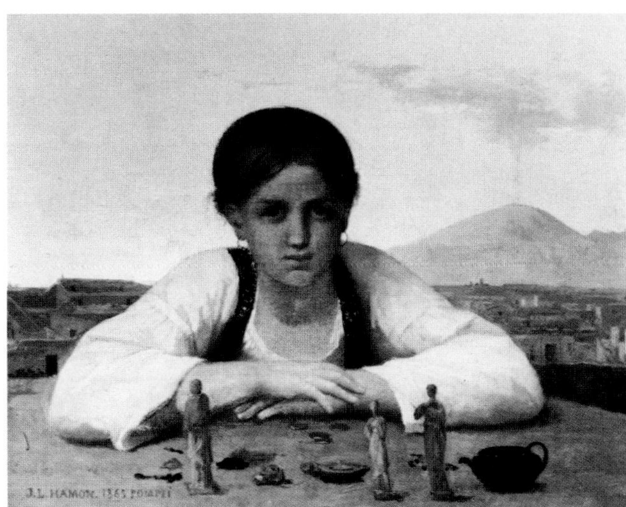

37.

38.
JEAN-JACQUES HENNER (French, 1829–1905)
A Bather
Oil on canvas
33⅛ x 27¾ in.
Signed l.l.: *JJ Henner*
The Metropolitan Museum of Art, New York, Bequest of Catharine Lorillard Wolfe, 1887, Catharine Lorillard Wolfe Collection

Provenance: Catharine Lorillard Wolfe, New York, by 1883

Exhibited at the 1883 *Pedestal Fund Art Loan Exhibition*, no. 20, *Listening Nymph*, loaned by Catharine Lorillard Wolfe

PLATE XIV

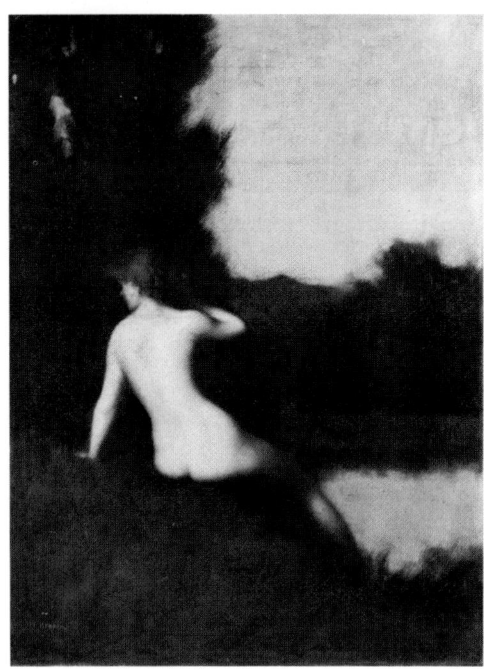

39.
JEAN-JACQUES HENNER
Reclining Nude
Oil on canvas
10¾ x 16⅜ in.
Signed u.r.: HENNER
National Gallery of Art, Washington, D.C., Timken Collection

Provenance: William R. Timken
J. S. Aron Sale, New York
Fishel, Adler & Schwartz, New York

Henner was described by Clarence Cook as an artist who had one theme: "The naked female figure in a rich gloaming ideal landscape."[1] *A Bather*, one of the paintings loaned to the *Pedestal Fund Art Loan Exhibition* by Catharine Lorillard Wolfe, and *Reclining Nude* are typical examples of Henner's "large nymph-family"[2] which gradually became known among American collectors following the artist's success at the 1878 *Exposition Universelle*. The vaporous contours of his figures were often compared with the *sfumato* of Giorgione and Correggio, whose work he had studied in Italy after winning the Prix de Rome in 1858. It may have been this old-master quality that appealed to collectors such as Wolfe, but his younger American colleagues admired the antiacademic anonymity of his evanescent nudes, the poetry of his tonalism, and the consistently painterly interpretation of a subject that was completely lacking in narrative.

1. Cook II, p. 129.
2. Strahan III, p. 53, used this term with regard to *The Nymph* in the collection of S. A. Coale, Jr., of Saint Louis. The Coale painting was described by Strahan as "one of Henner's nude figures, so admirable for their expression of flesh-texture and sharp impinging light—a strange unity of Correggio softness with Ribera definition."

40.
CHARLES-EMILE JACQUE (French, 1813–1894)
Sheep at the Entrance to a Forest
Oil on canvas
27⅜ x 39½ in.
Signed l.l.: *Ch. Jacque*
Allen Memorial Art Museum, Oberlin College, Oberlin, Ohio, Bequest of Mrs. Elisabeth Severance Allen Prentiss

Provenance: Mrs. Elisabeth Severance Prentiss, 1914–44
M. Knoedler & Co., New York
F. A. Bell, Saint Louis, 1898
Charles A. Dana, New York, by 1883
Chouanard, Paris

Exhibited at the 1883 *Pedestal Fund Art Loan Exhibition*, no. 7, *Sheep and Forest*, loaned by Charles A. Dana

PLATE XV

Charles Jacque was as well known in America for his etchings as for his bucolic paintings of shepherds and sheep. R. Swain Gifford, an organizer of the Pedestal Fund exhibition and a leader of the etching movement in America in the late 1870s, was one of several artists, including J. A. S. Monks, Peter Moran, and James D. and George F. Smillie, who acknowledged Jacque's influence on their graphic development.

In 1883 Jacque was one of the few surviving members of the original Barbizon group. He had personally instructed at least two Americans, J. Foxcroft Cole, the Boston painter, and Thomas H. Robinson, an important promoter of French painting in Providence and Boston.[1] Of the three works by Jacque loaned to the Pedestal Fund show, one, a painting of a shepherdess sleeping beneath a tree with her flock grazing nearby, involved the artist's reworking of a canvas by Georges Michel.[2] A second, loaned by William T. Evans, who later collected only American art, was a small sketch of sheep nibbling grass on a sunny hillside. The third, *Sheep at the Entrance to a Forest*, which was loaned to the Pedestal Fund show by Charles A. Dana, one of the founders of Brook Farm, was a large, fully developed work, a type generally preferred by American collectors. According to newspaper reporters, the "celebrated 'Sheep in the Forest,'"[3] as it was also called, sold for more than twice its original price at the Dana Sale of 1898, an indication of the "enduring and deserved popularity of 'the men of 1830' with the American art public."[4]

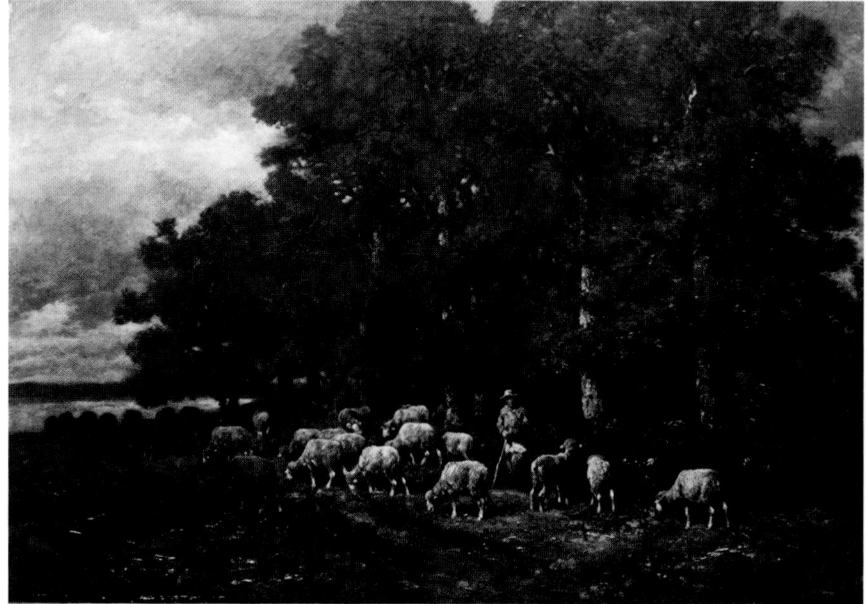

41.
CHARLES-EMILE JACQUE
Landscape with Sheep
Oil on canvas
26¼ x 38½ in.
Signed l.l.: *ch Jacque*
Detroit Institute of Arts, Bequest of Alfred J. Fisher

Provenance: Alfred J. Fisher

1. Robinson often acted as agent for the American dealer Seth Vose. See Peter Bermingham, *American Art in the Barbizon Mood* (Washington, D.C.: Smithsonian Institution Press, published for the National Collection of Fine Arts, 1975), p. 166; and Edward Allen, *Thomas Robinson: A Memoir* (Providence, Rhode Island: Privately printed, 1888).
2. Williams Sale, 1915, lot 38, Charles Jacque (in collaboration with Georges Michel), *Shepherdess*,

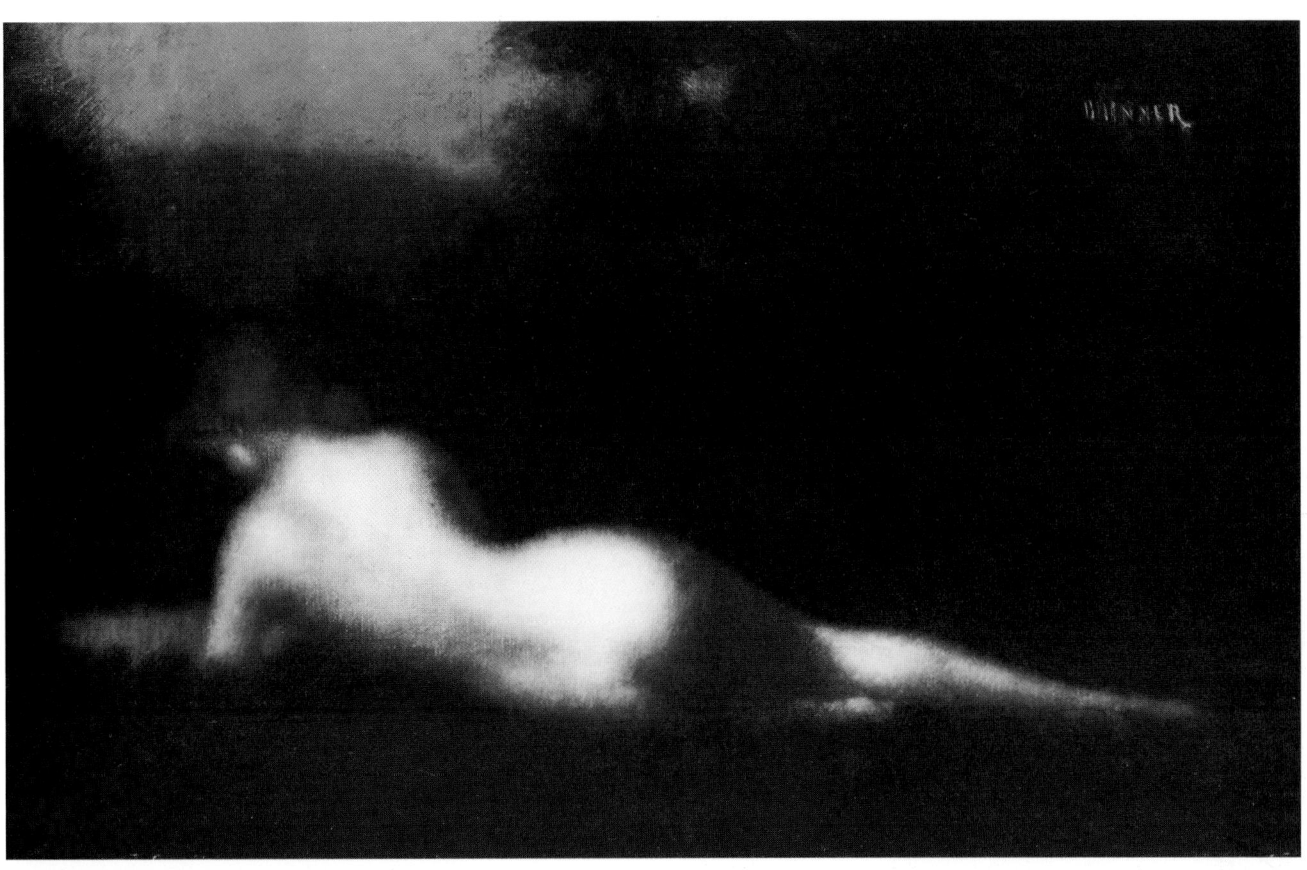

39.

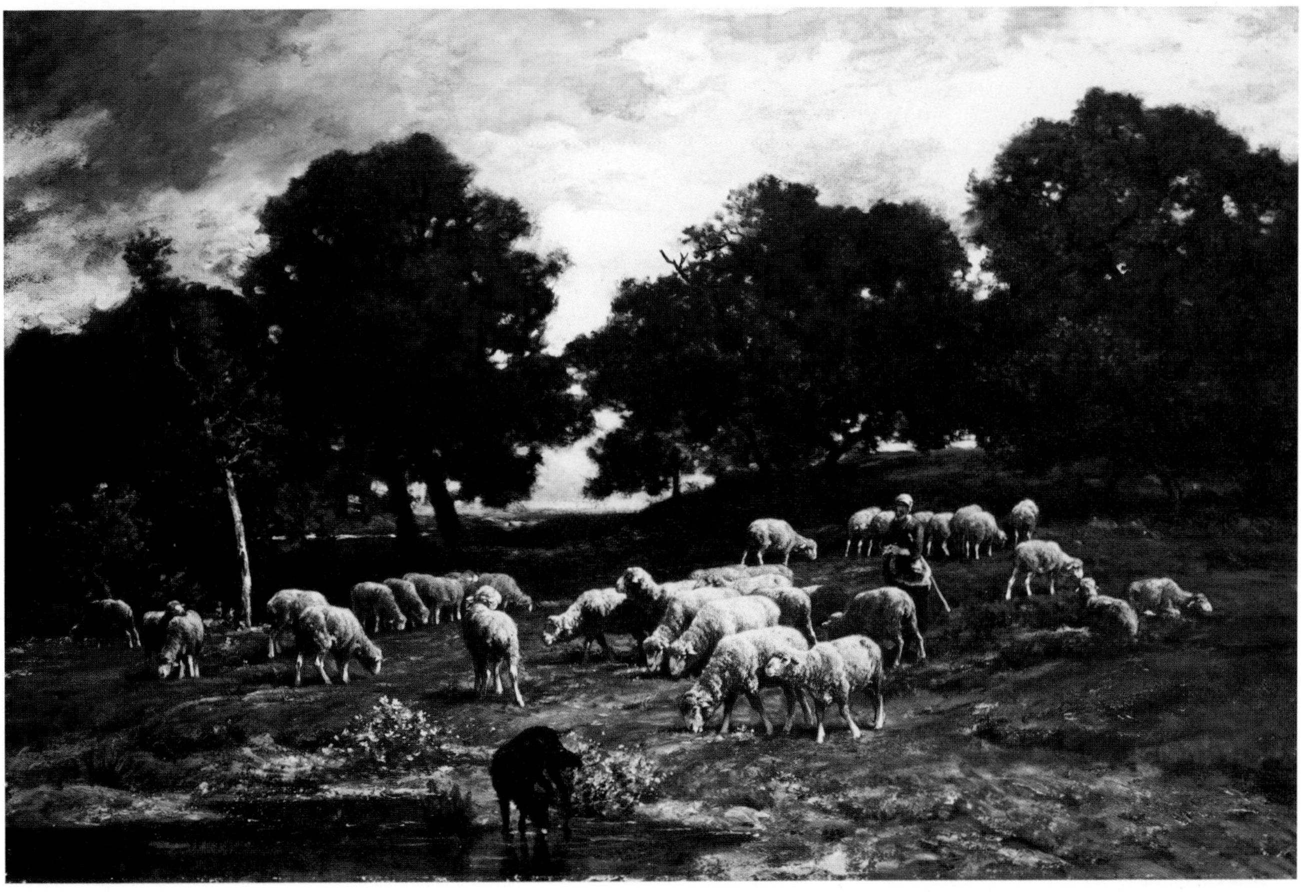

41.

Sheep and Landscape, 32 x 26 in., illus. Sold to W. W. Seaman, agent, $3,700.

3. "Art Treasures at Auction," *The New York Times*, January 21, 1898, p. 7.

4. "Fuller-Dana Picture Sale," *The New York Times*, February 26, 1898, p. 6.

42.
LUDWIG KNAUS (German, 1829–1910)
Pigs and Swineherd, 1878
Oil on canvas
18½ x 14 in.
Dated on tree trunk, l.: *1878*
Charles and Emma Frye Art Museum, Seattle, Washington

Provenance: Charles and Emma Frye
Josef Stransky, New York, 1916
Catholina Lambert, Paterson, New Jersey, 1888
Albert Spencer, New York, by 1883

Exhibited at the 1883 *Pedestal Fund Art Loan Exhibition*, no. 48, *Pigs,* loaned by Albert Spencer

PLATE XVI

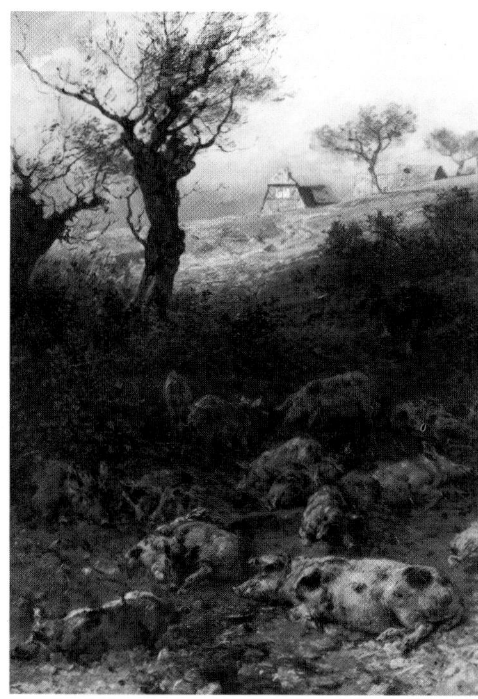

Ludwig Knaus, who was acknowledged in America as the "most famous of the German genre-painters and the head of the younger Düsseldorf school,"[1] had a secure position among American collectors by the early 1880s. *Pigs and Swineherd,* a twilight effect that was loaned to the *Pedestal Fund Art Loan Exhibition,* was one of at least four paintings in the New York collection of Albert Spencer.[2] Other owners of Knaus's paintings were William T. Walters and Catharine Lorillard Wolfe, whose *Holy Family* had been commissioned, and then rejected, by the Empress of Russia.

Although Knaus specialized in portraits and anecdotal scenes of country life that featured children, he was acknowledged in both Germany and France[3] as a naturalist who opposed the rigidity of the early Düsseldorf Academy. After spending seven years in Paris in the 1850s, Knaus returned to Düsseldorf where he was closely associated with the Achenbach brothers. His contact with Michael Munkácsy (see cat. no. 68), with whom he worked as an instructor, had the effect of further loosening his own technique, and by 1874, when he was awarded a professorship at the Berlin Academy, he had attracted a large following among younger German genre painters.

1. Cook III, p. 103.

2. Three others, *Les Amours et les roses, Head of a Brunette,* and *Le Salut des amours,* all very small pictures, were included in the Spencer Sale, 1888.

3. In 1882 Knaus was among the artists included in the *Exposition Internationale* at the rue de Sèze gallery of Georges Petit in Paris. His acceptance by a wide circle of contemporaries, including Giuseppe de Nittis, Alfred Wahlberg, Alfred Stevens, and Joseph Israels, and the appreciative review of his work by French critic Alfred de Lostalot ("Ludwig Knaus," *Gazette des Beaux-Arts*, vol. 25, per. 2 [April 1882], pp. 269–80) may have influenced the decision to include his work in the Pedestal Fund show.

43.
JEAN-PAUL LAURENS (French, 1838–1921)
Honorius, 1880
Oil on canvas
60½ x 42½ in.
Signed and dated l.r.: *Jn Paul Laurens. 1880*
The Chrysler Museum, Norfolk, Virginia, Gift of Walter P. Chrysler, Jr.

Provenance: Walter P. Chrysler, Jr., 1970
Darius O. Mills, New York

Jean-Paul Laurens's *Le Bas Empire: Honorius,* "a portrayal of imbecility in office," was exhibited at the Salon of 1880 and was acquired soon after by Darius O. Mills of New York and San Francisco.[1] Although Laurens had received considerable acclaim in France, and developed a following among the young artists of the Léon Bonnat atelier, there were few examples of his work in America in the 1880s.[2] Mural painter Edwin Howland Blashfield, who had observed Laurens's work during his own student days in Paris, was among those who admired the artist's brilliant colorism and often cynical selection of subjects from medieval history. He described *Honorius* as a grim satire that nevertheless represented a rare unbending of the artist's somber muse by depicting "the vacant-faced boy-emperor of the west, the very symbol of decadence and of a shrunken empire, a child muffled and lost in the imperial mantle, sitting stupid with inert dangling legs upon his throne, and unable to hold up the heavy globe and sceptre."[3]

1. Strahan II, p. 110, illus. p. 112. Strahan quotes the reaction to this painting of the Marquis de Chennevières (French Minister of Fine Arts at the time *Honorius* was exhibited at the 1880 Salon), who thought it "one of the most audacious *taches* or blots of color which even Laurens has hazarded." F. Thiollier, *L'Oeuvre de J. P. Laurens* (Saint-Étienne: J. Thomas & Cie, 1906) lists *Honorius* in the collection of "M. Vanderbilt."

2. In 1883, Laurens's *The Execution of the Duc d'Enghien* (1872) was in the G. B. Fearing collection, New York; a third painting, possibly *Benvenuto Cellini Visiting Charles VII* (a title attributed to N. A. Laurens by Strahan I, p. 140), was loaned to the *Pedestal Fund Art Loan Exhibition* by Theodore Havemeyer.

3. E. H. Blashfield in Van Dyke 1896, p. 85.

44.
JULES LESSORE (French, 1849–1892)
Boatyard in England, 1870
Watercolor on paper
10⅛ x 13⅝ in.
Signed and dated l.l.: *Jules Lessore 1870*
Courtesy Shepherd Gallery Associates, New York

Jules Lessore, a French expatriate in London and a close friend of Matthew Maris,[1] was promoted in and possibly brought to New York by Daniel Cottier. In 1877 Cottier exhibited a Lessore panorama entitled *Empire City,* which a reviewer described as "an enormous water-color, some 10 feet by 4, showing the lower portion of Manhattan Island, taken from a high point somewhere in the neighborhood of the Brooklyn pier of the bridge." He continued: "In the great expanse treated M. Lessore shows a wonderful grasp where most artists would have only got the unknit details of a panorama."[2] A painting of a similar subject,[3] *New York from Martin's Wharf, Brooklyn,* and two Venetian scenes were loaned by Cottier to the *Pedestal Fund Art Loan Exhibition* and were probably closer in scale and treatment to this 1870 watercolor, *Boatyard in England.*

Lessore was also represented in Cottier's private collection by a folio of nine watercolors of English cathedrals, twenty-one other watercolor views (including ten scenes of Glasgow), and oil paintings of Antwerp and Rouen.[4]

1. A portrait of Lessore by Maris was exhibited at The Hague, Gemeentemuseum, *Maris Tentoonstellung,* December 22, 1935–February 2, 1936, along with a painting of Lessore's son as a baby.

2. "The Cottier Gallery," *The New York Times,* March 1, 1877, p. 4. The reviewer questioned whether the scene had been painted from life when he noted that "the light and atmosphere do not strike us at all American, nor do we recognize the lines of our peculiar ferry-boats and shipping, nor can we agree that the water is good water, true to nature." The painting was offered for sale at the Cottier Sale, New York, 1878, but did not reach its reserve of $1,250.

3. No painting of monumental proportions is mentioned in contemporary reviews of the Pedestal Fund exhibition, so it must be assumed that Cottier sent a smaller version of this subject, possibly *The East River—New York* (Cottier Sale, New York, 1878, lot 162, 14 x 20 in.), bought in at the 1878 sale.

4. Cottier Sale, London, 1914.

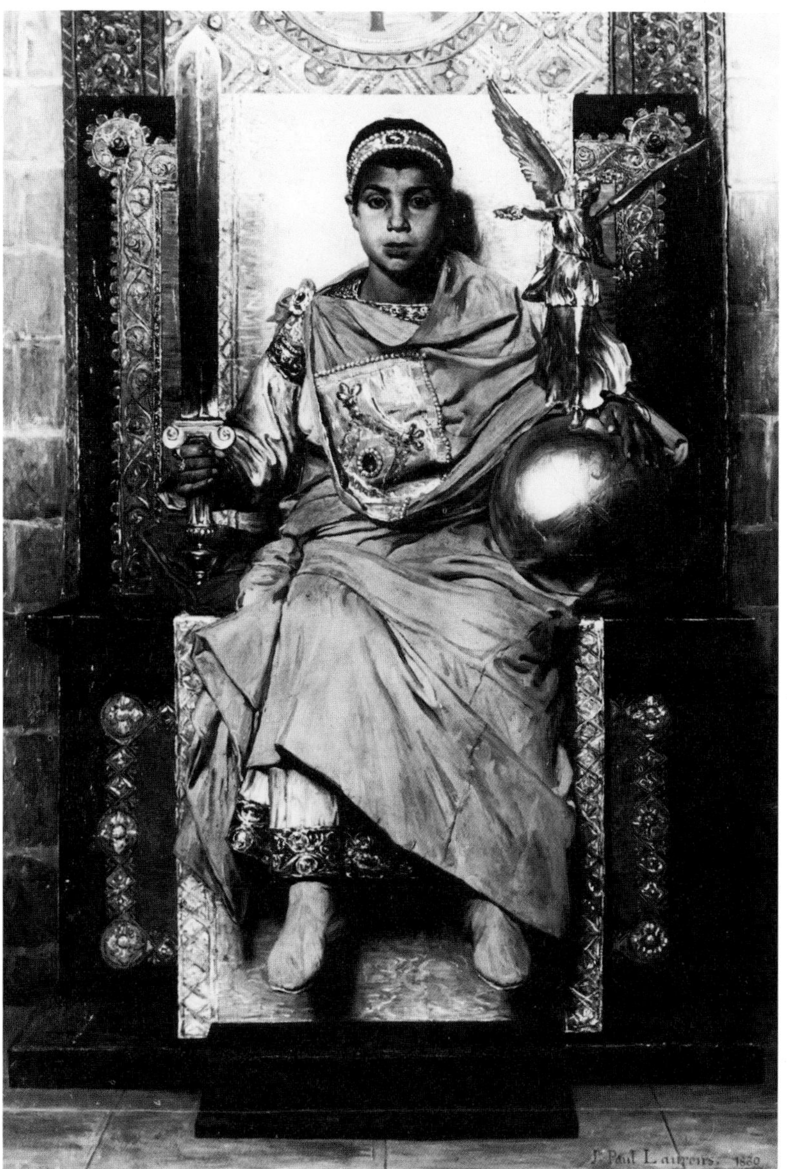

43.

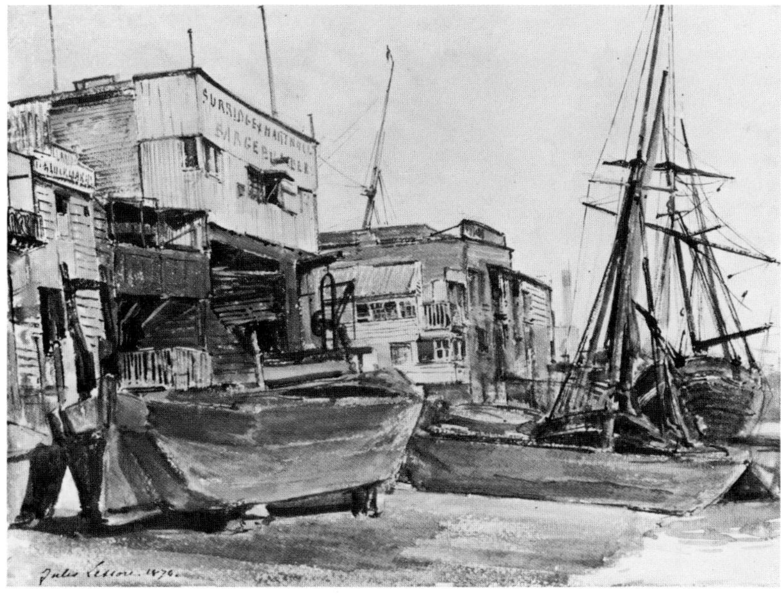

44.

45.
WILLIAM EWART LOCKHART (Scottish, 1846–1900)
Palace of the Duke of Montpensier, Seville
Watercolor on paper
9½ x 14½ in.
Signed l.r.: *W E Lockhart R S A*
Glasgow Art Gallery and Museum, Glasgow, Scotland
Provenance: Alan Teacher, 1898

William Ewart Lockhart was represented at the *Pedestal Fund Art Loan Exhibition* by the *View in Spanish Town* loaned by Daniel Cottier.[1] The painting was typical of Lockhart who, after studying at the life school of the Royal Scottish Academy, Edinburgh, in the 1860s, made frequent trips to Spain and exhibited numerous Spanish subjects. In 1878 Lockhart was elevated to full membership in the Academy, submitting the painting *Gil Blas and the Archbishop of Grenada*[2] to the annual exhibition that year. This watercolor, *Palace of the Duke of Montpensier, Seville,* proudly inscribed "W E Lockhart RSA," probably dates from the same period.

1. Cottier owned a number of Lockhart watercolors, including the following lots listed in the sale of his wife's collection (Cottier Sale, London, 1914): lot 43, *A Moorish Courtyard,* 17½ x 14¼; lot 44, *Cockburnspath,* 13½ x 20½; lot 45, *Porto del Vino, Alhambra,* 15 x 20½; lot 46, *Courtship* (sold with *On the Dunes* by N. Stacquet).
2. National Gallery of Scotland, Edinburgh. Oil on canvas, 59½ x 36½ in.

46.
ANTONIO MANCINI (Italian, 1852–1930)
Funeral Boy
Oil on canvas
38 x 28 in.
Signed l.l.: *Mancini / Roma*
Collection Gretchen Theobald and Sprague Theobald

Antonio Mancini was admired by a circle of contemporary American artists that included William Merritt Chase, Ralph W. Curtis, and John Singer Sargent. Chase owned four works by Mancini,[1] and Sargent, who, like Chase, admired his sharp value contrasts and generous impasto, declared him to be "the greatest living painter."[2]

Born in Rome and trained at the Academy in Naples, Mancini made his first visit to Paris in 1875 and worked for the international art dealer Goupil & Cie.[3] Elbert Jan van Wisselingh, also an employee at Goupil's Paris branch at the time, may have been responsible for introducing Mancini to the Hague School painter, Hendrik Mesdag, who eventually became his patron and supporter.[4]

Funeral Boy is typical of the picturesque but unsentimental figures exhibited by Mancini in the late 1870s and early 1880s and admired by the young Americans. Ralph W. Curtis was responsible for Isabella Stewart Gardner's purchase of a painting of a similar child posed as *The Standard Bearer of the Harvest Festival* before 1885.[5] A "painter's painter," Mancini was not well represented in New York collections in 1883. Daniel Cottier, who was probably familiar with Mancini through his contact with van Wisselingh, loaned a painting to the Pedestal Fund show entitled *Tired Out,*[6] which he had exhibited but apparently failed to sell in 1878.

1. Pisano 1979, p. 27.
2. Royal Cortissoz, "The Field of Art," *Scribner's Magazine*, vol. 80, no. 33 (1926), p. 456.
3. Goupil owned Mancini's *Les Frères saltimbanques,* one of six paintings representing the artist in the 1878 *Exposition Universelle,* Paris.
4. Although the financial arrangements of the relationship are unclear, Mesdag purchased many of Mancini's paintings and also arranged for his works to be exhibited in The Hague. See John Sillevis, "The Years of Fame (1885–1910)," in *The Hague School* 1983, p. 96. See also The Hague, Rijksmuseum H. W. Mesdag, *Catalogus der Schilderijen, Tekeningen, Etsen en Kunstvoorwerpen,* 1948, for a list of the paintings by Mancini in Mesdag's collection.
5. See Philip Hendy, *European and American Paintings in the Isabella Stewart Gardner Museum* (Boston, 1974), pp. 148–49, illus.
6. Cottier Sale, New York, 1878, lot 26, Mancini, Naples, *Tired Out,* 30 x 25 in. This painting probably was one of a woman resting while holding a large fan, Inglis Sale, 1909, lot 64, *The Fan,* 30½ x 24¼ in., illus.

47.
EDOUARD MANET (French, 1832–1883)
Boy with a Sword, 1861
Oil on canvas
51⅝ x 36¾ in.
Signed l.l.: *Manet*
The Metropolitan Museum of Art, New York,
Gift of Erwin Davis, 1889
Provenance: Erwin Davis, New York, 1881
Durand-Ruel, Paris, 1881
Feder, Paris, 1881
Edwards, Paris, 1881
Durand-Ruel, 1872
Fèbvre, Paris, 1872
Exhibited at the 1883 *Pedestal Fund Art Loan Exhibition,* no. 153, *Boy with a Sword,* loaned by Erwin Davis
PLATE XVII

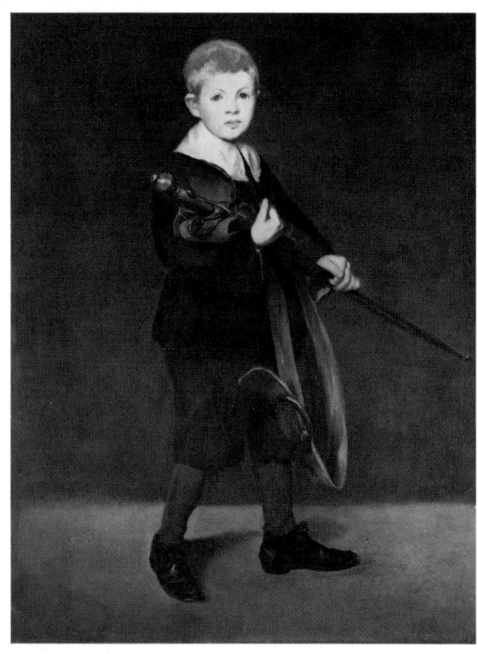

48.
EDOUARD MANET
Mlle V. . . in the Costume of an Espada
Pencil, ink, and watercolor on tracing paper, laid down
11⅞ x 8⅞ in.
Signed l.r.: *Manet*
Museum of Art, Rhode Island School of Design, Providence,
Gift of Mrs. Gustav Radeke, 1921
Provenance: Mrs. Gustav Radeke, Providence
Dr. Gustav Radeke, Providence

Three paintings by Edouard Manet appeared in the *Pedestal Fund Art Loan Exhibition*: *Boy with a Sword* (cat. no. 47), *Woman with a Parrot* (pl. XVIII), and *Toreador.*[1] Only the first two, owned by Erwin Davis and purchased on his behalf by Julian Alden Weir from Durand-Ruel, Paris, in 1881, attracted the attention of the New York critics. This could hardly have been avoided, as both were hung prominently on the south wall of the main picture gallery in an intentional gesture of homage to the leader of French Impressionism who had died only eight months earlier.

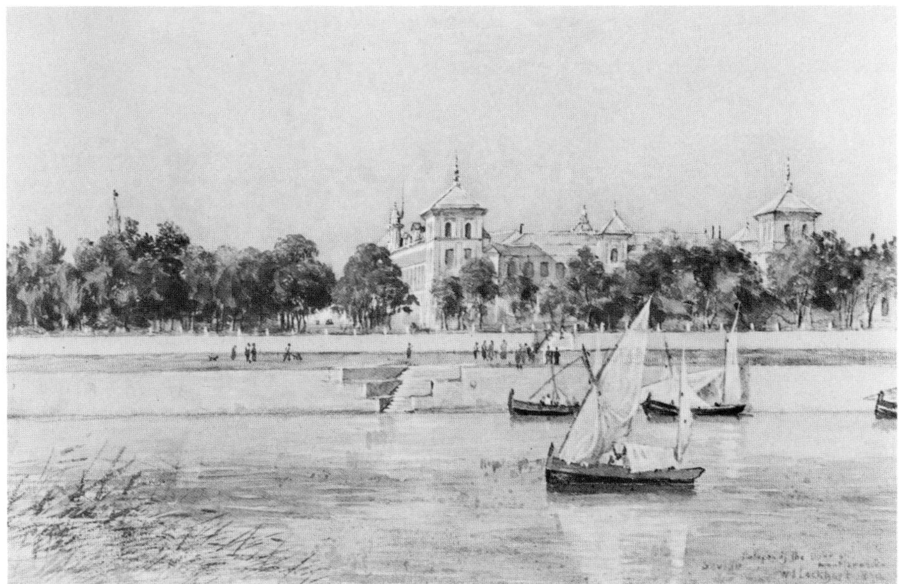

45.

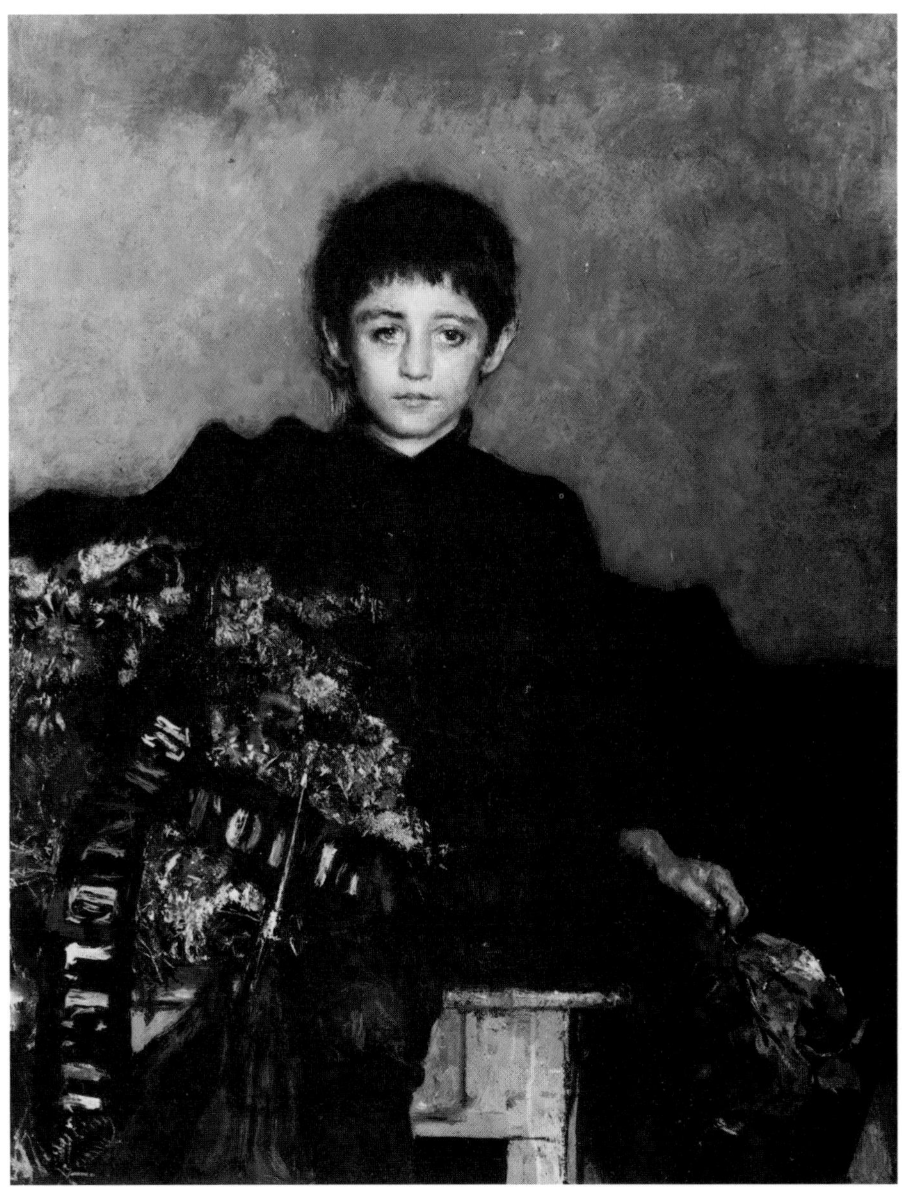

46.

The most thoughtful of reviewers made an effort to understand the qualities of this "peculiarly endowed painter,"[2] admitting that the "scrawny old maid with a parrot" and the "disreputable, dirty-looking boy holding a sword"[3] continued to draw the eye back to them, in the hope, perhaps, of grasping techniques that only artists could fully appreciate. To the general audience, which had no frame of reference for the style that had shocked Paris a good twenty years earlier, the paintings were simply ugly. Exhibited in New York twice more during the next six years—as loans to Durand-Ruel's 1886 *Special Exhibition: Works in Oil and Pastel by the Impressionists of Paris* and as entries in the 1889 Erwin Davis sale—they continued to elude the appreciation of the art public and entered the collection of The Metropolitan Museum of Art as gifts of Davis when he failed to find a buyer for them.[4]

Although "three important works"[5] by Manet are mentioned in a *New York Times* column that previewed the Pedestal Fund show, *Toreador,* loaned by Daniel Cottier, is never cited in later criticism. No major painting of this subject is known to have been in America in 1883, although Cottier's partner, James S. Inglis, subsequently owned both *Bullfight* (The Art Institute of Chicago) and the *Dead Toreador* (National Gallery of Art, Washington, D.C.).[6] In all likelihood, Cottier's loan was a watercolor, perhaps even the sketch *Mlle V. . . in the Costume of an Espada*, which was owned by an American by the early twentieth century and could easily have been called simply *Toreador*.[7] Cottier was a connoisseur of the medium and offered a number of watercolors, principally by artists of the Hague School, in his 1878 sale at the Leavitt Art Galleries, New York. As a member of a social circle that included artists Weir, Chase, and Albert Pinkham Ryder, and collectors Davis and Ichabod T. Williams, he was presumably among the art amateurs attending the reception for Manet's *Execution of Maximilian* (Städtische Kunsthalle, Mannheim) when it was exhibited at the Clarendon Hotel on Eighth Street and Broadway the following year, and it is possible that both his, and Inglis's, enthusiasm for Manet can be dated from this point.[8]

1. Pedestal Fund catalogue, 1883, no. 153, *Boy with Sword;* no. 182, *Portrait of a Lady;* no. 191, *Toreador.*
2. Mariana Griswold Van Rensselaer, "The Recent New York Loan Exhibition," *American Architect and Building News,* vol. 15, no. 421 (January 19, 1884), p. 30.
3. John C. Van Dyke, "The Bartholdi Loan Collection," *The Studio,* vol. 2, no. 49 (December 8, 1883), pp. 262–63.
4. See Frances Weitzenhoffer, "First Manet Paintings to Enter an American Museum," *Gazette des Beaux-Arts,* vol. 6, no. 98 (March 1981), pp. 125–29.
5. "The Pedestal Art Loan," *The New York Times,* December 2, 1883, p. 2. *The Art Interchange* (see Dinnerstein, n.42), reported only two Manets, raising the possibility that the third might have been withdrawn before the opening but also suggesting that the *Toreador* was a very small work in comparison to the others. Cottier may have withdrawn the *Toreador* in order to send it to Paris for the *Exposition Retrospective* of Manet's work at the Ecole des Beaux-Arts, Paris (January 6–28, 1884), but if so he could have removed the title from the Pedestal Fund catalogue, which was late in production.
6. According to records of The Art Institute of Chicago, the *Bullfight* was purchased by Inglis or his wife from Durand-Ruel in 1886, probably after it appeared in the *Special Exhibition: Works in Oil and Pastel by the Impressionists of Paris* held at the American Art Association and the National Academy of Design. In 1874 *The Dead Toreador* is known to have been owned by the opera singer Jean-Baptiste Faure, who sold it back to Durand-Ruel in 1892. Inglis purchased it from Durand-Ruel at this date, probably while in Paris to assist at the sale of Cottier's collection (May 27–28, 1892). Inglis loaned *The Dead Toreador* to the World's Columbian Exposition, Chicago, in 1893, and sold it to P. A. B. Widener the following year. Both *Bullfight* and *The Dead Toreador* appeared in the 1884 Paris retrospective, and were reproduced in installation photographs in Etienne Moreau-Nélaton, *Manet, raconté par-lui même,* vol. 2 (Paris, 1926). Similarly the *Majo Saluting, Young Man in the Costume of a Majo,* and the oil version of *Mlle V. in the Costume of an Espada* (all The Metropolitan Museum of Art, New York) were in French collections in 1883–84 and were exhibited at the Manet retrospective.
7. A watercolor of a male toreador is in the Burrell Collection, Glasgow Museums and Art Galleries, Glasgow, Scotland.
8. See Hans Huth, "Impressionism Comes to America," *Gazette des Beaux-Arts*, vol. 29, per. 6 (April 1946), pp. 225–52, for a discussion of this event.

49.
JACOB HENDRICUS MARIS (Dutch, 1837–1899)
View of a Dutch Town, 1873
Oil on canvas
14½ x 22½ in.
Signed l.r.: *J Maris ft 73*
Sterling and Francine Clark Art Institute, Williamstown, Massachusetts

Provenance: Robert Sterling Clark, 1939
M. Knoedler & Co. Inc., New York, 1938
Parish Watson & Co.
W. H. Woods, 1935
Mrs. James G. Shepherd, 1935
James G. Shepherd
S. von Denvies
Obach & Co., London, 1908

50.
JACOB HENDRICUS MARIS
View of Amsterdam (The Schreierstoren)
Oil on canvas
32 x 58½ in.
Signed l.l.: *J. Maris*
Philadelphia Museum of Art, Philadelphia, William L. Elkins Collection

Provenance: William L. Elkins, 1924
George James, London
James Staats Forbes, London

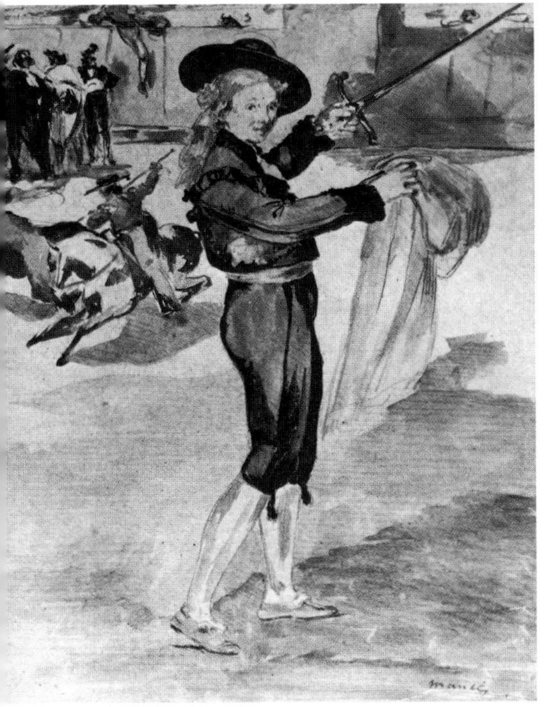

48.

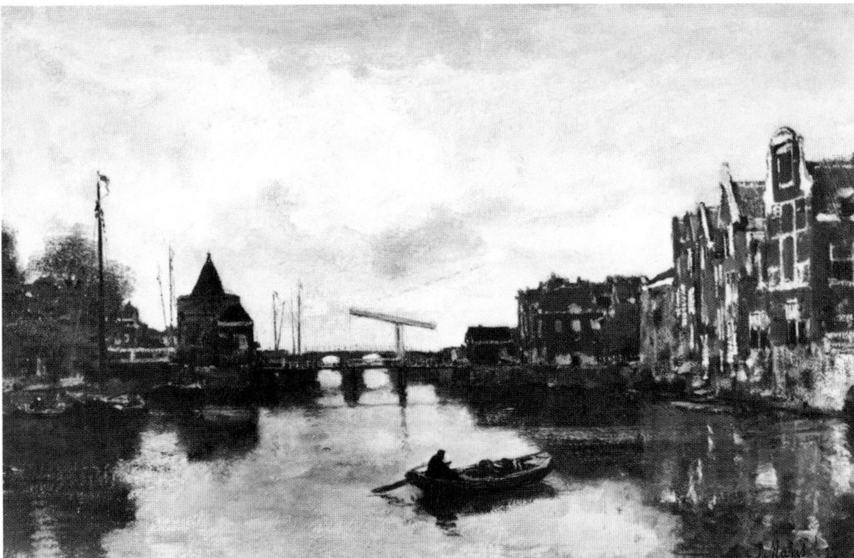

49.

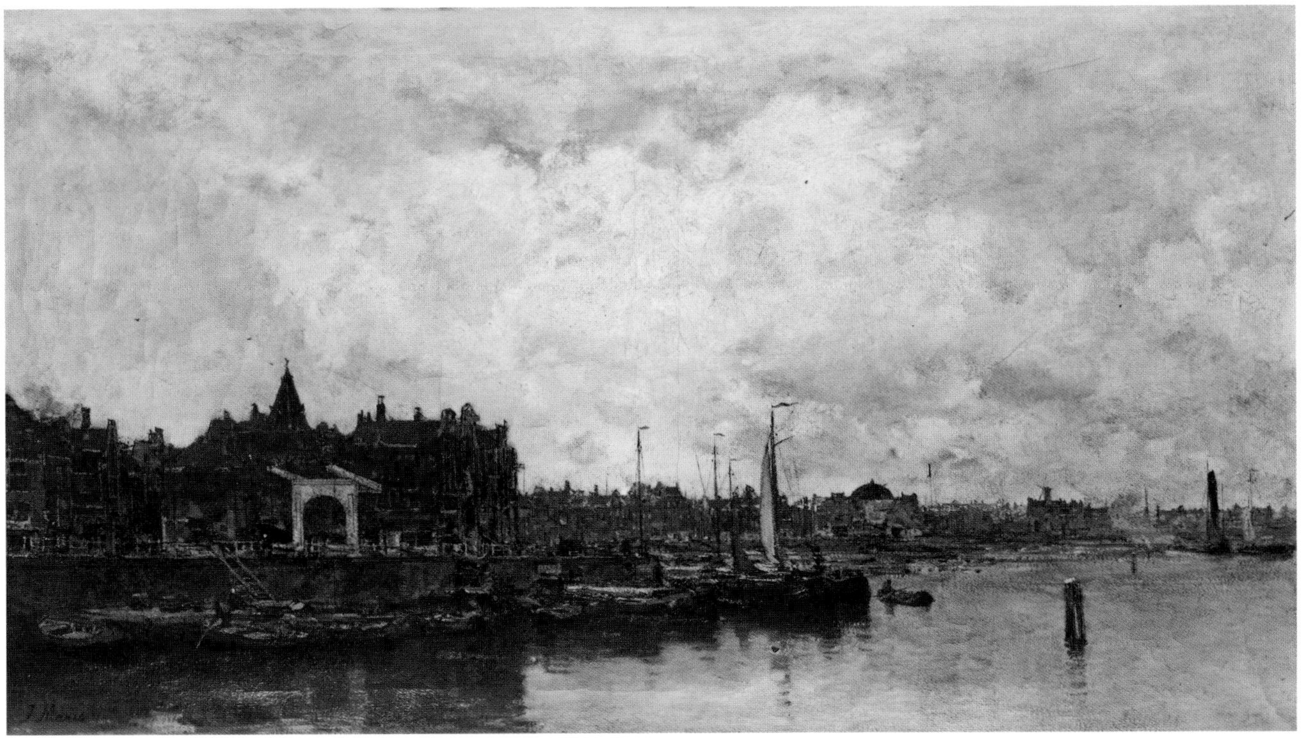

50.

Jacob Maris, like his younger brothers Matthew and Willem, was born in The Hague. In 1865, after sixteen years of study in that city and in Antwerp, he moved to Paris, where he remained until 1871. By the time of his departure, he had won the attention of French critic Paul Mantz, who praised Maris's *pinceau heureusement doué* ("talented paintbrush"),[1] as demonstrated in his submission to the 1872 Salon.

Around 1870, after exposure to the Barbizon School in France, Maris's early interest in figure painting shifted to landscape. Shortly after his return to Holland, he began to paint Dutch river scenes and townscapes, and appreciation of them spread among connoisseurs, including the Scottish art dealer Daniel Cottier. By 1877 Cottier had introduced Maris's "masterly landscapes"[2] to New York at his Fifth Avenue galleries; M. Knoedler and Co., also in New York, soon followed suit.[3] Cottier and his client, Ichabod T. Williams, each loaned two paintings to the *Pedestal Fund Art Loan Exhibition,* including a *Turkish Lady* "in emulation of Delacroix."[4]

View of Amsterdam (The Schreierstoren) was a subject Maris painted in several versions, one of which was in Cottier's persónal collection.[5] Like the smaller and sketchier (a trait that appealed to both Cottier and Williams) *View of a Dutch Town,* it includes the frequently repeated drawbridge motif and the cloud-scudded skies that characterized Maris's popular townscapes and eventually found favor with collectors in England and Scotland as well as in America.[6]

1. Paul Mantz, " Le Salon de 1872," *Gazette des Beaux-Arts,* vol. 6, per. 2 (July 1872), p. 45.
2. "The Fine Arts. Opening of The Cottier Gallery on Fifth Avenue," *The New York Times,* March 1, 1877, p. 4. Five paintings by Maris were offered at the Cottier Sale, New York, 1878.
3. "Notes," *The Art Journal,* vol. 5 (January 1879), pp. 31–32, referred to Maris and his colleagues as a "school of young men worthy of the great traditions of their country" and singled out the paintings in the 1878 Cottier Sale. M. Knoedler & Co., showing works by Maris and Anton Mauve, was also complimented for doing "unexpected service to the cause of high Art" by introducing contemporary Dutch work.
4. See fig. 40, p. 39; and O'Brien, n. 115.
5. See fig. 54, p. 45; and O'Brien, n. 183. See *The Hague School* 1983 for a discussion of this subject and its variations.
6. See Richard Marks et al., *The Burrell Collection* (London and Glasgow: Glasgow Art Gallery and Museum, 1983); Marta H. Hurdalek, *The Hague School: Collecting in Canada at the Turn of the Century* (Toronto: Art Gallery of Ontario, 1983); Charles Dumas, "Art Dealers and Collectors," in *The Hague School* 1983, pp. 125–36, with bibliography.

51.
MATTHEW MARIS (Dutch, 1839–1917)
A Corner of The Hague, 1860
Oil on panel
7⅝ x 11¾ in.
The Phillips Collection, Washington, D.C.
Provenance: James L. Phillips, Washington, D.C., 1915
Ichabod T. Williams, New York, by 1883
Daniel Cottier, New York
Exhibited at the 1883 *Pedestal Fund Art Loan Exhibition,* no. 42, *Corner of the Hague,* loaned by Ichabod T. Williams
PLATE XIX

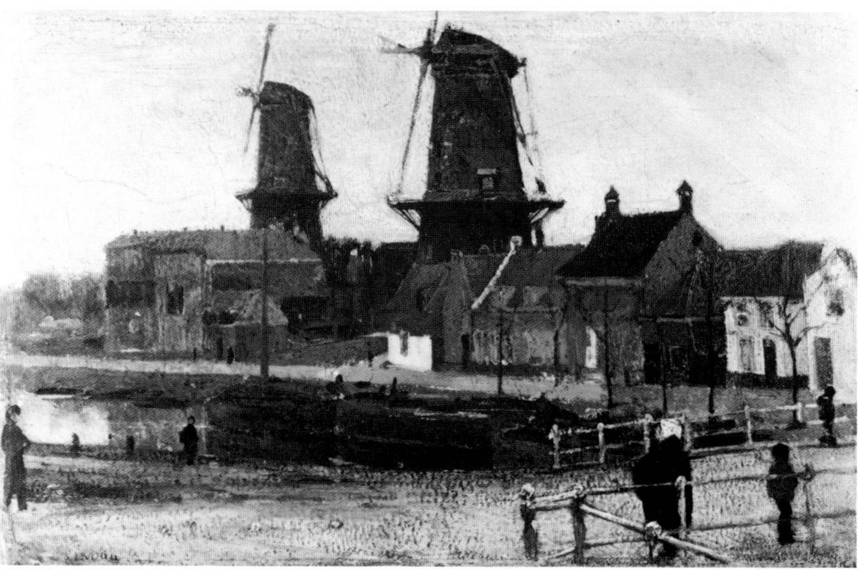

Matthew Maris was born in The Hague and studied painting in that city and in Antwerp. In 1869 he joined his older brother Jacob in Paris, establishing a friendship with a young Dutchman named Elbert Jan van Wisselingh, an employee of the international art dealers Goupil & Cie., who was later hired by Daniel Cottier to run his London gallery. Through van Wisselingh, Cottier met Maris and persuaded him to settle in London, where he worked as a gas-globe painter and a restorer of old-master paintings in order to supplement his income from his own work.[1]

Cottier introduced Matthew Maris's work to American collectors, as he had that of many of the Hague School painters. *A Corner of The Hague,* which was sold by Cottier to Ichabod T. Williams, was one of four paintings (and several other collaborations)[2] by Matthew Maris exhibited at the *Pedestal Fund Art Loan Exhibition.* Although the small townscape with its prominent windmills was a subject more frequently associated with Matthew's brother Jacob, two other paintings in the show, *Idyl* and *Flirtation,* revealed Matthew Maris as an artist of a more romantic sensibility whose loose stroke and harmonious color set him apart from his Hague School contemporaries and appealed to connoisseurs of "art of the imagination."

1. See Brian Gould, *Two Van Gogh Contacts: E. J. van Wisselingh, Art Dealer; Daniel Cottier, Glass Painter and Decorator* (Bedford Park: Naples Press, 1969), p. 4. Although the relationship with Cottier was apparently not a happy one for the artist (for a few years he even lived in the dealer's London home), an advantage of the collaboration was that the firm of Cottier & Co. published Maris's etchings. See D. Croal Thomson, *The Brothers Maris (James-Matthew-William)* (London, 1907), Special Summer Number of *The Studio.*
2. The painting of *Diana* (fig. 46, p. 41) was exhibited under the joint authorship of "Bellenger and M. Maris" in 1883. Adolphe Monticelli's *The Farmyard* (pl. XXXIV), also exhibited at the Pedestal Fund show, is now attributed to Monticelli and Maris, as is *Landscape with Figures* (cat. no. 67), formerly in the Ichabod T. Williams Collection.

52.
ANTON MAUVE (Dutch, 1838–1888)
Cattle, c. 1870
Oil on canvas
22¾ x 39¾ in.
Signed l.r.: *A Mauve*
Courtesy Schweitzer Gallery, Inc., New York
Provenance: California Palace of the Legion of Honor, San Francisco
Mildred Anna Williams, San Francisco
Boussod-Valadon, Paris

53.
ANTON MAUVE
The Timber Truck
Oil on canvas
49¾ x 33⅞ in.
Signed l.r.: *A Mauve*
Museum of Art, Carnegie Institute, Pittsburgh, Museum Purchase, 1911
Provenance: M. Knoedler & Co., New York, 1911

Anton Mauve's mature style was represented by a wide range of subjects at the *Pedestal Fund Art Loan Exhibition.* The art dealer Dan-

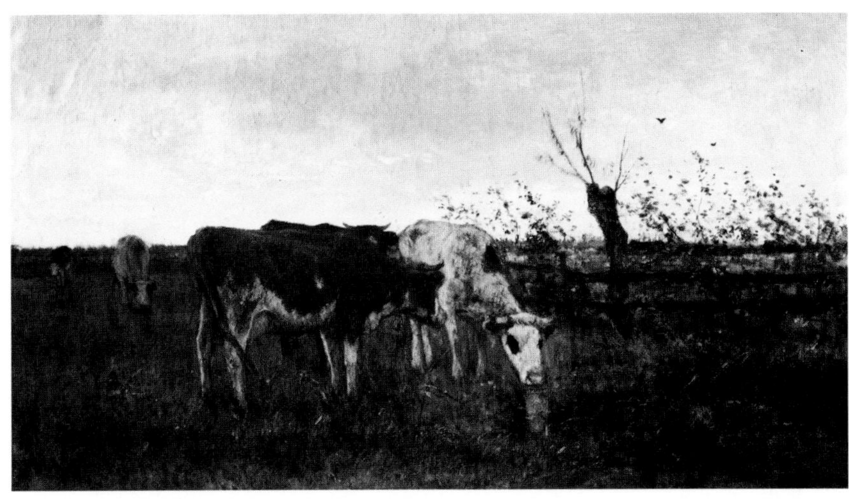

52.

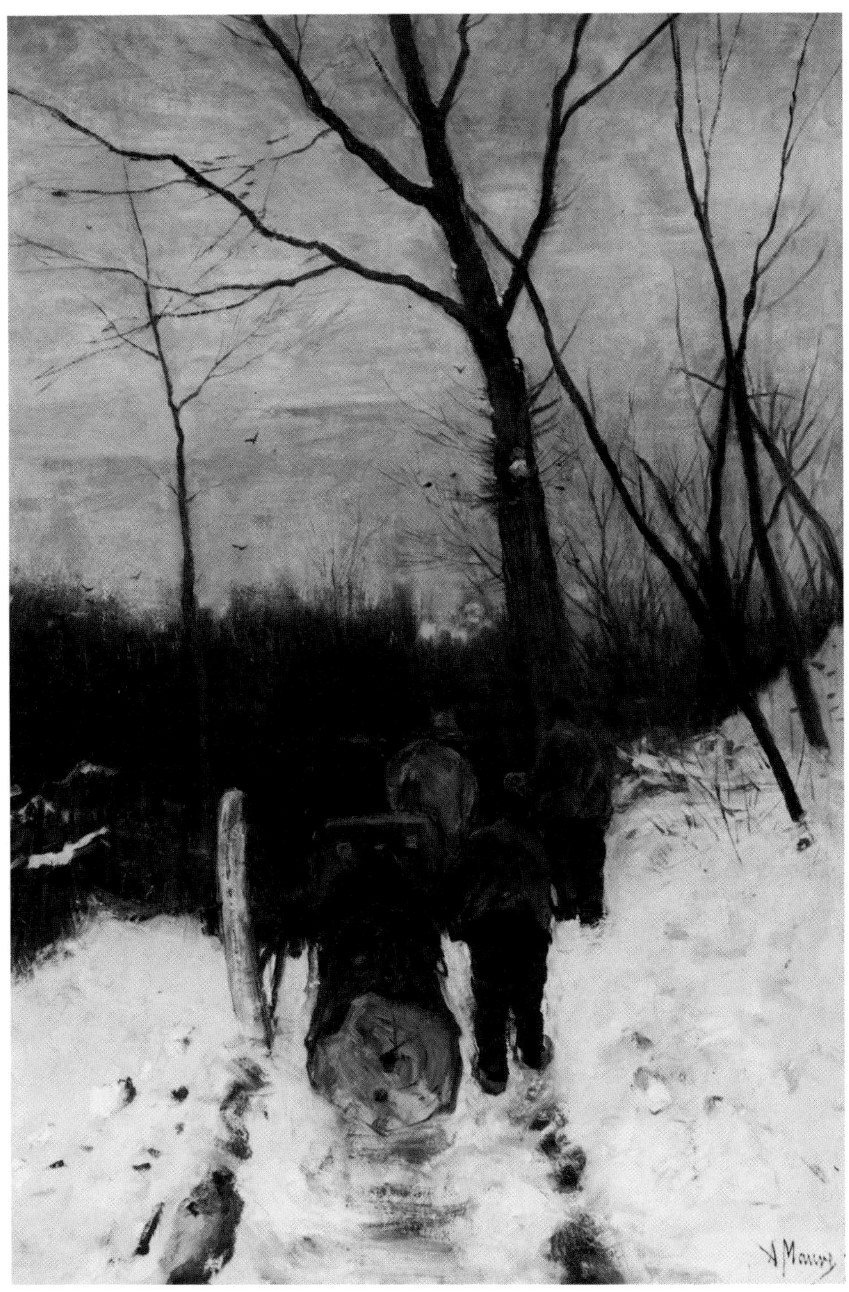

53.

iel Cottier, who had exhibited Mauve's landscapes and watercolors "of peculiar excellence"[1] at his New York gallery as early as 1877, loaned two cattle pieces, *Changing Pasture* (fig. 6, p. 25; pl. XX; The Metropolitan Museum of Art, New York) and possibly *Milking-Time* (fig. 52, p. 44), and two scenes of fishing boats on the Dutch coast (both called *Dutch Coast Scene*, figs. 3 and 5, pp. 24 and 25). Collector Erwin Davis sent a study of sheep[2] and *Twilight* (fig. 2, p. 24), a painting of a boy seated beneath a tree at dusk.

After winning a silver medal at the 1876 Philadelphia Centennial Exhibition with a painting called *Hauling up the Fishing Boat (Scheveningen*, fig. 53, pp. 44–45), a larger version of one of Cottier's Dutch coast scenes (fig. 5, p. 25), Mauve began to establish a solid reputation among American artists and critics for the truth and simplicity of his rural themes and for his exceptional watercolor technique. Particularly in works like *Timber Truck*,[3] a painting of Dutch foresters trudging alongside a horse-drawn logging cart in the snow, Mauve was admired for an ability to preserve "that fine natural sense of the expansiveness of Nature which Nature most often possesses and imparts when the sun is hidden and the sky is cold."[4] By 1888, the year of his death, Mauve was represented by a painting of sheep in the collection of The Metropolitan Museum of Art, and was acknowledged as an important influence on American painters in watercolor.[5]

1. "The Fine Arts. Opening of the Cottier Gallery on Fifth-Avenue," *The New York Times*, March 1, 1877, p. 4.
2. Possibly the watercolor in the Davis Sale, 1889, lot 45, *Watching the Flock*, 11 x 15 in.
3. A larger painting of this theme, entitled *The Forester's Team, Frosty Morning—Holland*, 42 x 48 in., was included in the Cottier Sale, New York, 1878, but was bought in when it did not meet a reserve of $3,000 (see "The Cottier Collection," *The New York Times*, April 24, 1878, p. 8).
4. "Notes," *The Art Journal* (January 1879), p. 32, regarding paintings then on view at M. Knoedler & Co., New York, which had also begun to show the works of Mauve.
5. Montezuma, "My Note Book," *The Art Amateur*, vol. 18, no. 5 (April 1888), p. 104.

54.
JEAN-LOUIS-ERNEST MEISSONIER
(French, 1815–1891)

The Cavalier: Portrait of the Artist, 1872
Gouache, watercolor, and wash on paper
13¼ x 8⅞ in.
Signed and dated l.r.: *E Meissonier 72*
The New-York Historical Society, New York, Robert L. Stuart Collection

Provenance: The New York Public Library, New York, 1892
Mrs. Robert L. Stuart, New York, 1882
Robert L. Stuart, New York, 1872, purchased at the sale of foreign paintings contributed by artists in aid of the Chicago Fire sufferers

Exhibited at the 1883 *Pedestal Fund Art Loan Exhibition*, no. 1, *The Cavalier*, loaned by Mrs. R. L. Stuart

PLATE XXII

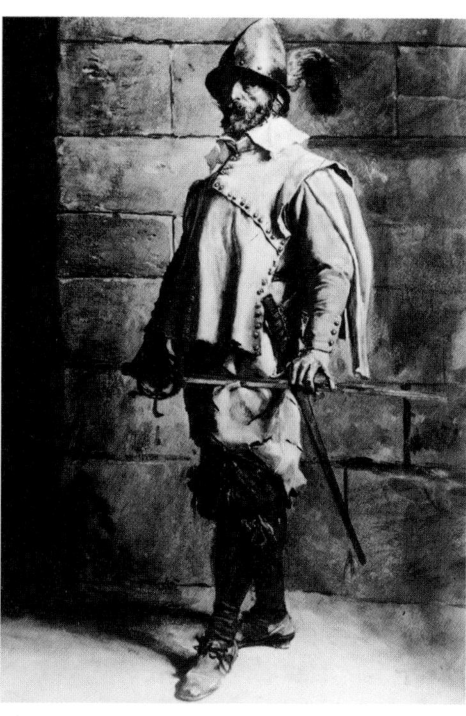

Questioning the longevity of Ernest Meissonier's fame, the American critic Clarence Cook wrote that "a man must be associated with his own time and his own experience" in order that his reputation endure.[1] Meissonier was one of the most popular painters in America in the 1880s and was represented in nearly every noteworthy collection by a carefully drawn study of historically costumed figures reading, smoking, playing cards, or engaged in military pursuits.[2] Cook attributed this success to the fact that the prices of his paintings were well publicized when sold from the studio or at auction and that "a mercantile community, especially one that has not enjoyed the advantage of seeing a great many pictures,"[3] has no better basis upon which to judge an artist.

Although several major works by Meissonier were in New York collections at the time of the *Pedestal Fund Art Loan Exhibition*, the selections committee chose to represent him by two small paintings: a watercolor of the artist as *A Cavalier*, which had been

Meissonier's contribution to an auction for the benefit of the 1872 Chicago fire victims, and the panel painting of *A General and His Aide-de-Camp* (pl. XXI; The Metropolitan Museum of Art, New York), a scene on the sun-drenched shores of Antibes, borrowed from Catharine Lorillard Wolfe. Despite this concession to Meissonier's consistently skillful execution and composition, both paintings were hung outside the main picture gallery at the exhibition, sharing in the company of Jean-Louis Hamon's *Etruscan Merchant* (fig. 15, p. 30) and Edouard Detaille's celebrated scene of the Franco-Prussian War, *Salut aux blessés* (fig. 19, p. 32).

1. Cook I, p. 68.
2. Edward Strahan lists forty-five paintings by Meissonier in the collections surveyed in *The Art Treasures of America* (1879–82).
3. Cook I, p. 69. Cook acknowledged that Meissonier had merits enough to earn him a distinguished name, but attributed his success to the fact that minuteness of finish, within a general aspect of largeness of effect, would always amuse a great many people.

55.
HENDRIK WILLEM MESDAG (Dutch, 1831–1915)
Departure of the Fishing Boats, Scheveningen
Oil on panel
20⅛ x 15½ in.
Signed l.r.: *H W Mesdag*
Worcester Art Museum, Worcester, Massachusetts, Bequest of Joseph Tuckerman, 1899
Provenance: Joseph Tuckerman, 1880

At the Paris Salon of 1872, a painting called *Le Départ des barques à Scheveningue* was found to have "an admirable verity of observation; one sees the white and sparkling water undulate under the dark boats."[1] The critic's praise confirmed the international reputation Hendrik Mesdag had established two years earlier when he won a gold medal at the Salon for *Les Brisants de la Mer du Nord.* By the mid-1870s he was chairman of Pulchri Studio, the art society of The Hague, and had begun plans to provide a permanent home for his growing collection of contemporary French and Dutch paintings.[2] The artist's taste, documented in the Mesdag Museum, which William Merritt Chase would visit with his students in 1903,[3] was mirrored by that of Daniel Cottier, who helped introduce Mesdag and his circle to America. Promoted by Cottier and by Mesdag, who served as head of the art committee for the Netherlands section of the World's Columbian Exhibition, Chicago, in 1893, the intimate genre scenes, painterly landscapes, and marines of the Hague School remained popular with collectors through the end of the century.

1. Paul Mantz, "Le Salon de 1872," *Gazette des Beaux-Arts,* vol. 6, per. 2 (July 1872), p. 47. He describes "une vérité d'observation admirable; on voit, sous les bateaux noirs, onduler l'eau blonde et vivante."
2. *The Hague School* 1983, p. 257.
3. Pisano 1979, p. 29.

56.
LOUIS METTLING (French, 1847–1904)
The Studio, 1874
Oil on canvas
17½ x 15¾ in.
Signed and dated l.l.: *L. Mettling* 74.
National Gallery of Canada, Ottawa
Musée des beaux-arts du Canada, Ottawa
Provenance: Cottier & Co., New York, 1911
E. J. van Wisselingh, 1892
Daniel Cottier, New York, by 1883
Exhibited at the 1883 *Pedestal Fund Art Loan Exhibition,* no. 114, *Among the Curios,* loaned by Daniel Cottier
PLATE XXIII

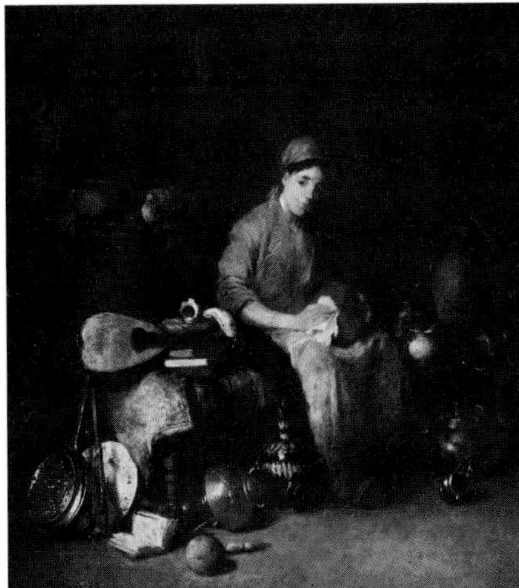

57.
LOUIS METTLING
The Peasant
Oil on canvas
24½ x 20½ in.
Signed u.l.: *L Mettling*
National Gallery of Canada, Ottawa
Musée des beaux-arts du Canada, Ottawa
Provenance: Wallis and Son, London, 1913

Louis Mettling, like his countryman Adolphe Monticelli, was introduced to America by the dealer Daniel Cottier. Admired by William Merritt Chase, who owned six of his paintings, and would have appreciated the Leibl-like analysis of the face of *The Peasant* (cat. no. 57), Mettling was disproportionately well-represented at the *Pedestal Fund Art Loan Exhibition* through seven loans from Cottier and two from the collection of Erwin Davis.

In 1877 Cottier had shown "a remarkable portrait in a few rich colors by Mettling"[1] at his Fifth Avenue gallery and expanded his selection to eight works the following year. At the 1878 sale of the Cottier collection, however, Mettling was said to suffer by "the increased number of specimens"[2] in which he could be studied, and all but one painting, the flower piece later loaned to the Pedestal Fund show by Erwin Davis,[3] failed to meet reserve prices and remained unsold. By 1883 critical opinion had again softened, and Mettling, "never seen before to such advantage," was praised for his "choice and fruity touch" and for "a most pleasing vaporous quality" in the copy after Rembrandt (fig. 8, p. 25) reproduced in the Pedestal Fund exhibition catalogue.[4] Cottier's loans included *The Studio,* a charming study of a young girl scouring a pot while seated "among the curios"[5] of an artist's atelier, as well as a selection of genre pieces and figure studies. *The Studio* was in Cottier's private collection until his death in 1891, and was among the works illustrated in the catalogue of his highly publicized sale in Paris in 1892.

1. "The Fine Arts. Opening of the Cottier Gallery on Fifth-Avenue," *The New York Times,* March 1, 1877, p. 4.
2. "The Cottier Collection of Paintings," *The New York Times,* April 17, 1878, p. 5.
3. Cottier Sale, New York, 1878, lot 43, *Flowers,* 16 x 13 in., was sold to J. A. Harper, and Davis purchased it at the J. A. Harper Sale, 1880. Cottier later sold another painting by Mettling from the 1878 sale (lot 108, *The Servant,* 16 x 13 in.) to H. O. Havemeyer.
4. "The Pedestal Art Loan," *The New York Times,* December 16, 1883, p. 5.
5. The painting was exhibited as *Among the Curios* (no. 114) at the Pedestal Fund show. The catalogue of the Cottier Sale in Paris, 1892, listed it as no. 85, *Le Récurage (Scouring).* It sold to Cottier's former associate, Elbert Jan van Wisselingh, for FF 2,700, and later reappeared at Cottier & Co., New York, to be included in the Inglis Sale, 1909 (lot 70, *Le Récurage,* "From the Collection of Daniel Cottier who purchased it from the artist").

58.
GEORGES MICHEL (French, 1763–1843)
The Windmill, c. 1820
Oil on panel
38 x 49⅝ in.
Herbert F. Johnson Museum of Art, Cornell University, Ithaca, New York, Robert Sterling Clark Foundation Fund
Provenance: Walker Art Galleries, Minneapolis, by 1927
Newmann Collection, Antwerp, Belgium

59.
GEORGES MICHEL (1763–1843)
Clouds and Landscape (The Hills of Montmartre), c. 1826
Oil on canvas
33½ x 46½ in.
The Heckscher Museum, Huntington, New York, Gift of August Heckscher

Provenance: August Heckscher, 1920
Mr. Cornell, 1915
Ichabod T. Williams, New York, by 1883
Daniel Cottier, New York

Exhibited at the 1883 *Pedestal Fund Art Loan Exhibition,* no. 38, *Hills of Montmartre,* loaned by Ichabod T. Williams

PLATE XXIV

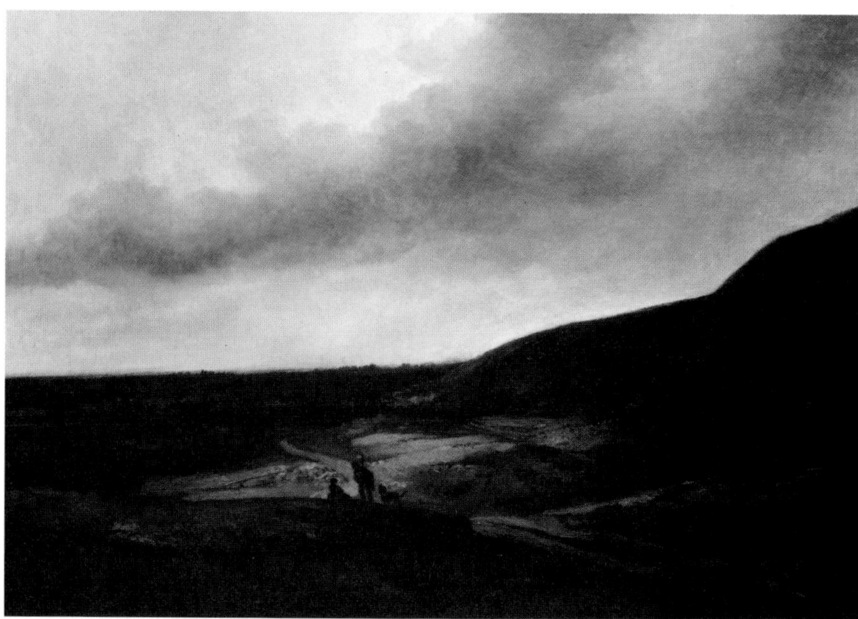

As landscape painting of the Barbizon School gained popularity in America, there emerged from obscurity the work of a predecessor, Georges Michel.[1] Described as "the French Ruisdael" for a style that emulated the seventeenth-century Dutch master, Michel specialized in later years in expansive views of the outskirts of Paris, sometimes breaking the low horizon with the silhouette of a picturesque windmill or populating the scene with solitary figures. Of the few works by Michel owned in America before 1883, most were concentrated in New England either in the collections of Martin Brimmer and Quincy Adams Shaw in Boston or of Beriah Wall in Providence. In New York, J. C. Runkle's modest collection included two works by Michel, who was otherwise known only among artists and connoisseurs.

The *Pedestal Fund Art Loan Exhibition* offered New Yorkers an impressive selection of five Michel landscapes—"powerful, broad, and carefully painted, like the old Dutchmen, sometimes like Old Crome"[2]—borrowed from the collections of Daniel Cottier,[3] Erwin Davis[4] and Ichabod T. Williams. *Clouds and Landscape,* which was loaned by Williams under the title *Hills of Montmartre,* was singled out by Clarence Cook in *Art and Artists of our Time* as an example of the simplicity of treatment, scorn for detail, and reliance upon vast perspectives that characterized a precursor of modern landscape painting.[5]

1. Michel's revival was actually precipitated by the interest of the Barbizon painters in his work, by the criticism of Thoré-Burger, and by Alfred Sensier's *Etude sur Georges Michel* (Paris, 1873).
2. "The Pedestal Art Loan," *The New York Times,* December 2, 1883, p. 2.
3. Cottier exhibited, but failed to sell, Michel's *Landscape–Coming Storm* (lot 106, 13 x 21 in.) at his 1878 New York sale, and described Michel in the introduction to the sale catalogue as one of the artists whose true worth and exalted place in the history of modern art was not yet comprehended. The sale of Cottier's collection after his death (Cottier Sale, Paris, 1892) included eight paintings by Michel.
4. A Michel watercolor, *Landscape,* 14 x 22 in., in the Davis Sale, 1889, may have been the painting he loaned to the *Pedestal Fund Art Loan Exhibition.*
5. Cook II, illus. opp. p. 205, as *Landscape.*

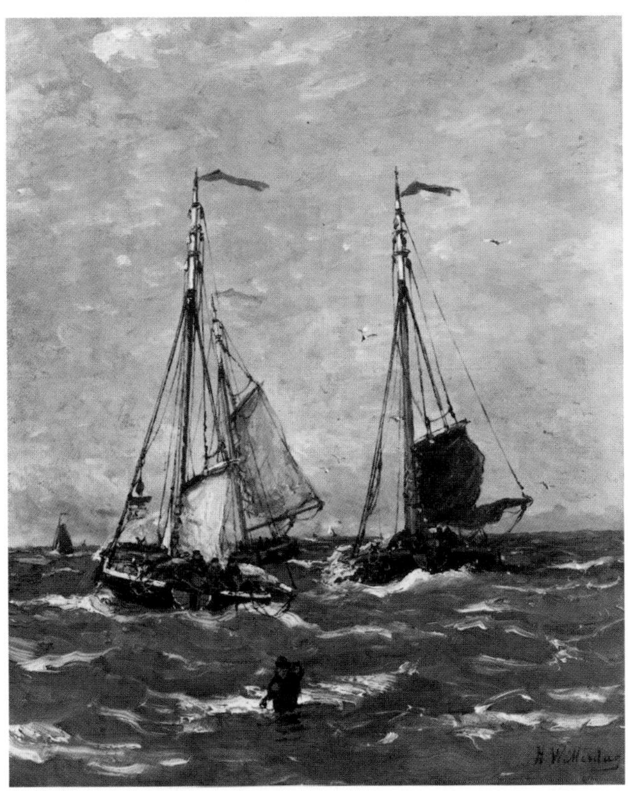

55.

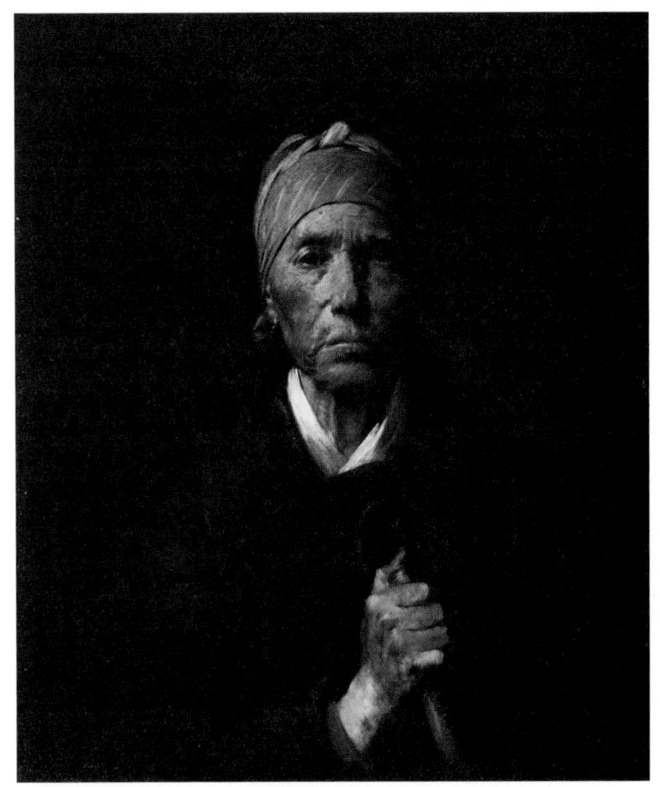

57.

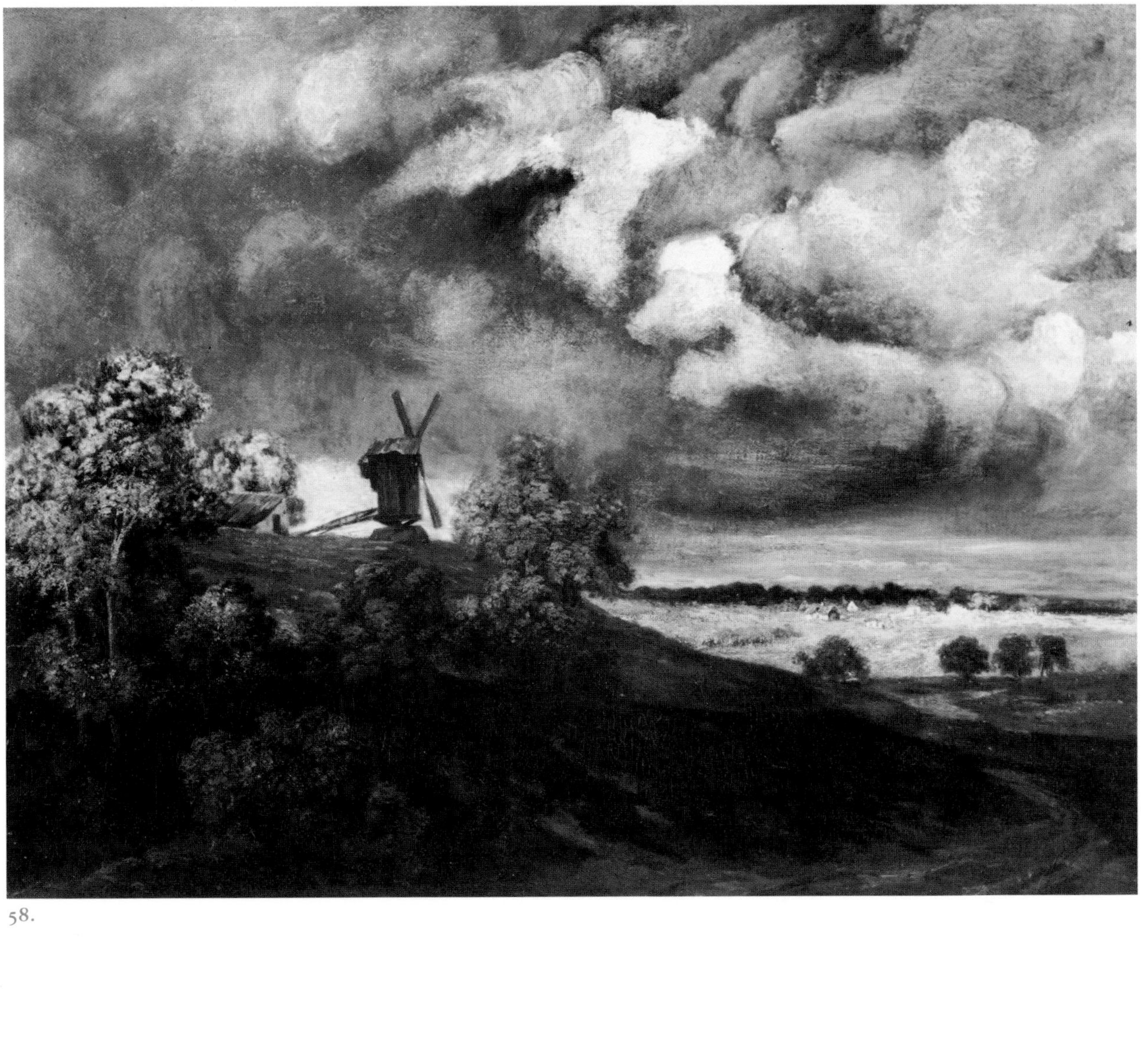

58.

60.
JEAN-FRANÇOIS MILLET (French, 1814–1875)
The Bather, c. 1846
Oil on canvas
12⅝ x 9⅝ in.
Signed l.r.: *J F Millet*
Yale University Art Gallery, New Haven, Connecticut, Anonymous Gift in Honor of Alan Shestack

Provenance: Arthur M. Barnhart
George Grey Barnard
Alfred Corning Clark, 1889
Erwin Davis, New York, by 1883

Exhibited at the 1883 *Pedestal Fund Art Loan Exhibition,* no. 165, *Woman Bathing,* loaned by Erwin Davis

PLATE XXV

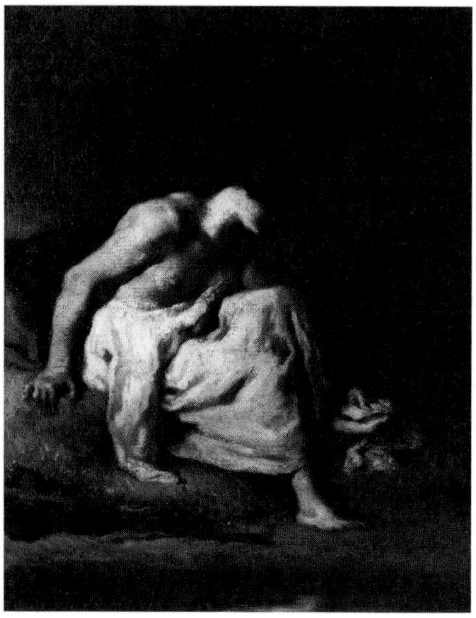

61.
JEAN-FRANÇOIS MILLET
The Quarriers, 1846–47
Oil on canvas
29 x 23½ in.
Millet Sale stamp l.r.: *J. F. Millet*
The Toledo Museum of Art, Toledo, Ohio, Gift of Arthur J. Secor

Provenance: Arthur J. Secor, Toledo, 1915–22
M. Knoedler & Co., New York, 1915
Ichabod T. Williams, New York, by 1883
Cottier & Co., New York, by 1878
Millet Sale, Paris, 1875

Exhibited at the 1883 *Pedestal Fund Art Loan Exhibition,* no. 36, *The Quarriers,* loaned by Ichabod T. Williams

PLATE XXX

62.
JEAN-FRANÇOIS MILLET
Après le bain, c. 1846–48
Oil on panel
5⅜ x 6¾ in.
Signed l.r.: *J F M*
Private Collection, Switzerland

Provenance: Richard Zinser
M. Knoedler & Co., Inc., New York
Frank Gair Macomber, 1919–20
J. Macomber, 1903
Durand-Ruel, 1903
Mrs. A. Esplen
Albert Spencer, by 1883
M. Perrau, Paris
Probably Alfred Serusier, Paris, 1877

Exhibited at the 1883 *Pedestal Fund Art Loan Exhibition,* no. 47, *Nude,* loaned by Albert Spencer

PLATE XXIX

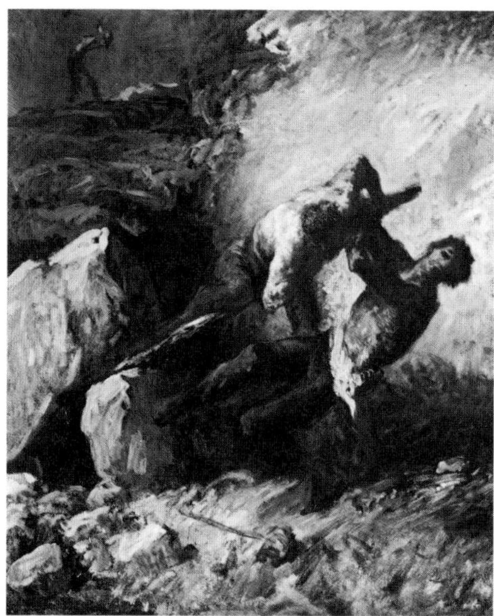

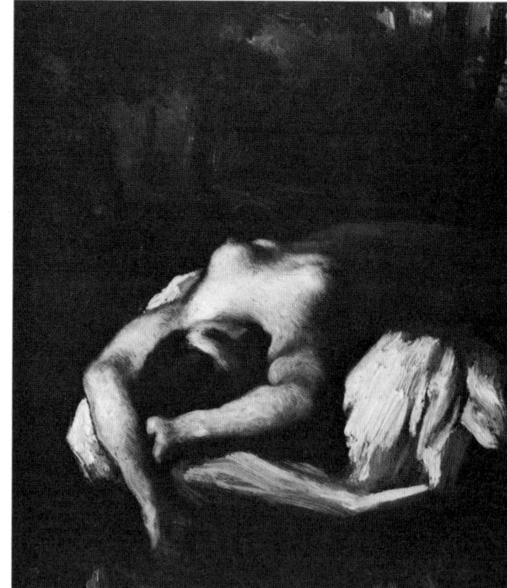

Eight years after the death of Jean-François Millet, his paintings were known and sought after by private collectors throughout the United States. Although the most important collections had been assembled in Boston in the 1860s and 1870s, when appreciation of Millet was fostered by William Morris Hunt and his circle, interest had spread to New York, Philadelphia, Cincinnati, Chicago, and Louisville by the early 1880s. Of the more that fifty works by Millet recorded in Edward Strahan's *The Art Treasures of America,*[1] the majority were paintings of sheepshearers, wool-carders, and spinners, which illustrated Edward Wheelwright's interpretation of the artist as a spiritual transcriber of peasant life.[2]

The image of Millet as a rural saint was apparently not the impression that the organizers of the *Pedestal Fund Art Loan Exhibition* wished to convey, however, nor did they conform to socio-political arguments on the meaning of his work. With an abundance of "typical" Millets from which to choose, the selections committee avoided anything that might lend itself to sentimental interpretation on the part of the press. It was no wonder, therefore, that *The New York Times* on the one hand complained that there were so many examples of Millet, "an artist for the select,"[3] and on the other deplored the absence of *The Sower,* a painting that had been brought to New York by Daniel Cottier and would easily have been available for loan.[4]

Dominating the show were eight paintings that ranged from female nudes of the 1840s to the late *Autumn Landscape with a Flock of Turkeys* (cat. no. 64; pl. XXXII). Rejecting any suggestion of narrative in all but the latter painting, in which a solitary figure is silhouetted against the sky in a melancholy, almost Symbolist setting, the selections were made from the highly personal collections of Charles A. Dana, Erwin Davis, Richard Morris Hunt, Albert Spencer, and Ichabod T. Williams. Five of the paintings involved studies of the nude, although two of these had religious or mythological connotations and a third was called *Peasant and Child* (now *The Whisper,* pl. XXVI; National Gallery, London) despite its references to Venus and Cupid. Davis's seated *Bather* (cat. no. 60; pl. XXV), crouched like a Michelangelesque sibyl on the ledge of a riverbank, was illustrated at the opening of the Paintings Section of the catalogue (fig. 1, p. 23). *Après le bain* (cat. no. 62; pl. XXIX), "a work that crushes all competition,"[5] caught the nude figure reclining in a position of abandon that reversed a gesture used by Delacroix for the wife of Sardanapalus. Drawn from the Old Testament, but painted with a similarly Romantic aggressiveness, was his *Susanna and the Elders* (pl. XXVIII; National Gallery of Victoria, Melbourne), "a tragedy almost too fearful to be looked at,"[6] from the collection of Hunt, the architect of the Pedestal. *Hylas and the Nymphs* (pl. XXVII; Rijksmuseum Kröller-Müller, Otterlo), loaned by Williams and later sold back to Daniel Cottier, so distorted the figures as to confuse their limbs with the landscape surrounding them.

After examining these paintings, the single forceful gesture of the *Woodchopper* (cat. no. 63), considered one of the "choicest hauls"[7] at M. Knoedler & Co., New York, in 1882, must have been a relief to viewers, although it would be hard to find poetic a

63.
JEAN-FRANÇOIS MILLET
The Woodchopper, c. 1850
Oil on canvas
15⅝ x 12½ in.
Signed l.r.: *J. F. Millet*
Ball State University Art Gallery, Muncie, Indiana, Elisabeth Ball Collection, Permanent Loan from George and Frances Ball Foundation

Provenance: Miss Elisabeth Ball, by 1957
Mr. and Mrs. George A. Ball, 1935
Mrs. James G. Shepherd, New York
Mr. James G. Shepherd, New York
John Levy Galleries, New York
Stendhal Galleries, Paris
M. Knoedler & Co., New York, by 1883
Probably Baron Papelon, Paris, 1859
Probably Baron Courtier, Paris, 1857

Exhibited at the 1883 *Pedestal Fund Art Loan Exhibition*, no. 76, *The Wood-Chopper*, loaned by Mr. Knoedler
PLATE XXXI

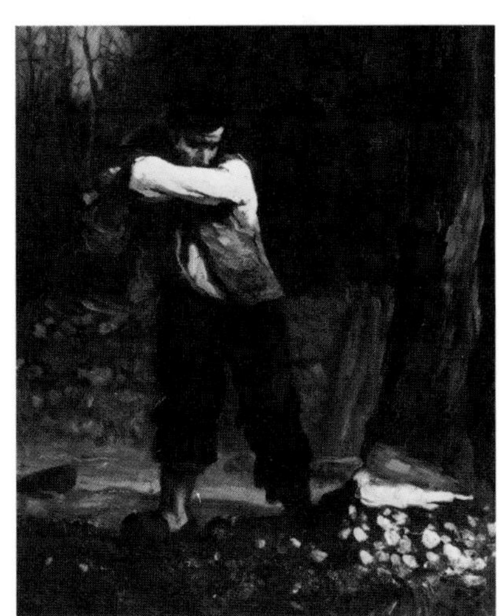

64.
JEAN-FRANÇOIS MILLET
Autumn Landscape with a Flock of Turkeys, c. 1870–74
Oil on canvas
31⅞ x 39 in.
Signed l.r.: *J. F. Millet*
The Metroplitan Museum of Art, New York, Bequest of Isaac D. Fletcher, 1917, Mr. and Mrs. Isaac D. Fletcher Collection

Provenance: Mr. and Mrs. Isaac D. Fletcher, New York, 1898
Hermann Schaus, New York, 1898
Charles A. Dana, New York, by 1883
M. M...., Marseilles, by 1874

Exhibited at the 1883 *Pedestal Fund Art Loan Exhibition*, no. 6, *The Turkey Guardian*, loaned by Charles A. Dana
PLATE XXXII

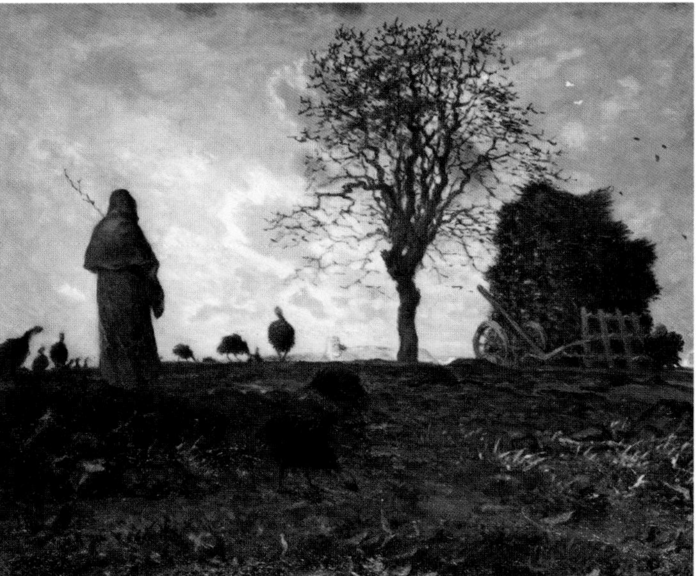

65.
ADOLPHE JOSEPH THOMAS MONTICELLI (French, 1824–1886)
Fête Galante, c. 1865–66
Oil on canvas
31⅞ x 46¼ in.
Private Collection, Chicago
Courtesy Pannonia Galleries, New York

Provenance: Pamela and Julian Beck, New York
Max Stern, Galerie Dominion, Montreal, 1971
Mr. Richard F. Angus, Montreal
Angus Collection, Montreal

rugged appearance that was no more refined than that of Courbet's *Stonebreakers*. An even more alienating alternative to the noble *Sower* was *The Quarriers* (cat no. 61; pl. XXX). Described when it was first shown in New York in 1877 as a sketch from the quarries near Paris,[8] it had an expressive brushstroke and gestural motif that appealed only to a small circle of connoisseurs.

This idiosyncratic, challenging selection of paintings by an artist who had been reverently brought to the attention of Americans by the English edition of Alfred Sensier's biography in 1881 did not alter the dominant critical analysis of Millet during the next twenty years. What it reveals, in retrospect, is the existence of an early core of American admirers who appreciated his art for qualities that ignored polemic and sentiment.

1. Strahan III, p. 139.
2. See Edward Wheelwright, "Personal Recollections of Jean-François Millet," *Atlantic Monthly*, vol. 38 (September 1876), pp. 257–76. The importance of Wheelwright's writings on America's interpretation of the work of Millet is analyzed by Laura Meixner in "The 'Millet Myth' and the American Public," *An International Episode: Millet, Monet and Their North American Counterparts* (Memphis: The Dixon Gallery and Gardens, 1982), pp. 68–91.
3. "The Pedestal Art Loan," *The New York Times*, December 16, 1883, p. 5.
4. "Art Notes: The Great Painting of 'The Sower,' by Millet," *The New York Times*, December 9, 1883, p. 6. The painting was already known by an etching by Matthew Maris and by an expensive heliotype published by Osgood and Co., Boston.
5. "The Pedestal Art Loan," *The New York Times*, December 2, 1883, p. 2.
6. *Ibid.*
7. *The New York Times*, December 31, 1882, p. 5.
8. "The Fine Arts. Opening of the Cottier Gallery on Fifth-Avenue," *The New York Times*, March 1, 1877, p. 4.

66.
ADOLPHE JOSEPH THOMAS MONTICELLI
Gateway to a Fort, c. 1867
Oil on panel
15¾ x 22⅞ in.
Signed l.l.: *Monticelli*
Montreal Museum of Fine Arts
Musée des beaux-arts de Montréal
Bequest of Miss Adaline Van Horne

Provenance: Adaline Van Horne, Montreal
Cottier & Co., New York

Exhibited at the 1883 *Pedestal Fund Art Loan Exhibition*, no. 128, *Gateway*, loaned by Daniel Cottier

PLATE XXXIII

In the fall of 1877, the work of Adolphe Monticelli attracted the attention of New York art critics through the exhibition of his painting *Don Quixote* at the Fifth Avenue galleries of Cottier & Co.[1] Although the American dealer Samuel P. Avery claimed credit for introducing Monticelli to New York,[2] it was Cottier who had the courage, even audacity, to stock and promote the exotic subjects of the Marseillaise artist.[3] Despite the limited audience for a talent characterized by an "effect of bewilderment, of gorgeous color, light yet effective drawing, brilliant but uninvolved composition,"[4] Cottier featured Monticelli at this gallery in 1878[5] and 1879,[6] and loaned eight of his paintings to the *Pedestal Fund Art Loan Exhibition*, including *The Farmyard* (pl. XXXIV), *Gateway to a Fort* (cat. no. 66; pl. XXXIII), and a number of *fêtes champêtres*. *Landscape with Figures* (cat. no. 67), a medieval scene that was "restored" by Matthew Maris, probably at Cottier's request, was owned by Ichabod T. Williams, another lender to the 1883 show.

Largely through Cottier's enthusiasm and persistence, major examples of Monticelli's work were owned by American collectors Catholina Lambert,[7] William A. Clark,[8] Clement Griscom,[9] and Herbert Terrell,[10] and the artist's reputation among connoisseurs was established in London, Scotland, and Canada prior to his popular recognition in Paris at the World's Fair of 1900.

1. "The Cottier Collection of Paintings," *The New York Times*, April 17, 1878, p. 5.
2. Samuel Avery, "The Artist Monticelli," letter to the editor dated September 5, 1879, *The New York Times*, September 29, 1879, p. 2. Comparing Avery's conservative buying of Monticelli to Cottier's daring, the critic Montezuma in *The Art Amateur*, vol. 2, no. 5 (April 1880), remarked: "Those at Avery's, I do not doubt, are the more marketable, but which one of them will stand in artistic value before 'The Scarf Dance?' [at Cottier's]."
3. Twenty-five paintings by Monticelli were included in the Cottier Sale, Paris, 1892 (lots 99–123).
4. *The New York Times*, April 17, 1878.
5. "Notes," *The Art Journal*, vol. 4 (March 1878), p. 4.
6. "An Impressionist's Work: The Pictures of Monticelli," *The New York Times*, May 20, 1879.
7. See New York, American Art Association, *Illustrated Catalogue of the Valuable Paintings and Sculpture by the Old and Modern Masters forming the Famous Catholina Lambert Collection*, 1916, which includes a commentary by W. Roberts, London, on the twenty-nine Monticellis in the collection.
8. A collection of twenty-one works by Monticelli was given to The Corcoran Gallery of Art, Washington, D.C., by Senator William A. Clark.
9. See Eliot Clark, "Adolphe Monticelli: 1824–1886," *Art in America*, vol. 3, no. 1 (December 1914), re: Cottier's role in the promotion of Monticelli and his reference to *La Cour de Henri Trois*, recently sold from the Griscom collection.
10. Regarding Monticelli's *Don Quixote*, see Samuel Isham, "The Herbert L. Terrell Collection," in La Farge and Jacacci 1907, p. 442.

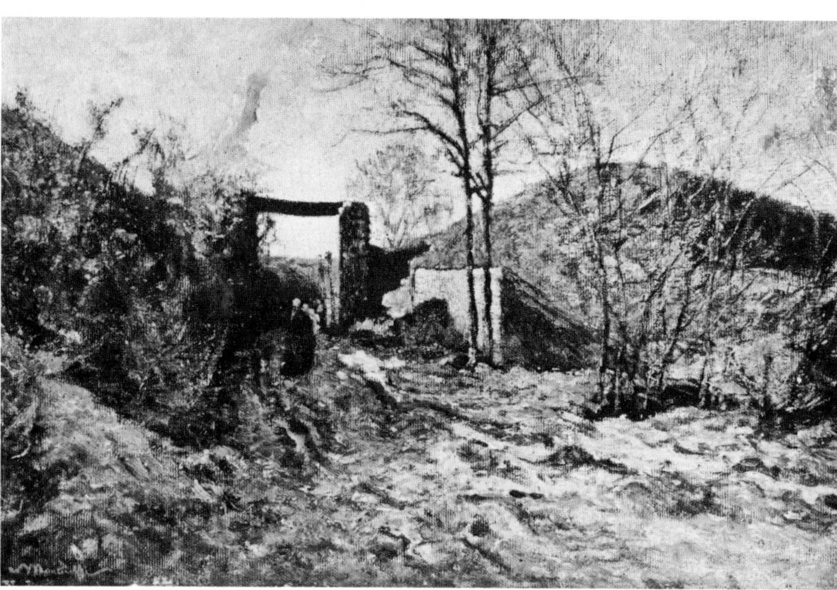

67.
ADOLPHE JOSEPH THOMAS MONTICELLI and MATTHEW MARIS
Landscape with Figures
Oil on panel
17½ x 31½ in.
The Phillips Collection, Washington, D.C.

Provenance: James L. Phillips, 1915
Ichabod T. Williams, New York
Daniel Cottier, New York

PLATE XXXV

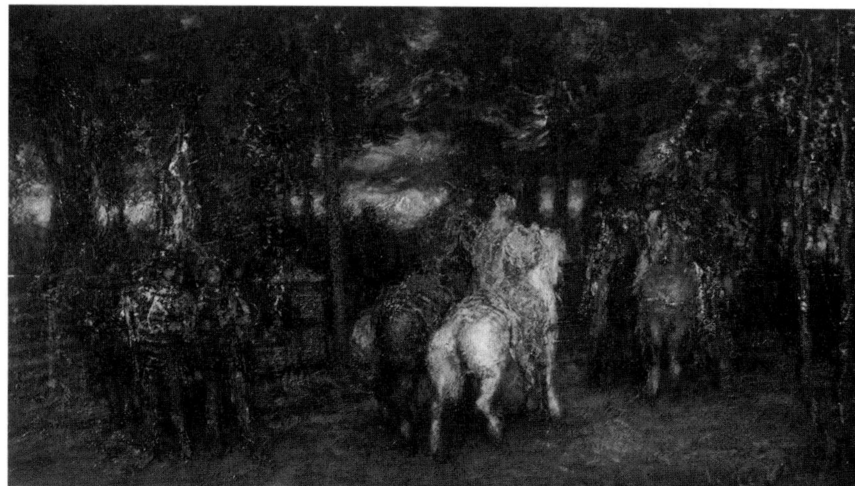

68.
MICHAEL MUNKACSY (Hungarian, 1844–1900)
Luncheon in the Garden
Oil on canvas
32 x 42 in.
Signed l.r.: *M. Munkacsy*
The New-York Historical Society, New York, Robert L. Stuart Collection

Provenance: The New York Public Library, 1892
Mrs. Robert L. Stuart, New York, 1882
Robert L. Stuart, New York, 1881

Exhibited at the 1883 *Pedestal Fund Art Loan Exhibition*, no. 2, *In the Garden*, loaned by Mrs. R. L. Stuart

Two of the most important early works by Michael Munkácsy were owned in America in 1883. *The Last Day of a Condemned Man*, the painting that introduced his dark realist style to the Paris Salon of 1870, had been commis-

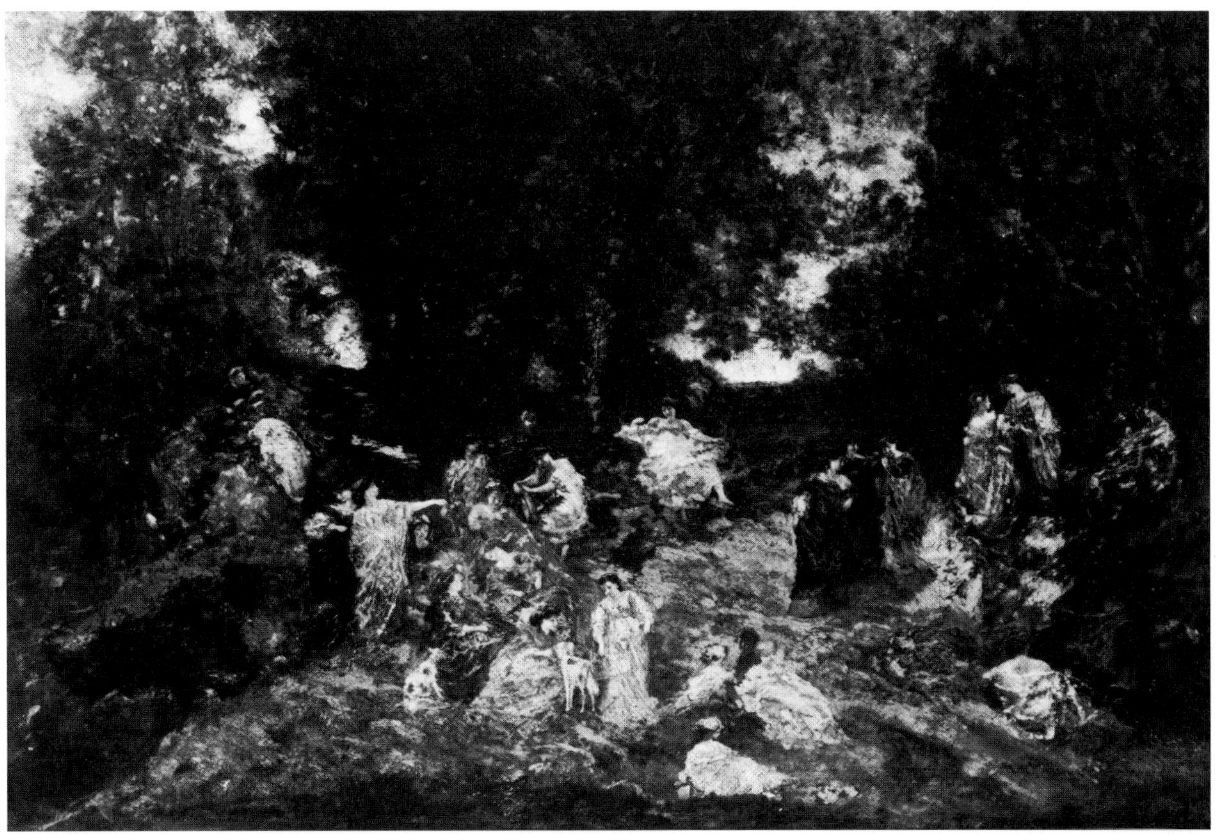

65.

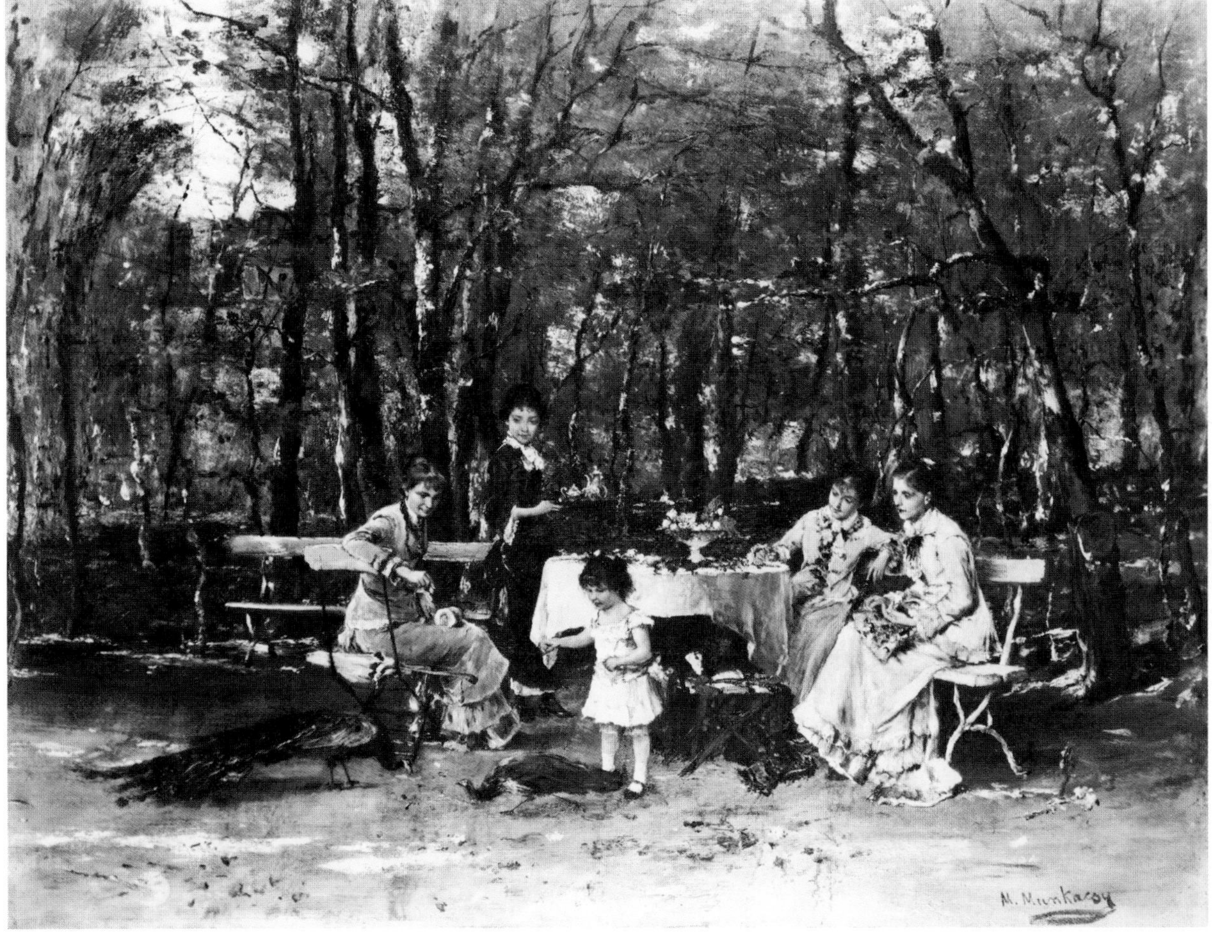

68.

sioned by W. P. Wilstach of Philadelphia and hung in his gallery there.[1] Munkácsy's *Milton Dictating "Paradise Lost" to his Daughters,* his award-winning contribution to the 1878 *Exposition Universelle,* was purchased by Robert Lenox Kennedy and presented to the New York Public Library where it received widespread critical attention.[2]

Born in Hungary, Munkácsy began his training in Budapest and Vienna, and briefly studied at the Munich Academy under Franz Adam. During his first visit to Paris in 1867, he was impressed with the paintings of Gustave Courbet and the Barbizon School; but, attracted by the presence of Ludwig Knaus, he returned to Germany and remained in Düsseldorf for the next four years. By the late 1870s, after he had returned to France, peasant customs had been replaced by bourgeois settings and Parisian interiors, and Munkácsy gradually adjusted his dark palette to the lighter tone of the Impressionists. An important example of this shift, *Luncheon in the Garden* (cat. no. 68),[3] was loaned to the *Pedestal Fund Art Loan Exhibition* by Mrs. Robert L. Stuart, whose husband, a New York collector and former president of the Museum of Natural History, New York, had purchased it in 1881.[4] A picture of fashionably dressed women and a child admiring peacocks in a park setting, it offered viewers a sharp contrast to Munkácsy's earlier narratives and demonstrated a brilliance in color and facility in brushstroke that appealed not only to William Merritt Chase but also to younger European contemporaries such as Max Liebermann and Fritz von Uhde.

1. John R. Tait, "Michael Munkácsy," *American Art Review,* vol. 2, part 1 (1881), pp. 235–43; vol. 2, part 2 (1881), pp. 13–20, noted that the painting was commissioned by Wilstach. Tait, an American, was a fellow student of Munkácsy's at Düsseldorf. George W. Sheldon, *Hours with Art and Artists* (New York: D. Appleton and Company, 1882), p. 12, also mentions that it was painted for an American in Düsseldorf in 1869. The painting won a gold medal at the 1870 Paris Salon. See Strahan III, illus. opp. p. 28, *The Last Day of a Malefactor.*
2. Tait, p. 18, noted that the extensive press received by the painting of Milton, which was among the works that won Munkácsy a medal of honor at the 1878 *Exposition Universelle,* was reprinted in the New York *Evening Post* when the painting was acquired by Robert L. Kennedy. It was also published in a booklet prepared by Munkácsy's Paris dealer, Charles Sedelmeyer, who presented a bust of Munkácsy to the New York Public Library (Tait, p. 236).
3. Reproduced in F. Walter Ilges, *M. von Munkacsy* (Bielefeld and Leipzig: Velhagen & Klasing, 1897), fig. 75, p. 84, *Mädchen im Park Pfaue fütternd;* and in a pencil sketch fig. 74, p. 83.
4. Stuart, who died in 1882, owned a Munkácsy *Study of Flowers,* purchased in 1881, and also had his portrait painted by Munkácsy, presumably in Paris. Both are mentioned by Sheldon, p. 12, but the portrait was not among the works bequeathed to the New York Public Library in 1892 by Mrs. Stuart.

69.
ALBERT NEUHUYS (Dutch, 1844–1914)
Mother and Children
Oil on panel
12¾ x 9¼ in.
Signed l.r.: *Albert Neuhuijs*
The Toledo Museum of Art, Toledo, Ohio, Gift of Edward Drummond Libbey

Provenance: Edward Drummond Libbey, Toledo, 1904
Henry Reinhardt, Milwaukee

Johannes Albert Neuhuys was born in Utrecht, Holland, and trained at the art academy of Antwerp. He returned to the Netherlands in the early 1870s and settled in The Hague in 1875. The peasant interiors upon which he established his reputation were begun during this period, when he associated with Jacob Maris, Anton Mauve, and Joseph Israels, the artist to whom he is most frequently compared. *Mother and Children,* which was owned by Milwaukee dealer Henry Reinhardt around the turn of the century, is typical of Neuhuys in both subject matter and soft atmospheric brushwork.

Neuhuys, one of the younger members of the Hague School, was not well known in America before his introduction by Daniel Cottier. A single painting, *The Broken Pitcher,* was included in Cottier's 1878 New York sale, but was bought in for lack of interest.[1] Cottier admired Neuhuys for his ability as a colorist and loaned two of his works, *Mending Sacks* (fig. 4, p. 24) and *The Lesson* (possibly fig. 56, p. 46), to the *Pedestal Fund Art Loan Exhibition.* Neuhuys was described by *The New York Times* critic as "a rarely seen painter ...whose vein with children and laboring folk is very pleasing."[2] A founder of the Laren School of painters, with whom American artist Gari Melchers would study, Neuhuys eventually developed an international following that included, in the 1880s, Erwin Davis and Mary Jane Morgan.[3] His reputation expanded toward the end of the century, and, after an initial trip to the United States in 1904, Neuhuys was invited to serve as a juror in 1908 and 1910 at the *Carnegie International Exhibition* in Pittsburgh.

1. Cottier Sale, New York, 1878, lot 10, 22 x 13 in.
2. "The Pedestal Art Loan," *The New York Times,* December 16, 1883, p. 5. Mary Jane Morgan Sale, 1886, lot 28, Albert Neuhuys, *The Reading Lesson,* 1874, 18 x 13 in.
3. Davis loaned Neuhuys's *Children* to the Pedestal Fund exhibition. The Davis Sale, 1889, contained the following paintings by Neuhuys: lot 37, *At Supper,* 20 x 25 in., watercolor; and lot 89, *Dressing the Baby,* 22 x 30 in.

70.
GIUSEPPE DE NITTIS (Italian, 1846–1884)
Return from the Races, 1875
Oil on canvas
22 x 45 in.
Signed and dated l.r.: *De Nittis 75*
Philadelphia Museum of Art, The W. P. Wilstach Collection, Given by John G. Johnson

Provenance: John G. Johnson, Philadelphia
Mrs. A. T. Stewart, New York
A. T. Stewart, New York

American critic Clarence Cook placed Italian painter Giuseppe de Nittis among "the best of modish painters of our day, the finest of the mirrors held up to the artificial life of our time ."[1] This praise easily fit his *Return from the Races,* a picture of fashionably dressed Parisians seated in the shade and parading in carriages in the Bois de Boulogne. Part of the collection of Mrs. A. T. Stewart, New York, in the 1880s (although not in the Pedestal Fund exhibition), it was one of a number of de Nittis's works in America at this time, including several of the costume pieces he made after arriving in Paris in 1867[2] and views of modern life that dated from his return to "nature" and his involvement in the first Impressionist show of 1874. *Che Freddo!,* a snowy scene of women who have descended from a carriage to test the ice on a frozen lake, was in the collection of Chauncey J. Blair of Chicago.[3] A third celebrated work, *Place de la Concorde* (possibly fig. 20, p. 32), was owned by the New York hotelier Samuel Hawk, who loaned it to the *Pedestal Fund Art Loan Exhibition.*[4]

De Nittis achieved considerable recognition in Paris in the late 1870s and early 1880s. The 1874 Salon success of *Che Freddo!* was followed by the distinction of exhibiting a dozen paintings at the 1878 *Exposition Universelle,* the subsequent purchase of one of his works by the French government, and the award of the Legion of Honor. Exhibitions at the galleries of the art publications *La Vie Moderne* and *L'Art* in 1879 and 1880, and personal involvement in the "petit Salon internationale" held at the Galerie Georges Petit in 1882 and 1883,[5] continued to bring his work to the attention of critics and artists, including William Merritt Chase, who owned a small de Nittis oil called *Winter.*[6]

1. Cook II, p. 137.
2. Strahan III lists eleven works by de Nittis, but does not mention *Place de la Concorde* in the Samuel Hawk collection.
3. Noted in Strahan III and reproduced, p. 65.
4. Described and illustrated by Cook II, pp. 135–36. When exhibited at the Pedestal Fund show, this painting was described as the "celebrated view" ("The Pedestal Art Loan," *The New York Times,* December 16, 1883, p. 5), which would lead one to believe that it was the painting of the Place de la Concorde in the rain (fig.

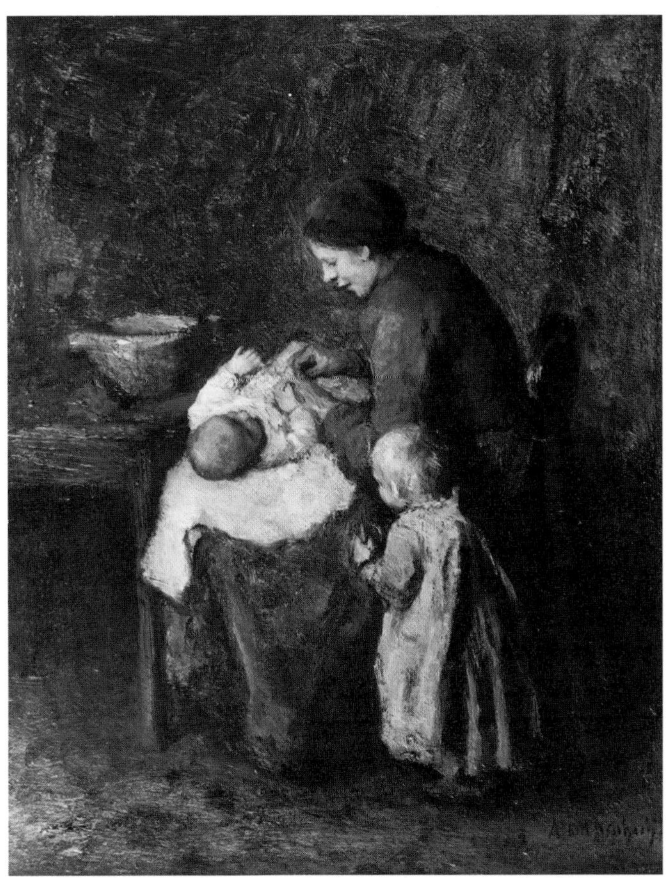

69.

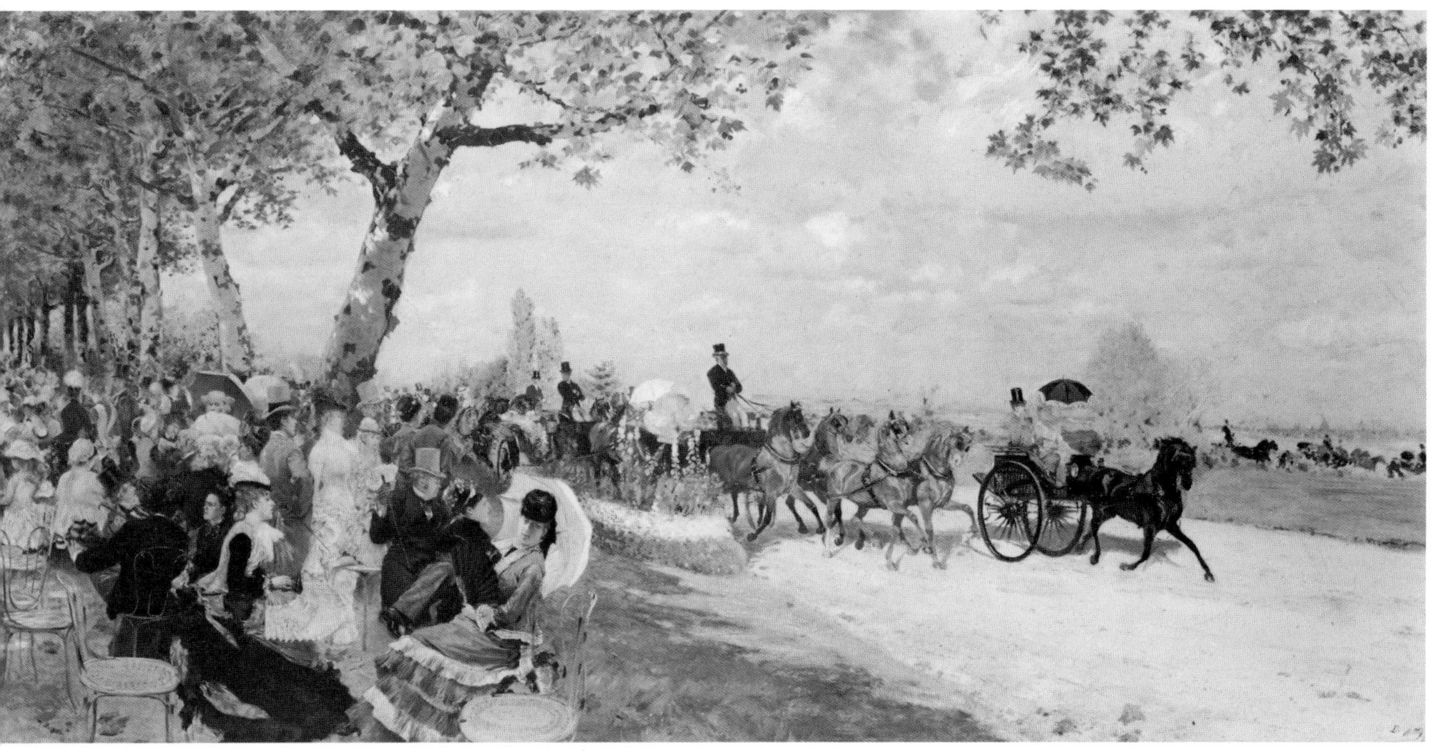

70.

20, p. 32) that was reproduced in two American publications in the 1880s; however, another painting of this site, a smaller, sunny view, was sold with the collection of William S. Hawk, Samuel Hawk's son, in 1931, and may be the work in question (see O'Brien, n.43).

5. See Emile Blémont, "Joseph De Nittis," in *Grands Peintres français et étrangers*, vol. 1 (Paris, 1884), pp. 113–28.

6. Pisano 1979, p. 30.

71.
ALBERTO PASINI (Italian, 1826–1899)
Mohammedan Market Scene (Constantinople), 1868
Oil on panel
10¹⁄₁₆ x 18¹⁄₁₆ in.
Signed and dated l.r.: *A. Pasini, 1868*
The Ackland Art Museum,
University of North Carolina at Chapel Hill,
Knapp Collection

Provenance: Joseph Palmer Knapp Collection, 1958

Alberto Pasini was represented by three paintings at the *Pedestal Fund Art Loan Exhibition,* escaping the general exclusion of such noted Orientalists as Jean-Léon Gérôme, his occasional traveling companion. Skilled at architectural subjects, Pasini was also a talented landscape painter who, in the 1850s, befriended Théodore Rousseau and made sketching trips with him along the Seine outside of Paris. He was known and admired by American collectors for paintings of Turkish mosques and markets, which had been inspired by an extended visit to Constantinople in 1868.[1]

Although capable of precise observation, Pasini could as easily capture a scene by recalling the vividness of local color and activity. Like a similar painting by Pasini that was exhibited at the *Pedestal Fund Art Loan Exhibition,* the *Mohammedan Market Scene (Constantinople)* is "luminous and vibrant... large in results."[2] Avoiding Orientalist anecdote, Pasini uses the market as a plein-air subject, documenting the atmosphere of the seaport, and conveying the daily commotion without laborious detail.

1. More than a dozen paintings by Pasini were owned in America in the early 1880s, including works in the collections of Catharine Lorillard Wolfe, Theodore Havemeyer, Henry C. Gibson, William T. Walters, and James H. Stebbins. The majority of these paintings were related to his trips to Persia and Turkey, but Havemeyer owned a painting of Venice that was probably made after Pasini returned there to live in 1878.

2. William T. Evans, who later became an important collector of American paintings, loaned *Constantinople,* another market scene, to the Pedestal Fund show. Although not illustrated, it was thoroughly described in the catalogue of the sale of his collection of European paintings in New York in 1890 (Evans Sale, 1890, no. 82, p. 59).

72.
THEODULE AUGUSTIN RIBOT (French, 1823–1891)
The Mandolin Player, 1862
Oil on canvas
28¾ x 23⅝ in.
Signed and dated l.r.: *t. Ribot, 1862*
Collection Joey and Toby Tanenbaum,
Toronto, Canada

Provenance: Mr. and Mrs. Joseph Tanenbaum, Toronto
Galerie André Watteau, Paris, 1975
Eduardo Mollard
R. Gerard

73.
THEODULE AUGUSTIN RIBOT
The Scullion, c. 1860–70
Oil on canvas
36⅜ x 20⅝ in.
Signed l.l.: *T. Ribot*
The Art Institute of Chicago, Mr. and Mrs. Lewis Larned Coburn Memorial Collection

Provenance: Mr. and Mrs. Lewis Larned Coburn
E. & A. Silberman Gallery, New York
Baron Adolphe Kohner, Budapest

Little known to American critics before the 1880s, Théodule Ribot was singled out by critics at the *Pedestal Fund Art Loan Exhibition* for *The Studio* (fig. 42, p. 40) from the collection of Ichabod T. Williams.[1] Acclaimed in Paris for an exhibition of his paintings at the galleries of the periodical *L'Art* in 1880,[2] Ribot, who had exhibited with Courbet and Manet in Munich at the 1869 *Internationale Kunstausstellung*,[3] was also greatly admired by Chase.[4]

Although Ribot's dark naturalistic canvases had been rejected by the Paris Salon juries of the 1850s, he attracted the attention of painter François Bonvin, who exhibited them in his own studio with the works of Henri Fantin-Latour, Antoine Vollon, and James Abbott McNeill Whistler. By 1861 Ribot had gained admission to the Salon, submitting several paintings of cooks and a still life of poultry. *The Scullion* (cat. no. 73), a knife protruding from the waist of his knotted apron and a steaming platter in his hands, is one of numerous figures of kitchen workers painted by Ribot during the 1860s. Posing comfortably with one slippered foot outstretched, the swarthy servant has unrefined features, laid in with wide flat strokes.

The scullion's counterpart, a street-elegant, Caravaggiesque *Mandolin Player* (cat. no. 72), is poised in song and dramatically lit against a neutral background, a cousin, as Gabriel Weisberg observes, to Manet's *Spanish Singer,* or *Guitarrero* (The Metropolitan Museum of Art, New York) of the 1861 Salon.[5] Like the cook's assistant, who was represented at the Pedestal Fund show by a humble colleague peeling potatoes, the musician belongs to a class of subjects that was frequently interpreted by Ribot. Daniel Cottier, who was the first to import Ribot's paintings to America, loaned a similar composition of a guitarist to the exhibition,[6] as well as a figure of *A Young Vendean* (pl. XXXVI; Montreal Museum of Fine Arts) with a hand resting on the barrel of a gun. Erwin Davis, the owner of Manet's *Boy with a Sword* (cat. no. 47; pl. XVII) and *Woman with a Parrot* (pl. XVIII), also owned several of Ribot's paintings, including one of "heavy strong heads of his children"[7] that was lent to the 1883 exhibition.

1. See O'Brien, n.118, for contemporary references to this painting. Another version, depicting the artist as a young man, is in the collection of the Munson-Williams-Proctor Institute Museum of Art, Utica, New York.

2. See Eugène Véron, "Th. Ribot Exposition générale de ses oeuvres dans les galeries de l'Art," *L'Art,* vol. 21 (1880), pp. 127–31, 155–61.

3. The 1869 Munich exhibition, which marked a turning point in German appreciation of French realist painting, particularly that of Courbet, included four paintings by Ribot: no. 211, *Portrait, junges Mädchen;* no. 212, *Männliches Portrait;* no. 1141, *Ein Mädchen Wein abziehend;* and no. 1522, *Die Philosophen.* Manet was also represented by two paintings: no. 1361, *Der Philosoph,* and no. 1384, *Spanischer Sänger* (Munich, *Katalog zur I. internationalen Kunstausstellung im königlichen Glaspalast zu München,* July 20–October 31, 1869).

4. Chase owned seven paintings by Ribot, comprising several small sketches and a large portrait of *The Artist's Daughter* (see Pisano 1979, p. 31, and his discussion in this catalogue of the paintings owned by Chase).

5. See Gabriel P. Weisberg, no. 53, Théodule Ribot, *The Mandolin Player,* in Louise d'Argencourt and Douglas Druick, eds., *The Other Nineteenth Century: Paintings and Sculpture in the Collection of Mr. and Mrs. Joseph M. Tanenbaum* (Ottawa: The National Gallery of Canada, 1978), p. 160.

6. Cottier's musician, titled *Guitarist* in the Pedestal Fund exhibition, may have been Cottier Sale, Paris, 1892, lot 134, *Le Joueur de mandoline,* 21¾ x 18 in.: "Standing, the bust half bare, dressed in a large black cloak which makes a great fold on his left arm and shoulder, he sings to his own accompaniment on a mandoline"; sold to Inglis. *A Young Vendean* (Montreal Museum of Fine Arts) was lot 131 in that sale.

7. Strahan III, p. 123. The Davis Sale, 1889, included *Portrait of His Children* (lot 92, 18 x 14 in.) and a small *Head* (lot 51, 13½ x 11 in.), which may have been the other Ribot loaned by Davis to the Pedestal Fund show. He also owned Ribot's *Portrait of the Artist* (lot 85, 17½ x 14 in.).

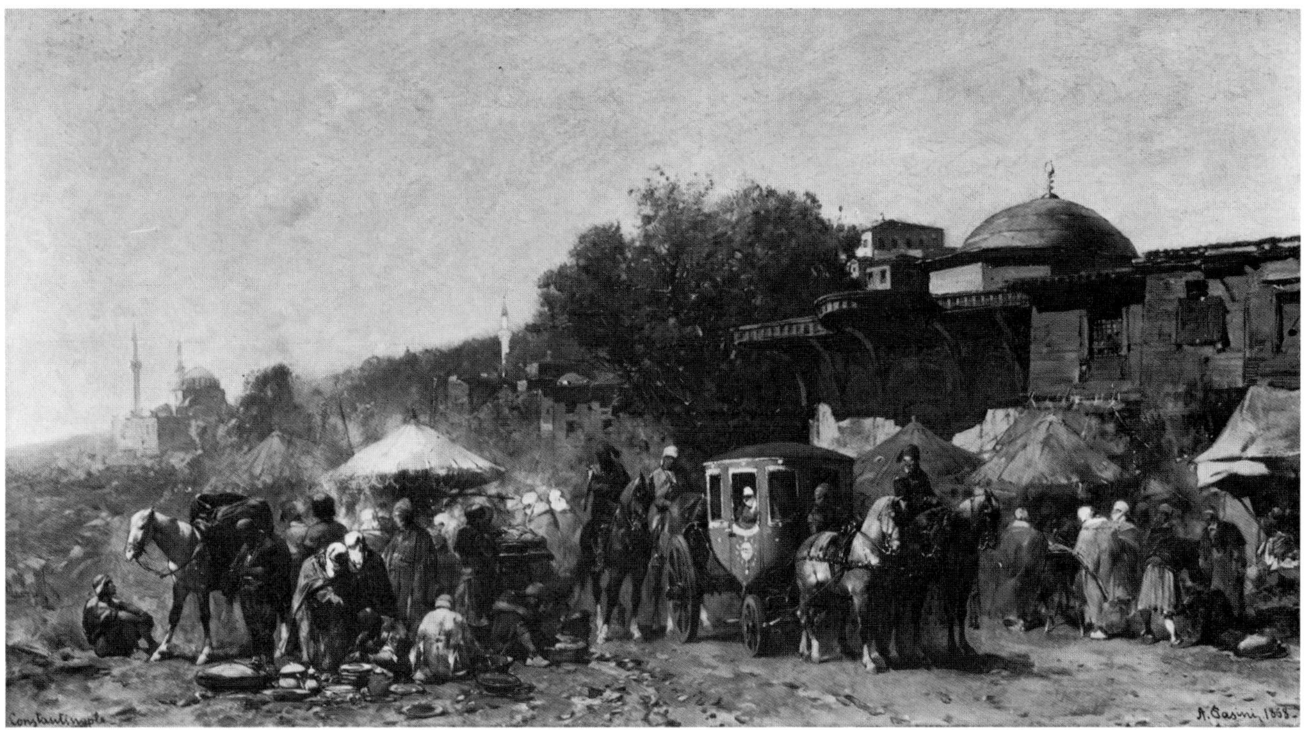

71.

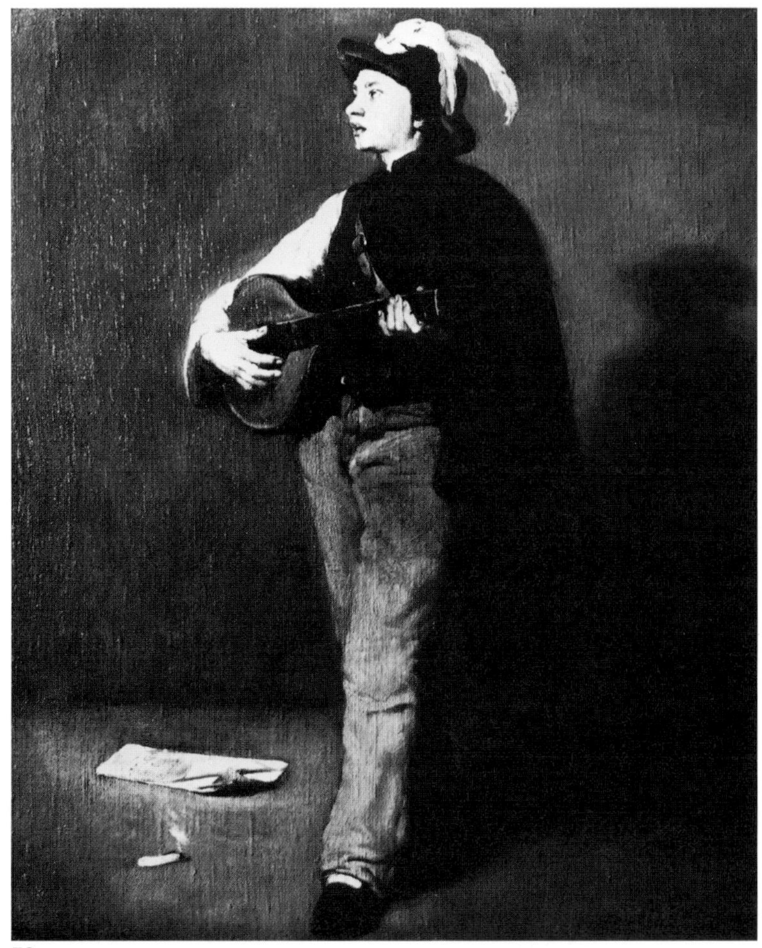

72.

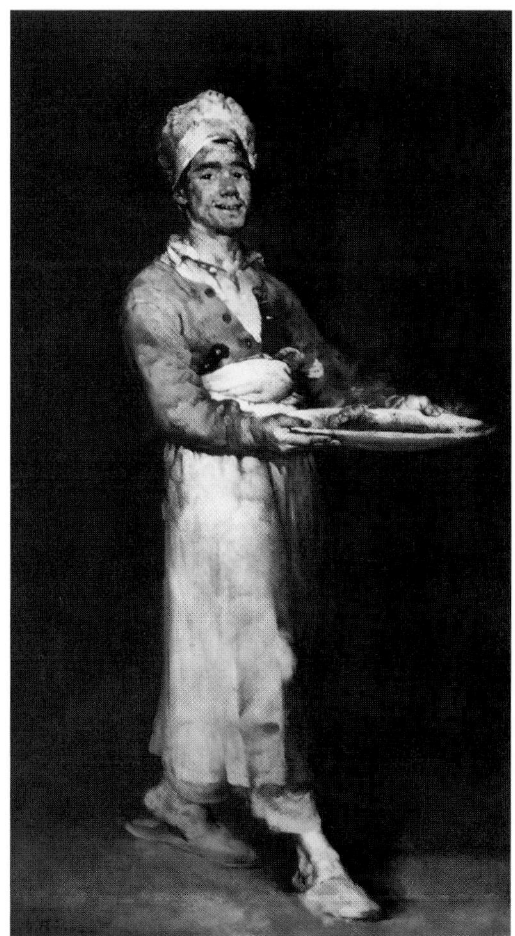

73.

74.
PHILIPPE ROUSSEAU (French, 1816–1887)
Still Life with Asparagus
Oil on canvas
14⅛ x 25½ in.
Signed l.l.: *Ph. Rousseau/à son ami A. Arago*
The Cleveland Museum of Art, Bequest of Noah L. Butkin

Provenance: Mr. and Mrs. Noah L. Butkin, Cleveland
Galerie Brame-Lorenceau, Paris

Philippe Rousseau's still lifes, compared by critics during his lifetime to the paintings of Chardin, were owned by only a few American collectors in the early 1880s, despite the attention given his work at the 1878 *Exposition Universelle.*[1] Clarence Cook called him a brother in the common household of Courbet, Manet, Mettling, and Vollon, an artist who "paints his fruits and salads as Velásquez painted them."[2]

Although Rousseau, also influenced by the Dutch and Flemish masters of the seventeenth century, frequently produced elaborate compositions of fruit, linens, and tableware, his simpler arrangements, such as *Still Life with Asparagus,* broadly painted and distinguished by sharp value contrasts and a dark romantic palette, appealed to the young painters of the Munich School.[3] Daniel Cottier, who loaned one of Rousseau's still lifes to the Pedestal Fund show, preferred these understated, realist impressions to the artist's larger, anecdotal paintings of nature's abundance.[4]

1. Rousseau was represented by twelve paintings at the 1878 *Exposition Universelle,* Paris, including works from the Barbedienne, Rothschild, and Alexandre Dumas collections.
2. Cook II, p. 186. William Merritt Chase also adopted Rousseau's vocabulary of fruit, vegetables, fish, oysters, and cheese, but owned and apparently preferred the still lifes of Vollon.
3. Rousseau was among the French realists whose work was included in the 1869 and 1879 *Internationalen Kunstausstellungen* in Munich.
4. Cottier exhibited three small works by Rousseau in his 1878 sale at the Leavitt Art Galleries, New York: lot 36, *Still Life,* 8 x 13 in.; lot 103, *A Well Provided Pantry,* 9 x 14 in.; and lot 109, *Landscape—Evening,* 9½ x 13 in. Only two paintings by Rousseau were named in Strahan III, p. 140: *Peaches,* Collection Mrs. W. P. Wilstach, and *Esmerelda's Window,* Collection C. H. Wolff, both of Philadelphia.

75.
PIERRE-ETIENNE-THEODORE ROUSSEAU (French, 1812–1867)
Valley of Tiffauge, 1837–44
Oil on canvas
25½ x 40½ in.
Signed l.l.: *TH. Rousseau*
Cincinnati Art Museum, Gift of Emilie L. Heine in Memory of Mr. and Mrs. John Hauck

Provenance: Emilie L. Heine, Cincinnati
Hauck Collection, Cincinnati
John Levy, New York, 1923
M. Knoedler & Co., New York
George Blumenthal, New York, 1921
Charles T. Yerkes, New York, 1910
Glaenzer Collection
Vever Collection, Paris, 1897
Frederick L. Ames, Boston
Peyrot Collection
Laurent-Richard, Paris, 1873
Goethals Collection, Brussels
Papeleu Collection, 1856
Baroilhet Collection, Paris, 1844

76.
PIERRE-ETIENNE-THEODORE ROUSSEAU
Forest Interior
Oil on canvas
16¾ x 22½ in.
Signed l.r.: *TH. R.*
National Gallery of Canada, Ottowa
Musée des beaux-arts du Canada, Ottowa

Provenance: Cottier & Co., New York, 1911

Théodore Rousseau, the preeminent painter of the forest of Fontainebleau, the fields of Barbizon, and the ravines of Apremont, died sixteen years before the *Pedestal Fund Art Loan Exhibition,* after achieving full recognition at the 1867 *Exposition Universelle.* Introduced to American collectors by Seth Vose in the 1850s, Rousseau, like his friend, Jean-François Millet, was first appreciated in New England, where his work could be seen in the Providence collections of Beriah Wall, John A. Brown, and Robert C. Taft. The *Valley of Tiffauge* (cat. no. 75), owned by Boston collector Frederick L. Ames, was described by the artist and critic William A. Coffin as "the best example I know of Rousseau's analytical manner,"[1] and was among the works loaned to the *Barye Monument Exhibition,* New York, in 1889–90.

Forest Interior (cat. no. 76), owned by Daniel Cottier's partner, James S. Inglis, represents the opposite pole of Rousseau's talent, the looser grasp of an impression of nature that appealed to his American admirers George Inness and Alexander Helwig Wyant.[2] Similar works, a study of trees loaned by Erwin Davis[3] and a woodland scene from Ichabod T. Williams,[4] represented Rousseau at the Pedestal Fund show, along with a broad, atmospheric *Harvest Field* (fig. 26, p. 35) from the collection of Charles A. Dana.

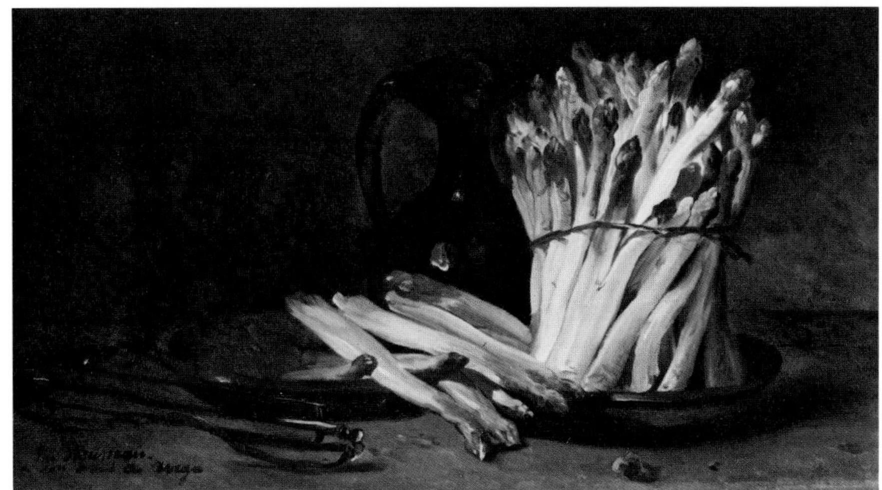

74.

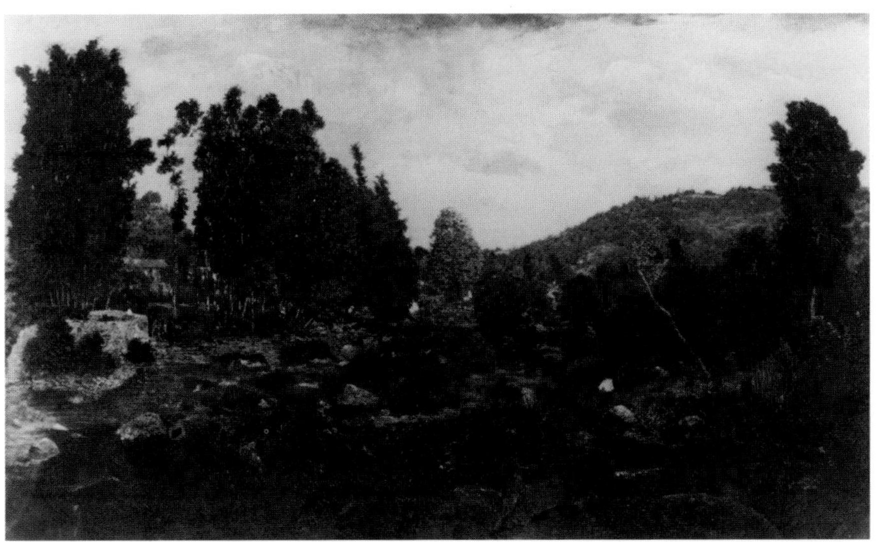

75.

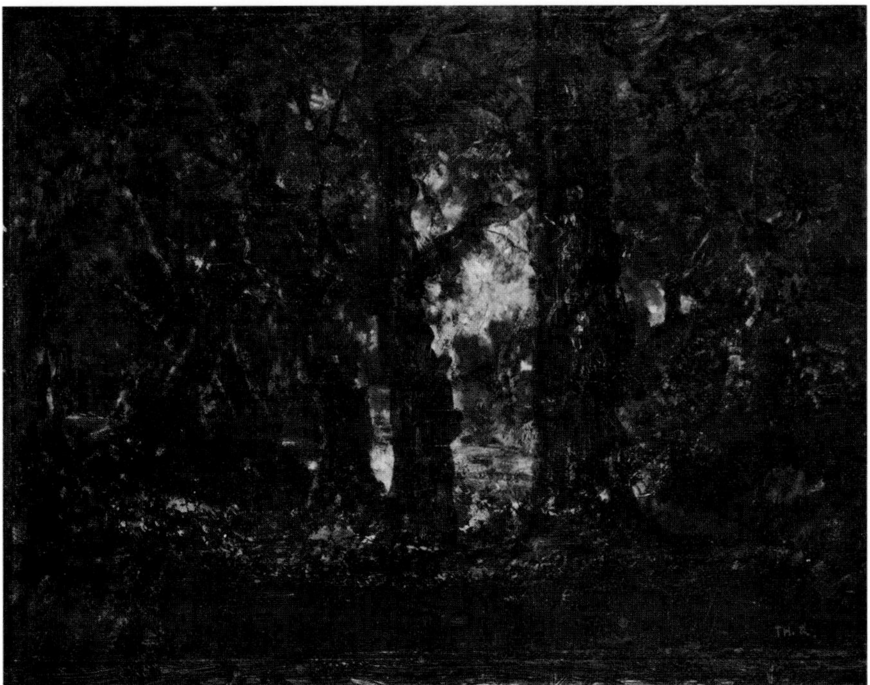

76.

1. William A. Coffin, "Pierre-Etienne Théodore Rousseau," in Van Dyke 1896, p. 121. Charles de Kay also cited this painting in "Theodore Rousseau," *The Century Magazine*, vol. 41, no. 4 (February 1891), p. 572, and found it a "noble work," but one that paid "too great attention to details."
2. See Peter Bermingham, *American Art in the Barbizon Mood* (Washington, D.C.: Smithsonian Institution Press, published for the National Collection of Fine Arts, 1975), p. 122.
3. Pedestal Fund exhibition catalogue, no. 146, *Trees*, which may correspond to Davis Sale, 1889, lot 52, *Landscape and Trees*, 14 x 21½ in., "From the Feder Collection, Paris."
4. Williams, who, like Daniel Cottier, often preferred the intimacy of a sketch to a highly finished painting, owned several works by Rousseau. Either *A Study of Sunlit Woods* (lot 63, 5¾ x 7¾ in.) or *Pool in the Woods* (lot 97, 16 x 25½ in.), both illustrated in the catalogue of the Williams Sale, 1915, may have been the Rousseau *Landscape* (no. 37) loaned by Williams to the Pedestal Fund show.

77.
FERDINAND ROYBET (French, 1840–1920)
The Brigand
Oil on canvas
13 x 16¼ in.
Signed l.l.: *F. Roybet*
Courtesy Schweitzer Gallery, Inc., New York
Provenance: Henri Robert, Paris

78.
FERDINAND ROYBET
A Cavalier
Oil on canvas
30¼ x 26½ in.
Signed u.r.: *F. Roybet*
Collection Lila and Herman Shickman, New York

Ferdinand Roybet's costume pieces of seventeenth-century cavaliers clearly appealed to William Merritt Chase,[1] who, like other members of the Munich School, found these picturesque figures suitable subjects for his own experimentation with the bravura technique of Frans Hals. Cavaliers were typical subjects of the genre paintings in the realist style favored by American collectors such as Henry C. Gibson, William H. Vanderbilt, and John Jacob and William Astor.[2] A painting entitled *Un Grand Seigneur—17th Century*[3] was loaned to the Pedestal Fund show by Moore & Clarke Co., one of several dealers that handled Roybet's work in the 1880s and the owner in 1884 of a variation of *The Brigand*.[4]

The popularity of Roybet's genre paintings, which were compared to the historical subjects of Ernest Meissonier,[5] obscures those characteristics of his work that were admired by artists and connoisseurs. In contrast to the elegant courtiers with their shiny halberds and starched ruffs, he produced a series of broadly painted figures such as *A Cavalier* (cat. no. 78), and paintings on literary and Orientalist themes, such as *The Favorite of the Harem*, which was in the A. E. Borie collection in Philadelphia,[6] and *Moorish Captive* (fig. 41, p. 40), which was loaned to the Pedestal Fund show by Ichabod T. Williams. Like Théodule Ribot, Roybet was influenced by the paintings of Dutch and Flemish masters as well as by Velásquez; but contrary to Ribot, he was acknowledged as a brilliant colorist who was also indebted to Delacroix.[7]

1. Pisano 1979, p. 31, notes Chase's admiration for Roybet and illustrates *Lady in Black*, p. 54, one of the four paintings by Roybet that was owned by Chase. See fig. 9, p. 68.
2. *The Connoisseurs*, which was owned by William Astor in 1883, is now in the collection of the John and Mable Ringling Museum of Art, Sarasota, Florida.
3. Listed in the Pedestal Fund catalogue as *En Grand Seigneur* (no. 64), the painting was sold in the Moore & Clarke Co. Sale, 1884, lot 101, 30 x 19 in. Roybet's *Masterless* (Pedestal Fund catalogue no. 65) was also in this sale, lot 255, 18 x 22 in.
4. Lot 209 in the Moore & Clarke Co. Sale, 1884, was also called *The Brigand*. Its size, 21½ x 14½ in., is close to that of a painting by this title depicting a man with a musket standing at the mouth of a cave, in the Montreal Museum of Fine Arts, Learmont Bequest, 1909.
5. Cook II, p. 164.
6. Illustrated in Strahan II, p. 23.
7. Discussing Roybet's *The Death of Roxana*, Strahan III, p. 20 (illus. p. 21), notes Roybet's "addiction to the hazardous splendours of coloring," a quality that was admired by Théophile Gautier. Strahan refers to "the hardy foreshortening, the confused adjustment, and the dashing rather than accurate drawing of the corpse of Roxana" as "an evident challenge to Delacroix."

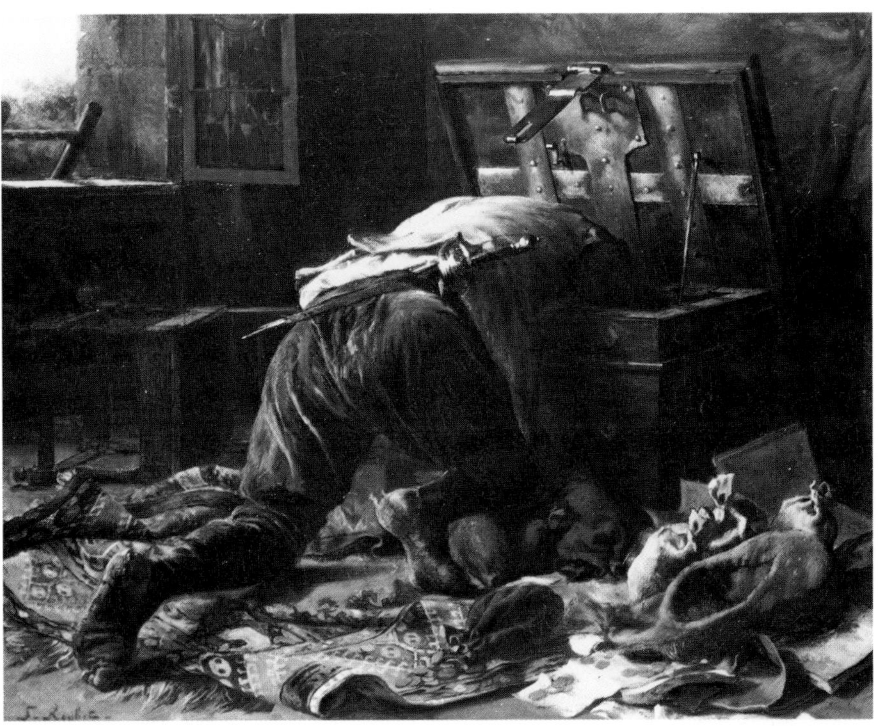

77.

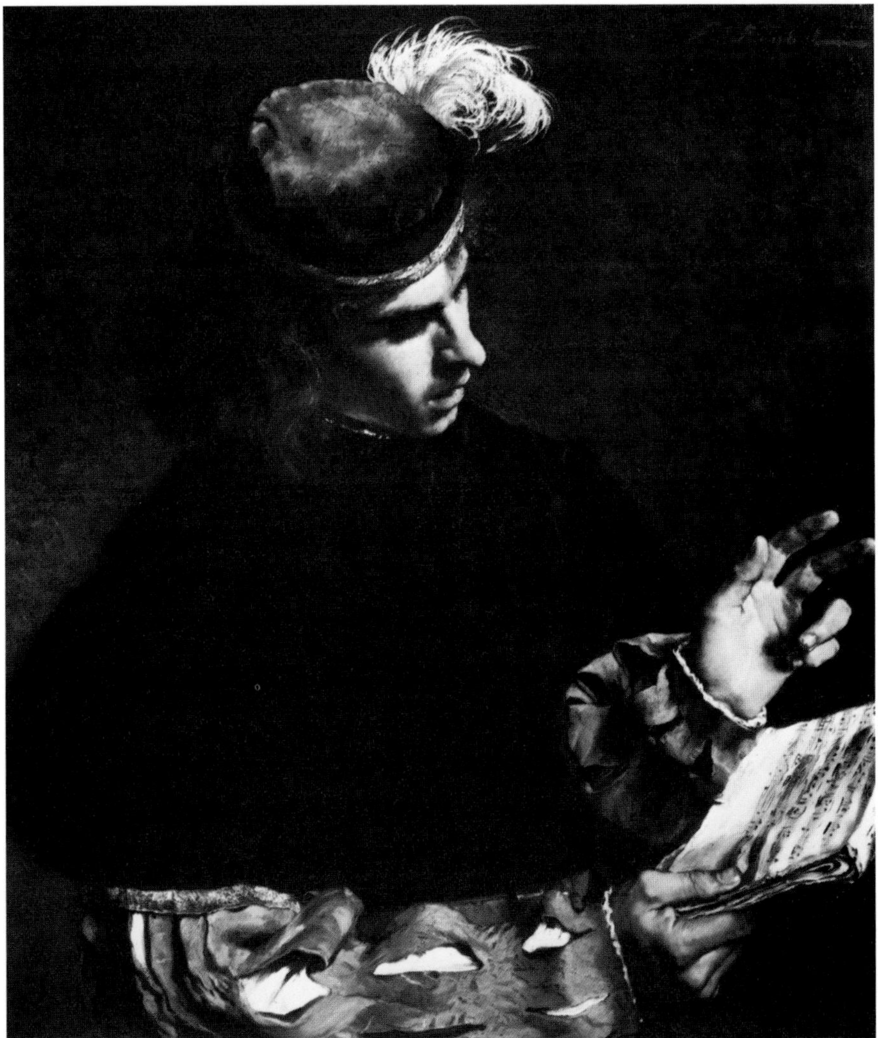

78.

79.
ALFRED EMILE LEOPOLD STEVENS
(Belgian, 1823–1906)
At the Pawnshop
Oil on panel
39¼ x 31½ in.
Signed and dated l.r.: *Alfred Stevens*
Museum of Art, Rhode Island School of Design, Providence, Gift of Mrs. Gustav Radeke

Provenance: Mrs. Gustav Radeke, Providence
Henry Schultheis, New York, 1914
Mrs. Emilie de Losey Havemeyer, New York, 1897
Theodore Havemeyer, New York, 1879

Exhibited at the 1883 *Pedestal Fund Art Loan Exhibition*, no. 24, untitled, loaned by Theodore Havemeyer
PLATE XXXVII

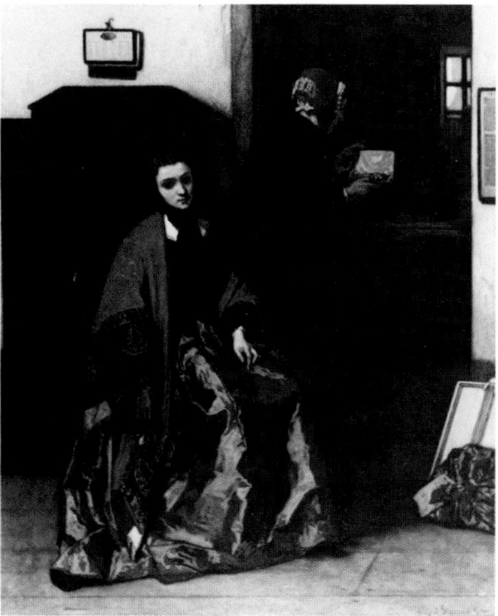

80.
ALFRED EMILE LEOPOLD STEVENS
La Jeune Mère
Oil on panel
25 1/16 x 16⅞ in.
Signed l.r.: *AStevens*
Worcester Art Museum, Worcester, Massachusetts

Provenance: Berlin Photographic Company, New York, 1913
William Merritt Chase, New York

81.
ALFRED EMILE LEOPOLD STEVENS
Seascape with Boats, c. 1880
Oil on panel
16½ x 13 in.
Signed l.r.: *A Stevens*
Private Collection

82.
ALFRED EMILE LEOPOLD STEVENS
Fedora (*Sarah Bernhardt*), 1882
Oil on canvas
45 x 34 in.
Signed and dated l.l.: *AStevens 82*
Private Collection, New York

Provenance: Millicent A. Rogers
Durand-Ruel, New York and Paris
Albert Sarens, Brussels, 1923
Baron de Mesnil, Paris
Prosper Crabbe, 1890

The young American painter Henry Bacon, who provided "Glimpses of Parisian Art" for the readers of *Scribner's Monthly* in 1880, wrote that Alfred Stevens, who possessed "all the strengths of nature obtained by Manet, through the mastery of lights and shadows, yet without the loss of the minutest detail," could have been a founder of the Impressionist school "had he not been so great a master."[1] Bacon's enthusiasm for the Belgian artist, who had won first-class medals in Paris at the *Expositions Universelles* of 1867 and 1878, was shared by a number of prominent American collectors[2] as well as by artist William Merritt Chase. The latter, who met Stevens in 1881 and eventually owned about a dozen of his works in various media,[3] including *La Jeune Mère* (cat. no. 80), chose a generous selection of Stevens's paintings for the *Pedestal Fund Art Loan Exhibition*, ranging from an early social realist subject, *At the Pawnshop* (cat. no. 79), then owned by Theodore Havemeyer,[4] to one of his recent French seascapes. On the advice of his physician, Stevens had begun in 1880 to make regular visits to the Normandy coast, where he painted broad, often impressionistic marines. *Seascape with Boats* (cat. no. 81) is typical of the rapidly sketched views painted in Le Havre.[5]

By the late 1870s, the actress Sarah Bernhardt had become a Stevens student and would also appear as his model during the next few years.[6] Although unlike the socially articulate interiors known to most collectors, *Fedora* (cat no. 85), which was exhibited at the Salon du Champ de Mars, Paris, in 1883, demonstrates at full strength the bravura brushstroke and gauzy surfaces that Chase would later emulate. A prototype of this single-figure study, without the individuality and presence of the Bernhardt portrait, was a bust-length painting entitled *Coquetry*, or *The Language of the Fan*, which was loaned to the Pedestal Fund show by New York collector Erwin Davis.[7]

1. Henry Bacon, "Glimpses of Parisian Art, I," *Scribner's Monthly*, vol. 21, no. 2 (December 1880), p. 170.
2. According to Strahan III, p. 141, between 1879 and 1882 there were at least seventeen paintings by Stevens among the collections of August Belmont, A. E. Borie, Robert L. Cutting, Henry C. Gibson, Robert Hoe, Mrs. Paran Stevens, Mrs. A. T. Stewart, William H. Vanderbilt, William T. Walters, W. P. Wilstach, Catharine Lorillard Wolfe, and John Wolfe.
3. Pisano 1979, p. 33. Chase loaned eleven works, including a watercolor and a pastel, to the Stevens exhibition at the Berlin Photographic Company, New York, in 1911. *La Jeune Mère*, one of several known versions of this subject (see also William A. Coles, *Alfred Stevens* [Ann Arbor: University of Michigan Art Museum, 1977], no. 10), has been identified with *Une Mère* (Coles no. 5), loaned by Chase to the 1911 exhibition. Coles suggests that it may be the painting listed by Strahan in the collection of A. E. Borie under the title *L'Accouché*, but also cautions that a photograph of Chase's picture, reproduced in Kenyon Cox, *Painters and Sculptors* (New York, 1907), opp. p. 64, varies slightly from the Worcester painting. In 1883, the New York collector George Campbell Cooper also owned a Stevens entitled *Mother and Child*, which he loaned to the Pedestal Fund exhibition.
4. See Havemeyer Sale, 1914, lot 75, Alfred Stevens, *The Last Resort*, 40 x 32 in.; sold to Schultheis, $200.
5. A painting entitled *At the Seashore* (*Havre*) was loaned to the Pedestal Fund exhibition by New York dealer L. Crist Delmonico, who also sent Stevens's *The Fortune Teller*.
6. See Coles nos. 35 and 37 for a discussion of the Bernhardt portraits and the Stevens-Bernhardt relationship. Chase owned Stevens's portrait of Sarah Bernhardt's sister, Jeanne (fig. 10, p. 69), which he loaned to the 1911 Stevens show in New York. See also Coles no. 38, illus.
7. Stevens's *Coquetry* was in the John Wolfe collection, New York, when it was described by Strahan I, p. 61, as a "characteristic, and better than beautiful, specimen.... A confirmed flirt of wily and experienced visage, all nerves and brains, without the softening mitigation of adipose tissue, has drawn one cream-colored glove and manages her dark Spanish fan with a world of provocative expression." It was sold to Erwin Davis at the John Wolfe Sale, 1882, lot 88, *Coquetrie*, or *The Language of the Fan*, 18¼ x 13, $1,000; several years later it appeared in the Davis Sale, 1889, lot 35, *Coquetry*.

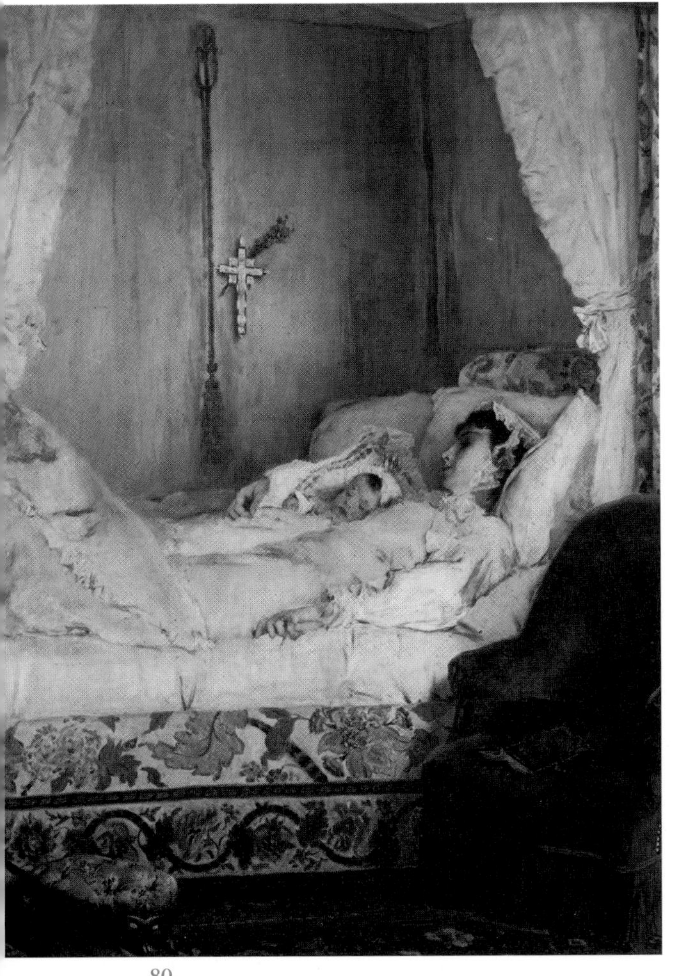

80.

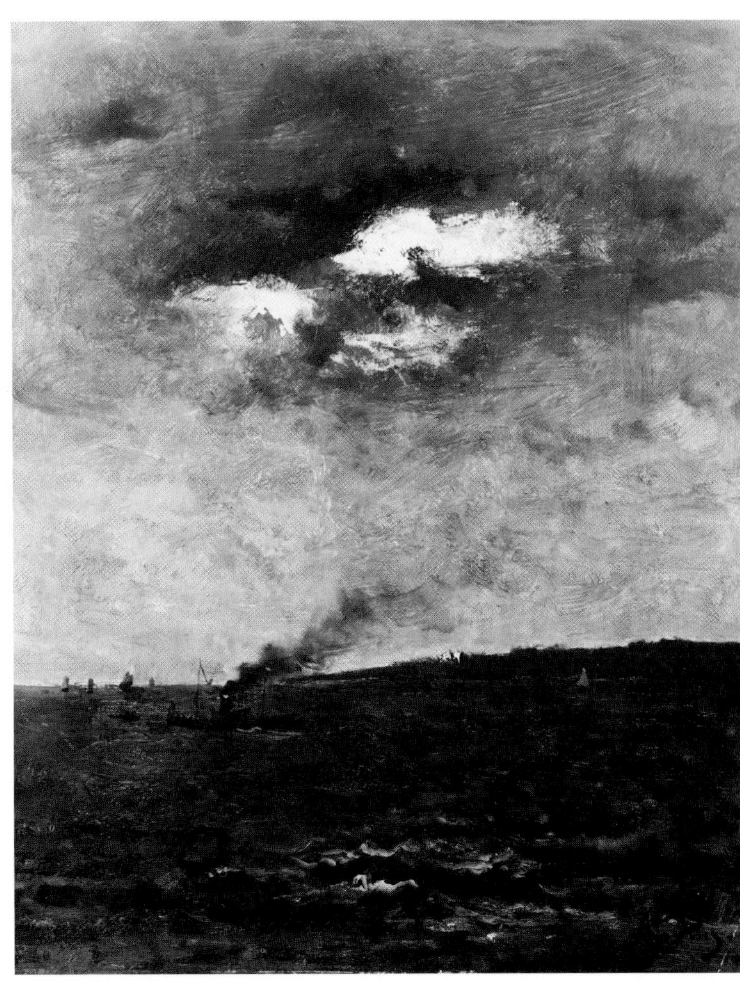

81.

83.
JAMES-JACQUES-JOSEPH TISSOT
(French, 1836–1902)
Richmond Bridge, c. 1878
Oil on canvas
14⅝ x 9¼ in.
Signed l.l.: *J. J. Tissot*
Collection William B. Ruger

Provenance: Stair Sainty Fine Art Inc., New York, 1982
Phillips, New York, 1982
George C. Cooper, New York, 1882
M. Knoedler & Co., New York, 1881

Exhibited at the 1883 *Pedestal Fund Art Loan Exhibition*, no. 81, *Richmond*, loaned by George C. Cooper

PLATE XXXVIII

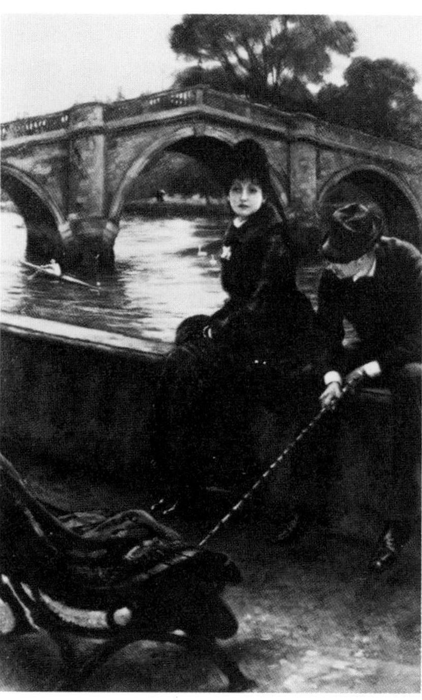

84.
JAMES-JACQUES-JOSEPH TISSOT
Visiteurs étrangers au Louvre, c. 1880
Watercolor on paper
24 x 15 in.
Indiana University Art Museum, Bloomington

Provenance: H. Shickman, New York

J.-J.-J. Tissot was represented at the *Pedestal Fund Art Loan Exhibition* by two paintings of modern life that featured his mistress Kathleen Newton in fashionable contemporary dress. *Richmond Bridge* (cat. no. 83), which lacks the narrative content of some earlier works by Tissot in American collections in 1883,[1] depicts a melancholy Mrs. Newton seated on the embankment of the River Thames in London with the artist at her side. It was loaned to the exhibition by George Campbell Cooper (nephew of the founder of Cooper Union, New York), a knowledgeable collector of prints, who had purchased the painting from M. Knoedler & Co., New York, in April 1882, only five months after it had been shipped from London.[2]

Visiteurs étrangers au Louvre (cat. no. 84), a watercolor version of a painting owned by George I. Seney of Brooklyn,[3] is related to the second Tissot in the Pedestal Fund exhibition, *Sculpture Gallery of the Louvre* (fig. 23, p. 34), loaned by M. Knoedler & Co.[4] As in the painting of Mrs. Newton at Richmond Bridge, the setting was read by a contemporary critic as "merely a background for a figure of a lovely English woman of the type more familiar to the artists than to London streets, a neatly and charmingly arrayed damsel, whose thoughts appear to be anywhere else rather than in the Louvre."[5] This oil painting was part of a series culminating in *L'Esthètique*, one of the subjects in Tissot's "La Femme à Paris" suite.

1. Two early paintings that show the influence of Baron Hendrik Leys and the German *kleine Meister* were *Penetrantes in Interiores Mortis*, 1860 (*Voie des fleurs, voie des pleurs* [*The Dance of Death*], oil on panel, Museum of Art, Rhode Island School of Design, Providence), owned by T. A. Dolan of Philadelphia (Strahan III, p. 2, illus.; Wentworth 1984, fig. 12); and *Marguerite at the Well*, 1861 (oil on canvas, collection Dr. and Mrs. Arthur C. Herrington; illus. Wentworth 1984, fig. 4). A painting by this title was owned by William T. Walters of Baltimore in 1883 (Strahan I, p. 94).
2. Information courtesy Michael J. Wentworth in a telephone conversation with the author, June 26, 1985: Knoedler purchased the painting from Tissot for £100 sterling and shipped it to New York aboard the *America* on November 14, 1881. Knoedler sold it to Cooper on April 17, 1882 for $900.
3. Seney Sale, 1891, lot 90, J. Tissot, *In the Louvre*, oil on canvas, 35½ x 19½; description p. 175; sold $700. There is also a smaller, more finished, watercolor version of this painting; see Matyjaszkiewicz 1985, no. 118, *Au Louvre* (*Visiteurs étrangers au Louvre*), c. 1879–80, 16¼ x 8¼, private collection, London.
4. Michael J. Wentworth, in a letter to the author, October 30, 1985, provided a history of the painting, now unlocated: painted c. 1879–80; purchased by Knoedler through Victor Bulla, agent, Paris, for FF 6,750, on or about August 16, 1880; sold by Knoedler to Mary J. Morgan, March 1, 1884; Mary Jane Morgan Sale, 1886, lot 178, *In the Louvre*, 28 x 18 in., sold to J. Sutton, $1,600. Before 1883, exhibited Liverpool, Walker Art Gallery, *10th Autumn Exhibition of Modern Pictures*, 1880, no. 1720. A smaller oil version of the Pedestal Fund painting is in a private collection, New York; see Matyjaszkiewicz 1985, no. 117, *Visiteurs étrangers au Louvre*, illus.
5. "The Pedestal Art Loan," *The New York Times*, December 16, 1883, p. 5.

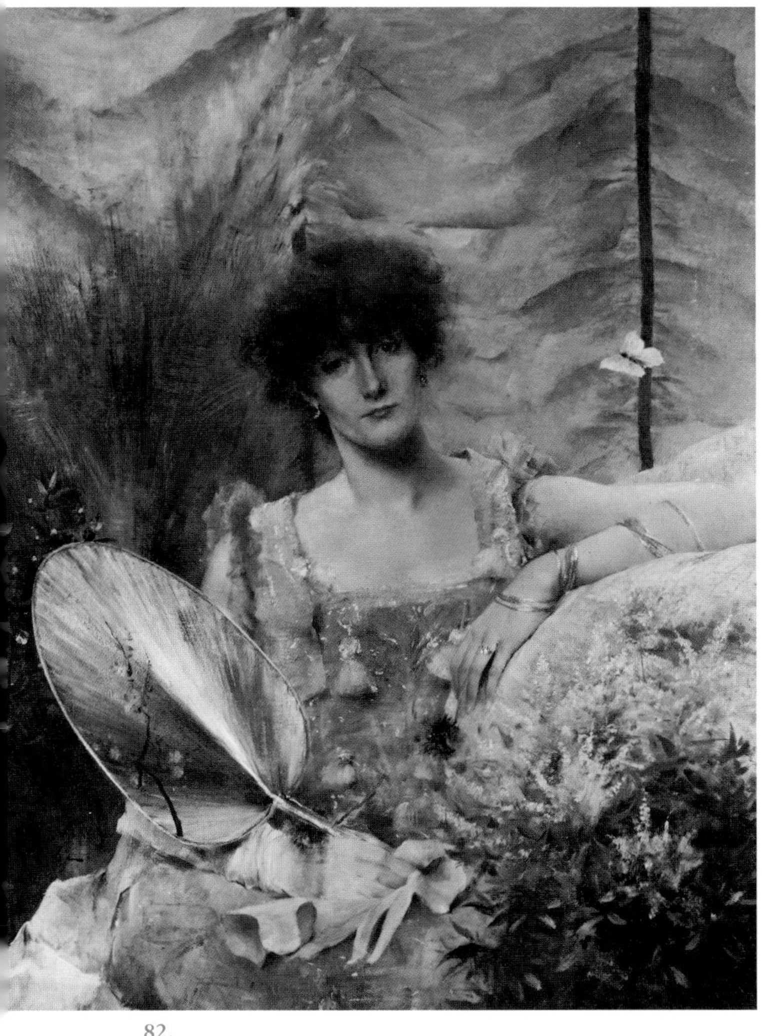

82.

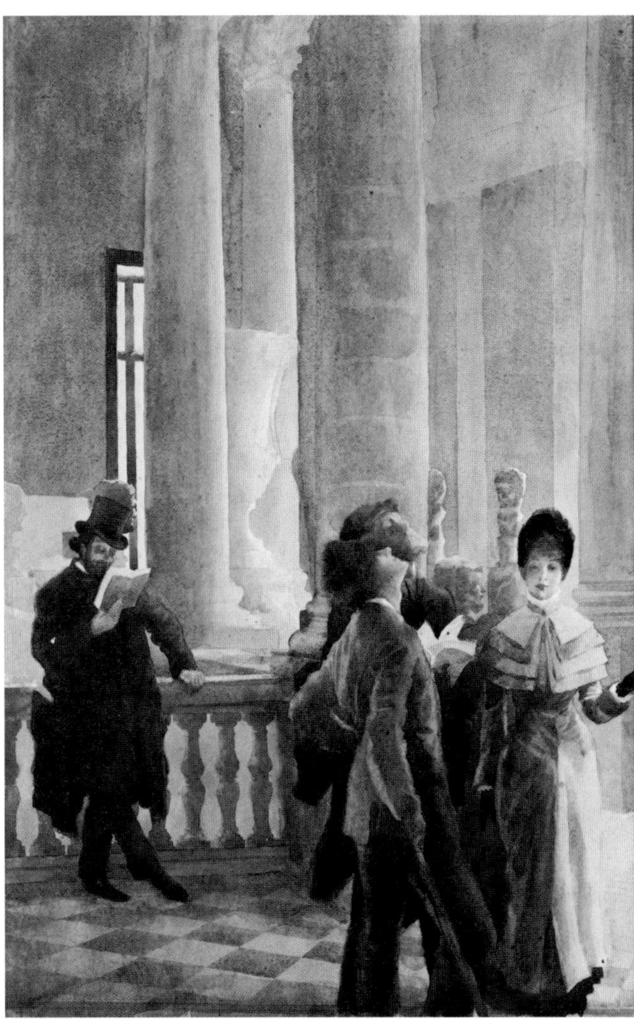

84.

85.
CONSTANT TROYON (French, 1810–1865)
Landscape with Cattle and Sheep
Oil on linen
38½ x 51½ in.
Signed l.l.: *C Troyon*
The Minneapolis Institute of Arts, Bequest of Mrs. Erasmus C. Lindley in Memory of Her Father, James J. Hill
Provenance: Mrs. Erasmus C. Lindley, 1949
James J. Hill, St. Paul

86.
CONSTANT TROYON
Vaches à l'abreuvoir
Oil on canvas
30¾ x 43⅞ in.
Signed l.l.: *C. Troyon*
The Taft Museum, Cincinnati, Ohio, Gift of Mr. and Mrs. Charles Phelps Taft
Provenance: Mr. and Mrs. Charles Phelps Taft, Cincinnati
Scott & Fowles, New York
Mrs. A. T. Stewart, New York
A. T. Stewart, New York

The admiration of American artists and collectors for Constant Troyon, "the first of modern animal-painters,"[1] was apparent in the selection of five of his works for the *Pedestal Fund Art Loan Exhibition.* The large *Holland Landscape with Cattle* (fig. 13, p. 29), similar to *Vaches à l'abreuvoir* (cat. no. 86), which in 1883 was in the collection of Mrs. A. T. Stewart, New York, was considered one of his finest paintings, clearly representing Troyon's appreciation of the seventeenth-century Dutch masters and his exceptional skill as a painter of both landscape and animals.[2] As an indication of the value placed on Troyon's works by contemporary American collectors, the *Drove of Cattle and Sheep* loaned to the Pedestal Fund show by Albert Spencer was sold to Cornelius Vanderbilt for $26,000 five years later, the highest price paid for any painting at the sale of the Spencer collection.[3]

Thomas Hicks, who loaned a painting called *Cattle and Landscape* to the 1883 exhibition, and William H. Howe, who contributed an essay on Troyon to John C. Van Dyke's *Modern French Masters* (1896), were only two of many American artists who acknowledged Troyon's influence on their own work.[4] His strength in modeling, well-developed pictorial sense, and atmospheric treatment of light and shadow contributed to his enduring reputation in America among animal and landscape painters alike.

1. Cook II, p. 225.
2. William H. Howe, "Constant Troyon," in Van Dyke 1896, pp. 148–49, illus. p. 147.
3. "A Big Sum for Paintings," *The New York Times,* February 29, 1888, p. 2. The painting went to Samuel P. Avery, who acquired it for Cornelius Vanderbilt. It was loaned by Vanderbilt to the *Barye Monument Exhibition,* 1889–90, no. 586, *A Drove of Cattle and Sheep,* 26 x 39 in.; current location unknown.
4. Among Troyon's other American admirers were Thomas Robinson, Carleton Wiggins, Thomas Craig, and J. Foxcroft Cole. See also Peter Bermingham, *American Art in the Barbizon Mood* (Washington, D.C.: Smithsonian Institution Press, published for the National Collection of Fine Arts, 1975), pp. 122–25.

87.
ANTOINE VOLLON (French, 1833–1900)
Portrait of a Man (Un Espagnol), c. 1878
Oil on canvas
29 x 23½ in.
Signed l.l.: *A. Vollon*
The Heckscher Museum, Huntington, New York,
Gift of August Heckscher
Provenance: August Heckscher, New York, by 1920
James Buchanan Brady, 1918
Cottier & Co., New York
P.-L. Everard, London, 1881

88.
ANTOINE VOLLON
Portrait of a Bearded Man
Oil on canvas
9⅝ x 7½ in.
Signed l.r.: *A. Vollon*
Private Collection

89.
ANTOINE VOLLON
Still Life with Fruit and Objects of the Hunt
Oil on panel
37½ x 27⅞ in.
Signed u.r.: *A. Vollon*
Private Collection

90.
ANTOINE VOLLON
Boats Moored on the River Oise
Oil on panel
12½ x 10¼ in.
Signed l.l.: *A. Vollon*
Private Collection

91.
ANTOINE VOLLON
Farmyard Landscape
Oil on panel
18⅛ x 26½ in.
Signed l.r.: *A. Vollon*
Collection Paul Underwood, New York

The broad representation of works by Antoine Vollon in the *Pedestal Fund Art Loan Exhibition* was undoubtedly influenced by William Merritt Chase, who owned at least twenty paintings by the French artist during his lifetime.[1] A member of the circle of realists who responded to Salon rejection in 1863 by organizing a Salon des Refusés, Vollon nevertheless won state recognition,

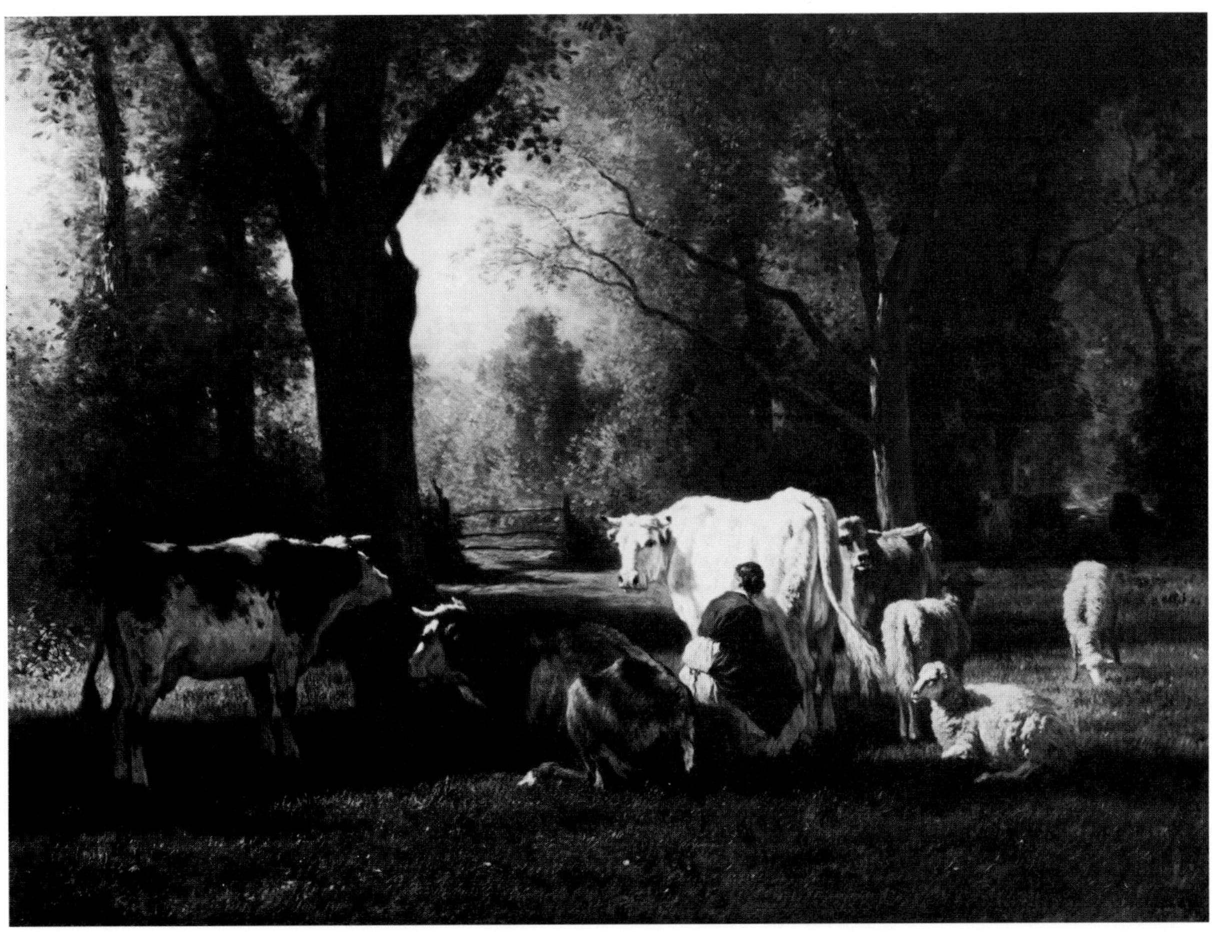

85.

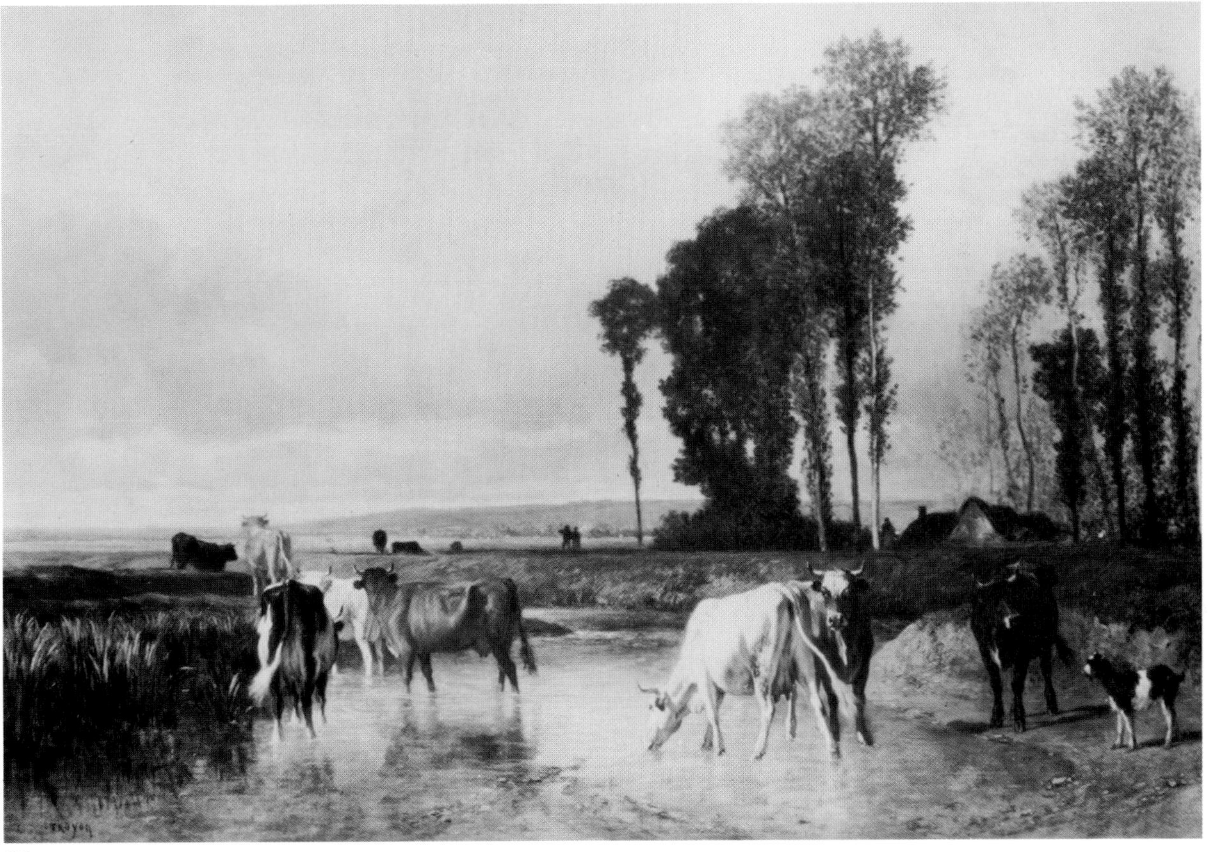

86.

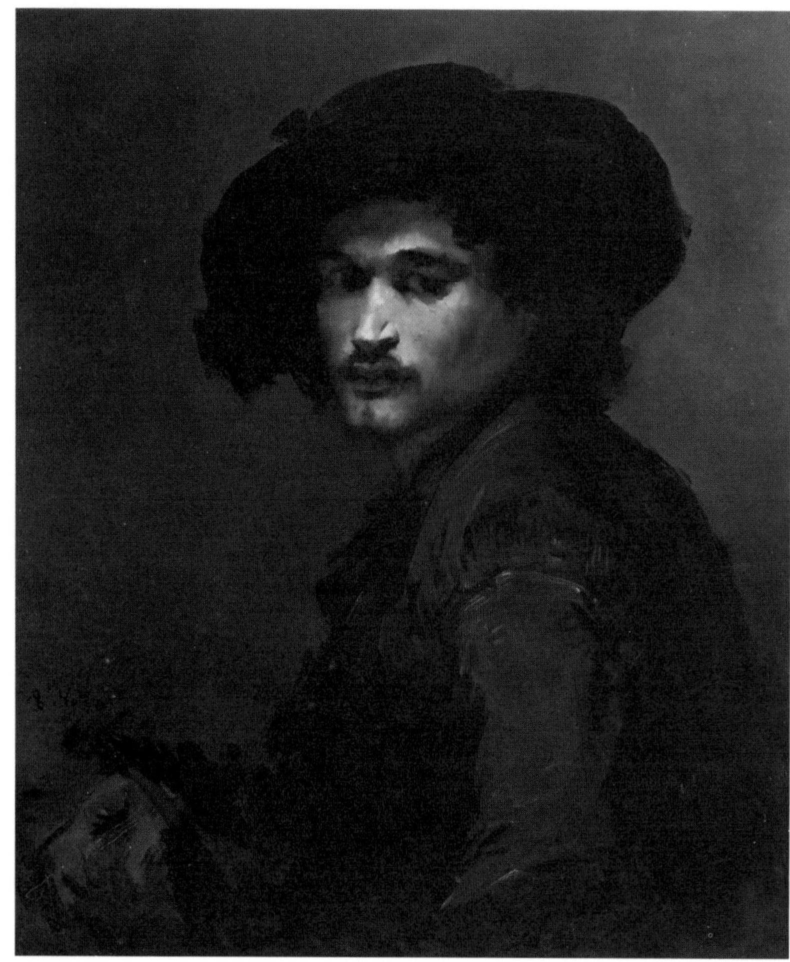

87.

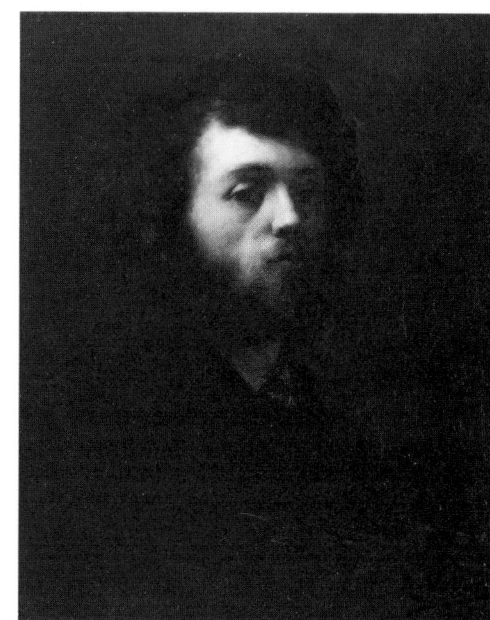

88.

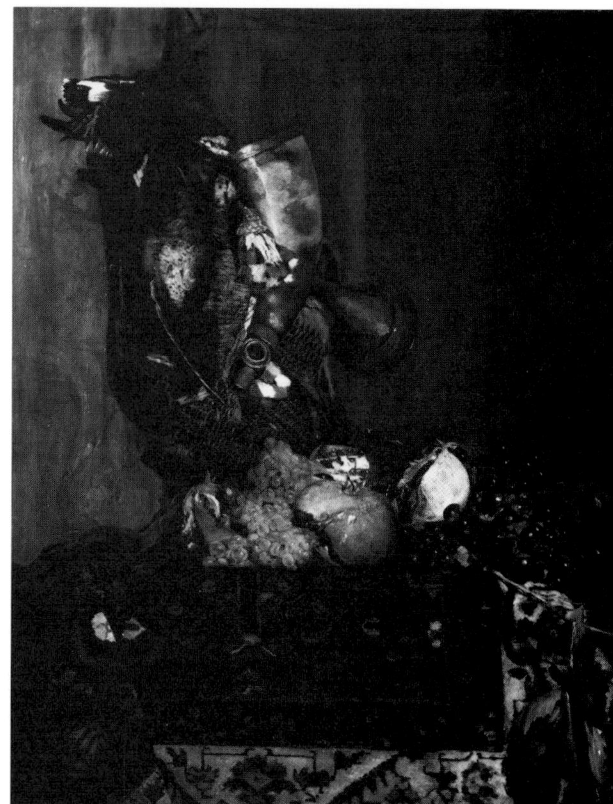

89.

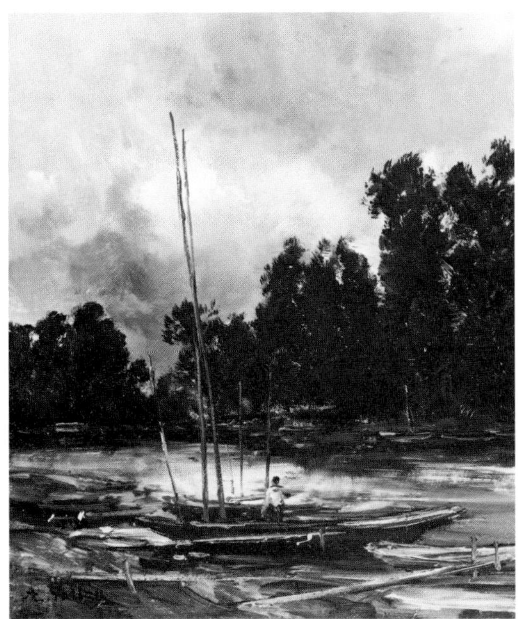

90.

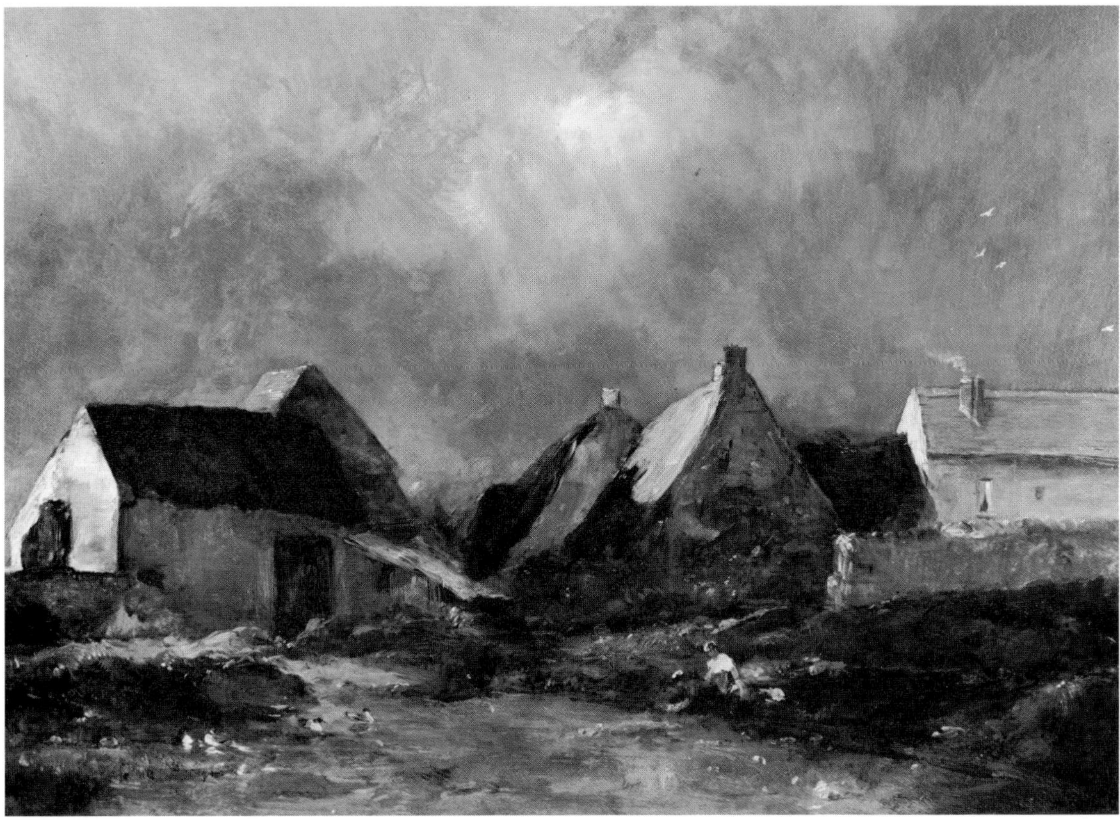

91.

and by the early 1880s had received awards at official Salons and at the 1878 *Exposition Universelle,* where he was named an officer of the Legion of Honor.

Vollon's widespread popularity was in large part based on lavish compositions such as *Still Life with Fruit and Objects of the Hunt* (cat. no. 89), which were emulated by Chase and sought by public and private patrons in France. A similarly rich arrangement, a covered Dresden bowl surrounded by fruit, was among the paintings by Vollon owned by Pedestal Fund exhibition lender Erwin Davis.[2]

Known to New York collectors by *French Farmyard* (fig. 17, p. 31), a large rural scene in the collection of Catharine Lorillard Wolfe,[3] Vollon was also an effective landscape painter whose smaller pieces, such as *Boats Moored on the River Oise* (cat. no. 90) and *Farmyard Landscape* (cat. no. 91), had a looseness and immediacy that caused American critics to view him as a leader of the Impressionists.[4] His great versatility, which must have appealed to Chase, extended to portraiture, as well. An admiration for the Dutch and Spanish masters, enhanced by his association with Théodule Ribot, was demonstrated in *Portrait of a Man (Un Espagnol)* (cat. no. 87) and *Portrait of a Bearded Man* (cat. no. 88). The latter, which may be a self-portrait in the guise of Rembrandt, closely resembles a painting that was submitted to the Pedestal Fund exhibition by Daniel Cottier and later owned by Ichabod T. Williams.[5]

1. Pisano 1979, p. 34. The Pedestal Fund exhibition included eight works by Vollon: *Portrait of the Artist's Sister* and *On the River* (figs. 34 and 38, pp. 37 and 39) from the collection of I. T. Williams; *French Farmyard* (fig. 17, p. 31) from the collection of C. L. Wolfe; still lifes from Erwin Davis and Moore & Clarke Co.; and two portraits (one of Rembrandt) and a sketch of a donkey (fig. 57, p. 46) from Daniel Cottier.
2. Described in Cook II, p. 181, as "a picture sufficient for fame."
3. Miss Wolfe's painting, which was described by Cook as one of Vollon's finest pictures, was formerly in the collection of The Metropolitan Museum of Art, Catharine Lorillard Wolfe Bequest of 1887. It was also noted in Strahan I, p. 133.
4. Strahan I, p. 133.
5. A painting entitled *Rembrandt* (lot 7, 11½ x 9 in.), "purchased from Messrs. Cottier & Co.," was included in the Williams Sale, 1915.

92.
ALFRED WAHLBERG (Swedish, 1834–1906)
Landscape, 1867
Oil on canvas
41¾ x 56⅜ in.
Signed and dated l.l.: *Alfred Wahlberg Paris, 1867*
The Brooklyn Museum, Brooklyn, New York,
Bequest of Charles Liebmann
Provenance: Charles Liebmann

Alfred Wahlberg was one of several Swedish painters who emigrated to Paris for study in the 1860s and 1870s. Like his countrymen Wilhelm von Gegerfelt, Oskar Törna, and Carl Frederik Hill, artists represented in the *Pedestal Fund Art Loan Exhibition* but not in this catalogue, Wahlberg was found appealing by French critics for his application of plein-air techniques, appropriated from the Barbizon painters, to native Scandinavian landscapes. Although Wahlberg, like Törna, had learned the descriptive style of the Düsseldorf School before settling in Paris, his contact with Jean-Baptiste-Camille Corot and Charles-François Daubigny led to the broader treatment that would characterize his signature moonlight marines and effects of changing seasons.

Known as a leader of the Swedish group in France, Wahlberg was named an Officer of the Legion of Honor in 1878, and was invited to participate in the first international exhibition at the Galerie Georges Petit, Paris, in 1882. Through exposure at the Paris Salons and *Expositions Universelles,* as well as at the Philadelphia Centennial Exhibition in 1876, Wahlberg attracted American patrons such as John Wolfe and his cousin Catharine Lorillard Wolfe, who purchased directly from the artist in Paris, on one instance commissioning paintings that were exhibited at the Salon before being shipped home.[1] Several dealers, including M. Knoedler & Co. and Daniel Cottier, carried his paintings in their New York galleries, catering to an admiring audience that included George I. Seney, Erwin Davis, Morris K. Jesup, and John Jacob Astor.

1. Two paintings bequeathed to The Metropolitan Museum of Art, New York, in 1887 by Catharine Lorillard Wolfe, *A Day in October near Waxholm, Sweden* and *Moonlight, Port of Waxholm near Stockholm, Sweden,* were painted to order for Miss Wolfe and exhibited at the Salon of 1873.

93.
JAMES ABBOTT MCNEILL WHISTLER (American, 1834–1903)
Winter Landscape
Pastel on paper
4½ x 11 in.
Private Collection,
Courtesy M. Knoedler & Co., Inc., New York
Provenance: Ira Spanierman, Inc., New York
E. B. Crocker Art Gallery, Art Museum of the City of Sacramento, California
Wyon Stansfield, Esq.
Mme Emilie Venturi

By the fall of 1883, American interest in the work of James Abbott McNeill Whistler had been heightened by a number of events that included his 1878 lawsuit against John Ruskin, the publication of William C. Brownell's 1879 *Scribner's* article "Whistler in Painting and Etching,"[1] and the exhibitions of prints from his French, Thames, and First Venice Sets at the galleries of The Pennsylvania Academy of the Fine Arts in 1879 and 1881.[2] Whistler's influence was strong among the participants in the American painter-etcher movement, and his importance to his younger countrymen, who acknowledged his position as one of the founders of Impressionism, was enhanced by his contact with American painter Frank Duveneck and his students in Venice during the summer of 1880.

During the 1870s, Whistler's etchings had been sought by American collectors James L. Claghorn, Howard Mansfield, C. L. Freer, and H. W. Whittemore. Although introduced to this growing audience by Samuel P. Avery, he was represented at the *Pedestal Fund Art Loan Exhibition* by a loan from the New York art dealer H. Wunderlich, who had opened a show of Whistler's etchings in New York on October 11, 1883. As if in tune with Whistler's interest in the small "perfect" oils, watercolors, and pastels which the artist would display in a one-man exhibition at the Dowdeswell Gallery, London, in May of 1884,[3] Wunderlich had purchased two watercolors from the artist in the summer of 1883.[4] It was presumably one of these, the watercolor *Snow Scene,* that was chosen by the selections committee of the Pedestal Fund show. Although not especially common in

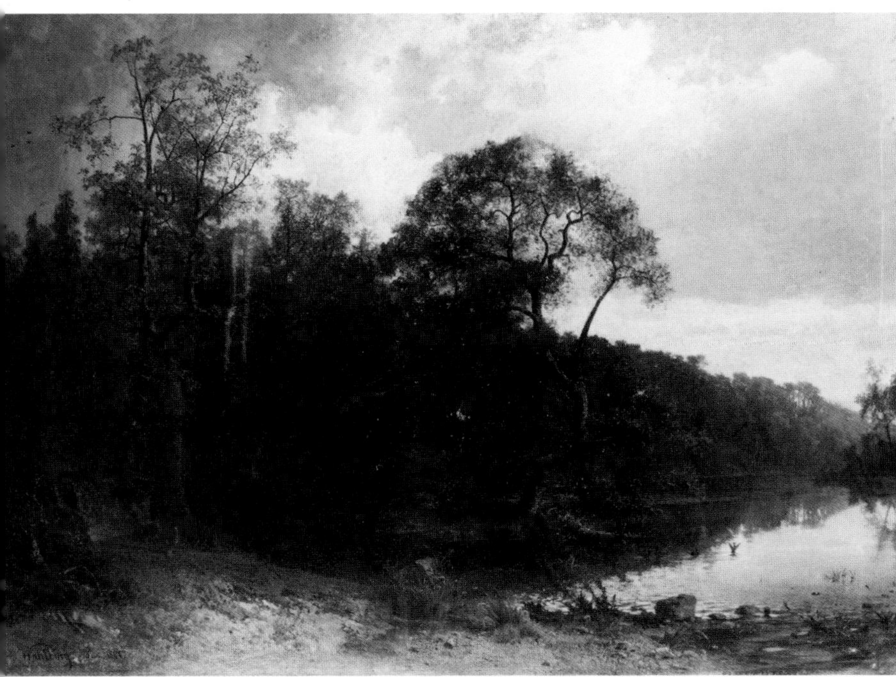
92.

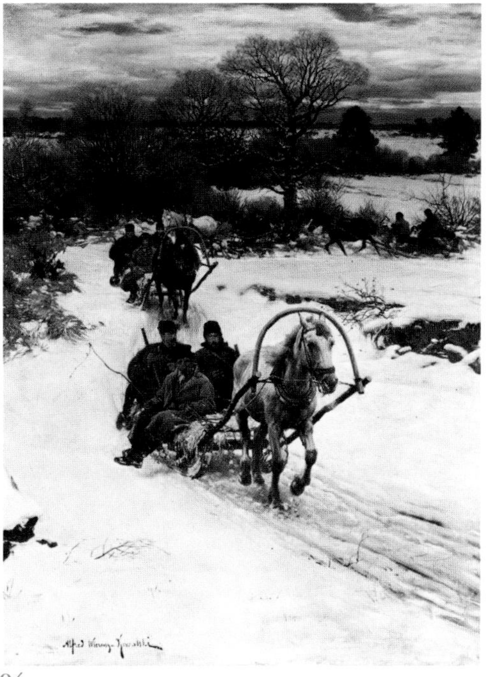
94.

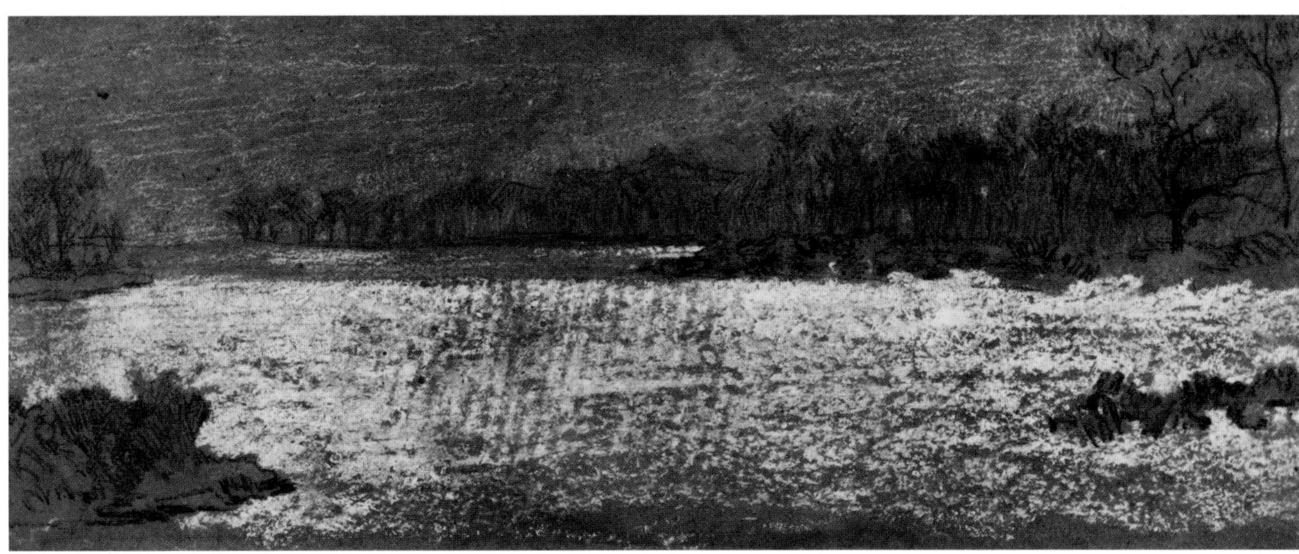
93.

Whistler's oeuvre, snow scenes, either rural or urban, provided excellent subjects for tonal experiments. *Winter Landscape* (cat. no. 93), a pastel on brown paper from the early 1870s, succinctly contrasts the textures of barren trees with the snowy surface of the frozen Thames. Other snow scenes of the 1870s include *Trafalgar Square, Chelsea* (Freer Gallery of Art, Washington, D.C.), and *Nocturne in Gray and Gold* (Fogg Art Museum, Cambridge, Massachusetts), both oil on canvas. During the winter of 1883, while visiting Amsterdam, Whistler again had an opportunity to study snowy landscapes. It is possible that the watercolors he sold to Wunderlich the following August included a snow scene on the Dutch canals.[5]

1. William C. Brownell, "Whistler in Painting and Etching," *Scribner's Monthly,* vol. 18, no. 1 (May 1879), pp. 481–95.
2. See M. Lee Wiehl, *A Cultivated Taste: Whistler and American Print Collectors* (Middletown, Connecticut: Davison Art Center, Wesleyan University, 1983), pp. 6–7, for a discussion of these exhibitions.
3. This exhibition is discussed by Margaret F. MacDonald in the introduction to *Notes Harmonies and Nocturnes, Small Works by James McNeill Whistler* (New York: M. Knoedler & Co., Inc., 1985).
4. Information courtesy Margaret F. MacDonald, in a letter to the author dated May 1, 1985: "Wunderlich's bought two watercolours from Whistler on 1 August 1883 for £50 according to a letter updating their accounts in January 1884 (Glasgow University W 1140)."
5. Margaret F. MacDonald, in a letter to the author dated April 1, 1985, cited Whistler's *Nocturne, Amsterdam, Winter,* a watercolor in the collection of the Freer Gallery of Art, Washington, D.C., showing skaters on a frozen canal, as an example of his work during this period. Mrs. MacDonald also suggested that an unlocated watercolor, *Winter Landscape,* 10 x 7¼ in., noted in the *Catalogue of Paintings, Prints, Sculpture and Objects of Art in the H. O. Havemeyer Collection,* Part II, Paintings and Prints (New York: Privately printed, 1931), and conceivably identifiable with the *Street Scene in Black and White* exhibited at the *Whistler Memorial Exhibition* held by the Copley Society, Boston, 1904, could have been the watercolor exhibited at the Pedestal Fund exhibition.

94.
ALFRED VON WIERUSZ-KOWALSKI
(Polish, 1849–1915)
Winter in Russia, before 1885
Oil on canvas
40¼ x 30 5/16 in.
Signed l.l.: *Alfred Wierusz-Kowalski*
Milwaukee Art Museum, Milwaukee, Wisconsin, Layton Art Collection, Gift of Frederick Layton, 1888

Provenance: Frederick Layton, Milwaukee, 1885
George I. Seney, Brooklyn

Alfred von Wierusz-Kowalski, a native of Poland, studied in Warsaw, Dresden, and Prague before following his countryman Maksymilian Gierymski (cat. no. 36) to Munich in 1876. Like William Merritt Chase, Wierusz-Kowalski first studied under Alexander von Wagner, soon establishing himself as one of the vigorous younger members of the Munich School.[1] A specialist in Polish and Russian genre scenes, Wierusz-Kowalski found appreciative audiences at international exhibitions in Munich, Berlin, Dresden, Paris, and Vienna.[2] By the mid-1880s his American patrons included New Yorkers Erwin Davis (who loaned a painting entitled *Napoleon in Russia* to the Pedestal Fund show),[3] Henry Hilton, Mary Jane Morgan, and George I. Seney, among a growing network of admirers that stretched from New England to the Midwest.[4]

Winter in Russia, purchased from the Seney Sale of 1885 by Frederick Layton of Milwaukee, demonstrates the balanced combination of incisive draftsmanship and fluid brushstroke that appealed not only to American collectors but also to contemporary painters such as Chase. Typical of the artist's fascination with the theme of horsedrawn sleds and snowy landscapes, a formula he used throughout his life, *Winter in Russia* is an example of the "folkloric" realism that retained its popularity with international juries through the end of the nineteenth century.[5]

1. See *Münchner Maler im 19. Jahrhundert,* vol. 4 (Munich: Bruckmann, 1983), p. 376. The present catalogue follows this reference work by using the form Wierusz-Kowalski; the artist's name may also be cited as Kowalski-Wierusz. Chase studied with Alexander von Wagner after arriving in Munich in 1872 but later worked under Karl von Piloty. Wierusz-Kowalski also studied with Josef von Brandt in Munich.
2. *Ibid.,* p. 379.
3. Davis's painting was acquired at the Nathan Sale, 1880, lot 11, *The Return from Moscow,* 21 x 11 in.
4. Strahan III, p. 137, also lists paintings by Wierusz-Kowalski in the collections of D. W. Powers, Rochester, and John D. Lakenau, Philadelphia. Cook VI, p. 335, briefly mentions "Kowalski-Wierutz [sic], residing in Paris," and illustrates, opp. p. 334, *On the Road—Poland,* noting that "his paintings are often seen in our American galleries."
5. Two of Wierusz-Kowalski's paintings, *In the Springtime* and *On the Way to the Wedding,* were illustrated in General Lew Wallace et al., *Famous Paintings of the World* (New York: Fine Art Publishers, 1895).

KEY TO ABBREVIATIONS IN CATALOGUE NOTES

American Art Annual 1898
American Art Annual, 1898. Florence N. Levy, ed. New York: The Macmillan Company, 1899.

Barye Monument Exhibition, 1889–90
New York, American Art Galleries. *Catalogue of the Works of Antoine-Louis Barye . . . His contemporaries and friends for the benefit of the Barye Monument Fund*. November 15, 1889–January 15, 1890.

Béraldi
Henri Béraldi. *Les Graveurs du XIXe siècle*. 12 vols. Paris: Librairie L. Conquet, 1885–92.

Blakeslee Sale, 1893
New York, Fifth Avenue Art Galleries. *Catalogue of . . . Trustees {Sale} of Blakeslee & Co*. April 4–5, 1893.

Boime
Albert Boime. *Thomas Couture and the Eclectic Vision*. New Haven, Connecticut: Yale University Press, 1980.

Brownell 1892
W. C. Brownell. *French Art: Classic and Contemporary Painting and Sculpture*. New York: Charles Scribner's Sons, 1892.

Champlin and Perkins
John D. Champlin and Charles C. Perkins. *Cyclopedia of Painters and Paintings*. 4 vols. New York: Charles Scribner's Sons, 1886–87.

Cook
Clarence Cook. *Art and Artists of Our Time*. 6 vols. New York: Selmar Hess, 1888.

Cottier Sale, London, 1914
London, Christie, Manson & Woods. *Catalogue of Modern Pictures and Water-Colour Drawings chiefly of the continental schools. The Property of Mrs. Cottier deceased*. May 1, 1914.

Cottier Sale, New York, 1878
New York, Leavitt Art Galleries. *Fine Oil Paintings by the Great Modern Classic Painters imported by Cottier & Co., 144 Fifth Avenue*. April 23–24, 1878.

Cottier Sale, Paris, 1892
Paris, Galeries Durand-Ruel. *Catalogue of the . . . Sale of the Pictures of the late Mr. Cottier of London*. May 27–28, 1892.

Dana Sale, 1898
New York, American Art Association. *Eastern Ceramics and other objects of Art belonging to the estate of the late Charles A. Dana*. February 24–26, 1898.

Davis Sale, 1889
New York, Fifth Avenue Art Galleries. *Catalogue of Modern Paintings belonging to Erwin Davis, Esq*. March 19–20, 1889.

Durand-Gréville 1886
E. Durand-Gréville. "Correspondance d'Amérique: Le Commerce des tableaux et la vente Morgan," *Gazette des Beaux-Arts*, vol. 33, per. 2 (June 1886), pp. 447–52.

Durand-Gréville 1887
E. Durand-Gréville. "La Peinture aux Etats-Unis: Les Galeries privées," *Gazette des Beaux-Arts*, vol. 36, per. 2 (July 1887), pp. 65–75, 252–55.

Evans Sale, 1890

New York, American Art Galleries. *Catalogue of Foreign Paintings . . . of the late Bernhard Stern . . . and William T. Evans, Jersey City*. March 6, 1890.

Fidell-Beaufort and Bailly-Herzberg 1975

Madeleine Fidell-Beaufort and Janine Bailly-Herzberg. *Daubigny*. Paris: Editions Geoffroy-Dechaume, 1975.

Forbes and Kelly

Christopher Forbes and Margaret Kelly. *War à la Mode: Military Pictures by Meissonier, Detaille, de Neuville and Berne-Bellecour from the FORBES Magazine Collection*. Introduction by Frank Anderson Trapp. Catalogue of exhibition, New York Cultural Center, 1975.

The Hague School 1983

The Hague, Haags Gemeentemuseum. *The Hague School: Dutch Masters of the 19th Century*. Edited by Ronald de Leeuw, John Sillevis, and Charles Dumas. Catalogue of exhibition, 1983. English edition: London, Royal Academy of Arts, in association with Weidenfeld and Nicolson, 1983.

Harper, J. A., Sale, 1980

New York, Leavitt Art Galleries. *Catalogue of Paintings . . . Private Collection of Mr. J. Abner Harper*. March 12–13, 1880.

Havemeyer Sale, 1914

New York, American Art Association. *Illustrated Catalogue of . . . {Mrs. Emilie de Losey Havemeyer Collection}*. November 16–23, 1914.

Hellebranth

Robert Hellebranth. *Charles-François Daubigny 1817–1878*. Morgues: Editions Matute, 1976.

Inglis Sale, New York, 1909

New York, American Art Galleries. . . . *Property of the Late James S. Inglis of Cottier & Company, New York*. March 11–12, 1909.

Joslyn 1982

Omaha, Nebraska, Joslyn Art Museum. *Jules Breton and the French Rural Tradition*. By Hollister Sturgis et al. Catalogue of exhibition, 1982.

La Farge and Jacacci 1907

John La Farge and August Jacacci, eds. *Noteworthy Paintings in American Private Collections*. 2 vols. New York: August F. Jacacci Co., 1907.

Landgren 1970

Marchal E. Landgren. In: College Park, Maryland, University of Maryland Art Gallery. *American Pupils of Thomas Couture*. 1970.

Lucas

The Diary of George A. Lucas: An American Art Agent in Paris, 1857–1909. 2 vols. Transcribed and with an introduction by Lilian M. C. Randall. Princeton, New Jersey: Princeton University Press, 1979.

Mather 1927

Frank Jewett Mather, Jr. *Modern Painting: A Study of Tendencies*. New York: Henry Holt and Co., 1927.

Matyjaszkiewicz 1985

Krystyna Matyjaszkiewicz, ed. *James Tissot*. New York: Abbeville Press, 1985.

Meyer

Julius Meyer, et al. *Allgemeines Künstler-Lexikon*. 3 vols. Leipzig: Wilhelm Engelmann, 1872–85.

Mireur

Doctor H. Mireur. *Dictionnaire des ventes d'art faites en France et à l'étranger pendant les XVIIIme et XIXme siecles*. 2 vols. Paris: Soullié, 1901–02.

Montgomery 1889
Walter C. Montgomery, ed. *American Art and American Art Collections*. 2 vols. Boston: E. Walker and Company, 1889.

Moore & Clarke Co. Sale, 1884
New York, Moore & Clarke Co. *247 High Class Paintings of the greatest European Painters Late the Property of Moore & Clarke Co., 290 Fifth Avenue, Retiring from the Art Business*. February 21–24, 1884.

Morgan, Mary Jane, Sale, 1886
New York, American Art Galleries. *Catalogue of the Art Collection formed by the late Mrs. Mary Jane Morgan*. March 8, 1886.

Nathan Sale, 1880
New York, Leavitt Art Galleries. *Collection of the Late Mrs. Benjamin Nathan and Others*. February 10, 1880.

Pisano 1979
Ronald G. Pisano. In: Southampton, New York, The Parrish Art Museum. *William Merritt Chase in the Company of Friends*. 1979.

Powers Sale, 1899
New York, American Art Association. *Valuable Paintings . . . from the Powers Art Gallery Collection*. January 18–20, 1899.

Seney Sale, 1885
New York, American Art Galleries. *Catalogue of Mr. George I. Seney's Collection of Modern Paintings . . . New York*. March 31–April 2, 1885.

Seney Sale, 1891
New York, American Art Association. *Catalogue of Modern Paintings . . . Belonging to the Estate of the Late George I. Seney.* February 11, 1891.

Smith 1903
S. Decatur Smith, Jr. "A Gallery of Modern Art," *The Booklovers' Magazine*, vol. 2, no. 3 (September 1903), pp. 256–73.

Spencer Sale, 1888
New York, Fifth Avenue Art Galleries. *Catalogue of the Albert Spencer Collection of Foreign Paintings*. February 28, 1888.

Sterling and Salinger
Charles Sterling and Margaretta M. Salinger. *French Paintings: A Catalogue of the Collection of The Metropolitan Museum of Art*, vol. 2, *XIX Century*. New York: The Metropolitan Museum of Art, distributed by New York Graphic Society, 1966.

Strahan
Edward Strahan [Earl Shinn], ed. *The Art Treasures of America*. 3 vols. Philadelphia: G. Barrie, 1879–82.

Van Dyke 1896
John C. Van Dyke, ed. *Modern French Masters: A Series of Biographical and Critical Reviews by American Artists*. New York: The Century Co., 1896.

Vente de Mme R., 1883
Paris, Vente de Mme R., February 3, 1883.

Wentworth 1984
Michael Wentworth. *James Tissot*. New York: Oxford University Press, 1984.

Williams Sale, 1915
New York, American Art Association. *Illustrated Catalogue of the Notable Collection of . . . the late Ichabod T. Williams, Esq., of New York*. February 3–4, 1915.

Wolfe, John, Sale, 1882
New York, Leavitt Art Galleries. *Catalogue of Mr. John Wolfe's Gallery of Valuable Paintings. . . .* April 5–6, 1882.

Bibliography

Alauzen, André M., and Pierre Ripert. *Monticelli, sa vie et son oeuvre.* Paris: Bibliothèque des Arts, 1969.

Allen, Edward. *Thomas Robinson: A Memoir.* Providence, Rhode Island: Privately printed, 1915.

American Art Annual, 1898. Florence N. Levy, ed. New York: The Macmillan Company, 1899.

Angell, Henry C. "Thomas Couture," *American Art Review*, vol. 2, part 2 (October 1881), pp. 239–46.

Ann Arbor, The University of Michigan Museum of Art. *Alfred Stevens.* Exhibition catalogue, text by William A. Coles, 1977.

"Anxious about Sunday, Why They Signed a Protest against the Sunday Art Show," *The Sun*, December 25, 1883, p. 1.

Bacon, Henry. "Glimpses of Parisian Art," *Scribner's Monthly,* vol. 21, no. 2 (December 1880), pp. 169–81; no. 3 (January 1881), pp. 423–31; no. 5 (March 1881), pp. 734–43.

Beckwith, James Carroll. Unpublished Diary, 1883. Collection, New York, National Academy of Design.

Béraldi, Henri. *Les Graveurs du XIXe siècle.* 12 vols. Paris: Librairie L. Conquet, 1885–92.

Bisanz, Rudolf M. *The Rene von Schleinitz Collection of the Milwaukee Art Center: Major Schools of German Nineteenth-Century Popular Painting.* Milwaukee: Milwaukee Art Center, University of Wisconsin Press, 1980.

Bogucki, Janus. *Gierymscy.* Warsaw: Wiedza Powszechna, 1959.

Boime, Albert. *Thomas Couture and the Eclectic Vision.* New Haven, Connecticut: Yale University Press, 1980.

Brooklyn, Brooklyn Art Association. *A Catalogue of Oil Paintings Exhibited by the Brooklyn Art Association in Aid of the Bartholdi Pedestal Fund, January 1884.* New York: De Vinne Press, 1884.

Brownell, William C. "Bastien-Lepage: Painter and Psychologist," *The Magazine of Art*, vol. 6 (1883), pp. 265–71.

———. *French Art: Classic and Contemporary Painting and Sculpture.* New York: Charles Scribner's Sons, 1892.

———. "Whistler in Painting and Etching," *Scribner's Monthly*, vol. 18, no. 4 (May 1879), pp. 481–95.

Brumbaugh, Thomas B. "Lost in Storage: Ludwig Knaus in America Collections, *Art Journal*, vol. 27, no. 3 (1968), pp. 262–65.

Buenos Aires, Argentina, Roldan y Cìa. *Importante y Excepcional Seleccion de Pinturas, Muebles, Objetos de Arte y Antiguedades.* Sale, June 3–7, 1974.

Carrington, Fitz Roy. *A Catalogue of the Engravings and Etchings formed by the late G. C. Cooper.* New York: Privately printed, 1897.

Carter, Susan N. "Street Life in Madrid," *The Century Magazine*, vol. 39, no. 1 (November 1889), pp. 32–41.

Catalogue of Paintings, Prints, Sculpture and Objects of Art in the H. O. Havemeyer Collection. Part II, Paintings and Prints. New York: Privately printed, 1931.

Champlin, John D., and Charles C. Perkins. *Cyclopedia of Painters and Paintings.* 4 vols. New York: Charles Scribner's Sons, 1886–87.

Champney, Elizabeth. *Witch Winnie's Studio.* New York: Dodd Mead & Co., 1892.

Chase, William Merritt. "Address of Mr. William Merritt Chase before the Buffalo Fine Arts Academy, January 28, 1890," *The Studio*, vol. 5, no. 13 (March 1, 1890), pp. 121–27.

———. "Painting," *The American Magazine of Art*, vol. 8, no. 2 (December 1916), pp. 50–53.

———. "The Two Whistlers: Recollections of a Summer with the Great Etcher," *The Century Magazine*, vol. 80, no. 2 (June 1910), pp. 218–26.

Chicago, The Art Institute of Chicago. *Dagnan-Bouveret: Exhibition of Works*. Exhibition catalogue, March 1–24, 1901.

Clarétie, Jules. *Peintres et sculpteurs contemporains*. 2 vols. Paris: Librairie des Bibliophiles, 1882–84.

Clark, Eliot. "Adolphe Monticelli, 1824–1886," *Art in America*, vol. 3, no. 1 (December 1914), pp. 14–23.

Clément, Charles. *Géricault: Etude biographique et critique avec le catalogue raisonné de l'oeuvre du maître*. Paris: Didier, 1879.

Coan, Titus Munson. "Gustave Courbet: Artist and Communist," *The Century Magazine*, vol. 27, no. 4 (February 1884), pp. 483–95.

Coffin, William A. "Dagnan-Bouveret," *The Century Magazine*, vol. 48, no. 1 (May 1894), pp. 4–15.

———. "Jean-Charles Cazin," *The Century Magazine*, vol. 55 (1898), pp. 393–99.

College Park, Maryland, University of Maryland Art Gallery. *American Pupils of Thomas Couture*. Exhibition catalogue, text by Marchal E. Landgren, March 19–April 26, 1970.

Cook, Clarence. *Art and Artists of Our Time*. 6 vols. New York: Selmar Hess, Publisher, 1888.

———. *The House Beautiful: Essays on Beds and Tables, Stools and Candlesticks*. New York: Scribner, Armstrong & Co., 1878.

———. "Recent House Decoration," *Scribner's Monthly*, vol. 15 (1877), p. 569.

Cortissoz, Royal. *John La Farge: A Memoir and Study*. Boston and New York: Houghton Mifflin, 1911.

———. "The Field of Art," *Scribner's Magazine*, vol. 80, no. 33 (1926), pp. 456–64.

Cox, Kenyon. "Antoine Vollon: A Painter's Painter," *The Manhattan*, vol. 2, no. 6 (December 1883), pp. 557–61.

———. *Painters and Sculptors*. New York, 1907.

De Kay, Charles. "Theodore Rousseau," *The Century Magazine*, vol. 41, no. 4 (February 1891), pp. 568–78.

De Taeye, E. L. *Les Artistes belgiques contemporains*. Brussels, 1894.

Detroit, Detroit Institute of Arts. *The Quest for Unity: American Art between World's Fairs*. Exhibition catalogue, 1983.

Donnelly, Michael. *Glasgow Stained Glass: A Preliminary Study*. Glasgow: Glasgow Museums and Art Galleries, 1981.

Durand-Gréville, E. "Correspondance d'Amérique: Le Commerce des tableàux et la vente Morgan," *Gazette des Beaux-Arts*, vol. 33, per. 2 (June 1886), pp. 447–52.

———. "La Peinture aux Etats-Unis: Les Galeries privées," *Gazette des Beaux-Arts*, vol. 36, per. 2 (July 1887), pp. 65–75, 252–55.

Eckford, Henry. "Antoine Louis Barye," *The Century Magazine*, vol. 31, no. 4 (February 1886), pp. 483–500.

———. "Eugene Fromentin," *The Century Magazine*, vol. 25, no. 6 (April 1883), pp. 829–38.

Engel, E. P. *Anton Mauve 1838–1888.* Utrecht: Academische Uitgeverig Haentjens Dekker & Gumbert, 1967.

Fernier, Robert. *La Vie et l'oeuvre de Gustave Courbet: Catalogue raisonné.* 2 vols. Lausanne and Paris: Bibliothèque des Arts, Fondation Wildenstein, 1978.

Fidell-Beaufort, Madeleine, and Janine Bailly-Herzberg. *Daubigny.* Paris: Editions Geoffroy-Dechaume, 1975.

Forbes, Christopher, and Margaret Kelly. *War à la Mode: Military Pictures by Meissonier, Detaille, de Neuville and Berne-Bellecour from the FORBES Magazine Collection.* Exhibition catalogue, introduction by Frank Anderson Trapp, New York Cultural Center, 1975.

Fromentin, Eugène. *Old Masters of Holland and Belgium (Les Maîtres d'autrefois).* Translated by Mrs. Mary Robbins. Boston: R. Osgood and Company, 1883.

Fuchs, Heinrich. *Eugen Jettel.* Vienna: Dr. Heinrich Fuchs Selbstverlag, 1975.

Geffroy, Gustave. *Claude Monet, sa vie, son temps, son oeuvre.* Paris: G. Crès et Cie, 1922.

Gilder, Richard W. "Bastien-Lepage," *Scribner's Monthly*, vol. 22, no. 2 (June 1881), pp. 230–35.

Girouard, Mark. *Sweetness and Light: The "Queen Anne" Movement, 1860–1900.* New York: Oxford University Press, 1977.

Gonse, Louis. *Eugène Fromentin: Peintre et écrivain.* Paris, 1881.

Goodrich, Lloyd. *Albert Pinkham Ryder.* New York: George Braziller, 1959.

Gould, Brian. *Two van Gogh Contacts: E. J. van Wisselingh, Art Dealer; Daniel Cottier, Glass Painter and Decorator.* Bedford Park: Naples Press, 1969.

Grands peintres français et étrangers, Ouvrage d'art publié avec le concours artistique des maîtres; text par les principaux critiques d'art. Paris: H. Launette, Goupil & Cie, 1884.

The Hague, Haags Gemeentemuseum. *Maris Tentoonstellung.* Exhibition catalogue, December 22, 1935–February 2, 1936.

________. *The Hague School: Dutch Masters of the 19th Century.* Edited by Ronald de Leeuw, John Sillevis, and Charles Dumas. Exhibition catalogue, 1983. English edition: London, Royal Academy of Arts, in association with Weidenfeld and Nicolson, 1983.

The Hague, Rijksmuseum H. W. Mesdag. *Catalogus der Schilderijen, Etsen en Kunstvoorwerpen.* Collection catalogue, 1948.

Hammond, Mason. "The Stained Glass Windows in Memorial Hall, Harvard University," Cambridge, Massachusetts, 1978 (unpublished ms. in Cottier File, American Arts Department, The Metropolitan Museum of Art, New York).

Harrison, Martin. "Contemporary Art Glass 100 Years Ago," *Glass*, vol. 6, no. 1 (January 1975), pp. 36–39.

Hart, Charles Henry. "The Collection of Mr. Henry C. Gibson, Philadelphia," *American Art Review*, vol. 1, part 1 (1880), pp. 231–35, and vol. 1, part 2 (1880), pp. 294–99.

Haskell, Francis, ed. *Salons, Galleries, Museums and Their Influence in the Development of 19th and 20th Century Art.* Bologna, Italy: Cooperativa Libreria Universitaria, 1979.

Held, Jutta. *Katalog der Gemälde des 19. Jahrhundert, Museum Folkwang, Essen.* Foreword by Paul Vogt. Essen, West Germany: Museum Folkwang, 1981.

Hellebranth, Robert. *Charles-François Daubigny 1817–1878.* Morgues: Editions Matute, 1976.

Hendy, Philip. *European and American Paintings in The Isabella Stewart Gardner Museum.* Boston: The Isabella Stewart Gardner Museum, 1974.

Hooper, Lucy A. "Art Notes from Paris," *The Art Journal*, n.s. 6 (1880), p. 253.

Huth, Hans. "Impressionism Comes to America," *Gazette des Beaux-Arts*, vol. 29, per. 6 (April 1946), pp. 225–52.

Ilges, F. Walther. *M. von Munkácsy.* Bielefeld and Leipzig: Velhagen & Klasing, 1897.

Jarvis, Robert. "Autumn Exhibition of the National Academy," *The Art Amateur*, vol. 10, no. 1 (December 1883), p. 8.

Johnson, Lee. *The Paintings of Eugène Delacroix: A Critical Catalogue, 1816–1831.* 2 vols. Oxford: The Clarendon Press, 1981.

Johnston, William R. "The Barye Collection," *Apollo*, vol. 100 (1974), pp. 56–63.

________. *The Nineteenth Century Paintings in the Walters Art Gallery.* Baltimore: The Trustees of the Walters Art Gallery, 1982.

________. "W. H. Stewart: The American Patron of Mariano Fortuny," *Gazette des Beaux-Arts*, vol. 77, per. 6 (1971), pp. 183–88.

K., G. "The Bartholdi Exhibition," *Harper's Weekly*, vol. 27, no. 1408 (December 15, 1883), pp. 799 and 804.

King, Moses. *Notable New Yorkers of 1896–1899.* New York: Moses King, 1899.

Klumpke, Anna. *Rosa Bonheur, sa vie, son oeuvre.* Paris: E. Flammarion, 1908.

Lacambre, Geneviève and Jean. *Champfleury, le Réalisme.* Paris, 1973.

La Farge, John. *The Higher Life in Art: A Series of Lectures on the Barbizon School of France Inaugurating the Scammon Course at the Art Institute of Chicago.* New York: The McClure Company, 1908.

________, and August Jacacci, eds. *Noteworthy Paintings in American Private Collections.* 2 vols. New York: August F. Jacacci Co., 1907.

Laffan, W. MacKay. "The Tile Club Ashore," *The Century Magazine*, vol. 23, no. 4 (February 1882), pp. 481–98.

________, and Edward Strahan [Earl Shinn]. "The Tile Club Afloat," *Scribner's Monthly*, vol. 19, no. 5 (March 1880), pp. 641–71.

________. "The Tile Club at Play," *Scribner's Monthly*, vol. 17, no. 4 (February 1879), pp. 457–78.

Lauderbach, Frances. "Notes from Talks by William M. Chase: Summer Class, Carmel by the Sea, California (Memoranda from a Student's Note Book)," *The American Magazine of Art*, vol. 8, no. 11 (September 1917), pp. 432–38.

Lemoisne, Paul André. *Degas et son oeuvre.* 4 vols. Paris: Paul Brame et C. M. Hauke, 1946–49.

London, Arts Council of Great Britain. *Jean-François Millet.* Exhibition catalogue, text by Robert Herbert, with Michel Laclotte and Roseline Bacon, Hayward Gallery, London, 1976.

London, Christie, Manson & Woods. *Catalogue of Modern Pictures and Water-Colour Drawings chiefly of the continental schools. The Property of Mrs. Cottier deceased.* Sale May 1, 1914.

London, Jan G. Milner, and Shepherd Gallery Associates, New York. *French 19th Century Paintings.* Exhibition, The Alpine Club Gallery, London, March 23–April 6, 1977.

London, Royal Academy of Arts. *The Orientalists: Delacroix to Matisse, European Painters in North Africa and the Near East.* Mary Anne Stevens, ed. London: Weidenfeld and Nicolson, 1984.

Lostalot, Alfred de. "Ludwig Knaus," *Gazette des Beaux-Arts*, no. 25, per. 2 (April 1882), pp. 269–80.

Low, Will H. *A Chronicle of Friendships 1873–1900.* New York: Charles Scribner's Sons, 1908.

________. *A Painter's Progress.* New York: Charles Scribner's Sons, 1910.

Lucas, George A. *The Diary of George A. Lucas: An American Art Agent in Paris,*

1857–1909. 2 vols. Transcribed and with an introduction by Lilian M. C. Randall. Princeton, New Jersey: Princeton University Press, 1979.

Mantz, Paul. "Le Salon de 1872," *Gazette des Beaux-Arts*, vol. 6, per. 2 (July 1872), pp. 33–66.

Marius, G. Hermine. *Dutch Painting in the Nineteenth Century*. Translated by Alexander Teixera de Mattos. London: Alexander Morning Limited, 1908.

Marks, Richard, et al. *The Burrell Collection*. London and Glasgow: Glasgow Art Gallery and Museum, 1983.

Mastowski, Maciej. *Maksymilian Gierymski I Jego Czasy*. Warsaw: Panstwowy Instytut Wydawniczy, 1970.

Mather, Frank J., Jr. *Modern Painting: A Study of Tendencies*. New York: Henry Holt and Co., 1927.

Matyjaszkiewicz, Krystyna, ed. *James Tissot*. New York: Abbeville Press, 1985.

Memphis, The Dixon Gallery and Gardens. *An International Episode: Millet, Monet and Their North American Counterparts*. Exhibition catalogue, text by Laura Meixner, 1982.

Meyer, Julius, et al. *Allgemeines Künstler-Lexikon, unter Mitwirkung der namhaftesten Fachgelehrten des In- und Auslandes*. 3 vols. Leipzig: Wilhelm Engelmann, 1872–85.

Middletown, Connecticut, Davison Art Center, Wesleyan University. *A Cultivated Taste: Whistler and American Print Collectors*. Exhibition catalogue, text by M. Lee Wiehl, 1983.

Mitchell, Peter. *Alfred Emile Léopold Stevens 1823–1906*. London: John Mitchell and Sons, 1973.

Montgomery, Walter C., ed. *American Art and American Art Collections*. 2 vols. Boston: E. Walker and Company, 1889.

Moran, John. "Studio Life in New York," *The Art Journal*, vol. 5 (1879), pp. 344–45.

Moreau-Nélaton, Etienne. *Manet, raconté par lui-même*. 2 vols. Paris: H. Laurens, 1926.

Münchner Maler im 19. Jahrhundert. 4 vols. Munich: Bruckmann Verlag, 1981–83.

Munich. *Führer durch die internationale Kunstausstellung in München*. Augsburg: Reichel Verlag, 1879.

———. *Katalog der I. internationalen Kunstausstellung im königlichen Glaspalast zu München*, 1869.

———. *Katalog der internationalen Kunst Ausstellung im kgl. Glaspalast zu München*. Munich: Verlag des Comités der internationalen Kunstausstellung in München, 1879.

———. *Offizieller Katalog der internationalen Kunst Ausstellung im kgl. Glaspalast in München*. Munich: Verlag des Comités, 1883.

Munich, Bayerische Staatsgemäldesammlungen und Ausstellungsleitung Haus der Kunst. *Die Münchner Schule 1850–1914*. Exhibition catalogue, Haus der Kunst, Munich, July 28–October 7, 1979.

Munich, Haus der Kunst. *München 1869–1958: Aufbruch zur moderner Kunst*. Including "Rekonstruction der ersten internationalen Kunstausstellung, 1869." Exhibition catalogue, June 21–October 5, 1958.

Muther, Richard. *The History of Modern Painting*. 4 vols. London: J. M. Dent & Co., 1907.

New York, American Art Association, *Catalogue of Modern Paintings . . . Belonging to the Estate of the Late George I. Seney*. February 11, 1891.

———. *Catalogue of the A. T. Stewart Collection of Paintings, Sculptures, and other objects of Art*. March 23–25, 1887.

———. *Catalogue of Valuable Paintings by Distinguished Artists of the Modern Schools, including: Estate of Mrs. Sarah B. Conkling (whose pictures were mostly selected by the late Dan-*

iel Cottier) . . . {and} The entire stock of L. Crist Delmonico, retiring from business. . . . February 8–9, 1905.

________. *The Charles T. Yerkes Collection of Very Valuable Paintings, Ancient Oriental Rugs and Beautiful Old Tapestries.* April 5–8, 1910.

________. *A Descriptive Catalogue of Paintings, Pastels and Water-Colors Collected by the late Mrs. S. D. Warren of Boston.* January 8–9, 1903.

________. *Eastern Ceramics and other objects of Art belonging to the estate of the late Charles A. Dana.* February 24–26, 1898.

________. *Illustrated Catalogue of Artistic Furnishings, Gallery of Modern Paintings, Rare Gobelin Tapestries, Costly Woodwork and other Interior Decorations of the Havemeyer Residence {Mrs. Emilie de Losey Havemeyer}.* November 16–23, 1914.

________. *Illustrated Catalogue of Notable Paintings by Great Masters Collected by the Late Clement A. Griscom, Esq., of Philadelphia.* February 26–27, 1914.

________. *Illustrated Catalogue of the Notable Collection of . . . the late Ichabod T. Williams, Esq., of New York.* February 3–4, 1915.

________. *Illustrated Catalogue of the Valuable Modern Paintings and Water Colors collected by the late Peter A. Schemm of Philadelphia.* March 14–17, 1911.

________. *Illustrated Catalogue of the Valuable Paintings and Sculptures by the Old and Modern Masters forming the famous Catholina Lambert Collection.* February 21–14, 1916.

________. *Valuable Paintings, Sculpture and Grand Clock selected from The Powers Art Gallery Collection (Daniel W. Powers), Rochester, New York.* January 18–20, 1899.

New York, American Art Association-Anderson Galleries. *Paintings of the XVI–XIX centuries from the Collection of William S. Hawk {and others}.* February 4–5, 1931.

New York, American Art Galleries. *Catalogue of the Art Collection formed by the late Mrs. Mary Jane Morgan.* March 8, 1886.

________. *Catalogue of the Art Collections of the American Art Association to be absolutely sold at auction to settle the estate of the late R. Austin Robertson.* April 7–8, 11, 1892.

________. *Catalogue of Foreign Paintings . . . Private Collections of the late Bernhard Stern, New York and William T. Evans, Jersey City.* March 6, 1890.

________. *Catalogue of Mr. George I. Seney's Collection of Modern Paintings. . . .* New York, March 31–April 2, 1885.

________. *Catalogue of the Private Collections of Modern Paintings belonging to Mr. Beriah Wall and Mr. John A. Brown of Providence, R. I..* March 30–31, April 1, 1886.

________. *Catalogue of the Works of Antoine-Louis Barye, Exhibited at the American Art Galleries under the auspices of the Barye Monument Association; also of paintings by . . . His contemporaries and friends for the benefit of the Barye Monument Fund.* November 15, 1889–January 15, 1890.

________. *Illustrated Catalogue of the Artistic Property, Fine Antique and Modern Furniture, Important Flemish Tapestries, Stained Glass, Textiles and other objects of household utility of the well-known house of Cottier and Company of New York.* November 19–26, 1913.

________. *Important Paintings belonging to the estate of George Crocker, Alice Newcomb. . . .* January 24, 1912.

________. *The Valuable Paintings and Other Art Property of the Late James S. Inglis of Cottier & Company, New York.* March 11–12, 1909.

New York, Anderson Galleries. *Drawings and Paintings from the Collections of Dr. J. Stedman Converse . . . the Late Dr. Harry R. Purdy . . . the Late Daniel Cottier of New York City.* November 7–8, 1923.

New York, Berlin Photographic Co. *Catalogue of the Work of Alfred Stevens on Exhibition at the Gallery of the Berlin Photographic Company.* February 27–March 11, 1911.

New York, Fifth Avenue Art Galleries. *Catalogue of a Valuable Collection of Modern Paintings to be sold by auction by order of the Trustees of Blakeslee & Co.*, April 4–5, 1893.

———. *Catalogue of Modern Paintings belonging to Erwin Davis, Esq.*. March 19–20, 1889.

———. *Catalogue of the Albert Spencer Collection of Foreign Paintings*. February 28, 1888.

———. *The S. P. Avery Collection of Oil Paintings*. March 20, 1902.

New York, Leavitt Art Galleries. *Catalogue of Mr. J. C. Runkle's Entire Collection of Foreign Cabinet Paintings*. March 8, 1883.

———. *Catalogue of Mr. John Wolfe's Gallery of Valuable Paintings. . . .* April 5–6, 1882.

———. *Catalogue of Paintings in Oil and Water Colors, The Private Collection of Mr. J. Abner Harper*. March 12–13, 1880.

———. *Collection of the Late Mrs. Benjamin Nathan and Others*. February 10, 1880.

———. *Fine Oil Paintings and Water-Color Drawings by the Great Modern Classic Painters imported by Cottier & Co., 144 Fifth Avenue*. April 23–24, 1878.

New York, Metropolitan Art Association. *Catalogue of Paintings, Art Objects, Books, Textiles, and Artistic Furniture comprising the entire stock of the firm of Cottier and Company of 718 Fifth Avenue, New York*. March 12, 1915.

New York, The Metropolitan Museum of Art. *Hand Book, no. 1, Part I, The Catharine Lorillard Wolfe Collection in the New Western Galleries*, 1889.

———. *Loan Exhibition of the Works of Gustave Courbet*. Exhibition catalogue, April 7–May 18, 1919.

New York, Moore & Clarke Co. *247 High Class Paintings of the greatest European Painters . . . Late the Property of Moore & Clarke Co., 290 Fifth Avenue, Retiring from the Art Business*, February 21–24, 1884.

New York, National Academy of Design. *Catalogue of Celebrated Paintings by Great French Masters, brought to this country for exhibition only*. New York: The American Association for the Promotion and Encouragement of Art, Managers, 1887.

———. *Catalogue of the Loan Exhibition in aid of the Society of Decorative Art, consisting of Gems of the Modern Foreign and American Schools of Painting and rare examples of various art industries*. 1877.

———. *Catalogue of the New York Centennial Loan Exhibition of Paintings, Selected from Private Art Galleries*. 1876.

———. *Catalogue of the Pedestal Fund Art Loan Exhibition*. December 1883.

———. *Special Exhibition: Works in Oil and Pastel by the Impressionists of Paris*. Exhibited under the management of the American Art Association of the City of New York, 1886.

New York, Parke-Bernet Galleries, Inc. *Distinguished Paintings by Old and Modern Masters . . . Frank D. Stout Collection, Chicago [and others]*. December 3, 1942.

New York, Stair Sainty Matthiesen. *The Macchiaioli: Tuscan Painters of the Sunlight*. Exhibition catalogue, preface by Cynthia V. Sainty, introduction by Erich Steingraeber, text by Giuliano Matteucci, 1984.

———. *Three Italian Friends of the Impressionists: Boldini, De Nittis, Zandomeneghi*. Exhibition catalogue, preface by Cynthia V. Sainty, introduction by Dario Durbe, essay and text by Enrico Piceni, 1984.

New York, New York University, Grey Art Gallery and Study Center. *Giovanni Boldini and Society Portraiture 1880–1920*. Exhibition catalogue, text by Gary A. Reynolds, 1984.

New Orleans, Isaac Delgado Museum. *Edgar Degas, His Family and Friends in New Orleans*. Essays by John Rewald, James B. Byrnes, Jean Sutherland Boggs. Published on the Occasion of an Exhibition of Degas's New Orleans Work, 1965.

Omaha, Nebraska, Joslyn Art Museum. *Jules Breton and the French Rural Tradition*. Exhibition catalogue by Hollister Sturges, with contributions by Annette Bourrut-

Lacouture, Gabriel P. Weisberg, Madeleine Fidell-Beaufort. Omaha: Joslyn Art Museum, in association with The Arts Publisher, Inc., New York, 1982.

Ottawa, The National Gallery of Canada. *The Other Nineteenth Century: Paintings and Sculpture in the Collection of Mr. and Mrs. Joseph M. Tanenbaum.* Organized and edited by Louise d'Argencourt and Douglas Druick. Ottawa: National Museums of Canada, 1978.

Pach, Walter. "Gericault in America," *Gazette des Beaux-Arts*, vol. 27, per. 6 (April 1945), pp. 227–40.

Paris, *Oeuvres de feu Barye*, February 5–6, 1876.

Paris, Galeries Durand-Ruel. *Catalogue of Ancient and Modern Pictures, Important Works of the French, English and Dutch Schools (Sale of the Pictures of the late Mr. Cottier of London).* May 27–28, 1892.

________. *Exposition retrospective de tableaux et dessins des maîtres modernes.* July 8, 1878.

Paris, Institut de France. *Catalogue des oeuvres de Dagnan-Bouveret.* Exhibition catalogue, 1930.

Paris, Musée du Louvre et des Galeries nationales d'exposition du Grand Palais. *Hommage à Claude Monet (1840–1926).* Paris: Editions de la Réunion des musées nationaux, 1980.

Paris, Palais de l'Industrie. *Catalogue des oeuvres de Th. Couture exposées au Palais de l'Industrie.* Exhibition catalogue, September 1880.

Pittsburgh, Museum of Art, Carnegie Institute. *Monticelli: His Contemporaries, His Influence.* Exhibition catalogue, text by Aaron Sheon, 1978.

Robaut, Alfred. *L'Oeuvre complet de Eugène Delacroix: Peintures, dessins, gravures, lithographies.* Commentary by Ernest Chesneau. Paris: H. Floury, 1885. Da Capo Press edition, 1969.

________. *L'Oeuvre de Corot, catalogue raisonné et illustré précédé de l'histoire de Corot et de ses oeuvres par Etienne Moreau-Nélaton.* 5 vols. Paris: Léonce Laget, 1965.

Robinson, John. "Personal Reminiscences of Albert Pinkham Ryder," *Art in America*, vol. 13 (June 1925), pp. 176–87.

Rochester, Memorial Art Gallery of the University of Rochester. *Orientalism: The Near East in French Painting 1800–1880.* Exhibition catalogue, text by Donald Rosenthal, 1982.

Roger-Miles, L. *Rosa Bonheur, sa vie, son oeuvre.* Paris: Société d'Edition Artistique, 1900.

Roof, Katherine Metcalf. *The Life and Art of William Merritt Chase.* New York: Charles Scribner's Sons, 1917.

Rosenblum, Robert, and H. W. Janson. *19th Century Art.* New York: Harry Abrams, Inc., 1984.

Rouart, Denis, and Daniel Wildenstein. *Edouard Manet: Catalogue raisonné.* 2 vols. Lausanne: Bibliothèque des Arts, Fondation Wildenstein, 1975.

Rowlands, Walter. "Art Sales in America," *The Art Journal*, vol. 50, n.s. 40 (1888), pp. 318–19.

________. "The Miss Wolfe Collection," *The Art Journal*, vol. 51, n.s. 41 (1889), pp. 12–15.

Sacramento, California, E. B. Crocker Art Gallery. *Munich and American Realism in the 19th Century.* Exhibition catalogue, text by Michael Quick, 1978.

Saint-Gaudens, Homer, ed. *Reminiscences of Augustus Saint-Gaudens.* 2 vols. London: Andrew Melrose, 1913.

St. Louis, Missouri. *Official Catalogue of Exhibitors, Universal Exposition, St. Louis, U.S.A., 1904, Department B, Art.* Halsey C. Ives, Chief. St. Louis: Published for the Committee on Press and Publicity by the Official Catalogue Company, Inc., 1904.

Sensier, Alfred. *Etudes sur Georges Michel.* Paris, 1873.

———. *La Vie et l'oeuvre de J.-F. Millet.* Paris: A. Quentin, 1881.

Sheldon, George W. *Hours with Art and Artists.* New York: D. Appleton and Company, 1882.

Silvestre, Armand, et al. *The Gallery of Contemporary Art: An Illustrated Review of the Recent Art Productions of All Nations.* Edited by Eugene Reed, A.M. Philadelphia: Gebbie & Co., Publishers, 1884.

Smith, S. Decatur, Jr. "A Gallery of Modern Art," *The Booklovers' Magazine*, vol. 2, no. 3 (September 1903), pp. 256–73.

"Society of American Artists," *Scribner's Monthly*, vol. 16, no. 1 (May 1878), p. 247.

Southampton, New York, The Parrish Art Museum. *William Merritt Chase in the Company of Friends.* Exhibition catalogue, text by Ronald G. Pisano, May 13–June 24, 1979.

Stepien, Halina. *Maksymilian Gierymski 1846–1874, Malarstwo I Rysunek.* Warsaw: National Museum of Warsaw, 1974.

Sterling, Charles, and Margaretta M. Salinger. *French Paintings: A Catalogue of the Collection of The Metropolitan Museum of Art*, vol. 2, *XIX Century.* New York: The Metropolitan Museum of Art, distributed by the New York Graphic Society, 1966.

Strahan, Edward [Earl Shinn], ed. *The Art Treasures of America, Being the Choicest Works of Art in the Public and Private Collections of North America.* 3 vols. Philadelphia: G. Barrie, 1879–82.

———. *Etudes in Modern French Art.* New York: Richard Worthington, Publishers, 1882.

———. *Mr. Vanderbilt's House and Collection.* 4 vols. Boston: G. Barrie, [c. 1883–84].

Stranahan, C. H. *A History of French Painting from Its Earliest to Its Latest Practice.* New York: Charles Scribner's Sons, 1893.

Sypher, Obadiah. "Bric-a-Brac," *The Curio*, vol. 1, no. 2 (October 1887), p. 192.

Tabarant, Adolphe. *Manet: Histoire catalographique.* Paris: Editions Montaigne, 1931.

Tait, John R. "Michael Munkacsy," *American Art Review*, vol. 2, part 1 (1880), pp. 235–43, and vol. 2, part 2 (1880), pp. 13–20.

Thiollier, Félix. *L'Oeuvre de J. P. Laurens.* Saint-Etienne: J. Thomas & Cie, 1906.

Thomson, D. Croal. *The Brothers Maris (James-Matthew-William).* London: Special Summer Number of *The Studio* (1907).

Toledo, Ohio, The Toledo Museum of Art. *European Paintings.* Collection catalogue. 1976.

Toronto, Art Gallery of Ontario. *The Hague School: Collecting in Canada at the Turn of the Century.* Exhibition catalogue, text by Marta H. Hurdalek, 1983.

Townsley, C. P. "A Leading Spirit in American Art," *Arts and Decoration*, vol. 2, no. 8 (June 1912), pp. 285–87, 306.

Truettner, William H. "William T. Evans, Collector of American Paintings," *The American Art Journal*, vol. 3, no. 2 (Fall 1971), pp. 50–79.

The United States Art Directory and Yearbook of 1884, vol. 2. Edited by Sylvester R. Koehler. New York, London and Paris: Cassell and Company, Limited, 1885.

United States Centennial Commission International Exhibition, 1876. Philadelphia: Published for the Centennial Catalogue Company by J. R. Nagle.

Van Dyke, John C. "The Bartholdi Loan Collection," *The Studio*, vol. 2, no. 49 (December 8, 1883), pp. 262–63.

———. *The Increase in the Appreciation of Serious Art in America: A Paper Read Before the Rembrandt Club, February 4th 1889.* Brooklyn: Published by the Club, 1889.

———, ed. *Modern French Masters: A Series of Biographical and Critical Reviews by American Artists.* New York: The Century Co., 1896.

van Gogh, Vincent. *The Complete Letters of Vincent van Gogh.* Greenwich, Connecticut: New York Graphic Society, n.d.

Van Rensselaer, Mariana Griswold. "American Etchers," *The Century Magazine*, vol. 25, no. 4 (February 1883), pp. 483–99.

———. *Book of American Figure Painters.* Philadelphia: J. B. Lippincott, 1886.

———. "Corot," *The Century Magazine*, vol. 38, no. 2 (June 1889), pp. 255–71.

———. "Courbet, the Artist," *The Century Magazine*, vol. 29, no. 5 (March 1885), pp. 792–94.

———. "The Recent New York Loan Exhibition," *American Architect and Building News*, vol. 15, no. 421 (January 19, 1884), pp. 29–30.

———. "William Merritt Chase—Second and Concluding Article," *American Art Review*, vol. 2 (February 1881), pp. 135–42.

Véron, Eugène. "Th. Ribot Exposition de ses oeuvres dans les galeries de *L'Art*," *L'Art*, vol. 21 (1880), pp. 127–31, 151–61.

Wallace, General Lew, et al. *Famous Paintings of the World.* New York: Fine Art Publishers, 1895.

Washington, D.C., The Corcoran Gallery of Art. *Of Time and Place: American Figurative Art from the Corcoran Gallery of Art.* Exhibition catalogue. Smithsonian Institution Traveling Exhibition Service and Corcoran Gallery of Art, 1981.

Washington, D.C., National Collection of Fine Arts. *American Art in the Barbizon Mood.* Exhibition catalogue, text by Peter Bermingham. Washington, D.C.: Smithsonian Institution Press for the National Collection of Fine Arts, 1975.

———. *1876: American Art of the Centennial.* Exhibition catalogue. Smithsonian Institution Press for the National Collection of Fine Arts, 1976.

Washington, D.C., National Gallery of Art. *The John Hay Whitney Collection.* Exhibition catalogue, text by John Rewald, 1983.

Weinberg, H. Barbara. "Thomas B. Clarke: Foremost Patron of American Art from 1872 to 1899," *The American Art Journal*, vol. 8, no. 1 (May 1976), pp. 52–83.

Weitzenhoffer, Frances. "First Manet Paintings to Enter an American Museum," *Gazette des Beaux-Arts*, vol. 6, no. 98 (March 1981), pp. 125–29.

Wentworth, Michael. *James Tissot.* New York: Oxford University Press, 1984.

Wheeler, Candace. *Yesterdays in a Busy Life.* New York and London: Harper & Brothers, 1918.

Wheelwright, Edward. "Personal Recollections of Jean-François Millet," *Atlantic Monthly*, vol. 38 (September 1876), pp. 257–76.

Wissman, Fronia, E. "Corot's *Hymn to the Sun*," *Elvehjem Museum of Art Bulletin 1983–1984.* Madison: University of Wisconsin, 1984.

World's Columbian Exposition 1893, Official Catalogue, Part X, Dept. K, Fine Arts. Halsey C. Ives, Chief. Chicago: W. B. Conkey Company, Publishers to the World's Columbian Exposition, 1893.

Young, Dorothy Weir. *Life and Letters of J. Alden Weir.* New Haven, Connecticut: Yale University Press, 1960.

Index of Artists

The following artists were represented in the Paintings Section of the 1883 *Pedestal Fund Art Loan Exhibition*. Those marked with an asterisk are not included in the current exhibition. Numbers refer to plates and catalogue entries.

PHOTOGRAPHY CREDITS

The majority of the photographs have been provided by the owners or custodians of the works reproduced. The following list applies to those photographs for which a separate acknowledgment is due.

Anne S. K. Brown Military Collection, Providence, Rhode Island (O'Brien, fig. 19)
Annmary Brown Memorial, Brown University, Providence, Rhode Island (Monkhouse, figs. 1, 3-5)
Christie's East, New York (cat. no. 10)
Ken Cohen, New York (cat. no. 93)
Richard Eells, Milwaukee (cat. no. 94)
Stanley L. Franzos, Pittsburgh (cat. no. 53)
Frick Art Reference Library, New York (O'Brien, figs. 21, 22, 57; Dinnerstein, fig. 8)
Harvard Law Art Collection, Cambridge, Massachusetts (Dinnerstein, fig. 1)
John Hay Library, Brown University, Providence, Rhode Island, (frontispiece: *Harper's Weekly*, December 6, 1884)
E. Heuker of Hoek (pl. XXVII)
T. McGinniss, New York (cat. no. 37)
Richard Margolis, Rochester, New York (cat. no. 20)
The Metropolitan Museum of Art, New York (O'Brien, figs. 1-9, 11, 26, 34, 38, 40, 41, 43, 47, 48, 52, 54, 55, 59; Dinnerstein, figs. 2, 4)
National Gallery Publications Department, London (O'Brien, fig. 27; pl. XXVI)
Otto E. Nelson, New York (cat. nos. 27, 58)
The New-York Historical Society (Dinnerstein, fig. 11)
The New York Public Library (Dinnerstein, figs. 9, 10)
Eric Pollitzer, New York (pl. X)
Clive Russ, Boston (pl. V)
Schwartz, Washington, D.C. (pls. XIX, XXXV; cat. nos. 51, 67)
Stair Sainty Fine Arts, Ltd., New York (pl. XXXVIII)
Ken Strothman and Harvey Osterhoudt, Bloomington, Indiana (cat. no. 84)
Studio 148, Buffalo, New York (cat. no. 17)
Joseph Szaszfai, New Haven, Connecticut (O'Brien, fig. 49; cat. no. 60; pls. XXV, XXXIV)
Robert Wallace (Pisano, fig. 1)

In Support of Liberty
was produced for
The Parrish Art Museum, Southampton, New York
by Perpetua Press, Los Angeles
Edited by Jane Fluegel
Designed by Dana Levy
Typeset in Garamond 3 by Continental Typographics
Printed in Japan by Nissha Printing Company, Kyoto